6. Can a local account be used in a trust relationship? Explain.

7. In a complete trust domain model that uses 4 different domains, what is the total number of trust relationships required to use a complete trust domain model?

Exam Questions

The following questions are similar to those you will face on the Microsoft exam. Answers to these questions can be found in section Answers and Explanations, later in the chapter. At the end of each of those answers, you will be informed of where (that is, in what section of the chapter) to find more information..

1. ABC Corporation has locations in Toronto, New York, and San Francisco. It wants to install Windows NT Server 4 to encompass all its locations in a single WAN environment. The head office is located in New York. What is the best domain model for ABC's directory services implementation?

   A. Single-domain model

   B. Single-master domain model

   C. Multiple-master domain model

   D. Complete-trust domain model

2. JPS Printing has a single location with 1,000 users spread across the LAN. It has special printers and applications installed on the servers in its environment. It needs to be able to centrally manage the user accounts and the resources. Which domain model would best fit its needs?

A. Single-domain model

B. Single-master domain model

C. Multiple-master domain model

D. Complete-trust domain model

5. What must be created to allow a user account from one domain to access resources in a different domain?

A. Complete Trust Domain Model

B. One Way Trust Relationship

C. Two Way Trust Relationship

D. Master-Domain Model

Answers to Review Questions

1. Single domain, master domain, multiple-master domain, complete-trust domain. See section, Windows NT Server 4 Domain Models, in this chapter for more information. (This question deals with objective Planning 1.)

2. One user, one account, centralized administration, universal resource access, synchronization. See section, Windows NT Server 4 Directory Services, in this chapter for more information. (This question deals with objective Planning 1.)

6. Local accounts cannot be given permissions across trusts. See section, Accounts in Trust Relationships, in this chapter for more information. (This question deals with Planning 1.)

Answers and Explanations: For each of the Review and Exam questions, you will find a thorough explanation located at the end of the section. The answers and explanations are easily identifiable because they are in blue type.

Exam Questions: These questions reflect the kinds of multiple-choice questions that appear on the Microsoft exams. Use them to become familiar with the exam question formats and to help you determine what you already know and what you need to review or study further.

Suggested Readings and Resources

The following are some recommended readings on the subject of installing and configuring NT Workstation:

1. Microsoft Official Curriculum course 770: *Installing and Configuring Microsoft Windows NT Workstation 4.0*

   • Module 1: Overview of Windows NT Workstation 4.0

   • Module 2: Installing Windows NT Workstation 4.0

2. Microsoft Official Curriculum course 922: *Supporting Microsoft Windows NT 4.0 Core Technologies*

   • Module 2: Installing Windows NT

   • Module 3: Configuring the Windows NT Environment

3. *Microsoft Windows NT Workstation Resource Kit Version 4.0* (Microsoft Press)

   • Chapter 2: Customizing Setup

   • Chapter 4: Planning for a Mixed Environment

4. Microsoft TechNet CD-ROM

   • *MS Windows NT Workstation Technical Notes*

     • MS Windows NT Workstation Deployment Guide – Automating Windows NT Setup

     • An Unattended Windows NT Workstation Deployment

5. Web Sites

   • www.microsoft.com/train_cert

Suggested Readings and Resources: The very last element in each chapter is a list of additional resources you can use if you want to go above and beyond certification-level material or if you need to spend more time on a particular subject that you are having trouble understanding.

Exam 70-098   Implementing and Supporting Microsoft Windows 98

PLANNING (CHAPTER 1)

OBJECTIVE	PAGE REFERENCE
Develop an appropriate implementation model for specific requirements in a Microsoft environment or a mixed Microsoft and NetWare environment. Considerations include the following: · Choosing the appropriate file system · Planning a workgroup	1)Body-of-text coverage—Section "Networking Windows 98" 2)Step by Steps—None 3)Exercises—1.1–1.3 4)Review Questions—1–3 5)Exam Questions—1–3
Develop a security strategy in a Microsoft environment or a mixed Microsoft and NetWare environment. Strategies include the following: · System policies · User profiles · File and printer sharing · Share-level access control or user-level access control	1)Body-of-text coverage—Section "Planning Windows 98 Security" (for general objective) 2)Step by Steps—None 3)Exercises—1.4–1.6 4)Review Questions—4–8 5)Exam Questions—4–10

INSTALLATION AND CONFIGURATION (CHAPTERS 2, 3, AND 4)

OBJECTIVE	PAGE REFERENCE
Install Windows 98. Install options include the following: · Automated Windows Setup · New · Upgrade · Uninstall · Dual-boot combination with Microsoft Windows NT 4.0	1)Body-of-text coverage—This whole chapter satisfies the objective. 2)Step by Steps—2.1–2.4 3)Exercises—2.1, 2.2 4)Review Questions—1–9 5)Exam Questions—1–8
Configure Windows 98 server components. Server components include the following: · Microsoft Personal Web Server 4.0 · Dial-Up Networking server	1)Body-of-text coverage—For objective as whole and for main part of objective, section "Configuring Windows 98 Server Components" 2)Step by Steps—3.18–3.20 3)Exercises—3.1–3.3 4)Review Question—1 5)Exam Questions—2, 9
Install and configure the network components of Windows 98 in a Microsoft environment or a mixed Microsoft and NetWare environment. Network components include the following: · Client for Microsoft Networks · Client for NetWare Networks · Network adapters · File and Printer Sharing for Microsoft Networks · File and Printer Sharing for NetWare Networks · Service for NetWare Directory Services (NDS) · Asynchronous Transfer Mode (ATM) components · Virtual Private Networking and PPTP · Browse Master	1)Body-of-text coverage—For objective as whole and for main part of objective, section "Installing and Configuring Network Components" 2)Step by Steps—3.2–3.4, 3.9–3.17 3)Exercises—3.4–3.6 4)Review Questions—2, 5, 7–11 5)Exam Questions—1, 5, 6, 8
Install and configure network protocols in a Microsoft environment or a mixed Microsoft and NetWare environment. Protocols include the following: · NetBEUI · IPX/SPX-compatible protocol · TCP/IP	1)Body-of-text coverage—For objective as whole and for main part of objective, section "Installing and Configuring Protocols" 2)Step by Steps—3.5–3.8 3)Exercise—3.7 4)Review Questions—None 5)Exam Questions—None

TROUBLESHOOTING (CHAPTER 8)

OBJECTIVE	PAGE REFERENCE
Diagnose and resolve installation failures. Tasks include the following: · Resolving file and driver version conflicts by using Version Conflict Manager and the Microsoft System Information utility	1)Body-of-text coverage—Section "Troubleshooting Installation Problems" 2)Step by Step—8.1 3)Exercises—8.1, 8.2 4)Review Questions—1–3 5)Exam Questions—1–3
Diagnose and resolve boot process failures. Tasks include the following: · Editing configuration files by using System Configuration utility	1)Body-of-text coverage—Section "Diagnosing and Resolving Boot Process Failures" 2)Step by Steps—None 3)Exercise—8.3 4)Review Questions—None 5)Exam Questions—None
Diagnose and resolve connectivity problems in a Microsoft environment and a mixed Microsoft and NetWare environment. Tools include the following: · WinIPCfg · Net Watcher · Ping · Tracert	1)Body-of-text coverage—Section "Diagnosing and Resolving Connectivity Problems" 2)Step by Steps—None 3)Exercises—8.4–8.6 4)Review Questions—4–7 5)Exam Questions—4–6, 10
Diagnose and resolve printing problems in a Microsoft environment or a mixed Microsoft and NetWare environment.	1)Body-of-text coverage—Section "Diagnosing and Resolving Printing Problems" 2)Step by Steps—8.2–8.4 3)Exercises—None 4)Review Question—9 5)Exam Questions—None
Diagnose and resolve file system problems.	1)Body-of-text coverage—Section "Diagnosing and Resolving File System Problems" 2)Step by Steps—None 3)Exercises—None 4)Review Questions—None 5)Exam Question—8
Diagnose and resolve resource access problems in a Microsoft environment or a mixed Microsoft and NetWare environment.	1)Body-of-text coverage—Section "Diagnosing and Resolving Resource Access Problems" 2)Step by Steps—None 3)Exercises—None 4)Review Question—10 5)Exam Questions—7, 9, 10
Diagnose and resolve hardware device and device driver problems. Tasks include: · Checking for corrupt registry files by using ScanReg and ScanRegW	1)Body-of-text coverage—Section "Diagnosing and Resolving Hardware Device and Device Driver Problems" 2)Step by Step—8.6 3)Exercise—8.7 4)Review Question—8 5)Exam Questions—None

| Create hardware profiles. | 1)Body-of-text coverage—Section "Working with Hardware Profiles"
2)Step by Steps—None
3)Exercise—6.3
4)Review Questions—7, 8
5)Exam Questions—8, 9 |

INTEGRATION AND INTEROPERABILITY (CHAPTER 3)

OBJECTIVE	PAGE REFERENCE
Configure a Windows 98 computer as a client computer in a network that contains a Windows NT 4.0 domain.	1)Body-of-text coverage—Section "Windows 98 on NT Networks" 2)Step by Steps—None 3)Exercise—3.8 4)Review Question—12 5)Exam Questions—None
Configure a Windows 98 computer as a client computer in a NetWare network.	1)Body-of-text coverage—Section "Windows 98 on NetWare Networks" 2)Step by Steps—3.21, 3.22 3)Exercises—None 4)Review Question—6 5)Exam Questions—None

Configure a Windows 98 computer for remote access by using various methods in a Microsoft environment or a mixed Microsoft and NetWare environment. Methods include the following:
   · Dial-Up Networking
   · Proxy server
	1)Body-of-text coverage—For objective as whole and for main part of objective, section "Windows 98 and Remote Access"
	2)Step by Steps—3.23–3.27
	3)Exercises—None
	4)Review Questions—3, 4, 13
	5)Exam Questions—3, 4, 7, 10

MONITORING AND OPTIMIZATION (CHAPTER 7)

OBJECTIVE	PAGE REFERENCE
Monitor system performance by using Net Watcher, System Monitor, and Resource Meter.	1)Body-of-text coverage—Section "Monitoring Your Windows 98 System" 2)Step by Step—7.1 3)Exercise—7.7 4)Review Questions—7, 8 5)Exam Questions—7–10

Tune and optimize the system in a Microsoft environment and a mixed Microsoft and NetWare environment. Tasks include the following:
   · Optimizing the hard disk by using Disk Defragmenter and ScanDisk
   · Compressing data by using DriveSpace 3 and the Compression Agent
   · Updating drivers and applying service packs by using Windows Update and the Signature Verification Tool
   · Automating tasks by using Maintenance Wizard
   · Scheduling tasks using Task Scheduler
   · Checking for corrupt files and extracting files from the installation media using the System File Checker
	1)Body-of-text coverage—Sections on optimization satisfy this objective.
	2)Step by Steps—7.2–7.4
	3)Exercises—7.1–7.6
	4)Review Questions—1–6
	5)Exam Questions—1–6

- Microsoft DLC
- Fast Infrared

Install and configure hardware devices in a Microsoft environment and a mixed Microsoft and NetWare environment. Hardware devices include the following: • Modems • Printers • Universal Serial Bus (USB) • Multiple display support • IEEE 1394 FireWire • Infrared Data Association (IrDA) • Multilink • Power management scheme	1)Body-of-text coverage—This objective is covered throughout the chapter. 2)Step by Steps—4.1–4.10 3)Exercises—4.1, 4.2 4)Review Questions—1–8 5)Exam Questions—1, 2, 4–10
Install and configure Microsoft Backup.	1)Body-of-text coverage—Section "Installing and Configuring Microsoft Backup" 2)Step by Steps—4.11–4.13 3)Exercises—4.3, 4.4 4)Review Questions—9, 10 5)Exam Questions—3, 11

CONFIGURING AND MANAGING RESOURCE ACCESS (CHAPTERS 5 AND 6)

OBJECTIVE	PAGE REFERENCE
Assign access permissions for shared folders in a Microsoft environment or a mixed Microsoft and NetWare environment. Methods include the following: • Passwords • User permissions • Group permissions	1)Body-of-text coverage—For objective as whole and for main part of objective, section "Assigning Access Permissions for Shared Folders" 2)Step by Steps—None 3)Exercises—5.1, 5.4 4)Review Questions—1–4 5)Exam Questions—3–5, 9
Create, share, and monitor resources. Resources include the following: • Remote computers • Network printers	1)Body-of-text coverage—Section "Creating, Sharing, and Monitoring Resources" 2)Step by Steps—5.1, 5.2 3)Exercises—5.2, 5.3 4)Review Questions—None 5)Exam Questions—1, 2, 6–8, 10
Configure hard disks. Tasks include the following: • Disk compression • Partitioning • Enabling large disk support • Converting to FAT32	1)Body-of-text coverage—For objective as whole and for main part of objective, section "Configuring Hard Disks" 2)Step by Steps—5.3–5.5 3)Exercise—5.5 4)Review Questions—5–8 5)Exam Questions—11, 12
Back up data and the Registry and restore data and the Registry.	1)Body-of-text coverage—Section "Backing Up Data and the Registry" 2)Step by Steps—5.6–5.8 3)Exercise—5.6 4)Review Questions—None 5)Exam Question—13
Set up user environments by using user profiles and system policies.	1)Body-of-text coverage—Sections "Setting Up User Environments through User Profiles" and "Setting Up User Environments through System Policies" 2)Step by Steps—6.1–6.5 3)Exercises—6.1, 6.2 4)Review Questions—1–6 5)Exam Questions—1–7, 10

MCSE
Windows® 98

Exam: 70-098

New
Riders

Joe Casad
Joe Phillips

MCSE Training Guide: Windows® 98

Copyright © 1999 by New Riders Publishing

International Standard Book Number: 1-56205-890-8

Library of Congress Catalog Card Number: 98-88580

Printed in the United States of America

First Printing: January, 1999

01 00 99   4 3 2 1

TRADEMARKS

WARNING AND DISCLAIMER

EXECUTIVE EDITOR
Mary Foote

ACQUISITIONS EDITORS
Sean Angus
Stacey Beheler

DEVELOPMENT EDITOR
Stacia Mellinger

MANAGING EDITOR
Sarah Kearns

COPY EDITOR
Daryl Kessler

INDEXER
Cheryl Landis

TECHNICAL EDITORS
Todd Brown
Danny Partain

SOFTWARE DEVELOPMENT SPECIALIST
Jack Belbot

PROOFREADER
Mary Ellen Stephenson

LAYOUT TECHNICIANS
Steve Geiselman
Brad Lenser
Eric S. Miller

Contents at a Glance

Table of Contents

Part II: Final Review

About the Authors

Joe Casad is an engineer who has written widely on PC networking and system administration. He is the author of *MCSE Windows NT Server and Workstation Study Guide*, *MCSE Training Guide: Networking Essentials*, and *Windows 98 Professional Reference*. He is the former managing editor of *Network Administrator* magazine.

Joe Phillips, MCSE, MCT, has been working as an independent trainer and consultant for the last six years throughout North America. He has contributed as a writer to various magazines and newspapers, and co-authored *MCSE TestPrep: Windows 95* and *MCSE TestPrep: Windows NT Server 4*. Before becoming an independent trainer, Joe taught for Columbia College, Chicago. When not teaching, consulting, or writing, Joe likes to fish, play chess, and take pictures of stuff. He can be reached via email at phillipsj@instructing.com.

About the Technical Reviewers

Todd C. Brown is a field systems engineer with Bell Industries / LMB Division in Indianapolis, Indiana. His primary activities are designing, implementing, and troubleshooting networks for clients throughout Indiana. He has been involved in operating system and PC network support for the past 12 years. In that time, Todd has had extensive experience with Windows (NT, 95, and 98), NetWare, Macintosh OS, and OS/2. Todd has completed his Microsoft Certified Systems Engineer (MCSE), Novell Master Certified Network Engineer (MCNE), and Compaq Accredited Systems Engineer (ASE) certifications. As an author and technical editor, Todd has worked with Macmillan Computer Publishing since 1992. He was a contributing author for *Absolute Beginner Guide to Networking*, *NetWare 4.1 Survival Guide*, and *Using NetWare 4.1*. He was the lead author for *Peter Norton's Maximizing Windows NT Server*. He has been the technical editor for many projects.

Danny E. Partain has been involved with NetWare since 1989. He is the MIS Manager for FOX 5— WAGA-TV in Atlanta, GA. He is also a member of the adjunct faculty at Gwinnett Technical Institute in the Business Information Sciences department. Danny teaches the following courses: Introduction to Networking (NetWare) and Advanced Networking (NetWare). On September 24, 1998, he received the "Division Adjunct Distinguished Service Award," for the 1998 school year from Gwinnett Technical Institute. He is a Certified NetWare Engineer (CNE), IntraNetWare CNE, and a Microsoft Certified Product Specialist (MCP) for Windows 95. He is a graduate of Southern Polytechnic State University and Gwinnett Technical Institute. He is a member of NetWare Users International and 3COM groups.

Dedication

From Joe Phillips

This book is dedicated to my 3-year-old son Kyle Joseph, who is always ready for a "buddy breakfast"—even at suppertime.

Acknowledgments

Joe Casad

I would like to thank Sean Angus and Stacia Mellinger for their confidence, patience, and good advice throughout this project. Thanks also to the tireless experts at Macmillan who brought these much-processed words to a more graceful and visible form. Thanks to my co-author Joe Phillips and to the other authors who contributed material to previous editions of this book, including Edward Tetz, Ed Wilson, Daniel Lauer, Michael Wolfe, Rob Tidrow, and Tim McLaren. In my years of writing acknowledgments, I am remiss for never having used this forum to thank my parents for their love and support through the years. A special thanks to Robert Casad and Sarah Casad.

Joe Phillips

I want to thank everyone involved with the creation of this book, including my co-author Joe Casad, Executive Editor Mary Foote, Acquisitions Editor Sean Angus, and Development Editor Stacia Mellinger—all of whom have been incredibly kind and patient throughout the process of creating this book. Thanks!

TELL US WHAT YOU THINK!

As the reader of this book, *you* are our most important critic and commentator. We value your opinion and want to know what we're doing right, what we could do better, what areas you'd like to see us publish in, and any other words of wisdom you're willing to pass our way.

As the Executive Editor for the Certification team at Macmillan Computer Publishing, I welcome your comments. You can fax, email, or write me directly to let me know what you did or didn't like about this book—as well as what we can do to make our books stronger.

Please note that I cannot help you with technical problems related to the topic of this book, and that due to the high volume of mail I receive, I might not be able to reply to every message.

When you write, please be sure to include this book's title and authors, as well as your name and phone or fax number. I will carefully review your comments and share them with the authors and editors who worked on the book.

Fax: 317-581-4663

Email: certification@mcp.com

Mail: Mary Foote
            Executive Editor
            Certification
            Macmillan Computer Publishing
            201 West 103rd Street
            Indianapolis, IN 46290 USA

How to Use This Book

New Riders Publishing has made an effort in the second editions of books in its Training Guide series to make the information as accessible as possible for the purposes of learning the certification material. Here, you have an opportunity to view the many instructional features that have been incorporated into the books to achieve that goal.

CHAPTER OPENER

Each chapter begins with a set of features designed to allow you to maximize study time for that material.

List of Objectives: Each chapter begins with a list of the objectives as stated by Microsoft.

Objective Explanations: Immediately following each objective is an explanation of it, providing context that defines it more meaningfully in relation to the exam. Because Microsoft can sometimes be vague in its objectives list, the objective explanations are designed to clarify any vagueness by taking advantage of the authors' test-taking experience.

OBJECTIVES

Microsoft provides the following objectives for "Connectivity":

Add and configure the network components of Windows NT Workstation.

▶ This objective is necessary because someone certified in the use of Windows NT Workstation technology must understand how it fits into a networked environment and how to configure the components that enable it to do so.

Use various methods to access network resources.

▶ This objective is necessary because someone certified in the use of Windows NT Workstation technology must understand how resources available on a network can be accessed from NT Workstation.

Implement Windows NT Workstation as a client in a NetWare environment.

▶ This objective is necessary because someone certified in the use of Windows NT Workstation technology must understand how NT Workstation can be used as a client in a NetWare environment and how to configure the services and protocols that make this possible.

Use various configurations to install Windows NT Workstation as a TCP/IP client.

▶ This objective is necessary because someone certified in the use of Windows NT Workstation technology must understand how TCP/IP is important in a network environment and how Workstation can be configured to use it.

CHAPTER 4

Connectivity

OUTLINE

Chapter Outline: Learning always gets a boost when you can see both the forest and the trees. To give you a visual image of how the topics in a chapter fit together, you will find a chapter outline at the beginning of each chapter. You will also be able to use this for easy reference when looking for a particular topic.

STUDY STRATEGIES

▶ Disk configurations are a part of both the planning and the configuration of NT Server computers. To study for Planning Objective 1, you will need to look at both the following section and the material in Chapter 2, "Installation Part 1." As with many concepts, you should have a good handle on the terminology and know the best applications for different disk configurations. For the objectives of the NT Server exam, you will need to know only general disk configuration concepts—at a high level, not the nitty gritty. Make sure you memorize the concepts relating to partitioning and know the difference between the system and the boot partitions in an NT system (and the fact that the definitions of these are counter-intuitive). You should know that NT supports both FAT and NTFS partitions, as well as some of the advantages and disadvantages of each. You will also need to know about the fault-tolerance methods available in NT—stripe sets with parity and disk mirroring—including their definitions, hardware requirements, and advantages and disadvantages.

Of course, nothing substitutes for working with the concepts explained in this objective. If possible, get an NT system with some free disk space and play around with the Disk Administrator just to see how partitions are created and what they look like.

You might also want to look at some of the supplementary readings and scan TechNet for white papers on disk configuration.

▶ The best way to study for Planning Objective 2 is to read, memorize, and understand the use of each protocol. You should know what the protocols are, what they are used for, and what systems they are compatible with.

As with disk configuration, installing protocols on your NT Server is something that you plan for, not something you do just because it feels good to you at the time. Although it is much easier to add or remove a protocol than it is to reconfigure your hard drives, choosing a protocol is still an essential part of the planning process because specific protocols, like spoken languages, are designed to be used in certain circumstances. There is no point in learning to speak Mandarin Chinese if you are never around anyone who can understand you. Similarly, the NWLink protocol is used to interact with NetWare systems; therefore, if you do not have Novell servers on your network, you might want to rethink your plan to install it on your servers. We will discuss the uses of the major protocols in Chapter 7, "Connectivity." However, it is important that you have a good understanding of their uses here in the planning stage.

Study Strategies: Each topic presents its own learning challenge. To support you through this, New Riders has included strategies for how to best approach your studies in order to retain the material in the chapter, particularly as it is addressed on the exam.

INSTRUCTIONAL FEATURES WITHIN THE CHAPTER

These books include a large amount and different kinds of information. The many different elements are designed to help you identify information by its purpose and importance to the exam and also to provide you with varied ways to learn the material. You will be able to determine how much attention to devote to certain elements, depending on what your goals are. By becoming familiar with the different presentations of information, you will know what information will be important to you as a test-taker and which information will be important to you as a practitioner.

Objective Coverage Text: In the text before an exam objective is specifically addressed, you will notice the objective listed and printed in color to help call your attention to that particular material.

Warnings: In using sophisticated information technology, there is always potential for mistakes or even catastrophes that can occur through improper application of the technology. Warnings appear in the margins to alert you to such potential problems.

EXAM TIP

Only One NTVDM Supports Multiple 16-bit Applications
Expect at least one question about running Win16 applications in separate memory spaces. The key concept is that you can load multiple Win16 applications into the same memory space only if it is the initial Win16 NTVDM. It is not possible, for example, to run Word for Windows 6.0 and Excel for Windows 5.0 in one shared memory space and also run PowerPoint 4.0 and Access 2.0 in another shared memory space.

Exam Tips: Exam Tips appear in the margins to provide specific exam-related advice. Such tips may address what material is covered (or not covered) on the exam, how it is covered, mnemonic devices, or particular quirks of that exam.

Notes: Notes appear in the margins and contain various kinds of useful information, such as tips on the technology or administrative practices, historical background on terms and technologies, or side commentary on industry issues.

---

8   Chapter 1   PLANNING

INTRODUCTION

Microsoft grew up around the personal computer industry and established itself as the preeminent maker of software products for personal computers. Microsoft has a vast portfolio of software products, but it is best known for its operating systems.

Microsoft's current operating system products, listed here, are undoubtedly well-known to anyone studying for the MCSE exams:

- ◆ Windows 95
- ◆ Windows NT Workstation
- ◆ Windows NT Server

NOTE

Strange But True Although it sounds backward, it is true: Windows NT boots from the system partition and then loads the system from the boot partition.

Some older operating system products—namely MS-DOS, Windows 3.1, and Windows for Workgroups—are still important to the operability of Windows NT Server, so don't be surprised if you hear them mentioned from time to time in this book.

Windows NT is the most powerful, the most secure, and perhaps the most elegant operating system Microsoft has yet produced. It languished for a while after it first appeared (in part because no one was sure why they needed it or what to do with it), but Microsoft has persisted with improving interoperability and performance. With the release of Windows NT 4 which offers a new Windows 95-like user interface, Windows NT has assumed a prominent place in today's world of network-based computing.

WINDOWS NT SERVER AMONG MICROSOFT OPERATING SYSTEMS

WARNING

Don't Overextend Your Partitions and Wraps It is not necessary to create an extended partition on a disk; primary partitions might be all that you need. However, if you do create one, remember that you can never have more than one extended partition on a physical disk.

As we already mentioned, Microsoft has three operating system products now competing in the marketplace: Windows 95, Windows NT Workstation, and Windows NT Server. Each of these operating systems has its advantages and disadvantages.

Looking at the presentation of the desktop, the three look very much alike—so much so that you might have to click the Start button and read the banner on the left side of the menu to determine which operating system you are looking at. Each offers the familiar Windows 95 user interface featuring the Start button, the Recycling

STEP BY STEP

5.1 Configuring an Extension to Trigger an Application to Always Run in a Separate Memory Space

1. Start the Windows NT Explorer.

2. From the View menu, choose Options.

3. Click the File Types tab.

4. In the Registered File Types list box, select the desired file type.

5. Click the Edit button to display the Edit File Type dialog box. Then select Open from the Actions list and click the Edit button below it.

6. In the Editing Action for Type dialog box, adjust the application name by typing **cmd.exe /c start /separate** in front of the existing contents of the field (see Figure 5.15).

FIGURE 5.15
Configuring a shortcut to run a Win16 application in a separate memory space.

Step by Steps: Step by Steps are hands-on tutorial instructions that walk you through particular tasks or functions relevant to the exam objectives.

Figures: To improve readability, the figures have been placed in the margins so they do not interrupt the main flow of text.

---

14   Chapter 1   PLANNING

You must use NTFS if you want to preserve existing permissions when you migrate files and directories from a NetWare server to a Windows NT Server system.

Windows 95 is Microsoft's everyday workhorse operating system. It provides a 32-bit platform and is designed to operate with a variety of peripherals. See Table 1.1 for the minimum hardware requirements for the installation and operation of Windows 95. Also, if you want to allow Macintosh computers to access files on the partition through Windows NT's Services for Macintosh, you must format the partition for NTFS.

MAKING REGISTRY CHANGES

To make Registry changes, run the REGEDT32.EXE program. The Registry in Windows NT is a complex database of configuration settings for your computer. If you want to configure the Workstation service, open the HKEY_LOCAL_MACHINE hive, as shown in Figure 3.22.

The exact location for configuring your Workstation service is

```
HKEY_LOCAL_MACHINE\System\CurrentControlSet\Services\
LanmanWorkstation\Parameters
```

To find additional information regarding this Registry item and others, refer to the Windows NT Server resource kit.

This summary table offers an overview of the differences between the FAT and NTFS file systems.

REVIEW BREAK

Choosing a File System

But if the system is designed to store data, mirroring might produce disk bottlenecks. You might only know whether these changes are significant by setting up two identical computers, implementing mirroring on one but not on the other, and then running Performance Monitor on both under a simulated load to see the performance differences.

This summary table offers an overview of the differences between the FAT and NTFS file systems.

In-Depth Sidebars: These more extensive discussions cover material that perhaps is not as directly relevant to the exam, but which is useful as reference material or in everyday practice. In-Depths may also provide useful background or contextual information necessary for understanding the larger topic under consideration.

Review Breaks: Crucial information is summarized at various points in the book in lists or tables. At the end of a particularly long section, you might come across a Review Break that is there just to wrap up one long objective and reinforce the key points before you shift your focus to the next section.

CASE STUDIES

Case Studies are presented throughout the book to provide you with another, more conceptual opportunity to apply the knowledge you are developing. They also reflect the "real-world" experiences of the authors in ways that prepare you not only for the exam but for actual network administration as well. In each Case Study, you will find similar elements: a description of a Scenario, the Essence of the Case, and an extended Analysis section.

CASE STUDY: REALLY GOOD GUITARS

ESSENCE OF THE CASE

Here are the essential elements in this case:

- need for centralized administration
- the need for WAN connectivity nation-wide
- a requirement for Internet access and e-mail
- the need for Security on network shares and local files
- an implementation of Fault-tolerant systems

SCENARIO

Really Good Guitars is a national company specializing in the design and manufacturer of custom acoustic guitars. Having grown up out of an informal network of artisans across Canada, the company has many locations but very few employees (300 at this time) and a Head Office in Churchill, Manitoba. Although they follow the best traditions of hand-making guitars, they are not without technological savvy and all the 25 locations have computers on-site which are used to do accounting, run MS Office applications, and run their custom made guitar design software. The leadership team has recently begun to realize that a networked solution is essential to maintain consistency and to provide security on what are becoming some very innovative designs and to provide their employees with e-mail and Internet access.

RGG desires a centralized administration of its

continues

Essence of the Case: A bulleted list of the key problems or issues that need to be addressed in the Scenario.

Scenario: A few paragraphs describing a situation that professional practitioners in the field might face. A Scenario deals with an issue relating to the objectives covered in the chapter, and it includes the kinds of details that make a difference.

Analysis: This is a lengthy description of the best way to handle the problems listed in the Essence of the Case. In this section, you might find a table summarizing the solutions, a worded example, or both.

CASE STUDY: PRINT IT DRAFTING INC.

continued

too, which is unacceptable. You are to find a solution to this problem if one exists.

ANALYSIS

The fixes for both of these problems are relatively straightforward. In the first case, it is likely that all the programs on the draftspeople's workstations are being started at normal priority. This means that they have a priority of 8. But the default says that anything running in the foreground is getting a 2-point boost from the base priority, bringing it to 10. As a result, when sent to the background, AutoCAD is not getting as much attention from the processor as it did when it was the foreground application. Because multiple applications need to be run at once without significant degradation of the performance of AutoCAD, you implement the following solution:

1. On the Performance tab of the System Properties dialog box for each workstation, set the Application Performance slider to None to prevent a boost for foreground applications.

2. Recommend that users keep the additional programs running alongside AutoCAD at a minimum (because all programs will now get equal processor time).

The fix to the second problem is to run each 16-bit application in its own NTVDM. This ensures that the crashing of one application will not adversely affect the others, but it still enables interoperability between the applications because they use OLE (and not shared memory) to transfer data. To make the fix as transparent as possible to the users, you suggested that two things be done:

1. Make sure that for each shortcut a user has created to the office applications, the Run in Separate Memory Space option is selected on the Shortcut tab.

2. Change the properties for the extensions associated with the applications (for example, .XLS and .DOC) so that they start using the /separate switch. Then any file that is double-clicked invokes the associated program to run in its own NTVDM.

EXTENSIVE REVIEW AND SELF-TEST OPTIONS

At the end of each chapter, along with some summary elements, you will find a section called "Apply Your Knowledge" that gives you several different methods with which to test your understanding of the material and review what you have learned.

CHAPTER SUMMARY

KEY TERMS

Before you take the exam, make sure you are comfortable with the definitions and concepts for each of the following key terms:

- FAT
- NTFS
- workgroup
- domain

This chapter discussed the main planning topics you will encounter on the Windows NT Server exam. Distilled down, these topics revolve around two main goals: understanding the planning of disk configuration and understanding the planning of network protocols.

◆ Windows NT Server supports an unlimited number of inbound sessions; Windows NT Workstation supports no more than 10 active sessions at the same time.

◆ Windows NT Server accommodates an unlimited number of remote access connections (although Microsoft only supports up to 256); Windows NT Workstation supports only a single remote access connection.

Key Terms: A list of key terms appears at the end of each chapter. These are terms that you should be sure you know and are comfortable defining and understanding when you go in to take the exam.

Chapter Summary: Before the Apply Your Knowledge section, you will find a chapter summary that wraps up the chapter and reviews what you should have learned.

Chapter 1   PLANNING   23

APPLY YOUR KNOWLEDGE

This section allows you to assess how well you understood the material in the chapter. Review and Exam questions test your knowledge of the tasks and concepts specified in the objectives. The Exercises provide you with opportunities to engage in the sorts of tasks that comprise the skill sets the objectives reflect.

FIGURE 1.2
The login process on a local machine.

Exercises

1.1   Synchronizing the Domain Controllerys

The following steps show you how to manually synchronize a backup domain controller within your domain. (This objective deals with Objective Planning 1.)

Estimated Time: Less than 10 minutes.

1. Click Start, Programs, Administrative Tools, and select the Server Manager icon.

2. Highlight the BDC (Backup Domain Controller) in your computer list.

3. Select the Computer menu, then select Synchronize with Primary Domain Controller.

2. Select the Policies menu and click Trust Relationships. The Trust Relationships dialog box appears.

4. When the trusting domain information has been entered, click OK and close the Trust Relationships dialog box.

12.2   Establishing a Trust Relationship between Domains

The following steps show you how to establish a trust relationship between multiple domains. To complete this exercise, you must have two Windows NT Server computers, each installed in their own domain. (This objective deals with objective Planning 1.)

Estimated Time: 10 minutes

1. From the trusted domain select Start, Programs, Administrative Tools, and click User Manager for Domains. The User Manager.

Review Questions

1. List the four domain models that can be used for directory services in Windows NT Server 4.

2. List the goals of a directory services architecture.

3. What is the maximum size of the SAM database in Windows NT Server 4.0?

4. What are the two different types of domains in a trust relationship?

5. In a trust relationship which domain would contain the user accounts?

Exercises: These activities provide opportunities for you to master specific hands-on tasks. Our goal is to increase your proficiency with the product or technology. You must be able to conduct these tasks in order to pass the exam.

Review Questions: These open-ended, short-answer questions allow you to quickly assess your comprehension of what you just read in the chapter. Instead of asking you to choose from a list of options, these questions require you to state the correct answers in your own words. Although you will not experience these kinds of questions on the exam, these questions will indeed test your level of comprehension of key concepts.

Exam Questions: These questions reflect the kinds of multiple-choice questions that appear on the Microsoft exams. Use them to become familiar with the exam question formats and to help you determine what you know and what you need to review or study further.

6. Can a local account be used in a trust relationship? Explain.

7. In a complete trust domain model that uses 4 different domains, what is the total number of trust relationships required to use a complete trust domain model?

Exam Questions

The following questions are similar to those you will face on the Microsoft exam. Answers to these questions can be found in section Answers and Explanations, later in the chapter. At the end of each of those answers, you will be informed of where (that is, in what section of the chapter) to find more information..

1. ABC Corporation has locations in Toronto, New York, and San Francisco. It wants to install Windows NT Server 4 to encompass all its locations in a single WAN environment. The head office is located in New York. What is the best domain model for ABC's directory services implementation?

   A. Single-domain model

   B. Single-master domain model

   C. Multiple-master domain model

   D. Complete-trust domain model

2. JPS Printing has a single location with 1,000 users spread across the LAN. It has special printers and applications installed on the servers in its environment. It needs to be able to centrally manage the user accounts and the resources. Which domain model would best fit its needs?

   A. Single-domain model

   B. Single-master domain model

   C. Multiple-master domain model

   D. Complete-trust domain model

5. What must be created to allow a user account from one domain to access resources in a different domain?

   A. Complete Trust Domain Model

   B. One Way Trust Relationship

   C. Two Way Trust Relationship

   D. Master-Domain Model

Answers to Review Questions

1. Single domain, master domain, multiple-master domain, complete-trust domain. See section, Windows NT Server 4 Domain Models, in this chapter for more information. (This question deals with objective Planning 1.)

2. One user, one account, centralized administration, universal resource access, synchronization. See section, Windows NT Server 4 Directory Services, in this chapter for more information. (This question deals with objective Planning 1.)

6. Local accounts cannot be given permissions across trusts. See section, Accounts in Trust Relationships, in this chapter for more information. (This question deals with Planning 1.)

Answers and Explanations: For each of the Review and Exam questions, you will find a thorough explanation located at the end of the section. These answers and explanations are easily identifiable because they are in blue type.

Suggested Readings and Resources: The very last element in every chapter is a list of additional resources you can use if you want to go above and beyond certification-level material or if you need to spend more time on a particular subject that you are having trouble understanding.

Suggested Readings and Resources

The following are some recommended readings on the subject of installing and configuring NT Workstation:

1. Microsoft Official Curriculum course 770: *Installing and Configuring Microsoft Windows NT Workstation 4.0*

   • Module 1: Overview of Windows NT Workstation 4.0

   • Module 2: Installing Windows NT Workstation 4.0

2. Microsoft Official Curriculum course 922: *Supporting Microsoft Windows NT 4.0 Core Technologies*

   • Module 2: Installing Windows NT

   • Module 3: Configuring the Windows NT Environment

3. *Microsoft Windows NT Workstation Resource Kit Version 4.0* (Microsoft Press)

   • Chapter 2: Customizing Setup

   • Chapter 4: Planning for a Mixed Environment

4. Microsoft TechNet CD-ROM

   • *MS Windows NT Workstation Technical Notes*

      • MS Windows NT Workstation Deployment Guide – Automating Windows NT Setup

      • An Unattended Windows NT Workstation Deployment

5. Web Sites

   • www.microsoft.com/train_cert

   • www.prometric.com/testingcandidates/ assessment/chosetest.html (take online

Introduction

MCSE Training Guide: Windows 98 is designed for advanced end-users, service technicians, and network administrators with the goal of certification as a Microsoft Certified Systems Engineer (MCSE). According to Microsoft's exam preparation guide, the "Implementing and Supporting Microsoft Windows 98" exam (#70-098) measures your ability to "implement, administer, and troubleshoot information systems that incorporate Windows 98 and measures your ability to provide technical support to users of Windows 98."

WHO SHOULD READ THIS BOOK

This book is designed to help you meet the goal of certification by preparing you for the "Implementing and Supporting Microsoft Windows 98" exam.

This book is your one-stop shop. Everything you need to know to pass the exam is in here, and Microsoft has approved it as study material. You do not *need* to take a class in addition to buying this book to pass the exam. However, depending on your personal study habits or learning style, you may benefit from taking a class in addition to studying this book.

This book also can help advanced users and administrators who are not preparing for an exam, but are looking for a single-volume reference on Windows 98.

HOW THIS BOOK HELPS YOU

This book guides you on a tour of all the areas covered by the "Implementing and Supporting Microsoft Windows 98" exam, and teaches you the specific skills you need to achieve your MCSE certification. You'll also find helpful hints, tips, real-world examples, exercises, and references to additional study materials. Specifically, this book is designed around four general concepts to help you learn:

◆ **Organization.** This book is organized first by major exam topic and then by individual exam objective. Every objective you need to know for the "Implementing and Supporting Microsoft Windows 98" exam is covered in this book. We attempted to make the information accessible in several different ways:

  • The full list of exam topics and objectives is included in this introduction.

  • Each chapter begins with a list of the objectives covered in that particular chapter.

  • Each chapter also includes an outline that provides an overview of the material in the chapter and notes the pages on which particular topics can be found.

  • To help you quickly locate where the objectives are addressed in the chapter, each objective is restated at the beginning of its corresponding section, and it appears in blue print.

  • The information on where in the book the objectives are covered is also conveniently condensed on the tear card at the front of this book.

◆ **Instructional features**. This book has been designed to provide you with multiple ways to access and reinforce the exam material. The book's instructional features include the following:

- *Objective explanations*. As mentioned earlier, each chapter begins with a list of the objectives covered in the chapter. Immediately following each objective is an explanation of it, in context that defines it more meaningfully.

- *Study strategies*. Each chapter also includes strategies for how to study and retain the material in the chapter, particularly as it is addressed on the exam.

- *Exam tips*. Exam tips appear in the margins to provide specific exam-related advice. Such tips might address what material is covered (or not covered) on the exam, how the material is covered, mnemonic devices, or particular quirks of that exam.

- *Reviews and summaries*. Crucial information is summarized at various points in the book in lists or tables. Each chapter provides a "Chapter Summary" section as well.

- *Key terms*. A list of key terms appears toward the end of each chapter.

- *Notes*. These appear in the margins and contain various kinds of useful information, such as tips on the technology or administrative practices, historical background on terms and technologies, or side commentary on industry issues.

- *Warnings*. When you use sophisticated information technology, there is always the potential that mistakes or even catastrophes can occur as a result of improper application of the technology. Warnings appear in the margins to alert you to such potential problems.

- *In-depth sidebars*. These more extensive discussions cover material that is, perhaps, not directly relevant to the exam, but is useful as reference material or in everyday practice. In-depth sidebars may also provide useful background or contextual information necessary for understanding the larger topic under consideration.

- *Step by Steps*. These are hands-on tutorial instructions that walk you through particular tasks or functions relevant to the exam objectives.

- *Exercises*. Found near the end of each chapter in the "Apply Your Knowledge" section, exercises may include additional tutorial material as well as other types of problems and questions.

- *Case studies*. Case studies are presented throughout the book. They provide you with another, more conceptual opportunity to apply the knowledge you are gaining. A case study includes a description of a scenario, the essence of the case, and an extended analysis section. It also reflects the "real-world" experiences of the authors in ways that prepare you not only for the exam, but for actual network administration as well.

◆ **Extensive practice test options.** The book provides numerous opportunities for you to assess your knowledge and practice for the exam. The practice test options include:

- *Review questions*. Review questions appear in the "Apply Your Knowledge" section near the end of each chapter. These open-ended questions allow you to quickly assess your comprehension of what you just read in the chapter. Answers to the questions are provided later in the chapter.

- *Exam questions*. These questions also appear in the "Apply Your Knowledge" section.

These questions reflect the kind of multiple-choice questions that appear on the Microsoft exams. Use them to practice for the exam and to help you determine what you know and what you need to review or study further. Answers and explanations for the questions are provided.

- *Practice exam.* A practice exam is included in the "Final Review" section of the book. The "Final Review" section and the practice exam are discussed later in this list.

- *Top Score software.* The Top Score software included on the CD-ROM provides further practice questions.

> **NOTE**
> **Top Score** For a complete description of New Riders' Top Score test engine, see Appendix D, "Top Score User's Manual."

◆ **Final review.** This part of the book provides you with three valuable tools for preparing for the exam.

- *Fast Facts.* This condensed version of the information contained in the book will prove extremely useful for last-minute review.

- *Study and Exam Prep Tips.* Read this section early on to help develop your study strategies. It provides you with valuable exam-day tips and information on new exam question formats, such as adaptive tests and simulation-based questions.

- *Practice Exam.* A full practice exam is included. Questions are written in the styles used on the actual exam. Use it to assess your readiness for the real thing.

This book also provides several valuable appendixes, including a glossary (Appendix A), an overview of the

Microsoft certification program (Appendix B), a description of what is on the CD-ROM (Appendix C), and a description of New Riders' Top Score test engine (Appendix D). These and all the other book features mentioned previously will prepare you thoroughly for the exam.

For more information about the exam or the certification process, contact Microsoft:

Microsoft Education: (800) 636-7544

Internet: `ftp://ftp.microsoft.com/Services/MSEdCert`

World Wide Web:
`http://www.microsoft.com/train_cert`

CompuServe Forum: `GO MSEDCERT`

WHAT THE "IMPLEMENTING AND SUPPORTING MICROSOFT WINDOWS 98" EXAM (#70-098) COVERS

The "Implementing and Supporting Microsoft Windows 98" exam (#70-098) covers the six main topic areas represented by the test objectives. The topic areas and accompanying objectives are covered in the following sections.

Planning

Develop an appropriate implementation model for specific requirements in a Microsoft environment or a mixed Microsoft and NetWare environment. Considerations include the following:

◆ Choosing the appropriate file system

◆ Planning a workgroup

Develop a security strategy in a Microsoft environment or a mixed Microsoft and NetWare environment. Strategies include the following:

- System policies
- User profiles
- File and printer sharing
- Share-level access control or user-level access control

Installation and Configuration

Install Windows 98. Installation options include the following:

- Automated Windows setup
- New
- Upgrade
- Uninstall
- Dual-boot combination with Microsoft Windows NT 4.0

Configure Windows 98 server components. Server components include the following:

- Microsoft Personal Web Server 4.0
- Dial-Up Networking server

Install and configure the networking components of Windows 98 in a Microsoft environment or a mixed Microsoft and NetWare environment. Network components include the following:

- Client for Microsoft Networks
- Client for NetWare Networks
- Network adapters

- File and Printer Sharing for Microsoft networks
- File and Printer Sharing for NetWare networks
- Services for NetWare Directory Services (NDS)
- Asynchronous Transfer Mode (ATM) components
- Virtual private networking and PPTP
- Browse Master

Install and configure network protocols in a Microsoft environment or a mixed Microsoft and NetWare environment. Protocols include the following:

- NetBEUI
- IPX/SPX-compatible protocol
- TCP/IP
- Microsoft DLC
- Fast Infrared

Install and configure hardware devices in a Microsoft environment and a mixed Microsoft and NetWare environment. Hardware devices include the following:

- Modems
- Printers
- Universal Serial Bus (USB)
- Multiple display support
- IEEE 1394 FireWire
- Infrared Data Association (IrDA)
- Multilink
- Power management scheme

Install and configure Microsoft Backup.

Configuring and Managing Resource Access

Assign access permissions for shared folders in a Microsoft environment or a mixed Microsoft and NetWare environment. Methods include the following:

- ◆ Passwords
- ◆ User permissions
- ◆ Group permissions

Create, share, and monitor resources. Resources include the following:

- ◆ Remote computers
- ◆ Network printers

Set up user environments by using user profiles and system policies.

Back up data and the Registry, and restore data and the Registry.

Configure hard disks. Tasks include the following:

- ◆ Disk compression
- ◆ Partitioning
- ◆ Enabling large disk support
- ◆ Converting to FAT32

Create hardware profiles.

Integration and Interoperability

Configure a Windows 98 computer as a client computer in a network that contains a Windows NT domain.

Configure a Windows 98 computer as a client computer in a NetWare network.

Configure a Windows 98 computer for remote access by using various methods in a Microsoft environment or a mixed Microsoft and NetWare environment. Methods include the following:

- ◆ Dial-Up Networking
- ◆ Proxy Server

Monitoring and Optimization

Monitor system performance by using Net Watcher, System Monitor, and Resource Meter.

Tune and optimize the system in a Microsoft environment and a mixed Microsoft and NetWare environment. Tasks include the following:

- ◆ Optimizing the hard disk by using Disk Defragmenter and ScanDisk
- ◆ Compressing data by using DriveSpace 3 and the Compression Agent
- ◆ Updating drivers and applying service packs by using Windows Update and the Signature Verification Tool
- ◆ Automating tasks by using Maintenance Wizard
- ◆ Scheduling tasks by using Task Scheduler
- ◆ Checking for corrupt files and extracting files from the installation media by using the System File Checker

Troubleshooting

Diagnose and resolve installation failures. Tasks include the following:

- ◆ Resolve file and driver version conflicts by using Version Conflict Manager and the Microsoft Information Utility.

Diagnose and resolve boot process failures. Tasks include the following:

◆ Editing configuration files by using System Configuration Utility

Diagnose and resolve connectivity problems in a Microsoft environment and a mixed Microsoft and NetWare environment. Tools include the following:

◆ WinIPCfg

◆ Net Watcher

◆ Ping

◆ Tracert

Diagnose and resolve printing problems in a Microsoft environment or a mixed Microsoft and NetWare environment.

Diagnose and resolve file system problems.

Diagnose and resolve resource access problems in a Microsoft environment or a mixed Microsoft and NetWare environment.

Diagnose and resolve hardware device and device driver problems. Tasks include the following:

◆ Checking for corrupt Registry files by using ScanReg and ScanRegW

HARDWARE AND SOFTWARE NEEDED

Intended as a self-paced study guide, this book was designed with the expectation that you will use Windows 98 as you follow along through the exercises. To install Windows 98 on your computer, you'll need a 486DX/66 or better processor and 16 MB of RAM. See Chapter 2, "Installing Windows 98," for more information about Windows 98 hardware requirements. If you

want to investigate all the exercises and procedures presented in this book, it will be helpful if your Windows 98 computer is part of a local area network.

Although Microsoft's exam objectives revolve almost exclusively around Windows 98 itself, on a few occasions this book makes reference to utilities found on the Windows 98 Resource Kit.

ADVICE ON TAKING THE EXAM

More extensive tips are found in the "Final Review" section in the chapter titled "Study and Exam Prep Tips." But keep the following suggestions in mind as you study:

◆ **Read all the material.** Microsoft has been known to include material on its exams that's not expressly specified in the objectives. This book has included additional information not reflected in the objectives in an effort to give you the best possible preparation for the examination and for the real-world network experiences to come.

◆ **Do the Step by Steps and complete the exercises in each chapter.** These features are designed to help you gain experience using the Microsoft product. All Microsoft exams are task- and experience-based and require you to have used the Microsoft product in a real networking environment.

◆ **Use the questions to assess your knowledge.** Don't just read the chapter content; use the questions at the end of the chapter to find out what you know and what you don't. Then study some more, review, and assess your knowledge again.

◆ **Review the exam objectives.** Develop your own questions and examples for each topic listed. If you can create and answer several questions for each topic, you should not find it difficult to pass the exam.

NOTE **No Guarantees** Although this book is designed to prepare you to take and pass the "Implementing and Supporting Microsoft Windows 98" certification exam, there are no guarantees. Study this book and work through the questions and exercises, and when you feel confident, take the Practice Exam and additional exams using the Top Score test engine. These self-tests should reveal whether you are ready for the real thing.

When taking the actual certification exam, make sure you answer all the questions before your time limit expires. Do not spend too much time on any one question. If you are unsure about an answer, answer the question as best you can and mark it for later review; you can return to it when you have finished the rest of the questions.

Remember, the primary objective is not to pass the exam—it is to understand the material. If you understand the material, passing the exam should be simple. Knowledge is a pyramid: To build upward, you need a solid foundation. This book and the Microsoft Certified Professional programs are designed to ensure that you have that solid foundation.

Good luck!

NEW RIDERS PUBLISHING

The staff of New Riders Publishing is committed to bringing you the very best in computer reference material. Each New Riders book is the result of months of work by authors and staff who research and refine the information contained within its covers.

As part of this commitment to you, the NRP reader, New Riders invites your input. Please let us know if you enjoy this book, if you have trouble with the information or examples presented, or if you have a suggestion for the next edition.

Please note, however, that New Riders staff cannot serve as a technical resource during your preparation for the Microsoft certification exams or for questions about software- or hardware-related problems. Please refer instead to the documentation that accompanies the Microsoft products or to the applications' Help systems.

If you have a question or comment about any New Riders book, you can contact New Riders Publishing in several ways. We will respond to as many readers as we

can. Your name, address, or phone number will never become part of a mailing list or be used for any purpose other than to help us continue to bring you the best books possible. You can write to us at the following address:

New Riders Publishing
Attn: Executive Editor
201 W. 103rd Street
Indianapolis, IN 46290

If you prefer, you can fax New Riders Publishing at 317-581-4663.

You also can send email to New Riders at the following Internet address:

`certification@mcp.com`

Thank you for selecting *MCSE Training Guide: Windows 98*.

EXAM PREPARATION

This chapter helps you to prepare for the Microsoft exam by covering the following objectives within the "Planning" category:

Develop an appropriate implementation model for specific requirements in a Microsoft environment or a mixed Microsoft and NetWare environment. Considerations include the following:

> **Choosing the appropriate file system**

> **Planning a workgroup**

▶ This objective will provide you with a foundation of Windows 98 file systems and networking strategies.

Develop a security strategy in a Microsoft environment or a mixed Microsoft and NetWare environment. Strategies include the following:

> **System policies**

> **User profiles**

> **File and Printer Sharing**

> **Share-level access control or user-level access control**

▶ Security is a crucial part of the Windows 98 exam. System policies and user profiles control what the user is allowed to do, while File and Printer Sharing and access level control what resources the user is allowed to access on a network.

CHAPTER 1

Planning

STUDY STRATEGIES

You must consider many variables when installing Windows 98. Will the machine be networked? If so, what kind of network will be implemented, or what network will it be joining? What file system will you use? What level of security will you provide for the network?

Throughout this chapter, take what is offered and apply it to real-world scenarios. The best way to study for your exam is to implement the principles in real situations.

If that's not feasible, then create your own environment on paper to better visualize how the various components will interrelate.

INTRODUCTION

Windows 98 is designed to be part of a network, and the networking theme is omnipresent in the Windows 98 exam. Almost all the sections in the objectives list relate somehow to networking. The "Planning" section is Microsoft's attempt to let you put all your knowledge of Windows 98 to work. Consequently, in some ways it might be more accurate to put the "Planning" section last instead of first. However, the "Planning" objectives provide a basis for some important definitions and introductions, and of course, you must plan a network before you install and configure it, so the "Planning" section is as good a place as any to begin a discussion of Windows 98. This chapter will discuss some of the factors you'll need to consider when planning a Windows 98 network. You'll also learn about Windows 98's file system options and about some concepts you'll need for planning a security strategy in Windows 98.

NETWORKING WINDOWS 98

Develop an appropriate implementation model for specific requirements in a Microsoft environment or a mixed Microsoft and NetWare environment.

Of all the objectives for the Windows 98 MCSE exam, the objective (or, rather, the sub-objective) "Planning a Workgroup" may be the most open-ended and the most difficult to prepare for. Almost anything you do in Windows 98 could conceivably have implications for how you plan your workgroup. The "Planning a Workgroup" topic is especially difficult to pin down because it isn't immediately evident what Microsoft means by "workgroup."

The term *workgroup* often refers to a group of computers in a peer-to-peer configuration (as described later in this section). A workgroup is also a configuration setting—defined through setup or the Network Control Panel—that associates the computer with a group in network browse lists. Microsoft, however, does not limit itself to peer-to-peer configurations and network browse lists in the MCSE exam. You should be prepared to answer questions about any of the following Windows 98 network models:

◆ Peer-to-peer networks

◆ Windows NT domains

◆ NetWare networks

If you're studying for the Windows 98 MCSE exam, chances are you've already faced the task of networking Microsoft-based PCs. Except for a few extra features, Windows 98's networking components are very similar to those of Windows 95.

What does it take for a PC (such as a standalone Windows 98 computer) to become part of a network? The first thing you'll need is some means of connecting the computer to other PCs on the network. On a Local Area Network (LAN), the connection usually occurs through a network adapter card installed in the back of each computer and connected to some form of networking cable. The Windows 98 exam does not directly cover network architecture options (such as 10Base-2 or 10Base-T), but you will need to know how to install and configure network adapters in Windows 98. A modem and a telephone line are another common means of physically connecting PCs.

There is more to networking, however, than a physical connection. The computers on a network must also be using software components that will allow them to communicate. In Windows 98, these software components are installed and managed through the Network Control Panel (see Figure 1.1).

Microsoft classifies Windows 98's networking components into the following four types:

◆ **Clients.** A component that enables a Windows 98 computer to request and receive services in a given network operating environment, such as a Microsoft or NetWare network.

◆ **Adapters.** A component consisting of the network adapter driver and other low-level protocol components related to the interface with the physical transmission medium.

NOTE

Networking Essentials Exam
Another exam in the MCSE exam series, the Networking Essentials exam, covers LAN architectures such as 10Base-2 and 10Base-T.

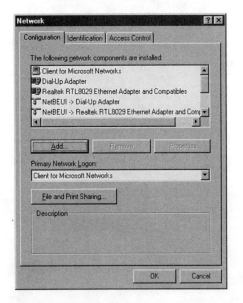

FIGURE 1.1
You can install and configure networking components through the Configuration tab of the Network Control Panel.

◆ **Protocols.** A component that supports network transmissions according to one of the common network protocol specifications. Network protocols in Windows 98 include TCP/IP, NetBEUI, and IPX/SPX-compatible protocol.

◆ **Services.** Network applications that provide services for the network.

You'll learn more about how to install and configure these networking components in Chapter 3, "Windows 98 Networking." For now, a simple illustration will provide you with some context to understand the concepts in this chapter.

Consider the simple network shown in Figure 1.2. The network consists of two Windows 98 PCs, each with a network adapter card, connected through some form of network cabling. Computer A contains a folder called Records that must be available to a user who requests access to it from Computer B. In this simple scenario, Computer A is acting as a *server* (making resources available for network access) and Computer B is acting as a *client* (requesting access to a network resource).

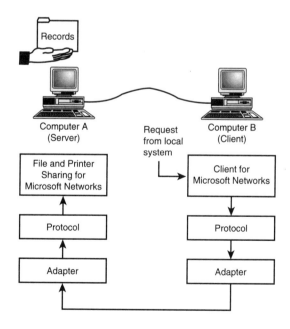

FIGURE 1.2

A network can be as simple as two Windows 98 computers with network adapter cards connected through a network cable.

Computer A uses a network server service—in this case Windows 98's File and Printer Sharing for Microsoft Networks—to listen for and fulfill incoming requests. (The Records folder on Computer A must also be shared, as described later in this chapter. *Sharing* is the deliberate act of making a resource available so that it can be accessed through a file and printer sharing service.)

When a user on Computer B requests access to the Records folder, the client networking component on Computer B (in this case, Client for Microsoft Networks) sends the request to the server service running on Computer A (in this case, File and Printer Sharing for Microsoft Networks). The request passes down through the protocol component on Computer B. Here the transmission will be staged and organized using a common set of procedures that will be understood by the corresponding protocol component on Computer A. The adapter component on Computer B then prepares the data for entry onto the transmission medium. Here it will be received by Computer A's adapter component, passed up through Computer A's protocol component, and then passed to the File and Printer Sharing service on Computer A, which will perform the tasks necessary to fulfill or deny the request.

Windows 98's simplest networking configuration, a *peer-to-peer* network, amounts to little more than the preceding description. In a peer-to-peer network, a small group of computers (usually 12 or fewer) basically operate independently but use the network to support resource requests, such as the request depicted in Figure 1.2. In a peer-to-peer network, each computer is responsible for its own security. Each computer provides (or may provide) its own local authentication at startup, and each computer provides security for its own resources. In Figure 1.2, Computer A could provide security for the Records folder by requiring a password. (You'll learn more about share-level security later in this chapter.)

As a network becomes larger, a peer-to-peer configuration becomes inefficient. For networks larger than 10 or 12 PCs, it is typically more efficient to provide some form of centralized management and security. Microsoft's answer to this problem is the Windows NT domain. A *domain* is a network centered within one or more Windows NT domain controllers. A *domain controller* is a Windows NT Server computer that maintains a database of user and group accounts for the network and uses that database to create a unified security framework for the network. When a user logs on from anywhere in the domain, the user's username and password are transmitted across the network to a domain controller, where the user's logon request is checked against information stored in the account database (see Figure 1.3). If the domain controller approves the user's logon request, the user logs on, and his identity is registered on the network. Because the user's identity is known to the network, permission to access resources can be assigned directly to users or groups of users. (You'll learn more about user-level security later in this chapter.)

This simple synopsis of Windows NT domain-based security, of course, does not begin to describe the complex issues surrounding life on a large Windows NT domain. Many of the important considerations regarding Windows 98 in a Windows NT domain are based around how Windows 98 interacts with some of the services included with Windows NT Server that provide support for network clients. Some of these important services are as follows:

◆ **Dynamic Host Configuration Protocol (DHCP).** Windows NT's DHCP service provides dynamic IP address assignment. The client can request a temporary IP address. This simplifies client configuration and reduces the number of IP addresses required for the network.

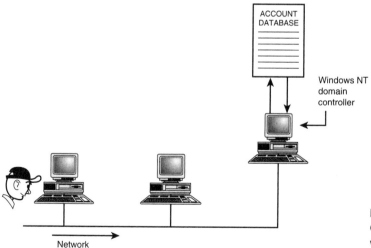

FIGURE 1.3

On an NT domain, the user's credentials are forwarded to an NT domain controller for authentication.

Windows 98 in Windows NT Domains
A Windows 98 computer does not
serve as a full, active member of a
Windows NT domain. It is often said
that a Windows 98 user logs on to
the domain, but the Windows 98 computer does not. Certain aspects of
Windows NT's domain security have
no equivalents in Windows 98. For
now, the two most important facts
about Windows 98 in a domain environment are as follows:

- The user logs on to the domain
  through Windows 98's Client for
  Microsoft Networks.

- The Windows 98 computer can
  use the domain's account database to control access to local
  resources through user-level
  access control and pass-through
  validation (described later in this
  chapter).

You'll develop a better understanding
of how Windows 98 operates in
Windows NT domains as you read
through the later chapters of this
book.

◆ **Windows Internet Name Service (WINS).** The WINS service maps IP addresses to NetBIOS computer names.

◆ **Domain Naming System (DNS).** Windows NT includes a
DNS server. DNS is the Internet's system for mapping IP
addresses to more human-friendly alphanumeric names, called
host names.

◆ **Remote Access Server (RAS).** Windows NT's Remote Access
Server service provides dial-up access for remote clients.

◆ **Internet Information Server (IIS).** Windows NT Server's
built-in Web server. Supports both Internet and intranet sites.

For the Windows 98 exam, you'll need to understand how Windows
98 interacts with these services in an NT domain-based environment. You'll learn more about Windows 98 on NT networks in
Chapter 3. You'll also need some background on Windows NT user
and group permissions, which are discussed in Chapter 5,
"Managing Resources in Windows 98."

Windows 98 can also participate in NetWare server-based networks.
Windows 98 adds support for NetWare 4.x's NetWare Directory
Services (NDS). Windows 98 can participate fully in NetWare 3.x
and NetWare 4.x networks, and can act as a peer server on NetWare
networks using Windows 98's File and Printer Sharing for NetWare
Networks (described later in this chapter). Microsoft, of course, is
not interested in making you an expert in NetWare, but you need to
know a little about NetWare to understand how Windows 98 operates in NetWare environments. Most of the NetWare-related questions will concentrate on the following:

◆ **Windows 98 NetWare client functionality.** Choosing which
NetWare client to use for each situation, configuring Windows
98 as a network client, and what you can and cannot do with
each Windows 98 NetWare client component.

◆ **IPX/SPX-compatible protocol.**

◆ **File and Printer Sharing for NetWare Networks.**

◆ **Windows 98's Service for NetWare Directory Services
(NDS).**

◆ **User-level access control using a NetWare computer as a security provider.**

See Chapter 3 for a discussion of Windows 98 in NetWare networks.

CHOOSING A FILE SYSTEM

In Windows 98, you can configure your hard disk partitions to use either the FAT16 or FAT32 file system format.

FAT16 is the 16-bit file system used with earlier versions of Windows. FAT16 is sometimes just referred to as *FAT*, and it appears in Disk Properties dialog boxes as FAT.

FAT32 is a newer file system that debuted in late versions of Windows 95. The principal benefits of FAT32 are as follows:

◆ **FAT32 supports larger partitions.** FAT16 partitions are limited to 2GB. FAT32 partitions can be as large as 2TB.

◆ **FAT32 provides better support for larger disks.** Some FAT16-compliant applications cannot determine the free or total disk space on a FAT16 disk when disk space exceeds 2GB. Also, FAT16 performance degrades for larger disks.

◆ **FAT32 uses a smaller cluster size.** A *cluster* is a chunk of data that is manipulated by the file system as a single unit. FAT32's smaller cluster size leads to better performance and more efficient use of space (as described later in this section).

FAT16 drives use a cluster size of 8KB for drives smaller than 511MB. For 511–1023MB, FAT16 uses 16MB clusters; for 1–2GB drives, FAT16 uses 32KB clusters. FAT32 uses 4KB clusters for up to 8GB drives, 8KB clusters for 8–16GB drives, and larger cluster sizes for drives larger than 16GB.

According to Microsoft, the smaller (4KB) cluster size for most FAT32 disks enables programs to load up to 50% faster. This smaller cluster size also has the effect of providing more efficient use of disk space.

> **NOTE**
>
> **FAT16 Still a Player** Just because FAT16 is older than FAT32 doesn't mean that FAT16 is old news or somewhat obsolete. FAT16 has been enhanced considerably since the early FAT (File Allocation Table) file system that was used in early versions of MS-DOS. The distinction between FAT16 and FAT32 has nothing to do with long filenames. Both FAT16 and FAT32 support long filenames.

Data is written to the disk in blocks that are sized according to the cluster size. If Windows 98 is writing a 3KB file (or a part of a file) to a 1.5GB FAT32 drive, the system will be left with 4KB – 3KB, or 1KB, of wasted space. The same operation on a 1.5GB FAT16 drive would produce approximately 32KB – 3KB, or 29KB, of wasted space. This example illustrates the added efficiency of FAT32. Overall, Microsoft contends that you can expect 10–15% more efficient use of space for larger drives with FAT32. (And, of course, drives larger than 2GB aren't even supported by FAT16.)

There are also some disadvantages to FAT32. Some reasons for not using FAT32 with Windows 98 are as follows:

◆ FAT32 is not compatible with many Windows operating systems. You can't access a FAT32 drive from Windows NT, Windows 3.x, MS-DOS, OS/2, UNIX, or early versions of Windows 95. In fact, you can access FAT32 only from Windows 95 OSR2 and Windows 98. The limited support for FAT32 is especially significant in dual-boot scenarios and in troubleshooting scenarios in which you may need to access the drive from a boot floppy disk.

◆ Disk utilities designed for FAT16 disks do not work with FAT32, although new FAT32 disk utilities are or will be available. You *cannot* compress a FAT32 drive using Microsoft's DriveSpace 3 compression utility.

◆ If you're operating in Windows 98 safe mode or MS-DOS mode, FAT32 is considerably slower than FAT16.

◆ FAT32 does not support drives smaller than 512MB.

◆ Windows 98 includes a utility that lets you convert a FAT16 partition to FAT32, but does not provide any means of changing a FAT32 partition back to FAT16. In other words, the conversion to FAT32 is irreversible.

It is important to remember that the local file system you choose for a Windows 98 computer does not affect network access to the file through File and Printer Sharing. A file on a FAT32 drive can still be accessed over the network by a client computer that doesn't support FAT32. Only the local computer interacts with the local file system. See Chapter 5 for more information about configuring hard disks in Windows 98.

NOTE

NTFS   Another Microsoft file system, NTFS, is important because it *isn't* a Windows 98 file system choice. NTFS, a Windows NT file system, is inaccessible from Windows 98. See Chapter 2, "Installing Windows 98," for more information about NTFS and its implications for Windows 98/Windows NT dual-boot.

PLANNING WINDOWS 98 SECURITY

Develop a security strategy in a Microsoft environment or a mixed Microsoft and NetWare environment.

Security is an important topic for any operating system, especially a system that is as accessible and "networkable" as Windows 98. Security considerations echo through all the objectives of the Windows 98 MCSE exam, and therefore the topic of security will appear frequently in the pages of this book.

The primary built-in methods for imposing security on a Windows 98 computer are as follows:

◆ **Authentication.** You can control who has access to the Windows 98 computer by requiring a username and password at startup.

◆ **Access control.** You can impose security on shared network resources by requiring a password (share-level security) or by directly providing or denying certain users or groups access to the resource (user-level security).

◆ **System policies and user profiles.** You can limit a user's access to the operating system through system policies and, to a lesser extent, user profiles.

As this chapter has already mentioned, Windows 98 can participate in a larger and more complex security scheme, such as a Windows NT domain or a NetWare network. Still, even in a domain or NetWare networking setting, the security on the Windows 98 computer itself typically comes down to authentication, access control, and some combination of system policies and user profiles.

The following sections introduce some important security considerations related to these topics. Each of these topics also comes up in later chapters of this book. See Chapters 3 and 5, and Chapter 6, "Managing Profiles and System Policies," for discussion of how these topics relate to Windows 98 configuration and management.

As you read through the following sections, be aware of how the information in these sections can affect the way you plan a security configuration. Also, remember that the following discussion of access control and File and Printer Sharing should be considered in the context of the greater discussion of passwords, permissions, and shares in Chapters 3 and 5. System policies and user profiles are described in greater detail in Chapter 6.

Authentication

Windows 98 provides two basic types of authentication:

◆ **Windows logon or the Windows Family logon.** You can log on directly to the Windows 98 computer using the Windows logon or the Windows Family logon. The Windows logon options can automatically execute any network logons if passwords are synchronized or if your Windows 98 computer is configured for password caching. (See Chapter 3.)

◆ **Network client logon.** You can log on to a network such as a Windows NT domain or a NetWare network at startup. You can select Client for Microsoft Networks or Microsoft Client for NetWare Networks as the primary network logon in the Configuration tab of the Network Control Panel.

You'll learn more about Windows 98 authentication in Chapter 3.

Shares and Sharing in Windows 98

Before entering a discussion of Windows 98 access control methods and file and printer sharing, it is best to pause for a look at an important Windows 98 concept: a share.

In Windows 98, a *share* is a network object containing a resource that has been made available for network access. The act of making a resource available for network access is called *sharing* the resource.

When you share a file folder, a drive, or a printer, you are configuring your Windows 98 computer to act as a file or print server and to respond to requests for access to that resource. To share drives, folders, and printers in Windows 98, you must install one of Windows 98's file and printer sharing services (discussed later in this chapter) and you must ensure that file and/or print sharing is enabled in the Configuration tab of the Network Control Panel.

N O T E   **No Sharing for Single Files** You cannot share an individual file in Windows 98. You can share file resources only by folder or drive. Because Windows 98's access control methods (described in the next section) apply to a share, you can't apply the access control methods described later in this chapter directly to a file.

To share a folder or printer, right-click on it and choose Sharing. Or, select the item in Windows Explorer or the Printers folder, choose Properties from the File menu, and click the Sharing tab.

When you share a resource, you must define a share name. The share name will appear in network browse lists, such as the list that appears in Network Neighborhood. Users will access the share by clicking on the icon beside the share name. You can also access a share by designating what is called the Universal Naming Convention (UNC) path to the share. UNC paths identify resources on networks that support NetBIOS. The UNC path to a file on a Windows 98 share could take the following form:

\\computer\share name\filename

If you want to share a resource but you don't want that resource to appear in network browse lists, you can create what is called a *hidden share* by ending the share name with a dollar sign (for example, *share$)*.

<table>
<tr><td>NOTE</td><td>**UNC Path**

A UNC path to a NetWare resource takes the form:

    \\server\volume

This path is equivalent to the NetWare path:

    server/volume</td></tr>
</table>

Share-Level and User-Level Security

In Windows 98, *access control* is the security applied to network resources. Windows 98 offers two options for controlling access:

◆ **Share-level access control.** Shares are protected with passwords. When you attempt to access a shared resource, a dialog box asks you to enter the password and doesn't give you access until you've entered the password correctly.

◆ **User-level access control.** Access to a resource is assigned through user and group permissions. Windows 98 user-level access is modeled on Windows NT's security system, in which specific users and groups are granted varying levels of access. Windows 98 does not have the capability to maintain its own user and group lists. If you decide to use user-level access control, you must configure Windows 98 to obtain an access list from a Windows NT computer or a NetWare server.

You can set the access control method for your Windows 98 computer in the Access Control tab of the Network Control Panel (see Figure 1.4). The access control setting applies to all the computer's

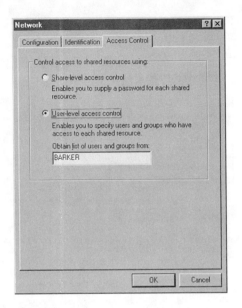

FIGURE 1.4
Use the Access Control tab in the Network Control Panel to configure share-level or user-level access control.

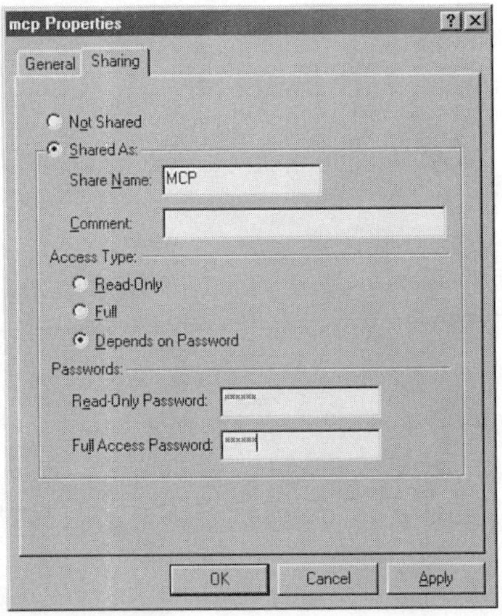

FIGURE 1.5
Enter a password in the Sharing tab of the Share Properties dialog box if share-level access control is enabled.

shared resources. You cannot decide to share one folder with user-level access control and another folder with share-level access control.

The following two subsections discuss some facts about Windows 98's access control methods that are relevant to the planning process. In real life (and on a real exam) the line between *planning* an access control method and *configuring* an access control method isn't as clear as it must be in this book. If on the exam you're faced with a question about access control, you should be prepared to use the information in these sections and also the Chapter 5 material about managing permissions and shares.

Share-Level Access

Share-level access lets you protect access to shared resources using a password. If your computer is configured for share-level access, when you share a folder, you'll be asked to specify an access type, as follows:

◆ **Read-only.** A network user accessing a file in the share can read but not change or delete the file

◆ **Full.** The network user has full control

◆ **Depends on password.** The network user's access depends on the password he enters. (See the discussion of passwords that follows.)

If you right-click on a folder and choose Sharing, the Sharing tab of the Share Properties box will appear (see Figure 1.5). Note that, depending on the access type you select, you can enter a read-only password and/or a full access password.

Share-level access is simpler and easier to implement than user-level access. Share-level access is designed specifically for peer-to-peer workgroup situations in which each PC is responsible for its own security and the network must function with minimal administrative overhead.

Some reasons for using share-level security are as follows:

◆ Share-level security is the only option if you don't have a Windows NT computer or a NetWare Server on your network.

◆ Share-level security does not require each user to have a pre-configured identity. As long as you know the password, you can access the resource.

There are also some reasons for not using share-level security. Share-level security can cause a proliferation of passwords. It is very difficult to control or systematize the spread of passwords around the network. (Windows 98's password-caching feature can help you organize and automate share-level authentication—see Chapter 3.) Also, the two gradations of share-level access (read-only or full access) provide fewer options than the range of access permissions available through user-level access.

User-Level Access

User-level security lets your Windows 98 computer use the security database of a Windows NT or NetWare system to check access requests for network shares. The Windows NT or NetWare machine serves as a *security provider*. The Windows 98 machine receives a list of user and group accounts in the security provider's account database. Permission to access a share can then be granted to those user and group accounts through Windows 98. However, Windows 98 is not capable of verifying the credentials of a user attempting to access the resource.

When a user attempts to access a shared resource on the Windows 98 machine, Windows 98 passes an authentication request to the security provider for validation. (This process is known as *pass-through* security.)

You can use user-level security to assign share permissions to specific users or groups of users. If user-level security is enabled, the Sharing tab of the Share Properties dialog box will appear as shown in Figure 1.6. In this figure, the permission level for each user or group that has been granted permission to the share is listed beside the assigned permissions. The Add button invokes the Add Users dialog box (see Figure 1.7), which lets you add additional users or groups to the access list.

User-level security lets you customize share permissions. You can click on the Edit button in the Sharing tab (refer to Figure 1.6) or the Custom button in the Add Users dialog box (refer to Figure 1.7) to invoke the Change Access Rights dialog box (see Figure 1.8). The

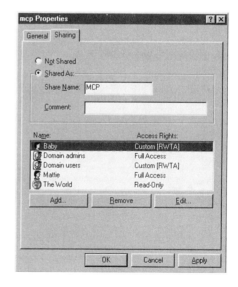

FIGURE 1.6
If user-level access control is enabled, choose the users or groups who have permission to access the share in the Sharing tab of the Share Properties dialog box.

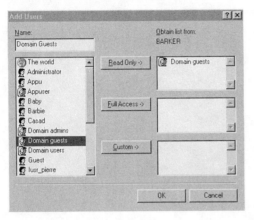

FIGURE 1.7

The Add Users dialog box lets you add users or groups to the list of those with permission to access the file.

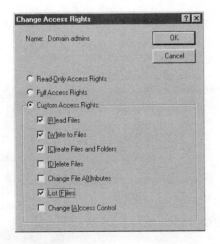

FIGURE 1.8

The Change Access Rights dialog box lets you customize access permissions.

Change Access Rights dialog box lets you customize access permissions. If you click on the Custom Access Rights option button, you can choose to assign any combination of the permissions. You'll learn more about the specifics of assigning user-level permissions to shares in Chapter 5.

User-level access is more complex and more versatile than share-level security. And user-level access is closer (than share-level security) to the user and group security systems of Windows NT domains and NetWare networks. To truly understand user-level access control, you must have an idea of how user and group permissions interrelate. Chapter 5 provides a discussion of user and group permissions. You should also remember the following important facts about user-level access:

◆ User-level access ensures that whoever accesses a share is registered on the network.

◆ User-level access lets you integrate the computer's security with the security of other computers on the network.

◆ If the Windows 98 computer will share files and folders on the NetWare network, you must use user-level access control.

◆ You must use user-level access control if you want your computer to support Windows 98 remote administration (either to connect to other computers or to receive remote administration connections). Windows 98 remote administration lets some of the key Windows 98 management utilities (such as Network Monitor, Registry Editor, and System Policy Editor) operate over the network.

The last bullet is an important point to remember for the "Planning" section of the MCSE exam. In order to use Network Monitor, Registry Editor, or System Policy Editor over the network, your computer and the remote computer must be configured for user-level access control. You'll learn more about these important management utilities in Chapters 5, 6, and 7.

File and Printer Sharing

Windows 98's file and printer sharing feature enables a Windows 98 computer to serve as a file server or a print server on the network.

In other words, users from the network can access files on a Windows 98 computer, and users from the network can access a printer that is attached to a Windows 98 computer.

Windows 98 comes with two ready-made services that provide file and printer sharing capabilities:

◆ File and Printer Sharing for Microsoft Networks

◆ File and Printer Sharing for NetWare Networks

Both file and printer sharing for Microsoft Networks and file and printer sharing for NetWare Networks have the same purpose: to accept and fulfill requests for file and print resources on the Windows 98 computer.

Like the access control methods discussed in the preceding section, these file and printer sharing services cannot really be viewed in isolation and must instead be considered in the context of configuring and managing shared resources.

On the subject of planning a security strategy, a few important points warrant mention. You can use your file and printer sharing configuration to control access to your Windows 98 computer in any of the following ways:

◆ By opting not to install one of the file and printer sharing services.

◆ By opting not to enable file and/or print sharing for one of the services.

◆ By choosing not to share a particular folder or printer. (See the discussion of sharing folders earlier in this chapter.) If a resource isn't shared, it can't be accessed over the network regardless of how you've configured the file and printer sharing service.

◆ By defining a share as a hidden share so it doesn't show up on network browse lists. (See the discussion of hidden shares earlier in this chapter.)

◆ By controlling access to the shared resource through share-level or user-level access control, as described in the preceding section.

◆ By selectively unbinding the file and printer sharing service from specific protocols.

The last bullet deserves some special attention. As you'll learn in Chapter 3, each protocol you install on your system must be *bound* to the services that will use the protocol. By choosing not to bind a particular service to a protocol, you prevent the users who access the computer through that protocol from accessing the network. This is often an effective security strategy. Consider the configuration shown in Figure 1.9.

A network administrator may want users on the local network to share files, but she may be extremely reluctant to let users from the Internet access files on the local network. Users connecting from the Internet will be using the TCP/IP protocol. The network administrator can remove the binding for file and print sharing under the TCP/IP protocol (refer to Figure 1.9) and retain the file and print service binding for a protocol that will be used on the local network, such as the NetBEUI protocol.

In Windows 98, as you'll learn in Chapter 3, a service is actually bound to a protocol/adapter combination; so, in effect, you can unbind file and printer sharing for a particular adapter even if both networks use the same protocol. In Figure 1.9, for instance, the local network can use file and print sharing bound to TCP/IP bound

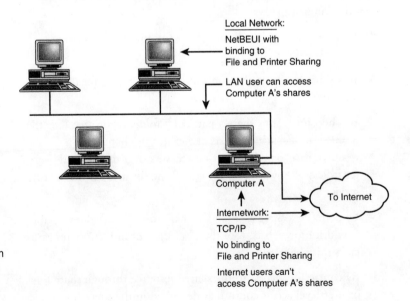

FIGURE 1.9

An installed protocol won't function on a given network unless it is bound to the appropriate network adapter.

to the computer's Ethernet adapter card and can disable File and
Printer Sharing for TCP/IP bound to the Dial-Up adapter.
When Computer A connects to the Internet through a dial-up
Internet service provider, Internet users will not be able to access
shares on Computer A.

See Chapters 3 and 5 for more information about configuring File
and Printer Sharing and managing shared resources. The following
sections provide some additional background on File and Printer
Sharing for Microsoft Networks and File and Printer Sharing for
NetWare Networks.

File and Printer Sharing for Microsoft Networks

File and Printer Sharing for Microsoft Networks is basically a *Server
Message Block (SMB)* server. SMB is the Microsoft Network file-sharing protocol. File and Printer Sharing for Microsoft Networks can
provide File and Print Services for network client systems that use
the SMB protocol. SMB systems include Windows 95/98, Windows
NT, Windows for Workgroups, LAN Manager, OS/2 Warp Server,
IBM LAN Server, Samba, and Digital Pathworks 32.

Microsoft provides the following summary of important facts about
File and Printer Sharing for Microsoft Networks. Keep these facts in
mind as you study for the "Planning" section of the Windows 98
MCSE exam:

◆ If you're using user-level security and you plan to implement
   File and Print Services for Microsoft Networks, a domain controller must be the security provider.

◆ If you're planning to use File and Printer Sharing for Microsoft
   Networks, you must also enable the client service Client for
   Microsoft Networks (see Chapter 3).

◆ You can't run File and Print Sharing for Microsoft Networks at
   the same time you're running File and Printer Sharing for
   NetWare Networks.

File and Printer Sharing for NetWare Networks

File and Printer Sharing for NetWare Networks provides File and Printer Sharing services for NetWare networks using the NCP file-sharing protocol. File and Printer Sharing for NetWare Networks can provide file and printer sharing services to any NetWare-compatible client.

Keep the following facts in mind as you study for the "Planning" section:

◆ If you're using File and Printer Sharing for NetWare Networks, you must use user-level security. The security provider (the computer supplying the user list) must be a NetWare server.

◆ File and Printer Sharing for NetWare Networks takes its user information from the NetWare bindery. (The bindery is a database that contains user information.) If the NetWare server is a NetWare 4.x server (which doesn't use a bindery), the NetWare server *must* be providing a bindery emulation context.

◆ The Windows 98 computer must access the NetWare security provider for pass-through validation of resource requests. You must create an account called Windows_Passthru (with no password) on the NetWare server that the Windows 98 machine can use to access the NetWare bindery.

◆ The computer using File and Printer Sharing for NetWare Networks must also be running Microsoft's Client for NetWare Networks as a network client. You *cannot* use an equivalent Novell client such as Novell Client for Windows 95/98 on a machine that is using File and Printer Sharing for NetWare Networks. (As stated earlier, however, a client using Novell Client for Windows 95/98 can *connect to* a Windows 98 computer that is running File and Printer Sharing for NetWare Networks).

See Chapter 3 for more information about how to configure File and Printer Sharing for NetWare Networks.

Planning System Policies

Windows 98's system policies feature lets a network administrator create a set of configuration settings that will override settings in the Registry. You can use system policies to limit user access to the system and to define certain aspects of the Windows 98 configuration.

Microsoft uses system policy templates to define a set of important and useful policy settings that you can configure using an interface tool called the System Policy Editor. Once again, Microsoft splits its coverage of system policies between the "Planning" section and the "Configuring and Managing Resources" section of the objective list. In this book, you'll find a description of system policies in Chapter 6. See Chapter 6 for a complete discussion of system policies and the System Policy Editor.

The policy settings you create using the System Policy Editor are saved to a file called `config.pol`. When the system starts, Windows 98 looks for the `config.pol` file. On a Windows NT domain, Windows 98 looks for the `config.pol` file in the `netlogon` share of the primary domain controller. You can also specify a local location for the `config.pol` system policy file.

If you're using Microsoft Service for NetWare Directory Services, you can implement system policies for a Windows 98 computer on an NDS-based NetWare network. (Again, see Chapter 6 for more information about implementing system policies.)

Most of the system policy settings have some relevance to security and the topic of developing a security strategy. The best way to study for system policy questions is to load the System Policy Editor on your computer and spend some time reviewing the various settings. (See Exercise 1.5 for a description of how to install and use the System Policy Editor.)

Some important system policy security settings are shown in Table 1.1.

TABLE 1.1

IMPORTANT SYSTEM POLICY SECURITY SETTINGS

Policy Setting	Setting Options
Computer Policies	
Access Control	Force User-Level Control Access
Logon	Logon Banner
	Require Validation from Network for Windows Access
	Don't Show Last User at Logon
	Don't Show Logon Progress
Password	Hide Share Passwords with Asterisks
	Disable Password Caching
	Require Alphanumeric Windows Password
	Minimum Password Length
User Policies	
Sharing	Disable File Sharing Controls
	Disable Print Sharing Controls
Windows 98 System/ Shell/Restrictions	(Several settings that remove features such as the Run command or Network Neighborhood from the user interface)
Control Panel/Display	Restrict Display Control Panel Settings
Control Panel/Network	Restrict Network Control Panel Settings
Control Panel/Passwords	Restrict Passwords Control Panel Settings
Control Panel/System	Restrict System Control Panel Settings
Restrictions	Disable Registry Editing Tools
	Only Run Allowed Windows Apps
	Disable Single-Mode MS-DOS Apps

Some system policy settings that Microsoft identifies as being particularly significant to planning a security strategy are the following computer policies in the Passwords subtree:

◆ **Disable Password Caching.** Password caching was discussed earlier in this chapter, and you'll learn more about password caching in Chapter 3. If password caching is disabled, Windows 98 will not cache the resource password the first time a user connects to a resource.

◆ **Require an Alphanumeric Windows 98 Logon Password.** A password that contains numbers and letters is harder to guess.

◆ **Require Minimum Windows 98 Logon Password Length.**
This policy lets you specify the minimum length for Windows
98 logon passwords.

◆ **Require Validation from Network for Windows Access.**
Through this setting, you can prevent users from bypassing the
Logon dialog box and force users to log on through the net-
work before accessing Windows 98. (See Chapter 3.)

The Control Panel and Shell system policy settings are also a powerful means of providing security by limiting the scope of the user's
activities. For instance, you can eliminate the Run command or the
DOS prompt so users will not be able to run unauthorized programs. Or, you can restrict the Control Panel applications, such as
the Network or Password applications, so users can't change their
configurations.

NOTE **Enable User Profiles** You must
enable user profiles if you want to
control user settings through system
policies. See Chapter 6.

User Profiles

Windows 98's user profiles feature lets each user customize the
Windows 98 operating environment. Each user's user profile can
contain custom settings for items such as the following:

◆ The Start menu

◆ Desktop settings

◆ Shortcuts

◆ Control Panel settings

A user profile is really a collection of settings that are saved under
the user's name when the user exits Windows, and are restored when
the user logs on again.

You enable user profiles through the User Profiles tab in the
Passwords Properties Control Panel (see Figure 1.10).

To enable user profiles, select Users Can Customize Their
Preferences and Desktop Settings. Note that you can elect to include
desktop icons and Network Neighborhood contents and/or Start
menu and Programs groups in the user profile.

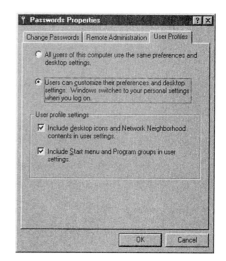

FIGURE 1.10
Configure Windows 98 for user profiles through
the User Profiles tab in the Passwords
Properties Control Panel.

When user profiles are enabled, you can make changes to your desktop configuration, and Windows 98 will save those changes (unless you're using mandatory profiles, which are described later).

Windows 98 supports three types of user profiles:

◆ **Local profiles.** User profiles stored on a single computer that are used only when the user logs on to that computer.

◆ **Roving (or roaming) profiles.** User profiles available through the network. The user's roving profile automatically follows the user to other computers on the network.

◆ **Mandatory profiles.** Profiles that users can't change. The network administrator can define user profile settings for the user, and those settings will automatically be invoked at logon.

As you'll learn in Chapter 6, Windows 98 creates a special directory for each user's user profile. The user profile directory includes a personalized copy of the Registry file user.dat (which contains profile-related settings). Depending on your configuration, the user profile directory may also contain other folders with configuration items such as the desktop shortcuts that will appear at logon. The user profile directory can also contain folders defining a personalized Start menu and shortcuts to recently accessed files. Windows 98 will use the information in the user profile to build an individualized user interface (wallpaper, Start menu, shortcuts, Favorites, and so forth) that will appear when you log on.

If you configure your Windows 98 computer for local profiles, you'll find the user profiles directories in the Windows/Profiles folder.

You can use network-based user profiles on either Windows NT domains or NetWare networks. If you're using roaming or mandatory profiles on a Windows NT domain, the profile information will be stored in each user's home directory, so make sure a home directory is defined for each user in Windows NT's User Manager for Domains.

If you're using roaming or mandatory profiles with a NetWare network, the user profile information is stored in a user's \Mail directory, unless your network uses Microsoft Service for NetWare Directory Services (NDS), in which case the profile information is stored in the user's home directory.

For full-featured roaming and mandatory profiles, the server with the profile information must support long file names. If the server doesn't support long file names, the user.dat file will still roam to the user's logon location, but other user-profile components, such as the Favorites list and the Start menu, may not download.

Microsoft also recommends that you use the same directory and hard drive letter for the Windows directory on all computers that will receive the roaming or mandatory profile. For instance, use C:\Windows for the Windows directory on all computers. Don't use C:\Windows on one computer, C:\W98 on another computer, and D:\Windows on another computer, for example.

Chapter 6 provides a complete discussion of user profiles in Windows 98. For purposes of planning a security strategy, pay particular attention to the following user-profile topics:

◆ **Mandatory profiles.** Mandatory user profiles are an important security tool. You can use mandatory profiles to force a user to use a specific desktop configuration. Be sure you know how to set up mandatory profiles (see Chapter 6).

◆ **User profile settings.** The User Profiles tab in the Passwords Control Panel lets you define what elements will be part of the user profile (refer to Figure 1.10).

◆ **System policies.** You can enable or disable user profiles through the Computer Policy/Windows 98 System/User Profile/Enable User Profiles settings. The User Policies/ Windows 98 System/Control Panel/Passwords/Restrict Passwords Control Panel setting lets you disable the Passwords Control Panel or hide the User Profiles page from the Passwords Control Panel.

Once again, see Chapter 6 for more on how User Profiles work and when you should use them.

Windows 98 Security

On any "networkable" operating system such as Windows 98, security is a major concern. Native Windows 98 security is implemented through some combination of the following elements:

- ◆ Authentication

- ◆ Access control

- ◆ System policies and user profiles

Windows 98 supports share-level or user-level access control for shared resources. Share-level access control protects the shared resource with a password. User-level access control protects the resource using user and group lists from a Windows NT computer or a NetWare server acting as a security provider.

System policies and user profiles help provide security by limiting the user's access to the Windows 98 operating environment.

Case Study: Best Distributors

ESSENCE OF THE CASE

Here are the essential elements of the case:

- Windows 98 installed on 45 computers

- Centralized server for data

- User policies for most users

- Mandatory profiles for the sales staff

- Printer sharing for two users

SCENARIO

Best Distributors, a vending machine distribution company, would like to implement Windows 98 throughout its office of 45 computers. The company requires a centralized server for data, which must be easy to learn and work with. Best Distributors would like to implement system policies for most of its users. All of the sales people, who are rarely in the office, share five PCs. The office manager would like to configure the five PCs so that the machines look and feel the same for all of the sales staff no matter which computer they are using. Two users will share

continues

CASE STUDY: BEST DISTRIBUTORS

continued

printers that are attached to their PCs. All other printers and data will be shared from the server.

ANALYSIS

Each computer would be installed with Windows 98. A Windows NT Server domain would probably be the best choice for this environment because of its ease of use and similar interface to Windows 98. (NetWare Servers would also satisfy the core requirements but Windows NT's interface is already similar to Windows 98.) The server, in addition to storing data, can be used

to host the user system policies, roaming profiles, and mandatory profiles for the office staff. The two Windows 98 machines that would share their printers would require the Microsoft File and Printer Sharing support to share out their printers.

Because the server is a Windows NT Server, it should be installed as a Primary Domain Controller so that all of the Windows 98 machines could be configured to log on to the domain for more security throughout the company.

CHAPTER SUMMARY

This chapter introduced some important concepts you'll need to understand in order to plan a Windows 98 configuration. You learned about Windows 98 networking models and about the FAT16 and FAT32 file systems. This chapter also examined File and Printer Sharing and discussed some Windows 98 components that help provide security for your system, such as user-level and share-level access control, user profiles, and system policies.

The Windows 98 exam is very scenario-based. For the most part, you won't see planning questions that simply ask you to recall basic facts. Instead, you'll use the facts and concepts explored in this chapter to navigate through network scenarios, and the trick will be determining which concepts are applicable to each situation. Be prepared to think. And be ready to sort through the details to isolate the critical fact or feature of Windows 98 that the question is really asking about.

KEY TERMS
- workgroup
- Peer-to-peer network
- domain
- FAT16
- FAT32
- system policies
- profile
- shared resource
- user-level security
- share-level security
- security provider

APPLY YOUR KNOWLEDGE

Exercises

1.1   Choosing Between a Domain and a Workgroup

This exercise will present six scenarios. Your task is to determine whether a workgroup or a domain would be appropriate for each scenario.

Estimated Time: 20 minutes

1. Global Marketing has 12 offices around the world. Each office has approximately eight employees. Employees need to share file resources only with the other employees in their own office. Communication between the offices is through email via an Internet service provider. Money is a major concern until the "big contract" comes through.

2. Tazwell Brothers Insurance Company has grown to 37 employees in one building. Currently the company is using Windows 98 but it is not networked. The Tazwell brothers want a reliable, secure network in which data can be centrally stored and users can access databases and applications on the network.

3. Gwen and John have just started a catering business. John has a Windows 98 machine that has all of the recipes in a database. Gwen handles all of the finances and marketing on her Windows 98 machine. They agree that their computers need to be networked. John thinks a domain is necessary to provide security for shared resources. Gwen disagrees. Who is correct?

4. Blue Screen Manufacturers has implemented Windows 98 throughout the company. It is currently using several peer-to-peer workgroups for the different departments in the company: Sales, Finance, Marketing, and so on. In all, the company has eight workgroups with a combined total of 250 users. Your job is to redesign the network and bring centralized administration to the job.

5. Maria, an outside sales rep, is upset because whenever she logs on to a different computer in your office, her profile is different from the one for the machine she logged on to earlier in the day. She threatens to quit and to take all of her high-paying accounts with her to your competition. You'll do anything to avoid that. What can you do to keep her happy?

6. You have just been hired as the new network administrator for a fast-growing publishing company. Right now the company has eight employees but is hiring five new people a week for the next year. Your first job is to implement a network that not only is capable of growing at a rapid pace but also will allow users to share data, access printers, and the Internet.

Answers to Exercise 1.1:

1. Global Marketing should create peer-to-peer workgroups in each office. A workgroup would allow users in each office to share data among themselves, send email to employees in other offices, and keep costs to a minimum. When that big contract comes through, a domain with Wide Area Network (WAN) inter-office connectivity would be ideal to centralize network administration and bring security up a level.

2. The Tazwell brothers want a domain. In a Windows NT domain, data and applications can be stored and accessed off the server, and Windows NT offers security, stability, and networking.

APPLY YOUR KNOWLEDGE

3. Gwen and John could get by on a workgroup. Because their new company has only two computers, they should take advantage of Windows 98's built-in networking, Microsoft backup, and the ability to join a domain if their network later requires it.

4. Blue Screen Manufacturers needs a domain. With 250 users, managing this network would be quite a task. A Windows NT domain would bring centralized administration, roaming profiles, and server-stored policies, and would create one unit to manage instead of several. Resources that are shared from Windows 98 workstations could now be managed through user-level management. But it is best to move as many resources as possible to the NT Servers. Windows NT would bring a new level of security and administration to Blue Screen's network.

5. Maria is upset because her profile is not a roaming profile. Her profile is being saved locally on an individual computer rather than being updated to a server. To keep Maria happy you'll have to implement a domain and then create a roaming profile for Maria so that any computer in the network that she uses will download her profile from the server.

6. You should implement a domain. Although in the short term a workgroup would suffice, things could become very complex very quickly. A domain allows for growth and for a large number of users. In addition to user management, a Windows NT Server acting as a PDC can also be used as a file and print server, an Intranet server, and a Web server.

1.2 Choosing Between FAT16 and FAT32

Exercise 1.2 will present several scenarios for which you will have to choose the best file systems, fully supporting your answers.

Estimated Time: 10 minutes

1. Mark wants to access a partition from either Windows 98 or Windows for Workgroups in a dual-boot configuration.

2. Mary has added a 4GB drive to her system. This drive will host a large database.

3. Julie wants to share data on her PC with a coworker who uses NT Workstation.

4. Rex never wants to use disk compression, but he also hates to waste space on his hard drive.

5. Sarah wants to use long filenames.

Answers to Exercise 1.2:

1. FAT16. To dual-boot, FAT16 is required because DOS, Windows 3.x, Windows 95a, and Windows NT 4.0 cannot recognize FAT32.

2. FAT32. FAT32 can format partitions up to 2TB.

3. FAT16 or FAT32. When sharing data over the network, it doesn't matter which file system is used.

4. FAT32. There is no disk compression on FAT32 and it uses smaller cluster sizes, therefore conserving space.

5. FAT16 or FAT32. Long filenames are supported on both file systems.

APPLY YOUR KNOWLEDGE

1.3 Converting a Drive to FAT32

This exercise walks you through the process of converting a FAT16 file system to a FAT32 file system. It requires Windows 98 and, naturally, a hard-drive partition formatted as FAT16 (sometimes just called FAT) that can be converted to FAT32. The built-in converter will be used during this exercise.

> **NOTE**
> **Remember:** You can't change back to FAT16 after you convert the partition to FAT32. Refer to the section "Choosing a File System" to ensure that FAT32 will meet your permanent needs.

Estimated Time: 10 minutes

1. To determine the file system currently in place, open Windows Explorer.

2. Right-click on the drive to be converted to FAT32 and choose Properties. On the General tab it should read FAT. Click OK and exit Explorer.

3. Choose Start, Programs, Accessories, System Tools, and then choose the Drive Converter (FAT32).

4. The Drive Converter (FAT32) Wizard appears. Read the directions on the wizard and then click Next.

5. Follow the wizard through the steps to convert your partition to FAT32. After rebooting, your partition will be FAT32.

6. Open Explorer and confirm that the partition selected is now the FAT32 file system.

1.4 Implementing User Profiles

This exercise shows you how to implement user profiles. It requires that Windows 98 be installed. The exercise is based on a standalone workstation, so all profiles and users are local to the Microsoft Windows 98 machine. If your workstation is configured to log on to a domain or NetWare server, you will want to add two test users, Fred and Sally, to your NetWare server or Windows NT domain. (The information covered in this exercise is not necessarily explored in detail within this chapter itself—that exploration takes place in Chapter 6. The following instruction, however, lets you really get your feet wet with user profiles.)

Estimated Time: 30 minutes

1. From Start, choose Settings, Control Panel.

2. In Control Panel, choose Passwords.

3. From the Passwords applet, choose the User Profiles tab. From this tab choose the option that allows users to customize their preferences and desktop settings.

4. At the bottom of the User Profiles tab, select both of the following options: Include Desktop Icons and Include Start Menu and Program Groups.

5. Choose OK and reboot your PC.

6. After you reboot, log on to Windows 98 as Fred.

7. You will be prompted that you (Fred) have not logged on to this PC before—would you like to save your settings? Choose Yes.

8. Right-click on your desktop and choose Properties.

9. Change your screensaver, color scheme, and wallpaper settings for Fred and then exit the Display applet.

10. From the Start menu, choose Log of Fred.

11. Now log on as Sally. Again, You will be prompted that you have not logged on to this PC before—would you like to save your settings? Choose Yes.

12. Notice that Fred's settings are not displayed. Log off as Sally and log back on as Fred.

13. Notice that Fred's environment is restored.

1.5   Implementing Local System Policies

This exercise will introduce you to the idea of creating system policies and storing your system policy on the local computer. A local policy is ideal if Windows NT or NetWare is not present on your network, or if your Windows 98 machine is a standalone computer. Make certain you have completed Exercise 1.4 before continuing with this exercise. System policies require that profiles be enabled. (The information covered in this exercise is not necessarily explored in detail within this chapter itself—that exploration takes place in Chapter 6. The following instruction, however, lets you really get your feet wet with system policies.)

Estimated Time: 40 minutes

1. Insert your Windows 98 CD-ROM.

2. Click Start, Settings.

3. Click on Control Panel.

4. Open the Add/Remove Programs applet.

5. Choose the Windows Setup tab and then click on Have Disk. Browse the CD-ROM and drill down to `<CD-ROM drive>\tools\reskit\ netadmin\poledit\poledit.inf`. Click OK when you've found it.

6. Click OK again to install the System Policy Editor. You'll be prompted to select the component you want to install. Select the System Policy Editor and click Install. Stay in the Add/Remove Program applet.

In addition to adding the policy editor, you also have to add the group policy support (grouppol.dll) to enable processing of group policies. To add group policy support, continue on with these steps:

7. From the Windows Setup tab, click on Have Disk. Browse the CD-ROM and drill down to `<CD-ROM drive>\tools\reskit\netadmin\ poledit\poledit.inf`. Click OK when you've found it.

8. From the list of components, select Group Policies and then click OK.

9. Click OK again to exit the Add/Remove Programs applet.

10. Close Control Panel.

11. The System Policy Editor has been installed and a shortcut for it has been created. To open the System Policy Editor, click Start, Programs.

12. Click Accessories, System Tools.

13. Click System Policy Editor.

14. The System Policy Editor opens. You must create a new file to begin. Click on File, New Policy; or click on the New Policy icon (it looks like a blank sheet of paper on the toolbar).

15. An untitled policy has been created. The default computer and the default user are displayed. The default computer affects the local computer, while the default user represents all users that log on to this machine. You want to work only with

APPLY YOUR KNOWLEDGE

the default values when you have a very wide system policy change that you want all users to have implemented.

16. On the toolbar, click the icon for adding a new user. This button looks like a single user with a star over his head.

17. Enter **Sam** as the name of the user you'd like to add to the policy and then press Enter.

18. Double-click the icon that represents Sam, and his properties will open. You can now restrict Sam's access on this computer.

19. Click the plus sign (+) by Windows 98 System, and a hierarchy of options will become available.

20. Click the plus sign by the Shell hierarchy and then click the plus sign by Restrictions. We are going to restrict Sam from doing several things on this PC.

NOTE

Box Shading Defined A gray box means that this particular setting is ignored in the Registry. A white box means to clear whatever setting is currently in the Registry. A white box with a check mark means to change this value in the Registry.

---

21. Check the following restrictions for Sam:

    • Remove the Run command.

    • Remove folders from Settings on the Start menu.

    • Hide Network Neighborhood.

    • Don't save these settings on exit.

23. Click the plus sign by Control Panel.

24. Click the plus sign by Display and then click the box next to the Restrict Display applet.

25. In the section at the bottom of Sam's properties, there are five settings you can implement for Sam's access to Control Panel. Select Hide Screen Saver Page and Hide Settings Page. Allow Sam access into all other sections of the Display applet.

26. Click the plus sign by the Printers section under Control Panel.

27. Click the Restrict Printer settings. Again notice there are choices across the bottom of Sam's properties. Because you don't want Sam to delete or add any printers to this computer, select both of these options.

28. Click the plus sign by the Desktop Display and then select the Color Scheme. For this exercise, you want Sam to always use the Rose 256 color scheme.

29. Click the plus sign by Restrictions.

30. You don't want Sam to be able to run any Registry editing tools. If you did want to, you could designate what applications Sam can run on this computer. The problem with this option, however, is that you must designate all the applications Sam can run, not the ones that Sam cannot run.

31. Click OK to close Sam's properties.

32. Click File to Save and then save the file as `config.pol` in the Windows directory.

33. Finally, to make the policy work, you must specify that the Registry not to look for a policy on the network, (which is the default), but rather look for one in the Windows directory.

34. Click on File, Open Registry. Double-click on the Local Computer icon.

35. Click the plus sign by Update and then click on the text `Remote Update`. The default is Automatic, which is to look out on the network for a `config.pol` file. You need to change this value to Local.

36. Click on Update Mode and change the value to Manual (use a specific path).

37. In the field path for manual update, enter `C:\windows\config.pol` (assuming your Windows directory is on the C: drive) and then click OK. Make certain that you enter the path including the file name `config.pol`, or your policy file will not work.

38. Exit the System Policy Editor.

39. Click on Start and then log off as whomever you are logged on as. Confirm that you do want to log off.

40. Log on to the system as Sam.

41. Observe that Sam's policy is in effect by testing out the restrictions you gave to Sam.

1.6 Implementing File and Printer Sharing with Share-Level Security for Microsoft Networks

This exercise will implement Windows 98's File and Printer Sharing mechanisms utilizing share-level security. Recall that share-level security is based on passwords to access resources. Share-level security is typically used in workgroup environments in which no central account database resides.

To complete this exercise successfully, you'll need at least two computers that are in the same network.

Estimated Time: 20 minutes

1. Click Start, Settings.

2. Click Control Panel, then open the Network applet.

3. On the Configuration tab, click the Add button.

4. A dialog box will appear prompting you to add a network component. Choose Service and then Click Add.

5. Another dialog box appears prompting you to choose a type of service. From the list of manufacturers, click Microsoft.

6. When Microsoft is selected, a list of available Network services will appear in the right pane of this dialog box. Choose File and Print Sharing for Microsoft Networks and then choose OK.

7. Choose OK again to confirm your selections. A System Settings Change warning will appear, prompting you to restart your system. Choose Yes and your PC will restart.

8. After your PC restarts, open Control Panel and then open the Network applet.

9. Select the Access Control tab and confirm that Share-Level Access Control is selected. Click OK to close the Network applet.

10. Click Start, Programs.

11. Click Windows Explorer to open Explorer.

12. On your C: drive, create a folder called `Sample`. Click on your C: drive to display its contents. Click on the File menu and Choose New, Folder. The folder will be created as `New Folder` on your C: drive.

APPLY YOUR KNOWLEDGE

(You can also create a new folder by right-clicking in the contents of C:, then choosing New and the folder.)

13. Type in `Sample`, press Enter, and the folder is renamed.

14. Right-click the folder named Sample. A shortcut menu appears from the shortcut menu; choose Sharing.

15. The Sharing tab of the Sample folder properties appears. The default is Not Shared. Select the attribute of Shared As.

16. When you select the attribute of Shared As, the share name field is filled in for you with the name of the folder. Click in the Comment field and type in `testing share-level security`.

17. In the Access Type, select Read Only.

18. Assign the password as `123` and then press Enter or click OK. You'll be prompted to confirm your password. Enter `123` and click OK.

19. `Sample` is now shared as Sample with a password of 123.

20. To test out the share, connect to that computer over the network and try to add a document to that share.

21. At a different computer on the network, double-click Network Neighborhood to open it.

22. Find the machine on which `Sample` resides and double-click the machine to open it.

23. Double-click the `Sample` share to access the directory. You will be prompted to supply a password to connect to the resource. Enter the password `123` and press Enter.

24. You are now connected to the `Sample` share. Right-click anywhere in the contents of the sample share windows and click New, Folder to attempt to create a folder. You cannot add anything to the folder because you only have read permissions on the folder.

Review Questions

1. Sam would like to dual-boot between DOS 6.22 and Windows 98. What file format should he use for his active partition?

2. Benjamin has 10 PCs that are going to be installed with Windows 98. He would like each user to maintain his own machine and network resources. What is the type of network Benjamin would like to install?

3. Holly, the Windows NT administrator, is in charge of migrating her 300 users from Windows 95 to Windows 98. She is concerned that she will have to reconfigure all network settings after Windows 98 is installed. Is this a valid concern?

4. Stephen wants to restrict users from changing their display settings and other hardware attributes with Microsoft Windows 98. What should he implement to restrict users from tinkering with their machines?

5. Donald is unhappy because his Start menu looks different on each machine he uses throughout the domain. He wants his Start menu to be the same on each machine he uses throughout the domain. What should you implement for him?

6. Virginia, the manager of the Sales department, wants all sales reps to have desktops that look the same throughout the Sales workgroup. How would you implement this for her?

APPLY YOUR KNOWLEDGE

7. What is a system policy?

8. You have created a system policy file and saved it in the home folder for each user. The policy is not implemented for the users in your Windows NT domain. What is the problem?

Exam Questions

1. Your new hard drive is a 6GB hard drive. You add it to the system but when you open FDISK to partition the drive, you get a warning message about large disk support. Why is the message important?

   A. It allows FDISK to interact with the BIOS of your computer.

   B. It enables Windows 98 to access drives larger than 512KB.

   C. It means that Windows 98 will use FAT32 to format any partitions created during that session of FDISK if you enable large disk support.

   D. It means that your hardware is not Plug and Play compatible.

2. How large can a FAT32 partition be?

   A. 2GB

   B. 4GB

   C. 2TB

   D. 16TB

3. You would like to implement FAT32 on several of your company's Windows 98 computers. David, your boss, is concerned though that the Windows 95 machines will not be able to access the shared folders on the Windows 98 machines because the Windows 98 machines are using FAT32 while the 95 machines are only using FAT. Is he right or wrong? Why?

   A. Right. FAT32 cannot be accessed by Windows 95.

   B. Wrong. FAT32 partitions work fine with Windows 95.

   C. Right. Windows 95 cannot detect partitions that are formatted with FAT32 if they are larger than 2GB in size.

   D. Wrong. On the network it doesn't matter what the file system of the machine sharing data is. The file format will be translated via the network.

4. Your company's network consists of five work-groups: Sales, Marketing, Research, Finance, and Production. Your boss complains that when he opens up Network Neighborhood he sees several computers, but not everyone's. To see the rest of the network, he has to open the entire network and then open the workgroup to get to the share he's after at that time. How would you explain this to him?

   A. Network Neighborhood always displays the list of computers in your workgroup first.

   B. His machine's network adapter card is dys-functional.

   C. He has not logged on to the Windows 98 machine. You must always log on first or you won't access all of the computers in the net-work.

   D. He needs to reboot his machine in safe mode.

5. Of the following, what are two reasons to choose a domain over a Windows 98 peer-to-peer workgroup?

   A. Domains can provide centralized administration of users.

   B. Workgroups cost more to provide than do domains.

   C. Domains offer security for data through the NTFS file system.

   D. Workgroups have security only if you are using the FAT32 file system.

6. What is the difference between user-level and share-level security?

   A. User-level security allows access based on a user's login ID, whereas share-level security is password based.

   B. User-level security is based on each user's password, whereas share-level security is based on each user's logon ID.

   C. User-level security is based on a NetWare account, whereas share-level security is based on a Windows NT account.

   D. User-level security is based on a Windows NT account, whereas share-level security is based on a NetWare account.

7. What are user profiles?

   A. User profiles are restrictions that are set up for a user and usually stored on a server.

   B. User profiles define the user environment that the user sees when he or she logs on to a Windows 98 machine.

   C. User profiles determine what applications a user is allowed to run on a Windows 98 machine.

   D. User profiles control what times a user can log on to a machine.

8. You are in charge of 70 users in a Windows NT domain. The 70 users are constantly changing their configurations of Windows 98 and they are adding screen savers, sounds, and other programs that are not supposed to be added to the 98 environment. In addition, you would like to force each user to agree to a logon statement warning them that the computers and data therein belong to your company. How can you implement this?

   A. Create a profile for each user. Put the logon statement in Notepad and save the file in the Startup folder. Finally, change the profile to a mandatory profile and save it in the `C:\Windows` directory of each Windows 98 machine.

   B. Create a profile for each user. Put the logon statement in Notepad and save the file in the Startup folder. Finally, change the profile to a mandatory profile and save it in the home folder of each user.

   C. Create a policy file with the appropriate restrictions for each group. Save the policy file in the `Netlogon` share of the domain controller.

   D. Create a policy file with the appropriate restrictions for each group. Save the policy file in the `Netlogon` share of the domain controller. You must also add group policy support on each of the client computers through Add/Remove programs.

APPLY YOUR KNOWLEDGE

9. Rosemary is a member of the Global Sales, Marketing, and Finance groups. She notices that Bob, who is also a member of the Sales group, has a slightly different Start menu than she does, and Bob cannot change his screensaver but she can. What would be controlling this behavior?

   A. Profiles.

   B. Policies.

   C. OEM installations of W98.

   D. Bob has a faulty installation of W98.

10. You would like to configure all of your Windows 98 computers to log on to the domain. You open the Network applet and configure your machine to log on to the Marketing domain. However, when you try to log on to the domain, your username and password cannot be found. What could be causing the problem? Choose all that apply.

    A. You do not have a user account in the domain.

    B. You have typed in your username incorrectly.

    C. Your account has been disabled from the domain.

    D. Your domain password is required to be changed at the first login.

Answers to Review Questions

1. Sam must keep his active partition formatted with FAT16 to dual-boot. DOS does not recognize FAT32. (For more information, refer to the section "Choosing a File System.")

2. Benjamin should install a peer-to-peer network. (For more information, refer to the section "Networking Windows 98.")

3. No. Holly's network settings will be preserved through the upgrade to Microsoft Windows 98. (For more information, refer to the section "Networking Windows 98.")

4. Stephen needs to implement system policies. (For more information, refer to the section "Planning Windows 98 Security.")

5. You would have to implement roaming user profiles in your network so that Donald could have his profile downloaded to each PC he logged on to. If you don't want Donald to be able to change his profile, use a mandatory user profile. (For more information, refer to the section "Planning Windows 98 Security.")

6. For Virginia to have a standard desktop, you would have to implement mandatory profiles for the Sales department users. (For more information, refer to the section "Planning Windows 98 Security.")

7. A system policy is a setting that enforces Registry restrictions that control what activities users are allowed to do, how their machines look and feel, and where system components, such as the Start menu items, are stored. (For more information, refer to the section "Planning Windows 98 Security.")

8. System policies must be stored in `%SystemRoot%\system32\Repl\Import\Scripts` (also called the `NetLogon` share) on Windows NT Domain Controllers if policies are to be enforced from a domain controller. (For more information, refer to the section "Planning Windows 98 Security.")

APPLY YOUR KNOWLEDGE

Answers to Exam Questions

1. **C.** FAT partitions are limited to 2GB in size. FAT32 allows partitions in sizes up to 2TB, or roughly 2,000GB. If you want to create partitions smaller than 2GB or partitions formatted with FAT, don't allow large disk support. (For more information on FDISK, refer to Chapter 5.)

2. **C.** FAT partitions are limited to 2GB in size. FAT32 allows partitions in sizes up to 2TB, or roughly 2,000GB. (For more information, refer to the section "Choosing a File System.")

3. **D.** David is wrong because it doesn't matter what file system is used when accessing network resources via the network. FAT32 is only an issue when attempting to access partitions formatted with FAT32 from operating systems on the same PC that are not FAT32-aware—such as Windows NT 4.0 and DOS. (For more information, refer to the section "Choosing a File System.")

4. **A.** Network Neighborhood, by default, and for convenience, always displays the list of computers that are in the same workgroup as the PC on which a user is working. (For more information, refer to the section "Planning Windows 98 Security.")

5. **A, C.** Domains provide centralized administration of users. Domains offer data security through the NTFS (New Technology File System), which Windows 98 workgroups cannot offer. Answer B is not valid because domains require Windows NT Server, which costs considerably more than Windows 98 and the associated hardware for that server is generally more expensive than a Windows 98 workstation would be.

Answer D is not valid because there is no local security with FAT32. (For more information, refer to the section "Planning Windows 98 Security.")

6. **A.** User-level security is based on the user's identification, whereas share-level security is based on passwords supplied to access resources. (For more information, refer to the section "Planning Windows 98 Security.")

7. **B.** Although profiles can be set up as mandatory profiles to control the user's environment (Answer A), Answer B is more accurate because not all profiles are mandatory. (For more information, refer to the section "Planning Windows 98 Security.")

8. **D.** You'll use the System Policy Editor to create a policy, and add the policy to the `Netlogon` share of the domain controller to enforce the policy. (For more information, refer to the section "Planning Windows 98 Security.")

9. **B.** Rosemary and Bob's machine are controlled based on system policies. Policies control what activity users are allowed to perform. (For more information, refer to the section "Planning Windows 98 Security.")

10. **A, B.** If you do not have an account in the domain you have configured your Windows 98 machine to use, you will not be allowed to log on to the domain. If you have incorrectly entered your username and password, you would not be allowed to log on to the domain. If your account had been disabled you would have been given a message stating so. Changing your domain password would not have an effect on this issue. (For more information, refer to the section "Planning Windows 98 Security.")

APPLY YOUR KNOWLEDGE

Suggested Readings and Resources

1. *The Windows 98 Resource Kit*; Microsoft Press

2. *The Windows 98 Professional Reference*, Hallberg and Casad; New Riders

This chapter helps you to prepare for the Microsoft exam by covering the following objective within the "Installation and Configuration" category:

Install Windows 98. Installation options include the following:
> **Automated Windows setup**
> **New**
> **Upgrade**
> **Uninstall**
> **Dual-boot combination with Microsoft Windows NT 4.0**

▶ This objective will establish the principles of installing Windows 98 under different scenarios and will introduce the concept of installing Windows 98 to dual-boot with Microsoft Windows NT.

CHAPTER 2

Installing Windows 98

OUTLINE

After reviewing this installation chapter, install Windows 98 from scratch using the various options described herein. Experiment with installing Windows 98 locally and across a network. Add variables to the installation process such as legacy hardware, faulty hardware (to see what Windows 98 will try to do with the hardware), and configure Windows 98 to dual-boot with Windows NT. The more experience you allow yourself with installing Windows 98, the more you'll recall during your exam.

INTRODUCTION

Microsoft has devoted considerable energy to making Windows 98 easy to install. A Windows 98 installation appears simple on the surface, but in the background, the Setup program executes hundreds of steps that check system components, identify hardware, copy files, and configure the Windows 98 system. In this chapter, you'll learn about Windows 98 installation, with a focus on the following topics:

◆ Hardware requirements

◆ Windows 98 installation concepts

◆ The Windows 98 setup process

◆ Installing Windows 98

◆ Automating Windows Setup

◆ Uninstalling Windows 98

◆ Dual-booting Windows 98 with Windows NT

HARDWARE REQUIREMENTS

Before you even consider a Windows 98 installation, you should ensure that your system meets the minimum Windows 98 hardware requirements. Some minimum requirements for installing Windows 98 system are as follows:

Processor: 486DX/66 or better. Pentium recommended.

Memory: 16MB.

Monitor: VGA (16-color). Super VGA recommended.

Some optional components are as follows:

Mouse: Windows 98-compatible mouse.

Modem: 28.8Kbps modem recommended.

CD-ROM drive: 1X CD-ROM drive minimum. 8X recommended.

Sound Card: Sound-blaster compatible.

The hard disk requirements depend somewhat upon your installation. A minimum of 120MB disk space is required for

---

EXAM TIP

Know the Requirements Be sure you know the minimum hardware requirements for the Windows 98 MCSE exam. The most important minimum requirements to remember are the RAM (16MB) and the processor (486/66 or better).

Windows 98—more space may be required depending on your configuration. Plus, you'll need up to 50MB if you want to save system files. Setup also requires some disk space to execute the installation. Microsoft's recommended disk space requirements are outlined in Table 2.1.

TABLE 2.1

WINDOWS 98 HARD DISK REQUIREMENTS (PER WINDOWS 98 RESOURCE KIT)

Installation method	Required disk space (MB)	Typical disk space (MB)
Windows 95 upgrade	120–295	195
Windows 3.1x and WFW upgrade	120–295	195
New Installation (FAT32)	140–255	175
New Installation (FAT16)	165–355	225
Network Installation	165–355	225
On server	170	170
On client	175–225	175–225

Microsoft also points out that, if you are installing Windows 98 to a drive that isn't the C: drive, Setup still needs 25MB of free disk space on the C: drive for system and log files.

Windows 98, like its predecessor Windows 95, supports a wide range of hardware. The Windows 98 installation CD includes device drivers for hundreds of hardware products, and Windows 98 can often find a generic driver if the correct driver isn't available. Microsoft maintains a document called the Windows 98 Hardware Compatibility List (HCL) with up-to-date information on Windows 98 hardware compatibility. You can obtain the Windows 98 HCL through the Microsoft web site: **www.microsoft.com**. The readme and setup.txt files on the Windows 98 CD also include information on Windows 98 hardware compatibility.

Windows 98 Installation Concepts

Installing Windows 98 can be as simple as sitting at your computer and plugging a CD into the drive. Or, it can be as complicated as rolling out 100 PCs from a network share point. The actual installation is the easy part—Windows 98's ubiquitous Setup program (setup.exe) does most of the work. The hard part is planning and preparing the best installation scheme for your situation.

As with every other aspect of Windows 98 configuration, Windows 98 Setup requires you to make choices. Some of these choices, such as the file system and the network type, are related to the long-term operation of your computer. You learn about some of those long-term choices in Chapter 1, "Planning." Other choices relate to the logistics of the installation itself. You learn about those choices in this chapter.

You can run Windows 98 Setup from MS-DOS 5.0 or later, Windows 3.1x, Windows for Workgroups 3.1x, or Windows 95. As discussed later in this chapter, you can dual-boot Windows 98 with Windows NT. If MS-DOS or Windows 3.x/95 is available on the Windows NT machine, you can Windows 98 through the Windows 3.x/95 side. Or, you can install Windows NT 4.0 after Windows 98 to configure a dual-boot through Windows NT Setup. You cannot run Windows 98 Setup from within Windows NT.

The following sections offer an introduction to some important installation concepts, including these:

- ◆ The setup command
- ◆ DOS installs, new installs, and upgrades
- ◆ Local and network installations
- ◆ Setup options
- ◆ Windows 98's Save System Files feature
- ◆ The Windows 98 Emergency Startup Disk

> **NOTE**
>
> **Dual-Booting Windows 98 with OS/2**
> You can also dual-boot Windows 98 with OS/2 if you install Windows 98 on the DOS end of an existing DOS + OS/2 dual-boot configuration.

The setup Command

Installation begins when you access the drive in which the Windows
98 files are located and execute the Windows 98 Setup program,
setup.exe. In Windows 95, for instance, if you're installing from the
Windows 98 CD and the CD-ROM drive is the D: drive, you enter
the following command from the Start Menu Run dialog box:

```
D:\Setup
```

If you're installing over the network, the Setup command would
include the network path to setup.exe on the installation share:

```
\\servername\sharename\setup
```

Or, you could browse to the `setup.exe` file in Windows Explorer
and double-click it. If `setup.exe` is located in some other directory
or on some other drive, provide the correct path with the `setup`
command.

The `setup` command also includes one or more command-line
options to control the installation process. These options, or *switches,*
are specified as arguments for the `setup` command (such as `setup`
`/?`). The specific option is preceded by a slash character (/), not the
backslash character used to specify directory mappings (\).

Some `setup` command-line switches are listed in Table 2.2.

> **NOTE**
>
> **Executing a Program in MS-DOS**
> The procedures for executing a pro-
> gram in MS-DOS or earlier Windows
> versions are similar. Enter the `setup`
> command from the DOS prompt or
> from the Windows 3.1 Run dialog box.

TABLE 2.2

WINDOWS 98 SETUP SWITCHES

Switch	Description
/?	Provides help with the syntax and use of Setup command-line switches.
/C	Instructs Windows 98 MS-DOS Setup not to load the SmartDrive disk cache.
/d	Instructs Windows 98 Setup not to use the existing version of Windows for the early phases of Setup.
/in	Instructs Windows 98 MS-DOS Setup not to run the Network Setup module when installing Windows 98.
/im	Instructs Windows 98 Setup not to check for the minimum conventional memory required to install Windows 98.
/id	Instructs Windows 98 Setup not to check for the minimum disk space required to install Windows 98.

continues

TABLE 2.2	*continued*

WINDOWS 98 SETUP SWITCHES

Switch	*Description*
/ie	Skips the prompt for a Windows 98 Startup disk.
/iq	Tells Setup not to check for cross-linked files.
/is	Instructs Windows 98 Setup not to run the ScanDisk quick check. You probably want to use this switch if you use compression software other than DriveSpace or DoubleSpace.
/ih	Instructs Setup to skip the Registry check.
/il	Loads the Logitech mouse driver. Use this option if you have a Logitech Series C mouse.
/nostart	Instructs Windows 98 Setup to install the required minimal DLLs used by the Windows 98 Setup, and then to exit to MS-DOS without installing Windows 98.
/domain:*domainname*	Tells Setup the name of a Windows NT domain to use for Client for Microsoft Networks logon validation.
File.inf	Instructs Windows 98 Setup to use settings in the specified script file to install Windows 98 automatically. For example, executing setup mybatch.inf specifies that the Setup program should use the settings in the mybatch.inf script file.
/IW	Lets you bypass the license agreement screen. It is very useful when creating an automated script file that will run without stopping. This switch must be entered in capital letters.
/t:tempdir	Specifies the directory where Setup is to copy its temporary files. Be aware that any existing files in this directory will be deleted.
/iv	Tells Setup to not display billboards during the setup process.

You can also include the name of an installation script with the setup command. An *installation script* provides configuration information for the Setup program. You can use an installation script to automate all or part of a Windows 98 installation. An installation script can save you from having to sit in front of your PC responding to screen prompts. (See the section "Automating Windows 98 Setup," found later in this chapter.)

An example of the setup command with switches and a Setup script is as follows:

```
D:\Setup /C /IE C:\script\W98scrpt.inf
```

DOS Install, New Install, or Upgrade

If your system is currently running Windows 3.1, Windows for Workgroups 3.1.1, or Windows 95, you can *upgrade* to Windows 98. If you perform an upgrade, the Setup program will preserve your current settings. Settings such as your computer name, network configuration settings, and desktop shortcuts will automatically be converted to Windows 98 settings. Previous optional components will be installed into Windows 98. Windows 3.1 or 3.1.1 program groups will appear as entries in the Windows 98 Start menu. To perform an upgrade from Windows 3.1, Windows 3.1.1, or Windows 95, you must run Setup from Windows.

UPGRADING WITHOUT PRESERVING SETTINGS

If you're installing Windows 98 on a Windows 3.1 or Windows for Workgroups 3.1.1 computer and you don't want to preserve the existing settings, exit the Windows interface and run the installation from MS-DOS.

If you're installing from Windows 95 and you don't want to preserve the existing settings, boot to MS-DOS mode to run the installation. To boot to MS-DOS mode, select Shut Down from the Start menu; in the Shut Down Windows dialog box, choose Restart the Computer in MS-DOS Mode and click on Yes.

You may also be able to boot to a previous version of MS-DOS by pressing F8 as the system starts and choosing a previous version of MS-DOS from the boot menu. See your Windows 95 documentation.

If Windows 3.1 or Windows 95 is present on your system but you choose to install Windows 98 from MS-DOS (refer to the preceding note), you can choose a new directory for the Windows 98 files. If you choose a directory that is different from the present location of Windows files, Setup will not migrate existing settings. Because Setup does not migrate settings, you'll have to input additional information during the installation process. (The Setup process is described later in this section.)

If you install Windows 98 to a different directory, you'll probably have to reinstall any Windows applications currently on your computer if you wish to use them with Windows 98.

The Windows Upgrade option, which automatically converts Windows 3.1, Windows 3.1.1, or Windows 95 settings, is not available for installation from Windows 3.0 or MS-DOS. If you're installing from Windows 3.0 or MS-DOS, you must run Setup from DOS.

You can't run Windows 98 Setup from OS/2 or Windows NT. If the Windows NT or OS/2 system is presently in a dual-boot configuration with MS-DOS or Windows, you can boot to DOS, Windows 3.1, or Windows 95 and run the installation accordingly.

Although the DOS-based Windows 98 installation does not typically migrate network settings, if real-mode network drivers are running when you begin the installation, Setup installs the required network client.

A Windows 98 installation from a DOS boot disk with active network drivers is common in network installation situations. See the section "Local or Network Installation" later in this chapter.

A *new installation* is a Windows 98 installation on a computer with a new or newly formatted hard drive. To perform a new installation of Windows 98, run Setup from MS-DOS using any of the following:

- ◆ **A CD-ROM-enabled boot floppy.** You can boot to a floppy disk that includes the system boot files and a CD-ROM driver. This will allow you to access the CD-ROM drive. You can then run Setup from the Windows 98 CD. The full version of Windows 98 includes a CD-ROM–enabled boot floppy. Some computer vendors may also provide a CD-ROM–enabled boot floppy with new computers.

- ◆ **The Windows 98 CD.** If your system supports CD-ROM boot, you can boot directly to the Windows 98 CD.

- ◆ **Windows 98 floppy disks.** If you happen to have the relatively rare Windows 98 floppy disk set, you can start your installation with the first floppy.

- ◆ **Network-enabled boot floppy.** If you're installing Windows 98 over the network (as described later in this chapter) you can boot to network-enabled boot floppy, then connect to the Windows 98 Setup files on a network share. This disk will need the system boot files as well as the real-mode network drivers. You can create a network-enabled boot floppy using Windows NT Server's Network Client Administrator Utility.

Local or Network Installation

A Windows 98 installation typically falls into one of two basic classifications:

◆ **Local installation.** The Windows 98 installation files reside on a local drive (almost always the CD-ROM drive).

◆ **Network installation.** The Windows 98 installation files reside on a shared folder somewhere on the network.

A local installation merely requires you to start the existing local operating system and execute the Setup program (setup.exe) as described in the preceding section. A network installation is a different story.

Network installation is an important feature of Windows 98, and Microsoft invests considerable effort in making sure the world knows about Windows 98's network installation capabilities.

To those who are accustomed to very small networks (or to no network) it may seem strange that anyone would want to use a network to perform installations. But, in fact, Windows 98's network installation is indispensable in situations in which a large number of workstations must be installed in a short time.

The purpose of a network installation is to save the network administrator from having to trot around the network with the Windows 98 CD and install Windows 98 locally at each workstation. In a network installation, the files can reside at one central location, and all workstations can connect to that location to access the files. Providing a central location for the installation files offers significant logistical advantages if you need to install Windows 98 onto several computers.

Although a network installation does not have to be an automated installation, the purpose of a network installation is to save time and effort. Consequently, in most cases, a network installation is implemented as an automated installation using a Windows 98 installation script. You'll learn more about automating Windows 98 Setup later in this chapter.

EXAM TIP

Network Installation Techniques Microsoft places considerable emphasis on network installation techniques. Be prepared, therefore, for questions on the exam about network installation. To understand the network installation scenarios on the MCSE exam, you'll need to integrate the information in this chapter with the basic networking concepts explored in Chapter 1 and Chapter 3, "Configuring Windows 98 Networking."

NOTE

Added Benefit Another benefit of a network installation is that Windows 98 remembers the location of the Windows 98 installation files. If Windows 98 needs to access the installation files to install a new component or driver, it will automatically check for the Windows 98 installation share.

The procedure for a network installation is basically the same as the procedure for a local installation. In a network installation, however, the installation files are located on another computer elsewhere on the network.

Before you can begin a network installation, you must create a share that contains the installation files. See Chapter 5, "Managing Resources," for a discussion of how to create a network share in Windows 98. You can share the installation files directly from the server's CD-ROM drive, but, in many cases, network administrators find it useful to copy the installation files to a hard drive. A hard drive is faster, and, if you have enough storage space, a hard drive can provide a permanent home for the installation files, so that workstations can access the files to implement changes to the configuration.

To launch a network installation, you must perform the following steps:

1. Connect to the share containing the Windows 98 installation files.

2. Execute the Setup program on the installation share. See the discussion of the setup command earlier in this section.

The most common way of initiating a network installation is to enter the setup command at the command prompt with the full network path to the installation files:

```
\\servername\sharename\setup W98script.inf
```

servername is the name of the computer where the Windows 98 installation files reside, and sharename is the name of the share containing the installation files. By default, setup.exe will look for the installation script in its own directory if you don't provide a full path for the installation script.

If you're performing a new installation and you wish to install over the network, you'll need to modify a boot floppy so that it contains the necessary network drivers.

If you're using a real-mode NetWare client to connect to installation files on a NetWare server, map a network drive to the installation files:

```
MAP X:=server/volume:path   or MAP X:=NDS volume Object
Name:path

X:setup X:W98scrpt.inf
```

<table>
<tr><td>N O T E</td><td>**Full Directory Path Needed**
If setup.exe is in a subdirectory within the share, you must provide the full directory path.</td></tr>
</table>

x is the drive letter of your choice for the mapped drive. *server* is the server containing the files. volume is the NetWare volume containing the files. path is the full directory path once you arrive on the server and volume. If you are using NDS Object paths, follow the second example.

W98scrpt.inf is the name of the installation script.

If you're upgrading from Windows 95 and you're using a protected-mode NetWare client (Windows 98's Client for NetWare Networks or Novell Client for Windows 95/98), you can't execute Setup directly because the NetWare login script processor will interfere with the installation. Instead, use Windows 95's Start command:

```
#Start\\server\W98\setup \\server\W98\W98scrpt.inf
```

Setup Options

Windows 98 includes four different setup options: Typical, Portable, Compact, and Custom. Each setup option is a design for a Windows 98 system with a unique collection of optional components. During Windows 3.x or MS-DOS installations, you'll be asked to choose one of these setup options. The Windows 98 setup options are defined in Table 2.3.

TABLE 2.3

SETUP OPTIONS

Setup Option	Description
Typical	The default option, which Microsoft recommends for most users with desktop computers. This option performs most installation steps automatically for a standard Windows 98 installation with minimal user action.
Portable	The recommended option for mobile users with portable computers. Installs the appropriate set of files for a portable computer. This includes installing Briefcase for file synchronization and the supporting software for direct cable connections to exchange files.
Compact	The option for users who have extremely limited disk space. Installs only the minimum files required to run Windows 98.

continues

TABLE 2.3	*continued*

SETUP OPTIONS

Setup Option	Description
Custom	The option for users who want to directly select application and network components. Custom installation also lets you select certain other aspects of the configuration, such as a keyboard layout and language support. This type of setup is recommended for advanced users who want to control all the various elements of Setup.

The component categories included with each of the setup options are detailed in Table 2.4.

TABLE 2.4

SOME COMPONENTS INCLUDED WITH EACH SETUP OPTION

Option	Component Categories	All or Some Components
Typical	Accessibility	Some
	Accessories	Some (includes most accessories)
	Internet Tools	Some
	Communications	Some (includes Phone Dialer, NetMeeting, and Dial-Up Networking)
	Outlook Express	All
	Multimedia	Some (includes most multimedia components)
	Online Services	All
	System Tools	Some (includes only FAT32 driver converter)
Portable	Accessibility	Some
	Accessories	Some (includes only Briefcase, scripting host, and Wordpad)
	Communications	Some (includes all but Dial-Up Server, Chat, and NetMeeting)
	Internet Tools	Some

Option	Component Categories	All or Some Components
	Outlook Express	All
	Multimedia	Some
	Online Services	All
	System Tools	Some (includes only FAT32 driver converter and disk compression tools)
Compact	Accessibility	Some
	Communications	Some
	Multimedia	Some
	Online Services	All
Custom	(Defaults are the same as for Typical. You can add or remove components in Setup.)	

If you choose the Custom option, you can select any optional components for your system. The Custom option also offers some additional choices. If you choose the Custom option, you'll have a chance to specify the following:

◆ A keyboard layout designed for a particular language or country.

◆ Language support for Baltic, Central European, Cyrillic, Greek, or Turkish. (The default is support for English and other Western European languages.)

◆ Regional languages and dialects.

◆ A user interface. The default Windows 98 configuration uses the Windows 95/98 interface (with the Start menu, Windows Explorer, Network Neighborhood, and so forth). The Custom option lets you choose to use a Windows 3.1-like interface instead.

You can always install Windows 98 components later by using the Windows Setup tab of the Add/Remove Programs Control Panel. For a quick look at the list of components available with Windows 98, browse through the component list (see Figure 2.1).

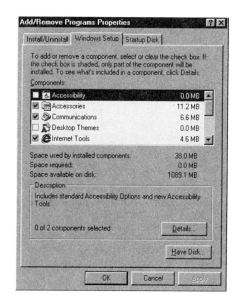

FIGURE 2.1
The Windows Setup tab of the Add/Remove Programs Control Panel displays a list of components available with Windows 98.

Saving System Files

When you install Windows 98, Setup will ask if you want to pre-serve the existing MS-DOS or Windows system files. If you choose to preserve the existing system files, the previous operating system will be stored in a hidden file called `winundo.dat` in the top directory of the hard drive. Two other hidden files, `winundo.ini` and `winklfn.ini`, contain additional information about your original configuration.

The reason for preserving the existing system files is that this makes it very easy to uninstall Windows 98. (You'll learn about uninstalling Windows 98 later in this chapter.)

Preserving existing Windows 95 files requires an additional 50MB of space on the hard drive.

Creating the Startup Disk

A *startup disk* is a Windows 98 bootable floppy disk that contains utilities you can use to troubleshoot a malfunctioning system. The startup disk loads the operating system and presents an MS-DOS command line. During Windows 98 installation, you'll be asked if you'd like to create a Windows 98 startup disk. It is a very good idea to create an Emergency Startup Disk during Windows 98 Setup.

Because of certain changes to the Windows 98 kernel, many Windows 95 Emergency Startup Disks *are not compatible* with Windows 98. You cannot count on being able to use an exist-ing Windows 95 startup disk to restart your Windows 98 system. It is better to create a new startup disk if possible.

You'll learn more about troubleshooting boot problems with a Windows 98 Emergency Startup Disk in Chapter 8, "Troubleshooting Windows 98."

> **NOTE**
>
> **Create at Least One Startup Disk**
> You should create at least one start-up disk during a Windows 98 setup. If you want to create a startup disk after the installation, you can use the Add/Remove Programs option in Control Panel to create one.

R E V I E W   B R E A K

Installation Concepts

The preceding sections introduced several Windows 98 installation concepts you'll need to know for the Windows 98 MCSE exam. As you prepare for the exam, make sure you understand the following:

◆ The operating systems that can run Windows 98 Setup

◆ The syntax of the setup command

◆ Windows 98 installation scripts

◆ The difference between a local and a network installation; how to implement a network installation

◆ The four Windows 98 Setup options (Typical, Portable, Compact, and Custom) and the reason of each option

◆ The reason for the Save System Files option

◆ The reason for creating an Emergency Startup Disk—even if you already have a Windows 95 startup disk for your PC

This list is a summary of important topics, but it is not a substitute for the information in the preceding sections. Study the "Installation Concepts" sections carefully—you're sure to see questions about these concepts on the Windows 98 MCSE exam.

After you've reviewed these concepts and planned your Windows 98 configuration (refer to Chapter 1), it is time to begin the installation. The next section describes the Windows 98 installation process.

THE WINDOWS 98 SETUP PROCESS

The Windows 98 setup process appears simple on the surface, but below the surface you'll find a complex collection of interdependent processes. In fact, the challenge of designing and coding a setup program that operates successfully over the vast range of devices and through all the possible software systems is the primary reason why Windows 98 is not called Windows 97.

The Windows 98 setup process is modular. The Setup program steps through this process, running only the modules either requested or needed. For example, the hardware detection phase identifies specific components on the computer, and the Setup runs only the installation modules that match those components. Some of the modules used by the Windows 98 Setup program are standard wizards, such as the setup for network components, modems, printers, and display monitors.

Microsoft divides the setup process into five phases. As you pass through each of the installation phases, Setup displays the name of the phase in a bar on the left side of the screen. The five setup phases are as follows:

◆ **Preparing to run Windows 98 Setup.** Setup checks for disk errors using ScanDisk. Setup also looks for existing Windows versions on your computer, prepares the Setup Wizard, and prompts you to accept the license agreement.

◆ **Collecting information about your computer.** Setup analyzes your system and asks for any additional information it will need to configure your computer. Setup begins finding and cataloging your system's hardware. In this phase, Setup will prompt you for decisions such as whether you'd like to save existing system files and whether you'd like to create an emergency disk. You may also be asked for a setup option (Custom, Compact, Typical, or Portable), a username and company name, a computer name, and other setup settings.

◆ **Copying Windows 98 files to your computer.** Setup copies the Windows 98 files to the new location on your hard drive. Windows 98 includes a new component called *Version Conflict Manager (VCM)*. VCM monitors whether a new file that is being copied with the installation is actually older than a copy already on the computer. If the file being installed is in fact older than the copy already on the computer, Setup still installs the file, but VCM backs up the existing (newer) file to the VCM folder of the Windows directory.

◆ **Restarting your computer.** Setup shuts down and reboots the computer.

◆ **Setting up hardware and finalizing settings.** Setup finishes configuring hardware devices, sets up Control Panel and desktop items, configures MS-DOS program settings, and completes system configuration.

Of all the tasks undertaken during Setup, hardware detection is perhaps the most complex and the most likely to stall or hang the Setup program. Setup first looks for Plug and Play devices. Then it uses an array of different techniques to find components that aren't Plug and

Play. For certain devices that are particularly difficult to locate and prone to hanging the system, Setup uses a feature called safe detection. *Safe detection* involves methodically searching the computer for software clues that can indicate the presence of certain devices. The config.sys, autoexec.bat, and all initialization (.ini) files are checked. Setup inspects memory locations for installed drivers and checks for other clues depending on the type of device. If these safe methods suggest the presence of a device, that device is configured.

Some classes of devices that are configured using safe detection include the following:

◆ CD-ROM drives (proprietary cards)

◆ Sound cards

◆ Network adapters

◆ SCSI devices

Give Windows 98 hardware detection a chance to work. Just because the computer locks up during the detection phase doesn't mean that Windows 98 will be unable to detect the hardware. You might have to turn the machine off two or three times to effect detection of all the hardware. However, patience during this phase of setup will pay dividends during later setup and configuration.

If your system stops during hardware detection, you can turn your computer off and restart. As you'll learn later in this chapter, Setup maintains a log of hardware detection events and can often circumvent the failure by skipping the driver that caused the crash when you restart the detection.

If Setup can't configure a legacy hardware device, try to configure it through the setup application that comes with the hardware. You might also check with the manufacturer to see if they have a compatible driver for Windows 98 that will allow Windows 98 to assign system resources, such as IRQs, to the device.

The next section takes a closer look at the Windows 98 installation process.

INSTALLING WINDOWS 98

Install Windows 98.

This section reviews the following important aspects of Windows 98 installation:

◆ Preparing for installation

◆ Upgrading from Windows 95

◆ Upgrading from Windows 3.1 or Windows for Workgroups 3.1.1

◆ DOS-based installs and new installs

◆ Setup failure detection and recovery

Preparing for Installation

Chapter 1 and the previous sections of this chapter outline some decisions you'll need to make about your configuration before you start to install Windows 98 (such as choosing a network type and choosing a file system). After you've made those decisions, you're ready for the last few preparatory tasks before you install. Microsoft recommends the following checklist of preliminary measures:

◆ **Ensure that the hardware is supported.** Check the readme file and the setup.txt file on the installation disk for hardware compatibility information. You can also check the Windows 98 Hardware Compatibility List (HCL). Refer to the discussion of the HCL earlier in this chapter.

◆ **Disable unnecessary Terminate and Stay Resident (TSR) programs.** Be careful not to disable TSRs necessary for hard disk control, network drivers, video drivers, CD-ROM drivers, and so on.

◆ **Disable time-out features, third-party display utilities, and antivirus software.** Time-out features are features common on portable PCs that suspend operation after a specific time-out period. Third-party display utilities should be disabled because if Setup can't recognize them, it stops the installation. Antivirus programs respond to changes in the configuration, such as changes to the master boot record, that take place during an installation. If you're upgrading from Windows 3.x, you should be especially wary of virus checkers because Windows 3.x virus checkers are incompatible with Windows 98 long filenames. Note that it isn't enough just to disable the virus software. You must make sure the virus software won't turn itself on when the system reboots because your system will restart itself while you're installing Windows 98.

◆ **Quit all applications.** You should close all current applications before running Setup.

◆ **Scan and defragment drives.** If you run Setup from MS-DOS, Setup will use ScanDisk during the installation to check the hard drive where Windows 98 will be installed. If you're running Setup from Windows 95, it is best to scan the disk before you start Setup. It is also a good idea to defragment all your drives before starting Setup. You'll learn more about ScanDisk and the Disk Defragmenter in Chapter 7, "Monitoring and Optimization." You can also use third-party scanning and defragmentation software. Consult your vendor documentation.

◆ **Back up key system files.** Several key system files should be backed up as a precaution. Back up config.sys, autoexec.bat and other key .bat files, .ini files, .grp files, Registry .dat files, .pwl password files, hardware drivers and other support programs referenced in config.sys and autoexec.bat, network configuration files, and logon scripts.

An easy way to back up these files is to create a batch file that performs the backup and executes that batch file from a network logon script. In fact, you could even carry it one step further and copy all .doc, .xls, and .ppt files as well.

◆ **Ensure that network software is working properly.** During setup, Windows 98 uses the current settings to help configure itself. If there are problems with the network wiring, interface card, configuration, security, or the like, Setup may not correctly configure Windows 98 networking.

Of course, an important unwritten addition to this checklist is to ensure that you have a backup copy of any important user files and applications. It is always a good idea to back up your files, but it is even more important to do so when you're about to begin a process as vast and unpredictable as an operating system upgrade.

Upgrading from Windows 95

When you upgrade from Windows 95 to Windows 98, Setup transfers most of the original settings and requires very little user input. During a Windows 95 upgrade, you'll be prompted for the following information:

◆ Your acceptance of the Windows 98 license agreement.

◆ Whether you want to save the existing system files. (Refer to the discussion of Setup's Save System Files features earlier in this chapter.)

◆ Your Windows 98 Product ID.

◆ An Internet channel set—a setting related to Windows 98's active channel feature. This setting controls which channel icons will appear in the channel bar of your Windows 98 Desktop. In most cases, just choose your home country from the list.

◆ Whether you want to create an Emergency Startup Disk. (Refer to the discussion of the Emergency Startup Disk earlier in this chapter.)

If you are planning an automated setup (as described later in this chapter) you can create a Windows 98 installation script that will provide responses to these prompts.

To upgrade from Windows 95 to Windows 98, perform the tasks outlined in Step by Step 2.1.

STEP BY STEP

2.1 Upgrading from Windows 95 to Windows 98

1. Initiate Windows 98 Setup using the setup command (as discussed earlier in this chapter) or by double-clicking the icon for setup.exe. You can run Setup locally or over the network. (When you place the CD-ROM in the CD-ROM drive, the Windows 95 autorun feature may automatically display the Windows 98 CD-ROM window and ask if you'd like to install Windows 98 or browse the CD.)

2. A message tells you that Setup is starting. When the Windows 98 license agreement appears, you must accept the license agreement to continue.

3. Setup asks if you'd like to save the existing system files. Choose Yes or No. (Refer to the discussion of Windows 98's Save System Files feature earlier in this chapter.)

4. Setup prompts for your Windows 98 Product ID. Enter the Product ID provided with your Windows 98 CD.

5. Choose an Internet channel set. (Refer to the discussion of the Internet channel set earlier in this section.)

6. Setup asks if you'd like to create an Emergency Startup Disk. Choose Yes. (It is a very good idea to create a startup disk. Remember that Windows 95 startup disks aren't compatible with Windows 98, so your old startup disk won't work after you finish the installation.)

7. Setup enters the file copy phase, in which it copies files to your Windows 98 directory. When the file copy is complete, Setup informs you that it is about to restart your computer.

8. After your computer restarts, Setup configures your hardware.

9. Your system again shuts down and restarts. Setup completes the hardware configuration and takes care of final configuration tasks, such as configuring Control Panel, Start menu, MS-DOS program settings, and system configuration settings.

10. The system again shuts down, and restarts in Windows 98.

Upgrading from Windows 3.1 or Windows for Workgroups 3.1.1

When you upgrade from Windows 3.1 or from Windows for Workgroups to Windows 98, Setup transfers system settings, program groups, and other configuration items to the new Windows 98 implementation. This upgrade option occurs when you run Setup from the Windows interface and install Windows 98 to the existing Windows directory. If you install Windows 98 to a different directory, Setup will not preserve existing settings. During a Windows 3.1x upgrade, you'll be prompted for the following information:

◆ Your acceptance of the Windows 98 license agreement.

◆ A Windows directory name. For the upgrade option, use the current Windows directory. If you install to a different directory, existing system settings will not migrate to Windows 98, and the Setup process will be more like an MS-DOS–based installation. You will probably also have to reinstall any existing applications to run them under Windows 98 if you install to a different directory.

◆ Whether you want to save the existing system files. (Refer to the discussion of Setup's Save System Files features earlier in this chapter.)

◆ Your Windows 98 Product ID.

◆ A setup option (Typical, Custom, Compact, or Portable). (Refer to the discussion of setup options earlier in this chapter. If you choose Custom, you'll also need to supply a keyboard layout, language support settings, regional settings, and Windows 98 components. You'll also have the chance to specify if you'd prefer to use the Windows 3.1 user interface with Windows 98 instead of changing to the Windows 95/98 interface.)

◆ An Internet channel set, a setting related to Windows 98's active channel feature. This setting controls which channel icons will appear in the channel bar of your Windows 98 desktop. In most cases, just choose your home country from the list.

◆ Whether you want to create an Emergency Startup Disk. (Refer to the discussion of the Emergency Startup Disk earlier in this chapter.)

If you are planning an automated setup (as described later in this chapter), you can create a Windows 98 installation script that will provide responses to these prompts.

To upgrade from Windows 3.1 or Windows for Workgroups 3.1.1 to Windows 98, perform the tasks outlined in Step by Step 2.2.

STEP BY STEP

2.2 Upgrading from Windows 3.1 or Windows for Workgroups 3.1.1 to Windows 98

1. Initiate Windows 98 Setup using the setup command (as discussed earlier in this chapter) or by double-clicking the icon for setup.exe. You can run Setup locally or over the network.

2. Setup checks your system using ScanDisk and prepares the Setup Wizard.

3. A message tells you that Setup is starting. When the Windows 98 license agreement appears, you must accept the license agreement to continue.

4. Setup asks for a Windows directory name. If you install to a directory that is different from the current Windows directory, Setup will not transfer existing settings. (Refer to the discussion earlier in this section.)

5. If you install to the current Windows directory, Setup asks if you'd like to save the existing system files. Choose Yes or No. (Refer to the discussion of Windows 98's Save System Files feature earlier in this chapter.)

6. Setup prompts for your Windows 98 Product ID. Enter the Product ID provided with your Windows 98 CD.

7. Setup prompts you to choose a setup option. Choose Typical, Compact, Portable, or Custom. (Refer to the discussion of setup options earlier in this chapter. If you choose Custom, you'll have several additional choices, such as a keyboard layout and Windows 98 components.)

   (If you're performing an upgrade (installing Windows 98 to the existing Windows directory), follow the remaining steps listed in the description of the Windows 95 upgrade. If you're installing to a different directory, follow the remaining steps listed in the description of the MS-DOS installation, discussed in the next section.)

DOS-Based Installs and New Installs

As discussed previously, if you perform the installation from MS-DOS, Setup does not migrate current settings, and you must enter more of the settings manually. You'll need to install from MS-DOS if you're installing onto a machine that uses MS-DOS, Windows 3.0, or Windows NT, or if you're installing Windows 98 onto a computer with a new or reformatted hard drive. During a DOS-based installation, you'll be prompted for the following information:

◆ Whether you accept the Windows 98 license agreement.

◆ A Windows directory name.

◆ Whether you want to save the existing system files. (See the discussion of Setup's Save System Files features earlier in this chapter.)

◆ Your Windows 98 Product ID.

◆ A Setup option (Typical, Custom, Compact, or Portable). See the discussion of Setup options earlier in this chapter. If you choose Custom, you'll also need to supply a keyboard layout, language support settings, regional settings, and Windows 98 components. You'll also have the chance to specify if you'd prefer to use the Windows 3.1 user interface with Windows 98 instead of changing to the Windows 95/98 interface.

◆ User information: your name and your company's name.

◆ Windows components. You'll have the chance to choose additional Windows components.

◆ Computer name, workgroup name, computer description—settings that will appear in the Identification tab of the Network Control Panel. You'll learn more about these settings in Chapter 3. The computer name must be a unique name of 15 characters or fewer with no embedded spaces. Computer names can consists of any letters A through Z, any digits 0 through 9, plus any of the following characters: ! @ # $ % ^ & ( ) -_' { } ~. The workgroup name is also 15 characters with a similar cast of characters. The computer description can be 48 characters and cannot contain any commas.

◆ An Internet channel set, a setting related to Windows 98's active channel feature. This setting controls which channel icons will appear in the channel bar of your Windows 98

Desktop. In most cases, just choose your home country from the list.

◆ Whether or not you want to create an Emergency Startup Disk. (See the discussion of the Emergency Startup Disk earlier in this chapter.)

If you are planning an automated setup (as described later in this chapter), you can create a Windows 98 installation script that will provide responses to these prompts.

To install Windows 98 from MS-DOS, perform the tasks outlined in Step by Step 2.3.

STEP BY STEP

2.3 Installing Windows 98 from MS-DOS

1. Initiate Windows 98 Setup using the setup command (as discussed earlier in this chapter). You can run Setup locally or over the network.

2. Setup checks your system using ScanDisk and prepares the Setup Wizard.

3. A message informs you that Setup is starting. When the Windows 98 license agreement appears, you must accept the license agreement to continue.

4. Setup asks for a Windows directory name.

5. Setup asks if you'd like to save the existing system files. Choose Yes or No. See the discussion of Windows 98's Save System Files feature earlier in this chapter.

6. Setup prompts for your Windows 98 Product ID. Enter the Product ID provided with your Windows 98 CD.

7. Setup prompts you to choose a Setup option. Choose Typical, Compact, Portable, or Custom. See the discussion of Setup options earlier in this chapter. If you choose Custom, you'll have several additional choices, such as a keyboard layout and Windows 98 components.

continues

continued

8. Setup asks for user information. Enter your name and your company's name. This information is optional. These entries will appear in the General tab of the System Control Panel.

9. Setup asks if you want to choose optional components. The Setup option you chose in step 7 is used as a default. You can add or remove components if you want.

10. Setup asks for a computer name, a workgroup name, and a computer description. See the discussion of these settings in Chapter 3. The computer name must be a unique name of 15 characters or fewer with no embedded spaces. Computer names can consist of any letters A through Z, any digits 0 through 9, plus any of the following characters: ! @ # $ % ^ & ( ) - _ ` { } ~. The workgroup name is also 15 characters with a similar cast of characters. The computer description can be 48 characters and cannot contain any commas.

11. Choose an Internet channel set. See the discussion of the Internet channel set earlier in this section.

12. Setup asks if you'd like to create an Emergency Startup Disk. Choose Yes. It is a very good idea to create a startup disk. Remember that Windows 95 startup disks aren't compatible with Windows 98, so your old startup disk won't work after you finish the installation.

13. Setup enters the file copy phase. You'll have to wait while Setup copies files to your Windows 98 directory. When the file copy is complete, Setup informs you that it is about to restart your computer.

14. After your computer restarts, Setup starts configuring your hardware.

15. Your system again shuts down and restarts. Setup completes the hardware configuration and takes care of final configuration tasks, such as configuring Control Panel, the Start menu, MS-DOS program settings, and system configuration settings.

16. The system again shuts down, and it restarts in Windows 98.

Setup Failure Detection and Recovery

If Setup fails unexpectedly, Microsoft recommends that you try the following steps (and in this order):

1. Press F3 or click on the Exit button.

2. Press Ctrl + Alt + Del.

3. Turn off your computer, wait 15 seconds, then restart.

Setup maintains a setup log (`setuplog.txt`), and if your system fails during installation, Setup can use the setup log to determine where the problem occurred. Setup also creates a hardware-detection log called `detcrash.log` (and a text-file equivalent called `detlog.txt`) if Setup fails during the hardware-detection phase. When you restart a failed Windows 98 installation, Setup may be able to work around the problem using information in `setuplog.txt` and `detcrash.log`.

If any previous attempt to install Windows 98 has failed, Setup gives you the option of using the Safe Recovery feature or running a full new Setup process. If the Safe Recovery dialog box appears when you start Setup, you should always select the Use Safe Recovery option. When you select this option, Setup can use various built-in methods to avoid problems that occurred previously.

You'll learn more about troubleshooting Setup problems in Chapter 8.

Windows 98 Installation

R E V I E W   B R E A K

You won't be required to memorize the order of the installation steps for the Windows 98 MCSE exam, but you should know about the phases of the installation process. You should also understand all the various bits of information that Setup may prompt you to supply in different situations, such as a computer name, workgroup name, user information, and Internet channel set.

You should also be aware of the steps for recovering from an installation failure. You'll learn more about installation troubleshooting later in this chapter.

AUTOMATING WINDOWS 98 SETUP

Microsoft continues to reduce the amount of user-supplied information necessary for setup. Windows 98 Setup requires relatively little user intervention. As you learned earlier in this chapter, however, even in the case of an upgrade, Setup requires input on a few key items, such as the product ID and a decision on whether you want to save the system files. DOS–based installations require even more user choices. You'll need to input a Windows directory name, a setup option, user information, and computer information such as a computer name. Anyone who has installed Windows knows you spend most of the time waiting in front of the computer, but that you still need to be available to answer the occasional screen prompts. Windows 98's automated setup lets you create a text file that will supply Setup with all the necessary configuration information. Automate setup lets you attend to other matters while Windows 98 is installing.

This chapter has already mentioned that the setup command can contain a reference to a Windows 98 installation script. An installation script is a text file that contains setup information.

Installation scripts are written in the inf file format that is often used to install devices or software components in Windows systems. An inf file looks a little like an old Windows ini file, with a few major categories enclosed in square brackets ([]) and individual settings on separate lines following the category marker. Following is a sample of some Windows installation script entries:

```
[BatchSetup]
Version=3.0 (32-bit)
SaveDate=01/28/98

[Version]
Signature = "$CHICAGO$"

[Setup]
Express=1
InstallDir="C:\WINDOWS"
InstallType=3
EBD=0
ShowEula=0
ChangeDir=0
OptionalComponents=1
Network=1
System=0
CCP=0
CleanBoot=0
```

```
Display=0
DevicePath=0
NoDirWarn=1
TimeZone="Central"
Uninstall=0
VRC=0
NoPrompt2Boot=1

[System]
Locale=L0409
SelectedKeyboard=KEYBOARD_00000409
DisplChar=16,640,480_

[NameAndOrg]
Name="Nicholas Rostov"
Org="Imperial Russia"
Display=0

[Network]
ComputerName="sonya"
Workgroup="BARKER"
Description="200 MHz Pentium"
Display=0
PrimaryLogon=VREDIR
Clients=VREDIR, NWREDIR
Protocols=NWLINK, MSTCP
Services=VSERVER
Security=NWSERVER
PassThroughAgent="BARKER"

[NWLINK]
Frame_Type=4
NetBIOS=0

[MSTCP]
LMHOSTS=1
LMHOSTPath="C:\WINDOWS\lmhosts"
DHCP=1
DNS=0
WINS=N

[NWREDIR]
FirstNetDrive=F:
ProcessLoginScript=1

[VREDIR]
LogonDomain="BARKER"
ValidatedLogon=1

[VSERVER]
LMAnnounce=0
MaintainServerList=2

[OptionalComponents]
"Accessibility Options"=0
"Enhanced Accessibility"=0
"Briefcase"=0
"Calculator"=1
```

Network administrators typically use the Windows 98 Resource Kit's Batch 98 utility to create and modify installation scripts. As stated previously, you specify a Windows 98 installation script name along with the setup command:

```
\\server\share\setup path\W98scrpt.inf
```

path is the full UNC path to the installation script W98scrpt.inf.

In addition to letting you automate setup, installation scripts let you fine-tune the configuration in ways that aren't otherwise possible. In a Windows 3.1 or Windows 95 upgrade, for instance, Setup automatically converts existing settings, and you don't have the option of making changes to the configuration. The DOS–based installation also only prompts for a subset of the total configuration possibilities. To specify elements such as an LMHOSTS file or a special printer configuration during setup, you'll need to use an installation script.

Examples of the settings you can configure using a Windows 98 installation script are as follows:

- ◆ **Installation Information.** Includes the name of the installation directory and the choice for whether you'd like to save existing system files.

- ◆ **Setup Prompt Information.** Includes whether you want to auto-accept the license agreement or whether you want to create an Emergency Startup disk. (Choose No if you want to configure an unattended installation.)

- ◆ **Regional Settings.** Includes a time zone or keyboard layout settings.

- ◆ **Desktop Icons.** Includes information about which icons you'd like to add to your desktop (for example, My Documents, Network Neighborhood, and Recycling Bin).

- ◆ **Printer Information.** Includes printer names, printer types, and printer ports.

- ◆ **Display Settings.** Includes resolution and color depth settings.

- ◆ **Optional Component Information.** Includes setup options (Typical, Portable, Compact, or Custom) and which specific components you'd like to include.

- ◆ **Network Information.** Includes detailed configuration for networking components, such as protocols, clients, adapters, and network services.

NOTE

Take a Look at an Installation Script
Although the Windows 98 exam probably won't require you to remember specific installation script entries, it is still helpful to spend some time examining an installation script so you'll have a sense of how they function. If you don't have access to the Windows 98 Resource Kit, check out the installation script msbatch in the Tools\sysrec directory of the Windows 98 CD. (Microsoft warns that "This inf is used for System Recovery Only," but you can still view this script as an example of INF format.)

See the Windows 98 Resource Kit for a detailed description of installation script entries. You probably won't be directly tested on the format of the installation script file on the MCSE exam, but having some familiarity with that format will help you understand how installation scripts work. You should be aware of the methods for creating an installation script (discussed in the following sections).

Creating Installation Scripts with Batch 98

The preferred method for creating Windows 98 installation scripts is to use the Batch 98 utility (batch.exe) included with the Windows 98 Resource Kit. Batch 98 provides a graphic interface that you can use to generate installation scripts (see Figure 2.2).

The system settings buttons lead to dialog boxes that will enable you to configure the various components of your installation script, such as Network components and Optional components. The General Setup Options button lets you configure items such as install settings, setup prompts settings, regional settings, display settings, and user profile settings. The Advanced Options button lets you include a Registry file (see Chapter 5) and/or a system policy file with the installation script.

After you've defined a configuration you'd like to use for the installation script, click Save Settings to INF to create an inf file. The default name for the inf file created by Batch 98 is msbatch.inf. You can also click on File (in the upper-left corner—see Figure 2.2) to invoke the File menu. The File menu's Save As option lets you give the file a different name.

The Gather Now button in the Batch 98 main dialog box creates an installation script with settings gathered from the Registry of the computer which you are now using. In other words, the Gather Now function lets you replicate the configuration of the computer on which you're now working through an installation script. This option leads to a scenario in which you can configure several identical systems:

1. Install Windows 98 manually on one PC.

2. Install the Windows 98 Resource Kit with the Batch 98 utility.

EXAM TIP

Optional Products Coverage
In the past, Microsoft has tended to avoid including optional products such as Resource Kit utilities in the MCSE exams. That trend, however, appears to be changing. Don't be surprised to see a question on the Resource Kit's Batch 98 utility. You may also see a question on the Resource Kit's INF installer, which is discussed in the next section.

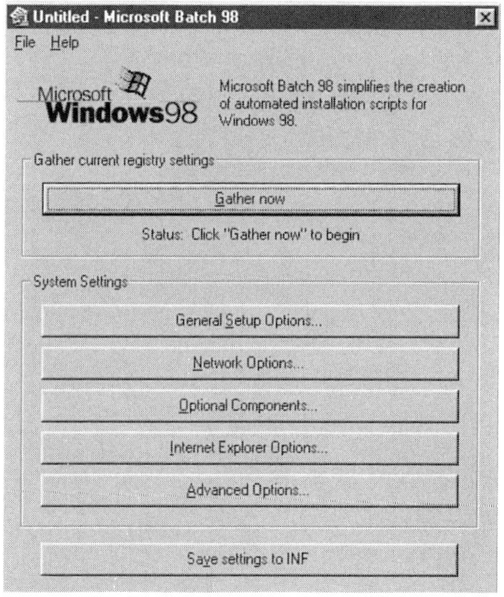

FIGURE 2.2
The Batch 98 tool provides an interface for creating Windows 98 installation scripts.

3. Configure the PC exactly the way you want it. (Configure network settings, system settings, display settings, and so on.)

4. Use Batch 98's Gather Now feature to create an installation script that reflects the current configuration.

5. Use the installation script created in step 4 to install Windows 98 on other computers. (Note that you'll have to manually edit computer-specific network settings in the installation script, such as the computer name and/or the IP address, so that you'll have a unique network configuration for each PC. Or you can use the Multiple Machine-Name Save option, described next.)

If you're installing over the network, you'll need to reconnect to the network share under the new configuration in order to complete the installation. To make that connection, your computer must have a unique computer name, and, if you're using TCP/IP, a unique IP address. The need for a unique network identity interferes with the ideal of using one installation script to install Windows 98 on multiple computers. One solution is to manually edit the installation script and change network name and address information for each computer you want to install. Another solution is to use Batch 98's Multiple Machine-Name Save option.

The Multiple Machine-Name Save option in the Batch 98 file menu lets you save a series of separate installation scripts with unique computer names and/or IP addresses. Multiple Machine-Name Save basically list-processes an installation script with a separate file that tabulates computer names (and optional IP addresses) for each computer on which you'd like to install Windows 98. The result is a series of scripts with identical configurations except that the computer names (and, optionally, IP addresses) are unique. The scripts will take the name `Bstp0001.inf`, `Bstp0002.inf`, `Bstp0003.inf`, and so forth, with one script for each computer in the name list.

INF Installer

Another utility provided with the Windows 98 Resource Kit, the INF Installer (*Infinst.exe*), lets you include device driver and network driver `inf` files with the Windows 98 installation files so that Setup will automatically add the drivers to the Windows 98 installation. The INF Installer main window is shown in Figure 2.3.

To add a new inf file to the Windows 98 installation files, enter the name of the inf file in the box labeled INF to Add to Windows 98 Setup. Enter the path to the Windows 98 installation share followed by Setup.exe in the box labeled Windows 98 Setup.exe:

```
\\server\share\setup.exe
```

Click on Add Inf to add the inf file to the share. INF Installer compares the specified inf files with current inf files that will be installed to the Wininf directory and updates the Windows 98 Installation files accordingly.

As you may have guessed, INF Installer works only if it can write to the installation files. For that reason, you must copy the installation files to a share on a hard drive for which you have write permissions if you're going to use INF Installer.

FIGURE 2.3
The INF Installer lets you include other inf files with the Windows 98 installation.

UNINSTALLING WINDOWS 98

If you elected to save system files during an upgrade to Windows 98, it is very easy to uninstall Windows 98.

As described previously, Setup copies the existing system files to the hidden file winundo.dat and creates hidden files called winundo.ini and winlfn.ini with information necessary to restore the system files.

To uninstall Windows 98 (after having saved the previous system files), perform the tasks outlined in Step by Step 2.4.

STEP BY STEP

2.4 Uninstalling Windows 98

1. Open the Add/Remove Programs Control Panel.

2. Select the Install/Uninstall tab (see Figure 2.4), select Uninstall Windows 98, then click on the Add/Remove button.

3. A dialog box appears, informing you that you are about to uninstall Windows 98. Click Yes.

continues

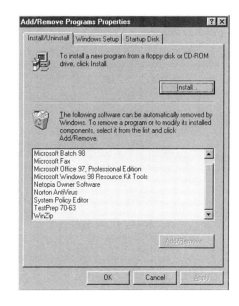

FIGURE 2.4
If you saved the system files, you can select the Install/Uninstall tab in Add/Remove Programs Control Panel to uninstall Windows 98.

continued

4. Subsequent prompts will inform you that the Uninstall program is checking your disk for errors. Click Yes to the prompts.

Your computer will shut down and reboot into MS-DOS mode to continue the Uninstall process.

For purposes of preparing for the Windows 98 MCSE exam, the most important thing to remember about Windows 98's uninstall feature—aside from the "how-to-do-it" steps outlined in the preceding procedure—is that the Uninstall feature *won't work* if either of the following took place during or after your Windows 98 installation:

◆ You converted your file system from FAT16 to FAT32.

◆ You compressed the system boot partition or any other partition on the disk that contains the winundo.dat file.

To uninstall Windows 98 if you did *not* save the system files at setup, you must boot to a previous operating system (if your PC is in a dual-boot configuration) or boot a bootable floppy and delete all Windows 98 system files. This makes your computer unbootable so you must use an MS-DOS 5.0 or 6.0 startup disk to reboot your computer. You can then use the MS-DOS sys command to restore system boot files.

N O T E

Deleting Uninstall Files To delete the uninstall files containing the previous operating system and uninstall information, select Delete Windows 98 Uninstall Information in the Install/Uninstall tab of the Add/Remove Programs Control Panel.

DUAL-BOOTING WINDOWS 98 WITH WINDOWS NT

Install Windows 98. Installation options include the following:

◆ Automated Windows setup

◆ New

◆ Upgrade

◆ Uninstall

◆ Dual-boot combination with Microsoft Windows NT 4.0

Microsoft officially states that you cannot install Windows 98 from Windows NT. However, Microsoft encourages and supports dual-boot configurations, in which NT and Windows 98 coexist on a single computer.

If your computer presently dual-boots Windows NT with another operating system, such as MS-DOS, Windows 3.x, or Windows 95, you can run Setup from the other operating system as described earlier in this chapter.

In case the Windows NT Loader (NTLDR) doesn't start after you install Windows 98, have a Windows NT Emergency Repair Disk ready so you can restore NT's boot files and the Windows NT Boot Sector.

If your system is running Windows NT only, you can boot to a network-enabled or CD-ROM–enabled DOS or Windows 95 start-up disk and run Windows 98 Setup from the startup disk. You will not be able to boot to Windows NT after installing Windows 98 from the startup disk. Use your Windows NT Emergency Repair Disk to restore the Windows NT startup files. You'll need to configure the boot menu to include Windows 98. See your Windows NT documentation for details.

Windows 98 Setup is supposed to automatically add Windows 98 to Windows NT's boot menu when you install Windows 98 with Windows NT; however, in some cases, you may need to edit Windows NT's boot.ini file using a text editor in order to update boot menu options. boot.ini is located in the top directory of the boot drive. Again, see your Windows NT documentation for further information.

If Windows 98 is already present on the system and you then install Windows NT to a different directory, the NT Setup program will take care of configuring the dual boot.

A few important points to remember about dual-booting Windows 98 with Windows NT are as follows:

◆ Windows NT 4.0 and earlier can't read FAT32 partitions and Windows 98 can't read NTFS partitions. The most important fact about NT dual-boot to remember for the Windows 98 exam is that any partitions you want to access from both operating systems must be FAT16.

◆ Microsoft strongly recommends that you install Windows 98 to a different disk or partition from Windows NT. Sometimes Microsoft says you *must* install Windows 98 to a different partition.

Know Windows 98/Windows NT Dual-Boot Requirements
Memorize the preceding list of Windows 98/Windows NT dual-boot requirements. You're very likely to need something from this list on the Windows 98 MCSE exam.

◆ You can't install Windows 98 to a directory that currently holds a Windows 3.x/Windows NT dual-boot configuration. Windows 98 must be installed in a different directory (which would be the case anyway if you heed the warning in the preceding bullet).

◆ The active partition should be a FAT16 partition.

DUAL-BOOTING WINDOWS 98 WITH MS-DOS, WINDOWS 3.1, OR WINDOWS FOR WORKGROUPS

If you have a previous version of MS-DOS on your Windows 98 computer, you can configure Windows 98 to dual-boot to the previous DOS version. If you installed Windows 98 from Windows 3.x and you elected to install to another directory, your Windows 3.x files will remain unchanged. You can start Windows 3.1 from MS-DOS using the Win command.

If your Windows 98 computer is configured to dual-boot with MS-DOS, you can boot to the previous operating system in either of two ways:

◆ By pressing F4 as the system starts

◆ By pressing F8 to invoke the Windows 98 boot menu and selecting Previous Version of MS-DOS from the list of choices.

If MS-DOS is present on your system but your system is not configured to dual-boot, go to the [Options] section of the file msdos.sys and change the value of the parameter BootMulti to BootMulti=1. You'll have to change the read-only and hidden attributes of the msdos.sys file in order to find it and edit it. Use the following command:

```
attrib -h -s -r msdos.sys
```

If you don't have MS-DOS on your Windows 98 system, you can add the MS-DOS system files from an MS-DOS 5.0 or later system disk and configure Windows 98 to dual-boot. After you've made the preceding change to the Bootmulti setting in the msdos.sys file, copy the files io.sys, msdos.sys, and command.com from the system disk to the root directory of the boot drive and give the files the

*.DOS extension in the new location. (You'll have to turn off the hidden and Read-only attributes for io.sys and msdos.sys, as described previously.) Then, create files called autoexec.doc and config.dos to include any DOS commands that would normally go in the DOS system files autoexec.bat and config.sys.

CASE STUDY: QUALITY TITLE COMPANY

ESSENCE OF THE CASE

Here are the essential elements in this case:

- Windows 95 upgrade for 32 identical Pentiums

- Windows 3.1 upgrade for 16 486s

- New install on eight laptops

- Windows NT/Windows 98 dual-boot on two workstations

SCENARIO

Quality Title Company plans to upgrade the workstations on its network to Windows 98. The network consists of the following:

◆ Two Windows NT Server 4.0 systems serving as domain controllers. These systems will not be converted to Windows 98.

◆ 32 identical Pentium 100 PCs with 16MB memory and 1GB hard drives running Windows 95.

◆ 16 identical 486/66 PCs with 8MB RAM and 300MB hard drives running Windows 3.1. These PCs use a rare network adapter card for which Windows 98 doesn't have a built-in driver. You have obtained an inf file from the adapter manufacturer with a Windows 98 driver and accompanying files.

◆ Eight new laptop PCs with 24MB RAM and 1GB hard drives with newly formatted hard drives.

◆ Two PCs, used by high corporate officials who must sometimes use NT's enhanced security features, that will dual-boot Windows 98 with Windows NT.

continues

CASE STUDY: QUALITY TITLE COMPANY

continued

You need to get all the systems running in a hurry, because an important client will be visiting the office, and that client has already remarked to several of your marketing personnel that any company that isn't using Windows 98 is "living in the Stone Age."

ANALYSIS

The Windows 95 upgrade will be the easier part of the installation. The systems are ready for Windows 98 now. One of the objectives is to carry off the installation quickly, and with 32 PCs, a network installation seems like an appropriate solution. Use the Windows 98 Resource Kit's Batch 98 utility to create an installation script for an automated installation, and copy the Windows 98 installation files to a share point on one of the Windows NT domain controllers.

The 486 PCs do not have enough RAM to run Windows 98. You must upgrade the RAM for the 486 PCs to 16MB. You can then use the installation share you created (refer to the preceding paragraph) to upgrade the Windows 3.1 PCs to Windows 98 over the network. Use the Windows 98 Resource Kit's INF Installer to include the installation files for the network adapter with the Windows 98 installation.

The laptops require a clean installation. If the laptops are equipped to participate in the network, you can create a network-enabled boot disk using Windows NT Server's Network Client Administrator utility. Or, if creating a network-enabled boot floppy is too much trouble for just eight PCs, you can perform a local installation. Boot to a boot floppy that contains CD-ROM drivers and install Windows 98 from the local CD-ROM drive. Because you're in a hurry, use the Portable Setup option for a collection of optional components designed to accommodate portable PCs.

If the two PCs that will dual-boot with Windows NT already have NT dual-booting with DOS, Windows 3.x, or Windows 95, you can install Windows 98 through the other operating system. If these are new machines, or if NT is not presently installed, the easiest solution may be to install Windows 98 first and then install Windows NT to a different directory. NT Setup will configure the dual-boot. Remember that the active partition should be a FAT16 partition, and that Microsoft strongly recommends you install Windows 98 and Windows NT to different partitions.

CHAPTER SUMMARY

KEY TERMS

- dual-boot
- Emergency Startup Disk
- hardware detection
- INF
- installation script
- local installation
- network installation
- Safe Recovery
- setup option
- uninstall
- upgrade

This chapter discussed the various options and features of Windows 98 installation. You learned about DOS installations and Windows upgrades, local installations and network installations, setup options, and the Save System Files feature. This chapter also discussed some preliminary steps that should precede an installation and took a step-by-step look at the installation process. Lastly, this chapter looked at automating the Windows 98 installation, uninstalling Windows 98, and dual-booting Windows 98 with Windows NT.

If you're studying for the MCSE exam, it is more important to remember how and why to use the various installation options and methods than it is to memorize step-by-step procedures. Pay particular attention to Windows 98's safe recovery feature, Windows 98's Uninstall option, network installation methods, and the rules for dual-booting Windows 98 with Windows NT.

APPLY YOUR KNOWLEDGE

Exercises

2.1   Installing Windows 98 Across the Network

This exercise walks you through the process of installing Windows 98 across the network.

Estimated Time: 60 minutes

1. Insert the Microsoft Windows 98 CD into the CD-ROM drive of a Windows NT, Windows 95, or Windows 98 computer. (Not the computer on which you plan to install Windows 98.)

2. Create a network share for the CD-ROM drive. Right-click on the CD-ROM drive in Windows Explorer and select Sharing (see Chapter 5). Record the computer name of the computer and the name of the CD-ROM share. Make sure the share permissions are set so you can access the share in step 3.

3. From a command prompt or Run dialog box of another computer, type the full path to the setup program (setup.exe) on the shared CD-ROM drive. For instance, if the computer is a Windows 95 computer, click the Start button and choose Run; then enter the following:

   `\\server\share\setup.exe`

   server is the computer name of the computer with the shared CD-ROM drive and *share* is the name of the CD-ROM share.

4. If you're just doing this as a test, exit Setup. If you wish to install Windows 98 at this time, follow the instructions on your screen. See the description of the installation process earlier in this chapter. Don't forget to create an Emergency Startup Disk. And, if you have the disk space for it, don't forget

to save the existing system files. A typical network installation scenario would set up several computers at once and would probably make use of Windows 98 installation scripts. See the discussion of automated installation earlier in this chapter.

2.2   Exploring Windows 98/DOS Dual-Boot

This exercise describes the process of enabling MS-DOS dual-boot on a Windows 98 PC. The procedure provides the steps for adding DOS dual-boot capability to your system. The complete process may require some coordination and troubleshooting of the autoexec.dos and config.dos DOS boot files (see step 6), so if your goal is to prepare for the MCSE exam, you may wish to just work through steps 1–4 without completing undergoing the full reconfiguration.

Estimated Time: 20 minutes

1. The first task is to find the file msdos.sys and check the BootMulti setting. In Windows 98, open Explorer. In the Explorer View menu, select Folder Options and choose the View tab. Under Hidden Files, choose Show All Files. This setting will make hidden files appear in the Explorer directory tree.

2. Go to the root directory of the boot drive and look for the file msdos.sys. Double-click on the MSDOS.SYS icon, and when the Open With dialog box appears, choose NotePad. Or, open Notepad (in the Accessories group), choose Open from the File menu, and choose MSDOS.SYS.

3. In msdos.sys, look for the BootMulti setting in the Options section. If BootMulti is set to 1, DOS dual-boot is already configured for your system. If you'd like to add DOS dual-boot to your system, you must change the setting to 1

APPLY YOUR KNOWLEDGE

and resave `msdos.sys`. You may need to change the Read-only attribute for `msdos.sys` in order to make the change. Right-click on the file icon and choose Properties, then uncheck the read-only checkbox.

4. Browse through the root directory of your boot drive. If your system supports DOS dual-boot, you'll see DOS boot files with a `.dos` extension (`io.dos`, `msdos.dos`, `command.dos`, `autoexec.dos`, `config.dos`). If you don't want to make changes to your system, you're finished. Otherwise, follow the remaining steps to add MS-DOS boot files to your configuration.

5. If these DOS files aren't present and you wish to configure dual-boot, copy the files `io.sys`, `msdos.sys`, `command.com`, `autoexec.bat`, and `config.sys` from an MS-DOS 5.0 or later boot disk. Remember to change the extension to `.dos`. (Files such as `io.sys` and `msdos.sys` are used in the Windows 98 boot process. If you don't change the extension of the DOS boot files you copy from the disk, you will overwrite your Windows 98 boot files.)

WARNING

Do Not Use the DOS SYS Command
Do *not* use the DOS SYS command to copy the files from the boot disk. SYS will not change the names of the boot files and will overwrite your Windows 98 boot files.

---

6. Make any necessary changes to the `autoexec.dos` and `config.dos` files so that they will work on your system. Change any references to the A: drive, make sure all drivers are present, and so on.

7. Change the attributes of the new DOS files in the root directory of the boot drive (and in the host drive if you're using disk compression) to hidden, read-only, and system with the following command:

```
attrib +r +h +s *.dos
```

8. If you're using disk compression, copy the new DOS files to your host drive. To view the host drive in Explorer, right-click on the boot drive and choose Properties. Then, select the Compression tab and click on the Advanced button. In the Advanced Properties dialog box, uncheck the Hide Host Drive checkbox.

9. Shut down Windows 98. As the system boots, press F4 to boot to MS-DOS.

Review Questions

1. How much RAM is required to install Windows 98?

2. What is the minimum processor required to install 98?

3. How will Windows 98 treat shortcuts created within Windows 95 when doing an upgrade?

4. How does Windows 98 treat legacy hardware during the setup phase of Windows 98?

5. What will Windows 98 do when a file existing on your system is newer than the version Setup is attempting to install?

6. If a user forgets to add a component to Windows 98 how can she add it back to the system?

7. What should a user do if Setup hangs during the installation process?

8. What are the four setup options used with Windows 98?

9. What does NT 4.0 require of your active partition to dual-boot?

Exam Questions

1. A user informs you that he is trying to upgrade Windows for Workgroups to Windows 98, but he cannot. What is the problem?

    A. He only has 4MB of RAM.

    B. He cannot upgrade Windows for Workgroups to Windows 98.

    C. He does not have a computer account in the domain, which is required before they upgrade their Windows for Workgroup computer to Microsoft Windows 98.

    D. All of the above.

2. Bob has installed Windows 98 and Windows NT on his help desk computer. When in Windows NT he can see all of the files on all of his partitions. When he boots to Windows 98 he can only see the files on his C: drive. What do you suspect is the problem?

    A. Windows NT uses a different partition table than Windows 98.

    B. Windows NT can use the NTFS file system, which Windows 98 cannot see.

    C. Windows 98 can only see one primary partition at a time, whereas Windows NT can see four.

    D. Windows 98 will only support the FAT32 file system.

3. You suspect that Windows 98 Setup has overwritten some files that were needed by a program you ran in 95. What log file will help you determine what files were overwritten?

    A. `setup.log`

    B. `setuplog.txt`

    C. `system.log`

    D. `setupvcm.log`

4. You have 40 machines that need to be upgraded to 98. What is the best method to install Windows 98 onto these machines?

    A. Use sysdiff.exe to copy an image of one machine and then duplicate that image to all machines.

    B. Use SMS to push the operating system down to each machine.

    C. Use the Batch 98 tool to create a script for the install.

    D. You must visit each machine and install Windows 98 from the CD.

5. You are installing Windows 98 on a user's workstation that currently has Windows 95. The user will continue to log into your NT domain, use all of the installed software, and use dial-up networking. What will you have to do to configure the Setup program so that all of the current settings will convert to Windows 98?

    A. Use the `setup /ox` command.

    B. Use the `setup /o` command.

    C. Run group convert.exe after the installation.

    D. Do nothing but install Windows 98. The Setup program will convert all of the current settings to 98.

APPLY YOUR KNOWLEDGE

6. Your Windows 98 installation has stopped responding and appears to hang. You have tried pressing F3, clicking on Exit, and pressing Ctrl + Alt + Del, but your computer still won't respond. What should you do to continue with the install?

   A. Boot from your Windows 95 boot disk.

   B. Boot from your Windows 98 boot disk.

   C. Boot off of the Windows 98 CD-ROM.

   D. Power down and then power up the PC.

7. A user calls to tell you that she cannot access her D: drive when she boots into NT 4.0, but she can access it while in Windows 98. What do you suspect is the problem?

   A. Windows NT cannot access FAT32 partitions. Drive D: is probably formatted as FAT32.

   B. Windows NT cannot recognize any partitions created in Microsoft Windows 98.

   C. Windows NT cannot see the FAT partition because there can only be one primary partition at a time.

   D. The D: drive is probably on a controller card that is not supported by Windows NT.

8. You have installed Windows 98 on your PC. All hardware was found except for a sound card that you recently added to your computer. Upon further investigation you realize that the sound card is not Plug and Play compatible. How can you add the card to work with Windows 98?

   A. Windows 98 cannot use cards that are not Plug and Play compatible.

   B. Use the Add Legacy Hardware Wizard in Control Panel.

   C. You will have to manually add the card by using a setup program for the sound card to assign or confirm resources and then you will have to add the card through the Add New Hardware Wizard with a compatible driver.

   D. The sound card needs to be converted to Plug and Play mode.

Answers to Review Questions

1. 16MB of RAM. Note that this RAM requirement is considerably higher than Windows 95's 4MB minimum. The availability of low-price RAM in today's market has caused Microsoft to discontinue support for low-end systems. (For more information, refer to the section "Hardware Requirements.")

2. 486DX/66 or higher. (For more information, refer to the section "Hardware Requirements.")

3. Microsoft has gone to great effort to make the Windows 95 upgrade as simple and invisible as possible. User settings, such as shortcuts, will be preserved during setup. (For more information, refer to the section "Upgrading from Windows 95.")

4. Legacy hardware is detected last through a query of system settings and hardware resources in use, and by examining areas of memory that these devices may be using. (For more information, refer to the section "The Windows 98 Setup Process.")

5. The Version Conflict Manager will automatically save a copy of the newer file when it replaces the file with the version included on the Windows 98 CD. The file will be saved to the `\windows\VCM` subdirectory. (For more information, refer to the section "The Windows 98 Setup Process.")

6. She can add system components through the Add/Remove Programs Control Panel. (For more information, refer to the section "Setup Options.")

7. First try F3 and Exit, then Ctrl + Alt + Del, then restart the computer; Setup will attempt to recover using information in the Setup log files when the machine is restarted. (For more information, refer to the section "Setup Failure Detection and Recovery.")

8. Typical (for normal installations), Portable (for portable computers), Compact (for computers with limited disk space), and Custom (for custom configurations). (For more information, refer to the section "Setup Options.")

9. NT 4.0 requires the active partition to be formatted with FAT16. (For more information, refer to the section "Dual-Booting Windows 98 with Windows NT.")

Answers to Exam Questions

1. **A.** Windows 98 requires 16MB RAM. (For more information, refer to the section "Hardware Requirements.")

2. **B.** Windows NT can use the NTFS file system, which cannot be seen by Windows 98. Bob probably has NTFS partitions on his PC. (For more information, refer to the section

"Dual-Booting Windows 98 with Windows NT.")

3. **B.** The log file `setuplog.txt` contains a record of installation events. (For more information, refer to the section "Setup Failure Detection and Recovery.")

4. **C.** The Microsoft Resource Kit includes the Batch 98 tool to automate the installation of Windows 98 to many PCs. (For more information, refer to the section "Creating Installation Scripts with Batch 98.")

5. **D.** As part of the upgrade of Windows 95 to Windows 98, the users' settings will also be converted. (For more information, refer to the section "Upgrading from Windows 95.")

6. **D.** If your Windows 98 machine has stopped responding during the installation of Windows 98, power down and then power up the machine. Setup will examine the `setuplog.txt` file and will create a workaround for the problem. Most likely, the hang was due to resource arbitration during the hardware detection phase of the installation. (For more information, refer to the section "Setup Failure Detection and Recovery.")

7. **A.** Windows NT 4.0 cannot access FAT32 partitions. (For more information, refer to the section "Dual-Booting Windows 98 with Windows NT.")

8. **C.** If you can't configure a legacy hardware through Windows 98, try to configure it through a setup application that comes with the hardware. You might also check whether the manufacturer has a compatible driver for Windows 98 that will allow Windows 98 to assign system resources, such as IRQs, to the device. (For more information, refer to the section "The Windows 98 Setup Process.")

APPLY YOUR KNOWLEDGE

Suggested Readings and Resources

1. The *Windows 98 Resource Kit*; Microsoft Press

2. *The Windows 98 Professional Reference,* Hallberg and Casad; New Riders

This chapter helps you to prepare for the Microsoft exam by covering the following objectives within the "Installation and Configuration" and "Integration and Interoperability" categories:

Configure Windows 98 server components. Server components include the following:

> **Microsoft Personal Web Server 4.0**
>
> **Dial-Up Networking Server**

▶ Windows 98 can serve as an Intranet server and as a dial-up server for various types of clients dialing into the dial-up server. Your knowledge of these components will be tested on the Windows 98 exam.

Install and configure the network components of Windows 98 in a Microsoft environment or a mixed Microsoft and NetWare environment. Network components include the following:

> **Client for Microsoft Networks**
>
> **Client for NetWare Networks**
>
> **Network adapters**
>
> **File and Printer Sharing for Microsoft Networks**
>
> **File and Printer Sharing for NetWare Networks**
>
> **Service for NetWare Directory Services (NDS)**
>
> **Asynchronous Transfer Mode (ATM) components**
>
> **Virtual private networking and PPTP**
>
> **Browse Master**

▶ Windows 98 includes networking features that support both Microsoft and NetWare environments. Your knowledge of how to create a network from the adapter card to sharing resources on either a Microsoft or NetWare network, or even a mixed

CHAPTER 3

Windows 98 Networking

environment, is crucial to passing the Windows 98 exam. In addition to local networking, you will also need an operational understanding of Asynchronous Transfer Mode, Virtual Private Networks, and the Point to Point Tunneling Protocol (PPTP).

Install and configure network protocols in a Microsoft environment or a mixed Microsoft and NetWare environment. Protocols include the following:

> **NetBEUI**
>
> **IPX/SPX-compatible protocol**
>
> **TCP/IP**
>
> **Microsoft DLC**
>
> **Fast Infrared**

▶ Windows 98 networking can use a variety of protocols. You will need to know the attributes of each protocol, how to configure each protocol, and why a particular protocol should be used in a given situation.

Configure a Windows 98 computer as a client computer in a network that contains a Windows NT 4.0 domain.

▶ Windows 98 can be configured to log in to a Windows NT domain. You will need to understand what an NT domain is, what its components are, and how Windows 98 interacts with the domain.

Configure a Windows 98 computer as a client computer in a NetWare network.

▶ Windows 98 can act as a client in a NetWare Environment. You'll need to have a working knowledge of the NetWare components included with Windows 98 to configure the Windows 98 machine to participate in the NetWare environment.

Configure a Windows 98 computer for remote access by using various methods in a Microsoft environment or a mixed Microsoft and NetWare environment. Methods include the following:

> **Dial-Up Networking**
>
> **Proxy server**

▶ Windows 98 can act as a dial-up client to a number of different servers: Windows NT RAS Servers, NetWare servers, Internet servers, and even other Windows 98 machines. You will need to understand how to set up this process on a Windows 98 machine.

A proxy server can act as a go-between—between the Windows 98 host and the Internet. You will need to know what a proxy server is and how to configure Windows 98 to interact with one.

OUTLINE

STUDY STRATEGIES

To study effectively for these test objectives, complete the review questions, read the chapter content, complete the networking exercises, and test yourself with the exam questions. It would also benefit you to create a Windows 98 network from the ground up to joining a Windows NT Domain or a NetWare environment. Investigate all of the settings within the Network applet. Pay close attention to the attributes of each protocol and when you should use one protocol rather than another. Know how to configure the Windows 98 machine to act as a client in a variety of different networks: Dial-Up, NetWare, and Windows NT. Understand what a proxy server is, how it works, and why a company might use one.

INTRODUCTION

Networking is at the heart of Windows 98, and it is therefore at the heart of the Windows 98 MCSE exam. Microsoft warns that you should be prepared to plan, configure, manage, and troubleshoot Windows 98 in all its most common networking environments, including peer-to-peer networks, Windows NT domains, dial-up networks, and Novell NetWare networks.

Windows 98's modular networking architecture lets you easily adapt Windows 98 to different network environments and configurations. As you learned in Chapter 1, "Planning," your Windows 98 networking configuration consists of four important component types:

◆ Adapters

◆ Protocols

◆ Clients

◆ Services

Stated briefly, an *adapter* (and the accompanying adapter software) interfaces the computer with the transmission medium. A *protocol* carries out the rules and procedures for communicating over the network under a given protocol specification. A *client* sends requests to the network and manages responses to those requests. Finally, a *service* is an application that listens for and fulfills network requests.

Windows 98 includes several adapter drivers that you can install and configure to match your driver hardware. Windows 98 also includes several protocols, clients, and services that are useful in specific situations. A major part of configuring Windows 98 networking consists of deciding on the right components so that your computer will interact appropriately in a given networking environment. This chapter will discuss the protocols, clients, and services included with Windows 98 and will show you which components to use for a workgroup, NetWare network, or Windows NT domain.

> NOTE
> **NIC**   The form of adapter used on Ethernet local area networks is commonly called a Network Interface Card, or NIC.

In addition to deciding which components to install and configure, you must also configure a few other networking settings. Some of those settings include the following:

◆ **Primary network logon.** Tells Windows 98 how to authenticate a user who is logging on to the system. You'll learn more about Windows 98 Logon in an upcoming section.

◆ **Identification.** You can choose a computer name and workgroup for your Windows 98 computer. You'll learn more about computer names and workgroup names, and their roles in identifying a Windows 98 computer on the network, later in this chapter.

◆ **Access Control method.** If your computer will be sharing its own resources with the network, you'll need to decide whether to use share-level or user-level security. Chapter 1 described Windows 98's access control methods. You'll see how to configure access control later in this chapter.

Of course, there are many other factors you'll have to consider when configuring Windows 98 networking. This chapter provides some details on the many Windows 98 networking components. In addition to adapters, protocols, clients, and services, you'll learn about some Windows 98 server components, such as Personal Web Server (PWS) and Dial-Up Networking Server, and you'll learn about new networking features included with Windows 98, such as multilink and PPTP. This chapter also takes a look at how Windows 98 fits in a NetWare network and a Windows NT domain. Finally, you'll learn about remote access in Windows 98.

The chapter is organized into the following main networking sections, and in the following order:

◆ Understanding Windows 98 Logon

◆ Browsing and Identifying in Windows 98

◆ Windows 98 Networking Configuration: A Quick Tour of the Control Panel

◆ Configuring Network Components

◆ Windows 98 Server Components

◆ Windows 98 on NT Networks

◆ Windows 98 on NetWare Networks

◆ Windows 98 and Remote Access

UNDERSTANDING WINDOWS 98 LOGON

A first step in establishing a network connection is often a network logon. Most networking environments—including Microsoft NT and NetWare environments—support some form of network logon, and if Windows 98 is to act as a client in these environments, it must provide network logon capability. Networks also require some form of authentication for access to network resources, such as file and printer resources. (Chapter 1 introduced user-level access control; you'll learn more about it in Chapter 5, "Managing Resources in Windows 98.") The logon scheme must also provide some means of defining the user environment on the local computer through Windows 98's user profile feature (see Chapter 6, "Managing Profiles and System Policies"). Before beginning a study of Windows 98's networking components, it is best to pause for a quick look at Windows 98 logon and its effect on network connectivity.

A simple description of Windows 98 logon is that you can define a Primary Network Logon in the Network Control Panel's Configuration tab, and this Primary Network Logon setting will define what logon dialog box appears at startup. Options include the following:

◆ **Windows Logon.** Not a network logon at all (at least not directly). The local Windows 98 validates your logon information and uses your username to assign the correct user profile. (See Chapter 6 for more information about user profiles in Windows 98.) Although Windows logon is validated locally, it can provide you with network access through password synchronization and password caching, as described later in this section.

◆ **Network Client Logons.** You can configure Windows 98 to display a network client logon dialog box at startup. Network-based authentication is an important feature of many network systems, such as NT domains and NetWare networks. Windows 98's most commonly used built-in Clients—Client for Microsoft Networks and Client for NetWare Networks—both provide primary network logon options. As you'll learn later in this section, network administrators use the client logon to force the user to log on to the network before being granted access to the system.

- **Windows Family Logon.** Windows Family Logon, a new Windows 98 feature, is similar to Windows Logon except the user must select a username from a menu rather than entering a username in a text box.

If you have configured your system through a network client, you can configure Windows 98 to log you on to that network even if you don't choose the client as the Primary Network Logon. By definition, Windows 98 logs you on to the network defined as the Primary Network Logon network. Windows 98 may also be able to connect you automatically to a network that isn't the Primary Network Logon network, however. You can configure Windows 98 to log on to other networks (in addition to the network defined in the Primary Network Logon) in the following ways:

- **Synchronizing passwords.** If the Windows 98 password or the password for another network matches the Primary Network Logon password, Windows 98 automatically uses the Primary Network Logon password to log you on to Windows 98 or to the other network. For instance, if the Windows 98 PC for a user named Kevin is configured to log Kevin on to a Windows NT domain, Kevin could use the Windows logon to access the system; likewise, if the Windows logon password matched the NT domain password, Windows 98 will log Kevin on to the domain automatically.

- **Password caching.** Windows 98 includes a feature called password caching that lets you store passwords and reuse them automatically to restore connections and log on to networks. Password caching lets you automatically connect to a network even if the passwords aren't synchronized.

Password caching is enabled by default in Windows 98. You can use password caching to store passwords that will provide access to the following:

- Windows NT domains, when the domain client is *not* specified as the primary network logon

- NetWare servers

> **NOTE**
>
> **Changing Your Windows Password**
> The Change Passwords tab in the Passwords Control Panel lets you change your Windows password or the password Windows will use to access another resource (see Figure 3.1).

◆ Local Windows NT systems

◆ Network resources protected with Windows 95/98 share-level
security

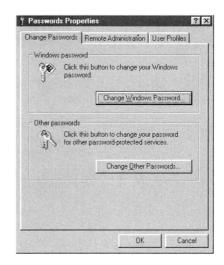

When you access a password-protected resource, you'll see a checkbox labeled Save This Password in your password list. If you check
the checkbox, the password will be added to the password list. The
password list is a file with a PWL extension stored in the Windows
directory. Each user on the system has a password list file that contains cached passwords the user has saved. When the user logs on
through the primary network logon, the password list is *unlocked*
and becomes accessible to the user. If the user bypasses the primary
network logon at startup by clicking Cancel in the logon dialog box,
the password list will remain locked and the user will not be able to
access any cached passwords.

FIGURE 3.1
You can change your Windows password using
the Change Passwords tab in the Passwords
Control Panel.

Passwords are stored in an encrypted format in the password list file.
The Windows 98 CD includes a tool called Password List Editor
that lets you view entries in the password list file. You cannot view
actual passwords but you can remove items from the list and view
the resources with entries in the password list.

To install Password List Editor, perform the tasks outlined in Step by
Step 3.1.

STEP BY STEP

3.1 Installing Password List Editor

1. Start the Add/Remove Programs Control Panel and select
the Windows setup tab.

2. Click on Have Disk.

3. In the Install from Disk dialog box, click on Browse.

4. Place the Windows 98 CD in the CD-ROM drive and
enter the path to the file `tools\reskit\Netadmin\`
`Pwledit\pwledit.inf`. Click on OK and OK again.

5. Select Password List Editor in the Have Disk dialog box
and click on Install.

After Password List Editor is installed, you can run it by typing **pwledit** in the Start menu's Run dialog box.

Password caching is very convenient, but it is also a risk in many secure environments. Password caching could mean, for instance, that anyone who happens upon your Windows logon password could obtain access to any or all of your network connections. Many network administrators prefer to disable password caching. You can disable password caching through System Policy Editor using the Local Computer Policy Windows 98 Network/Passwords/Disable Password Caching. See Chapter 6 for more on System Policy Editor.

The Windows Logon Authentication option is a simple way to process the logon locally and match the user to a local user profile. As described earlier, the Windows logon can also provide access to network connections through password caching.

One disadvantage of the Windows logon is that it only applies to one computer. You can't roam to other computers on the network and automatically access the same network-based account. You also can impose the same centralized security through the Windows logon that you can with a network-based Primary Network Logon. On server-based networks such as NetWare Networks and Windows NT domains, a practical approach is to designate the primary network client as the Primary Network Logon and then use system policies to require that the user logon to the network before accessing Windows 98. To require network validation, enable the default computer policy Windows 98 Network/Logon/Require validation from network for Windows access. The user will thus be required to identify herself to the network before accessing Windows 98, and network-based environment features such as user profiles and system policies (see Chapter 6) will follow the user to other locations on the network.

The Windows logon does not really secure the system (although it does secure a particular user's profile and password). You can bypass the Windows logon by clicking Cancel in the logon dialog box, or you can simply enter a new username and password and Windows will create a new user profile and let you log on.

The Microsoft Family logon is similar to the Windows logon except it requires the user to choose a username from the list of users already configured for the system. A user is thus required to use an existing profile, and users who haven't been configured for the system cannot log on. New users can be added to the system using the Users Control Panel, which invokes the User Settings dialog box (see Figure 3.2).

BROWSING AND IDENTIFYING IN WINDOWS 98

Windows 98's Network Neighborhood lets you conveniently browse for computers and their shared resources. Browsing vastly simplifies the task of connecting to network resources, and it is an extremely important feature of PC networking systems. Microsoft goes to considerable trouble to support browsing on Windows 98 systems. Network Neighborhood and the other features of Windows 98 that support browsing use the NetBIOS program interface. NetBIOS began with PC-based networks and remains an important feature in Windows 98. The NetBIOS interface provides a means for locating resources on the network, either through network browsing or through text-based commands using the Universal Naming Convention (UNC).

NetBIOS identifies computers by computer name. A computer name is an alphanumeric name of 15 or fewer characters with no blank spaces. The characters can be letters, numerals, or any of the following special characters: !@#$%^&()-_{}~. The computer name must be unique.

Because NetBIOS is not a network protocol but is, instead, a program interface that rests above the network protocol in Windows 98 modular architecture, NetBIOS supports a variety of underlying protocols. If you're using TCP/IP, Windows 98 supports a number of methods for resolving computer names with IP addresses. You'll learn more about NetBIOS name resolution later in this chapter.

You can define a computer name for your computer during Windows 98 Setup. Or you can add or change the computer name after Windows 98 is installed by using the Network Control Panel's Identification tab.

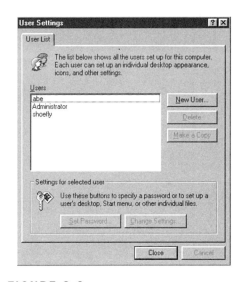

FIGURE 3.2
The User Settings dialog box lets you add additional Windows users.

The Identification tab of the Network Control Panel also lets you define a workgroup name. The workgroup name follows the same naming conventions as the computer name except that it doesn't have to be unique, and, in fact, shouldn't be unique if it is to be of any practical use. The *workgroup* is a group under which the computer will be organized in network browse lists. Computers with the same workgroup name will be grouped together in Network Neighborhood and other browse lists.

According to Microsoft, the browse list can contain "the names of domains, workgroups, and computers running the file and printer sharing service." The list can contain the following:

- ◆ Windows 95/98 computers
- ◆ Windows NT computers
- ◆ Windows for Workgroups computers
- ◆ LAN Manager 2.x servers
- ◆ Workgroup Add-on for MS-DOS peer servers
- ◆ NT domains
- ◆ LAN Manager domains
- ◆ Workgroups comprised on Windows 95/98, Windows NT, and Windows for Workgroup PCs

A browse list looks very simple and appears seamlessly beneath the Network Neighborhood icon in Windows Explorer as if it were another directory of files, but, in fact, an invisible interaction of process and services makes browsing possible in Windows 98.

On a Microsoft network, one computer in a workgroup serves as *browse master*. The browse master maintains the browse list for the workgroup and makes the browse list available to other computers. Microsoft sometimes uses the term *master browse server* for the browse master PC, and this term is perhaps more appropriate because it reminds you that the browse master is acting as a *server*— a computer that fulfills network requests. In addition to master browse server, the subnet may contain one or more backup servers. Backup browse servers receive copies of the browse list from the master browse server at periodic intervals and assist with resolving browse client requests.

When a Windows 98 computer starts, it checks whether a master browse server exists in the workgroup. If the workgroup does not have a master browse server, a browser election takes place. A *browser election* is a procedure, invisible to the user, in which the computers in the workgroup determine which computer will become the master browse server. The decision of which computer will serve as the master browse server depends on a number of criteria, including the operating system, the operating system version, and the present browser role. A Windows NT server system will be chosen before a Windows NT workstation system, which will be chosen before a Windows 95 or Windows 98 PC. A backup browser is more likely to become browse master than a computer with no browser role.

When the ratio of computers to browsers in a workgroup exceeds some predefined threshold (typically one browser per 15 computers), an additional computer is selected as a backup browse server.

> NOTE
>
> **Not Much of an Election**   A browser election isn't really much like an election. It is more of a war council or, perhaps, a bragging contest. The winner is chosen not through suffrage but by a direct comparison of credentials.

Although browser elections are invisible to the user, you can influence the election by manually configuring the Browse Master setting for a Windows 98 PC. You can set the Browse Master setting to Disable (which disqualifies the PC from serving as the browse master). Another option is to set the Browse Master setting to Enabled (which gives the computer a higher priority over other Windows 95/98 PCs in the browser election). You also can place the Browse Master setting on Automatic (the default), which basically lets the network determine whether the PC should serve as a browse master.

On larger networks with routers and multiple subnets, the interactions necessary to support network browsing become more complex. You'll learn more about browsing on NetWare networks in section "Windows 98 on NetWare Networks." Routed Windows NT networks typically use the TCP/IP protocol, and Microsoft networks include a number of features that provide the name resolution functions necessary to support browsing and NetBIOS addressing in TCP/IP. You'll learn more about NetBIOS name resolution in TCP/IP later in this chapter.

The Browse Master feature is a server role, and you configure the Browse Master setting through the active file and printer sharing service.

To access the browser configuration options for a computer running File and Printer Sharing for Microsoft Networks, perform the tasks outlined in Step by Step 3.2.

STEP BY STEP

3.2 Configuring Browser Options with File and Printer Sharing for Microsoft Networks

1. In the Configuration tab of the Network Control Panel, select File and Printer Sharing for Microsoft Networks in the component list.

2. Click the Properties button to invoke the File and Printer Sharing for Microsoft Networks dialog box.

3. In the Advanced tab, select the Browse Master property. In the box labeled Value, click on the down arrow to select one of the following choices:

   • Select Automatic to have Windows 98 automatically determine whether the computer is needed as a browse server.

   • Select Disabled to prevent the computer from maintaining browse lists for the network.

   • To give the computer a higher priority for the browse elections, select Enabled. This computer will then be preferred over other Windows 98 computers that have the Automatic value for the browse elections.

4. Click OK twice, and then restart the computer.

To access the browser configuration options for a computer running File and Printer Sharing for NetWare Networks, perform the tasks outlined in Step by Step 3.3.

STEP BY STEP

3.3 Configuring Browser Options with File and Printer Sharing for NetWare Networks

1. Choose the Network Control Panel. In the Configuration tab, select File and Printer Sharing for NetWare Networks from the component list.

2. Click Properties and select the Workgroup Advertising property (see Figure 3.3).

3. Choose one of the following options from the drop-down list:

- To have Windows 98 automatically determine if the computer is needed as a browse server, select Enabled: May Be Master.

- To prevent the computer from maintaining browse lists for the network, select Enabled: Will Not Be Master.

  The Enabled: Will Not Be Master option doesn't prevent the computer from browsing the network resources; it prevents the computer from maintaining a browse list for itself and other computers. (Select the Disabled option to prevent the computer from using the browse service.)

- To give the computer a higher priority for the browse elections, select Enabled: Preferred Master. This computer will then be preferred over other Windows 95 computers that have Automatic set for the Browse Master value for the browse elections.

- To prevent the computer from using the browser service to browse network resources, select Disabled. The computer will not be added to the browse list and therefore will not be seen by other browsing computers.

- To allow the computer to send SAP broadcasts announcing its presence to real-mode NetWare clients, select the SAP Advertising property and change the value to Enabled.

4. Click OK twice, and then restart the computer.

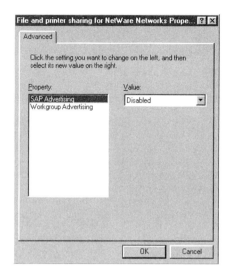

FIGURE 3.3
You can set browser options in the File and Printer Sharing for NetWare Networks Properties dialog box.

N O T E

The SAP Advertising Disabled Option
Selecting the Disabled option for the SAP Advertising property doesn't prevent the computer from browsing the network resources. Rather, it prevents the computer from maintaining a browse list for itself and other computers. As long as at least one computer on the network is a browser, other computers can use the browsing service.

Handling Browser Failures

A number of things can go wrong with the browser operations on a Microsoft network. If you are aware of the problems, it's easy to compensate for them. Table 3.1 lists some of the most common problems and solutions, a reference that will get you through the rough parts.

TABLE 3.1

DIAGNOSING BROWSER PROBLEMS

Problem	*Solution*
Computers appear on the browse list but are not accessible.	When a computer shuts down properly, it notifies the master browser, which removes the computer from the browse list. It may take up to 15 minutes for the master browser to let the backup browser know that the computer is gone. If a computer is shut down improperly, it must fail at three of its 12-minute announcements before the master browser removes the computer from the browser list. Wait for it to fix itself, or reboot the master browser.
DOS clients and Windows clients receive different browse lists.	DOS browser clients don't know how to deal with backup browsers. Windows browser clients always receive their server lists from the backup browser. Because the DOS client always gets its list from the master browser, its list will be more current than the Windows list. Wait 15 minutes, and the lists should be the same. This is not a problem. The Windows clients try to reduce the workload on the master browser.
Windows 98 reports the error `Network unavailable` when attempting to browse the Network Neighborhood.	This will happen if there is no master browser for your workgroup. You should either change your workgroup name to match a workgroup that has a master browser or install File and Printer Sharing and configure your workstation to maintain the browse list.
No other workgroups or domains are listed in the Network Neighborhood.	If your master browser has just started up, it will make workgroup announcements in addition to the default announcements every 15 minutes. This allows the master browser to show up on other workgroup browse lists.

Problem	*Solution*
	However, the master browser will have to wait until the other servers reach their 15-minute announcement period before it knows about other domains.

Most problems with the browse list will be solved on their own if you just wait. To be sure that you don't have a problem with network connectivity, choose Start, Run and type *server_name* for a known server that is currently running. If you are presented with a share list, you're on the network.

WINDOWS 98 NETWORKING CONFIGURATION: A QUICK TOUR OF THE CONTROL PANEL

The Network Control Panel is the center for Windows 98 networking configuration. To access the Network Control Panel, choose Start, Settings, Control Panel and double-click on Network in the Control Panel window. You can also access the Network Control Panel by right-clicking on the Network Neighborhood desktop icon and choosing Properties.

In order to use the Network Control Panel wisely, you have to know what components and settings you wish to configure, and this will depend on the type of network and the role you want Windows 98 to play on that network. Later sections in this chapter will show you which networking components to install for various situations. This section provides a brief tour of the Network Control Panel so you'll see how everything fits together.

The Network Control Panel is shown in Figure 3.4. The currently installed components appear in the box at the top of the Configuration tab. Select any component and click on the Properties button to configure settings for that component. You'll learn more about how to configure the various networking components later in this chapter.

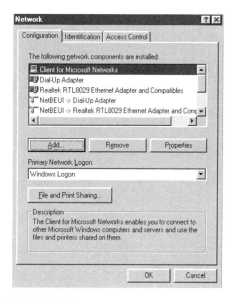

FIGURE 3.4

The Network Control Panel is the center for Windows 98 networking configuration.

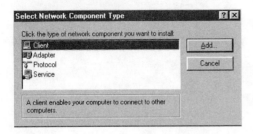

FIGURE 3.5
The Select Network Component Type dialog box lets you choose what type of component you'd like to install.

Click on the Add button to invoke the Select Network Component Type dialog box (see Figure 3.5), which lets you add a component to your configuration. Note that the components fall into the four categories described earlier in this chapter (clients, adapters, protocols, and services). Double-click on an icon in the Select Network Component Type dialog box to select a component. For example, double-clicking on the Client icon invokes the Select Network Client dialog box (see Figure 3.6). In this dialog box, select a manufacturer in the left box and the available client components associated with that manufacturer appear in the right box. Or, click on the Have Disk button to provide a disk containing a specific software package you want to install.

The Configuration tab also lets you configure the primary network logon. The primary network logon (as described earlier in this chapter) tells Windows 98 how to validate the user's username and password at logon.

The File and Print Sharing button lets you enable or disable file sharing and printer sharing (see Figure 3.7). You'll need to enable file and printer sharing on your computer if you want to share files and printers on the network. You'll learn more about Windows 98's file and printer sharing later in this chapter.

The Network Control Panel's Identification tab (see Figure 3.8) lets you configure a computer name and workgroup name.

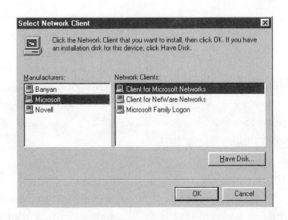

FIGURE 3.6
Choose a manufacturer and component from the list, or click on Have Disk to install a component from another source.

The Access Control tab (see Figure 3.9) lets you configure either share-level or user-level access control for your PC. These settings are important if you want to make resources available for network access. Chapter 1 described share-level and user-level access control, and you'll learn more about how to configure access control later in this chapter in the discussion of file and printer sharing. Note that the user-level access control option lets you enter the name of a security provider—a Windows NT or NetWare computer that will provide Windows 98 with a list of user and group names. See Chapter 5 for more information about user and group permissions.

This quick tour should give you an idea of how the Network Control Panel is organized. Upcoming sections refer often to the ubiquitous Network Control Panel as they walk you through the actual processes of configuring network components.

FIGURE 3.7
Clicking the File and Print Sharing button invokes the File and Printer Sharing dialog box.

INSTALLING AND CONFIGURING NETWORK COMPONENTS

Install and configure the network components of Windows 98 in a Microsoft environment or a mixed Microsoft and NetWare environment.

As this chapter has already mentioned, Windows 98 classifies network components as adapters, protocols, clients, and services. These components work together to form a pathway for data traveling from the local machine to the network and back again. In the Network Control Panel, these components appear jumbled together in a common component list, but in fact, the networking components interact with each other in specific, predetermined ways.

If you've taken the Networking Essentials MCSE exam, or if you've studied networking in the past, it may be helpful to consider that, although only one of the components is called the *protocol* component, in fact, all the Windows 98 networking components are part of what is known in common networking terminology as a *protocol stack*. Note that what Windows 98 calls a *"protocol"* is a component that performs services at the Network and Transport layers of the protocol stack. The adapter component at the Media Access layer (or

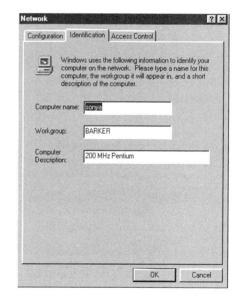

FIGURE 3.8
The Identification tab lets you specify a computer name and workgroup name.

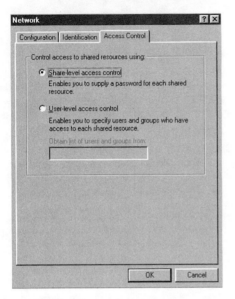

FIGURE 3.9
The Access Control tab lets you specify share-level or user-level access control.

Manually Configuring Bindings As you'll learn in later sections, you can manually disable or enable bindings to limit the interaction of networking components. The Bindings tab in the Protocol Properties dialog box or the Adapter Properties dialog box lets you manually configure bindings.

Data Link/Physical layers in OSI terminology), and the Services and Clients occupy the upper layers of the protocol stack.

In reality, the arrangement of modular components in Windows 98 networking is somewhat more complicated than the one just discussed and includes several internal components that assist in interfacing Windows 98 applications with the network. One component that is particularly essential is the NDIS component (ndis.vxd), which lets you interface multiple Network/Transport protocols with multiple network adapters. NDIS and other internal Windows 98 mechanisms work with the installable adapter, protocol, client, and service components to create Windows 98's seamless and integrated networking capability.

In order for Windows 98 networking components to behave like a stack, Windows 98 must define a potential channel or pathway that links one component with another component in the layers above or below it. This potential pathway is known as a *binding*. A binding establishes a link between an adapter component and a protocol component, or between a protocol component and a service component. You'll learn more about bindings in the following sections, which describe how to configure adapters, protocols, clients, and services in Windows 98.

Installing and Configuring Adapters

In Windows 98, a *network adapter* is a device that provides access to the network medium. More to the point, when you install and configure an adapter component in Windows 98 networking, you are really installing and configuring a software component that interacts with the adapter device. This software component is commonly referred to as the *adapter driver*.

It is important to note that the network adapter can be, but does not have to be, an adapter card for a local area network (such as an Ethernet or Token Ring card). Windows 98's Dial-Up Adapter is an adapter component designed to provide connectivity through a dial-up modem connection. Other adapters provide access to media such as ISDN and ATM.

Windows 98 includes drivers for many of the most popular network adapters. Additional network adapter drivers may be supplied by the network adapter vendor for use with Windows 98. Before you can install any other Windows 98 networking components, you must install a network adapter driver through the Network Control Panel.

You can configure an installed network adapter driver by selecting the adapter from the component list in the Network Control Panel and choosing Properties. If the network card supports the Plug and Play standard, Windows 98 can install a new adapter automatically. Otherwise, install the adapter according to the manufacturer's documentation or as outlined in Step by Step 3.4.

> **NOTE**
>
> **Microsoft Dial-Up Adapter Driver**
> If you don't have an actual network card in the computer, you can use the Microsoft Dial-Up Adapter driver, along with a compatible modem, for network connectivity.

STEP BY STEP

3.4 Installing an Adapter

1. Open the Network Control Panel and choose the Configuration tab.

2. Click the Add button and choose Adapter.

3. Click the Add button.

4. Choose the manufacturer and adapter you want to install, as shown in Figure 3.10. If your adapter is updated or unlisted, click the Have Disk button, provide the path to the `oemsetup.inf` file, and choose the adapter you want. Then click OK.

5. Click OK to close the Network dialog box. You will be prompted for the Windows 98 CD.

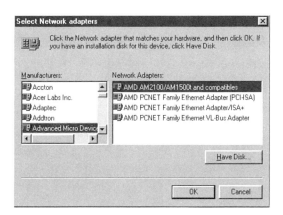

FIGURE 3.10
Microsoft provides drivers for a wide range of network cards from most major card manufacturers.

Sometimes, network adapters must be manually configured. Because every network adapter is different, you should consult the card's documentation to find out what settings are required. You can configure network adapter settings in either the Network Control Panel or in Device Manager (see Chapter 5). Network adapter settings usually include the following:

◆ Driver type

◆ Bindings

◆ Advanced configuration

◆ Resources

All of these settings are accessible through the Network Control Panel. If you choose to access the settings on the network card through the Network Control Panel, select the installed adapter in the components list and click on the Properties button.

The following sections discuss these network adapter settings. You'll also take a quick look at the following topics related to installing and configuring network adapters:

◆ Installing Plug and Play adapters

◆ Installing legacy adapters

◆ Installing adapter cards that aren't in the Windows 98 distribution

Choosing a Driver Type

To configure a driver type for a network adapter, select the adapter in the Components list of the Network Control Panel's Configuration tab and click on Properties. In the Driver Type tab (see Figure 3.11), select a driver type. Three driver types may be used: enhanced-mode (32-bit and 16-bit) NDIS, real-mode (16-bit) NDIS, and real-mode (16-bit) ODI. As described earlier in this chapter, NDIS is a standard that lets you interface one adapter with multiple protocols or one protocol with multiple adapters. ODI is an equivalent standard developed by Apple and Novell.

Whenever it is available, you should use the enhanced-mode NDIS driver, because it will load in protected memory, which frees up conventional memory for DOS sessions. If the drivers are 32-bit, they will also give you an added advantage of increased speed.

16-bit drivers are a second choice. Use the 16-bit NDIS driver if you need it for a real-mode Microsoft network client. Use the ODI driver with a real-mode NetWare client.

Configuring Bindings

To configure bindings for a network adapter, select the adapter in the components list of the Network Control Panel Configuration tab and click on Properties. Select the Bindings tab. The Bindings tab, shown in Figure 3.12, lists the connections to an adapter by various protocols. As described previously, a binding is a potential pathway. For instance, if a network adapter is bound to the NetBEUI protocol, Windows 98 will be able to use the adapter to send and receive NetBEUI transmissions. The Bindings tab always lists the items on the next level up in the Windows 98 Network model (discussed later in this chapter).

The Bindings tab lists all the protocols that are connected or "bound" to the adapter you're viewing. You can unbind a protocol by clearing its check box. In order to improve the overall speed of your computer's network access, you should unbind all unnecessary network protocols.

You can also disable protocol bindings as a security feature. For instance, if your computer is connected to the Internet through an ISDN line, you could disable the TCP/IP binding for the local LAN Ethernet card to ensure that Internet users won't be able to access the local network. If a protocol is installed on your computer but not bound to any adapters, you won't be able to use the protocol.

Configuring Advanced Settings

The Advanced tab of the Adapter Properties dialog box, shown in Figure 3.13, lists a series of advanced settings for the network adapter. This list of settings varies from one adapter driver to another. The Advanced tab often includes settings such as the maximum transmission size for network packets and buffer settings for the

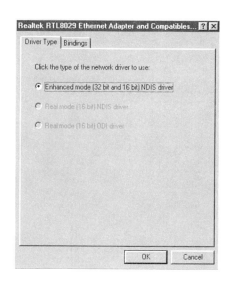

FIGURE 3.11
Choosing the driver type incorrectly can affect the system's overall network access.

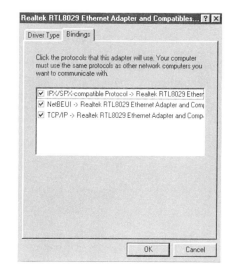

FIGURE 3.12
By making only necessary bindings, you can decrease the amount of time that it takes for your computer to establish a connection with a server.

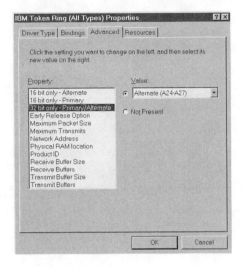

FIGURE 3.13
Many network adapters have advanced settings that can be modified to provide support of specific features.

> **NOTE**
>
> **Restrictions** Some network adapters cannot be configured through Device Manager.

adapter. If possible, it is best to use the default values. If you need to make a change, consult the adapter manufacturer.

Configuring Adapter Resources Through Device Manager

You can change resource settings for your network adapter (such as IRQ and Input/Output Range) through the Device Manager tab of the System Control Panel. Your network adapter should be located under the Network Adapters section of Device Manager's device tree. Select your adapter and click on Properties. In the Adapter Properties dialog box, click on the Resources tab. The Resources tab (see Figure 3.14) lets you see and—depending on your adapter— change the resources being used by the adapter. The resources used by the adapter may include the IRQ and I/O address. See Chapter 5 for more information about configuring resource settings through Device Manager.

If your network adapter does not support Plug and Play, you may have to choose resource settings that are consistent with the jumper settings on the card itself. Consult the manufacturer's documentation.

Installing Plug and Play Adapters

If a network card is Plug and Play compliant, it can be automatically detected and configured with Windows 98. Simply plug the card into the appropriate expansion slot and start Windows 98. The model of card will be detected, and the appropriate Windows driver will be installed. Windows 98 then assigns an available interrupt request (IRQ) line and memory or I/O address range to the network card as appropriate and configures the card to use these settings.

Installing Legacy Adapters

Some legacy adapters support software configuration for IRQ and I/O addresses, but many in this class allow configuration changes only by changing jumpers or dip switches. The Windows 98 resource settings must be consistent with the jumper or dip switch settings. Also, legacy cards don't always support 32-bit drivers; therefore, you might need to use 16-bit (possibly real-mode) drivers with legacy adapter cards.

Installing Adapters That Aren't in the Windows 98 Distribution

You might find that some network adapters aren't listed in the default distribution files that ship with Windows 98. When this happens, you have to work through the installation of the network adapter until you are prompted to choose a manufacturer and adapter type. Instead of choosing an adapter from the list, click the Have Disk button and provide the path to the unlisted drivers.

Installing and Configuring Protocols

Install and configure network protocols in a Microsoft environment or a mixed Microsoft and NetWare environment.

Protocol components in Windows 98 (more or less) provide the services associated with the OSI Network and Transport layers. The word *protocol* can have many meanings in the networking business. In this case, it is important to note that Windows 98's protocol components are not *protocols* in the strict sense (a protocol is a system of rules defining a means of communication) but are instead software components designed to transmit and receive data according to the protocol's rules.

Windows 98 includes built-in support for several network protocols. Microsoft highlights the following protocols as being important for the Windows 98 MCSE exam:

◆ NetBEUI

◆ IPX/SPX-compatible protocol

◆ TCP/IP

◆ Microsoft DLC

◆ Fast Infrared

The first three protocols in the preceding list (NetBEUI, IPX/SPX-compatible, and TCP/IP) are by far the most common and the most important protocols used with Windows 98.

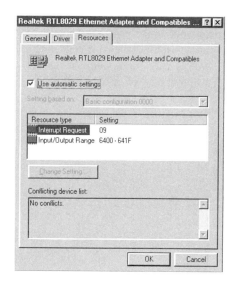

FIGURE 3.14

You can change adapter resource settings in the Device Manager's Adapter Properties dialog box.

NOTE

Protocols and OSI The comparison of Windows 98 protocol components with the OSI Network/Transport layers works better with Windows 98's full-featured protocols (such as TCP/IP and IPX/SPX-compatible) than with some of the more limited protocols. NetBEUI, for instance, doesn't support routing and therefore isn't much of a Network/Transport layer protocol. DLC is even more limited. However, the analogy with the Network/Transport layers is still apt in that the Windows 98 protocol component rests above the hardware-related layers (associated with the adapter component) and below the service-related layers (associated with the client and service components).

N O T E **Network Traffic** Another disadvantage of NetBEUI is that it creates relatively levels of network traffic higher than that created by other protocols.

NetBEUI is a fast protocol designed for small local networks. NetBEUI is simple to configure. (In fact, except for a few options discussed in the next section, you can't really configure it.) The biggest disadvantage of NetBEUI is that it isn't routable. NetBEUI can't be used on complex networks that require routing.

The IPX/SPX-compatible protocol is Microsoft's version of Novell's IPX/SPX protocol, which is used on NetWare networks. The IPX/SPX-compatible protocol is designed to provide connectivity with NetWare networks, but the IPX/SPX-compatible protocol is a fully functioning, routable network protocol system. You don't have to have a NetWare network in order to use IPX/SPX-compatible protocol.

TCP/IP is the protocol of the Internet, and for that reason, it is quickly becoming the world's protocol. TCP/IP supports a huge variety of software and hardware products, and TCP/IP works well on both large and small networks. Routed Windows NT networks tend to use TCP/IP, and Windows NT Server includes a collection of TCP/IP-related services that extend TCP/IP functionality and simplify TCP/IP configuration. You'll learn about some of those services later in this chapter.

The following sections describe how to configure network protocols in Windows 98. As you read through the following sections and work through the accompanying procedures, notice that in Windows 98 a separate protocol component is actually linked to each network adapter. Protocol configuration information, such as TCP/IP addressing information, applies to an adapter, not to the computer itself. Protocol components listed in the Network Control Panel's Configuration tab show the protocol and also the adapter to which the protocol is linked. For instance, the TCP/IP component configured for the dial-up adapter will be listed as *TCP/IP→Dial-Up Adapter*.

NetBIOS Extended User Interface (NetBEUI)

The NetBIOS Extended User Interface (NetBEUI) protocol is relatively easy to implement, because it doesn't require the configuration of additional network settings for each computer other than the computer name and domain or workgroup name.

The advantages of the NetBEUI protocol include the following:

◆ Communication is fast on smaller networks.

◆ Performance is dynamically self-tuned.

◆ The only configuration required is a NetBIOS computer name and a workgroup or domain name.

As was mentioned in the preceding section, NetBEUI is nonroutable and is therefore suitable only for local area networks. An interesting exception to this non-routability rule is that NetBEUI can access a remote network through the Windows NT Remote Access Server (RAS) NetBIOS gateway. You'll learn more about NT's NetBIOS gateway later in this chapter.

Besides the computer name and workgroup name, only two other settings can be changed. These two settings are found on the Advanced tab of the Protocol-to-Adapter Properties screen (see Figure 3.15). To reach the Advanced tab, click on a Protocol/Adapter entry in the Network Control Panel's Configuration tab and click on Properties. The Advanced tab settings are as follows:

◆ **Maximum Sessions.** Identifies the maximum number of network sessions that your computer can keep track of. These include both inbound and outbound sessions.

◆ **NCBS (Network Control Block Size).** Identifies the size or number of Network Control Blocks that Windows 95 will use. These blocks are used to transfer or carry NetBIOS information for the NetBEUI protocol.

Because these are the only two configuration settings that can be changed, NetBEUI is an easy protocol to configure. Even if you wanted to change other settings, you cannot.

Bindings, as with adapters, can be configured for each protocol. Protocols are bound to items on the next layer up in the Windows 98 Network model. The next major layer above the protocols includes both clients and services, as shown in Figure 3.16.

Bindings will be listed on the Bindings tab for any clients or services that can work using NetBEUI. Because the NetWare client requires the IPX/SPX-compatible protocol, it isn't listed on the Bindings tab for NetBEUI. As with bindings on the network card, any bindings that aren't used should be removed.

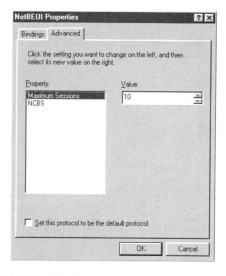

FIGURE 3.15

NetBEUI protocol advanced settings allow for only two options to configure the protocol.

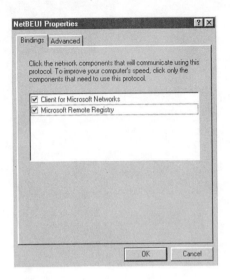

FIGURE 3.16
NetBEUI bindings allow you to disable clients or services for the protocol.

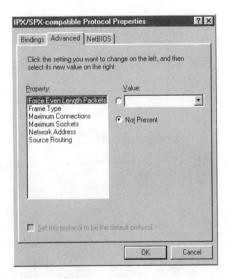

FIGURE 3.17
IPX/SPX-Compatible Protocol Properties' advanced settings let you modify several settings for the protocol.

IPX/SPX-Compatible Protocol

The IPX/SPX-compatible protocol is a routable network protocol that provides connectivity with NetWare IPX/SPX networks. The IPX/SPX-compatible protocol is more complex than NetBEUI. If you have multiple network segments on your network, you will require a routable protocol. The IPX/SPX-compatible protocol is required for communication with most NetWare servers. The IPX/SPX-compatible protocol must be installed if you're planning to use Client for NetWare Networks. The IPX/SPX is not required for the Client for Microsoft Networks, but it can be used under Client for Microsoft Networks as the primary or only protocol. If the IPX/SPX-compatible protocol is used with Client for Microsoft Networks, the optional NetBIOS support should be enabled.

To configure settings for the IPX/SPX-compatible protocol, select the IPX/SPX-compatible protocol in the Network Control Panel's Configuration tab and click on Properties. A number of settings can be adjusted through the Advanced tab of the IPX/SPX-Compatible Protocol Properties dialog box (see Figure 3.17):

◆ **Force Even Length Packets.** Used for compatibility with older NetWare Ethernet drivers with monolithic protocol stacks and on some older IPX routers.

◆ **Frame Type.** IPX supports several variations on standard network packets. The different frame specifications are referred to by frame type. You can talk only to servers or clients that are using the same frame type as yours. If a frame type isn't specified, Windows 98 will go with the detected frame type, or 802.2. Here are the frame types from which you can choose:

  • 802.2

  • 802.3

  • ETHERNET II

  • ETHERNET_SNAP

  • Token_Ring

  • Token_Ring_Snap

◆ **Maximum Connections.** Allows you to set the maximum number of network sessions that Windows 98 will support.

◆ **Maximum Sockets.** Specifies the number of IPX Socket connections that may be made to or from the server. This is excluded from NetBIOS traffic.

◆ **Network Address.** The four-byte IPX network address.

◆ **Source Routing.** Specifies the cache size to be used with source routing. This setting is only applicable to Token Ring networks.

With the number of settings that can be modified, and the loss of network connectivity if the settings are configured incorrectly, IPX/SPX-compatible protocol is a more difficult to work with than the NetBEUI protocol. The Maximum Connections, Maximum Sockets, and Network Address settings are configured dynamically in Windows 98.

NetBIOS is required in order for Microsoft network clients to communicate with Microsoft servers. NetBIOS is also used to create and maintain lists of servers on the network. By default, IPX/SPX doesn't use NetBIOS, but it can be enabled on the NetBIOS tab of the IPX/SPX-Compatible Protocol Properties, as shown in Figure 3.18.

The IPX/SPX-Compatible Protocol Properties dialog box also includes a Bindings tab, in which you can enable and disable bindings with network clients and services (see Figure 3.19).

TCP/IP

Windows 98 comes with the Microsoft 32-bit TCP/IP protocol, related utilities, and an SNMP client. TCP/IP gives Windows 98 an industry-standard, routable, enterprise-level networking protocol. TCP/IP is the transport protocol of the Internet. Along with TCP/IP's versatility comes a certain amount of complexity. TCP/IP is more difficult to configure than other protocols. Many server-based systems (including Windows NT Server) provide services that extend and simplify TCP/IP. You'll learn more about some of these services, such as DHCP, WINS, and DNS, in the following sections.

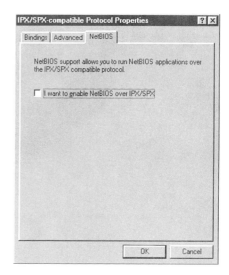

FIGURE 3.18
IPX/SPX-compatible protocol NetBIOS settings can be enabled or disabled.

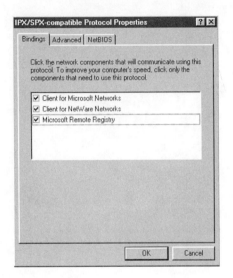

FIGURE 3.19
You can enable and disable bindings for
IPX/SPX-compatible protocol in the Bindings tab
of the IPX/SPX-compatible Protocol dialog box.

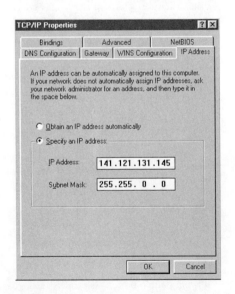

FIGURE 3.20
After you install TCP/IP, the TCP/IP Properties
sheet appears.

To install the TCP/IP protocol on a Windows 98 computer, perform the tasks outlined in Step by Step 3.5.

STEP BY STEP

3.5 Installing the TCP/IP Protocol on a Windows 98 Computer

1. Select Start, Settings, Control Panel, and then double-click the Network icon.

2. Click the Add button in the Network Properties sheet. The Select Network Component Type dialog box appears.

3. Select Protocol and click Add to open the Select Network Protocol dialog box.

4. Select Microsoft from the Manufacturers list and TCP/IP from the Network Protocols list.

5. Click OK to return to the Network Properties sheet.

After you install TCP/IP, the TCP/IP Properties sheet will appear. There may be six or seven tabs on this sheet (see Figure 3.20), including some or all of the following:

◆ IP Address

◆ Gateway

◆ DNS Configuration

◆ WINS Configuration

◆ NetBIOS

◆ Advanced

◆ Bindings

Which of the many settings you need to configure depends on your network configuration.

The upcoming sections explain how to use each tab to configure TCP/IP settings.

IP Address

The IP Address tab in the TCP/IP Properties dialog box lets you specify an IP address and subnet mask. The IP address uniquely identifies a computer (actually, a network adapter) on a TCP/IP network. The IP address is a 32-bit binary address that is usually expressed in what is called *dotted decimal* format. In dotted decimal format, the series of four 8-bit octets is expressed as a series decimal equivalents separated with periods (for example, 141.121.200.14, or 109.156.114.112). No two computers on the network can have the same IP address.

Another parameter that often accompanies the IP address is the subnet mask. The *subnet mask* specifies which part of the IP address describes the host ID and which part describes the network and subnet ID. Subnet masking is powerful tool that lets you subdivide the network into smaller subnets for more efficient delivery and more efficient use of available addresses.

The IP Address tab of the TCP/IP Properties dialog box lets you choose to enter an IP address and subnet mask directly or receive a temporary IP address configuration automatically through *Dynamic Host Configuration Protocol (DHCP)*. DHCP is a protocol that lets a server machine (called a DHCP server) temporarily assign a TCP/IP configuration to a workstation that is configured for dynamic IP address assignment (called a DHCP client).

When Windows 98 is configured as a DHCP client and then restarted, it broadcasts a message looking for a DHCP server. The DHCP server provides the client with an IP address to use for a predetermined length of time, the *lease* of the IP address. This lease, and other information passed from DHCP client to server, is configured by the server administrator.

A DHCP server can be configured to pass all the necessary IP address information to a DHCP client. This includes the IP address leased to the client, as well as the IP addresses of the default gateway, subnet mask, DNS servers, and WINS servers.

The centralized management of IP configuration, ensuring correct IP address assignments, is a major advantage of DHCP. In the case of TCP/IP addressing errors, there is one centralized location to troubleshoot instead of trying to track down a single troublesome

> NOTE
>
> **Unique for the Network** Even on the Internet (the world's largest TCP/IP network), IP addresses are supposed to be unique. If your computer will be part of the Internet, you can only use an IP address that has been duly assigned to your organization. If your computer will not be part of the Internet, you can assign any IP address you want, but the system of IP address, subnet masks, and gateways you use on your network must be compatible and must follow the rules of IP addressing.

workstation. DHCP also allows for quicker TCP/IP setup by eliminating the need to enter a separate 12-digit IP address for each workstation.

An incorrect IP address can cause TCP/IP communication problems, not only with the misconfigured workstation, but also possibly with other machines. DHCP greatly reduces this problem by keeping track of which IP addresses it has leased and not leasing them to other workstations.

DHCP is also useful in cases in which a large number of computers must share a limited number of IP addresses. If each user uses an IP address only occasionally, a group of users can share the pool of available IP addresses through DHCP. A notable example of this technique is the case of Internet service providers. Internet providers typically use DHCP to assign IP addresses to dial-up customers.

Now, the current IP addressing scheme, version 4, uses a 32-bit number divided into four 8-bit octets. This results in four numbers, each in the range of 0 to 255, separated by periods. For instance, the IP address of the **whitehouse.gov** server, 198.137.241.30, is expressed in four binary octets as follows:

    11000110.10001001.11110001.00011110

Each Internet-connected device has its own unique IP address, although numbers are starting to run short. Any other Internet-connected computer can contact your local workstation if the remote computer knows your IP address.

On a TCP/IP network, each host must be able to determine if a message can be delivered to the local subnet, or if it must be sent to a router for delivery elsewhere on the network.

A basic IP address actually consists of two parts: a network ID and a host ID. The *network ID* identifies the network; the *host ID* identifies the computer on the network. If the network ID (or the subnet ID, in the case of a subnetted network) is the same for the source and destination of a message, the message can be delivered locally. Otherwise, the data must be sent to the greater network through a gateway (a router).

The set of possible IP addresses is divided into address classes. Each address class divides the IP address differently (see Table 3.2).

NOTE

Routers and Gateways Because no computer can directly contact all the possible IP addresses on the Internet, intermediary devices called routers forward communications when your computer tries to communicate with a workstation not located on the local subnet. A TCP/IP data packet might pass through many routers, each one examining your data packet for address information, before reaching its destination. A router is sometimes called a *gateway* in the TCP/IP community. (This definition of a gateway as an everyday router is a little different from the definition used elsewhere in the networking industry, where the term typically refers to a router that also performs some kind of protocol translation.)

TABLE 3.2

IP ADDRESS CLASSES AND SUBNET MASKS

Class	First Octet Range	Default Mask
Class A	1 to 126	255.0.0.0
Class B	128 to 191	255.255.0.0
Class C	192 to 223	255.255.255.0

On Class A networks, the first eight bits of the IP address refer to the network ID. On Class B networks, the first 16 bits (the first two octets) refer to the network ID. On Class C networks, the first 24 bits (the first three octets) refer to the network ID and only the last eight bits are used for the host ID. The first number in the IP address determines the address class (refer to Table 3.2). By looking at the first number in the IP address you can determine the address class and, therefore, you'll be able to determine the network ID and the host ID given the IP address.

The IP address classes offer a means for assigning and organizing IP addresses on the greater Internet, but within a given network, additional levels of the addressing hierarchy are helpful and sometimes necessary. TCP/IP accomplishes this further logical division through subnetting. A subnet is a logical division of the network.

In a typical scenario, routers divide the network into segments and each segment is configured as a separate subnet. The subnet is specified in the IP address by taking part of the address that would nominally (according to the address class) be used for the host ID and using it for a subnet ID. A parameter called the subnet mask tells TCP/IP which address bits define the network and subnet IDs and which bits define the host ID. The subnet mask is a 32-bit binary value that basically acts as a key to the IP address. A bit position that is used in the IP address to represent a network or subnet ID is represented in the subnet mask with a 1. A bit position that is used in the IP address for the host ID is represented with a 0 in the subnet mask.

The rightmost column in Table 3.2 shows the default mask for each address class (assuming no subnetting). Note the reoccurrence of the number 255. A quick foray into binary math will show you that the decimal number 255 is equivalent to the binary 11111111 (all one bits). Thus, a 255 in the default mask represents an octet that is part of the network ID. Note that a Class B network saves two octets (16 bits) for the host ID. These 16 bits can provide unique addresses for 65,534 hosts. A single network segment with 65,534 hosts is very impractical. You can use subnetting to divide the smaller and more manageable units. For instance, you could use the third octet to specify a subnet ID and the fourth octet to specify hosts on each subnet. In this scenario, the subnet mask would be 255.255.255.0. You would thus divide the address space into 254 subnets with 254 possible host IDs on each subnet.

Because humans have difficulty remembering lists of 12-digit numbers, TCP/IP provides a means of assigning friendly names to computers. TCP/IP's native friendly-name system, the *Domain Name System (DNS)*, is used on the Internet and throughout the TCP/IP community. In DNS, a system of name servers, or DNS servers, resolve name service queries from DNS clients. Microsoft has also invested considerable effort in devising ways for using NetBIOS computer names (described earlier in this chapter) on TCP/IP networks. Windows 98 supports several methods for mapping NetBIOS computer names with IP addresses. You'll learn more about DNS and NetBIOS name resolution later in this chapter.

N O T E

Masking Bits The subnet mask does not have to divide the IP address into even octets. For instance, the subnet mask 255.255.240.0 divides the subnet ID and the host ID at the fourth bit of the third octet. (240 is binary 11110000.)

Gateway

After you have an IP address and subnet mask, your Windows 98 computer is ready to talk to other workstations on the local network, but it still has no way to reach the internetwork beyond the local network. A gateway provides the connectivity to the rest of the networked world.

When your workstation tries to communicate with an IP address that isn't located on the local network, the message is forwarded to the default gateway. The *default gateway* is a router connected to other network segments. Each router has a table of IP information (called a *routing table*) that allows it to move your message closer to its final destination. Multiple gateways can be configured to provide routing backup. If a gateway is unavailable, perhaps due to hardware failure, the next gateway on the list is used.

To configure a default gateway, perform the tasks outlined in Step by Step 3.6.

STEP BY STEP

3.6 Configuring a Default Gateway

1. Select Start, Settings, Control Panel. Double-click the Network icon.

2. Double-click the TCP/IP protocol in the Installed Network Components window.

3. Select the Gateway tab on the TCP/IP Properties sheet, as shown in Figure 3.21.

4. Enter your default gateway IP address in the New Gateway box.

5. Click Add. The new default gateway will appear in the Installed Gateways window. Add additional gateways to the Installed Gateways list if you want.

6. Click OK twice. Windows 98 will prompt you to restart with your new gateway information.

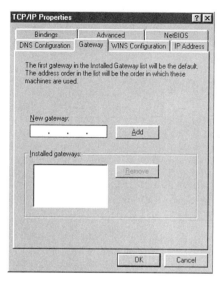

FIGURE 3.21
The Gateway tab of the TCP/IP Properties sheet lets you configure a gateway.

Name Resolution

Name resolution is the process of converting alphanumeric friendly names to or from IP addresses. Name resolution enables you to reference computers on a TCP/IP network by DNS host name or NetBIOS computer name rather than having to enter the complete IP address. As described earlier, Windows 98's TCP/IP implementation supports two name service systems:

◆ **DNS.** The name service method used on the Internet.

◆ **NetBIOS.** The system of computer names native to Microsoft operating systems such as Windows 98.

The *Domain Name System (DNS)* is a hierarchical name space that provides a naming scheme for TCP/IP hosts. Historically, these hosts have been UNIX workstations and servers, but with the growing popularity of the Internet in the early 1990s, desktop computers needed easy access to DNS as well.

A Fully Qualified DNS name consists of a host name appended to a domain name. For example, the host www would be appended to microsoft.com to give the Fully Qualified Domain Name **www.microsoft.com**. In order to participate on the Internet, organizations must register their domain names with InterNIC. InterNIC registers domain names based on the top-level domains listed in Table 3.3.

TABLE 3.3

INTERNET TOP-LEVEL DOMAIN NAMES

Domain Name	Type of Organization
com	Commercial organization
edu	Educational institution
gov	Government institution
mil	Military group
net	Network service provider
org	Other organizations, often nonprofit
Country code, such as .jp for Japan	A country

DNS provides a static, centrally administrated database for resolving domain names to IP addresses. If a DNS client encounters a reference to a network host expressed as a DNS name, the DNS client sends a query to its DNS server asking for the IP address associated with the referenced DNS name. The DNS server either provides the name resolution or sends the query to another DNS server in the name server hierarchy. The query may travel through a chain of DNS servers until the name is finally resolved.

Windows 98 can be configured to use DNS with the DNS Configuration tab on the TCP/IP Properties sheet (see Figure 3.22).

The Enable DNS fields on the DNS Configuration page allow Windows 98 to take advantage of several DNS services:

◆ **Host.** The local computer's registered DNS name.

◆ **Domain.** The organization's InterNIC-registered domain name.

◆ **DNS Server Search Order.** Allows backup DNS servers to be configured in case the primary fails.

◆ **Domain Suffix Search Order.** Tells TCP/IP utilities what domains to append and search if only a host name is given to the utility.

To configure a Windows 98 computer to use DNS, perform the tasks outlined in Step by Step 3.7.

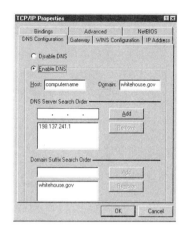

FIGURE 3.22
You can enable DNS through the TCP/IP Properties DNS Configuration tab.

STEP BY STEP

3.7 Configuring a Windows 98 Computer to Use DNS

1. Select Start, Settings, Control Panel. Double-click the Network icon.

2. Double-click the TCP/IP protocol in the Installed Network Components window.

3. Select the Enable DNS option button.

4. Enter your computer's registered name and domain in the appropriate fields.

5. Enter your primary DNS server's IP address in the DNS Server Search Order box, and click Add.

6. Repeat step 5 for each secondary DNS server.

7. As each is added, the DNS servers' IP addresses will appear in the DNS Server Search Order window.

8. Enter your primary domain in the Domain Suffix Search Order box, and click Add.

9. Repeat step 8 for secondary domains you might use often.

10. As each domain is added, it will appear in the Domain Suffix Search Order window.

If a DNS server isn't available, or if your situation does not warrant the effort and expense of maintaining a DNS server, your Windows 98 computer can use a HOSTS file to resolve DNS names. A HOSTS file is a text file that contains a table of IP-address-to-DNS-name associations. The HOSTS file should be named HOSTS (with no extension) and stored in the Windows directory. The Windows 98 HOSTS file is compatible with the UNIX HOSTS file. For a sample of the HOSTS file format, see the file HOSTS.SAM in Windows 98's Windows directory.

A HOSTS file is convenient for small and very permanent networks, but as the network becomes bigger, and as configurations become more transient, the HOSTS file becomes extremely inefficient because you have to manually reconfigure every HOSTS file on the network whenever there is a change.

In order to use a HOSTS file in Windows 98, you must enable DNS for Windows 98 by clicking on the Enable DNS option button in the TCP/IP Properties DNS Configuration tab.

Again, name resolution enables you to reference computers on a TCP/IP network by DNS host name or NetBIOS computer name. As described earlier in this chapter, the Microsoft operating system family has had a longstanding relationship with the application programming interface NetBIOS. NetBIOS locates resources according to computer name. Microsoft provides the following methods for resolving computers' names to IP addresses, so that a computer name can be used rather than an IP address on TCP/IP networks:

◆ **WINS (Windows Internet Name Service).** Provides dynamic NetBIOS-to-IP name resolution through one or more WINS server systems operating on the network.

◆ **LMHOSTS.** A text file (similar in concept to the HOSTS file) that provides a table of NetBIOS-to-IP associations.

◆ **Broadcast.** Microsoft operating systems such as Windows 95, Windows 98, and Windows NT can resolve NetBIOS names on the local subnet through broadcast.

Of these methods, WINS is the most versatile and convenient. A Windows NT Server system can act as a WINS server. A WINS server allows centralized resolution and dynamic registration of NetBIOS names to IP addresses. When a new NetBIOS-capable device is first brought online, it attempts to broadcast its NetBIOS name and IP address to a WINS server. If a WINS server is found, the new device will automatically be registered and will almost immediately be available for name resolution.

WINS allows a Windows 98 user to use a human-friendly NetBIOS name in network utilities—for instance, using a UNC path to access a share. Then Windows 95 can query the WINS server to resolve the NetBIOS name to an IP address, allowing TCP/IP communication to take place.

It is important to keep in mind the differences between WINS and DNS:

◆ WINS uses a dynamic registration system. DNS relies on static tables.

◆ DNS resolves Fully Qualified Domain Names into IP addresses. WINS resolves NetBIOS computer names into IP addresses.

◆ DNS is a hierarchical system. WINS uses the flat NetBIOS name space.

Windows 98 is configured to use a WINS server through the WINS Configuration tab of the TCP/IP Properties sheet (see Figure 3.23).

There are three choices of WINS configuration for a Windows 98 TCP/IP client:

◆ **Disable WINS Resolution.** If WINS is disabled, an alternative form of NetBIOS name resolution, such as an LMHOSTS file, is necessary.

◆ **Enable WINS Resolution.** If WINS resolution is enabled, the IP address of a primary WINS server is required. A secondary WINS server can be configured to provide backup.

◆ **Use DHCP for WINS Resolution.** If the Windows 98 client is using DHCP to configure IP numbers, you can select this option to use the WINS servers specified by the DHCP server.

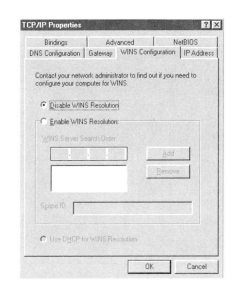

FIGURE 3.23
You can enable or disable WINS through the TCP/IP Properties' WINS Configuration tab.

You can also provide computer-name-to-IP-address mappings by using a text file called LMHOSTS (with no extension). The LMHOSTS file should be located in the \Windows directory. A sample file called LMHOSTS.SAM in the \Windows directory provides a sample of LMHOSTS format. Like the HOSTS file, an LMHOSTS file is convenient for very simple networks but quickly becomes inconvenient for larger networks because a separate copy of the LMHOSTS file must reside on each workstation and must be continually updated to reflect changes in the network. Also, note that an LMHOSTS file is of no use if you're assigning IP addresses dynamically through DHCP.

Computers running Microsoft TCP/IP can also use broadcast for NetBIOS name resolution. A client computer makes IP-level broadcasts to register its name by announcing it on the network. Each computer in a broadcast area is responsible for challenging attempts to register a duplicate name and for responding to name queries. Broadcasts are generally filtered at routers, so broadcast across subnets might not be possible.

If WINS is enabled on a Windows 98 computer, the computer first queries the WINS database and then, if it is unsuccessful, uses broadcast for name resolution (this is known as h-node name resolution). If WINS is not enabled, the computer uses broadcast (this is known as the b-node condition).

Data Link Control (DLC)

The other Microsoft-written network protocol included with Windows 98 is Microsoft *Data Link Control (DLC)*. However, this protocol is used only for communicating with certain network interface printers and mainframe systems. DLC is not used for peer-to-peer networking of Windows 98 computers. Due to DLC's limited use, you should consult the documentation for the items you are connecting to with DLC to determine the best settings for items listed on the Advanced tab, shown in Figure 3.24.

Fast Infrared

Windows 98 supports several infrared standards including the Infrared Data Association (IrDA) 1.1 specification for Fast Infrared Devices (FIR). FIR-compliant devices can send and receive data at up to 4MBPS over wireless, infrared connections.

FIGURE 3.24
Advanced settings for Microsoft DLC allow for many configuration modifications.

Fast Infrared Protocol is a protocol available through the Network Control Panel Configuration tab. (Click Add in the Configuration tab, choose Protocol and click on Add, and then in the Select Network Protocol dialog box, choose Microsoft as a manufacturer and click on Fast Infrared Protocol.) In Windows 98, however, the software necessary for supporting infrared devices is installed automatically when a Plug and Play infrared device is installed. Because all Fast Infrared devices are Plug and Play, the easiest way to install Fast Infrared capability is to install a Fast Infrared device and reboot, as outlined in Step by Step 3.8.

STEP BY STEP

3.8 Installing a Fast Infrared Device

1. Attach the device and boot Windows 98. Windows 98 infrared software will be installed.

2. An Infrared icon should appear in Control Panel. Double-click the Infrared Control Panel to activate the infrared device. If you don't see the Infrared Control Panel, press F5.

Windows 98 includes several other features that support infrared networking. The Microsoft Infrared Transfer application, for example, helps you quickly transfer files across an infrared connection.

The Infrared Monitor application helps you manage and monitor infrared connections. To reach Infrared Monitor, double-click on the Infrared Control Panel. Infrared Monitor also appears as an icon in the system tray when infrared networking is active.

Installing and Configuring Clients

The client component enables a Windows 98 computer to act as a network client. In other words, a *client* component lets your computer request and receive services from a computer that is acting as a server. A client is what is sometimes known as a redirector. A *redirector* is a software component that listens for I/O requests on the local machine and, checks to see if those requests belong on the network, and, if so, redirects the requests from the local machine to the network. In Windows 98, redirectors take the form of file system drivers.

Windows 98 supports several network clients, but the most common, and the most important for the MCSE exam, are the following:

◆ Client for Microsoft Networks

◆ Client for NetWare Networks

You'll learn about these important network client packages and how to configure them in the following sections. Later in this chapter, you'll learn about some of the alternative network client options available for NetWare networks.

The modular architecture of Windows 98 allows Windows 98 components written by other network vendors to be installed. Many network vendors of 16-bit network clients now have 32-bit network equivalents that can function in conjunction with the network components that ship with Windows 98.

To add a new network client, perform the tasks outlined in Step by Step 3.9.

NOTE

How Many Clients? Windows 98 can have only one 16-bit network client installed at a time, but it can run multiple 32-bit clients. The 32-bit clients that come with Windows 98 are Microsoft Client for Windows Networks and Microsoft Client for NetWare Networks.

STEP BY STEP

3.9 Adding a New Network Client

1. Open the Network Control Panel and choose the Configuration tab.

2. Click the Add button and select Client.

3. Click the Add button.

4. Select the manufacturer and client you want to install. If this is an updated or unlisted client, click the Have Disk button and provide the path to the client setup files. Click OK.

5. After you click OK again, you might be prompted for the Windows 98 CD while the client files are copied to your hard drive.

Client for Microsoft Networks

Windows 98's Client for Microsoft Networks (Vredir.vxd) is the client of choice for Windows 95/98 workgroups or Windows NT domains. Actually, Client for Microsoft Networks is designed to support any Microsoft networking product that uses the Server Message Block (SMB) protocol. SMB-compliant systems include Windows NT, Windows 98, Windows 95, Windows for Workgroups, LAN Manager, and Workgroup Add-On for MS-DOS.

Client for Microsoft Networks does most of its work behind the scenes. To use Client for Microsoft Networks, you must make sure it is installed (see procedure for adding a client in the preceding section) and you must make sure it is bound to the protocols you want to use it with.

The user configuration options for Client for Microsoft Networks apply to the way Client for Microsoft Networks establishes a network connection at logon. Specifically, you can configure the following options:

> ◆ **Logon Validation.** You can specify whether you want Client for Microsoft Networks to automatically log the user on to a Windows NT domain, LAN Manager domain, or a Windows NT computer at startup.
>
> ◆ **Network Logon Options.** You can choose whether you want Client for Microsoft networks to restore connections to network drives automatically when you log on, or you want to use a *Quick Logon*, which does not automatically restore network drive connections at logon. (The connection to the drive will be restored at the time you access the drive.)
>
> ◆ **Primary Network Logon.** You can choose Client for Microsoft Networks as the primary network logon. The Client for Microsoft Networks logon dialog box would then become the initial logon dialog box you see at startup.

See the section "Understanding Windows 98 Logon," earlier in this chapter, for more on Windows 98 client logon.

To configure Client for Microsoft Networks Properties, perform the tasks outlined in Step by Step 3.10.

NOTE

Checking Bindings   Note that the protocol bindings for clients and services are configured with the protocol properties, rather than with the client or service properties. To check whether a protocol (for example, TCP/IP) is bound to Client for Microsoft Networks, select TCP/IP→*adapter_name* in the Configuration tab of the Network Control Panel, then choose the Bindings tab and make sure the box for Client for Microsoft Networks is checked.

STEP BY STEP

3.10 Configuring Client for Microsoft Networks Properties

1. Choose Client for Microsoft Networks in the Configuration tab of the Network Control Panel. Click on Properties.

2. In the Client for Microsoft Networks Properties dialog box (see Figure 3.25), check the checkbox labeled Log On to a Windows NT Domain if you want Client for Microsoft Networks to log on to a domain at startup and enter the domain name in the box provided. Although this fact is not noted in the dialog box, you can also enter the name of a LAN Manager domain or the name of a Windows NT (version 3.1 or later) computer on which you have a user account.

3. In the Network logon options area, choose whether you'd like a Quick Logon (which verifies the user's credentials but does not automatically re-establish connections to network drivers) or whether you'd like to log on to the network and also re-establish network connections at logon.

4. When you're finished configuring Client for Microsoft Network Properties, click on OK.

5. In the Network Control Panel Configuration tab, click on the down arrow beside the box labeled Primary Network Logon and choose Client for Microsoft Networks if you want to make Client for Microsoft Networks the primary network logon. See the discussion of logon options earlier in this chapter.

6. When you are finished, click on OK in the Network Control Panel. If you made changes to your configuration, Windows 98 will prompt you to restart.

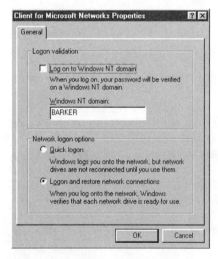

FIGURE 3.25
Configure logon properties in the Client for Microsoft Networks Properties dialog box.

If you're configuring the Windows 98 computer to log on to a Windows NT domain, make sure you check the checkbox labeled

Log On to a Windows NT Domain and enter the domain name (see step 2 of the preceding procedure). You don't have to specify Client for Microsoft Networks as the primary network logon in order to log on to a domain. If you check the Log On to Windows NT Domain option, Windows 98 will prompt you to log on to the domain after the primary network logon. If password caching is enabled, and if the primary network logon is successful, Windows 98 will attempt to log you on to the domain automatically.

Network administrators often choose to make Client for Microsoft Networks the primary network logon when the computer will be logging on to a Windows NT domain for the following reasons:

◆ You force the user to register himself with the network before doing anything else on the Windows 98 PC.

◆ You can prohibit users who don't have domain accounts from accessing the computer. (See the earlier discussion of logon options and the Require Network Logon System Policy setting.)

◆ You can provide the user with a roaming, custom user environment through network-based user profiles (see Chapter 6).

If you plan to use the Quick Logon option (see step 3 of the earlier procedure), password caching must be enabled. Password caching is enabled by default, but you must make sure it isn't disabled through System Policies if you want to use Quick Logon.

Although Windows 98 can use a DOS real-mode client to operate on a Microsoft network, Microsoft recommends Client for Microsoft Networks for the following reasons:

◆ It can be installed with other 32-bit clients.

◆ It has full support for mapping, remapping, and browsing network resources.

◆ It frees up conventional memory in all Virtual DOS Machines before loading Windows 98.

◆ Faster 32-bit programming yields better network response.

Client for Microsoft Networks computers can communicate using one or more of the following network protocols:

◆ Microsoft NetBEUI

◆ Microsoft TCP/IP

◆ Microsoft IPX/SPX-compatible

As mentioned earlier, check the Bindings tab of the protocol's Properties dialog box to make sure the protocol is bound to Client for Microsoft Networks.

Client for NetWare Networks

Windows 98 provides the 32-bit Client for NetWare Networks to support networking in Novell NetWare environments. Client for NetWare Networks is one of several NetWare client options supported by Windows 98. You'll learn more about the alternative NetWare clients in the section entitled "Windows 98 on NetWare Networks."

Microsoft claims that Client for NetWare Networks is superior to Novell's 32-bit NetWare client, and Novell, predictably, disagrees. (You can guess which viewpoint will inform the choice of questions for the Windows 98 MCSE exam.)

Client for NetWare Networks is compatible with NetWare 3.x and NetWare 4.x networks. If you want to support NetWare Directory Services (NDS) on NetWare 4.x networks, you'll need to also install Windows 98's Microsoft Service for Directory Services. (You'll learn more about Microsoft Service for NetWare Directory Services later in this chapter.)

To install Client for NetWare Networks, perform the tasks outlined in Step by Step 3.11.

> **NOTE**
>
> **IPX/SPX with Microsoft Network Client** The last protocol in the preceding list is worth a moment's reflection. Although the IPX/SPX-compatible protocol is designed for NetWare networks, it is fully functional on Microsoft networks and does not require the NetWare-oriented Client for NetWare Networks.

STEP BY STEP

3.11 Installing Client for NetWare Networks

1. Click on the Add button in the Configuration tab of the Network Control Panel

2. Choose Client and click Add.

3. In the Select Network Client dialog box, choose Microsoft and select Client for Microsoft Networks. Click OK.

You must use Client for NetWare Networks with the IPX/SPX-compatible protocol. Also, check the Bindings tab in the IPX/SPX-Compatible Protocol dialog box to ensure that the IPX/SPX-compatible protocol is bound to Client for NetWare Networks.

Like Client for Microsoft Networks, Client for NetWare Networks does much of its work behind the scenes. You can configure NetWare logon properties through the Client for NetWare Networks Properties dialog box. For instance, you can specify a preferred server. The *preferred server* is the server that appears automatically in the logon dialog box. The preferred server is also the server in which Windows 98 will look for network-based system policies and user profiles.

To configure Client for NetWare Networks logon properties, perform the tasks outlined in Step by Step 3.12.

STEP BY STEP

3.12 Configuring Client for NetWare Networks

1. Select Client for NetWare Networks in the Configuration tab of the Network Control Panel and click on Properties.

2. In the Client for NetWare Networks Properties General tab (see Figure 3.26), enter a preferred server and a first network drive. You can also elect to enable logon script processing.

3. Click on OK to return to the Configuration tab. In the Configuration tab, click the arrow to the right of the box labeled Primary Network Logon if you want to select Client for NetWare Networks as the Primary Network Logon.

4. When you're finished configuring Client for NetWare Networks settings, click on OK. Windows 98 will prompt you to restart if you made changes.

You don't have to configure Client for NetWare Networks as the Primary Network Logon in order to log on to a NetWare Network. (See the discussion of Windows 98 logon features, such as password synchronization and password caching, earlier in this chapter.)

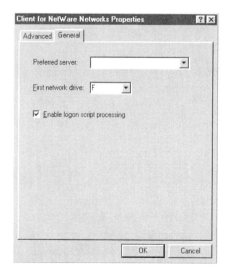

FIGURE 3.26
The Client for NetWare Networks Properties General tab lets you configure logon settings.

Designating Client for NetWare Networks as the Primary Network Logon has the following advantages:

- Users must be registered with the network before they do anything else.

- Network-based system policies and user profiles will follow the user, and will accompany the logon.

- The last login script executed will run from the NetWare server.

NDIS and ODI As you learned earlier in this chapter, NDIS and ODI are competing standards that define an interface between adapter components and protocol components. Microsoft supports NDIS, and that is one reason why NDIS is the default driver type in the Adapter Properties Driver Type tab. Novell supports ODI, and that is one reason why ODI might work better in some cases for communicating with Novell NetWare networks. The real-mode ODI driver, however, will not support some of the features provided with the protected-mode NDIS driver.

Microsoft recommends that you use a 32-bit protected-mode adapter driver with Client for NetWare networks, but the 32-bit NDIS-compliant driver may not be compatible with all NetWare versions and configurations. In some situations, you may want to use Client for NetWare Networks with a real-mode ODI driver. Change the adapter driver in the Driver Type tab of the Properties dialog box for the network adapter. See the discussion of network adapter configuration earlier in this chapter.

Installing and Configuring Services

A *service* is a process that listens for requests and fulfills those requests. It is no coincidence that the term *service* is closely related to the term *server*. A *server*, such as a file server, a print server, or an application server, is a computer running one or more services that support network activities. In the Windows 98 MCSE exam objectives, Microsoft makes a point of highlighting the following two services:

- File and Printer Sharing for Microsoft Networks
- File and Printer Sharing for NetWare Networks

These important services let a Windows 98 computer act as a network file server or print server. You'll learn more about Windows 98's file and printer sharing services and how to configure them in the following sections. You'll learn more about Windows 98's Service for NetWare Directory Services, and about some of Windows 98's server components such as Dial-Up Server and Personal Web Server, later in this chapter.

File and Printer Sharing for Microsoft Networks

File and Printer Sharing for Microsoft Networks lets your computer act as a file server or a printer server on Microsoft network. As you learned earlier in this chapter, File and Printer Sharing for Microsoft Networks also enables your computer to act as a master browse server on Microsoft networks.

File and Printer Sharing for Microsoft Networks does not automatically provide network access to your computer. It is merely a background process that supports access to resources that have been shared through Windows 98's share-level or user-level security. (See Chapters 1 and 5 for more information about sharing resources in Windows 98.) After you've installed File and Printer Sharing for Microsoft Networks and enabled file and printer sharing through the Configuration tab of the Network Control Panel (as described later in this section), you still have to *share* the resource (as described in Chapter 1) before it is available to network users.

File and Printer Sharing for Microsoft Networks supports any client PCs that use the *Server Message Block (SMB) protocol* . SMB systems include Windows for Workgroups, Windows 95, Windows 98, Windows NT, LAN Manager, IBM LAN Server and OS/2 Warp, Samba, and Digital Pathworks 32. The client PC must, of course, use some suitable client software component that supports SMB, such as Windows 98's Client for Microsoft Networks.

Microsoft stresses three important things to remember if you plan to use File and Printer Sharing for Microsoft Networks on a Windows 98 PC:

◆ You cannot use File and Printer Sharing for Microsoft Networks and File and Printer Sharing for NetWare Networks at the same time. You can install one or the other.

◆ Your computer must install Client for Microsoft Networks in order to use File and Printer Sharing for Microsoft Networks.

◆ If your computer uses user-level security (see Chapter 1), you must designate a Windows NT domain controller as the security provider.

To install File and Printer Sharing for Microsoft Networks, perform the tasks outlined in Step by Step 3.13.

STEP BY STEP

3.13 Installing File and Printer Sharing for Microsoft Networks

1. Select Start, Settings, Control Panel. Choose the Network icon to display the Network Control Panel.

2. Click the Add button to open the Select Network Component Type dialog box.

3. Select Service and click the Add button. You see the Select Network Service dialog box.

4. From the Manufacturers list, select Microsoft. From the list of Network Services, select File and Printer Sharing for Microsoft Networks.

5. Click OK. File and Printer Sharing for Microsoft Networks is added to your installed network components. When you click OK back on the Network Properties sheet, the system updates itself and might prompt you for the location of required files.

6. Restart Windows 98.

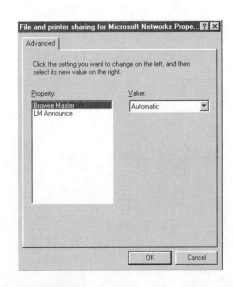

FIGURE 3.27
Configure a browser role in the Advanced tab of the File and Printer Sharing for Microsoft Networks Properties dialog box.

File and Printer Sharing for Microsoft Networks must be bound to the protocol you want to use with it. See the discussion of bindings earlier in this chapter. When you install File and Printer Sharing for Microsoft Networks, it will automatically be bound to the active protocols that support it (NetBEUI, IPX/SPX-compatible, and TCP/IP). To verify protocol bindings, select the appropriate protocol→adapter in the Configuration tab of the Network Control Panel, click on Properties, and choose the Bindings tab.

After you install File and Printer Sharing for Microsoft Networks, there isn't much to configure within the service itself. If you select File and Printer Sharing for Microsoft Networks in the Configuration tab of the Network Control Panel and click on Properties, you'll see the Advanced tab of the File and Printer Sharing for Microsoft Networks Properties dialog box (see Figure 3.27). In this tab, you can config-ure a browse master setting (Automatic, Enabled, or Disabled, as described earlier in this chapter), or you can set the

LM Announce property. The LM Announce property specifies whether you want your Windows 98 computer to perform periodic announcements of its file and printer sharing services in order to support a LAN Manager 2.x domain. (This value should be set to No unless your network includes a LAN Manager 2.x domain.)

The Configuration tab of the Network Control Panel includes a button labeled File and Printer Sharing. Click on this button to invoke the File and Printer Sharing dialog box. This dialog box includes checkboxes that let you enable or disable file sharing, print sharing, or both on your PC. When you install File and Printer Sharing for Microsoft Networks, file and printer sharing will automatically be enabled in the File and Printer Sharing dialog box. You can selectively disable file sharing, printer sharing, or both, by unchecking the appropriate boxes.

As mentioned earlier, you not only must install and configure File and Printer Sharing for Microsoft Networks (and the other components necessary for Microsoft networking: Client for Microsoft Networks, one or more protocols, and one or more adapters). You still have to configure Windows 98 security and make the deliberate decision to share some resource in order for your computer to provide file and printer sharing services on the network. See Chapter 1 for more on security and resource sharing.

File and Printer Sharing for NetWare Networks

The File and Printer Sharing for NetWare Networks service lets you share directories and printers on NetWare networks. Like File and Printer Sharing for Microsoft Networks, File and Printer Sharing for NetWare Networks enables sharing, but it doesn't automatically cause any resources to be shared. After File and Printer Sharing for NetWare Networks is installed and properly bound to an active protocol, you must still deliberately *share* any resource before it is available for network access.

There are four very important points to keep in mind when considering using File and Printer Sharing for NetWare Networks:

◆ You can't have File and Printer Sharing for NetWare Networks and File and Printer Sharing for Microsoft Networks installed simultaneously. Only one can be configured on a particular Windows 98 workstation.

◆ File and Printer Sharing for NetWare Networks must use the user-level security model. The security provider specified in the Access Control tab of the Network Control Panel must be a NetWare server operating in a bindery context. If the server is a NetWare 4.x server, it must be using bindery emulation. (See Chapter 1 for more on user-level security.)

◆ The NetWare server that is acting as a security provider must have a Windows_Passthru account (no password) that will be used for pass-through validation (see Chapter 1).

◆ Microsoft's Client for NetWare Networks (described earlier in this chapter) must be installed on the Windows 98 system. Microsoft warns that the Novell client component alternatives (such as Novell Client for Windows 95/98) do not support File and printer sharing for NetWare Networks.

As described in Chapter 1, under user-level security, the server that is acting as a security provider is queried any time a network user tries to access a shared resource. The username or group membership must be on the NetWare server's account list and must have the necessary rights to gain access to the resource.

It is important to note that, even though the computer that is using File and Printer Sharing for NetWare Networks must use Microsoft's Client for NetWare Networks client component, other computers accessing shared resources on the Windows 98 machine can use any of several NetWare-compatible clients. File and printer sharing for NetWare Networks uses the NetWare Core Protocol (NCP). NetWare-compatible clients that use NCP can access resources on the Windows 98 machine that are shared through File and printer sharing for NetWare Networks. The compatible clients include, in addition to Client for NetWare Networks, NETX, VLM, and Novell Client for Windows 95/98. You'll learn more about NetWare clients later in this chapter.

File and Printer Sharing for NetWare Networks can be set up as outlined in Step by Step 3.14.

STEP BY STEP

3.14 Setting Up File and Printer Sharing for NetWare Networks

1. Select Start, Settings, Control Panel. Double-click the Network icon.

2. Click the Add button in the Network Properties sheet. The Select Network Component Type dialog box appears.

3. Double-click Service. The Select Network Service dialog box appears.

4. From the Manufacturers column, choose Microsoft.

5. From the Network Services column, choose File and Printer Sharing for NetWare Networks.

6. Click OK. The File and Printer Sharing for NetWare Networks service will be installed in the Network Properties sheet.

7. Choose the Access Control tab of the Network Properties sheet.

8. Choose the User-Level Access Control option.

9. Enter the name of the NetWare server that contains the account list in the Obtain List of Users and Groups From field.

10. Click OK. Windows 98 might ask for the location of needed files. It will prompt you to restart when it is done copying files.

After File and Printer Sharing for NetWare Networks is installed, you can choose between a pair of options for how the Windows 98 computer will advertise its services on the network (in other words, how File and Printer Sharing for NetWare Networks will make itself visible for browsing). To configure an advertising option, perform the tasks outlined in Step by Step 3.15.

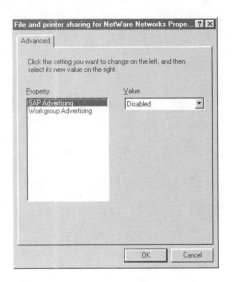

FIGURE 3.28
You can select an advertising method in the File and Printer Sharing for NetWare Networks Properties dialog box.

STEP BY STEP

3.15 Configuring an Advertising Option

1. Select File and Printer Sharing for NetWare Networks in the Component list of the Network Control Panel's Configuration tab. Click on Properties.

2. In the File and Printer Sharing for NetWare Networks Properties dialog box (see Figure 3.28), select either of the following options:

   - **SAP Advertising.** The browser-advertising method used on NetWare 2.15 and later networks. You must enable this option if you want shared resources on the Windows 98 computer to be available to VLM and NETX clients.

   - **Workgroup Advertising.** Compatible with the broadcast-oriented browser notification used for workgroups on Microsoft networks.

3. After you choose an advertising property, choose a value for the property in the box labeled Value.

You'll learn more about sharing resources on NetWare networks later in this chapter.

Configuring Asynchronous Transfer Mode (ATM)

Asynchronous Transfer Mode (ATM) is one of several emerging Wide Area Network (WAN) technologies that can transfer network data over vast distances at very high speeds. ATM requires specialized equipment, and is considerably different in design from other networking technologies supported by Windows 98.

ATM communicates through what is known as a virtual circuit. A *virtual circuit* is a pre-established virtual message path between the two communicating computers. ATM is so different from the other networking technologies supported by Windows 98 that it does not fit easily into the Windows 98 networking component structure described earlier in this chapter. To support ATM in Windows 98, Microsoft implements what is known as LAN emulation. *LAN emulation* translates Ethernet addresses into ATM addresses, thus allowing protocol components to communicate through ATM as they would through a more traditional medium.

Windows 98 includes the following components for ATM support:

◆ **User Network Interface (UNI) 3.1 Call Manager.** A component that provides media-specific signaling for the virtual circuit connection.

◆ **ATM LAN Emulation 1.0.** A component that communicates with the LAN Emulation Service on an ATM to provide LAN emulation.

Microsoft also points out that Windows 98 includes ATM miniport drivers and also an API for interfacing kernel-mode drivers with an ATM network.

To configure your Windows 98 computer for an ATM network, you must install the ATM Call Manager component, the ATM Emulated LAN component, and the ATM LAN Emulation Client component, all of which are classified as Protocol components in the Network Control Panel.

To install ATM networking support, perform the tasks outlined in Step by Step 3.16.

STEP BY STEP

3.16 Installing ATM Networking Support

1. In the Configuration tab of the Network Control Panel, click on Add.

2. In the Select Network Component Type dialog box, choose Protocol and click on Add.

3. In the Select Network Protocol dialog box, choose Microsoft and select ATM Call Manager. Click on OK.

4. When the foreground returns to the Configuration tab, click on the Add button again.

5. In the Select Network Component Type dialog box, choose Protocol and click on Add.

6. In the Select Network Protocol dialog box, choose Microsoft and select ATM Emulated LAN. Click on OK.

7. When the foreground returns to the Configuration tab, click on the Add button again.

8. In the Select Network Component Type dialog box, choose Protocol and click on Add.

9. In the Select Network Protocol dialog box, choose Microsoft and select ATM LAN Emulation Client. Click on OK.

10. Click on OK in the Configuration tab. Windows 98 will prompt you to restart your computer.

A Windows 98 computer can support more than one ATM Emulated LAN. If you wish to configure your computer to participate in an ATM-emulated LAN that is different from the default, select the LAN Emulation Client for the desired adapter, click on Properties, and enter the name of the emulated LAN in the Value box.

Virtual Private Networking and PPTP

Point to Point Tunneling Protocol (PPTP) is a secure Wide Area Network (WAN) protocol that is starting to receive wide acceptance as a secure protocol over the Internet. The purpose of PPTP is to offer users the privacy of a private network with convenience (and low cost) of a public network such as the Internet. PPTP lets you establish a secure connection from a remote location over the Internet.

PPTP works by encapsulating the local networking protocol (TCP/IP, NetBEUI, or IPX/SPX) into a PPP packet and then encapsulating the PPP packet into a TCP/IP packet for delivery on the

Internet. PPTP can thus produce Internet-ready transmissions that take advantage of the advanced encryption features of PPP. Another interesting feature of PPTP is that it lets you transmit networking protocols other than TCP/IP over the Internet. For instance, to IPX-based NetWare, LANs can communicate over the Internet using PPTP.

PPTP is implemented through an adapter component called Microsoft Virtual Private Networking Adapter and an accompanying protocol called NDISWAN. NDISWAN is a modified version of TCP/IP that allows for carrying other packets in the data section of the IP packet.

To install PPTP virtual private networking components, perform the tasks outlined in Step by Step 3.17.

STEP BY STEP

3.17 Installing PPTP Virtual Private Networking Components

1. From the Configuration tab of the Network Control Panel, click on the Add button.

2. In the Select Network Component Type dialog box, choose Adapter and click on Add.

3. In the Select Network Adapters dialog box, choose Microsoft in the Manufacturers list and select Microsoft Virtual Private Networking Adapter. Click on OK.

4. Click on OK in the Configuration tab. When you install the Virtual Private Networking Adapter (see step 3), Windows 98 will also install the NDISWAN protocol. You may be asked to specify the location of the Windows 98 CD. You must restart your computer for the changes to take effect.

The Advanced tab on the VPN Properties sheet (see Figure 3.29) allows for a log file (similar to the PPP or modem log files) to track and troubleshoot connections to remote servers. The advanced

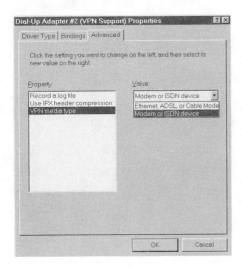

FIGURE 3.29
Dial-Up Adapter #2 (VPN Support) advanced
properties allow you to specify the log file
creation and PPTP media types.

settings also allow you to identify the physical media that you will be
running the PPTP connection over.

To effectively use PPTP and VPN, you need some or all of the following components installed:

◆ Client for Microsoft Networks.

◆ Optional second client for use on remote LAN.

◆ Dial-up adapter if making the VPN connection through an
Internet service provider (ISP).

◆ NDISWAN protocol installed for packet encapsulation.

◆ TCP/IP to act as a transport for the NDISWAN protocol.

◆ Optional second protocol to be used on the remote LAN. This
would include NetBEUI or IPX/SPX if you will not be using
TCP/IP on the remote LAN.

You create a PPTP connection through Windows 98 Dial-Up
Networking (described later in this chapter). Basically, you create a
Dial-Up Networking document and specify the Microsoft VPN
Adapter as a connection device instead of a modem (see Figure
3.30). Rather than specifying a phone number, you will enter the IP
address of the network adapter on the remote access server (see
Figure 3.31).

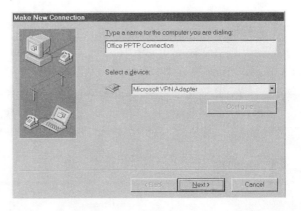

FIGURE 3.30
The Microsoft VPN Adapter takes the place of a
modem during a PPTP connection.

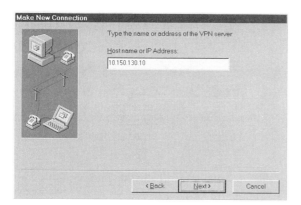

FIGURE 3.31
The VPN or PPTP connection has an IP address as a destination.

Before establishing a PPTP connection, you must first establish a connection to a TCP/IP network. PPTP then operates through that connection. The TCP/IP connection may be a dial-up connection to an ISP. It may, however, be a direct Internet connection or a connection to any other TCP/IP network. In other words, even though you're using Dial-Up Networking to make the PPTP connection, the connection does not have to be through a dial-up medium. After that connection to the TCP/IP network is in place, you will open the PPTP dial-up connection (see Figure 3.32). This connection will have the IP address of the PPTP adapter on the RAS server as the destination.

> NOTE
> **Why DUN?** It may seem strange that you use Dial-Up Networking (DUN) to make a PPTP connection even if the connection isn't through a dial-up medium. You use Dial-Up Networking because of its built-in support for PPP. PPP is an essential ingredient in a PPTP connection.

CONFIGURING WINDOWS 98 SERVER COMPONENTS

Configure Windows 98 server components.

Windows 98 is primarily designed to act as a network client, but Microsoft has included some other server components (in addition to the useful file and printer sharing components) that provide increased functionality for Windows 98 as a server machine. Microsoft highlights two of those server components in the Windows 98 exam objectives, as follows:

- ◆ Microsoft Personal Web Server (PWS) 4.0
- ◆ Dial-Up Networking Server

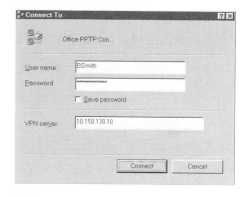

FIGURE 3.32
The dial-up connection leaves previous connections open.

The following sections discuss these important server components and how to configure them.

Personal Web Server (PWS)

Windows 98's *Personal Web Server (PWS)* is a scaled-down Web server application. PWS lets you post HTML documents for access from the network.

PWS is designed primarily for small-scale intranet traffic. Although in theory, you could use it on the open Internet, PWS supports only very light use (two or three connections at a time) and thus isn't really hearty enough for the open Internet. The principal use for PWS is to post HTML documents for access by users on a local network. Microsoft also points out that PWS can be used to develop and test Web pages that will eventually be posted on your corporation's or your ISP's main Web server.

To install Microsoft Personal Web Server, perform the tasks outlined in Step by Step 3.18.

STEP BY STEP

3.18 Installing Microsoft Personal Web Server

1. Double-click on the Add/Remove Programs Control Panel icon.

2. Insert the Windows 98 CD in the CD-ROM drive. In the Add/Remove Programs Control Panel, click on Install.

3. Click on Browse. Browse to the \add-ons\pws directory of the Windows 98 CD.

4. Double-click on Setup.exe. Windows 98 will install PWS.

5. Windows 98 will prompt you to restart your PC.

When you finish the installation, an icon labeled Publish should appear on your desktop. This icon will open Personal Web Manager, an application that manages your Personal Web Server configuration (see Figure 3.33). You can also reach Personal Web Manager by choosing Start, Programs, Internet Explorer, Personal Web Server, Personal Web Manager.

Personal Web Manager is a central interface for managing your PWS Web site. The icons in the left pane present different configuration options, as follows:

◆ **Main.** The Main window displays the home page and home page directory and provides statistics on your Web site. Click on the Stop button to stop Web service.

◆ **Publish.** The Publish icon launches the Publishing Wizard, which guides you through the process of making your HTML pages available for Web access. The Home Page Wizard button lets you create a home page. (You must run the Home Page Wizard one time before running the Publishing Wizard.)

◆ **Web Site.** The Web Site icon lets you view your Web site. If you don't have a Web site yet, you'll reach the Home Page Wizard.

◆ **Tour.** The Tour icon provides a brief tour of Personal Web Manager options.

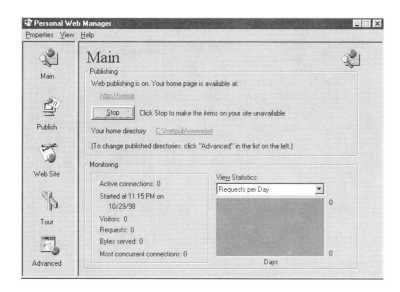

FIGURE 3.33
Personal Web Manager provides an interface for managing your Web resources.

◆ **Advanced.** The Advanced icon lets you view virtual directories on your PC (see Figure 3.34). You can also configure a default document, choose whether to allow Web users access to directory browsing, and choose whether to save a log of Web activity.

Dial-Up Server

Windows 98 includes a Dial-Up Server application that lets your Windows 98 computer receive dial-up connections. In other words, you can call in to a Windows 98 computer that has Dial-Up Server enabled and make a remote network connection to the Windows 98 computer.

It is best to think of Dial-Up Server—and its client counterpart Dial-Up Networking, described later in this chapter—as another form of network connection. To use Dial-Up Server, you must have a modem or another similar adapter device, and that modem must be bound to whatever protocol(s) you intend to use. If you plan to share files from the machine that is acting as the dial-up server, you must install the appropriate file and printer service (described earlier in this chapter), and you must make sure it is bound to whatever protocol you plan to use.

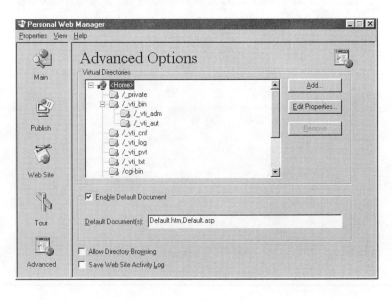

FIGURE 3.34
Personal Web Manager's Advanced icon lets you view virtual directories and configure security settings.

To install Dial-Up Server, perform the tasks outlined in Step by Step 3.19.

STEP BY STEP

3.19 Installing Dial-Up Server

1. Double-click on the icon for the Add/Remove Programs Control Panel.

2. Click on the Windows Setup tab.

3. Double-click on the component group labeled Communications.

4. In the Communications dialog box, check the checkbox for Dial-Up Server. Click on OK.

5. Click on OK in the Add/Remove Programs Properties dialog box. Windows 98 will attempt to install Dial-Up Server. You may be asked to supply the Windows 98 CD. Windows 98 will prompt you to restart your PC.

After Dial-Up Server is installed, you can configure it through the Dial-Up Networking folder in My Computer.

To configure Dial-Up Networking, perform the tasks outlined in Step by Step 3.20.

STEP BY STEP

3.20 Configuring Dial-Up Networking

1. Double-click on My Computer.

2. In the My Computer window, double-click on the Dial-Up Networking folder.

3. In the Dial-Up Networking window, pull down the Connections tab and choose Dial-Up Server.

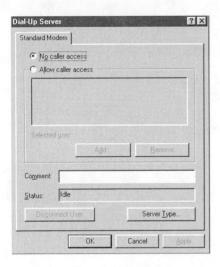

FIGURE 3.35
The Dial-Up Server dialog box lets you configure Dial-Up Server settings.

4. The Dial-Up Server dialog box will appear on your screen (see Figure 3.35). The Dial-Up Server dialog box lets you configure Dial-Up access settings.

5. To enable the Windows 98 computer to receive dial-up connections, select the option button labeled Allow Caller Access.

6. If the Windows 98 computer is configured for user-level security (as described earlier in this chapter), click on the Add button to add users to the list of those who have permission to initiate dial-up connections to the Dial-Up Server machine.

   If your computer is configured for share-level access, click on Change Password to enter an access password for dial-up users.

7. For additional options, click on the button labeled Server Type in the Dial-Up Server dialog box. The Server Types dialog box will appear.

8. In the Server Types dialog box, choose whether the dial-up server will use Point to Point Protocol (PPP)—the common Internet line protocol that is also used by Windows 95/98 and recent versions of NT) or the Windows for Workgroups and Windows NT 3.1 dial-up protocol. If you choose the Default option, Dial-Up Server will automatically assume PPP mode and will switch to WfW/NT3.1 if PPP doesn't work. The Server Types dialog box also lets you specify whether to use software compression and whether to require encrypted passwords. Click on OK.

9. In the Dial-Up Server dialog box, click on Apply to save any changes. Choose OK to close the Dial-Up Server dialog box.

You'll learn more about Dial-Up Networking later in this chapter.

For the purpose of the Windows 98 exam, one important thing to remember is that, like Windows NT's Remote Access Service (RAS),

Dial-Up Server can act as a NetBIOS gateway. In other words, a client using the NetBEUI protocol can connect through the Dial-Up Server to a local network using NetBEUI, TCP/IP, or IPX/SPX-compatible protocol.

WINDOWS 98 ON NT NETWORKS

Configure a Windows 98 computer as a client computer in a network that contains a Windows NT 4.0 domain.

Windows 98 on NT networks is a huge topic. In fact, it is arguably the main topic of the Windows 98 exam. Most of the questions on Windows 98 in NT domains won't deal specifically with the act of configuring Windows 98 to let you log on to a domain, but will instead ask you to apply a wide range of topics discussed elsewhere in this book to the context of Windows 98 in an NT environment.

This chapter has already discussed all the steps you'll need to configure Windows 98 to log on to an NT domain. The following is a summary:

1. Make sure Client for Microsoft Networks is installed and properly bound to a protocol that is used on the domain and make sure the protocol is properly bound to the necessary network adapter.

2. Select Client for Microsoft Networks in the Configuration tab of the Network Control Panel and click on Properties. Check the checkbox labeled Log On to Windows NT Domain and enter the name of the NT domain. Click on OK.

3. If you want to make the domain logon the primary network logon (see the discussion of logon options earlier in this chapter), in the Configuration tab, click on the arrow to the right of the box labeled Primary Network Logon and select Client for Microsoft Networks.

4. To use the domain's user lists to provide user-level security for the Windows 98 computer's shared resources, click on the Access Control tab in the Network Control Panel and select user-level access control. Enter the name of the domain in the box provided. Click on OK.

Beyond these simple configuration steps, you'll need to understand how Windows 98 operates within the complete ecosystem of an NT domain. The questions on NT domains will draw from the following topics:

◆ See Chapter 1 for an introduction to Microsoft networking and a discussion file sharing and user-level versus share-level access control.

◆ See the discussion of Windows 98 logon options earlier in this chapter.

◆ See the discussion of Windows 98 networking components, especially Client for Microsoft Networks and File and Printer Sharing for Microsoft Networks.

◆ See the discussion of browsing earlier in this chapter. Be sure you know how browsing works on Microsoft networks and how to configure a browser role for a Windows 98 PC.

◆ *(Very important)* See the discussion of TCP/IP earlier in this chapter. Be sure you understand TCP/IP addressing and NetBIOS name resolution. Make sure you know how Windows 98 interacts with all the TCP/IP-related services provided with Windows NT server, such as WINS, DHCP, and DNS.

◆ See Chapter 6 for discussions of Windows 98 with network-based user profiles and system policies.

WINDOWS 98 ON NETWARE NETWORKS

Configure a Windows 98 computer as a client computer in a NetWare network.

Many existing LANs make use of Novell NetWare servers for application serving or File and Printer Sharing, as well as for their directory database. Microsoft Windows 98 includes the IPX/SPX-compatible protocol (described earlier in this chapter) for integration into existing NetWare LANs.

For interoperability with NetWare 2.x and 3.x networks and NetWare 4.x networks with servers using bindery emulation, Windows 98 includes the following:

- ◆ The 32-bit client for NetWare Networks, using the NWREDIR.VXD driver

- ◆ Support for older 16-bit NetWare clients

- ◆ A NetWare logon script processor

- ◆ The IPX/SPX-compatible protocol

- ◆ The IPX ODI protocol for compatibility with older NetWare networks

- ◆ The File and Printer Sharing for NetWare Networks service

In order for Windows 98 to operate on NetWare networks, you must install the IPX/SPX-compatible protocol and ensure that it is bound to the necessary adapter (discussed earlier in this chapter).

Windows 98 also includes Services for NetWare Directory Services (NDS), which enables a Windows 98 computer to interact with a NetWare 4.x NDS-based network. The File and Printer Sharing for NetWare Networks service (described earlier in this chapter) allows Windows 98 to act as a peer-to-peer server on a NetWare network. In addition to Microsoft's own Client for NetWare Networks, Windows 98 includes other optional clients for accessing NetWare networks. You'll learn more about NetWare client options in a later section.

Configuring Windows 98 to Access a NetWare Bindery

To take advantage of the IPX/SPX-compatible protocol and allow connections to NetWare servers with binderies, you must install Client for NetWare Networks or another NetWare-compatible client. (You'll learn more about NetWare client options in an upcoming section.)

To install a NetWare client, perform the tasks outlined in Step by Step 3.21.

STEP BY STEP

3.21 Installing a NetWare Client

1. Select Start, Settings, Control Panel. Double-click the Network icon.

2. Click the Add button in the Network Properties sheet. The Select Network Component Type dialog box appears.

3. Double-click Client. The Select Network Client dialog box appears.

4. If you wish to install Client for NetWare Networks, choose Microsoft from the Manufacturers list and select Client for NetWare Networks. Click on OK.

5. If you wish to install a Novell client, choose Novell from the Manufacturer's list and select Novell NetWare (Workstation Shell 3.X 9NETX) or Novell NetWare (Workstation Shell 4.x and above). See the upcoming section for more information about alternative NetWare clients. Or, click on the button labeled Have Disk to install a client that isn't present on the Windows 98 CD. Click on OK.

6. Click on OK in the Configuration tab. Windows 98 may prompt you for the location of the Windows 98 CD. You'll need to restart your computer for the changes to take effect.

Configuring Windows 98 to Access an NDS Tree

Windows 98 provides the Service for NetWare Directory Services (NDS) service to allow access to NetWare 4.x NDS "trees."

NDS is an X.500-compliant directory service that provides a hierarchical, distributed directory service. NDS allows an initial authentication to a particular NDS "tree" using a user object with associated password. This authentication can then be used, if the user object has sufficient permissions, to gain access to shared resources. This allows a single point of login for network services.

Services for NDS must be accompanied by Microsoft's Client for NetWare Networks client component. You can't use Services for NDS with the alternative 16-bit NetWare clients described in the next section. If an alternative client is already installed on your system, you must remove it and install Client for NetWare Networks if you want to use Services for NDS.

To configure the Microsoft NDS client, perform the tasks outlined in Step by Step 3.22.

> **NDS Needs Client for NetWare Networks** This service can only be configured on Windows 98 workstations that *already* have the IPX/SPX-compatible protocol and the Client for NetWare Networks installed. When you install Services for NDS, the Client for NetWare Networks will automatically be installed if it isn't present on your system.

STEP BY STEP

3.22 Configuring the Microsoft NDS Client

1. Select Start, Settings, Control Panel, and then double-click the Network icon.

2. Click the Add button in the Network Properties sheet. The Select Network Component Type dialog box appears.

3. Double-click Service. The Select Network Service dialog box appears.

4. In the Manufacturers column, choose Microsoft.

5. In the Network Services column, choose Service for NetWare Directory Services.

6. Click OK. The NetWare Directory Services service will be installed.

7. On the Configuration tab of the Network sheet, double-click NetWare Directory Services.

8. The Services for NetWare Directory Services Properties sheet appears, as shown in Figure 3.36.

   You have the following options:

   • **Preferred Tree.** This is the NDS tree where the user will access shared resources.

   continues

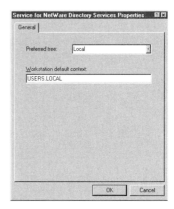

FIGURE 3.36
The NetWare Directory Services Properties General tab lets you configure NDS options.

continued

- **Workstation Default Context.** The default context where the user's NDS user object can be found.

9. After you close the Network Properties sheet, Windows 98 might ask you for the location of necessary files. You will need to restart.

With Microsoft's NDS client, a user can log in to only one tree and context at a time. Changing your tree and context requires that Windows 98 be restarted.

Also, the Windows 98 NDS user can't make a bindery connection to a NetWare server using a username or password different from his or her NDS user object.

Understanding NetWare Client Options

In addition to Microsoft's own Client for NetWare Networks client, Windows 98 comes with the following NetWare clients:

- **NetWare VLM.** A 16-bit, real-mode NetWare Client by Novell. NetWare VLM supports NetWare 3.x and 4.x servers.

- **NetWare NETX.** A 16-bit, real-mode client by Novell. NETX supports NetWare 3.x and NetWare 4.x in bindery mode.

- **Novell Client for Windows 95/98.** Novell's 32-bit NetWare client. Client for Windows 95/98 supports NetWare 3.x and NetWare 4.x servers and includes support for NDS.

Microsoft recommends the 32-bit Client for Windows 95/98 over the other Novell client options, but, as you might guess, Microsoft recommends its own Client for NetWare Networks over any of the NetWare or third-party options. Basically, Client for NetWare Networks provides tighter integration with the Windows 98 environment. The Novell clients may, in some cases, provide better integration with NetWare. For instance, you may need to load additional files supplied by Novell in order to run certain NetWare-based utilities.

Microsoft clearly enumerates the advantages of Client for Microsoft Networks over the VLM and NETX 16-bit clients. Those advantages include the following:

◆ Client for Microsoft Networks runs in protected-mode memory and thus doesn't use any conventional memory.

◆ The 32-bit architecture offers a 50–200% increase in network file I/O operations over the 16-bit versions running on Windows 3.x.

◆ Client for Microsoft Networks allows additional network clients to be used at the same time.

The advantages of Client for NetWare Networks over Novell's 32-bit Client for Windows 95/98 are not as pronounced. One important advantage of Client for NetWare Networks over the Novell 32-bit client is that you must use Client for NetWare Networks if you want to use File and Printer Sharing for NetWare Networks (described earlier in this chapter).

A Novell client is required if any of the following are used:

◆ NCP packet signature security (requires VLM).

◆ NetWare IP protocol (which doesn't use Microsoft's TCP/IP as it tunnels IPX/SPX through the IP protocol).

◆ Helper Terminate and Stay Resident (TSR) applications loaded from DOS (such as 3270 emulators).

◆ Custom Virtual Loadable Modules (VLMs) with functionality not provided by the Windows 95 components, such as Personal NetWare (PNW.VLM).

◆ Novell utilities, such as NWADMIN and NETADMIN. Most of the DOS-based 3.x utilities will still work, such as SYSCON, RCONSOLE, and PCONSOLE.

◆ IPX ODI protocol.

◆ Monolithic IPX (IPX.COM) or ARCnet protocols.

Putting It All Together: Windows 98 in NetWare

The experts who write questions for the Windows 98 exam are good at devising scenarios that draw from a full range of topics within a network environment. As you prepare for questions on Windows 98 in NetWare environments, you'll need to look beyond this section to sections and chapters of this book that provide details on NetWare configuration. Take advantage of the following references:

◆ See Chapter 1 for a discussion of user-level security. Be sure you know how to configure a NetWare server as a security provider.

◆ See earlier sections of this chapter for a discussion of networking components, including Client for NetWare Networks and File and Printer Sharing for NetWare Networks.

◆ See the discussion of Dial-Up Server earlier in this chapter. Remember that Dial-Up Server can act as a NetBIOS gateway to an IPX/SPX network such as a NetWare network.

◆ See the discussion of Dial-Up Networking later in this chapter. Dial-Up Networking can connect to a NetWare Dial-Up Server using IPX-compatible protocol.

◆ See Chapter 6 discussions of how to implement roaming profiles and system policies on NetWare networks.

WINDOWS 98 AND REMOTE ACCESS

Configure a Windows 98 computer for remote access by using various methods in a Microsoft environment or a mixed Microsoft and NetWare environment.

The term *remote access* can mean many things in networking. Sometimes it refers to basic network access; sometimes it refers to access to the greater network (beyond the LAN); and sometimes it refers specifically to dial-up access. In the Windows 98 exam objectives, Microsoft highlights the following remote access topics:

◆ **Dial-Up Networking.** Dial-Up Networking (DUN) is primarily used for dial-up modem access. Dial-Up Networking sometimes can be used for other types of network connections, such as connections through a null modem cable or PPTP connections (described earlier in this chapter).

◆ **Proxy server.** A proxy server, as you'll learn in a later section, is a computer that acts as an Internet proxy for a client PC.

You'll learn more about these features in the following sections.

Dial-Up Networking (DUN)

Dial-Up Networking is one of Windows 98's most important networking features. Even home users who aren't part of a local network and have no need for Ethernet cards and file and printer sharing will need a Dial-Up Networking connection if they want to check email or search the Web through a modem connection to an Internet service provider (ISP).

Windows 98's Dial-Up Networking (DUN) is a handy and simple means of connecting to the Internet through a modem. You can also use DUN to connect to a remote LAN or even to call a single computer that is using Windows 98's Dial-Up Server (described earlier in this chapter) or some other dial-up server service.

To configure a dial-up connection, perform the tasks outlined in Step by Step 3.23.

STEP BY STEP

3.23 Configuring a Dial-Up Connection

1. Double-click the My Computer icon on the client computer.

2. Double-click the Dial-Up Networking icon to display the Dial-Up Networking folder.

continues

NOTE **Installing Dial-Up Networking**   If Dial-Up Networking isn't installed on your PC, you can install it through the Windows Setup tab of the Add/Remove Programs Control Panel. Click on the Communications group and select Dial-Up Networking.

continued

3. Double-click the Make New Connection icon to start the Make New Connection Wizard, shown in Figure 3.37. Enter a name for the connection in the Type a Name for the Computer You Are Dialing field, such as the name of your ISP.

4. In the Select a Device drop-down list, choose the modem you want to use to dial out using the new Dial-Up Networking connection. Click the Next button.

5. In the Make New Connection screen, enter the area code and telephone number of the host computer. Click the Next button.

6. Click Finish to create a new Dial-Up Networking connection. A new icon for that connection is added to the Dial-Up Networking folder.

Configuring Dial-Up Properties

After you create a Dial-Up Networking connection, right-click on the connection icon in the Dial-Up Networking folder and choose Properties to configure connection properties. The following sections examine the various configuration options available through the Connection Properties dialog box and look at a few other important topics related to Dial-Up Networking connections. Topics include the following:

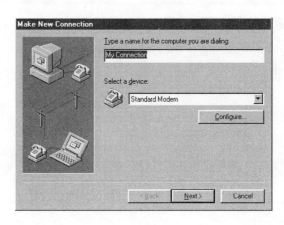

FIGURE 3.37
The Make New Connection Wizard lets you create a new dial-up connection.

- ◆ Configuring general properties
- ◆ Configuring server types
- ◆ Configuring scripting
- ◆ Configuring multilink
- ◆ Password authentication schemes
- ◆ Configuring network protocols through DUN

Configuring General Properties

The Connection Properties General tab (see Figure 3.38), provides a chance to edit the phone number and country code properties you entered when you created the dial-up connection. You can also configure modem properties for the connection. In the box labeled Connect Using, select a modem. The Configure button lets you configure modem properties. If you click on the Configure button, the subsequent Modem Properties dialog box is similar to the dialog box of the same name invoked through the Modems Control Panel. However, the Options tab of the Standard Modem Properties dialog box, invoked by clicking on the Configure button (see Figure 3.39), offers some additional options related to dial-up connections. In the Modem Properties Options tab, you can choose whether to bring up a terminal window before or after dialing. A terminal window is necessary in some environments to support text-based logon to the dial-up server.

Configuring Server Types

The Connection Properties Server Types tab (see Figure 3.40) provides settings that let you define parameters used in the connection with the server machine. The box labeled Type of Dial-Up Server specifies the type of server that will receive the connection.

The server type setting is associated with a line protocol. A *line protocol* is a protocol used for communication between point-to-point devices such as modems. The connection shown in Figure 3.40 is configured for the *Point to Point Protocol (PPP)*. PPP is the default line protocol for Windows 98 Dial-Up Networking connections. PPP was originally designed for the TCP/IP environment, but it is capable of transporting TCP/IP, NetBEUI, or IPX/SPX-compatible protocol in Windows 98. PPP also supports a variety of dial-up servers. PPP allows the following:

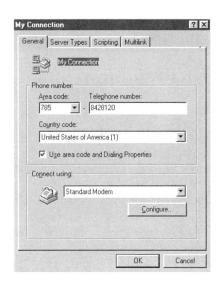

FIGURE 3.38
The Connection Properties General tab provides dialing options and lets you configure modem properties.

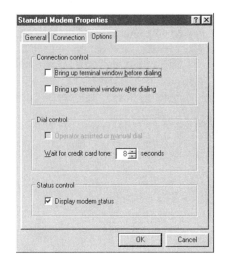

FIGURE 3.39
In the Standard Modem Properties Options tab, you can decide whether to bring up a terminal window.

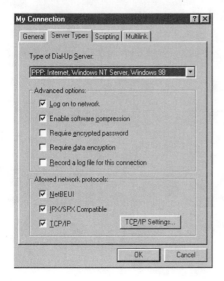

FIGURE 3.40
The Connection Properties Server Types tab
lets you choose the server type and configure
protocol settings and advanced settings.

NOTE **Supporting Protocols** NetBEUI,
IPX/SPX-compatible, and TCP/IP are
supported by DUN only in their 32-bit
implementations as provided with
Windows 98. For example, you can't
use DUN with a real-mode IPX protocol, such as that provided by Novell
and installed through a batch file.

◆ Multiplexing of sessions across a single serial link, allowing
multiple network applications to appear to communicate
simultaneously

◆ Multiple network protocols to be transported simultaneously
over a single link

◆ Software compression to increase throughput

◆ Automatic negotiation of addressing, allowing DHCP to
assign a dynamic IP address to Windows 95

◆ Error detection

In addition to PPP, DUN supports the following line protocols and
server types:

◆ CLSIP: UNIX connection with IP header compression

◆ NetWare Connect Version 1.0 and 1.1

◆ SLIP: UNIX connection

◆ Windows for Workgroups and Windows NT 3.1

Another line protocol that requires some notice (in addition to PPP)
is *Serial Line Internet Protocol (SLIP)*. SLIP is an older, UNIX-based
line protocol that exists primarily on the (still numerous) dial-up
server systems that were bought and paid for before PPP was widely
available. SLIP supports only the TCP/IP network protocol. SLIP
has the following limitations:

◆ It doesn't support dynamic IP addressing.

◆ It doesn't support multiple protocols.

◆ It doesn't have error detection or correction.

Even though PPP is more powerful and versatile than SLIP, many
older dial-up server system require SLIP.

As shown in Figure 3.40, DUN also includes several other protocol
options and advanced options. Note that all server types do not support all these options. Select a network protocol to use for the connection. If you will use the TCP/IP protocol, click on the TCP/IP
Settings dialog box to enter settings.

Configuring Scripting

The Scripting tab (see Figure 3.41) lets you specify a script file that DUN will use to connect to the server and logon to the remote network. A dial-up script is only necessary if the dial-up server requires a manual logon. (Most ISPs and most NT RAS dial-up servers do not require manual logon.)

Windows 98 includes sample scripts that provide examples of the dial-up script format. These sample scripts are located in the \Program Files\Accessories directory. The Windows directory contains a file called scripts.doc that describes how to write dial-up scripts.

After you create a script, save it to the \Program Files\Accessories directory with the .scp extension.

Configuring Multilink

The Connection Properties Multilink tab (see Figure 3.42) lets you configure the connection to support PPP Multilink. PPP Multilink is a feature that lets you combine two or more devices into a single connection. The purpose of Multilink is to increase the bandwidth for a connection by using multiple devices. The devices don't have to be the same model or even the same type. You can use modems and ISDN channels. In order to use Multilink, the server to which you're connected must be configured to support multilink connections.

When you place a multilink connection, the connection is first established through the primary device, then other devices are added to the connection.

To configure a Dial-Up Networking connection for Multilink, perform the tasks outlined in Step by Step 3.24.

STEP BY STEP

3.24 Configuring a Dial-Up Networking Connection for Multilink

1. Right-click on a dial-up connection in the Dial-Up Networking folder and click on Properties.

2. Choose the Multilink tab.

continues

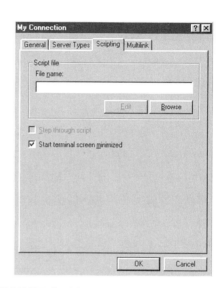

FIGURE 3.41
Enter the name of an optional dial-up script file in the Connection Properties Scripting tab.

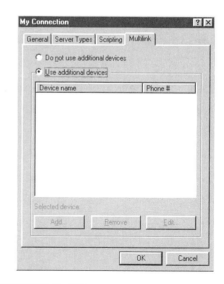

FIGURE 3.42
You can use the Connection Properties Multilink tab to configure a connection to use Multilink.

continued

3. In the Multilink tab, select the option button labeled Use Additional Devices. Click on the Add button.

4. Select the devices you'd like to add to the connection.

Password Authentication Schemes

PPP supports several password authentication schemes, which are used by different servers and have different features. The DUN connection automatically negotiates which of the following authentication protocol schemes to use:

◆ **Password Authentication Protocol (PAP).** Uses a two-way handshake to establish identity. This handshake occurs only when the link is originally established. Passwords are sent over the media in text format, offering no protection from playback attacks.

◆ **Challenge Handshake Authentication Protocol (CHAP).** Periodically verifies the identity of the peer using a three-way handshake. CHAP provides protection from playback attack, and the password is never sent over the media, protecting against illicit snooping. Windows 95 and NT don't support ongoing challenges with CHAP, but they implement Microsoft's version of CHAP, MS-CHAP.

◆ **Shiva Password Authentication Protocol (SPAP).** Offers encryption of PAP passwords and Novell NetWare bindery access for user account information.

A PPP server that doesn't support PAP or MS-CHAP might require that you use a terminal window to log on. Dial-Up Networking has an option that allows a terminal window to be displayed after dialing. Without PAP or CHAP, encrypted passwords can be used to improve security.

Configuring Network Protocols Through DUN

Three network protocols are supported by Windows 98 DUN: NetBEUI, IPX/SPX-compatible, and TCP/IP. These three protocols are configured through the Server Types Properties sheet. NetBEUI and IPX/SPX-compatible are enabled and disabled through the provided check boxes. In order to increase the speed of your connection, it's a good idea to have only the necessary protocols enabled. TCP/IP can be further configured through the TCP/IP Settings button, which invokes the TCP/IP Setting dialog box (see Figure 3.43). The IP address the ISP assigns, plus DNS and WINS information, can be configured in the TCP/IP Settings dialog box. Or, you can configure DUN to receive a dynamically assigned IP address from the dial-up server. (ISPs typically provide dynamic assignment of IP addresses.)

There are also two other checkboxes in the TCP/IP settings: one to allow higher throughput by enabling IP header compression, and one to use the default gateway on the remote network. IP header compression might not work with some dial-up servers and might need to be disabled if you experience connection difficulties.

DUN with NT RAS

On the Windows 98 exam, Microsoft pays particular attention to scenarios in which a Windows 98 client connects to a Windows NT system that is using the Remote Access Service (RAS) service. A RAS server can provide connectivity to a network and supports NT domain features such as automatic IP address assignment through DHCP.

You can also use RAS to connect to a LAN-based network from a remote location. RAS supports the following routing features:

◆ **IPX/SPX routing.** You can connect to a RAS server using the IPX/SPX-compatible protocol and gain access to an IPX/SPX network

◆ **TCP/IP routing.** You can connect to a RAS server using TCP/IP and gain access to a TCP/IP network.

◆ **NetBIOS gateway.** RAS's NetBIOS gateway feature lets a remote client connect to a RAS server using the NetBEUI protocol and gain connect to a LAN that is using IPX/SPX, TCP/IP, or NetBEUI.

The NetBIOS gateway feature is an important feature that Microsoft likes to work into exam questions. Remember that a remote client

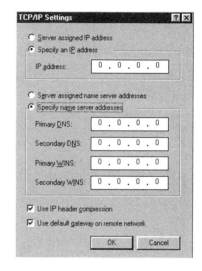

FIGURE 3.43
Configure TCP/IP setting for the dial-up connection in the TCP/IP Settings dialog box.

Configure Through DUN Microsoft recommends that you configure IP address information for dial-up connections through DUN, although you could also configure IP addressing information for the TCP/IP→Dial-Up adapter protocol in the Network Control Panel. Configuring address information through DUN lets you maintain separate address configurations for multiple dial-up connections.

using NetBEUI can connect to a TCP/IP or IPX/SPX network (or a NetBEUI network) using NT RAS. This is similar to the routing features provided with Windows 98's Dial-Up Server (discussed earlier in this chapter).

Dialing Locations

Windows 98 lets you create multiple Dialing Locations entries so that you can initiate modem connections from different locations with specific call settings. This feature is especially useful for portable PCs. A salesperson for a company with several branch offices can create a dialing location for each of the company's branch offices, for example. When she visits each office, she can switch to the local set of dialing properties rather than having to re-enter settings such as the area code or an access code.

To create a new dialing location, perform the tasks outlined in Step by Step 3.25.

STEP BY STEP

3.25 Creating a New Dialing Location

1. Click on the Telephony Control Panel. In the My Locations tab of the Dialing Properties dialog box (see Figure 3.44), click on the New button.

2. A new dialing location will be created. The name New Location will appear in the box to the left of the New button. Change the name New Location to the name you wish to use for the dialing location.

3. Enter the information in the My Locations tab that applies to the new location.

To edit the properties for an existing dialing location, click on the arrow to the right of the box labeled I Am Dialing From and choose the dialing location you wish to edit. The settings will appear in the My Locations tab. Make any changes, and click on Apply to save the new settings.

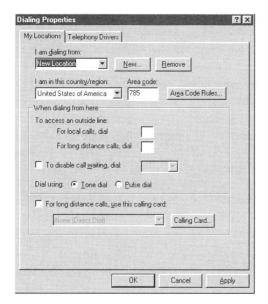

To initiate a Dial-Up Networking connection, perform the tasks outlined in Step by Step 3.26

STEP BY STEP

3.26 Initiating a Dial-Up Networking Connection

1. Double-click on a connection icon in the Dial-Up Networking folder. (You may wish to create a shortcut to the connection icon and place the shortcut on your desktop.)

2. In the subsequent Connect To dialog box (see Figure 3.45), click on the Dial Properties button if you wish to change the dial location for the connection. The My Locations tab will appear. Choose a dialing location from the drop-down list and click on OK.

3. Click on Connect to connect to the dial-up server.

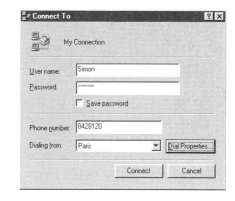

Proxy Server

A *proxy server* is a computer that receives requests from network clients, forwards those requests to the Internet, and forwards responses to those requests back to the network client. In other words, the proxy server acts as a proxy for the network client on the Internet. A proxy server can simplify configuration and also security on a local network. Only the proxy server needs to be connected directly to the Internet. The other computers on the local network send their Internet requests through the proxy server.

A proxy server is often implemented as part of a firewall system. The proxy server acts as a barrier that prevents Internet users from accessing the local network.

For the most part, Microsoft leaves its high-profile Web browser, Internet Explorer, out of the Windows 98 exam objectives. The only objective that relates directly to Internet Explorer is "Configure a Windows computer for remote access by various methods…Methods include…Proxy Server."

To configure Windows 98 to use a proxy server, perform the tasks outlined in Step by Step 3.27.

NOTE

One Small Step In keeping with Microsoft's tendency to claim the generic, the proxy server included with Microsoft's BackOffice suite is called Proxy Server.

STEP BY STEP

3.27 Configuring Windows 98 to Use a Proxy Server

1. Open Internet Explorer, by clicking on the magic *e* in the taskbar or desktop, or by choosing Start, Programs, Internet Explorer.

2. In Internet Explorer, pull down the View menu and choose Internet Options.

3. In the Internet Options dialog box, click on the Connection tab (see Figure 3.46).

4. In the Connection tab, find the area labeled Proxy Server and check the checkbox labeled Access the Internet Using a Proxy Server. Enter the IP address or NetBIOS name of the proxy server and the port address to use for the connection.

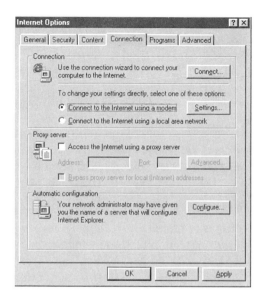

FIGURE 3.46

The Connection tab in the Internet Options dialog box lets you configure a proxy service.

5. Click on the Advanced button to invoke the Proxy Settings dialog box (see Figure 3.47). The Proxy Settings dialog box lets you configure separate proxy server addresses for different Internet services and components, such as HTTP, FTP, and Gopher. In the Exceptions box, you can enter specific IP addresses or domain names (which may include the wild card character *) for which the proxy server will not be used. This feature lets you bypass the proxy server for local transmissions. Click on OK.

6. Click on OK in the Internet Options dialog box.

You can also reach the Connection tab, which is used to configure a proxy server (as described in the preceding procedure), through the Internet Control Panel.

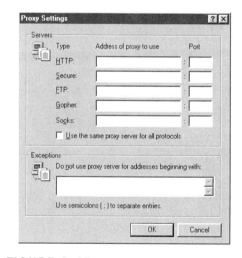

FIGURE 3.47

The Proxy Settings dialog box lets you bypass the proxy server-specific addresses or configure separate proxy settings for different services.

CASE STUDY: TRAKTONE TRAILER AGENCY

ESSENCE OF THE CASE

Here are the essential elements in this case:

- All users must be able to use the Internet simultaneously.

- All users must be restricted from certain Internet sites that are not work-related.

- Users' Web activity must be monitored and recorded.

SCENARIO

Elliot, the MIS Manager for Traktone Trailer Agency, does not have enough IP addresses for all of his users to use the Internet connection at one time. He would also like to manage where users are allowed to go on the Internet.

ANALYSIS

A proxy server can allow all users to access the Internet at one time. Through filters on the proxy server, specific domain names can be blocked from users' access. All user activity can be monitored and recorded.

CHAPTER SUMMARY

<table>
<tr><td>

KEY TERMS

- bindings
- Plug and Play cards
- legacy cards
- NetBIOS
- IPX/SPX
- frame type
- TCP/IP
- subnet mask
- IP address
- gateway
- NetBEUI
- DLC
- Fast Infrared
- file and printer sharing services
- Asynchronous Transfer Mode
- Virtual Private Networking
- PPTP
- PWS
- DUN locations
- proxy server

</td><td>

This chapter guided you through the spectrum of Windows 98 networking. You learned about Windows 98 networking components and about network browsing. You also learned about Windows 98 logon options. This chapter also discussed Windows 98's principle networking protocols, described some server components included with Windows 98, and outlined some of the information you'll need to answer questions on Windows 98 in NT and NetWare environments. Lastly, you learned about Dial-Up Networking and you learned how to configure Windows 98 to access a proxy server.

It is a good idea to get as much hands-on experience as possible with Windows 98 networking. Set up different networking scenarios. Work through the exercises in this chapter and become familiar with the tools and procedure.

</td></tr>
</table>

Exercises

3.1 Configuring the Personal Web Server

This exercise will examine the installation and configuration of the Personal Web Server.

Estimated Time: 30 minutes

1. Insert your Windows 98 CD-ROM and click Start to Run.

2. In the Run dialog box, **insert X:\ add-ons\pws\setup.exe** (substitute *X* with your CD-ROM's drive letter) and then press Enter.

3. Personal Web Server setup starts. Click Next to continue.

4. Read and accept the End User License Agreement.

5. Click on the Typical Installation button to continue.

6. By default, Personal Web Server will use `C:\InetPub\wwwroot` as the folder your Web service will publish HTML documents from. Accept this default by selecting the Next button.

7. The Web Server Setup will install the required application files.

8. To finish setup, click on the Finish button. You'll be prompted to restart your computer.

9. Upon restarting you computer, click Start and then point to Programs, Microsoft Personal Web Server, Personal Web Manager.

10. A tip of the day is displayed. Click it to begin configuring your Intranet.

11. The Personal Web Manager offers many choices for creating and maintaining an intranet. For this exercise, choose the Tour button to walk through an interactive tour to learn what Personal Web Server can do for you. After the tour, resume this exercise.

12. To begin publishing your Web site, click once on the Web Site button.

13. The Home Page Wizard is activated to publish a home page on your intranet. Click once on the wizard.

14. You are presented with several template options for your home page. Choose the Journal template for this exercise; you can reconfigure your site later. Choose the Advance button to continue with the setup.

15. You are prompted to create a guest book for visitors to sign into your Web site. Accept the default that you do want a guest book and then click the Continue button.

16. You have the option to add a drop box on your site. For this exercise choose No and then continue.

17. You've set the ground rules for your home page. Now you can personalize the home page. Choose the Continue button.

18. Internet Explorer will open and you'll be prompted to fill in some information about your site in the form supplied.

19. Enter the appropriate information in each field and then choose the Enter New changes button at the bottom of the page.

20. After entering the changes, your home page is configured and displayed.

21. To edit your home page, note that the Home Page Wizard is minimized on your taskbar and that you can open it up and edit your home page. Click on the Personal Web manager to activate it. Click on Edit Your Home Page.

22. Change the template to Gunmetal, make any necessary text changes, and then enter the changes you've made.

23. The changes you have made are again displayed in Explorer for you to review. Close Explorer and bring the Personal Web Manager to the foreground.

24. Click on the Main button and you'll see information about your Web site—everything from what your home directory is to the current statistics on your Web page.

25. From the Main dialog box you can also see how others on your network can access this page through the network. Go to another machine and enter the path to your computer in the Internet Explorer Address field to see your published page.

3.2 Publishing Files on Your Web Server

This exercise will walk you through the process of creating and publishing files on your Intranet Server.

Estimated Time: 15 minutes

1. Open Windows Explorer. Before you can publish any files on your intranet you first have to make certain that you have some files to publish.

2. On your C: drive, create a folder called **Data** and then open it up. (To create a new folder, right-click anywhere there is not an object while viewing the contents of your C: drive and choose New Folder.)

3. Create two notepad documents in this new folder. Call the documents Test1 and Test2. Enter a few lines of text into each document.

4. After you have created and added text to the two documents, close Windows Explorer and open the Personal Web Manager.

5. Click on the Publish button to start the Publishing Wizard. Click on the Continue button to begin the process.

6. The Publishing Wizard prompts you to enter a path to the file you want to publish, or you can click on the Browse button to find the file. For this exercise, click on the Browse button.

7. You'll be prompted to find the folder in which your files are located. On your C: drive, find the Data folder that was created earlier in this exercise. Click the folder to display the contents of the folder.

8. Select the Test1.txt document and choose OK. You are returned to the Publishing Wizard. Type a description of the file. This description is what your users will see before they access the file.

9. Click on the Add button. Test1.txt is added to the list of files to publish.

10. Click the Browse button and add Test2.txt to the list of files to publish. Click Continue when you are finished.

11. The Publishing Wizard tells you that the files were published on your Web site.

APPLY YOUR KNOWLEDGE

12. Open the Internet Explorer and go to your Web site by entering your computer's name.

13. On the right side of your Web page you'll see a hyperlink that reads `View my published document`. Click on this link.

14. Your published files are listed with the description you entered. Click on the link to view Test1.txt.

15. The published document is viewed through Explorer. Click the Back button on Explorer to return to the list of published files.

16. View Test2.txt. Again your document is displayed.

3.3   Configuring a Dial-Up Server

This exercise will walk you through the steps to create a Windows 98 Dial-Up Server.

Estimated Time: 10 minutes

1. Open the Dial-Up Networking folder in My Computer.

2. From the Connections menu choose Dial-Up Server.

3. The Dial-Up Server dialog box appears. Each modem you have installed on Windows 98 machine is represented by a tab for that modem.

4. Click the option button Allow Caller Access. You can also set a layer of security on the access type by choosing the users who can connect to your machine if you are using user-level security. If you are not using user-level security, you can set a password for the modem access.

5. Click on the Server Type button.

6. From the list of Server Types choose PPP: Internet, Windows NT Server, and Windows 98.

7. From the advanced options confirm that both selections are checked: Enabled Software Compression and Require Encrypted password.

8. Click OK.

9. Allow caller access on each modem you have installed on your machine and then choose OK to save your work.

3.4   Adding the Client for Microsoft Networks

This exercise will add the Client for Microsoft Networks so that you can participate in either a domain or workgroup environment.

Estimated Time: 10 minutes

1. Open the Network applet in Control Panel.

2. Click Add and then double-click Client.

3. From the list of Manufacturers, choose Microsoft and then choose the Client for Microsoft Networks.

4. Click OK to install the Client for Microsoft Networks.

5. Select the Client for Microsoft Networks and then choose Properties.

6. On the General tab, check the box Log On to Windows NT Domain.

7. In the Windows NT Domain field, enter the name of the domain to which you will be logging on.

8. At the bottom of this dialog box are two options for types of Network logons:

   • **Quick Logon.** This option logs you on to the network but does not restore network, or mapped, drives until you access the resource. You will want to use this option if you are configuring Windows 98 to log on to a Windows NT domain from a laptop that will dial into the server to log on.

   • **Logon and Restore Network Connections.** This option will log you on to the network and restore network connections. This option is what you will use if the computer you are configuring is logging on through the network rather than through a RAS connection.

9. Once your logon selections have been made, click OK, and then OK again.

10. After rebooting, you will be prompted to log on to the domain. You will need to supply the user name and password of the account that has been created for you through the User Manager for Domains.

3.5   Configuring the Client for NetWare Networks

This exercise will configure the Client for NetWare networks to log in to a NetWare Server.

Estimated Time: 10 minutes

1. Open the Network applet in Control Panel.

2. Confirm that you have a network adapter card and the IPX/SPX protocol.

3. Choose Add and then double-click Client.

4. From the list of Manufacturers, choose Microsoft and then choose the Client for NetWare Networks.

5. Choose OK and the Client for NetWare Networks is installed.

6. Open the Network applet in Control Panel.

7. On the Configuration tab, choose the Client for NetWare Networks and then choose Properties.

8. In the Preferred Server field, enter the name of your NetWare server where your logon account resides.

9. Choose the first network drive letter that should be used for resources.

10. Choose OK. After restarting, you'll be prompted to log on to your NetWare Server as identified here.

3.6   Enabling File and Printer Sharing for Windows 98

This exercise adds the File and Printer Sharing service for Microsoft Networks. You'll need to be using the Client for Microsoft Networks as described in Exercise 3.4.

Estimated Time: 10 minutes

1. Click Start, Settings, Control Panel.

2. Open the Network applet.

3. On the Configuration tab, click Add.

4. From the list of Network Components, choose Service and click Add.

5. From the list of Models choose File and Printer Sharing for Microsoft Networks.

APPLY YOUR KNOWLEDGE

6. Click OK.

7. On the Configuration tab click the File and Printer Sharing button.

8. Check both boxes, which will allow you to share your files and your printers on your network.

9. Choose OK and OK again. You can now begin sharing your resources on your Microsoft network.

3.7   Adding Protocols to Windows 98

This exercise shows you how to add additional protocols to your Windows 98 machine.

Estimated Time: 10 minutes

1. Click Start, Settings, Control Panel, and open the Network applet.

2. In the Configuration tab, take note of what protocols you may currently have installed.

3. Click Add and double-click Protocols.

4. From the list of Manufacturers, choose Microsoft.

5. From the list of Network Protocols, choose a protocol that is not currently installed on your system and choose OK. You may be prompted for your Windows 98 CD.

6. Based on what protocol you have selected, you may be prompted to configure the protocol. You should check with your network administrator to determine what attributes will need to be assigned with the selected protocol to begin communication with other machines that are using the same protocol.

3.8   Configuring a Windows 98 Machine to Log On to a Windows NT Domain

This exercise will configure your Windows 98 machine to log on to a Windows NT domain. The exercise assumes that you have a Windows NT domain with a valid user name and password so that you can log on to the domain. If you do not, you can still walk through most of the steps presented here.

Estimated Time: 10 minutes

1. Click Start, Settings, Control Panel, and open the Network applet.

2. On the Configuration tab, double-click the Client for Microsoft Networks.

3. The Client for Microsoft Networks Properties sheet is displayed. Check the box that says, Log On to Windows NT Domain and then enter the name of your Windows NT Domain.

4. In the bottom section of this dialog box, confirm that Logon and Restore Connections is selected. This selection is used when you are on a LAN. The option to do a quick logon should be used when you are logging on through a dial-up connection.

5. Click OK and OK again.

6. After restarting your system, enter your Windows NT domain password to log on to the Windows NT domain.

Review Questions

1. What tool can you use with Windows 98 that allows you to publish Web pages and create an intranet?

APPLY YOUR KNOWLEDGE

2. What protocol is required to browse the Internet?

3. What tool allows Windows 98 to accept dial-up users?

4. How can you restrict which users can dial into your dial-up server?

5. What is a protocol?

6. What does the Client for NetWare Networks allow you to do?

7. What are three ways you can add a network adapter card to your Windows 98 system?

8. How many characters can you have in your Windows 98 computer name?

9. To Windows 98, what is a gateway?

10. Before you can share files on a NetWare network, what service must you add to your computer?

11. What is a browse list?

12. What is a Windows NT domain?

13. What does a proxy server do for Windows 98 clients?

Exam Questions

1. Tom would like to configure his Windows 98 machine to act as a file and printer server in his 98 workgroup. Nancy doesn't think it can be done without a Windows NT Server. Who is correct, and why?

    A. Tom is correct, because Windows 98 has file and printer sharing built in; he just has to enable the service and start sharing resources.

    B. Tom is correct because Windows 98 has file and printer sharing built in. All he has to do is use the share as command in Windows Explorer.

    C. Nancy is correct. Windows 98 can do file and printer sharing as long as there is a Windows NT Server on the network.

    D. Nancy is correct. Windows 98 has no file and printer sharing capabilities.

2. You are in charge of developing your company's intranet. Your boss informs you that you have to spend as little money as possible in the development of this project. You currently are using all Windows 98 machines and the Microsoft Office products throughout your fairly large workgroup. What is the best route to take to implement this intranet?

    A. You must purchase Windows NT Server and use the Internet Information Server.

    B. You must purchase a dedicated computer for the Intranet server, using Personal Web Server, which is included with Windows 98.

    C. You must purchase the Personal Web Server add-on package to create the Intranet.

    D. Purchase nothing additional. Use a Windows 98 machine as the Intranet server; install the Personal Web Server and begin publishing pages.

3. You are a consultant for several companies in your city. You would like to configure their computers so that you could dial into their servers remotely for troubleshooting, for file and printer access, and to upload files to their machines. How can you do this with Windows 98?

A. You cannot do this with Windows 98.

B. Use the Dial-Up Networking tool to configure your clients' 98 machines as dial-up servers.

C. Purchase the Dial-Up Networking add on feature for Windows 98 and configure the machines appropriately.

D. Do nothing. All Windows 98 machines are pre-configured to accept phone calls.

4. Several sales reps from your company travel throughout the country to visit clients. Recently they have complained that they are configuring their Dial-Up Networking properties for each city that stay in. Is there anything you could do to streamline the Dial-Up Networking configuration?

A. Create a batch file that would automate each city's properties.

B. Through the Modems applet, configure the dialing properties for each city and save the locations so they can use them repeatedly.

C. Through the Dial-Up Networking tool, configure the dialing properties for each city and save the locations so they can use them repeatedly.

D. Through the Dial-Up Networking tool, configure a script for each location that would set up the modem to dial the appropriate numbers.

5. You use two computers in your Windows NT domain. One is a Windows NT Workstation, the second is a Windows 98 computer. Whenever you open the Network Neighborhood in

Windows NT you see all of the domain; when you do the same on Windows 98 you only see the current workgroup. Why?

A. You do not have the correct client installed for Windows 98. You must use the Client for Microsoft Networks.

B. You do not have the Windows 98 machine configured to log in to the domain. Windows NT workstations are configured to log in to the domain by default.

C. Windows 98 machines are always members of a workgroup. They will always display only the contents of the workgroup they belong to.

D. Windows NT machines are the only members of a domain. To configure Windows 98 to see the contents of a domain as Network Neighborhood, change the name of the workgroup to the name of the domain and restart the Windows 98 machine.

6. You are the administrator for a large Windows 98 workgroup. You can see all members of the workgroup except for one computer. From that computer, you should be able to access printers and shares throughout the workgroup, but no one can access this computer. What do you suspect is the problem?

A. Bad network adapter card

B. Incorrect permissions

C. No file and printer sharing service installed

D. No Client for Microsoft Networks installed

APPLY YOUR KNOWLEDGE

7. Polly and Sarah are adding multiple modems to take advantage of multilink abilities with Windows 98. Sarah is certain that all of the modems have to be the exact same brand, whereas Polly thinks the modems can be different brands. Who is correct and why?

   A. Polly is correct. You can add modems of different brands.

   B. Polly is correct. You can add modems of different brands as longs as they are of the same speed.

   C. Sarah is correct. You cannot mix modem brands because they have to use the exact same driver.

   D. Sarah is correct. You cannot mix modem brands, speed, or type due to the instruction set and memory stack required for each modem.

8. You are a consultant for an accounting firm. This accounting firm uses a Windows 98 workgroup only. You have configured one machine to serve as their file and printer server for the entire workgroup. What service could you configure to ensure that this machine would keep the list of resources to keep network traffic at a minimum?

   A. The browser service through the Registry: `HKEY_LOCAL_MACHINE\Services\MaintainServerList:YES`.

   B. The browser service through the Network applet. Check that the properties on the Client for Microsoft Networks are configured for Browser:Enabled.

   C. The browser service through the Network Applet. Check that the properties on the File and Printer Sharing for Microsoft Networks are configured for Browser:Enabled.

   D. The browser service through the Network applet. Check that the properties on the File and Printer Sharing for NetWare Networks are configured for Browser:Enabled.

   E. You cannot configure this service on Windows 98, as it is always automatic.

9. You are a computer consultant for a small, but growing, insurance agency. Currently they have 50 workers in their Windows 98 workgroup. The owner of the agency has told you he would like to quit printing so many memos, handbooks, and new changes in the insurance agency and just send the changes out over email. Of the following, which are valid options that could reduce the number of his printed internal communications?

   A. Do as he plans to: email the new manuals, handbooks, and memos.

   B. Use directory replication to disperse the data.

   C. Use Microsoft Personal Web Server to distribute the data.

   D. Install Internet Information Server to distribute the data.

10. Mark, a field agent for an accounting agency, often needs files from his computer while he is at a client's office. Currently, he has Rebecca, his assistant, email the files to his email account, and then he retrieves them through his laptop in the field. What might you suggest for Mark to make things easier to work with?

APPLY YOUR KNOWLEDGE

A. Use Dial-Up Networking to connect to his computer in the office to retrieve his data.

B. Create an FTP site with PWS and FTP into his computer to retrieve the files.

C. Use Infrared technology to remotely retrieve his documents.

D. Use NetMeeting to retrieve his data through the Internet.

Answers to Review Questions

1. Microsoft Personal Web Server can be used to create an Intranet and publish Web pages. (For more information, refer to the section "Configuring Windows 98 Server Components.")

2. TCP/IP is the protocol required to browse the Internet. (For more information, refer to the section "Installing and Configuring Network Components.")

3. Dial-Up Server. (For more information, refer to the section "Windows 98 and Remote Access.")

4. Password security can be configured for each modem in use on your Windows 98 machines that is serving as a dial-up server. (For more information, refer to the section "Windows 98 and Remote Access.")

5. A protocol is a language that allows computers to talk to another on a network. (For more information, refer to the section "Installing and Configuring Network Components.")

6. The Client for NetWare Networks allows Windows 98 to log in to a NetWare Environment. (For more information, refer to the section "Windows 98 on NetWare Networks.")

7. Plug and Play, Find New Hardware Wizard, and the Network applet in Control Panel. (For more information, refer to the section "Installing and Configuring Network Components.")

8. Fifteen characters is the limit for computer names on a Microsoft network. (For more information, refer to the section "Installing and Configuring Network Components.")

9. A router to another network segment. (For more information, refer to the section "Installing and Configuring Network Components.")

10. A File and Printer Sharing for NetWare Networks service. (For more information, refer to the section "Installing and Configuring Network Components.")

11. A browse list is the list of shared resources on a network. (For more information, refer to the section "Browsing and Identifying in Windows 98.")

12. A domain is a collection of Windows NT computers that are configured to be validated by a central Windows NT Server, called the Primary Domain Controller (PDC). (For more information, refer to the section "Windows 98 on NT Networks.")

13. A proxy server acts as a "proxy," or go-between, for Windows 98 clients and the Internet. Microsoft Proxy Server can be used to monitor Internet access and activity. (For more information, refer to the section "Windows 98 and Remote Access.")

APPLY YOUR KNOWLEDGE

Answers to Exam Questions

1. **A.** Tom is correct. Windows 98 has file and print-er sharing capabilities, but he has to enable the service and then share out the necessary directo-ries or printers. (For more information, refer to the section "Installing and Configuring Network Components.")

2. **D.** You do not have to purchase any additional equipment or software to use Personal Web Server. In some environments, IIS or a dedicated Windows 98 machine for Personal Web Server may be more practical, but this scenario does not require anything additional to get the network up and running. (For more information, refer to the section "Configuring Windows 98 Server Components.")

3. **B.** Dial-up servers in Windows 98 can solve this problem quickly and easily. (For more informa-tion, refer to the section "Windows 98 and Remote Access.")

4. **B.** Create a location for each city the sales reps will be visiting to streamline their time spent con-figuring their connections. You will use the modems' dialing properties to create locations for each machine. (For more information, refer to the section "Windows 98 and Remote Access.")

5. **C.** Windows 98 machines always see the work-group that they belong to first in the Network Neighborhood. Windows NT workstations will see the resources in the domain they belong to first. (For more information, refer to the section "Browsing and Identifying in Windows 98.")

6. **C.** Your machines will not show up in the Network unless they have a file and printer service installed. (For more information, refer to the section "Browsing and Identifying in Windows 98.")

7. **A.** Polly is correct. You can add modems of differ-ent brands and of varying speeds. (For more information, refer to the section "Windows 98 and Remote Access.")

8. **C.** You can configure one machine to always be the Master Browser through the Network applet's properties on file and printer sharing service. (For more information, refer to the section "Browsing and Identifying in Windows 98.")

9. **C.** The most effective plan would be to create an intranet to disseminate the information. Through Personal Web Server, the information could be displayed on-screen, for future reference, easy access, and updating. Users would only have to check the appropriate intranet sites for updates of the information. The update alerts could be sent out to users via email with hyperlinks to the intranet sites that have been updated. (For more information, refer to the section "Configuring Windows 98 Server Components.")

10. **A.** Mark and Rebecca should configure Mark's workstation as a dial-up server through Dial-Up Networking. Mark could then create a connec-tion on his laptop to his workstation to retrieve whatever files he needed in the field without dis-rupting Rebecca at the office. For security, Mark could password-protect his computer's dial-up connection. (For more information, refer to the section "Windows 98 and Remote Access.")

APPLY YOUR KNOWLEDGE

Suggested Readings and Resources

1. *The Windows 98 Resource Kit*; Microsoft Press

2. *The Windows 98 Professional Reference*, Hallberg and Casad; New Riders

This chapter helps you to prepare for the Microsoft exam by covering the following objectives within the "Installation and Configuration" category:

Install and configure hardware devices in a Microsoft environment and a mixed Microsoft and NetWare environment. Hardware devices include the following:

> **Modems**
>
> **Printers**
>
> **Universal Serial Bus (USB)**
>
> **Multiple display support**
>
> **IEEE 1394 FireWire**
>
> **Infrared Data Association (IrDA)**
>
> **Multilink**
>
> **Power management scheme**

▶ The ability to install and configure hardware devices is crucial not only to passing the exam but also to your day-to-day work with Windows 98. Hardware devices can be added to Windows 98 through a variety of ways; you'll need to become familiar with all of the different ways to add hardware to Windows 98.

Install and configure Microsoft Backup.

▶ Microsoft Backup is used to keep your working data secure. Your knowledge of how to install and configure Microsoft Backup to work in a number of scenarios is essential to passing the Windows 98 exam.

CHAPTER 4

Installing and Configuring Hardware

STUDY STRATEGIES

To study for these exam objectives, test yourself with the review questions, read the content matter, reinforce your knowledge with the hands-on exercises, and challenge yourself with the exam questions. You may also find it beneficial to invest additional time experimenting with hardware devices in a Windows 98 machine. Dig into the Device Manager to troubleshoot system resource and possible conflicts. Learn what all of the different system resources are: IRQs, I/O Ports, DMA, and memory. You would also benefit from learning the default IRQs for COM ports because you'll likely encounter system conflicts on the Microsoft exam.

INTRODUCTION

Hardware devices are an essential element of every PC. An everyday PC is likely to have (in addition to basic system devices such as a keyboard and hard disk), a video adapter and monitor, sound card, modem, CD-ROM drive, and possibly a printer or a network adapter. Devices were part of the original design for PC-compatible computers since the early days of MS-DOS, and Windows 98 provides support for older, legacy devices as well as newer models. In fact, Microsoft originally envisioned Windows 95/98 as a low-maintenance operating system for home users and low-budget corporate users, and one of the major design objectives was to provide support for the widest possible variety of devices.

This chapter examines some features of Windows 98 that help you install, configure, and manage hardware devices. First you'll learn some general concepts for supporting hardware in Windows 98. You'll then learn about some specific hardware configuration issues, such as issues relating to Universal Serial Bus (USB), multiple display, modems, and printers. Lastly this chapter examines Windows 98's Backup utility, which works with a backup device, such as a tape backup device, to back up your hard drive and protect you from catastrophic data loss.

PLUG AND PLAY VERSUS NON-PLUG AND PLAY

Theoretically, the devices supported by Windows 98 fall into two main categories:

- ◆ **Plug and Play devices.** The Windows 98 computer can configure automatically with little or no user input.

- ◆ **Legacy devices.** These devices do not support Plug and Play technology and must therefore be manually installed and configured by the user.

Like most categories in the real world, these categories are not as simple as they appear. The level of auto-configuration provided with Plug and Play can vary from device to device. And, as you learned in Chapter 2, "Installing Windows 98," Windows 98's Setup program can sometimes detect and configure devices that aren't even considered Plug and Play. Still, plug and play is more than marketing—it is a design concept, a set of specifications, and an important part of the Windows operating system.

Microsoft describes a Plug and Play system as consisting of the following three components:

◆ A Plug and Play operating system

◆ A Plug and Play BIOS

◆ Plug and Play devices and drivers

Plug and Play functionality depends on the presence of these components.

Windows 98 can use an information file called an `inf` file to install and configure a device, a program, or the Windows operating system itself. (You learned about `inf` files in the discussion of Windows 98 installation scripts in Chapter 2.) At startup, Windows 98 automatically looks for Plug and Play hardware. If Windows 98 finds a Plug and Play device, it receives an identifier from the device called the device ID. Windows 98 uses the device ID to search the `Windows\INF` directory for an `inf` file that will provide automated installation information for the device.

Windows 98 can recognize and configure some devices without requiring you to restart your system. These devices are called *hot-pluggable* devices. Some hot-pluggable devices include PC card devices and Universal Serial Bus (USB) devices.

To install a Plug and Play device, perform the tasks outlined in Step by Step 4.1.

NOTE

Plug and Play Popularity Most Windows-compatible devices on the market today have some form of Plug and Play functionality.

STEP BY STEP

4.1 Installing a Plug and Play Device

1. Turn off your PC, insert or plug in the device, and then turn your PC back on (unless the device is hot-pluggable, in which case you can just plug in the device while the PC is still on).

continues

continued

   2. Windows 98 should locate the device and install it. If
      Windows 98 identifies the device and has the necessary
      software, the installation will proceed automatically. If
      Windows 98 does not have the required driver, it may
      attempt to configure the device using a generic driver, or
      you may be asked to insert the Windows 98 CD.

If your computer does not detect the device, Microsoft recommends
that you look for the new device in the Unknown Devices section of
Device Manager and, if necessary, install the driver for the device
through Device Manager. (A later section describes Windows 98's
Device Manager.)

If the device you want to install is not a Plug and Play device, you'll
need to play a bigger role in the installation. To install a legacy
device, you may need to configure hardware resource settings (such
as an IRQ setting) on the card itself using jumpers or dip switches.
You'll also need to initiate the installation process, and you may need
to supply Windows with resource settings and troubleshoot any
resource conflicts.

To install a legacy (non-Plug and Play) device, perform the tasks
outlined in Step by Step 4.2.

STEP BY STEP

4.2 Installing a Legacy Device

   1. Turn off your system, insert or plug in the device, then
      turn on the PC and restart Windows 98.

   2. Double-click Add New Hardware in Control Panel. The
      Add New Hardware icon launches the Add New
      Hardware Wizard.

   3. The Add New Hardware Wizard first checks for new Plug
      and Play devices. If it finds new Plug and Play devices, it
      lists all the devices and asks if the device you want to
      install is listed. You are then asked to select the devices to
      install and click Yes or No.

4. If you currently have disabled devices or devices with resource conflicts, the wizard may ask if you want to repair the configuration.

5. If the Add New Hardware Wizard does not find a new Plug and Play device (which will most likely be the case if you're installing a new non-Plug and Play device), the wizard will ask if you want Windows 98 to search for non-Plug and Play devices. You have two options:

   - **Yes (recommended)**. Searches for non-Plug and Play hardware.

   - **No, I want to select the hardware from a list.** Presents a list of hardware device types (such as a display adapter, modem, keyboard, mouse, or global positioning device) and lets you choose which type of device you'd like to install.

6. If you answered Yes in step 5, Windows 98 will attempt to locate the device and install it. If Windows 98 fails to detect and install the device, or if you chose No in step 5, the Add New Hardware Wizard will ask you to choose a device type. Click Next.

7. Select the device manufacturer and model from the list, and then click on Have Disk.

8. Enter the path to the driver files and click OK. Click Next in the Model/Manufacturer dialog box that appears.

You do not need the Add New Hardware Wizard to install certain devices. Modems and printers can be installed directly through the Modems and Printers Control Panels. (You'll learn more about installing modems and printers later in this chapter.) Network adapters can be installed through the Network Control Panel, which you learned about in Chapter 3, "Windows 98 Networking."

WINDOWS 98 HARDWARE RESOURCE SETTINGS

In order for the devices in your PC to interact successfully with the operating system, the operating system must provide a means for each device to communicate and share information with the processor. In Windows 98 (and all of its PC-compatible predecessors) a device's connection with the processor is often defined through one or more hardware resource settings. Some of the resource settings used in Windows 98 include the following:

◆ **IRQ.** An interrupt request line the device can use for contacting the processor.

◆ **DMA.** Direct memory access. Lets the device transfer data directly to or from memory.

◆ **I/O.** A memory address that marks the beginning of the memory area used to transfer data between the device and the CPU.

◆ **Memory.** A memory address that marks the beginning of the memory buffer used by the device.

Every device does not need all of these resource settings. For some devices, especially Plug and Play devices, you might not ever need to know what these settings are. The beauty of Plug and Play is that if it is working right, you don't have to get involved with the details of which device is using which resources. Sometimes there are conflicts, however—especially when all or some of the devices do not support Plug and Play. A *resource conflict* is a malfunction that occurs when two or more devices attempt to use the same system resources. For instance, two devices attempting to use the same IRQ channel would result in a resource conflict.

At startup, when Windows 98 configures the Plug and Play devices, it attempts to assign resource settings so as to avoid conflicts. If the device you're installing does not support Plug and Play, you may be prompted to supply resource settings when you install the device. In some situations, Windows 98 may be able to find free settings and assign them to the device. In MS-DOS and early (pre-Windows 95) Windows, resource settings were typically defined through the start-up configuration files. In Windows 95/98, resource settings reside with other hardware configuration information in the Registry. You can configure and manage resource settings using Device Manager, which is described in the next section.

For many non-Plug and Play devices, in addition to configuring resource settings through the operating system, you may also need to physically configure jumpers on the card itself. Consult your vendor documentation for more details.

DEVICE MANAGER

Device Manager (see Figure 4.1) is the center for configuring, managing, and troubleshooting devices in Windows 98. Through Device Manager, you can remove or disable a device, update a driver, or change resource settings. Like other Control Panel applications, Device Manager is essentially an interface to the Registry. When you change a setting in Device Manager, you are editing the Registry information for that device. Device Manager reports on devices currently configured for the system, which means that, if you are using hardware profiles (see Chapter 6, "Managing Profiles and System Policies"), Device Manager will reflect the configuration of the current hardware profile.

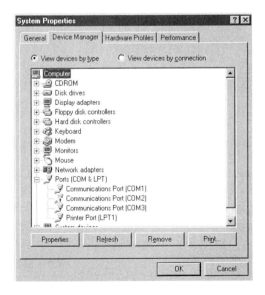

FIGURE 4.1
Device Manager provides an interface for editing device settings.

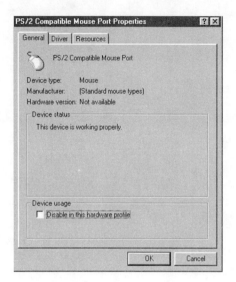

FIGURE 4.2

Selecting a device in Device Manager and clicking on the Properties button invokes the device's Properties dialog box.

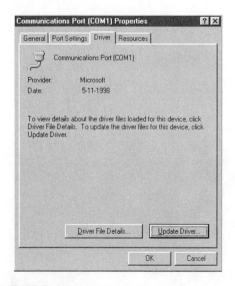

FIGURE 4.3

The Device Manager Driver tab lets you view driver information or update the current driver.

To access Device Manager, double-click on the System Control Panel and choose the Device Manager tab. Devices are listed hierarchically (refer to Figure 4.1). Using the option buttons at the top of the Device Manager tab, you can view the devices by type (as shown in Figure 4.1) or by the connection through which they access the system. (Connection categories include COM port, printer port, Plug and Play BIOS, System board, and so forth.) Type view is the default, and it is generally the most convenient because you usually use Device Manager to obtain information about a specific device. Click on the device you want to investigate, and then click on Properties. A dialog box such as the one shown in Figure 4.2 appears.

The tabs present in the device Properties dialog box vary somewhat depending on the device. The tabs shown in Figure 4.2 are probably the most common, and are described as follows:

◆ **General.** Every device has a General tab, which provides a summary of device information, such as the device type and manufacturer. The Device Status box states whether the device is working properly, or, if not, makes a guess at a possible remedy. If hardware profiles are enabled for your PC, the Device Usage box lets you enable or disable the device in the current profile. See Chapter 6 for more on hardware profiles and device usage settings.

◆ **Driver.** Every device has a Driver tab (see Figure 4.3). The Driver tab lets you view information on driver files for the device and also lets you update the driver. Click on the Update Driver button to launch the Update Device Driver Wizard.

◆ **Resources.** The Resources tab (see Figure 4.4) lets you configure hardware resource settings such as IRQ, I/O, and DMA settings (described earlier in this chapter). You can view or change the current settings. To change the current settings, clear the Use Automatic Settings checkbox, select a resource, and click on the Change Settings button. Note the Conflicting Device List at the bottom of the Resources tab; it lists any devices with conflicting resources.

Again, to view device information in Device Manager, select a device and click on the Properties button. (Remember to click on the plus sign (+) beside the device category to reveal the devices within that category.) The Properties dialog box for the selected device lets you view and configure settings for that device.

If a device on your system is disabled or otherwise unable to function because of a configuration problem such as a resource conflict, Device Manager will mark that device with a yellow exclamation point. (See Communications Port (COM2) in Figure 4.1.) Check the Device Status box in the device Properties General tab for more information about the problem. If the device is in conflict with other devices, Windows 98 may not have assigned resources to the device. In this case, the device Properties Resources tab may give you the option of configuring resources manually (see Figure 4.5). Click on the Set Configuration Manually button to configure resource settings. The Set Configuration Manually button transforms the Resources tab into a format similar to that shown in Figure 4.4. Conflicting devices will appear in the Conflicting Device List. Clear the Use Automatic Setting checkbox, select a resource, and click on the Change Settings button.

To remove a device, select the device in the Device Manager tab (refer to Figure 4.1) and click on the Remove button. Removing a device prevents the device from loading and also frees resources assigned to the device. (Disabling, on the other hand, prevents a non-Plug and Play device from loading but does not release resources. See the discussion of Device Usage in the General tab bullet, earlier in this section.) Refer to Chapter 6 for more on disabling and removing devices in a hardware profile.

You can use the Print button in the Device Manager tab (refer to Figure 4.1) to print a report on device settings. You can print a system summary, a report on a class or device, or a report on all devices (with a system summary included).

WINDOWS 98 DEVICE CONFIGURATION ISSUES

Install and configure hardware devices in a Microsoft environment and a mixed Microsoft and NetWare environment.

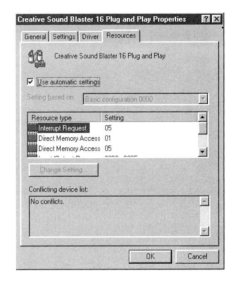

FIGURE 4.4
The Device Manager Resources tab lets you view and configure resource settings for the device.

EXAM TIP

Device Manager Exam Coverage
Spend some time exploring Device Manager. You're sure to see some Device Manager questions on the MCSE exam.

NOTE

Resource Settings Not to Be Shared
Remember that devices should not share resource settings. If two devices are in conflict, you'll need to change one device to an unused setting.

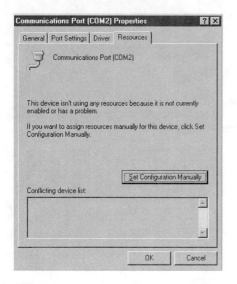

FIGURE 4.5
If resources aren't assigned because a device is in conflict, Device Manager may ask if you want to configure the device manually.

> **NOTE**
>
> **System Information Utility** A new utility included with Windows 98, Microsoft System Information Utility, provides a summary of hardware resources listed by resource (IRQ, DMA, and so on). The System Information Utility also provides information on hardware resource conflicts. The System Information Utility is primarily an informational utility and does not provide the same configuration features included with Device Manager. You can, however, directly access other utilities, such as the Version Conflict Manager and the System Configuration Utility, through the System Information Utility's Tools menu.

You can use Device Manager, the Add New Hardware Wizard, and Windows 98's Plug and Play to install and configure a wide assortment of devices in Windows 98. Certain devices, because of their importance or some unique requirements or options, receive special attention elsewhere in Control Panel. Some of the other Control Panels that include device installation or configuration options include the following:

◆ **Display.** Lets you configure video adapter and monitor settings.

◆ **Keyboard.** Lets you define keyboard properties.

◆ **Modems.** Lets you add and remove modems and configure modem properties.

◆ **Mouse.** Lets you configure mouse settings such as the double-click speed and the primary mouse button.

◆ **Multimedia.** Lets you configure audio, video, MIDI, and CD music settings. Also provides an Explorer-like view of multimedia devices (similar to Device Manager) from which you can view and configure device properties.

◆ **Network.** Lets you add and remove network adapters.

◆ **Printers.** Lets you add, remove, and configure printers.

Click on Start, Settings, Control Panel and double-click on any of these Control Panels to explore their configuration features. You'll learn more about the Modems and Printers Control Panels later in this chapter.

Microsoft highlights some special device-related issues in the Windows 98 MCSE exam objectives. Those special issues include the following:

◆ Universal Serial Bus (USB)

◆ Multiple display support

◆ IEEE 1394 FireWire

◆ Infrared Data Association (IrDA)

◆ Multilink

◆ Power management scheme

The following sections discuss these device-related issues. Microsoft also highlights modems and printers as important configuration topics. Modems and printers require a bit more explanation than the preceding topics. You'll find sections about Windows 98 modems and printers later in this chapter.

Universal Serial Bus (USB)

A system bus standard is a specification that defines how hardware devices should connect to a computer and the electronic details of passing information in and out of the system. Windows 98 supports several bus standards found in previous versions of Windows, such as ISA, EISA, SCSI, PCI, and PC Card (or PCMIA). Windows 98 also supports a pair of new bus standards that make use of some of the advanced features of the new Windows Driver Model (WDM). The new bus standards included with Windows 98 are IEEE 1394 FireWire (discussed later in this chapter) and Universal Serial Bus (USB).

Part of the purpose of USB is to extend the convenience of Plug and Play to external devices connected through a standard connector. Some of the features of USB are as follows:

◆ USB can provide power to external devices.

◆ USB lets you daisy-chain up to 127 devices with cables up to 15 feet.

◆ USB is hot-pluggable. You don't have to restart your computer to install a USB device through Plug and Play.

◆ USB provides a data transfer rate of 12Mbps for devices that require high bandwidth (such as scanners, speakers, and printers). Devices that don't require high bandwidth can operate at a lower rate of 1.5Mbps.

To install a USB device, just plug it into a USB port on your computer. You don't restart your system or provide additional configuration (unless Windows 98 is missing a necessary driver or software component for the device, in which case you may be asked to supply a disk with the necessary software).

An important feature of USB is that USB devices can be *daisy-chained* (connected together in a string).

USB components are classified into two basic categories:

◆ **Devices.** Hardware devices connected to the PC through USB.

◆ **Hubs.** Ports that serve as connection points for USB devices.

The key to USB daisy-chaining is that some devices can also serve as hubs. A special hub known variously as the *root hub*, *root tier*, or *host* is built into the motherboard or installed in the computer by way of an adapter card. The root hub controls all transmissions that pass onto the bus.

Many of the complications associated with USB are a result of USB's daisy-chain feature and of the ability of USB to actually supply power to a hub through the USB connection. A hub that gets its power directly from the USB connection is called a *bus-powered hub*. Conversely, a hub that gets its power from some external source is called a *self-powered hub*. A few rules for USB devices in Windows 98 are as follows:

◆ You cannot connect a bus-powered hub to another bus-powered hub.

◆ A bus-powered hub cannot support more than four down-stream ports.

◆ A bus-powered hub cannot support a bus-powered device that draws more than 100mA.

◆ You can plug a self-powered hub into a bus-powered hub.

◆ The USB bus cannot support more than five tiers (layers of hubs).

EXAM TIP

Know the Rules Remember the preceding USB configuration rules and be prepared to interpret these rules in a troubleshooting situation as you prepare for the Windows 98 MCSE exam.

Multiple Display Support

One of the more interesting new features of Windows 98 is its support for multiple monitors. According to Microsoft, a single Windows 98 PC can support up to nine monitors. Each monitor requires a video adapter, however, and in everyday life you'll rarely have a PC with enough free slots for nine video adapters. A second monitor could indeed be helpful for many users, and most working motherboards can accommodate a second video adapter. When you have multiple monitors installed on your system, the virtual desktop spans all the monitor space. Each monitor displays a part of the desktop.

In order to use Windows 98's multiple monitor feature, both video adapters must be PCI. When you install a second adapter, the system BIOS decides which of the two adapters will be the *primary* video adapter. (The primary video adapter will be the one that runs the Power On Self Test as the system boots.) To change the card that will be primary, switch the positions of the cards in the PCI slots. Almost any Windows 95/98-compatible video adapter can serve as the primary adapter. Not all adapters, however, can serve as Windows 98 secondary adapters. Consult your vendor documentation for details.

After you've installed a second (or third or fourth) video adapter on your computer, plug a monitor into the adapter and reboot. Windows 98 will display a message on the secondary adapter stating that it has successfully initialized the adapter. To use the additional monitor, open the Display Control Panel and select the Settings tab. In the Settings tab (see Figure 4.6), you'll see an icon for each monitor installed on the system. Select the monitor you want to add to the display and check the checkbox labeled Extend My Windows Desktop onto This Monitor. Adjust the color and screen settings, and click on Apply. Click OK to close the Display Properties Control Panel.

Windows 98 and IEEE 1394 FireWire

Windows 98 supports another new system bus standard known as IEEE 1394 FireWire. IEEE 1394 is designed for extremely high data transfer rates and is intended for devices such as digital videodisc players and digital video recorders. Windows 98's support for IEEE 1394 FireWire, like its support for USB, is built around the new Windows Driver Model (WDM).

IEEE 1394 is designed for data transfer rates ranging from 98Mbps to 393Mbps. Like USB devices, IEEE 1394 devices are hot-pluggable and daisy-chainable (up to 63 devices). If your system supports IEEE 1394, you can install an IEEE 1394 device by plugging it into the IEEE 1394 port on your computer.

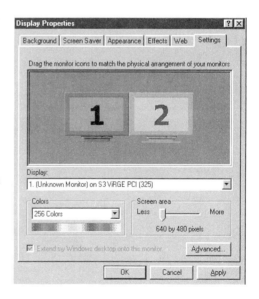

FIGURE 4.6
You can configure multiple display support in the Settings tab of the Display Properties dialog box.

Windows 98 and Infrared Data Association (IrDA)

Windows 98 includes improved support for infrared wireless networking. Windows 98's Microsoft Infrared 3.0 supports the Infrared Data Association (IrDA) Standard 1.0 for serial devices and IrDA 1.1 for fast infrared.

If you install a Plug and Play infrared device, Windows 98's Infrared 3.0 software installs automatically onto your system. You can then use the Infrared Control Panel to activate and configure the infrared device.

To install a non-Plug and Play infrared device, perform the tasks outlined in Step by Step 4.3.

STEP BY STEP

4.3 Installing a Non-Plug and Play Infrared Device

1. Attach the device.

2. Double-click on the Add New Hardware Control Panel, launching the Add New Hardware Wizard.

3. In the Add New Hardware Wizard, choose No when asked whether you want to choose the device from the list.

4. Choose No when asked whether you want Windows 98 to search for your hardware.

5. When asked to choose a hardware type, choose Infrared devices.

6. When prompted for a device, choose the default option: Generic Serial Port or Dongle.

7. When asked for additional input, such as the COM port the device will use, accept the default if you are unsure of the settings.

Windows 98 also includes an application called Infrared Monitor that lets you monitor the status of infrared connections. After you've installed an infrared device, you can start Infrared Monitor through the Infrared Control Panel or by clicking on the infrared icon in the system tray.

Multilink

Multilink is a feature that lets you combine multiple communication channels into a single connection. For instance, you can combine two single 64Kbps ISDN lines to create a dual-channel 128Kbps line. You can also combine two modems (if they are connected to separate lines), or you can combine a modem and an ISDN line. The devices participating in a multilink connection can be different makes, models, or types. The connection is initiated through one of the channels, and after the connection is established, the other channels are added to the connection.

Multilink is configured through Windows 98 Dial-Up Networking. See Chapter 3 for a discussion of Windows 98's Dial-up Networking and how to use multilink with dial-up connections.

Power Management in Windows 98

Windows 98 includes some sophisticated power management features. Windows 98 supports the Advanced Configuration and Power Interface (ACPI), Advanced Power Management (APM), and Simply Interactive PC (SIPC) standards. The primary purpose of Windows 98's power management features is to conserve power on battery-powered portable PCs, but the same power management features can be used on any PC to reduce power consumption.

Windows 98 implements power management through the OnNow feature. You can use OnNow to configure conditions in which your PC will go into what is called *sleep mode*, a low-power condition in which the PC's only function is to wait and listen for specific wake-up events (such as the pressing of a key on the keyboard). If a wake-up event occurs, the PC returns to the *on* state.

The rules you define for when and how your computer goes into sleep mode are called a *power management scheme*. You can create, configure, and manage power management schemes using the

NOTE **ACPI and APM** To fully implement ACPI through Windows 98's OnNow, you must have a BIOS that supports the ACPI specification. Some systems may support an older power-management specification known as Advanced Power Management (APM) instead. APM is managed directly by the BIOS and is configured using the BIOS Setup menu when your system starts.

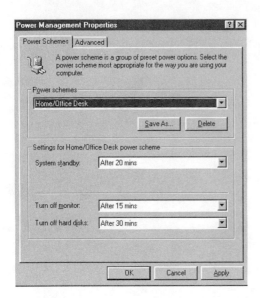

FIGURE 4.7
The Power Schemes tab in the Power
Management Properties dialog box lets you
select and configure a power management
scheme.

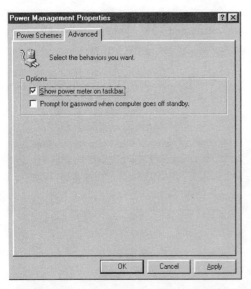

FIGURE 4.8
The Power Management Properties Advanced
tab offers additional power management
options.

Power Management Control Panel. Double-click on the Power
Management icon in Control Panel to reveal the Power Management
Properties dialog box (see Figure 4.7). Depending on your hardware,
the Power Management Properties dialog box on your computer
may contain additional tabs and settings not shown in Figure 4.7.

Windows 98 comes with three built-in power management schemes,
as follows:

- ◆ **Home/Office.** Designed for home and office desktop systems.

- ◆ **Portable/Laptop.** Designed to conserve battery power on
  portable PCs.

- ◆ **Always On.** Designed for server systems and other PCs that
  must remain in constant operation.

Click the down arrow beside the Power Schemes box (refer to Figure
4.7) to select one of these built-in power schemes. You can also create a new power scheme by saving a scheme under a different name
(using the Save As button), selecting the new scheme, and configuring new settings.

The power scheme is essentially a set of rules for how long to wait
before putting the system on standby and when to turn off the monitor and hard disks. After you select a power scheme, you can
configure these power scheme settings by using the System Standby,
Turn Off Monitor, and Turn Off Hard Disks boxes in the lower portion of the Power Schemes tab. On a portable PC, you may see two
columns of boxes to configure separate settings for the *plugged-in*
state and the battery-powered state.

On certain PCs (primarily laptops), you'll see an Alarm tab in the
Power Management Properties dialog box that will let you configure
an alarm that will sound when the battery power slips below a minimum threshold. You may also see a Power Meter tab. The power
meter gives the current status of battery usage (% of total power).

The Advanced tab (see Figure 4.8) lets you choose whether to
include an icon for the power meter in the taskbar and whether
the system should prompt for a password when returning from
the standby.

Devices

Windows 98 offers support for a vast range of devices. The preceding sections discussed Plug and Play and non-Plug and Play devices. You learned how to install devices in Windows 98, and you learned about Device Manager, a tool that helps you configure and troubleshoot devices. You also learned about some recent device features that Microsoft considers important enough to highlight in the Windows 98 exam objectives:

◆ Universal Serial Bus (USB)

◆ Multiple display support

◆ IEEE 1394 FireWire

◆ Infrared Data Association (IrDA)

◆ Multilink

◆ Power management scheme

Be sure you're familiar with these features when you take the Windows 98 exam.

INSTALLING AND CONFIGURING MODEMS UNDER WINDOWS 98

Windows 98 makes installing and configuring your modem a simple process. If you have a modem installed in your computer, for example, the Windows 98 Setup program will attempt to detect the modem brand and speed and then install the proper driver files.

If you want to change your modem or install a new modem after you're already running Windows 98, you have various options for how to invoke the Install New Modem Wizard. If you attach a Plug and Play modem to your computer, Windows 98 will detect it at Startup (or without restarting if the modem is hot-pluggable) and will launch the Install New Modems Wizard. You can also launch the Install New Modem Wizard through the Add New Hardware

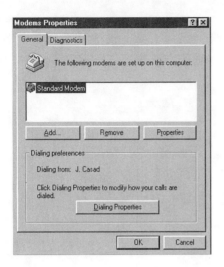

FIGURE 4.9
The Modems Properties dialog box lets you add
or remove a modem or configure modem properties.

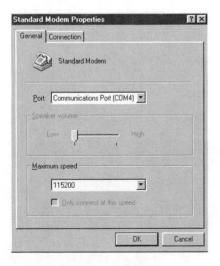

FIGURE 4.10
A specific modem's Properties dialog box offers
configuration options.

Wizard (described earlier in this chapter) or the Modems Control
Panel. Or, according to Microsoft, a communications application
that requires the modem may cause Windows 98 to launch the
Install New Modems Wizard. The Modems Control Panel is the
center for modem configuration. You can use the Modems Control
Panel to reconfigure an existing modem.

To display the Modems Properties dialog box, which you use to add,
remove, or modify a modem, perform the tasks outlined in Step by
Step 4.4.

STEP BY STEP

4.4 Getting to the Modems Properties Dialog Box

1. Select Start, Settings, Control Panel.

2. Double-click the Modems icon to display a General tab of
   the Modems Properties dialog box, shown in Figure 4.9.

To reconfigure an existing modem from this sheet, perform the steps
outlined in Step by Step 4.5.

STEP BY STEP

4.5 Reconfiguring an Existing Modem

1. In the Modems Properties dialog box, click the Properties
   button to display the Properties sheet for the selected
   modem, as shown in Figure 4.10.

2. The Modem Properties General tab lets you set the COM
   port, speaker volume, and maximum speed for the
   modem. Change modem settings as required.

3. The Connection tab lets you can change stop bits, parity,
   and data bits, and call preferences (see Figure 4.11).

Installing a new modem is just as easy. Perform the tasks outlined in
Step by Step 4.6.

STEP BY STEP

4.6 Installing a New Modem

1. Click the Add button on the Modems Properties sheet (refer to Figure 4.9). A Windows wizard guides you through the process of installing the new modem.

2. The Install New Modem Wizard states that Windows 98 will attempt to detect your modem. If you would prefer to select the modem from a list, check the checkbox labeled Don't Detect My Modem. I Will Select It from a List. Click Next.

3. If you chose to select the modem from a list, choose the modem manufacturer and model from the list and click on Next. If the modem manufacturer and model aren't listed, click on the Have Disk button and supply vendor software. If you chose to let Windows 98 detect your modem in step 2, the wizard will attempt to detect your modem and will prompt you for additional information.

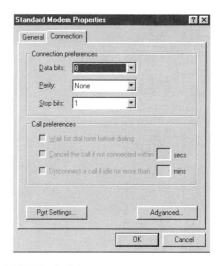

FIGURE 4.11
The Modem Properties Connection tab provides connection preference and call preference settings.

MODEMS IN WINDOWS 98

A *modem* is a special piece of computer hardware that converts the data coming from your computer to a signal that can be transmitted through normal telephone lines. This process is called *modulation*. The modem also converts signals from the phone line into data that your computer can understand through a process called *demodulation*. From these two processes (modulation and demodulation) comes the term *modem*.

Most computers now come with modems already installed. If your computer doesn't already have a modem, however, you can purchase one separately. Many brands and varieties of modems are available today, although most fall into one of a few main categories: internal, external, PCMCIA format (for notebook computers), and portable.

continues

continued

Modems also have a variety of attributes and features, such as error correction, compression, and flow control. Perhaps the most important attribute, however, is the speed with which the modem can transfer data over the telephone line. This speed is measured in bytes per second. As might be expected, a faster transfer rate is generally better. As recently as five years ago, 1200Bps was considered standard, and 2400Bps was fast. Currently, 28800Bps, 33600Bps, and 56000Bps are standard. However, for true 56KB communications, the sender and receiver, as well as the physical phone lines, must support 56KB.

Windows 98's Dial-Up Networking supports modems supported by the miniport driver. This includes modems that use the standardized set of modem commands, called the *AT command set*. Some of the advanced modem features that Dial-Up Networking supports include MNP/5 and v.42bis compression and error controls, as well as RTX/CTS and XON/XOFF software follow control.

As mentioned in the preceding paragraph, Windows 98 supports v.42bis and MNP/5 compression and v.42 error correction. *Flow control*, which regulates data traffic between communication devices, is a key component of implementing data compression and error correction in modem devices.

Examining COM Ports

Modems are configured to transfer data to and from your computer through connections called COM ports (communication ports). COM ports are connected to your computer's main motherboard and allow communications devices to pass data into and out of the computer.

The Windows 98 Setup program automatically detects your COM ports and attempts to configure any devices (such as modems) attached to those ports. Alternatively, you can select a specific COM port for your modem from the General tab of a modem's Properties sheet. Windows 98 attempts to communicate with the COM port and creates the computer files and connections necessary to allow data to flow from the computer to the device.

To manually configure a COM port (without a modem attached), open the Control Panel, double-click the System icon, and select the

Device Manager tab. You see a list of all the computer devices in your computer.

Double-click the COM port you want to configure. You see a Communications Port Properties dialog box with several tabs, as shown in Figure 4.12.

From this Properties sheet, you can configure the port to any specifications you need. These settings include port settings, device driver setup, and resource allocation information.

WINDOWS 98 PRINTING FEATURES

Windows 98 includes the following printing features, many of which are inherited from Windows 95:

- Plug and Play (PnP) printers
- Extended Capabilities Ports (ECPs)
- Image Color Matching (ICM)
- A unidriver/minidriver printer driver model
- Point and Print setup
- Drag-and-drop printing
- Enhanced Metafile (EMF) spooling
- Improved conflict resolution
- Deferred printing

The following subsections take a closer look at each of these Windows 98 printing features.

Plug and Play (PnP) Printers

Windows 98 can take full advantage of the automatic configuration features of Plug and Play (PnP) printers. Windows 98 automatically detects and configures devices complying with PnP standards each time the operating system initializes. Thus, when a PnP-compliant printer is plugged into a port on the computer, and Windows 98 is

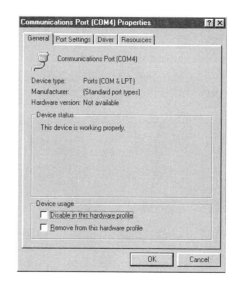

FIGURE 4.12
The Communications Port Properties dialog box lets you configure COM port settings.

NOTE

Modem Diagnostics Tool You can run the Modem Diagnostics tool in Windows 98 to identify and solve modem problems. Open the Modems Control Panel and click the Diagnostics tab. Next, choose the modem you want to troubleshoot and click More Info. Windows displays a message letting you know that the diagnostics process might take a few minutes. After the Modem Diagnostics tool runs, you see a window with information about your modem, including the port it uses, resources, highest speed, and command set configured for it. However, note that you can't run this utility while you're using the modem.

started, the operating system can detect the model of printer and set up the printer in the Printers folder.

The PnP setup uses bidirectional communication through the printer cable to obtain information on the printer, including the following:

◆ Manufacturer and model

◆ Memory installed

◆ Font cartridges installed

The printer model is reported as a device ID defined in the IEEE 1284 PnP standards. If Windows 98 has a printer driver for that specific device ID, it installs the driver and creates a printer in the Printers folder for that printing device.

If Windows 98 doesn't have the exact driver for that device ID, a dialog box appears, giving the following options:

◆ The user can insert a floppy disk with a Windows 98 driver for the printer.

◆ The user can select a driver for a printer that Windows 98 has determined to be compatible.

◆ The user can choose not to install the printer.

Bidirectional printer capability allows printers to send unsolicited messages to Windows 98, such as messages announcing that the printer is out of paper or low on toner.

To enable the bidirectional printing features of Windows 98, including PnP configuration, you must have the following:

◆ A printer that supports bidirectional communication.

◆ A printer with a PnP BIOS (if PnP is to be used).

◆ An IEEE 1284-compliant printer cable (this has "1284" stamped on the cable).

◆ A port configured for two-way communication in the Windows 98 Device Manager. For example, if the port is in AT-compatible mode, change it to PS/2-compatible mode.

Extended Capabilities Port (ECP)

An Extended Capabilities Port (ECP) allows Windows 98 to use data compression to speed the data transfer to an attached printer. The improvements in printing speed are even greater if the printer is also ECP compliant.

Image Color Matching (ICM)

A problem that has always been associated with color printing is that you can never be too sure what a color will look like when it's printed, or how closely it will match what you see onscreen. A traditional solution was to use hard-copy color samples, printed on the color printer so that you could see exactly what shade the red would be or how blue the blue really was. Unfortunately, this required a hard copy for each printer to be used, which could be cumbersome, especially if you were working with 64 million colors.

To solve this problem, a group of industry hardware vendors (chiefly Kodak, Microsoft, Apple Computer, Sun Microsystems, and Silicon Graphics) created a color-matching specification known as InterColor 3.0. Windows 98 implements Kodak's Image Color Matching (ICM) technology, which conforms to the InterColor 3.0 specification to ensure that the colors displayed on a monitor closely match colors printed from any ICM-supporting printer.

Each color monitor, printer, and scanner supporting ICM has a color-matching profile stored in the *systemroot*\SYSTEM\COLOR directory (where *systemroot* is WINDOWS, for example). This profile takes into account how closely the device matches various colors to the international (CIE) color reference standards. The Windows 98 operating system then takes these color-matching capabilities into account and makes any modifications necessary when displaying that color on the monitor, so what you see is as close as possible to the color that is printed.

For example, if printer A generally prints a darker red than printer B, the ICM profile for printer A tells Windows 98 to display a darker red on screen when the driver for printer A is selected. In addition, if that document is open at another computer whose monitor displays colors slightly differently, the ICM profile for that monitor causes Windows 98 to adjust the on screen colors so that they look the same as in the original document.

In summary, the benefits of ICM are as follows:

◆ The color on screen closely matches the color of the printout if ICM devices and applications are used.

◆ The colors used are consistent on any ICM-compliant devices, ensuring colors that match the international standards regardless of which ICM device they are printed to or displayed on.

Printer Drivers

The Windows 95/98 printer driver architecture is similar to that used with Windows NT. Printing is controlled through a Microsoft-written universal driver, along with a small machine-specific minidriver supplied by the printer manufacturer. Thus, a printer manufacturer needs to write only a small amount of code to customize the driver to the particular requirements and features of that printer.

Unidrivers

Windows 98 uses two universal drivers (unidrivers): one for PostScript printers and one for non-PostScript printers.

Non-PostScript Universal Driver

The non-PostScript universal driver has built-in support for almost all the existing printer control languages, such as the following:

◆ HP PCL

◆ Epson ESC P/2

◆ Canon CaPSL

◆ Lexmark PPDS

◆ Monochrome HP-GL/2

◆ Most dot-matrix technologies

The non-PostScript driver also supports device-resident Intellifont and TrueType scalable fonts, as well as downloading TrueType fonts for rasterizing by the processor of a PCL printer.

PostScript Universal Driver

The Windows 98 PostScript universal driver supports PostScript Level 2 commands for advanced PostScript printing support. In addition, Adobe PostScript Printer Description (PPD) files are supported for version 4.2 and older PPDs. Another feature of the Windows 98 PostScript universal driver is the off-loading of ICM processing to the printer's PostScript processor. This reduces the processor load on the computer, which improves system performance.

Minidrivers

Windows 98 includes a large number of minidrivers for the most common printers. In addition, because of the Windows 98 driver architecture, a manufacturer can create a minidriver for its printer much more quickly and easily. Furthermore, because most of the driver code is in the universal driver, the possibility of the minidrivers needing to be updated to fix programming bugs is decreased.

Point and Print Setup

A network printer serving as a Windows 98, Windows NT, or NetWare print server can be configured as a Point and Print printer. When a Windows 98 client on the network first attempts to print to the network printer or "points" to the printer by opening the print queue in Network Neighborhood, the printer driver files can be automatically copied to and installed on the Windows 98 client. In addition, if the printer is on a Windows 95/98 server, such settings as printer memory, paper size, and so on can be automatically configured on the client. The Windows 98 .INF files define the files required for a particular printer.

With a printer configured for Point and Print setup, a Windows 98 user can have the printer drivers automatically installed on the Windows 98 client, without having to worry about what the printer model is, what driver to use, and so on. The information obtained from a printer when you enable Point and Print can include the following:

◆ The printer driver name and file information.

◆ Model information about the printer.

> **NOTE**
>
> **File and Print Sharing Required** You must have File and Print Sharing for Microsoft Networks or File and Print Sharing for NetWare Networks enabled in order for Point and Print to work.

◆ Which printer driver to retrieve from the Windows folder on a local or network computer. Printer driver files are located in the \WINDOWS\SYSTEM folder.

◆ The server name on which the printer files are stored.

The \WINDOWS\SYSTEM folder is automatically set up as a read-only share when you share a printer under Windows 98. It uses the share name PRINTER$ and has no password. It is part of the UNC (Universal Naming Convention) share name of the computer that shares the printer. So, if a computer named \\PEART is sharing a printer, Windows 98 automatically creates a share named \\PEART\PRINTER$. You can't see this share in Explorer because it's hidden. You can, however, map to the hidden share using the NET USE command. This hidden PRINTER$ share is needed for Point and Print support so that the printer driver files can be available across the network.

When a print server supports Point and Print and UNC names, the remote printer doesn't have to be associated with any of the local computer's printer ports. On the other hand, if the server doesn't support UNC names, you can set up one of the local printer ports with the network printer. In fact, the printer port can be a *virtual port*—that is, a port that isn't physically part of the computer. This means, for example, that you can associate LPT3 up to LPT9 to a remote printer.

For information about how to configure and use a printer for Point and Print setup, refer to the section "Connecting to a Network Printer Using Point and Print Setup" later in this chapter.

Drag-and-Drop Printing

Do you have a document that you want to quickly send to a printer without having to manually open the document in an application? Simply click the document and keep holding down the mouse button while dragging the document over to the printer icon. When you release the mouse button, the application associated with the document opens, the document is sent to the printer, and the application then automatically closes.

Most applications support this feature. If an application doesn't support this feature, you must open the file in the application and then print the file.

Enhanced Metafile (EMF) Spooling

For non-PostScript printing, Windows 98 generates an Enhanced Metafile (EMF). Spooling to an EMF allows control to be returned to an application approximately twice as fast as if the data is spooled with the RAW format. Thus, the printing process time that makes your computer inaccessible is much shorter in Windows 95/98 than in Windows 3.1.

With Windows 98, the Graphical Device Interface (GDI) generates an EMF using the document information generated by the application. The *EMF* is a collection of commands for creating an image, such as commands to draw a rectangle and put some text underneath it. The EMF print API has a command to draw a rectangle and instructions on placing the text beneath it. After the EMF is created, the application no longer is busy, and the user can continue to work in it.

The EMF is interpreted in the background by the 32-bit printing subsystem, which translates the EMF into printer data that can be sent to the printer (called *rasterizing*). EMF spooling adds an intermediate step in the print process but returns control to an application much more quickly.

Windows 98 provides an alternative RAW spool data format for cases in which the EMF format isn't supported or isn't functioning. The RAW format completes the rasterizing earlier—before the data is sent to the spooler. This eliminates the step of creating and interpreting the EMF file, which simplifies the printing process, but it also means that Windows 98 must take more time to process the print data before returning control to the application. PostScript printers use the RAW spool data format by default. A PostScript printer handles the rasterizing process itself, so EMF isn't necessary when you print to a PostScript printer.

Figure 4.13 illustrates the differences between the Windows 3.x and Windows 95/98 print processes.

To set the spooler settings for a printer, open the Printers folder (from My Computer or Control Panel), right-click the printer you want to examine, and choose Properties from the context menu. The Properties page for that printer appears. Select the Details tab and click the Spool Settings button to display the Spool Settings dialog box, shown in Figure 4.14.

NOTE

Right-Clicking Alternative If you right-click a document and select Print from the context-sensitive menu that appears, the same process occurs as with drag and drop printing, except that the document is sent to the default printer. If you want to print to a different printer, you can use the drag and drop method if the application supports printing to a non-default printer.

NOTE

GDI Is Key The GDI in Windows 98 is the key to understanding EMF. The GDI handles most graphical I/O tasks in Windows 98. These tasks include painting the screen, sending output to printers, and rendering graphical objects and text. The EMF file that is created when you send a print job to a printer set up for EMF contains GDI commands, a color palette, and additional data used to render the image defined by the GDI commands.

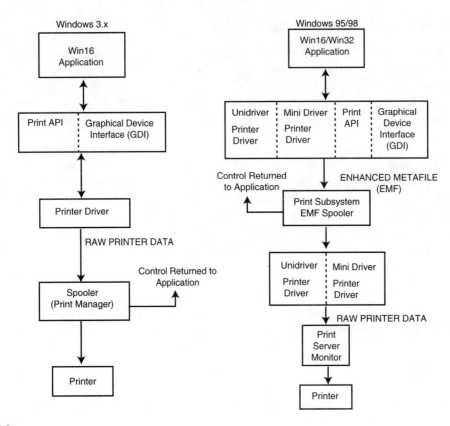

FIGURE 4.13
The Windows 95/98 print process provides several new components not present in Windows 3.x.

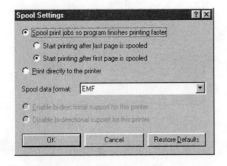

FIGURE 4.14
The Spool Settings dialog box lets you configure a spool data format and other important settings.

From this dialog box, you can choose a spool data format and control when the system begins printing. The following options control when printing starts:

❖ Start Printing After Last Page Is Spooled

❖ Start Printing After First Page Is Spooled

Some options in the Spool Settings dialog box might be disabled, depending on the printer driver installed.

EMF spooling works with most Windows applications. However, some applications might be capable of printing using only raw printer data. For these applications, you might need to use the RAW format. The steps outlined in Step by Step 4.7 show you how to disable EMF spooling.

STEP BY STEP

4.7 Setting the Spool Data Format

1. Right-click the Printer icon and select Properties. The Properties sheet for the printer appears.

2. Select the Details tab and choose Spool Settings. The Spool Settings dialog box appears.

3. In the Spool Data Format list box, select RAW and click OK. Data sent to this printer no longer will be spooled using an EMF file.

In most situations, using EMF is a good idea if your system can handle the additional background tasks. If your computer suffers in performance due to background tasks like this, you might want to follow the preceding steps to disable EMF. If you encounter a problem with EMF, run ScanDisk to check for disk integrity and free disk space. If you still experience problems after running ScanDisk, switch to RAW printing.

> **NOTE**
> **DOS and EMF** DOS applications don't benefit from EMF spooling. However, as you'll see in the next section, DOS applications can use Windows 98's spooling feature so as not to encounter conflicts with other applications when sending print jobs to the printer.

Conflict Resolution

The Windows 95/98 printing subsystem handles conflicts between different MS-DOS and Windows applications trying to print to a printer port simultaneously. This functionality is an improvement over the Windows 3.1 printing subsystem.

In Windows 3.1, conflicts usually occurred when you tried to print from an MS-DOS–based application and a Windows-based application simultaneously, because the DOS application couldn't use the Windows 3.1 Print Manager. The Print Manager set up a spooler to spool all print jobs. Because a DOS application couldn't use the Print Manager, the DOS print job went straight to the printer, conflicting with other jobs.

Under Windows 95/98, however, printer spooling is automatically set up for DOS applications (in other words, the user doesn't need to manually configure this support). Now when you send a print job from a DOS application, it goes to the spooler first and then to the printer. This spooling action also has the benefit of turning control back over to the DOS application sooner under Windows 95/98 than under Windows 3.1.

Deferred Printing

The spooling capabilities of Windows 98 allow a job to be spooled to a printer even if the printer is currently unavailable. For a remote user, Windows 98 automatically detects that the laptop is not connected to a local or network printer and sets the printer to Work Offline mode. The job is still sent to the printer, but it doesn't print until a connection to that printer is detected. For example, when the user returns to the office, attaches to the printer or the network, and starts Windows 98, the jobs can be sent to the printer as a background process.

You can also manually set a printer to hold print jobs by right-clicking the printer icon and selecting Pause Printing. This might be useful if you want to hold the jobs until later in the day, for example. To resume sending jobs to the printer, right-click the printer icon and deselect Pause Printing.

THE WINDOWS 98 PRINTING PROCESS

The printing model for Windows 98 is made up of modular components, which allow a great deal of flexibility because individual components can be substituted. To illustrate the Windows 98 printing model, the following list contains the three different printing processes that can occur:

- ◆ Printing from a non-Windows application
- ◆ Printing from a Windows application to a non-PostScript printer
- ◆ Printing from a Windows application to a PostScript printer

Regardless of which print process is used, the print job is eventually formatted into raw printer data.

Before describing each of these printing alternatives, the following section describes an important component of Windows 98 printing: the print spooler.

Print Spooler

A *print spooler* essentially is an internal print queue in which the print job data is written while the print job is being processed. Any printing done in Windows 98 uses the local print spooler on the Windows 98 client. If the network printer is used, the local print spooler passes the print job to the spooler on the network print server.

As the print jobs are spooled, they are written to a temporary file on the hard disk. For Windows 95/98 computers, the print jobs are queued in *systemroot*\SPOOL\PRINTERS—for example, C:\WINDOWS\SPOOL\PRINTERS.

When a job begins to spool, it is the responsibility of the Print Monitor to decide when to send the information to the printer. Using the default settings, and assuming that the printer is available to accept a new print job, the Print Monitor starts sending the job to the printer after the first page has spooled. To change this, choose Spool Settings from the Details tab of the Properties sheet for the printer. The Print Monitor writes the spooled data to either a port (if the printer is locally connected) or a print spooler on a network print server.

After the job has printed, the Print Monitor can display a pop-up message informing the user that the job has printed.

Printing from a Non-Windows Application

For non-Windows (that is, DOS) applications, the application sends information to the printer driver, which converts the information into raw printer data using a printer control language that the printer understands. For example, to print a circle, an HP LaserJet driver would send an HPPCL command to the printer specifying the size of the circle and the location on the page. The raw data is then sent to the print spooler, and control is returned to the application after all the raw data has been submitted to the print spooler.

Printing from a Windows 98 Application to a Non-PostScript Printer

When you select a network printer in a Windows application, Windows 98 can copy the printer driver to the local directory *systemroot*\SYSTEM (for example, C:\WINDOWS\SYSTEM). If the file has already been copied, the print server driver is not copied to the local computer unless the local driver is a version older than that of the driver on the print server. Similarly, if a local printer is selected, the driver already is on the local computer.

When the client has the correct printer driver on the hard drive, the driver is loaded into RAM. The Windows application can then query the printer driver for the current print settings (such as page orientation) to produce a What-You-See-Is-What-You-Get (WYSIWYG) image on screen.

To print the document, the Windows 98 GDI (which is responsible for displaying how the screen looks—for example, drawing the text in a certain font) sends a series of commands to the Windows 98 graphics engine. The Windows 98 graphics engine then translates the GDI commands into an EMF. After the EMF has been created, control is returned to the application. The spooler then processes the EMF information in the background and sends it to the print router. The print router routes the print job either to the local print provider or to the network in the case of a network printer. The print data then passes through a universal printer driver and to a hardware-specific minidriver, where it is converted to raw printer data.

Printing from a Windows Application to a PostScript Printer

This process is the same as for non-PostScript printers, except that the GDI doesn't generate commands for an EMF file. Instead, the PostScript driver generates a series of printer commands to tell the printer how to print the specified pages. The printer data (in the PostScript language) is then sent to the print spooler.

INSTALLING A LOCAL PRINTER IN WINDOWS 98

A local printer can be installed in Windows 98 using either PnP hardware detection or the Add Printer Wizard, if the printer isn't PnP-compliant.

Installing a Plug and Play Printer

If a Plug and Play (PnP)-compliant printer is connected to the Windows 98 computer at startup, the printer is detected, and the appropriate printer driver is automatically installed. If Windows 98 can't determine the proper driver to be used, it prompts the user to specify the correct driver.

Installing a Printer Using the Add Printer Wizard

The Add Printer Wizard is used to install a printer driver in Windows 98. The Add Printer Wizard can be accessed from the Printers folder. To access the Printers folder, select Start, Settings, Printers, or open it after opening My Computer.

The steps outlined in Step by Step 4.8 show you how to use the Add Printer Wizard to install a locally attached printer.

STEP BY STEP

4.8 Using the Add Printer Wizard to Install a Locally Attached Printer

1. Open the Printers folder in Control Panel.

2. Double-click the Add Printer Wizard and choose Next.

3. You are asked whether the printer is attached directly to the computer or is accessed from the network. Select Local Printer and click Next.

continues

> **NOTE**
>
> **The Printers Folder**   The Printers folder can be used to perform the following functions:
>
> - Install a printer
> - Share a printer on a network
> - Set permissions for accessing a printer
> - Connect to a network printer
> - Manage printers
> - Change printer properties such as page size

continued

N O T E

Printing to FILE: If you don't have an actual printer attached to your computer, you can still perform the following steps and select FILE: as the port to print to. When you print to FILE:, you are prompted for a filename and path to which to save the output. Printing to FILE: is usually used with the Generic/Text Only printer driver to create text output in a file.

4. Select the printer manufacturer from the Manufacturers list.

5. Select the printer model from the Printers list. If you do not have an actual local printer, you may select the Generic/Text Only driver after selecting Generic as the manufacturer. Click on Next.

6. From the list of Available ports, select the port to which the printer is connected. For example, for a parallel port, you might need to select LPT1:. If you don't have a local printer attached, select FILE:.

7. Choose Next and assign the printer a printer name. You can accept the default name, or you can use a more descriptive name, such as "LaserJet II in Room 312."

8. If you want print jobs to be sent to this printer by default, click Yes and then click Next. Otherwise, click No and then Next.

9. The Add Printer Wizard asks whether you want to print a test page, and then it copies the files from the Windows 98 distribution media. If Windows 98 can't find these files, you are prompted for the path.

10. An icon for the printer is created in the Printers folder. To configure the printer, see the following section.

CONFIGURING A PRINTER IN WINDOWS 98

The settings on a printer are controlled through the Properties dialog box for that printer. To access the Properties sheet, right-click the Printer icon in the Printers folder and choose Properties.

The contents of the Printer Properties dialog box can vary depending on your printer. The Properties sheet can contain the following tabs:

- ◆ General
- ◆ Details
- ◆ Paper
- ◆ Graphics
- ◆ Fonts
- ◆ Device Options
- ◆ PostScript

These tabs are described in the following sections.

Selecting General Properties

In the General tab, you can specify the printer name and any additional descriptive comments. In addition, if you want to print a separator page between print jobs, this instruction can be specified in the General tab.

Selecting the Details

In the Details tab (see Figure 4.15), you can specify the printer driver to be used, as well as various port settings. You can specify a print driver and select a port for the printer. The Capture Printer Port button lets you map a local port to a network path. This option is sometimes useful for printing from MS-DOS applications. If you change the Transmission Retry setting, Windows 98 will wait that number of seconds before reporting a timeout error if the printer is not responding. This is helpful in remote printing situations. Additionally, you can access the Spool Settings dialog box from the Details tab.

Selecting Paper Properties

The type of information on this tab varies depending on the printer driver used. The Paper tab may contain configuration settings for some of the following items:

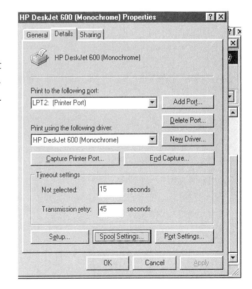

FIGURE 4.15

The Printer Properties Details tab offers several printer configuration options.

- Default paper size

- Default orientation (for example, landscape or portrait)

- Paper source (for example, tractor feed or upper paper tray)

- The number of copies to print for each print job

Selecting Graphics Settings

The configurable information in the Graphics tab varies depending on the printer driver used. This tab may contain settings such as the following:

- **Resolution.** Specifies the number of dots per inch (dpi) used for printing graphics or scalable fonts.

- **Dithering.** Specifies how the colors are blended together for a color printer.

- **Intensity.** Specifies the degree of lightness or darkness of the print job.

Selecting Fonts Options

The Fonts tab is usually available for laser printers. If cartridges are installed on the printer, they can be specified here. In addition, you can specify whether to use TrueType fonts or built-in printer fonts. In general, the fonts built into the printer can be rendered more quickly. For PostScript printers, a font substitution table can be configured to substitute TrueType fonts for PostScript fonts.

Selecting Device Options

If the Device Options tab is available, it can be used to configure information specific to the printer. For example, the printer manufacturer might include options to specify the amount of memory installed or other printer-specific features.

Selecting PostScript Settings

The PostScript tab is available on PostScript printers and can be used to configure the PostScript options, such as the following:

◆ **Output format.** Used for file compatibility.

◆ **Header.** By default, a PostScript header containing printer-specific configuration information is sent with each print job. If the printer is accessed only locally, you might want to change this setting so that a header need not be sent with each print job.

◆ **Error information.** Allows the printer to print error messages.

◆ **Advanced.** Additional information, such as the PostScript language level and data format, can be specified. Windows 98 supports PostScript Levels 1 and 2.

WINDOWS 98 NETWORK PRINTING

One of the principal reasons for PC networking is to share resources, and a printer is one of the resources most often shared. In Windows 98, a network printer is a printer that is attached to another computer on the network. When you print to a network printer, the print data is forwarded across the network to the spooler on the print server machine.

Windows 95/98 network printing support includes the following features:

◆ **A modular architecture.** Allows for different print providers for different types of networks

◆ **Point and Print installation.** Allows printer drivers to be automatically installed over the network

◆ **The capability to assign network permissions to print queues.** Can prevent unauthorized changes to the print queues or print jobs

◆ **Support for different network print servers.** Includes HP JetDirect printers and DEC PrintServer printers

Architecture

The modular format of the Windows 95/98 printing subsystem uses a layered model. The four layers are as follows:

◆ Print Application Programming Interfaces (APIs)

◆ Print router

◆ Print Provider Interface

◆ Print providers

Print Application Programming Interfaces (APIs)

The Print Application Programming Interfaces (APIs) are used to pass information to and from the Windows application and the print router. Windows 98 includes the 16-bit Win16 API for use with WIN16 applications, as well as the 32-bit Win32 API for use with WIN32 applications. The print APIs provide such functions as opening, writing, and closing print jobs. The print APIs are also used for print queue management.

Print Router and Print Provider Interface

The print router passes printing requests from the print APIs to the proper Print Provider Interface (PPI). The PPI in turn passes this information to the correct print provider. For example, if the printing request is for a local printer, the print router sends the information through the PPI to the Windows 98 Local Printing Print Provider.

Print Providers

A print provider is a 32-bit dynamic link library (DLL) that contains code for printing and network support, as appropriate. The print providers translate requests from the PPI to the appropriate network or local printer requests.

The following print providers are included with Windows 98:

◆ Local Printing Print Provider

◆ Microsoft 32-bit Network Print Provider

◆ Microsoft 16-bit Network Print Provider

◆ NetWare Network Print Provider

In addition, third-party network vendors can supply their own print providers, which can be designed to fit in with the modular Windows 98 printing subsystem.

Local Printing Print Provider

The Local Printing Print Provider is found in the `spoolss.dll` file, along with the print router. This print provider handles the local print queue and manages print jobs that are sent to local printers.

Microsoft Network Print Provider

Two print providers for Microsoft Network printing support exist. The 32-bit print provider, known as WinNet32 Network Print Provider, is contained in the file `mspp32.dll`. The 16-bit print provider, WinNet16 Network Print Provider, is actually a part of `mspp32.dll`, which translates PPI requests into 16-bit WinNet16 requests for backward compatibility with 16-bit Microsoft Network drivers.

When a print job is submitted to a Microsoft Network printer, the PPI interacts with the Microsoft Network Print Provider (`mspp32.dll`) and the Microsoft Network support library (`msnet32.dll` if a 32-bit network client is used and `msnet16.dll` if a 16-bit network client is used). It sends the print job to the network printer using the Installable File System (IFS) Manager (`ifsmgr.vxd`). The IFS Manager then interacts with the network redirector (`vredir.vxd`) to send the job over the network.

For printer management (for example, viewing a print queue), the print provider and network support library send requests directly to the network redirector.

The Registry subkey that contains information about the print provider for the Microsoft Network is as follows:

```
HKEY_LOCAL_MACHINE\System\CurrentControlSet\Control\Print\
Providers\Microsoft Networks Print Provider
```

NetWare Network Print Provider

Similar to the Microsoft Network Print Provider, the NetWare Network Print Provider (nwpp32.dll) uses the IFS Manager (the ifsmgr file) to submit jobs to the network redirector. nwpp32.dll also interacts with the nwnet32.dll file, which is the NetWare Network Support library. For a NetWare network, the network redirector is nwredir.vxd.

The NetWare Network Print Provider can also translate print requests into 16-bit calls if a real-mode (16-bit) NetWare client is used. When a 32-bit network DLL, such as nwpp32.dll or nwnet32.dll, accesses a NetWare service, the file nw16.dll provides the translation and thunking necessary for real-mode NetWare clients. nw16.dll then sends the call to NETX or VLM via VNETWARE.386.

The Registry subkey that contains information about the print provider for NetWare is as follows:

```
HKEY_LOCAL_MACHINE\System\CurrentControlSet\Control\Print\
Providers\Microsoft Print Provider for NetWare
```

Third-Party Network Print Providers

Third-party network vendors can write their own print providers and print provider interfaces that communicate with their own network redirector software. A third-party network print provider can be installed using the Control Panel Network applet.

Printing to a Network Printer

To connect to a network printer, you must first install, configure, and share the printer on the network server. For information about installing and configuring the driver on the network server, refer to the preceding sections on local printer installation and configuration.

After the Windows 98 printer driver has been configured on the network print server attached to the printer, the printer must be shared to allow other users to access it. To share a printer in Windows 98, the network print server must be running a 32-bit protected-mode client, and a file and printer sharing service must be enabled. The steps outlined in Step by Step 4.9 demonstrate how to share a network printer.

STEP BY STEP

4.9 Sharing a Network Printer

1. Right-click the Printer icon and select Properties to open the Properties sheet.

2. Select the Sharing tab to display the Sharing configuration settings, shown in Figure 4.16.

3. Select Shared As and enter a share name and an optional descriptive comment for the printer. Windows 98 doesn't allow a share name to contain invalid characters, including spaces. The share name also must not exceed 12 characters.

4. You must grant permissions to access this printer. If share-level permissions are used, you must assign a password to the printer. To access the print queue, users must supply the correct password. If user-level permissions are used, you must add the users who will be granted access to this print queue. For example, to allow everyone to print to the print queue, you would add the Everyone group and give it the Print access right. (See Chapter 5, "Managing Resources in Windows 98," for more information about Windows 98 permissions.)

5. Click OK to share the printer. The printer icon now appears as a hand holding or sharing the printer with others. Remote users with the correct permissions can now access the printer after installing the printer as a network printer on their own computers.

When the printer has been configured and shared on the network print server, a Windows 98 client can be configured to connect to the print server and print to the printer over the network. This configuration can be done either manually with the Add Printer Wizard or by configuring the network printer for Point and Print setup.

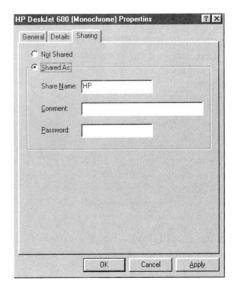

FIGURE 4.16

The printer's Sharing tab lets you share a printer on the network.

Connecting to a Network Printer Using the Add Printer Wizard

To manually configure a Windows 98 client to print to the network printer using the Add Printer Wizard, follow the steps outlined in Step by Step 4.10.

STEP BY STEP

4.10 Manually Configuring a Windows 98 Client to Print to the Network Printer Using the Add Printer Wizard

1. Start the Add Printer Wizard from the Printers folder.

2. Select the option button for a Network Printer and click Next.

3. Enter the Universal Naming Convention (UNC) path of the network printer—for example, \\SARAH\HP4, or click on the Browse button to select the printer from a network browse list.

4. If you won't be using MS-DOS applications to print to this printer, you can select No under Do You Print from MS-DOS-Based Programs?. To have the printer be associated with a printer port, such as LPT1:, you should select Yes for this option. Click Next.

5. If you have specified that you will print to this printer using MS-DOS-based applications, you are prompted to select the desired port from the Capture Printer Port dialog box. Click Next to continue. If the printer driver cannot be delivered automatically by the server, you may be asked to supply printer make and model information and provide the disk with the necessary files.

6. If you want to see whether you can print properly to the network printer, click Send Test Page. Click Finish to complete the installation. If Windows 98 can't find the files, you are prompted to enter the path to the Windows 98 distribution files.

7. An icon for the network printer is created in the Printers folder. If desired, you can drag a copy of this icon to the Desktop to create a shortcut.

Connecting to a Network Printer Using Point and Print Setup

To connect to a network printer that is *not* configured for Point and Print setup, a client must know the correct printer driver to be used. In addition, the client must know other information, such as the share name and network server name. However, after a network printer has been configured to enable Point and Print setup, the printer driver installation on the client is greatly simplified. The Point and Print printer supplies the client with information such as the UNC path and the printer driver to be used.

To install the printer drivers for the Point and Print printer on a Windows 98 client, locate the icon for the printer in Network Neighborhood. Then, drag the printer icon onto the Desktop. Alternatively, you can right-click the network Printer icon and select Install.

In addition, if you try to drag and drop a document onto the network printer icon, the printer driver will be installed on the Windows 98 client if it hasn't already been installed. If the driver version on the network printer is more recent than the version on the client, the later printer driver version will be copied to the client.

A Point and Print printer can be configured on any of the following servers:

◆ Windows 95/98 server

◆ Windows NT Server (including both Windows NT Server and Windows NT Workstation servers)

◆ NetWare bindery-based or NDS-based server

A Windows 95/98 server is simply a computer running Windows 95 or 98 that has a file and printer sharing service enabled. Any printers directly connected to the Windows 95/98 server are automatically enabled for Point and Print setup. No further configuration is required.

> NOTE
>
> **Setting Up a Printer from Network Neighborhood** In Network Neighborhood, if you double-click the name of a network printer not set up on your computer, Windows 98 displays a Printers message asking if you want to set up the printer now. Click Yes to start the Add Printer Wizard and walk through the wizard to set up the printer.

When you use Point and Print over a Windows 95/98 server, printer information is communicated between the client (the computer sending the print job) and the server (the computer to which the printer is attached) using VREDIR and VSERVER drivers. VREDIR initiates a request for Point and Print printer setup. VSERVER replies to VREDIR with the name of the printer. Then the following events take place:

1. The Windows client displays the name to the user.

2. VSERVER receives a message from VREDIR, asking which files are needed on the client machine and where those files are located.

3. In response, VSERVER tells VREDIR the name of the files and that they are in the *server_computername*\PRINTER$ folder.

4. VREDIR connects to the *server_computername*\PRINTER$ folder and makes copies of the necessary printer files. If the client machine already has a printer driver or other software that matches the files in *server_computername*\PRINTER$, Windows 98 asks the user if she wants to keep the existing files. The user should respond Yes to make sure that the latest files are copied to the client computer.

5. VREDIR terminates the connection to the *server_computername*\PRINTER$ folder.

6. A new icon pointing to the network printer displays in the Printers folder on the client computer.

Any settings that have been configured for the server printer (such as memory) are also copied to the Windows 98 client.

REVIEW BREAK

Printing

You'll see several questions on printing on the Windows 98 exam. The preceding sections discussed the components of the Windows 98 printing process and described how to install and configure local and network printers. An understanding of Windows 98's printing components will help you with printer troubleshooting. Work through the Add Printer Wizard and the Printer Properties dialog box, and become familiar with the configuration choices. You should also become familiar with the differences between Windows 98's EMF and RAW spool data formats, and make sure you know how Windows 98 prints from MS-DOS applications.

INSTALLING AND CONFIGURING MICROSOFT BACKUP

Install and configure Microsoft Backup.

Any systematic PC administration scheme should include a backup plan. Windows 98 includes an improved Backup utility that you can use to back up and restore important files. The Microsoft Backup utility (which was actually developed by Seagate Software) is not included in the Typical Windows 98 installation.

To install Microsoft Backup, perform the steps outlined in Step by Step 4.11.

STEP BY STEP

4.11 Installing Microsoft Backup

1. Click on the Add/Remove Programs Control Panel.

2. Select the Windows Setup tab.

3. Double-click on the System Tools group.

4. Check the checkbox next to Backup and click on OK.

5. Click on OK in the Windows Setup tab. Be prepared to supply the Windows 98 CD if necessary.

Microsoft Backup is not a full-featured backup utility. The principal limitation is that you cannot conveniently schedule backups to happen automatically. Even the Windows 98 Task Scheduler (see Chapter 7, "Monitoring and Optimization") cannot automate Backup because of user intervention necessary to operate the Microsoft Backup utility.

According to Microsoft, the Microsoft Backup utility supports backup devices such as QIC 80 and 80 Wide; 3010 and 3010 Wide; 3020 and 3020 Wide; TR1,2,3 and 4; DAT (DDS1 and 2); DC 6000; 8mm; DLT; and other removable media such as floppy disks and Jaz drives. Other devices are also supported. Windows 98's Microsoft Backup utility does not support QIC-40 devices. You can use Microsoft Backup to restore backup jobs created using the Windows 95 backup utility. You can't use Microsoft Backup to restore jobs created with MS-DOS v6.0 or earlier.

If your computer doesn't have a tape backup device, you can use Microsoft Backup to back up your files over the network.

Each file or folder in Windows 98 has an attribute known as the archive attribute or archive bit. When a file or folder is created, the archive bit is turned on. Microsoft Backup uses the archive bit to decide whether or not to back up the file under a given backup scheme and resets the archive bit after the backup according to the rules of the backup scheme. Microsoft classifies backup schemes as follows:

◆ **Full backup.** Backs up all selected files and directories regardless of the status of the archive bit. Clears the archive bit on all files and directories after the backup. The result of a full backup is a complete copy of all selected files and directories.

◆ **Incremental backup.** Backs up only the files with the archive bit set and clears the archive bit of files included in the backup.

◆ **Differential backup.** Backs up only the files with the archive bit set and does not clear the archive bit after the backup. These files will continue to be backed up in subsequent differential backups until a full backup or an incremental backup is performed.

The difference between an incremental and a differential backup is subtle but significant. If you perform an occasional full backup and intermediate incremental backups, each incremental backup will contain only the files changed or added since the last incremental backup. If you perform an occasional full backup and intermediate differential backups, each differential backup will contain all files

EXAM TIP

Incremental versus Differential Backups Be sure you know the difference between incremental and differential backups for the Windows 98 exam.

added or changed since the last full backup. A differential backup
takes longer and uses more space than an incremental backup, but
restoring from a differential backup can be faster and simpler than
restoring from an incremental backup. If you don't remember exactly
when a file was changed, you may need to hunt through several
incremental backup sets to find a copy of the file.

If Microsoft Backup is installed on your system, you can open it
by clicking on Start, Programs, Accessories, System Tools, Backup.
When you first start Microsoft Backup, a dialog box appears in the
foreground asking if you'd like to create a new backup job, open an
existing backup job, or restore backed up files (see Figure 4.17). You
can choose one of these options to start an appropriate wizard, or
you can click on the Close button to reach the Microsoft Backup
main window.

The Microsoft Backup main window (see Figure 4.18) lets you configure and manage the backup process.

To back up files, launch the Backup Wizard from the Microsoft
Backup Tools menu (or from the Wizard dialog box—refer to Figure
4.17), or else perform the tasks outlined in Step by Step 4.12.

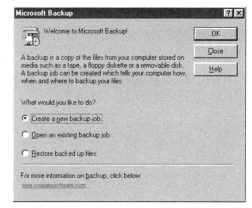

FIGURE 4.17
Microsoft Backup first asks if you'd like to create a backup, open a backup job, or restore a
file.

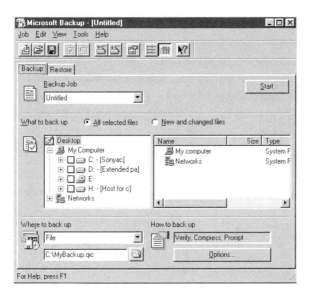

FIGURE 4.18
The Microsoft Backup main window is an alternative to the Backup and Restore Wizards.

STEP BY STEP

4.12 Backing Up Files

1. Select the Backup tab in the Microsoft Backup main window.

2. Enter a name for the backup job in the box labeled Backup Job.

3. Using the option buttons below the Backup Job box, choose whether to back up all selected files, or only the files in the selected file group that are new or changed.

4. In the Explorer-like boxes in the center of the Backup tab (refer to Figure 4.18), select the files and directories you'd like Backup to consider for backup. If you choose to back up new and changed files (refer to step 3) only the selected files that have changed will be backed up. To reveal files and subdirectories, click the plus sign (+) beside the drive or directory. The box immediately to the left of the drive, directory, or filename is a checkbox you can use to select the item. If you select a drive or directory, all subdirectories and files beneath that directory will automatically be selected. Click on a checked item to uncheck it.

5. In the box in the lower-left corner of the Backup tab, enter the path to the backup destination. Click on the folder icon to browse for a destination. Note that you can choose to back up the files to another computer on the network.

6. Click on the Options button to configure backup job options. The Backup Job Options dialog box is shown in Figure 4.19. The tabs of the Backup Job Options dialog box are as follows:

   • **General.** (See Figure 4.19.) Lets you configure verification and compression options. You can also choose whether to append or overwrite the backup to the backup media.

   • **Password.** Lets you set a password for the backup job. You'll need the password to restore the files.

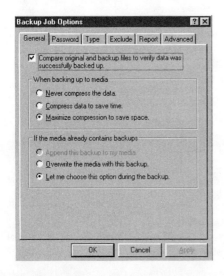

FIGURE 4.19
The Backup Job Options dialog box lets you configure backup options.

- **Type.** (See Figure 4.20.) Lets you choose a full, differential, or incremental backup.

- **Exclude.** Lets you exclude specific file types from the backup set.

- **Report.** (See Figure 4.21.) Lets you define what information will be included in the report that accompanies the backup. You can also choose to perform an unattended backup. An unattended backup does not display message boxes or prompts during the backup process.

- **Advanced.** Lets you choose whether to back up the Windows Registry.

7. When you've finished configuring backup options, click the Start button in the Microsoft Backup tab (refer to Figure 4.18) to begin the backup.

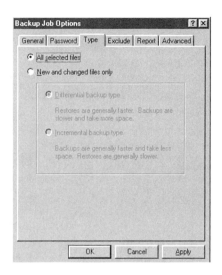

FIGURE 4.20
The Backup Job Options Type tab lets you select a backup type.

The Restore tab in the Microsoft Backup main window (see Figure 4.22) lets you restore files from existing backup sets.

To restore files, launch the Restore Wizard from the Microsoft Backup Tools menu (or from the Wizard dialog box—refer to Figure 4.17), or else perform the tasks outlined in Step by Step 4.13.

STEP BY STEP

4.13 Restoring Files

1. Select the Restore tab in the Microsoft Backup main window.

2. In the Restore tab (see Figure 4.22), enter the medium of the backup job in the box under the heading Restore From. In the box at the right, type the name of the backup file.

3. Click on Refresh to open the backup job specified in the Restore From boxes.

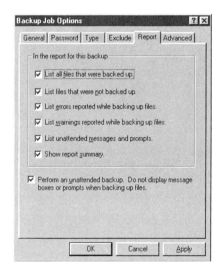

FIGURE 4.21
The Backup Job Options Report tab lets you define what information will be included in the backup report.

FIGURE 4.22
The Microsoft Backup Restore tab lets you restore an existing backup.

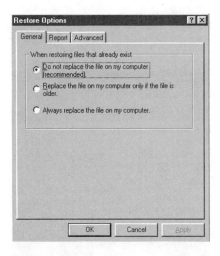

FIGURE 4.23
The Restore Options dialog box lets you config- ure restore options.

4. Select a location for the restored files in the box labeled Where to Restore.

5. Click on the Options button to select restore options. The Restore Options dialog box is shown in Figure 4.23. The General tab specifies options for what to do if the restore procedure attempts to restore a file that already exists on the system. The Report and Advanced tabs are similar to the Backup Options Report and Advanced tabs (see step 5 of the preceding Step by Step). Click on OK to return to the Microsoft Backup main window.

6. Click on the Start button to begin the restore.

A text file with a history of backup and restore operations or your computer, report.txt, is located in the Program Files\ Accessories\Bckup\Reports directory.

CASE STUDY: ALPHA PRINTING CORPORATION

ESSENCE OF THE CASE

Here are the essential elements in this case:

- All users in the company must be able to print to network printers that are managed through the Windows NT Server.

- Michelle has to add the printers to nearly 140 different Windows 98 machines that are already configured to log in to the Windows NT domain.

- Time is of the essence. She must quickly add the printers with as little downtime as possible.

SCENARIO

Michelle, the MIS Director for Alpha Printing Corporation, is responsible for connecting all of the Windows 98 machines to the printer in the Windows NT Domain. She has configured all of the Windows 98 machines to log in to the domain.

ANALYSIS

Michelle would need to share the printers from the Windows NT Server and assign the appropriate rights. From the Windows 98 machines, she will simply drag and drop the shared printers to the Printers folder. Because she has shared the printers from the Windows NT Server, the Windows 98 drivers will already exist on the server and will be copied down to Windows 98 machine.

CHAPTER SUMMARY

KEY TERMS

- Plug and Play hardware
- legacy hardware
- Device Manager
- hardware resources
- USB
- IEEE 1394 FireWire
- IrDA
- multilink
- Extended Capabilities Port
- Image Color Matching
- unidrivers
- Point and Print Setup
- Enhanced Metafile spooling

This chapter described the Windows 98 components and features that help to support hardware devices. You learned about Plug and Play and non-Plug and Play devices and how to install them. You also learned about hardware resource settings in Windows 98 and how to configure them using Device Manger. This chapter toured through the special hardware configuration issues highlighted in the Windows 98 exam guidelines, such as Universal Serial Bus (USB), multiple display, IEEE 1394 FireWire, and power management. This chapter also described how to install and configure modems and printers in Windows 98. Lastly, you learned about how to back up files to a backup device using the Microsoft Backup utility.

All the information in this chapter is important for the MCSE exam, but pay particular attention to Device Manager and to the special issues highlighted in the exam objectives (USB, multiple display, power management, and so on). Also, be sure you know how to install and configure printers, and be prepared to apply the concepts described in this chapter to troubleshooting printers in real situations.

APPLY YOUR KNOWLEDGE	

Exercises

4.1   Installing Modems

This exercise will introduce you to adding modems through the Add New Hardware Wizard and the Add New Modems Wizard. (Before you can begin using Dial-Up Networking, you must add a modem to your machine. You may already have a valid modem installed in your machine but for this exercise you are going to add several modem drivers so your machine can be configured to work with multilink. You do not actually need several physical modems, or any modems for that matter.)

Estimated Time: 15 minutes

1. Open the Add New Hardware Wizard applet in Control Panel.

2. Choose Next to start adding modems to your machine. Click the Next button and the wizard will begin searching for new hardware installed in the computer.

3. If the wizard found new hardware, for now choose No the Device Isn't in the List, and click Next.

4. If the wizard did not find hardware choose No, I Want to Select the Hardware from a List.

5. From the type of hardware to be installed, choose Modems.

6. The Add New Hardware Wizard will start. Choose the option Don't Detect My Modem; I Will Select It from a List.

7. From the list of Manufacturers, choose your preferred manufacturer and model to add the desired modem driver, then click Next.

8. You are now prompted to select the port that the modem is installed on. Choose an available port and click Next.

9. You may be prompted to insert your Windows 98 CD to add the modem driver. Supply the CD if needed, then click Finish.

10. Repeat these steps to add two additional modems. The modems you add need not necessarily all use the same driver, nor operate at the same speed.

4.2   Creating a Power Management Scheme

This exercise will create a power management scheme for your Windows 98 computer. Your computer must support the Advanced Configuration and Power Interface (ACPI) or Advanced Power Management (APM) feature. Most computers within the last few years have this system built in. If you are uncertain about your machine, please check the documentation before continuing.

Estimated Time: 10 minutes

1. Click Start, Settings, and choose Control Panel.

2. From the Power Schemes Control Panel, click the drop down list for the power schemes selection.

3. For this exercise, choose Home/Office Desk.

4. From the Turn Off Monitor category, choose After 1 Minute.

5. From the Turn Off Hard Disk category, choose After 3 Minutes.

6. Click on the Advanced tab and choose the option to Show Power Meter on Taskbar.

7. Choose OK and wait one minute for your power schemes to go into effect.

APPLY YOUR KNOWLEDGE

8. When you're finished with the exercise, return to the Power Schemes Control Panel and reset the power management settings to their original values.

4.3 Using Microsoft Backup to Back Up a File

This exercise will walk you through the basics of backing up a file. You will create a file and back it up to floppy; typically, however, you would back up multiple files to tape, a server, or some type of removable media.

Estimated Time: 20 minutes

1. Create a folder on your C: drive called January. In the January folder, create a text document called Sales.

2. Click Start, Programs, Accessories, System Tools, Backup.

3. You may be prompted by Windows 98 to search for backup drives. For this exercise, choose No so that the Add New Hardware Wizard will not launch.

4. Microsoft Backup launches and asks what you would like to do. Choose Create a New Backup Job and click OK.

5. The Backup Wizard appears. Click on the option to Back up selected files, folders, and drives, and then click Next.

6. Click the plus sign (+) by your C: drive (you do not want a check mark in C:—that represents backing up the entire drive).

7. From the list of folders, check to back up the January folder you created in step 1 and then choose Next.

8. The Backup Wizard will prompt you on what to back up—either all files or new and changed files. Because you just created a folder and file choose All Selected Files and then click Next.

9. The Backup Wizard asks you where the backup files should be placed. Click on the folder icon to choose a new destination for your backup file. Insert a floppy disk into drive A: and then choose drive A: from the dialog box.

10. Click Open to select drive A: and then click Next to continue.

11. The Backup Wizard will ask you how the backup should occur. Choose Compare Original and Backup Files to Verify Data Was Successfully Backed Up, and choose to compress the data to save space. Choose Next to continue.

12. The Backup Wizard prompts you to name the job. Call the job January Sales and then click Start.

13. After the Backup Wizard has backed up the folder and file it reports that the job has been completed. Click OK and review the details of the Backup Progress dialog box.

14. Click Report to see the backup details through Notepad.

15. Click OK to close this dialog box, and then exit Microsoft Backup.

4.4 Restoring Data from a Microsoft Backup

This exercise is based on the completion of Exercise 4.2. If you have not completed that exercise, do so before continuing here. This exercise shows you how to restore data from a Microsoft Backup.

Estimated Time: 15 minutes

APPLY YOUR KNOWLEDGE

1. Open Explorer and delete the folder C:\January. Empty your Recycle Bin so that the document cannot be retrieved through Windows 98.

2. Open Microsoft Backup through System Tools in Accessories.

3. Choose to restore backed up files and then click OK.

4. The Restore Wizard will ask where the backup file exists. Make certain the floppy created in Exercise 4.2 is in the A: drive and click Next.

5. The option to select backup sets is displayed. Confirm that January Sales is selected and then click OK.

6. The Restore Wizard will ask which folder should be restored. Click the plus sign (+) by your C: drive and then check the folder Backup. Choose Next to continue.

7. You are given the option to restore to your original location or to choose an alternate location. Choose Original Location and click Next to continue.

8. You are prompted on how to overwrite existing files, if any, on your computer. Accept the default not to override existing files on your computer and then click Start.

9. You are prompted to enter media January Sales. Choose OK to continue.

10. Microsoft Backup restores the files and reports that the restore has been completed. Choose OK and then click Report to view the report through Notepad.

11. Exit Notepad and then exit Microsoft Backup.

12. Open Explorer and confirm that the folder January and the text document inside of it exists.

13. Exit Windows Explorer.

Review Questions

1. What are three ways to add a modem to Windows 98?

2. How can a printer be added to Windows 98?

3. What is EMF?

4. What is a USB?

5. How many display adapters can a Windows 98 computer support?

6. What is an IEEE 1394 FireWire?

7. What is multilink?

8. Why use power management schemes on Windows 98?

9. Will Windows 98 Backup support backups to another computer on a network?

10. Is a tape drive required to use Microsoft Backup? Why or why not?

Exam Questions

1. You have just added a legacy network card to your Windows 98 computer. The card is not acting properly and you suspect that there is a conflict with another piece of hardware. You would like to see what IRQs are currently in use on your system. What Windows 98 tools will allow you to see all of the hardware resources that are currently in use?

APPLY YOUR KNOWLEDGE

A. The Microsoft Systems Information utility

B. The Device Manager

C. The System Resource Meter

D. The System Troubleshooter

2. A worried user reports that he has added a new video adapter card to his Windows 98 computer. The video adapter is Plug and Play compliant but his Windows 98 computer did not detect the adapter. What do you suspect is the problem?

A. The user's computer has not been restarted.

B. The user does not have a computer with a Plug and Play BIOS.

C. The card is not Plug and Play unless you enable Plug and Play in Device Manager.

D. The user can only have one video card within his Windows 98 machine.

3. Todd and Mary own a small bakery. They keep all of their crucial business operations information on one Windows 98 computer. They do have a removable drive that they hardly ever use. They would like to start using Microsoft Backup but are uncertain if they can back up their information to this removable drive. Todd thinks that they can, but Mary believes all backups have to go onto a tape drive—which means they will have to purchase and add a tape drive to their system. Who is correct and why?

A. Todd is correct. Microsoft Backup allows backups to various forms of media, including removable drives.

B. Todd is correct. Microsoft Backup allows backups to tape drives and removable drives only.

C. Mary is correct. Microsoft Backup will not back up to anything other than a fixed taped drive.

D. Mary is correct. Microsoft Backup will only back up to tape drives and to floppy disks.

4. You have added a new sound card to your system and Windows 98 did not recognize the card through Plug and Play. What can you do now to add the sound card to your system?

A. Use the Add New Hardware Wizard.

B. Restart your computer with the Shift key down to use a more invasive Plug and Play search.

C. Use the Sounds applet in Control Panel to detect the sound card.

D. Use the Device Manager in the System applet to add the hardware.

5. Ned has just added a modem and everything is working great—except that his colleagues are complaining about the loud noise that his modem makes whenever he dials into a RAS server. What can you do about the problem?

A. Use the Sounds applet to disable all system sounds from his machine.

B. Use the Modems applet to turn down the volume of his modem.

C. Use the Device Manager to disable the speaker on his modem to silence the modem.

D. Because this is hardware dependent, there is nothing you can do within Windows 98.

APPLY YOUR KNOWLEDGE

6. Of the following, which are valid options you could use to install a printer on Windows 98?

   A. Plug and Play. Attach the printer and start Windows 98.

   B. Add New Hardware Wizard. Attach the printer and let the Add New Hardware Wizard find it.

   C. Add a Printer Wizard. Use this option to add a printer.

   D. Drag and drop a printer on the network into your Printers folder to start the install.

7. Richard is still using many DOS applications. Two of his DOS applications cannot print to network printers. Why is this, and how would you resolve the problem?

   A. Many DOS applications cannot print to UNC names of printers. There is nothing you can do to get the printers and the DOS applications to work together.

   B. Many DOS applications cannot print to UNC names of printers. You will have to capture a printer port to the network printer and then tell the DOS applications to print to the port you have captured.

   C. Many DOS applications cannot print under Windows 98. You will have to restart the computer in DOS mode and then print.

   D. Many DOS applications cannot print under Windows 98. You will have to restart the computer in DOS mode, capture the printer, and then print to the captured port.

8. Your company has just purchased 50 new computers that have Universal Serial Buses installed. How can this help your company be more productive? Choose all that apply.

   A. USB-compatible devices can be hot-swapped without interrupting the status of the operating system.

   B. USB and IEEE 1394 devices can be interchanged on the same port without interrupting the system.

   C. Devices can be added without having to open the workstation units panel covers.

   D. System resource assignment is automatic.

9. Polly and Sarah are adding multiple modems to take advantage of multilink abilities with Windows 98. Sarah is certain that all of the modems have to be of the exact same brand, whereas Polly thinks the modems can be of different brands. Who is correct and why?

   A. Polly is correct. You can add modems of different brands.

   B. Polly is correct. You can add modems of different brands as long as they are of the same speed.

   C. Sarah is correct. You cannot mix modem brands because they have to use the exact same driver.

   D. Sarah is correct. You cannot mix modem brands, speed, or type, due to the instruction set and memory stack required for each modem.

APPLY YOUR KNOWLEDGE

10. Mary complains that whenever she leaves her machine alone for more than a minute the monitor blacks out. Her machine is still running but the monitor is not active. What do you suspect is the problem?

    A. Mary has a bad monitor.

    B. Mary has a bad video adapter.

    C. Mary has set power management schemes on her computer.

    D. Mary has a set power management schemes to be invoked when there is a power surge.

11. You are a consultant for a small business that as three networked Windows 98 machines. The clients would like to back up their data, but their budget will not allow them to purchase a tape drive. What would you recommend?

    A. They cannot back up without a tape drive.

    B. They should back up all files to floppies.

    C. They should back up all data to one computer over the network. Then this computer should be configured to back up its data to another machine on the network for redundancy.

    D. They should back up all data to one computer on the network and then back up the backup file to floppy disks.

Answers to Review Questions

1. Plug and Play, Modems Applet, and Add New Hardware Wizard. (For more information, refer to the section "Plug and Play versus Non-Plug and Play.")

2. The Printers Applet, Add New Printer Wizard. (For more information, refer to the section "Installing a Local Printer in Windows 98.")

3. EMF is an Enhanced Metafile format. The EMF format returns control to the Windows applications sooner, while the print job is processed in the background. (For more information, refer to the section "Windows 98 Printing Features.")

4. USB is Universal Serial Bus, a new device specification that allows devices to be added or removed without your having to restart Windows 98 each time. (For more information, refer to the section "Universal Serial Bus (USB).")

5. Windows 98 has been tested for up to nine display adapters. (For more information, refer to the section "Windows 98 Device Configuration Issues.")

6. IEEE 1394 FireWire is a specification for very high bandwidth devices such as digital video recorders. Like USB, IEEE 1394 FireWire is hot-pluggable and supports daisy-chaining. (For more information, refer to the section "Windows 98 Device Configuration Issues.")

7. Multilink is a feature that lets you use multiple communications devices for a single connection. (For more information, refer to the section "Windows 98 Device Configuration Issues.")

8. Power management schemes help Windows 98 machines conserve electricity when the machine is not in use. (For more information, refer to the section "Windows 98 Device Configuration Issues.")

9. Windows 98 Backup can back up network drives just as it can back up any other drive in the computer. (For more information, refer to the section "Installing and Configuring Microsoft Backup.")

APPLY YOUR KNOWLEDGE

10. Windows 98 does not require a tape drive to complete a backup. Backups can be done to various forms of media including floppies, removable drives, and, of course, tape drives. (For more information, refer to the section "Installing and Configuring Microsoft Backup.")

Answers to Exam Questions

1. **A, B.** You can use the Systems Information utility and the Device Manager to check out what IRQs are currently in use. (For more information, refer to the section "Device Manager.")

2. **B.** The user's computer does not have a Plug and Play BIOS to participate in Plug and Play hardware detection. (For more information, refer to the section "Plug and Play versus Non-Plug and Play.")

3. **A.** Microsoft Backup allows users to back up data to various forms of media, including floppy disks, networks drives, and removable drives. (For more information, refer to the section "Installing and Configuring Microsoft Backup.")

4. **A.** Use the Add New Hardware Wizard to search for Plug and Play drivers and non-Plug and Play drivers, and then to manually add the sound card drivers if necessary. (For more information, refer to the section "Plug and Play versus Non-Plug and Play.")

5. **B.** Open the Modems applet in Control Panel, choose properties on the modem, and then turn the sound down. (For more information, refer to the section "Installing and Configuring Modems under Windows 98.")

6. **A, B, C, D.** Like most things in Windows 98, there are many different ways to do the same job. (For more information, refer to the section "Plug and Play versus Non-Plug and Play.")

7. **B.** If a DOS application cannot print to a network printer, it's usually because the DOS application must print to a local printer port and can't recognize the UNC network path. Capture the printer through the Printer Properties and then point the DOS application to the port you've captured. (For more information, refer to the section "Windows 98 Printing Features.")

8. **A, C, D.** USB devices can offer many fast, easy-to-manage and easy-to-configure solutions for your Windows 98 machines; they cannot, however, be connected to IEEE 1394 ports. (For more information, refer to the section "Windows 98 Device Configuration Issues.")

9. **A.** Polly is correct. You can add modems of different brands, and of different speeds to participate in multilink sessions. (For more information, refer to the section "Installing and Configuring Modems under Windows 98.")

10. **C.** Mary has Power Management set on her computer. She should adjust the timings to a longer delay. (For more information, refer to the section "Windows 98 Device Configuration Issues.")

11. **C.** Microsoft Backup allows files to be backed up over the network. By backing up data to one machine over the network and then backing up files on that machine to another, the data is secure in case of a machine failure. (For more information, refer to the section "Installing and Configuring Microsoft Backup.")

APPLY YOUR KNOWLEDGE

Suggested Readings and Resources

1. *The Windows 98 Resource Kit*; Microsoft Press

2. *The Windows 98 Professional Reference*, Hallberg and Casad; New Riders

This chapter helps you to prepare for the Microsoft exam by covering the following objectives within the "Configuring and Managing Resource Access" category:

Assign access permissions for shared folders in a Microsoft environment or a mixed Microsoft and NetWare environment. Methods include the following:

> **Passwords**

> **User permissions**

> **Group permissions**

▶ You will need an operational understanding of how permissions work with share- and user-level security. User-level security will include user accounts and group accounts from NetWare environments and from Windows NT Domains.

Create, share, and monitor resources. Resources include the following:

> **Remote computers**

> **Network printers**

▶ The Windows 98 exam will include questions on sharing, monitoring, and creating resources on a Windows 98 computer. You will need to be able to create, monitor, and troubleshoot resources through a Windows 98 network.

Configure hard disks. Tasks include the following:

> **Disk compression**

> **Partitioning**

> **Enabling large disk support**

> **Converting to FAT32**

▶ Disk management will be covered on the Windows 98 exam. Know how to create partitions with FAT32, convert FAT partitions to FAT32, and compress existing partitions.

CHAPTER 5

Managing Resources in Windows 98

Back up data and the Registry, and restore data and the Registry.

▶ The Windows 98 exam will cover Microsoft Backup. Know the particulars of Microsoft Backup, such as media types that Backup can use. Also know how to back up the Registry files and what the Registry files are used for.

Configuring and managing resources can be time-consuming. The best way to learn the material herein is to read it thoroughly first, then go and implement the strategies described. After some initial practice, you'll have a good foundation of the concepts and soon managing resources will be second nature. Know the difference between FAT and FAT32 and the idiosyncrasies of each. Resource access and networking have always been crucial to Microsoft exams, so have an operational understanding of the different tools to manage resource access. Pay close attention to Microsoft Backup and the rules that govern how it can be used.

INTRODUCTION

In this chapter, you'll learn about how to configure and manage some important Windows 98 resources. You learn about Windows 98 access permissions—a subject that builds upon the introduction to Windows 98 security in Chapter 1, "Planning." You'll also learn about remote administration, about Windows 98 hard disk resources, and about the Windows 98 Registry.

ASSIGNING ACCESS PERMISSIONS FOR SHARED FOLDERS

Assign access permissions for shared folders in a Microsoft environment or a mixed Microsoft and NetWare environment.

As you learned in Chapter 1, a *share* is a logical entity representing a resource that has been made available to the network. In Windows 98, the act of making a resource available for network access is called *sharing*. Even after your computer is fully connected to the network and you have installed and configured File and Printer Sharing, you still must *share* a given folder, printer, or drive before it is available for network access. And when you share a resource, you'll need to decide on access permissions that will restrict access to that resource. The Windows 98 exam objectives list three forms of access permissions:

◆ Passwords

◆ User permissions

◆ Group permissions

The first form, passwords, is not really a form of permission at all, but it *is* a means of restricting access to a network share, so Microsoft classifies it with the others. (You could argue, I suppose, that you are assigning *permission* for a user to access a share by telling the user the password, but that is not generally how Microsoft uses the word.) As Chapter 1 explained, a Windows 98 computer that assigns permissions to users and groups must rely on a Windows NT or NetWare computer to validate access requests through what is known as user-level access control.

Before you assign any access permissions at all, you must create a network share, and to create a network share, you must ensure the following:

◆ The computer must be connected to the network, and the computer must have the necessary network components so that it may communicate with other computers on the network. For instance, the computers must be using a common networking protocol. See Chapter 3, "Windows 98 Networking," for more information about network components.

◆ A File and Printer Sharing service must be present on the computer on which you'd like to create the share. The File and Printer Sharing services must be compatible with the client and protocol software on the computers that will be accessing the share. For instance, you would use File and Printer Sharing for NetWare networks to share files in a NetWare environment. See Chapter 3 for more information about file sharing services, network clients, and network protocols.

◆ File and/or printer sharing must be enabled on the computer. To enable file and/or printer sharing, click on the File and Print Sharing button in the Configuration tab of the Network Control Panel (see Figure 5.1) and make sure the appropriate box(es) are checked in the File and Print Sharing dialog box (see Figure 5.2). These boxes are enabled by default when you install File and Printer Sharing.

After you've configured networking and enabled File and Printer Sharing, you can share a folder on the network. The easiest way to share a folder is to right-click on the folder in Explorer or My Computer and click on Sharing. (Or, select a folder and choose Sharing from the Explorer of My Computer Files menu.) The subsequent Sharing dialog box can take one of two forms depending on whether your computer is configured for share-level access control (passwords) or user-level access control (user and group permissions). As you learned in Chapter 1, the access control setting for your computer is defined through the Access Control tab of the Network Control Panel (see Figure 5.3).

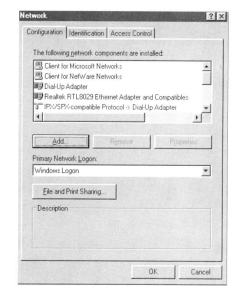

FIGURE 5.1

Click on the File and Print Sharing button in the Network Control Panel to make sure file and/or printer sharing are enabled.

NOTE **System Policies and File and Printer Sharing** If your network uses system policies, you should make sure the active system policy file does not disable File and Printer Sharing for your Windows 98 computer.

FIGURE 5.2

If you want to share printers and file resources, make sure the appropriate boxes are checked.

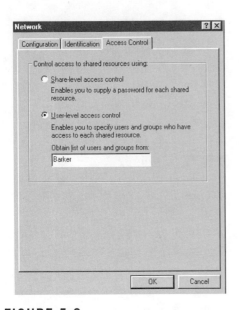

FIGURE 5.3

Select an access control method in the Access Control tab of the Network Control Panel

Net Watcher You can also share folders through Windows 98's Net Watcher utility. You'll learn more about Net Watcher later in this chapter, in Chapter 7, "Monitoring and Optimization," and in Chapter 8, "Troubleshooting Windows 98."

The following sections explore the options for restricting access to shared folders and files under share-level and user-level security. The exam objective specifies access *permissions,* so the information focuses primarily on the permissions that are available through user-level security.

Assigning Passwords Through Share-Level Security

As you learned in Chapter 1, the simplest method for controlling access to network resources is through share-level security. This method relies on each resource being assigned a password, which is then given to users requiring access. This method has several disadvantages (discussed later in this section), but it requires no additional services from the network.

To enable the password security method, you have to enable the Share-Level Access Control in the Access Control tab of the Network Control Panel. This is the default setting for Windows 98. After the Share-Level Access Control is enabled, whenever you share a resource, you will be asked to enter a Full Control access password and/or a Read-only password (see Figure 5.4). Users who attempt to access the resource will be asked to enter a password before gaining access.

The advantage of this security method is that it doesn't require other support devices elsewhere on the network. However, share-level security is generally considered less effective than user-level security in all but the simplest environments. The principal disadvantages of share-level security are as follows:

◆ You have to distribute the password to the user somehow—this is inconvenient and sometimes causes a whole new set of security concerns, with users jotting down passwords on post-its and emailing passwords to each other in clear-text messages.

◆ If you have multiple shared folders on your network, the users have to remember lots of passwords. Windows 98 has the password-caching feature (described in Chapter 3), but the password cache helps only if you access the resource from a specific computer that you've used to access the resource before.

◆ You can't control who accesses the resource. Anyone with the password can gain access. (It is true that someone could also obtain a user's logon password and access the resource if it is configured for user-level security, but users are often more protective of their logon password than they are of the miscellaneous passwords they need to access miscellaneous folders.)

◆ The user does not have to register himself with the network.

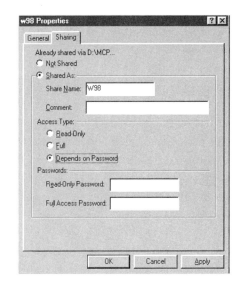

FIGURE 5.4
When implementing share-level security, passwords are assigned to resources.

User Permissions

To implement user permissions, you first have to enable user-level security in the Access Control tab of the Network Control Panel. As you learned in Chapter 1, after you've enabled user-level security, access requests pass to *a security provider* for authentication. A security provider is a Windows NT computer or a NetWare server that holds a list of network users and groups. If you enable user-level security, the user list you see when you assign permissions to a share will be the user list obtained from the security provider. The security provider can be any of the following:

◆ Microsoft Windows NT Domain

◆ Microsoft Windows NT Server

◆ Microsoft Windows NT Workstation

◆ Novell NetWare 3.x or 4.x Server

As mentioned previously, the security provider is responsible for supplying a list of users when you want to share a resource. The security provider is also responsible for verifying username and password pairs for Windows 98 when users attempt to access resources.

When sharing resources, Windows 98 provides a list of users to which you might grant access (see Chapter 1). You can select from the list the users to whom you want to grant access. These users don't need to provide any additional information before accessing the resource. When a user attempts to connect to the resource, the

EXAM TIP

Know Your Providers Learn all the different computer systems that can serve as a Windows 98 security provider. (Refer to the list in the left column.)

network client passes his network username and password to the Windows 98 computer to which he is connecting. The Windows 98 computer then connects to its security provider and verifies the client's username and password. When the username and password are verified, the Windows 98 computer determines what level of access has been defined for that user.

Group Permissions

Both Microsoft and NetWare networks employ the concept of a *group* for assigning permissions to network resources. A group is nothing more than a collection of users. Typically, the users in a group are classified together because they have some common duties or needs, and because they access the same resources. For instance, the users in a company's accounting department might all be members of a group called *Accounting*. The advantage of a group is that you can assign permission to a folder once for the group, rather than having to assign permission to each user individually. For instance, you could assign permission to the shared directory called Accounts to the Accounting group, so that anyone who is a member of Accounting would have access to Accounts. Members of the Accounting group may also have a common need to access other folders, and those folders can similarly be assigned to the Accounting group. Group permissions greatly simplify the task of assigning permissions to shared resources.

Implementing group permissions is similar to implementing user permissions. The first step is to enable user-level security on your Windows 98 system. After user-level security is enabled, you can share information with users on the network based on their group membership in your security provider.

All the security providers listed in the preceding section also support the creation of groups of users. Just as you can share with other users, you can share your resources and assign permissions to groups. When a client on the network attempts to connect with your Windows 98 computer, he provides his username and password. The Windows 98 computer then connects to its security provider and checks whether the user's name and password are valid. It also verifies the groups to which the user belongs. If the user is a member of any groups that have access to the resource, he will be granted access.

NOTE

Assigning and Creating Groups Like the network user accounts used with user-level security, group assignments are defined and maintained on the security provider system. For instance, on a Windows NT domain, the User Manager for Domains lets you create and configure user accounts—and this includes defining the groups to which the user will belong. You can also create and delete groups through User Manager for Domains.

Both user permissions and group permissions provide an important benefit: ease of implementation. If your network has a computer that can act as a security provider, you no longer have to maintain a list of passwords for your computer or for anyone else's. To access a resource on a computer, you need to know only your username and password on the security provider. This should be your only username and password for the network.

Understanding Permissions on Microsoft Networks

As you learned in Chapter 1, you can set various levels of access permission for users or groups through Windows 98's user-level access control.

You may be wondering what happens when one user belongs to several groups, and each group has different permissions for a particular share. On Microsoft networks, user and group permissions are cumulative. That is, except for one important exception, the total permissions assigned to a user is the sum of permissions assigned directly to the user and permissions assigned through the user's group affiliations. If Bill receives the Read permission (R) permission to a share through his affiliation with the Accounting group and the Execute (X) permission through his affiliation with the Budgeting group, Bill will have both Read and Execute permissions for the share. The important exception is the No Access permission. The No Access permission supersedes all other permissions. If Bill receives the No Access permission through his affiliation with the Peon group, Bill will not be able to access the share regardless of the access Bill receives through his other affiliations.

When you assign permissions for users to a directory share, these permissions are termed *Explicit*. Each subdirectory automatically has the same permissions applied to the directory share. For subdirectories, however, the permissions are called *Implicit* or *Inherited*.

These Explicit and Implicit permissions enable you to control access to your directory structure on a folder-by-folder basis.

Given the directory structure C:\DATA\MYFILES, you can share the DATA directory with a group of users and can grant them read access. The read permission you grant them at this level is Explicit. Suppose

NOTE

NT Permissions On Windows NT systems, the file and directory permissions available through the NTFS file system add another dimension to the problem of interacting permissions. Unlike the FAT16 and FAT32 file system supported by Windows 98, NT's NTFS file system supports file and directory permissions that are independent of the share permissions. Although you can't set these permissions on a Windows 98 share, you should learn a little about how these NT permission interact because a Windows 98 system can access NT-based shares as a network client. Remember these facts:

- NTFS file permissions take precedence over NTFS directory permissions.

- NTFS user and group permissions are like share permissions in that they are cumulative. The total permissions are the sum of user and group permissions except that the No Access permission overrides all other permissions.

- If a file or folder has been assigned both share permissions and NTFS permissions, the most restrictive permissions apply.

you do not want the users (with the exception of your user account) to have read access to MYFILES. Initially, the MYFILES directory has Implicit permissions that are the same as the DATA directory. In the Sharing tab of the folder properties, however, you can change the permission list without sharing the folder, thus changing the access to subfolder MYFILES.

CREATING, SHARING, AND MONITORING RESOURCES

Create, share, and monitor resources.

In Chapter 1 and earlier in this chapter, you learned about creating shares and assigning permissions to shared resources. The "Create, Share, and Monitor Resources" objective seems to reach beyond the topic of simply creating shares. The resources indentified with this objective included the following:

◆ Remote Computers

◆ Network Printers

It is likely that this objective centers on Windows 98's remote administration features. You must configure a Windows 95/98 computer for remote administration if you want to administer its files and printers from a remote PC.

Windows 98 provides several additional tools that help you administer remote Windows 95/98 computers. These tools also require remote administration. The tools supply a number of important remote-management features, and you have seen or will see these tools mentioned elsewhere in this book. Specifically, Windows 98's remote administration tools include the following:

◆ **Net Watcher.** Net Watcher lets you create and monitor shares on the local computer and also on remote computers. This tool also helps you track connections to shares and open files. You'll learn more about Net Watcher in Chapters 7 and 8, and also in the next section.

◆ **System Policy Editor.** System Policy Editor lets you create system policies that will override Registry settings. System Policy

Editor also contains a Registry mode, which lets System Policy Editor serve as a Registry interface. You can use the Connect option in System Policy Editor to connect to the Registry of a remote computer. You'll learn more about System Policy Editor in Chapter 6, "Managing Profiles and System Policies."

◆ **Registry Editor.** Registry Editor lets you browse the Registry directly to view or edit Registry settings. The Connect Network Registry option in Registry Editor's Registry menu lets you connect to the Registry of a remote Windows 95/98 computer. You learned about Registry Editor in Chapter 4, "Installing and Configuring Hardware."

◆ **System Monitor.** System Monitor lets you view and record performance parameters for a Windows 95/98 computer. The Connect option in System Monitor's File menu lets you connect to another computer to view performance data.

Each of these remote administration tools requires that you configure user-level security and enable remote administration on every computer you wish to monitor and administer remotely.

To enable remote administration, perform the tasks outlined in Step by Step 5.1.

STEP BY STEP

5.1 Enabling Remote Administration

1. Open the Passwords Control Panel.

2. Select the Remote Administration tab.

3. If your computer is configured for share-level access control, the Remote Administration tab will appear as shown in Figure 5.5. Enable remote administration for this server. Enter a password that will be required of anyone who wants to administer this computer's files and printers from a remote PC. (Note that, if you want to use the administration tools in the preceding bulleted list, you must configure user-level access control.)

continues

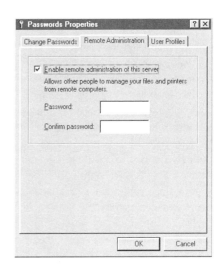

FIGURE 5.5

If your computer is configured for share-level access control, enter a remote administration password.

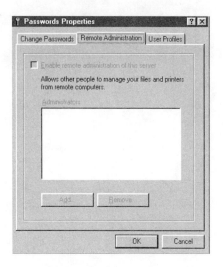

FIGURE 5.6
If your computer is configured for user-level access control, click on Add to add additional users or groups to the Administrator list.

continued

4. If your computer is configured for user-level access control, the Remote Administration tab will appear as shown in Figure 5.6. Check the checkbox labeled Enable Remote Administration of This Server. To add a user or group name to the list of those who have permission to administer this computer's files and printers from a remote PC, click on the Add button and choose additional users and groups from the subsequent list.

To use System Policy Editor, Registry Editor, or System Monitor to monitor a remote computer, you must also install the Remote Registry Service on both the computer that will be monitoring and the computer you wish to monitor.

To install the Remote Registry Service, perform the tasks outlined in Step by Step 5.2.

STEP BY STEP

5.2 Installing the Remote Registry Service

1. Open the Network Control Panel.

2. In the Configuration tab, click on Add.

3. In the Select Network Component Type dialog box, select Service and click on Add.

4. In the Select Service dialog box, click on Have Disk.

5. Place the Windows 98 CD in the CD-ROM drive and enter the path to the `Tools\Reskit\Netadmin\remotereg` directory. Click on OK.

6. Click on Microsoft Remote Registry and click on OK.

7. Windows 98 will install the Remote Registry service. You may be asked to give the location of additional files. Enter the path to the Windows 98 CD. When Windows 98 finishes installing the Remote Registry service, you be asked to reboot. Shut down and restart your system.

N O T E

Windows NT and NetWare If you have enabled user-level security with a Windows NT domain as a security provider, remote administration is enabled by default and the Domain Administrator account appears automatically in the Administrators list in the Remote Administration tab of the Passwords Control Panel. If the security provider is a NetWare server, remote administration is enabled. For a NetWare 3.x server, the Supervisor account appears in the Administrators list. For a NetWare 4.x server, the Admin account appears in the Administrators list.

Note that when user-level access is enabled, the Remote Administration tab prompts you to specify the users who are granted permission to administer the computer remotely. Only users and groups listed in the Remote Administration tab can access the computer for any task that requires remote administration.

Net Watcher is a very useful tool for administering shared resources on computers that have been configured for remote administration. Net Watcher requires that both computers be configured for user-level security, but it does not require the Remote Registry Service. (The Remote Registry Service is required for other tools such as System Monitor and System Policy Editor.) You can use Net Watcher to view connections, shared folders, or open files. You can also add new shares, stop sharing a folder, or view shared folder properties. See Chapter 7 for a complete discussion of the Net Watcher utility.

You must enable Remote Administration on a computer if you wish to manage the computer's printers remotely. To view print jobs other than your own, and to pause or cancel other users' print jobs on a printer attached to a remote PC, you must supply the remote administration password or be listed as an Administrator in the user-level Remote Administration Administrator's list.

CONFIGURING HARD DISKS

Configure hard disks.

Microsoft knows that anyone who claims to be an expert in managing Windows 98 resources had better know something about configuring hard disks. Hard disks are an essential part of the Windows 98 ecosystem, and objectives related to hard disks and file storage occur in several places in the Windows 98 exam guidelines. Chapter 1 discussed the differences between the FAT16 and FAT32 file systems and the reasons for choosing FAT16 or FAT32. This chapter provides some information on other important facets of hard disk configuration. You'll learn about the following:

◆ Disk compression

◆ Partitions

◆ Converting FAT16 to FAT32

◆ Long filenames

Chapter 7 continues the discussion of hard disks with additional information on some Windows 98 disk utilities such as ScanDisk, Disk Defragmenter, and Compression Agent.

Disk Compression

Windows 98 implements a form of disk compression known as on-the-fly compression. *On-the-fly compression* is so named because the compression/decompression process occurs automatically in the background and is transparent to the user. On-the-fly compression intercepts normal MS-DOS read/write calls and compresses the data before writing it to the hard disk. This enables the data to consume less space. When the data is read back, it automatically is uncompressed before being transferred to the application or process that requested it.

Disk compression, as implemented in Windows 98 (and in the version released with MS-DOS 6.x), consists of two processes:

◆ Token conversion

◆ Sector allocation granularity

Token conversion replaces repetitive patterns in a given piece of data with a token, which takes up less space. *Sector allocation granularity* changes the way data is stored on a hard drive by circumventing the large amounts of wasted space often created under a normal FAT file system. FAT file systems operate based on a cluster being the smallest traceable unit of measure. If the cluster size is 4KB, for example, and a 2KB file is stored in that cluster, 2KB are wasted. If 1,000 such files exist on a hard drive, 1,000 × 2KB are wasted. With disk compression in place, the smallest allocation unit shrinks to one sector (or 512 bytes), which can greatly reduce the amount of wasted space on a drive.

Disk compression can enhance, degrade, or leave system performance at the same level. If you work on a system with large amounts of RAM (24–32MB) and have a slow hard drive with a fast CPU, you might notice disk compression improving system performance. With disk compression, you gain by reading smaller amounts of data (the compressed data) from the hard drive; you then must decompress that data in RAM. If the time spent decompressing the data is less than the time you would have spent reading the data, you perceive a performance increase. Most new computers have fast CPUs and more RAM. They also have fast hard drives, however, which lowers or even reverses the speed benefit. On new computers, you likely will notice that the system performance decreases. Performance likewise will decrease on systems that are low on RAM or that have slow CPUs.

The utility that performs these actions in Windows 98 is called DriveSpace.

DriveSpace Structure

Microsoft first included disk compression with MS-DOS version 6.0, and the disk compression was called DoubleSpace. It later was re-released as DriveSpace in MS-DOS version 6.2. This new version contained some changes to the compression routines and a major new feature: the capability to uncompress a drive. The compression structure has since remained fairly consistent.

After disk compression is installed and the files are initially compressed, the files are stored in the Compressed Volume File (CVF). This actually is a large hidden file sitting on the physical drive C:. When the system boots up, however, the CVF is assigned drive letter C:. The physical C: drive, which now contains only a few files because everything else is compressed inside the CVF, is assigned a higher drive letter, typically H:. This higher-letter drive is called a *host* drive and is hidden from normal view by default. The process of switching the drive letters and making the CVF available for viewing in MS-DOS and Windows is called *mounting*. From this point on, any file operation is handled through the disk compression routines. These routines are responsible for compressing and uncompressing files as disk I/O requests are made by the operating system.

You learn more about disk compression and the Windows 98's built-in DriveSpace utility in the next section.

N O T E

Compression and the Compressed
When a floppy is compressed, the DriveSpace drivers only load when the floppy is in the drive. In general, DriveSpace drivers only load when compressed media (hard drive or floppy) are detected.

N O T E

FAT32 and Disk Compression It may seem like a shortcoming that Windows 98 does not provide a means of compressing drives that are formatted with the new, improved, and advanced FAT32 file system. The reasons for this are many. The main reason why Windows 98 does not presently support FAT32 disk compression may be that FAT32 is still relatively new, and all the utilities haven't caught up with it yet. Officially, Microsoft says that the version of DriveSpace included with Windows 98 "recognizes FAT32 drives but does not compress them." It is also important to point out, however, that FAT32 naturally stores data more efficiently than FAT16, so disk compression offers a smaller reward for the overhead.

Compressing Drives with DriveSpace

Windows 98's built-in compression utility DriveSpace 3 lets you compress FAT16 drives. (You can't use DriveSpace 3 on FAT32 drives.) Windows 98 also includes a utility called Compression Agent that helps you manage and optimize disk compression. You'll learn more about Compression Agent in Chapter 7.

You can access DriveSpace either by starting the DriveSpace application (which is in the Accessories, System Tools group), or by right-clicking on a FAT16 drive in Explorer, selecting Properties, and choosing the Compression tab.

To configure DriveSpace compression settings, perform the tasks outlined in Step by Step 5.3.

STEP BY STEP

5.3 Configuring DriveSpace Compression Settings

1. Choose Start, Programs, Accessories, System Tools, DriveSpace.

2. In the DriveSpace main window (see Figure 5.7), select the drive for which you'd like to modify compression properties. In the figure, note that drive C: is already compressed and drive H: is designated as a host drive for drive C:.

3. Pull down the Drive menu (see Figure 5.8). The menu options include the following:

    - **Compress.** Lets you compress the drive.

    - **Uncompress.** Lets you uncompress the drive. When you uncompress a compressed drive, the drive will lose some of its free space. The host drive's files will be copied to the main drive, and the host drive will be deleted.

    - **Adjust Free Space.** Lets you transfer free space from the main drive to the host drive. By default, the free space on the compressed drive is maximized, and the host drive is typically at or near capacity. Some applications and even Windows 98 will sometimes issue prompts saying the drive is full because the host drive has insufficient free space. The Adjust Free Space option lets you add or remove free space on the host drive.

- **Properties.** Invokes the Compression Properties dialog box. Shows the capacity of the drive, the amount of free space and used space, and the compression ratios.

- **Upgrade.** Lets you upgrade a previously compressed drive from an earlier version of DoubleSpace or DriveSpace to DriveSpace 3.

- **Format.** Lets you format a drive. Formatting destroys all the data on the drive. You cannot format your startup drive or a host drive.

4. Pull down the Advanced menu and choose Change Ratio. The Compression Ratio dialog box appears (see Figure 5.9). The Compression Ratio dialog box lets you change the estimated compression ratio that Windows 98 uses to calculate how much space remains on the disk.

5. The Advanced menu's Create Empty option lets you create a new empty compressed drive using free space available on an existing drive.

6. The Advanced menu's Settings option invokes the Disk Compression Settings dialog box, which lets you choose the compression method DriveSpace will use to compress a disk (see Figure 5.10). Note that you can also choose to use no compression until the disk reaches a certain percent of its capacity and then to use standard compression. See the discussion of Compression Agent in Chapter 7 for more on HiPack versus Standard compression.

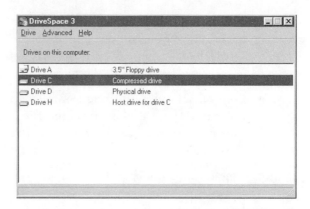

FIGURE 5.7

Select the drive you want to compress in DriveSpace's main window.

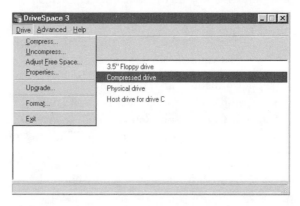

FIGURE 5.8

DriveSpace's Drive menu offers several configuration options.

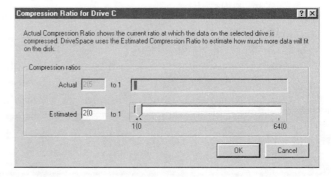

FIGURE 5.9

The Compression Ratio dialog box lets you change the compression ratio used in disk space estimates.

You can also configure disk compression directly from the drive Properties dialog box in Explorer. Right-click on the icon for a FAT 16 drive and choose Properties. In the Properties dialog box, select the Compression tab. The Compression tab (see Figure 5.11) provides a convenient summary of compression statistics for the drive, showing the amount of space compressed at each of the compression levels and the space gained by using compression as opposed to leaving the drive uncompressed. (This display is similar to the information you'll generate using Compression Agent, which is discussed in Chapter 7.) You can start Compression Agent by clicking on the button labeled Run Agent.

The Advanced button invokes the Advanced Properties dialog box (see Figure 5.12), in which you can opt to hide the host drive. Note that you can invoke the DriveSpace utility by clicking on the Run DriveSpace button.

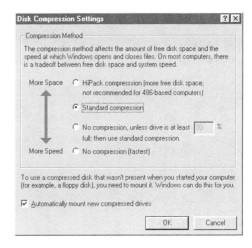

FIGURE 5.10
The DriveSpace Advanced menu's Settings option invokes the Disk Compression Settings dialog box.

Windows 98 File System Architecture

Windows 98's modular design enables it to adapt to developing technologies. In this modular design, generic features of Windows 98 subsystems—such as networking, printing, and communications—are implemented by a universal component (for example, the universal printer driver). The universal driver then passes control to a type-specific driver (for example, the printer mini-driver for a Hewlett-Packard LaserJet). Microsoft also uses a modular architecture for Windows 98 file systems. All I/O requests first are handled by a universal file-system manager. All that is necessary to accommodate a new file system type is a file-system driver that can communicate with the universal file-system driver.

File operations are handled by the installable file system (IFS) components of Windows 98. These components include the following:

- ◆ IFS Manager
- ◆ File-system drivers
- ◆ I/O Supervisor
- ◆ Volume Tracker
- ◆ Type-specific drivers
- ◆ Port drivers

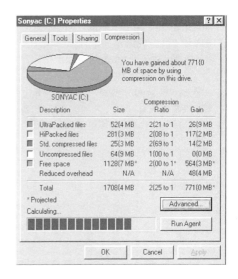

FIGURE 5.11
The Drive Properties Compression tab provides a summary of compression statistics.

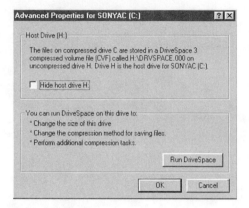

FIGURE 5.12
The Compression tab's Advanced Properties dialog box lets you hide the host drive or launch the DriveSpace utility.

> **Installable File Systems** Windows 95/98 file systems are known as *installable* file systems because they can be loaded into and removed from the system memory as needed. This is another indication of the modularity of the Windows 95/98 file-system components.

IFS Manager

The IFS Manager analyzes incoming I/O requests from applications and other processes and determines which file-system driver can fulfill the requests. When you install a new file-system driver, it registers itself with the IFS Manager. The driver informs the IFS Manager what types of I/O requests it can process. Note that the file-system driver does not need to know how to communicate with applications or other processes directly. The driver needs to know only how to communicate with the IFS Manager.

File-System Drivers

File-system drivers enable I/O requests to be sent to and from the installed file systems. Windows 98 includes support for the following file system drivers (although you can add others using third-party drivers):

◆ 32-bit virtual FAT (VFAT)

◆ 32-bit CD-ROM file system (CDFS)

◆ 32-bit network redirectors

◆ 32-bit Universal Disk Format (UDF)

The VFAT file-system driver (FSD) is the primary FSD for the system and cannot be disabled. It is responsible for all local hard disk I/O requests (including SCSI). VFAT is responsible for interacting with the file system present on the storage medium, which in the case of Windows 98 may be FAT16 or FAT32. Like all FSDs, VFAT supports long filenames (LFNs). (LFNs are discussed in more detail later in this chapter.)

In the case of SCSI drives, after the FSD for hard drives determines that a given I/O request is intended for a SCSI drive, a number of sublayers come into play. The TSD passes the request to either a SCSI translator for hard drives or one for CD-ROM drives. The translator is responsible for translating generic I/O commands into commands the SCSI bus can understand. These are known as SCSI command descriptor blocks.

The SCSI Manager then takes control and acts as the intermediary between the SCSI translator and the lowest layer—the miniport drivers, which are responsible for communicating with specific brands of SCSI adapters. There might be a specific miniport driver, for example, for all Adaptec SCSI controllers, or for one particular product line.

Because data on a CD-ROM is stored and accessed differently than data on a hard drive, a separate FSD for CD-ROM file access is required. The *CDFS driver* passes on the CD-ROM I/O request to a specific device driver based on one of the following four CD-ROM configurations:

◆ **IDE CD-ROM.** With this configuration, the CD-ROM typically is attached to the IDE hard drive controller of the computer. The I/O request is passed on to the ESDI_506.PDR port driver, which is the same driver used to communicate with IDE hard drives.

◆ **SCSI CD-ROM.** This type of CD-ROM is connected on the SCSI bus of the computer, along with any SCSI hard drives or other SCSI devices. It is supported through the various SCSI driver layers previously mentioned (refer to the section "VFAT File System Driver").

◆ **Proprietary CD-ROM controller.** This type of CD-ROM controller often is integrated on a sound card. Windows 98 currently ships with protected-mode drivers for proprietary controllers from Sony, Panasonic, and Mitsumi. Any other type of proprietary CD-ROM controller must be supported through protected-mode drivers from the OEM or through real-mode CD-ROM drivers until protected-mode drivers become available.

◆ **Real-mode CD-ROM drivers specified in `config.sys` or `autoexec.bat`.** All CD-ROM drives that do not fall into the preceding categories are supported by MS-DOS–based drivers specified in `config.sys` or `autoexec.bat`. The CD-ROM drive is said to be operating in MS-DOS compatibility mode.

Network redirectors are responsible for forwarding I/O requests to the network. A network redirector is, therefore, an essential part of client-networking capability. In Windows 98, a redirector is implemented as a form of file system driver. If the IFS Manager determines that an I/O request cannot be satisfied locally and that it likely is intended for a remote device, it attempts to pass the request

NOTE **Not with DOS** VFAT is used only for hard drives with 32-bit disk-access components installed. If a drive is accessed through real-mode drivers (for example, an Ontrack Disk Manager driver in `config.sys`), the drive is accessed through MS-DOS compatibility mode and does not take advantage of the 32-bit VFAT.

NOTE **Use Smartdrive with MS-DOS Compatibility Mode** Any hard drive or CD-ROM drive running in MS-DOS compatibility mode cannot take advantage of protected-mode caching. The MS-DOS disk cache Smartdrive must be used instead.

to one of the network redirectors (if any Windows 98 networking components have been installed).

The Universal Disk Format (UDF) driver provides access to devices that conform to the UDF specification. This driver supports read-only access to devices such as DVD disks.

I/O Supervisor

The I/O Supervisor oversees all local I/O requests (as opposed to network-based requests). When the IFS Manager determines that a given I/O request can be fulfilled on the local computer, it passes the request to the I/O Supervisor.

The I/O Supervisor's other duties include registering port and mini-drivers when a new device is installed and sending dynamic messages to drivers as necessary (for example, in the case of a Plug and Play event).

Volume Tracker

The Volume Tracker identifies and monitors removable media, such as CD-ROMs, floppies, and removable hard drives. It ensures that the correct media type is present and that it is not removed or inserted at the wrong time. The Volume Tracker enables CD-ROMs to autoexecute when inserted, for example, by polling the CD-ROM drive constantly for new insertions. When the Volume Tracker detects such an event, it scans the CD-ROM for a file called `autorun.inf`. If it finds this file, it executes the commands in the file.

The Volume Tracker also identifies disk geometry; it notes, for example, when a 1.44MB floppy is removed and a 720KB floppy is inserted.

Type-Specific Drivers

Type-specific drivers (TSDs) are intermediate to the I/O Supervisor and the physical device drivers (port drivers) that actually communicate with the hardware. TSDs are responsible for all functions associated with a particular type of hardware, such as CD-ROMs, floppy drives, or hard disks. A TSD for CD-ROM drives, for example, handles functions specific to CD-ROMs, but not those specific to SCSI CD-ROMs.

Port Drivers

Port drivers, last in the chain of command, translate logical I/O requests (for example, "put this data on the CD-ROM") into physical requests (for example, "put these bytes on track 9, section 5 of the CD-ROM").

Partitions in Windows 98

A file system imposes an organized structure on the hard disk so that Windows 98 can read, write, and locate data stored on the disk. In the simplest situation, especially on the smaller disks of older machines, a single organized file system structure can include the entire hard disk. However, it is not necessary for the organizational structure imposed by the file system to serve an entire disk. It is possible, and often advantageous, to have two or more file system structures on a single disk. PC-based operating systems, therefore, depend on two important concepts to subdivide the storage space on a physical disk:

◆ **Partitions.** A partition is a physical division of the disk into separate areas.

◆ **Logical drive.** A logical drive is a logical division within a partition that receives a separate drive letter and is treated as a separate entity within Windows 98.

In Windows 98, a hard disk can include one primary partition and one extended partition. The primary partition can be marked as active and, therefore, can be used to boot Windows 98. The extended partition can contain multiple logical drives. Each logical drive receives its own drive letter and can be formatted and managed separately.

You can use Windows 98's FDISK utility to create and manage partitions. FDISK is a simple, DOS-based application that is extremely powerful, so use it carefully. The purpose of FDISK is to create and delete partitions and logical drives. After you have created a partition or logical drive, you must format it for the file system you want to use (in the case of Windows 98, you must format the file system as FAT or FAT32). You'll learn more about formatting a partition or logical drive later in this section.

To create a partition or logical drive using FDISK, perform the tasks outlined in Step by Step 5.4.

STEP BY STEP

5.4 Creating a Partition of Logical Drive with FDISK

1. Go to the MS-DOS prompt and enter **FDISK**. If you are accessing FDISK in a troubleshooting situation, which is a common use for FDISK, you may need to start FDISK from an MS-DOS or Windows 98 startup disk.

2. The first screen asks if you'd like to enable large disk support. As you learned in Chapter 1, Windows 98's FAT32 file system supports drives larger than 512MB. Choosing Yes for this option tells FDISK to prepare any new drives you create to use the large disk support provided by FAT32. If you plan to format the new drive with FAT32, choose Y for this option. If you don't plan to use FAT32, choose N. Note that this option does not format the new drive with FAT32. You must format the drive after you create it using the FORMAT utility.

3. The main FDISK menu offers the following options:

   - Create DOS Partition or Logical DOS Drive

   - Set Active Partition

   - Delete Partition or Logical DOS Drive

   - Display Partition Information

4. Enter the number for the menu option you wish to select and follow the subsequent prompts. For this exercise, choose 1 to create a partition or logical drive. FDISK will ask if you wish to create a primary partition, an extended partition, or a logical drive in the extended DOS partition. FDISK will not let you create a primary partition if you already have one. Nor will FDISK let you create an extended partition if you already have one. To create a logical drive on the extended partition, you must have free space available on the extended partition.

If the hard disk is used as the boot disk, and if you create more than one partition, you must mark the primary partition Active. The active partition is the partition that Windows 98 accesses at startup. You can use FDISK to mark a partition as the active partition. (See item 2 in the main FDISK menu—step 3 of the preceding Step by Step.)

When you create a new partition or drive, FDISK will assign a drive letter to it. After you've created the partition or logical drive, you must format it. You can format a disk by entering the FORMAT command at the DOS prompt and specifying the drive letter. If the drive letter of the new drive is D:, you would enter the following:

FORMAT D:

You can also format a drive from within Explorer. Right-click on a drive icon and select Format. The Format dialog box will appear on your screen (see Figure 5.13). Select format options and click on Start. You will not be able to reformat the disk with the Windows 98 system files.

Formatting the drive deletes all data on the drive. Don't format a drive unless you're willing to lose all data that may be on the drive. Of course, if you just created the drive using FDISK, the drive won't contain any data.

Windows 98 includes a utility that lets you convert a FAT16 drive to FAT32 without reformatting the drive. The Drive Converter utility is discussed in the next section.

Converting a FAT16 Drive to FAT32

Windows 98 provides a utility that lets you convert a FAT16 partition to FAT32. If you use the Drive Converter utility to convert a FAT16 drive to FAT32, you won't have to reformat the drive and you won't lose any data on the drive (at least, theoretically—Microsoft still recommends you back up data on the drive before starting the conversion).

The Drive Converter utility only converts FAT16 drives to FAT32. It doesn't convert FAT32 drives to FAT16 and it cannot convert other file system formats that aren't accessible from Windows 98, such as NTFS. Before you use the Drive Converter utility to convert an existing drive to FAT32, be sure the drive is a suitable candidate

> **EXAM TIP**
>
> **Know the Enable Large Disk Support Option** Be sure you know about FDISK's Enable Large Disk Support option. Microsoft mentions this option in the exam objectives, and you are likely to see an exam question about it.

FIGURE 5.13
The Format dialog box lets you format an existing drive.

for the FAT32 file system. See Chapter 1 for more on when to use FAT16 and when to use FAT32.

To convert a FAT16 drive to FAT32, perform the tasks outlined in Step by Step 5.5.

STEP BY STEP

5.5 Converting a FAT16 Drive to FAT32

1. Choose Start, Programs, Accessories, System Tools, Drive Converter (FAT32).

2. The Drive Converter Wizard appears on your screen (see Figure 5.14). Click on the Details button to learn more about Drive Converter. To proceed with the conversion, click on Next and respond to subsequent prompts.

Drive Converter cannot convert a DriveSpace–compressed FAT16 drive (or its host drive) to FAT32. See Chapter 1 for additional issues concerning FAT16 to FAT32 drive conversion.

Long Filenames

Windows 98 supports long filenames (LFNs). Windows 98 supports descriptive filenames up to 255 characters, which includes blank spaces. A file's path can have up to 260 total characters. If both the path and the filename are specified, however, the total still can be only 260 characters.

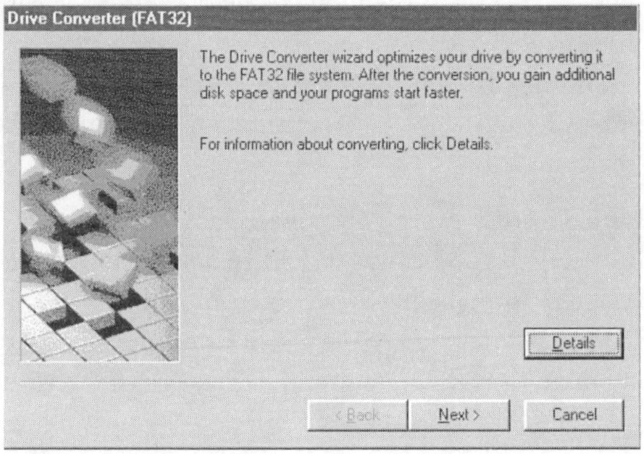

NOTE

The Added Number   The number is added to ensure unique short filenames. Two files named November Sales Forecast and November Marketing Report, for example, would both have aliases that start with the characters Novemb~. The first file created is named Novemb~1 and the next is named Novemb~2. If more than nine similar files exist, the first five characters are used, plus the tilde (~) and a two-digit number.

FIGURE 5.14
The Drive Converter Wizard lets you convert a FAT16 drive to FAT32 without reformatting.

To remain backward compatible with Windows 3.1 and DOS applications, Windows 98 automatically generates an 8.3-format short filename (known as the *alias*) for each LFN. The algorithm for the auto-generation of this short filename is as follows:

1. Remove any characters that are illegal in MS-DOS filenames, such as spaces.

2. For the eight-character name, take the first six remaining characters of the LFN, add a tilde character (~), and add an incremental number beginning with 1.

3. To create the three-character extension, take the first three remaining characters after the last period. If the long filename contains no period, the extension is omitted.

Table 5.1 shows how sample long filenames convert to short filenames. Each of the files in the table is assumed to be saved in the same folder; the files were created in the order shown.

NOTE **Matters of Case** Long filenames preserve the case of characters, but they are not case sensitive. When you copy long filenames to floppy disks, they are preserved. The shorter 8.3 filenames also are not case sensitive, but they do not preserve the case of characters.

TABLE 5.1

CONVERTING LONG FILENAMES TO SHORT FILENAMES

Long Filename	*Converted Short Filename*
Fiscal Report Quarter 1.XLS	fiscal~1.xls
Fiscal Report Quarter 2.XLS	fiscal~2.xls
Fiscal Report Quarter 4.XLS	fiscal~3.xls
Employee Benefits 1997.DOC	employ~1.doc
Employee Benefits 1998.DOC	employ~2.doc
Taxes.Mdb	taxes.mdb

The following subsections discuss the long filenames concept even further:

◆ Rules for the construction of long and short filenames

◆ Long filename data structure

◆ Issues with long filenames

◆ Adding long filename support for Novell NetWare

Rules for the Construction of Long and Short Filenames

The following rules apply when creating a long filename and when generating a short filename alias:

◆ The symbols \ / : * ? " < > ¦ are illegal in both long and short filenames.

◆ The symbols + , ; = [ ] are permitted in a long filename, but not in a short filename alias.

◆ Lowercase characters in a long filename are converted to uppercase characters in a short filename alias.

EXAM TIP

Know Long Filenames   Microsoft doesn't mention long filenames in the exam objectives, but you'd still be wise to know the rules for creating filename aliases for the Windows 98 exam.

Long Filename Data Structure

In a standard FAT-based operating system, the root directory of a hard disk can contain a maximum of 512 directory entries. In MS-DOS, each file or subdirectory typically takes up an entry. In the case of long filenames, however, each requires a minimum of two directory entries: one for the alias and one for every 13 characters of the long filename. A long filename with 79 characters, for example, requires seven entries (78 / 13 = 6, plus 1 for the alias). Because LFNs use up multiple directory entries, you'll run out of available root directory entries faster if you're using LFNs.

Issues with Long Filenames

When working in an environment that accepts both long and short filenames, you should be aware of the following issues:

◆ LFNs are active only when Windows 98 is running. Because they are integrated with the 32-bit file system native to Windows 98, LFNs are not visible, for example, when Command Prompt Only is selected from the Boot menu when the system boots. (LFNs are visible, however, from a DOS prompt inside Windows 98).

◆ Even if you do not add an extension to a file when you create it, the application you are using might automatically add an extension. (WordPad, for example, adds the extension .doc to any saved file by default.) Filenames enclosed in double quotes usually do not have the extension added.

◆ Using file utilities that are not long filename aware (such as those in MS-DOS 6.x and earlier) to copy or rename a long filename destroys the long filename and leaves only the alias.

◆ If you are using a Windows 3.1 application and choose Save As (effectively renaming the file), the long filename is lost. If you choose Save, however, the long filename is preserved because the existing name is reused.

◆ Using a disk-repair utility that is not long filename aware (such as MS-DOS 5.x ScanDisk or Norton Disk Doctor) on a volume containing LFNs might destroy the LFNs. The utility interprets the new long filename data structure as errors in the file system that must be corrected. The file utilities SCANDISK.EXE, CHKDSK.EXE, and DEFRAG.EXE that shipped with MS-DOS 6.x do not harm long filenames on your hard drive.

◆ Windows 98 can interpret LFNs from an NTFS volume but only at a remote location (across a network). Windows 98 does not read local NTFS volumes at all.

◆ Windows 98 can read LFNs from a NetWare server, but only at a remote location (across a network). The NetWare server needs to be running OS/2 Name Space to store LFNs using HPFS rules (not Windows rules) for the naming of the 8.3 alias.

◆ If you perform a search on a group of files, Windows 98 searches both the long filename and the alias for occurrences of the given search criteria.

NOTE **The LFNBK.EXE Utility** If you need to remove long filenames from a disk, such as to run hard disk utilities released prior to Windows 98, run the LFNBK.EXE utility. (The DriveSpace utility included with Windows 98 is compatible with long filenames; you can use it to manage compressed disks that have been created with older versions of DriveSpace or DoubleSpace.) The LFNBK utility is located on the Windows 98 CD-ROM in the \tools\reskit\file\LFNBACK folder. When the LFNBK utility runs at the command prompt with the /B switch, it renames each file with an alias. After running LFNBK and restarting Windows, the Start menu appears with its default settings rather than with your custom Start menu. You can restore your custom Start menu by restoring long filenames—run the LFNBK utility with the /R switch.

Adding Long Filename Support for Novell NetWare

When you run Windows 98 on a version 4.10 or earlier NetWare volume, you must install a module called OS2.NAM (the OS/2 Name Space feature) to activate long filenames. NetWare does not support long filenames by itself. To install the OS/2 Name Space feature, type the following at the file server console:

```
LOAD OS2
ADD NAME SPACE OS2 TO VOLUME volume_name
```

In the preceding command, the *volume_name* parameter should be replaced by the name of the volume on which you want Name Space to be added. You also need to add the following to the startup.ncf configuration file:

```
LOAD OS2
```

Then, shut down the NetWare server and copy the file os2.nam from your NetWare disk to the directory that contains SERVER.EXE.

In some cases, it may not be necessary to add the preceding LOAD OS2 statement to startup.ncf. Some versions of NetWare automatically load the OS/2 module when a volume containing the OS/2 Name Space is mounted. If you don't know for sure, this LOAD statement will ensure that the OS/2 module is loaded.

On NetWare 4.1x and later servers, you can enable long filenames by entering the following at the console prompt:

```
LOAD LONG
ADD NAME SPACE LONG TO SYS
```

After you make these changes, shut down the server and bring it back up to make the long filename feature functional at the server. In general, the Name Space feature places additional memory burdens on your server; if you're light on memory, you may want to add more server RAM.

> **NOTE**
>
> **LFNs in NetWare** Novell NetWare 3.1x, 4.0, and 4.1 use OS/2 Name Space to support long filenames, although it actually only supports 254 characters. With the introduction of IntraNetWare 4.11, the name of the support file is now long.nlm, and it supports filenames up to 255 characters in length.

REVIEW BREAK

Disks

You can expect to see questions on configuring and managing disks and partitions on the Windows 98 exam. The preceding sections discussed Windows 98 file system architecture and described how to use the FDISK utility to create partitions and logical drives. You also learned how to convert a FAT16 drive to FAT32 and you learned about Windows 98's support for long filenames.

As you prepare for the Windows 98 exam, pay special attention to FDISK, to the FAT32 conversion utility (and to the differences between FAT16 and FAT32, which are outlined in Chapter 1) and to the rules for how Windows 98 creates aliases for long filenames.

BACKING UP DATA AND THE REGISTRY

Back up data and the Registry, and restore data and the Registry.

Windows 98 provides a backup utility called Microsoft Backup that you can use to configure, manage, and execute backup and restore operations. See Chapter 4 for a discussion of how to back up and restore files using Microsoft Backup.

The Backup objective in the "Configuring and Managing Resource Access" exam section also specifies that you should know about backing up and restoring the Registry. This chapter summarizes some of the ways you can back up and restore Registry data in Windows 98. But first, the following sections provide a brief introduction to the Registry and show how and when you might need to edit the Registry.

Understanding the Windows Registry

The Windows Registry is a database of configuration information. Applications and Windows 98 itself use the Registry to obtain information about your computer's hardware and software. Windows 98 generates the Registry at boot time based on the contents of the Registry files system.dat and user.dat and on other information Windows 98 obtains on the state of your computer.

The files system.dat and user.dat are the central source of Registry information. system.dat contains computer-specific settings and user.dat contains user-specific information. system.dat resides in the Windows directory. user.dat is also in the Windows directory unless user profiles are enabled for the computer, in which case each user will have an individual user.dat file.

The Registry is organized into trees of information that Microsoft calls *hives* (as in bee hives, believe it or not).

The six hives for the Windows 98 Registry are as follows:

◆ HKEY_LOCAL_MACHINE

◆ HKEY_CLASSES_ROOT

NOTE **config.pol** The System Policy file, config.pol, is a little like a Registry file because it provides settings that override Registry files and, therefore, becomes part of the Registry. See Chapter 6 for more information about system policies and the config.pol file.

◆ HKEY_CURRENT_CONFIG

◆ HKEY_DYN_DATA

◆ HKEY_USERS

◆ HKEY_CURRENT_USER

The following sections discuss these hives of the Windows 98 Registry. Later sections will talk about how to edit the Registry using Windows 98's Registry editor regedit.exe.

HKEY_LOCAL_MACHINE

HKEY_LOCAL_MACHINE is the most extensive key in the Windows 98 Registry (see Figure 5.15).

HKEY_LOCAL_MACHINE is a repository of software and hardware configuration information for the local computer. HKEY_LOCAL_MACHINE contains several subtrees, including:

◆ **HKEY_LOCAL_MACHINE\Enum.** Contains information on hardware devices.

◆ **HKEY_LOCAL_MACHINE\Security.** Has information on network security and remote administration.

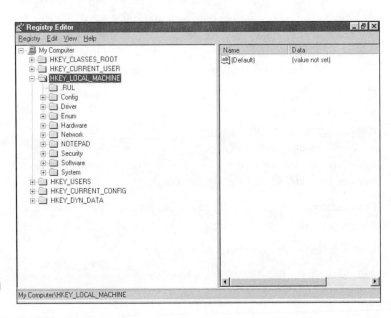

FIGURE 5.15
HKEY_LOCAL_MACHINE contains several subtrees with configuration information for the local system.

◆ **HKEY_LOCAL_MACHINE\Software.** Contains computer-specific settings for software installed on the system.

◆ **HKEY_LOCAL_MACHINE\Software\Classes.** Provides file extension registration information. (This subtree is aliased to HKEY_CLASSES_ROOT.)

◆ **HKEY_LOCAL_MACHINE\Config.** Stores information on hardware profiles. (The subtree for the active hardware profiles is aliased to HKEY_CURRENT_CONFIG.)

HKEY_CLASSES_ROOT

HKEY_CLASSES_ROOT contains software registration and OLE (Object Linking and Embedding) information. HKEY_CLASSES_ROOT is actually an alias of the key HKEY_LOCAL_MACHINE\Software\Classes. The reason for creating a separate key for OLE registration information is to provide backward compatibility with old Windows 3.1 programs.

When you click on the plus sign (+) beside HKEY_CLASSES_ROOT in Registry Editor (described later in this chapter), you will open up a long listing of file extensions Windows 98 recognizes. Although many will just have default types associated with them (such as .ani will say it is an ani file), others will have much more information contained in their keys.

HKEY_CURRENT_CONFIG

HKEY_CURRENT_CONFIG is drawn from the HKEY_LOCAL_MACHINE\Config and points to the current hardware profile.

HKEY_DYN_DATA

HKEY_DYN_DATA provides dynamic data that must be accessed quickly, and is, therefore, stored in RAM. This information comes from hardware devices that were detected when the machine started up, and the drivers associated with them. This information is pulled from RAM whenever you select this key in the Registry Editor, and consequently it is never out-of-date. Other information found here includes information for the bus enumerator and performance statistics gleaned from various network components.

HKEY_USERS

HKEY_USERS stores information on users who access the local computer, including both default user information and also user-specific settings.

HKEY_CURRENT_USER

HKEY_CURRENT_USER contains user settings for the user who is currently logged on to the system. The HKEY_CURRENT_USER tree points to the subtree of HKEY_USERS with settings for the current user.

Editing the Registry

Windows 98 and Windows 98 applications constantly modify the Registry as necessary to incorporate new settings and adapt to new situations. Installing a device (either Plug and Play or non-Plug and Play) will cause Windows 98 to modify the Registry. Adding a file type association through View, Folder Options in Explorer or creating a desktop shortcut will alter the Registry's contents. Installing a new driver or new font or changing logon settings will affect the Registry. In many cases (such as the case of installing a new Plug and Play device), Windows 98 updates the Registry automatically. At other times, you may want to change some configuration settings yourself—in most cases, this will entail changing the Registry.

Windows 98 provides a variety of methods for changing the contents of the Registry. The simplest, and usually the most practical, way to change the Registry is through Control Panel. Each Control Panel application is an interface to the Registry that controls a predefined collection of settings. Most of the time, when you make a change in Control Panel, you are changing a Registry setting. Although Control Panel provides access to only a fraction of the possible Registry settings, Control Panel was specifically designed to control many of the most common and most important settings. (For evidence of the importance of Control Panel, just look at how many times the term *Control Panel* appears in this book.)

Another built-in interface to the Windows 98 Registry is System Policy Editor. As you'll learn in Chapter 6, System Policy Editor's Registry mode lets you change Registry settings. System Policy Editor's Policy mode also, in effect, lets you alter the Registry by overriding the contents of the system.dat and user.dat Registry files. Again, see Chapter 6.

The most direct and comprehensive method for editing the Registry is through Windows 98's Registry Editor utility REGEDIT.EXE. Registry Editor (refer to Figure 5.10) provides an Explorer-like, hierarchical view of Registry trees and subtrees, and lets you selectively alter Registry settings.

Registry Editor's main window provides a folder-like icon for each of the Registry hives described in the preceding section. Click on the plus sign (+) beside an icon to explore subtrees within the hive. When you reach the lowest level of the subtree, Registry settings within the selected subtree will appear on the right side of the screen (see Figure 5.16). To change a setting, click on the setting you wish to change and choose Modify from the Edit menu. The Edit String dialog box will appear (see Figure 5.17). Enter the new value and click on OK. To add a new value to a subtree, select the subtree and choose New from the Edit menu. You'll be asked to choose a data type for the new value.

A Registry entry can be in any of the following data types:

◆ **String.** A string of characters enclosed in quotation marks

◆ **Binary.** A binary number represented in hexadecimal format

◆ **DWORD.** A binary number of up to four bytes expressed as a hexadecimal number with the decimal equivalent in parentheses.

Opinions on the act of editing the Registry with Registry Editor range from "routine and appropriate" to "incredibly dangerous and reckless." The fact is, if you make a mistake when editing the Registry, you can mess up your whole configuration and render your computer unbootable. However, many would say that the lesson from this is not that you shouldn't edit the Registry, but that you *shouldn't make a mistake*. (You can also render your computer unbootable by dropping it on the floor, but no one says you shouldn't pick up your computer.)

Typically, you can make most of the normal Registry modifications through Control Panel or System Policy Editor. Most network administrators only use Registry Editor if they know exactly what setting they wish to change. Microsoft and other vendors often distribute tips and fixes that require changes to specific Registry values. Certain optimizations also take the form of documented or undocumented Registry settings.

NOTE

Registry Editor and Remote Administration You can use Registry Editor to connect to a remote computer's Registry if both computers have the Remote Registry Service installed and if the remote computer is configured for remote administration. Remote administration was described earlier in this chapter. To access a remote Registry, pull down the Registry menu and select Connect Remote Registry.

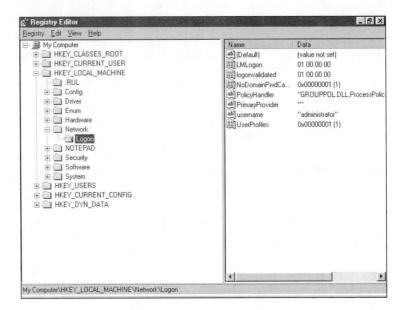

FIGURE 5.16
Registry settings appear in the right pane of
Registry Editor's main window.

In general, some occasions when you might have to make direct
modifications to the Registry include the following:

◆ You removed a program or device from your computer, and
the uninstall program did not do a good job, or the uninstall
failed. In this instance, hopefully, you have some good
information from the maker of the device, or the company
that wrote the application. In this instance, you use the Find
utility to search for specific words until you can remove ves-
tiges of the old application.

◆ You need to make a change to enhance performance, or fix a
bug, and you read about the fix in the Microsoft Knowledge
Base or TechNet. Occasionally Microsoft posts a bug fix that
requires direct editing of the Registry. You should not make
such changes, however, unless your machine is exhibiting the
problems the fix is designed to correct. In these instances, it
might be best to not fix something that is not broken.

◆ You want to change the behavior or enhance a feature of
Windows 98, and there is no other way to make the modification without editing the Registry. A word of caution here:
Be especially wary of Registry hacks that do not come from
reputable sources. One can find thousands of neat tricks on
the Internet, for example, but many of these have no place in a
business-production environment.

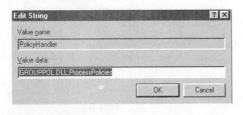

FIGURE 5.17
When you select Modify from Registry Editor's
Edit menu, the Edit String dialog box will prompt
you to enter a new value.

Backing Up the Registry

Microsoft provides several methods for backing up the Registry. The preferred method is to use the Registry Checker utility (ScanReg and ScanRegW). Registry Checker backs up the Registry once a day when the system starts, but you can also initiate a manual backup through Registry Checker.

To access Registry Checker, perform the tasks outlined in Step by Step 5.6.

STEP BY STEP

5.6 Accessing Registry Checker

1. Choose Start, Programs, Accessories, System Tools, System Information.

2. In the System Information utility, pull down the Tools menu and select Registry Checker.

See Chapter 8 for more information on Windows 98's Registry Checker utility.

Another method for backing up the Registry is through Windows 98's Microsoft Backup utility. The Advanced tab in Microsoft Backup's Backup Job Options dialog box lets you include the Windows Registry in a backup (see Figure 5.18). See Chapter 4 for more information about Microsoft Backup.

The Registry Editor utility (described in the preceding section) lets you export a file with a complete record of settings for all or part of the Registry. This exported Registry file can be sent to a remote help desk in troubleshooting situations, or it can be used to incorporate Registry setting with Windows 98 Setup using the Batch98 installation script utility (see Chapter 2, "Installing Windows 98"). You can also import an exported Registry file into the Registry.

To export a Registry file, perform the tasks outlined in Step by Step 5.7.

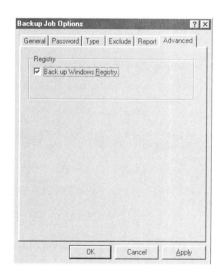

FIGURE 5.18
Microsoft Backup lets you include the Registry in a backup job.

STEP BY STEP

5.7 Exporting a Registry File

1. In Registry Editor, select a subtree you'd like to include in the exported Registry file. To include the entire Registry, select the My Computer icon.

2. Pull down the Registry menu. Select Export Registry File.

3. In the Export Registry File dialog box (see Figure 5.19), select a location and enter a name for the Registry file.

Restoring the Registry

Each method for backing up the Registry has a corresponding method for restoring the Registry. Just as the Advanced tab of the Backup utility's Backup Options dialog box has an option for backing up the Registry, the Restore Options Advanced tab has an option for restoring the Registry. (Refer to Chapter 4.)

The Registry Checker will attempt to restore the Registry automatically on reboot if it detects problems with the Registry. (See Chapter 8.)

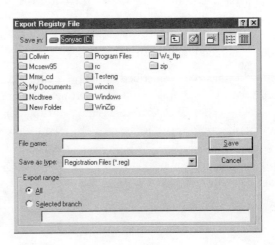

FIGURE 5.19
The Export Registry File dialog box lets you save a file that contains Registry information.

And just as you can export a Registry file through the Registry Editor, you can also import a previously exported Registry file. To import a Registry file, perform the tasks outlined in Step by Step 5.8.

STEP BY STEP

5.8 Importing a Registry File

1. In Registry Editor, pull down the Registry menu and select Import Registry file.

2. In the Import Registry File dialog box, select the Registry file you wish to import. The file should have a `.reg` extension.

3. When you import a Registry file, Registry Editor checks to ensure that the file is a valid Registry file. If so, a dialog box will appear informing you that the file was successfully imported. Click on OK.

> **NOTE**
>
> **The `.reg` Extension** `.reg` is a registered file extension in Windows 98. This means that you can also import a Registry file by double-clicking on the file (which must have a `.reg` extension) in Explorer.

The Registry

REVIEW BREAK

No discussion of Windows 98 is complete with out a description of the Registry and the Registry Editor utility. The preceding sections provide a brief tour of the major Registry trees and show how to navigate through the Registry using the Registry Editor (REGEDIT.EXE).

The wording of the exam objective covers a bit narrower field than the whole Registry. Microsoft states the you should know how to "back up data and the Registry and restore data and the Registry." It is likely that Microsoft added this objective because it wants you to know about the Registry Checker utilities (ScanReg and ScanRegW—see Chapter 8) and the Registry backup option of the Microsoft Backup utility (see Chapter 4). But the Registry is too important to depend on Microsoft to stay within this narrow subject. Learn the basic structure of the Registry, and spend some time with Registry Editor. Don't forget to be very careful when you're using Registry Editor—and don't make any changes unless you're sure about the change.

CASE STUDY: TOTAL QUALITY CONSULTANTS

ESSENCE OF THE CASE

Here are the essential elements in this case:

- All changed data must be backed up over the network.

- Backups will occur nightly.

- Mike would like to configure the backups to continue without prompting him for information about files that are being backed up.

- Speed is of utmost importance.

SCENARIO

Total Quality Consultants has 14 Windows 98 machines all networked in a peer-to-peer environment. Mike, the owner, would like to back up all data to a central tape backup drive. In addition, he would like to back up only the data that has changed since the last tape backup, in the interest of saving time.

This scenario provides an example of how Registry backup can be part of a routine backup process.

ANALYSIS

Each Windows 98 computer should share out its C: drive with a password that only Mike knows for security. Mike would then map a drive to each Windows 98 computer's C: drive. Each mapped drive can be configured to reconnect at logon so that Mike would not have to map the drives repeatedly. When Mike creates the first backup job through Microsoft Backup, he should save all of his preferences and settings so that he will have the backup options for the next backup. From the options tab, Mike should choose the following:

- To secure the backup with a password.

- To make this backup an incremental backup to save on backup time.

- To make this backup an unattended backup.

- To back up the Windows Registry.

For more information about Windows 98's Backup utility, refer to Chapter 4.

CHAPTER SUMMARY

This chapter looked at access permissions in Windows 98. You learned about user and group permissions and how they interact. You also learned about remote administration in Windows 98 and how you can use Windows 98's remote administration features to manage resources such as remote computers and printers. This chapter also looked at hard disk support, describing compression, partitioning, and Windows 98's FAT32 conversion utility. And you learned about some methods for backing up and restoring data and the Registry.

KEY TERMS

- share-level security
- user-level security
- DoubleSpace
- DriveSpace
- IFS Manager
- partitions
- FAT16
- FAT32
- Registry

APPLY YOUR KNOWLEDGE

Exercises

5.1 Utilizing Share-Level Security

In this exercise, you will work with share-level security in a Windows 98 workgroup. Share-level security is based on passwords. This security is easily compromised because passwords can be discovered and access to inappropriate resources can occur. You will need at least two network computers to do this lab.

Estimated Time: 20 minutes

1. Open the Control Panel and then choose the Network applet.

2. Confirm that the computer is configured for network access (see Chapter 3). Confirm that the Client for Microsoft Networks is currently installed. If it is not installed, choose Add.

3. From the Select Network Component dialog box, choose Client and then choose Add.

4. From the list of Manufacturers, choose Microsoft and then choose the Client for Microsoft Networks from the Network Clients.

5. Click OK. The Client for Microsoft Networks software will be added to your PC. You may be prompted to supply the Microsoft Windows 98 CD and then you'll have to restart your computer to continue.

6. Also in the Network applet, confirm that you have the File and Printer Sharing for Microsoft Networks installed. If you do not, choose Add, Service, and Add again.

> **NOTE**
>
> **File and Printer Sharing Service**
> Remember that your computer only allows one instance of a File and Printer Sharing service. In other words, you cannot have the file and printer service for both NetWare networks and Microsoft networks. For this exercise, you should use the File and Printer Sharing Service for Microsoft Networks because you are going to work with share-level security.

7. From the Manufacturers list, choose Microsoft, and then choose the File and Printer Sharing Service from the File and Printer Sharing Service for Microsoft Networks. Choose OK. You will have to supply the source files from the CD and the restart your computer to update the files.

8. Finally, in Control Panel's Network applet, choose the Access Control tab and confirm that share-level security is being used. If not, select it now.

9. Choose OK to exit the Network applet and approve these changes to the system.

10. Open Windows Explorer and create three folders on your C: drive. Name the first folder Sales, the second folder Marketing, and the third Finance. You'll need these folders to share and for a future exercise.

11. Right-click the Sales folder and choose Sharing from the pop-up menu. The Sharing dialog is displayed.

APPLY YOUR KNOWLEDGE

12. Choose Shared As and the name Sales is automatically entered into the Share Name field. In the Comment field, type **For Sales Reps only!**.

13. Under Access Type, assign the access type as Full Control. Assign a full control password of **abc** and choose OK to approve your changes.

14. You'll be prompted to confirm your password, so again enter **abc** and then choose OK to confirm your password.

15. You have just shared out the Sales folder. Notice that the folder appears in Explorer with a hand under the folder to represent that is being shared out on the network.

16. Right-click Marketing and share it as Read-only with a password of **xyz**.

17. Go to another computer on the network and open Network Neighborhood. Double-click the computer where the Sales and Marketing shares reside.

18. Double-click the Sales folder and you'll be prompted to supply the password for Sales. Enter the wrong password to see what happens.

19. Enter the correct password and you'll se the contents of the Sales folder. Right-click in the contents of Sales and choose New Text Document. Create and name the document October.

    Why can you create this document over the Network in the Sales share?

20. Open the share for Marketing and try to create a text document.

    Can you create a document in this share?

    Why or why not?

21. Close Explorer and return to the computer where the Sales and Marketing shares are to continue with Exercise 5.2.

5.2   Creating and Monitoring Remote Shares

In this exercise, you will create and modify a remote share through Net Watcher. Through Net Watcher you can monitor users, resources, and share permissions from a remote computer. This exercise assumes that you have completed Exercise 5.1 to enable sharing, creating folders, and shares. For more on Net Watcher, see Chapter 7.

Estimated Time: 25 minutes

1. On the computer where the Sales and Marketing shares reside, open the Control Panel's Passwords applet.

2. Click on the Remote Administration tab. Because you are using share-level security, you must provide a password for others to remotely administer this computer. (With user-level security you would simply identify what users could administer this machine.)

3. Check the Enable Remote Administration of This Server checkbox, and then enter the password of **pencil** and choose OK.

4. Move to the another Windows 98 computer on your network.

5. Click Start, Programs, Accessories, System Tools. From System tools, select the Net Watcher tool.

6. You are going to monitor the resources on your first computer where the Sales and Marketing shares reside; then you'll share out another folder from this PC.

7. From the Administer menu, choose Select Server. You can either type in the NetBIOS name of the remote computer, or you can browse and find the remote computer through a Network Neighborhood interface. After you have found the remote computer, choose OK to verify that you want to monitor this computer from your PC through the network.

8. When you first connect to this server, you are viewing the users connected to this computer. From the View menu, choose View by Shared Folders to see a list of folders that are shared on this server. You can also click the Show Shared Folders button on the toolbar. You should see the Sales and Marketing folders that you created in Exercise 5.1 in the list of shared folders.

9. Click on the Sales folder. From the Administer menu, choose Shared Folder Properties. The standard Sharing dialog box appears. Change the attribute of the folder from Full Control to Read and change the password from 123 to **purple** and choose OK.

10. You have just changed the access permissions for the share Sales on a remote computer.

11. Click on Administer from the menu bar, and then choose Add Shared Folder.

12. Click Browse to view the shares and the C$ share to view the folders on the machine you are remotely administering.

13. Click the plus symbol (+) by the C$ share. The tree of the remote computer is displayed. From the list of folders, find the folder you created in Exercise 5.1 called Finance. Select Finance and then choose OK.

14. Choose OK again to confirm the path of the resource you want to share out.

15. The Standard Sharing dialog box appears. Click the Shared As button, and the shared name of Finance is provided for you.

16. Under Access Type, choose Full Control and assign a password of **Jupiter**. Click OK to confirm these sharing properties.

17. Confirm your password and then click OK.

18. Exit Net Watcher and open Network Neighborhood.

19. Open the remote computer from the list of servers.

20. Open the share Finance, supply the password "Jupiter," and click OK.

21. The folder is displayed and you have full control permission to the folder on the network.

5.3 Creating a Network Printer

In this exercise, you will create and share a network printer of your Windows 98 machine.

Estimated Time: 15 minutes

1. Click Start, Settings, Printers.

2. Open the Add Printer Wizard and click Next to begin.

3. Select the option that this printer is connected locally to your machine.

4. From the Manufacturers, choose HP.

5. From the list of Printers, choose HP LaserJet 4SI.

6. If you are prompted for your Windows 98 CD, insert the CD to add the print drivers.

7. Click Next to continue.

8. When prompted to choose what port the printer is on, choose an available port and then click Next.

9. Assign the printer the name **TESTING**, and choose Next.

10. When prompted to print a test page, choose No, and then click Finish.

11. Your printer has been installed on your Windows 98 machine.

12. To begin sharing the printer, right-click on the printer and choose Sharing.

13. The Sharing tab of the Printer's properties appears. Click on the Shared As option button.

14. In the Comment field, enter the text **This is only a test.** and then enter a password if you are using share-level security. If you are using user-level security, identify three users that will have print permissions to this printer.

15. Click OK. If you entered a password, you will need to confirm your password.

16. Your printer has been shared.

5.4   Connecting to a Shared Printer

This exercise builds on Exercise 5.3 and connects to the printer that was shared.

Estimated Time: 10 minutes

1. On another Windows 98 machine in your network, open the Printers folder.

2. Open the Add a Printer Wizard and choose Next.

3. Click on the Would Like to Add a Network Printer button and then click Next.

4. To find the network printer, click on the Browse button. Find the name of the computer name from which the printer is shared and choose the network printer.

5. Click Next to continue with the installation.

6. Assign the printer the name **Testing2** and click Next.

7. When prompted to print a test page, choose No.

8. Click Finish and the printer has been installed.

9. Open your **Printers** folder, and you will see that the network printer Testing2 has been added.

5.5   Converting to FAT32

This exercise walks you through the steps of converting to FAT32. It will require that Windows 98 be installed on a computer that has a FAT or FAT16 partition. If you do not have a machine with a FAT partition, you can still complete the major steps of the exercise, but an actual drive will not be converted.

Estimated Time: 10 minutes

1. Click Start, Programs, Accessories, System Tools, and then click Drive Converter (FAT32).

2. The Drive Converter Wizard appears and will begin the process of converting your drive to FAT32.

3. Click the Details button to view the FAT32 Help information. Review the material and then close the Help dialog box.

4. Click Next and you are prompted to choose a partition to convert to FAT32.

APPLY YOUR KNOWLEDGE

If you do not have any FAT32 partitions, you are given the message that there are no drives that can be converted to FAT32 at this time.

If you do have a FAT or FAT16 partition, choose that partition and then choose Next.

5. The FAT32 Wizard will begin the conversion. After you reboot, your drives will be converted to FAT32.

5.6   Backing Up the Windows 98 Registry and Data

Microsoft Backup allows the operator to back up the Registry and restore the Registry files if needed. This exercise will explore that possibility.

Estimated Time: 15 minutes

1. Click Start, Programs, Accessories, System Tools, Backup.

2. The Backup program opens. Choose the option to create a new backup job and then click OK.

3. Choose the option to back up selected files and folders and then click Next.

4. Click the plus sign (+) by your C: drive and then select the folder called Windows to get to the files it contains. (Do not *check* the folder called Windows, or all contents of the Windows directory will be backed up.)

5. Find the bitmap file called sandstone.bmp (if you do not have this file, choose another small bitmap image). Check the box next to the file to select it for backup and then choose Next.

6. Accept the option to back up all selected files. Choose where this file should be backed up to: your floppy drive, a tape, or a removable hard disk. Choose Next when ready.

7. Select the options to verify backup and to compress data.

8. For the name of the job, type in **Data** and click Start.

9. The backup will continue, and then you'll see the job details of Data.

10. From How to Back Up Sections, click on the Advanced tab and then choose to back up the Windows Registry. Click OK and then click Start.

11. You may be prompted to save the data job before continuing. Click OK to save the job.

12. You may be prompted to overwrite the existing backup set. Click OK to do so that the new settings are enforced to back up the bitmap image and the Registry files.

13. Exit Backup when the job is complete.

Review Questions

1. How are folders shared?

2. What is user-level security?

3. What is share-level security?

4. Where are passwords changed for access to resources when using share-level security?

5. How many primary partitions can be on one physical disk within Windows 98?

6. What tool is used in Windows 98 to create logical drives?

7. What Windows 98 tools are used for disk compression?

8. How can FAT32 be enabled if a drive is already formatted with FAT?

APPLY YOUR KNOWLEDGE

Exam Questions

1. You are the administrator for a Windows 98 and Windows NT workgroup. There are 17 workstations in the workgroup; all of the workstations have constantly changing directories that others need access to, and three of the workstations have printers that others will need to access. In this scenario, which of the following choices would be best?

   A. Move all the shares to one Windows 98 machine. Create a master directory called SHARES, put all resource directories into this master directory, and share out just the SHARES directory. Leave the printers where they are and share them from the machine to which they are attached.

   B. Share the directories and printers from each machine on which the resource resides.

   C. Share the directories from each machine on which they reside, but move the printers to one Windows 98 machine and create a printer pool.

   D. Implement an intranet environment and share all resource through the intranet.

2. Amelia is having trouble connecting to a resource on Joe's machine. She was certain that the password was "carrots" but she is still denied access. What do you suspect is the problem? Choose all that apply.

   A. The password has changed and Amelia doesn't know the new password.

   B. Amelia is typing the password incorrectly.

   C. Amelia does not have permission to view the resource.

   D. The resource no longer exists on Joe's machine so the password is incorrect when she tries to connect.

3. Virginia, the administrator of a small workgroup, is sharing a directory for which some users need only Read-only permission and others need Full Control permissions. What is the best way to share this resource in this share-level security environment?

   A. Create two shares—one with Read-only permissions and the other with Full Control.

   B. Create two shares—one with Read-only permissions and the other with Full Control. To the share that has Full Control permission, add a dollar symbol ($) to the end of the share name so that user will not see it in the browse list.

   C. Use the option Depends on Password to create varying levels of access to shares.

   D. Use the option Depends on User ID to create varying levels of access to shares and then identify users that have Read-only rather than Full Control permissions.

4. You are the administrator for a Windows NT domain. Most of your clients are Windows 98 users and they have File and Printer Sharing turned on with user-level security. Some users, however, cannot access resources on other users' machines. Upon further investigation, you discover that these users are not logging in to the domain. Why does this have an impact on access to resources?

   A. It doesn't have an impact. The users simply do not have permission to access the resources.

B. If the user does not log in to the domain, there is no authentication of the account to verify that the user has permission to access the shared resources.

C. If a user does not log in to the domain, he can still provide his credentials when he goes to access the resource. The user simply does not have permission to access the resources.

D. The user will receive an ACL (Access Control List) from the Primary Domain Controller each time he logs in to the domain. The ACL will be compared to resources the user is trying to access to verify that he has rights to the resource. If the user does not log in to the domain, there is no ACL assigned to the user; therefore, he cannot access any shared resources.

5. You are attempting to share out resources from your Windows 98 machine. Your Windows 98 machine is configured to log in to the NetWare server NWEast. You would like to create a share and assign the password "oaktree" to the resource. However, the option to assign the password is missing from the Share dialog box. What do you suspect is the problem and how would you resolve it?

A. You are not looking at the Share dialog box. Right-click on the resource and choose Sharing and then you can implement the password.

B. There is no problem. If your machine is configured to log in to a NetWare server, you are required to use user-level security.

C. You are using user-level security. Open the Network applet, choose Access Control, and then change from user-level to share-level security. After rebooting your machine, log in to your NetWare server, where you can share out the resource with the password desired.

D. Your machine has a system policy implemented that prevents you from sharing resources with passwords. There is nothing you can do to resolve the problem—without changing the system policy.

6. You are the administrator for a Windows 98 workgroup. You have just launched Net Watcher to monitor shares on remote computers in your network. Whenever you attempt to connect to another computer, you receive an error message that Net Watcher cannot connect to share ADMIN$. What do you suspect is the problem and how can you fix it?

A. Net Watcher has to be installed on every remote machine that you want to connect to. To resolve the problem, install Net Watcher on each of the remote computers.

B. You must have a share created called ADMIN$ on each machine before running Net Watcher. Create the share on each machine you want to monitor, restart each machine that has the share, and then launch Net Watcher again.

C. The ADMIN$ is hidden to Net Watcher. Before starting Net Watcher, you have to edit the Registry through HKEY_LOCAL_MACHINE\ Services\CurrentControlSet\Services\ NetWatcher\AllowedHiddenShares. The REG_DWORD value is set to 0; change it to 1, restart your computer, and then Net Watcher will work with Windows 98.

D. Remote Administration must be enabled on all remote computers to use Net Watcher to monitor these resources. Open Control Panel's Passwords, choose Remote Administration, and then enable Remote Administration. With share-level security, supply a difficult password; with user-level security, identify the users or groups that should have the rights to perform remote administration.

7. Mark, the sales manager, has a color printer that he is sharing on the network. He is already using user-level security in your NetWare environment and has identified that only the Sales group has rights to the printer. Other users, however, are continuing to ask if they, too, can print to the printer. What can Mark do so that his colleagues will not continue to ask to print to his printer, yet keep it so that only the Sales group will have permission to the resource?

   A. Implement system policies so that his colleagues will get a standard message stating that the printer is reserved only for the Sales group when they try to connect to the printer through Network Neighborhood.

   B. Quit sharing the printer; all sales people will copy the documents they need printed to a share on Mark's machine called SALES and then Mark will print the documents for the sales reps.

   C. Share the printer out with a dollar symbol ($) behind the share name so that no one can see the printer on the network; users will be less likely to request access to the resource through the network. Sales reps will connect to the printer by supplying the UNC path to the printer when they install the printer on their machines.

   D. Create and share a second printer in Mark's system that would print to his printer only at certain times of the day. That way all users could print to the printer, but only during certain hours.

8. Roger, an accountant for your company, has just switched his computer from share-level security to user-level security. However, users in his department now claim that all of his shares are now missing from the network. What is the problem?

   A. Roger stopped sharing all folders during the process of converting to user-level security. He must now re-create the shares and identify each user or group that has permission to access the share.

   B. Roger has changed his computer name so his shares are no longer showing up in the network under his computer name.

   C. The shares are still available, but Roger has not identified the users with user-level security.

   D. Roger has inadvertently turned off File and Printer Sharing during his conversion to user-level security.

9. You have created the following directory structure on your Windows 98 machine:

   C:\Public

   \Sales

   \Marketing

   \Finance

   \Announcements

   \News

   \Suggestions

APPLY YOUR KNOWLEDGE

You have shared the Public directory with everyone who has the Read permission. You have also shared out the Sales, Marketing, and Finance directories so that the managers have full control over these folders. However, when Tom, the marketing manager, opens the Marketing folder, he cannot change the files inside of the share. What is the problem and how can it be resolved?

A. Tom is accessing the folder through the Public share where he will only receive Read permission on the resource. He'll need to access the resource through the Marketing share to get full control of the folder.

B. Permissions are always most restrictive, so Tom will always receive Read permissions in the Marketing folder with this directory tree.

C. Permissions are always accumulative on resources, so Tom should receive Full Control on the resource. Tom is probably not a member of the Managers group and so does not receive the desired permissions.

D. You cannot share a folder inside of another folder, so there is no resolution to this problem.

10. Marie would like to share out her fax modem as a fax server from her Windows 98 computer. Michael doesn't think it's possible to share out a fax modem from Windows 98. Who is correct, and why?

A. Marie is correct because you can share out the fax modem through the Device Manager.

B. Marie is correct because you can share out the fax modem just like you would share out a printer.

C. Michael is correct because you can share out hardware devices like modems, scanners, and CD-ROM drives.

D. Michael is correct because fax modems require a local driver and interface because of the new Unimodem driver model.

11. Your computer is set up to dual-boot with Windows NT Workstation 4.0 and Windows 98. During a Windows 98 session, you created another partition through FDISK and formatted it FAT32. Whenever you restart your computer in Windows NT Workstation, you cannot access this partition. What do you suspect is the problem?

A. Windows NT cannot access FAT32 drives.

B. Windows 98 and NT use distinct naming conventions so they cannot share drives.

C. In dual-boot situations, you must create all partitions through Windows NT Workstation's Disk Administrator.

D. You have not changed the boot.ini file on Windows NT to reflect the presence of a new partition.

12. You have just added a new 8GB hard disk to your Windows 98 computer. When you go to partition the drive, you are prompted to enable large disk support. Why is this message an issue?

A. If you enable large disk support, you are using FAT16 only.

B. If you enable large disk support, you are enabling FAT32 for any partition created during that session of FDISK.

APPLY YOUR KNOWLEDGE

C. You are using a SCSI drive, which uses sector translation. Windows 98 cannot use sector translation unless large drive support is enabled.

D. Your controller card is not WD_1003, so Windows 98 will create a work-around for the controller card.

6. FDISK (For more information, refer to the section "Configuring Hard Disks.")

7. DriveSpace3, Compression Agent (For more information, refer to the section "Configuring Hard Disks.")

8. Drive Converter (FAT32) (For more information, refer to the section "Configuring Hard Disks.")

Answers to Review Questions

1. To share a folder, right-click on the folder and choose Sharing; assign the appropriate level of permissions, identify the users or assign a password to access the resource. (For more information, refer to the section "Assigning Access Permissions for Shared Folders.")

2. User-level security is a mechanism to restrict users' access to resources based on their logon identification. (For more information, refer to the section "Assigning Access Permissions for Shared Folders.")

3. Share-level security is a mechanism to allow access to shared resources based on passwords. (For more information, refer to the section "Assigning Access Permissions for Shared Folders.")

4. Passwords are changed within the share properties for each shared resource. (For more information, refer to the section "Assigning Access Permissions for Shared Folders.")

5. One primary partition per physical disk is allowed within Windows 98. (For more information, refer to the section "Configuring Hard Disks.")

Answers to Exam Questions

1. **B.** Share each directory and printer from the machine on which the resource resides. In a workgroup environment, this is the most practical. Choice A might have been a good answer, except that the idea of a master shared directory complicates the task of varying levels of access for the subdirectories.

2. **A, B.** Choice C does not identify the problem because Amelia is supplying a password for access, so the resource must be controlled by share-level, rather than user-level, security. Choice D could not be correct because Amelia would receive the message stating that the network path was not found when she tried to access the resource. (For more information, refer to the section "Assigning Access Permissions for Shared Folders.")

3. **C.** Virginia should use the option Depends on Password to assign a Read-only password, and a Full Control password. (For more information, refer to the section "Assigning Access Permissions for Shared Folders.")

APPLY YOUR KNOWLEDGE

4. **B.** With user-level security enabled, the user must log in to the domain to be recognized as a valid user in the network. The Windows 98 machine will pass the validation to the domain controller to verify that the user is valid to grant the appropriate level of access to the shared resource. Option D is incorrect because the user does not receive the ACL (Access Control List) from the Domain Controller. The ACL is actually on each shared resource. The ACL is a listing of what users and groups have what level of access to a shared resource. (For more information, refer to the section "Assigning Access Permissions for Shared Folders.")

5. **B.** In a NetWare Server environment, if you are using the Microsoft Client for NetWare Networks, you must use user-level security to share resources. (For more information, refer to the section "Assigning Access Permissions for Shared Folders.")

6. **D.** Remote Administration must be enabled on each machine that is to be monitored by Net Watcher. (For more information, refer to the section "Creating, Sharing, and Monitoring Resources.")

7. **C.** Mark should create a hidden share so that users will not see the printer in the browse list. All though this answer does not stop users from requesting to use the printer, users will be less aware that the printer is shared out. (For more information about configuring printers, refer to Chapter 4. For more information about creating hidden shares, refer to Chapter 1.

8. **A.** Roger has stopped sharing all of his folders when he switched from share-level to user-level security. He will have to share out his resources again using user-level security. (For more information, refer to the section "Assigning Access Permissions for Shared Folders.")

9. **A.** Tom cannot get Full Control to the resource if he accesses it through the Public share. He will need to access the resource through the Marketing share directly. (For more information, refer to the section "Assigning Access Permissions for Shared Folders.")

10. **B.** Marie is correct. You can share out the fax modem in the same as you would a printer. Users would connect to the shared fax modem in the same way they would to a printer. (For more information about configuring printers, refer to Chapter 4.)

11. **A.** FAT32 partitions are not accessible through Windows NT 4.0. (For more information, refer to the section "Configuring Hard Disks." Refer to Chapter 1 for more information about Windows 98 file systems.)

12. **B.** If you enable large disk support, all partitions that you created during that FDISK session will be formatted with FAT32. (For more information, refer to the section "Windows 98 File System Architecture.")

APPLY YOUR KNOWLEDGE

Suggested Readings and Resources

1. *The Windows 98 Resource Kit*; Microsoft Press

2. *The Windows 98 Professional Reference*, Hallberg and Casad; New Riders

This chapter helps you to prepare for the Microsoft exam by covering the following objectives within the "Configuring and Managing Resource Access" category:

Set up user environments by using user profiles and system policies.

▶ Windows 98 profiles allow users to have personalized settings such as shortcuts, Start menu items, colors, and more. You can control users' profiles by creating roaming profiles or even mandatory profiles to control what users' machines look and feel like. System policies take the concept of controlling users one step further. System policies allow you to control what users are allowed to do on a Windows 98 machine. You can restrict activities and prevent access to system components into which you do not want users to pry.

Create hardware profiles.

▶ Hardware profiles allow users to control how hardware interacts with Windows 98 based on thee physical location of their hardware, the job at hand, or available system resources for given hardware. Typically, hardware profiles are used for machines that may participate both on and off a network.

CHAPTER 6

Managing Profiles and System Policies

To study effectively for these exam objectives, complete the review questions, read the content of this chapter, complete the exercises, and then test your knowledge with the exam questions. In addition, you may find it valuable to experiment with your own profiles, system policies, and hardware profiles.

INTRODUCTION

Windows 98 includes some advanced features that you can use to customize the user interface and the operating environment the user sees when starting the system. This chapter discusses the three following important features:

- ◆ **User profiles.** Provide a set of custom, user-specific environment settings, such as a custom desktop or a custom Start menu.

- ◆ **System policies.** Let the network administrator selectively impose settings that limit a user's access to operating system and supercede changes the user might make to the Windows 98 environment.

- ◆ **Hardware profiles.** Let you design a separate configuration for each hardware state in which the computer will operate.

These features are the most powerful tools the administrator has for customizing the Windows 98 environment. The owner of a single-user, standalone computer could go for years without needing to implement these features, but in organizational environments—even on small networks—these features are important enough to be a part of the everyday routine. Microsoft places a great deal of emphasis on user profiles, system policies, and hardware profiles, and it is clear that Microsoft doesn't want anyone installing Microsoft networks who doesn't know how to implement these features.

This chapter describes these three important customization features of Windows 98.

SETTING UP USER ENVIRONMENTS THROUGH USER PROFILES

Set up user environments by using user profiles and system policies.

A *user profile* is a bundle of user-specific configuration settings. You can use user profiles to create a custom user environment for each user who accesses a Windows 98 system. A user profile can contain settings such as the following:

◆ Wallpaper and desktop settings

◆ Mouse tracking speed and button settings

◆ Desktop icons

◆ Start menu icons

◆ Application settings such as Microsoft Office 97 Settings

This section examines how Windows 98 supports user profiles, both on standalone and networked computers.

As you learned in previous chapters, Windows 98 configuration settings reside in a large database called the Registry. When the user logs out, active Registry settings are saved into a pair of files called system.dat and user.dat. The information in these files is used to restore the Registry upon startup. The fact that the Registry is saved into these two files instead of one file is the secret behind Windows 98's user profiles feature. system.dat contains settings that apply to all users who access the computer. user.dat contains settings that apply to a user's personal configuration (such as the settings in the preceding bulleted list).

When user profiles are enabled, each user on the Windows 98 computer has a personal user.dat file with user-specific configuration settings. When the system starts, Windows 98 uses the common system.dat file (in the Windows directory) along with the user's custom user.dat file to generate the Registry. In addition to a custom user.dat file, the user's user profile can also contain a custom desktop, Start menu, and other custom features. As you'll learn later in this section, the user profile can either be stored locally, or it can be placed on the network for Windows 98 to download automatically upon network logon.

After you enable user profiles for your computer, Windows 98 does most of the work of maintaining user profiles automatically. You can make changes to your configuration, and those changes are automatically stored in your user profile. (An exception to this is the mandatory profile, which is *not* saved when you log off. Mandatory profiles are described later in this chapter.)

As described in Chapter 1, "Planning," user profiles are enabled through the User Profiles tab of the Password Control Panel (refer to Figure 1.10). To enable user profiles, the correct choice is Users Can

Customize Their Preferences and Desktop Settings. This option keeps a separate user.dat file for each user that logs on to the computer. The user.dat file for each user initially is copied from the user.dat file in the Windows directory to a subdirectory bearing the name of the user in the Windows\Profiles directory.

Two additional settings can be included in each user profile: Include Desktop Icons and Network Neighborhood Contents in User Settings, and Include Start Menu and Program Groups in User Settings. If you include the Start menu and program groups in the user profile, applications installed by one user do not show up in the Start menu for other users. Additional subfolders for items such as application data, desktop shortcuts, and Start menu contents may also be included in a user's profile directory, depending on the user profile settings you specify.

In a network environment, a user profile can be copied automatically from a central network share to any computer from which you log in. This process enables the user profile to move with a user from computer to computer. This type of user profile is called a *roaming user profile*. The following criteria must be met to implement roaming user profiles:

◆ You must be using a 32-bit, protected-mode network client. (Both Client for Microsoft Networks and Microsoft Client for NetWare Networks are 32-bit, protected-mode clients.)

◆ For Windows NT networks, your Windows 98 computer must be configured with the Log On to Windows NT Domain option enabled. This is configured in the Client for Microsoft Networks, on the Configuration tab of the Network Control Panel. Also, you must specify Client for Microsoft Networks as the Primary Network Logon.

◆ You must set a home directory for the user account through User Manager for Domains on your Windows NT Domain Controller.

◆ For full user profile support, make sure the network server that holds the user profile directory supports long filenames.

The Windows 98 user profile automatically is copied from the local hard drive to the user's home directory when the user logs out. Any changes he makes during the session are copied to his roaming user profile.

Step by Step 6.1 describes how to implement roaming profiles on a Windows NT domain. You'll learn more about user profiles on NetWare networks later in this section.

STEP BY STEP

6.1 Implementing Roaming Profiles on a Windows NT Domain

1. Open the Passwords Control Panel. In the User Profiles tab, make sure the option button is set to User Can Customize Their Preferences and Desktop Settings. Select the checkboxes for Desktop Icons and Network Neighborhood, Start menu, and Program Groups as desired. Click on OK.

2. In the Network Control Panel, make sure Client for Microsoft Networks is selected as the Primary Network Logon (see Chapter 3, "Windows 98 Networking").

3. On the NT domain controller, use User Manager for Domains to make sure every user who will receive a roaming profile is set up with a home directory.

4. Log off from the Windows 98 computer and restart the system. Set user-specific configuration settings the way you want them and log off again. The user profile settings will be saved to your home directory.

Windows 98 supports another kind of network-based user profile called a mandatory profile. A *mandatory profile* is like a roaming profile, except that the user cannot make permanent changes to a mandatory profile. When the user logs off, a copy of the current profile is not saved to the profile directory. You can use mandatory profiles to enforce a predefined set of desktop settings for some or all network users. To create a mandatory profile, copy an existing user profile directory (including all subdirectories, such as Start Menu, Favorites) to the user's home directory; then change the name of the user.dat file to user.man. A good procedure for creating a mandatory user profile is offered in Step by Step 6.2.

NOTE

User Manager and the User Profile Path User Manager for Domains includes an option for specifying a user's user profile path. It is important to note that this option doesn't apply to Windows 98. You can't specify a user profile path for a Windows 98 computer. Network-based user profiles should reside in the user's home directory, which is also specified through User Manager for Domains.

STEP BY STEP

6.2 Creating a Mandatory User Profile

1. Make sure user profiles are enabled for the Windows 98 PC (refer to Figure 1.10).

2. Make sure your configuration meets all the requirements for a roaming user profile (discussed earlier in this chapter).

3. Log on locally to the Windows 98 machine using the Windows logon and specify a new username, such as *profile1*.

4. Configure the Windows 98 machine the way you would like it to appear with the mandatory user profile.

5. Log off. A user profile directory for the username you used (*profile1*) is created in the Windows\Profiles directory.

6. Log back on with administrative privileges for the network. Copy the contents of the user profile directory you just created to the home directory of the user for whom you are creating the mandatory profile.

7. Go to the user's home directory and change the filename of the file user.dat to user.man. Set the file attributes of user.man to read-only.

Sometimes a user profile (local, roaming, or mandatory) becomes corrupted. If a profile becomes corrupted or unusable, log on as a different user and delete both the local and network-based copies of the profile.

When a user logs in, profile existence is checked in the following order:

1. If there is a server copy, it is copied to the local hard drive.

2. If there is not a server copy, the local copy is used.

3. If there is not a local copy, a new copy is created from the default files in the Windows directory. This new local profile is copied to the server when the user logs out.

If you are implementing user profiles on a Novell NetWare network and you aren't using Microsoft Services for NetWare Directory Services (refer to Chapter 3), the user profile is stored in the user's NetWare Mail directory. This directory within the SYS:MAIL directory is generated when the user account is created; it is assigned a random number as a directory name. If your Windows 98 computer uses Microsoft Services for NetWare Directory Services on an NDS-based NetWare 4.x network, roaming profiles are stored in the user's home directory.

If you are having problems with user profiles, see Table 6.1 for possible solutions.

TABLE 6.1

TROUBLESHOOTING USER PROFILES

Problem	*Solution*
User profiles are downloaded onto some computers; other computers download only part of the profile. The computers that do not take the entire profile leave out the desktop icons.	Make sure user profiles are enabled on all computers and that they have been set to include all the same settings, such as desktop icons and Start menu folders.
User profiles work on your current computer and are downloaded when you move to another computer. The settings, however, do not follow you back to your own computer.	Check to see whether all your computers have the same system time. Windows 98 will not download a server-based profile if it has been saved with a future date. The date stamp placed on the file is the local date and time from the Windows 98 computer. On Windows NT networks, the NET TIME command can be used to synchronize time on all your computers.
Errors are generated when the profile is saved to the server when you log out of your computer; the profile does not function properly afterward.	If you are using a Novell NetWare server, make sure OS/2 Name Space or LONG Name Space has been enabled to support the long filenames used as part of the user's profile. If you are using a Windows NT server, make sure the user's home directory has not been compressed.

User Profiles

User profiles provide a method for customizing user settings such as Start menu items, display settings, shortcuts, and network drives. If a Windows 98 computer supports several users, each user can have a personal user profile. User profile settings are saved in a personalized copy of the user's user.dat Registry file.

A *roaming profile* is a network-based user profile. A roaming profile is stored on a network server or in the user's home directory on a Windows NT domain. When the user logs on from any computer on the network (assuming the computer is configured to support roaming profiles) the user's network-based user profile is copied to the machine from which the user is logging on.

By default, a user can change user-specific configuration settings during a session and the new settings are saved to the user profile when the user logs off. A special user profile called a *mandatory profile* is similar to a roaming profile, except that changes to the profile are *not* saved. The same preconfigured profile loads every time the user restarts Windows 98.

For the Windows 98 exam, be prepared to implement both local and roaming user profiles, and be ready to decide what kinds of things you can and can't do with user profiles.

SETTING UP USER ENVIRONMENTS THROUGH SYSTEM POLICIES

Chapter 1 introduced the important topic of system policies in Windows 98. System policies are configuration settings that override the settings stored in the Windows 98 Registry files system.dat and user.dat. A network administrator can use system policies to secure and limit the Windows 98 operating environment.

System policies are a much more versatile and powerful tool for controlling the user environment than user profiles. Mandatory user profiles (described earlier in this chapter) can control the configuration the user sees when the system starts, but user profiles are not as effective as system policies for controlling what the user does once he or she logs on.

Also, a user profile must be taken as a complete set of user-related profile settings. Using system policies, you can selectively control specific settings and leave other settings alone.

Another important difference between user profiles and system policies is that user profiles let you predefine only user-related settings; system policies let you predefine either user-related or computer-related settings. In addition to user and computer policies, you can impose system policies on a *group* of users defined through Windows NT or NetWare network security.

NOTE **System Policies Require User Profiles** Chapter 1 includes several important notes and tips on using system policies. One important fact to remember is that you must enable user profiles in order to use system policies.

SYSTEM POLICIES REDUCE TCO

One goal of system policies is to help reduce the *total cost of ownership (TCO)* for computers on your network. Each computer has hardware and software costs, and these costs are fixed. Each computer also has a support cost, which often varies depending on how the computer is managed. Studies have shown that, in a corporate setting, much support time is spent fixing silly mistakes made by the operators of the computers. System polices reduce the TCO by limiting access to controls that can cause mistakes. Five common operational problems are a major source of lost money and wasted support hours. The top support time-wasters are as follows:

1. Changes in video settings or the display adapter type that cause the display not to work

2. Changes to network settings (such as the removal of required protocols or clients) or the addition of conflicting components that cause network access to fail

3. Installation of unsupported or untested software that causes problems with required applications

4. Removal of required applications

5. Modification to or deletion of required configuration files such as config.sys

continues

continued

System policies let you restrict access to the system's configuration tools so that ambitious users won't inadvertently introduce errors such as these that will require later troubleshooting.

The following sections describe Windows 98 system policies and show you how to use system policies to shape the user environment. First you learn how system policies work and how to enable system policies for your Windows 98 computer. You then learn how to use the System Policy Editor to configure system policy settings, and you get a guided tour of system policy user and computer settings. Topics include the following:

◆ Understanding system policies

◆ Where to place the system policy file

◆ Enabling group policies

◆ Using the System Policy Editor

◆ Changing user settings

◆ Changing computer settings

◆ Creating policy settings for users, groups, and computers

◆ Using policy template files

Understanding System Policies

The effect of system policies in Windows 98 is shown in Figure 6.1. In Windows 98, system policy settings are stored in a file called config.pol. You can think of config.pol as a third Registry file (in addition to user.dat and system.dat) because it plays a part in defining the contents of the Windows 98 Registry. But config.pol plays a slightly different role in the startup process.

When Windows 98 boots, if your computer is not using system policies, the contents of system.dat and user.dat (or user.man, if you're using mandatory profiles) are used to create the settings in the Windows 98 Registry. If you are using system policies (refer to Figure 6.1), the settings in config.pol overwrite certain settings that

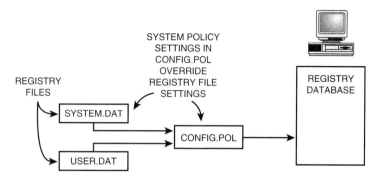

FIGURE 6.1

`config.pol` overrides settings in the Registry files.

would have been copied to the Registry from `user.dat` or `system.dat`. Parameters that have no equivalent setting in `config.pol` pass directly to the Registry without alteration. Parameters for which values are set in `config.pol`, on the other hand, are overwritten so that the Registry will contain the values defined in `config.pol`. No matter what values you set in the Registry (through a Registry user-interface tool such as Registry Editor or the Control Panel applets), the actual contents of the Registry at startup (and hence, the configuration of your computer) will include the settings you have predefined in the `config.pol` system policy file.

Managing system policy settings is really a matter of managing the contents of the `config.pol` system policy file. Windows 98 includes a tool called the System Policy Editor that you can use to create system policy files and change policy settings within a system policy file. You must start with a predefined collection of parameters to which you'd like to assign values. These parameters must correspond to specific entries in the Windows 98 Registry. This predefined collection of parameters is known as a *system policy template*.

The method for creating a `config.pol` system policy file is as follows. Load one or more system policy templates into the System Policy Editor, assign values to the various parameters defined in the policy template using the System Policy Editor user interface, and then save the results to a file called `config.pol`. You can also open an existing policy file in the System Policy Editor and change the settings in the file.

The default system policy template is the file `Windows.adm` in the `Windows\INF` directory. (System policy templates have the .adm extension.) The `Windows.adm` template includes an assortment of useful entries that will help you secure the Windows 98 operating environment. Later in this chapter, you'll find an extensive discussion of the various configuration options available through the System Policy Editor with the default `Windows.adm` policy template. You can also create your own System Policy template with a custom collection of parameters to which you can assign values in the System Policy Editor. You'll learn more about creating system policy templates later in this chapter.

Special system policy templates are sometimes created by vendors for specific software packages and distributed with the software. Windows 98's `Windows\INF` directory actually includes other system policy templates that provide settings for features such as Internet Explorer, Outlook Express, and active desktop. The template `common.adm` contains policy settings common to Windows 95/98 and Windows NT computers that aren't included in `Windows.adm` or the Windows NT default policy template `winnt.adm`. You can load multiple system policy templates into the System Policy Editor. When you load a new template, the additional policy settings merge into the user and computer trees of the System Policy Editor user interface. For instance, if you load the system policy template `Chat.adm` (located in the `Windows\INF` directory), a new subtree with policy settings for the Microsoft Chat application will appear in the Default User tree.

Where to Place `config.pol`

By default, when you are logging on to a Windows NT domain, Windows 98 looks for the `config.pol` file in the `Netlogon` share on the primary domain controller. `Netlogon` is the share name of the Windows NT primary domain controller's `<winntroot>\system32\ repl\import\scripts` directory. Place `config.pol` in this directory if the Windows 98 computer will log on to a Windows NT domain. Microsoft states that you should create the Windows 98 `config.pol` file in Windows 98 and then copy it to the Windows NT server machine, rather than using Windows NT's System Policy Editor to create the `config.pol` file. If the Windows 98 machine will log on to a NetWare network, place the `config.pol` file in the Public directory of the user's preferred server.

A pair of important system policy settings available through the Default computer/Windows 98 Network/Update subtree of the `windows.adm` template will let you modify the default `config.pol` location described in the preceding paragraph. Both these settings are discussed later in this chapter:

◆ **Load balancing.** On a Windows NT domain, if Enable the Load Balancing setting, Windows 98 will retrieve the `config.pol` system policy file from whatever domain controller processed the logon (either a primary domain controller or a backup domain controller). You can use load balancing only when you're using a 32-bit protected-mode client that is using automatic (rather than manual) downloading.

◆ **Manual update.** The manual update setting lets you enter the UNC path to the `config.pol` file. The file can be located on the network or on the local computer.

Enabling Group Policies

Both Windows NT domains and NetWare networks support user groups. A *group* is a collection of users. You can assign specific permissions and rights to the group. This saves you the trouble of separately configuring the permissions and rights for each individual user. (See Chapter 5 "Managing Resources in Windows 98," for more information about groups in Windows 98.) You can create system policies for a group in Windows 98 if you install group policies support on every machine that will use group policies.

To enable group policies on your Windows 98 computer, perform the tasks outlined in Step by Step 6.3.

NOTE

Configuring Manual Update You may be wondering how it helps to provide the location of the `config.pol` file through a system policy setting. (How will Windows 98 read the setting if it hasn't already located the policy file?) To implement the manual update setting through system policies, the computer must use an automatic update first to read the manual update location into the Registry. Another way to enter the manual update location is to switch to Registry mode in the System Policy Editor. In Registry mode (described later in this chapter), the System Policy Editor changes the Registry directly (as opposed to creating a file that will change the Registry at startup). Exercise 6.2, later in this chapter, shows how to configure a manual update through System Policy Editor's Registry mode.

STEP BY STEP

6.3 Enabling Group Policies

1. In the Start menu, select Settings, Control Panel.

2. Open the Add/Remove Programs Control Panel.

3. Select the Windows Setup tab, and click the Have Disk button.

4. Enter the path to the Windows 98 CD's `tools\reskit\ netadmin\poledit` directory. Select the file `grouppol.inf` and click OK. Then, click OK in the Install from Disk dialog box.

5. Enable the check box for the Group Policies, then click the Install button.

Using the System Policy Editor

As mentioned, the System Policy Editor is the a tool that assigns values to parameters specified in one or more system policy templates and saves those values to a system policy file.

To start the System Policy Editor, click on the Start menu and select Programs, Accessories, System Tools, System Policy Editor. If the System Policy Editor isn't installed on your PC, you can install the System Policy Editor as detailed in Step by Step 6.4.

STEP BY STEP

6.4 Installing the System Policy Editor

1. In the Start menu, select Settings, Control Panel.

2. Open the Add/Remove Programs Control Panel.

3. Select the Windows Setup tab, and click the Have Disk button.

4. Enter the path to the Windows 98 CD's `tools\reskit\ netadmin\poledit` directory. Select the file `poledit.inf` and click OK. Then, click OK in the Install from Disk dialog box.

5. Check the check box for System Policy Editor. If you'd
like to enable group policies for your PC, check the check
box for Group Policies. Then click the Install button (see
Figure 6.2).

When you start the System Policy Editor, it opens with a blank window. The first thing you should do is check which system policy
templates are currently loaded in the System Policy Editor. The system policy templates define the options that will be available when
you create a new policy file.

To load or remove a policy template, or to check the current tem-
plate(s), perform the tasks outlined in Step by Step 6.5

STEP BY STEP

6.5 Working with Policy Templates

1. Pull down the Options menu and choose Policy Template.
The Policy Template Options dialog box appears on your
screen (see Figure 6.3).

2. To add a new template, click on Add. Browse through the
available policy template (`*.adm`) files. If you want to add a
template file included with Windows 98, make sure the
Open Template File dialog box is set on the `Windows\INF`
directory. Click on a template file and choose Open.

3. To remove a template file, select the file in the Policy
Template Options dialog box and click on Remove.

4. When you're finished making changes to your policy template configuration, click on OK in the Policy Template
Options dialog box.

FIGURE 6.2
You can install group policies and the System
Policy Editor through the Add/Remove Programs
Control Panel.

To create a new policy file, select New from the File menu. Two
icons appear in the System Policy Editor main window:

◆ Default User

◆ Default Computer

FIGURE 6.3
The Policy Template Options dialog box lets you
load a policy template.

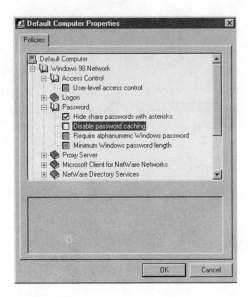

FIGURE 6.4

System policy settings inhabit a hierarchical tree.

The default user settings override settings in the user-specific user.dat file. The default computer settings override settings in the computer-specific system.dat file. Double-click on one of the icons and you see how the system policies settings appear within the System Policy Editor interface. Each icon becomes the top of an Explorer-like tree structure, with individual policy settings in sub-trees beneath the main heading (see Figure 6.4).

The Default User and Default Computer icons provide default policies for all computers that will process the policy file you create. You can also add policies targeted at specific users, computers, or groups.

To add a user, computer, or group icon, pull down the Edit menu in the System Policy Editor main window and select Add User, Add Computer, or Add Group. Windows 98 prompts you for the name of the user, computer, or group and creates an icon with that name to the System Policy Editor window. Double-clicking that icon leads to a collection of policy settings that apply to the user, computer, or group. The user and group icons provide the same collection of policy options available with the Default User icon. The icon for a specific computer provides the same policy options included within the Default Computer icon.

Double-click on any icon to browse the policy tree and configure system policy settings. At the lowest level of the hierarchical structure, you'll find check boxes representing specific policy settings. Each check box has three possible settings:

- ◆ **On (checked box).** Represents the On position. It turns the setting on for all computers processing this policy. If the setting already was on, there is no change; if the setting was off, however, it now is turned on. Checking the Logon Banner option under Default Computer\Network\Logon, for example, turns the banner on for everyone.

- ◆ **Off (clear box).** Represents the Off position. It turns the setting off for all computers processing this policy. If the setting was on, it now is set to the off position; if the value already was off, it remains off.

- ◆ **Neutral (gray box).** Represents a setting that is not affected by the system policy file. In other words, you are going to leave this setting alone. If the value currently is on, it remains on; if the value currently is off, it remains off. Gray is the default for all values in Default User and Default Computer.

The following sections provide a guided tour of settings available through the `Windows.adm` system policy template. Browse through the system policy options and configure policies as required for your system. When you're ready to save the settings to a system policy file, pull down the File menu and select Save As. The Save As dialog box appears. If you're ready to make this policy file operational, enter the name `config.pol`. The System Policy Editor saves the current policy settings to a `config.pol` file. You must locate the `config.pol` file in the appropriate directory (as described earlier in this chapter) so that Windows 98 can find the file when the system starts.

In some cases, it may be useful to save the current policy settings to a different filename and then rename the file `config.pol` when you're ready to implement it. For instance, you may want to develop several system policy files and test them one at a time.

See Exercise 6.2 for a step-by-step procedure of how you can create and save a system policy file.

NOTE **Irreversible Change** An example of a change that is irreversible (if somewhat trivial) is the assignment of one wallpaper to all users. After the wallpaper has been assigned, you cannot return the users' computers to their original wallpaper. You have two options: clear the check box or gray the check box. A clear check box removes or turns off the wallpaper for all users. If you assign a new wallpaper through the Display Control Panel while this policy is in effect, the new wallpaper is turned off at the next logon. A gray check box leaves the wallpaper as it is and does not override any future changes the user makes.

Changing the User Settings in the System Policy Editor

This section examines the user settings that can be adjusted or enforced in a system policy. To access user-specific system policy settings, double-click Default User in the System Policy Editor. Or, create a user or group icon (as described in the preceding section) and double-click on that user or group icon.

The user settings described in the following sections override settings stored in the user's `user.dat` file. The settings described in these sections are found in the default `Windows.adm` system policy template. As described in the previous section, you can also load other policy templates into the System Policy Editor that produce entirely different system policy options. The upcoming sections cover the following user-related system policy subtrees:

◆ Control Panel settings

◆ Desktop settings

◆ File and Printer Sharing settings

◆ Shell settings

◆ System restrictions

FIGURE 6.5
Control Panel settings affect only the major
Control Panel applets.

Control Panel Settings

Control Panel settings enable you to control or restrict access to some important Control Panel applets. Microsoft's default Policy Template file targets the Control Panel applets offered in the following list. You can find the Control Panel settings in the Default User/Windows 98 System/Control Panel subtree (see Figure 6.5).

Restrictions can be applied to the following Control Panel applets:

◆ Display

◆ Network

◆ Passwords

◆ Printers

◆ System

The following subsections examine the effects of each type of restriction.

Display Control Panel Restrictions

The restrictions for the Display Control Panel are as follows:

◆ **Disable Display Control Panel.** This setting disables all access to the Display Control Panel. It is useful if there is a justifiable reason for the user not to have access to any settings in the Display Control Panel. You might want to restrict access to the Wallpaper, Screen Saver, and Appearance tabs if your company has a corporate image policy and wants to enforce it. Restricting the Settings tab prevents users from setting screen resolutions and color-depth values beyond the capabilities of their monitors; these changes usually prompt a support call.

◆ **Hide Background Page.** This setting removes the Background tab from the Display Control Panel. Access to these settings does not tend to cause additional support problems. If, however, your company has created a corporate wallpaper to be implemented on all workstations, for example, this prevents users from changing it.

◆ **Hide Screen Saver Page.** This setting removes the Screen Saver tab from the Display Control Panel. As with the Background tab, access to these settings does not tend to cause support problems. If, however, your company has created a corporate screen saver, for example, you might want to limit access to this tab. Limiting access to this tab also prevents users from disabling the Password Protect option.

◆ **Hide Appearance Page.** This setting removes the Appearance tab from the Display Control Panel. Having access to the color schemes can cause support problems. People with vision problems might require a special color scheme, but most users should be fine using the Windows default scheme. Limiting access to this tab prevents users from creating new color schemes such as the black-on-black color scheme—black menu bar, black menu text, black active window, black inactive windows, and so on.

◆ **Hide Settings Page.** This setting removes the Settings tab from the Display Control Panel. Access to this tab can cause many support problems. If a user decides to create a larger viewing area or greater color depth, the changes can be effected on this tab. Windows 98 attempts to test the settings, but it is not always able to do so. Improperly configured display settings require a trip out to the offending workstation.

Network Control Panel Restrictions

The following settings enable you to modify restrictions to the Network Control Panel:

◆ **Disable Network Control Panel.** This setting prevents all access to the Network Control Panel. Most users do not require any access to the Network Control Panel. If you have a reason to limit access to the Network controls, do not disable them; rather, use the following settings to limit access.

◆ **Hide Identification Page.** This setting hides the Identification properties of the Network Control Panel.

◆ **Hide Access Control Page.** This setting hides the Access Control (user-level versus share-level) properties of the Network Control Panel. For network security on the File and Printer Sharing service, you should implement user-level access control if your network supports it. Preventing users from changing back to the less secure share-level Access Control is a must.

Passwords Control Panel Restrictions

Users often need some form of access to the Passwords Control Panel, although full access is rarely required. The following is a list of restrictions that can applied:

♦ **Disable Passwords Control Panel.** This setting prevents all access to the Passwords Control Panel. Because access to this Control Panel is necessary to change the Windows password and many server passwords, this option is probably too restrictive for most environments.

♦ **Hide Change Passwords Page.** This setting hides the Change Passwords properties of the Passwords Control Panel. This prevents changing passwords, which might be necessary in your environment.

♦ **Hide Remote Administration Page.** This setting hides the Remote Administration properties of the Passwords Control Panel. Remote Administration leaves your computer open for full access to other users across the network, which could lead to users configuring this option incorrectly. In user-level environments, Network Administrators (Domain Admins on Windows NT) automatically are added to the Remote Administration list. In denying access to this tab, you prevent a user from removing people from the administration list.

♦ **Hide User Profiles Page.** This setting hides the User Profiles tab of the Passwords Control Panel. To properly implement system policies, user profiles must be enabled. If you hide this tab, users cannot turn user profiles off in an attempt to bypass security. They also cannot add or remove elements (such as Start menu, program groups, or desktop settings) from the user profile.

Printers Control Panel Restrictions

The following list describes the restrictions that can be placed on the Printers Control Panel:

♦ **Hide General and Details Pages.** This setting hides the General and Details properties for the printer icons in the Printers folder. This prevents users from changing their drivers, assigned printer ports, and spool settings. It also prevents users from switching to a printer you do not want them to use, such as a color printer that costs more per page to operate.

◆ **Disable Deletion of Printers.** This setting prevents the deletion of installed printers. This prevents you from having to repeatedly reinstall printers that have been deleted accidentally.

◆ **Disable Addition of Printers.** This setting prevents the installation of printers. Some users attempt to do what they can without calling for help. If the wrong printer driver is selected for a printer, you can run into several printer problems that can be time consuming to troubleshoot. You also can prevent users from adding the drivers that enable them to use a printer that is more expensive to operate.

System Control Panel Restrictions

The System Control Panel offers more dangers than most other Control Panels. The default policy template, however, does not include an option to disable this Control Panel entirely. The following is a list of restrictions that should be applied to this den of dangers:

◆ **Hide Device Manager Page.** This setting hides the Device Manager properties of the System Control Panel. With one quick press of the Delete key, users can accidentally remove required devices (or at least the drivers) from their workstations, including network cards, drive controllers, and keyboards. Even if devices are not completely deleted, settings on the devices might be modified to leave the devices in an unusable state. This is a major restriction.

◆ **Hide Hardware Profiles Page.** This setting hides the Hardware Profiles properties of the System Control Panel. As you'll learn later in this chapter, hardware profiles enable users to have several sets of device manager settings for different hardware configurations. In some cases, multiple hardware profiles are implemented to prevent users from accessing certain devices at the same time, such as modems and network cards.

◆ **Hide File System Button.** This setting hides the File System button from the Performance properties in the System Control Panel. The File System button invokes the File System Properties dialog box, which you can use to optimize and troubleshoot your hard disk and file system configuration (refer to Chapter 5 for more information about the File System Properties dialog box). Changes to file system settings should be made cautiously to avoid creating new problems and to prevent degradation in system performance.

◆ **Hide Virtual Memory Button.** This setting hides the Virtual Memory button from the Performance properties in the System Control Panel. Improper virtual memory settings can severely hamper system performance.

Desktop Settings

The User Policy desktop settings are fairly straightforward. Many companies implement these settings to force users to comply with corporate-image standards. The following settings can be enforced:

◆ **Wallpaper Name.** Enables you to select a wallpaper for the user.

◆ **Display Method.** Lets you specify whether to center the wallpaper or to stretch the wallpaper to fill the screen.

As mentioned, these settings can help enforce corporate-image standards by implementing specific color schemes and wallpapers. If the Display Control Panel has been restricted, users cannot change any of these settings. If users can access the Display Control Panel, they can change its settings. The settings reset to the corporate standards, however, the next time the user logs in. Because any changes made are lost at the next logon, most users stop changing their settings because it's a losing battle.

File and Printer Sharing Settings

In some cases, you may need to enable File and Printer Sharing even though you don't really need to share files and/or printers from the Windows 98 PC. For instance, you may have installed File and Printer Sharing because you want to enable Remote Administration. Or, you may want your Windows 98 computer to act as a printer server without sharing files. The following two policy entries enable you to keep the service installed but to selectively remove from the users the ability to share files or printers. You'll find these policy settings in the Default User/Windows 98 Network/Sharing subtree:

◆ **Disable File Sharing Controls.** Hides all the file sharing controls from Windows Explorer Folder property sheets.

◆ **Disable Print Sharing Controls.** Hides all the print sharing controls from Windows Explorer Printer property sheets.

Shell Settings

The System Policy Editor provides several security features for the Windows 98 user interface in the form of custom folders and shell restrictions. These settings are located in the User/Windows 98 System/Shell/Custom Folders subtree.

The settings for these two security features can be found in the following two lists. The first list contains the custom folders that can be configured:

◆ **Custom Programs Folder.** This option enables you to specify an alternate location for a folder that contains the contents of the Programs directory. This folder should contain items or shortcuts you want to display in the Programs section of the Start menu. The folder can be stored locally on the workstation, or it can be located on a network drive and accessed through a UNC path such as the following:

`\\NTSERVER\MENUS\FINANCE\STARTMENU`

◆ **Custom Desktop Icons.** This option enables you to specify an alternate location for a folder that contains the contents of the Desktop directory. This folder should contain items or shortcuts you want to display on the desktops of the computers on your network.

◆ **Hide Start Menu Subfolders.** This option enables you to hide the default Start menu folders. If this option is not selected, users see the normal Start menu folders.

◆ **Custom Startup Folder.** This option enables you to specify an alternate location for a folder that contains the contents of the Startup directory. This folder should contain items or shortcuts that you want to start automatically when the desktop shell loads.

NOTE

Turn On the Hide Start Menu Subfolders Option If your policy uses a custom Start menu, Programs folder, or other custom folders, you must turn on the Hide Start Menu Subfolders option. If you do not enable this option, users do not see the effect of your custom folders in their Start menus; they see the normal Start menu.

❖ **Custom Network Neighborhood.** This option enables you to specify an alternate location for a folder that contains the contents of Network Neighborhood. This folder should contain items or shortcuts you want to display in Network Neighborhood. Users are prevented from browsing the entire network for resources; instead, you provide a list of resources for them to use.

❖ **Custom Start Menu.** This option enables you to specify an alternate location for a folder that contains the contents of the Start Menu directory. This folder should contain items or shortcuts you want to display in the root of the Start menu. These items appear at the top of the Start menu.

In addition to custom folders, several restrictions can be applied to the user's desktop shell. The following list describes these restrictions, which are located in the User/Windows 98 System/Shell/Restictions subtree:

❖ **Remove Run Command.** This option removes the Run command from the Start menu. This helps prevent users from running executables for which shortcuts are not provided in the Start menu.

❖ **Remove Folders from Settings on Start Menu.** This option hides the Printers and Control Panel folders from the Settings folder in the Start menu. It also removes the copies of these folders from the My Computer window.

❖ **Remove Taskbar from Settings on Start Menu.** This option hides Taskbar from the Settings folder in the Start menu. It also disables the properties from the menu when you right-click the taskbar.

❖ **Remove Find Command.** This option removes the Find command from the Start menu. As with removing the Run command, this option helps prevent users from running other executables.

❖ **Hide Drives in My Computer.** This option removes all drive icons from My Computer.

❖ **Hide Network Neighborhood.** This option removes Network Neighborhood from the desktop.

◆ **No Entire Network in Network Neighborhood.** If you decide to leave Network Neighborhood on the desktop, you can hide the Entire Network icon to prevent network browsing outside the current workgroup.

◆ **No Workgroup Contents in Network Neighborhood.** If you choose to leave Network Neighborhood on the desktop, you can hide the current workgroup contents. This forces browsing resources through the Entire Network icon.

◆ **Hide All Items on Desktop.** This option removes all icons from the desktop, including both user- and OS-created icons.

◆ **Disable Shut Down Command.** This option removes Shut Down from the Start menu. Because the Shut Down dialog box also is used for logging out, this prevents the user from doing so. If you install Internet Explore 4.x's Shell Enhancements, Log On as a Different User is removed from the dialog box and a new Start Menu Logout command is added.

◆ **Don't Save Settings at Exit.** This option prevents desktop changes from being saved when exiting Windows. This includes any Explorer windows left open.

In addition to the desktop shell settings, additional restrictions are applied to other applications, as you see in the next section.

System Restrictions

System restrictions are put in place to prevent the user from escaping the Windows 98 graphical user interface (GUI) and the controlled environment. If a user is allowed to close the Windows 98 GUI, none of the policy changes you have implemented (such as program restriction) will affect the user. All these restrictions are enforced by either the GUI or EXPLORER.EXE (the default shell). If the user is allowed to leave this environment, you lose control of the user. System restrictions are not limited to the shell itself but to the operating system. System restriction policies are located in the Default User/Windows 98 System/Restrictions subtree. They are as follows:

◆ **Disable Registry Editing Tools.** This option prevents the use of any Registry editing tools on the system.

◆ **Only Run Allowed Windows Applications.** This option lets you specifically define which applications the user can run. The only application you can't exclude is EXPLORER.EXE because it is required as a shell. This means you can prevent applications such as SETUP.EXE or INSTALL.EXE from running on computers.

◆ **Disable MS-DOS Prompt.** This option prevents the DOS prompt from being launched because no shell restrictions take effect in DOS.

◆ **Disable Single-Mode MS-DOS Applications.** This option prevents applications from running in MS-DOS mode, in which the Windows shell is unloaded from memory.

Changing Computer Settings in the Policy File

Computer-specific system policy settings override settings in the `system.dat` Registry file. You can view and implement computer policies by double-clicking on the Default Computer icon in the System Policy Editor window or by creating an icon for a specific computer (by using the Add Computer option in the Edit menu) and double-clicking on the icon for the specific computer. Computer settings are applied to the computer regardless of which user logs on. The upcoming sections describe settings in the following computer-related policy subtrees.

◆ Windows 98 Network settings

◆ Windows 98 System settings

Network Settings

The network settings subtree of the computer policy covers configuration options for most of the Windows 98 network interface. The network settings subtree is covered in the following order:

◆ General Network settings

◆ Logon settings

◆ Microsoft Client for NetWare Networks

◆ Microsoft Client for NetWare Directory Services

◆ Microsoft Client for Windows Networks

◆ Password settings

◆ File and Printer Sharing for Microsoft Networks

◆ Update settings

For step-by-step instructions on creating your own system policy file, see Exercise 6.2.

Configuring General Network Settings

Following are general Network policy categories, each with only a single configuration option:

◆ **Access Control.** This option enables you to require user-level access control for the PC. When checked, you also must specify a security provider and the type of network operating system the security provider is running. This setting overrides access control settings in the Network Control Panel.

◆ **File and Printer Sharing for NetWare Networks.** This option enables you to disable SAP advertising. This stops the server advertising protocol from being used for File and Printer Sharing for NetWare Networks. With this option turned off, your computer advertises itself in the same fashion as the NetWare servers on your network, which can lead to confusion for users.

◆ **Dial-Up Networking.** This option enables you to disable dial-in and stops dial-up server from working on this computer. This can turn out to be a preemptive strike. If the user is not running dial-up server, nothing happens; if the user installs dial-up server, it is disabled at the next restart and logon. The only way to re-enable dial-up server is to reinstall it. The change does not take effect until the next reboot, at which time dial-up server is disabled again.

◆ **Proxy server**. This setting lets you disable the automatic location of a proxy server. This option keeps Windows 98 from accepting proxy server location information provided by a DHCP server. Refer to Chapter 3 for more information about using Windows 98 with a proxy server.

Configuring Logon Settings

The Logon section enables you to set additional warnings and security on Windows 98. This is done through the following settings:

◆ **Logon Banner.** You can set an option that causes a logon banner to display prior to the presentation of the Logon dialog box. This enables you to satisfy legal issues of informing unauthorized users of your system that they are not allowed. You are able to specify both a window title and a message.

◆ **Require Validation by Network for Windows Access.** This option forces users to validate their usernames and passwords before they can access the Windows 98 desktop. If this option is enabled, all desktop computers (and docked laptops) must be successfully logged in by a network server before the desktop shell will be loaded. This setting is not enforced for undocked laptops.

◆ **Don't Show Last User at Logon**. By default, the Logon dialog box shows the username of the last user who logged on. Many believe displaying a valid username reduces security. (Why give an unauthorized user a head start?) This setting requires that the User Name field in the Logon dialog box appear blank.

◆ **Don't Show Logon Progress**. Logon progress information could provide unnecessary hints to an unauthorized user who is looking for a way into the system.

Configuring the Microsoft Client for NetWare Networks

Several configuration changes can be made for the Microsoft Client for NetWare Networks. These configurations are as follows:

◆ **Preferred Server.** This option specifies the name of your preferred NetWare server or the server on which your user account resides.

◆ **Support Long Filenames.** This option enables Windows 98 to determine what to do when working with long filenames on your network. You can opt to support long filenames on NetWare servers version 3.12 and greater, or you can specify support for all NetWare servers that support long filenames, including NetWare 3.11 servers that have had a patch applied.

◆ **Disable Automatic NetWare Login.** This option prevents Windows 98 from using the credentials of the Primary Network Logon to authenticate the user on the NetWare network. This forces separate logins for each client installed on your computer, but it increases security by forcing a user to know all the passwords.

Configuring the Microsoft Client for NetWare Directory Services

The Default Computer/Windows 98 Network/NetWare Directory Services subtree offers several options for configuring Windows 98 NDS settings. You can specify a preferred tree and a default name context. You can also impose restrictions that limit the user's access to the NDS environment. Some of those restrictions are as follows:

◆ Disable Automatic Tree Login

◆ Don't Show Servers that Aren't NDS Objects

◆ Don't Show Server Objects

◆ Don't Show Container Objects

◆ Don't Show Printer Objects

◆ Don't Show Print Queue Objects

◆ Don't Show Volume Objects

Configuring the Microsoft Client for Windows Networks

As with the NetWare client, many configuration changes can be implemented for the Microsoft Client for Windows Networks. You can use these settings to enforce a network configuration for the Windows 98 PC. These configurations are explained in the following list:

◆ **Log On to Windows NT.** This option enables the domain logon for Windows NT networks. If you fill in a domain name, the user can override the domain name during logon, but it reverts back to the one configured in the policy at the next logon.

◆ **Display Domain Logon Validation.** This option informs users whether they were logged on to the domain and what security level they were granted.

◆ **Disable Caching of Domain Password.** This option disables the caching of the domain password in the local password list file (*.PWL).

◆ **Workgroup.** This option specifies a workgroup name for the computer.

◆ **Alternative Workgroup.** This option specifies a workgroup name to use for network browsing. If your workgroup does not have a computer running the Computer Browser service, you can use the browse list from another workgroup.

Configuring Password Settings

Configuring password settings can greatly increase security on your computer. The following settings in the Computer/Windows 98/Passwords subtree explain how Windows 98 works with passwords:

◆ **Hide Share Passwords with Asterisks.** This option applies to passwords listed in the Sharing tab of Folder properties. The default value in Windows 98 is to hide passwords with asterisks. If you disable this option, you can confirm the current password on forgotten shares without having to reset. Unfortunately, other people who with access to your computer also can see the current passwords.

◆ **Disable Password Caching.** This option disables caching of network and other passwords in the local Password List file. If this option is enabled, the Quick Logon feature of the Microsoft network client cannot be used. Unfortunately, this option forces confirmation of a Windows password at every logon.

◆ **Require Alphanumeric Windows Password.** This option forces users to choose Windows passwords that are a combination of letters and numbers. This increases security by forcing users to have more complex Windows passwords.

◆ **Minimum Windows Password Length.** This option sets a minimum length for Windows passwords. This increases security because it prevents people from leaving their Windows password blank.

Configuring File and Printer Sharing for Microsoft Networks

The Default Computer/Windows 98 Network/File and Printer Sharing for Microsoft Networks subtree lets you disable file sharing and/or print sharing for the computer. The options are as follows:

◆ **Disable File Sharing.** This option enables you to turn off file sharing. This differs from the user policy setting Disable File Sharing Controls, which only hides the controls. This option actually stops the service.

◆ **Disable Print Sharing.** This option enables you to turn off print sharing. This differs from the user policy setting Disable Print Sharing Controls, which only hides the controls. This option actually stops the service.

Configuring Update Settings

The Update options enable you to move the active policy file to another location (one other than the default location). You can specify either Automatic or Manual update mode. If you specify Automatic, the policy file is downloaded from the default path (overriding a manual setting in the local Registry). If you specify Manual, you can enter a path for the system policy file. The following list describes the options for updates:

◆ **Remote Update.** This option sets the update method for future downloads of the System policy.

◆ **Update Mode.** This option can be either Automatic (for policies in the default location) or Manual (for policies stored in an alternate location).

◆ **Path for Manual Update.** This option requires a UNC path to the alternate location for the policy file. This enables certain computers to execute a different policy file than the rest.

- ◆ **Display Error Message.** This option enables the display of an error message if the policy is not available on the network when the user logs in.

- ◆ **Load-Balance.** This option is extremely important because it enables Windows 98 to process policy files from the Backup Domain Controller on a Windows NT network. If this option is disabled, Windows 98 processes policy files only from the Primary Domain Controller. This can cause slower logons and more network traffic.

This concludes the Network settings that can be configured as part of the policy file. The next section examines changes in the System settings.

System Settings

System settings enable you to configure basic options for Windows 98, including various methods of starting applications at boot time. The following list describes these settings:

- ◆ **Enable User Profiles.** This option enables user profiles. Before any settings in the User tree of the system policy are enabled, user profiles must be turned on. This option turns user profiles on and keeps turning them back on if users turn them off.

- ◆ **Network Path for Windows Setup.** This option enables you to specify a UNC path to the network location of the Windows 98 Setup program. This location is used when Windows 98 needs to load new drives instead of prompting for the Windows 98 CD.

- ◆ **SNMP**. For companies that use Simple Network Management Protocol (SNMP), Windows 98 offers a series of SNMP policy settings that configure communities, managers, traps, and Internet MIB contact information.

- ◆ **Programs to Run.** This option specifies a list of applications to run after the Windows shell loads. This is similar to including items in the Startup folder or to adding Load or Run lines to win.ini. The list of applications is stored in the Registry in the HKEY_LOCAL_MACHINE\SOFTWARE\MICROSOFT\WINDOWS\ CURRENTVERSION\RUN key. The applications are executed in order of Value Name.

◆ **Run Once.** This option specifies a list of applications to run before the Windows shell loads. These applications run one at a time, and the Windows shell does not load until the last application has finished. The list of applications is stored in the Registry in the `HKEY_LOCAL_MACHINE\SOFTWARE\MICROSOFT\WINDOWS\CURRENTVERSION\RUNONCE` key. After each application completes, its Registry entry is removed so it does not execute the next time Windows 98 loads. If you add these entries to the System policy, each time Windows 98 loads the policy (at each logon), it re-adds the entries to the Run Once key in the Registry.

◆ **Run Services.** This option specifies the list of applications to execute as services when Windows 98 loads. These applications start up first when Windows 98 loads. They execute when the Logon dialog box displays.

◆ **Install Device Drivers**. This subtree lets you specify that Windows 98 should automatically check for a valid digital signature when installing a device driver. See Chapter 8, "Troubleshooting Windows 98," for more information about digital signatures and Windows 98's Signature Verification tool.

◆ **Windows Update**. The Windows Update subtree lets you disable or override settings related to Windows 98's Windows Update feature. (See Chapter 8.) You can disable the Windows update feature, or you can specify a different local or Internet Windows Update site.

NOTE

Run, Run Once, Run Services   The Run, Run Once, and Run Services entries are similar. The difference lies in when and how they execute:

· **Run Services.** This option starts first and executes at the same time the user logon screen appears. All services start, and you do not have to close or exit the services to continue.

· **Run Once.** These commands execute one at a time, in order, after the logon is complete. You have to exit each Run Once command before the next one is called. Run Services continue to run through this entire process.

· **Run.** These commands execute after all Run Once commands are finished and the desktop shell is loaded. These commands all execute at the same time. Run Services continue to run through this process.

System Policy Settings

REVIEW BREAK

System policies are a very powerful tool for controlling the Windows 98 user environment. The preceding sections presented a guided tour of system policy settings available with Windows 98's `Windows.adm` policy template. You won't need to memorize all these settings for the Windows 98 exam, but the preceding discussion should give you an idea of the kinds of changes you can make to the system through system policies. Many system policy settings mirror Registry settings available through the Control Panel applications, although a system policy setting is different from a Registry setting in that a system policy setting will override any Registry changes when the system restarts. A few important settings to which you may want to give some special attention are as follows:

◆ **Password restrictions.** In the Computer/Windows 98 Network/Password subtree. You can disable password caching (refer to Chapter 3), require an alphanumeric password (in this case, *alphanumeric* means the password must contain *both* letters and numbers), and set a minimum password length.

◆ **Logon policies.** In the Computer/Logon subtree. The most significant is the setting Require Validation from Network for Windows Access, which forces the user to undergo network authentication before accessing Windows. Refer to Chapter 3 for more information about Windows 98 logon.

◆ **Custom folders.** In the User/Windows 98 System/Shell/ Custom Folders subtree. You can create custom Start Menu folders, desktop icons, and Network Neighborhood.

◆ **User restrictions.** In the User/Windows 98 System/Shell/ Restrictions subtree. You can remove items from the user interface, such as the Run and Find commands. You can also hide other items, such as Network Neighborhood, drives in My Computer, and all desktop items. Finally, you can disable the Shut Down command.

◆ **Control Panels.** In the User/Windows 98 System/Control Panel subtree. You can disable the Display, Network, Passwords. Printers, or System Control Panels or you can hide key elements of these Control Panels.

◆ **System restrictions.** In the User/Windows 98 System/ Restrictions subtree. You can prevent the user from accessing Registry editing tools. You can also disable the MS-DOS prompt, disable single-mode MS-DOS applications, or prevent the user from running any Windows applications except the applications you specify.

Creating Policies for Users, Groups, and Computers

As mentioned earlier in this chapter, when you create a policy file, you have the option of adding individual icons for users, groups of users, or computers on your network. To add additional entries to your policy, choose Add User, Add Computer, or Add Group from the Edit menu. If your system is configured for user-level access control, you can browse a list of users, groups, and computers; otherwise, you have to type the name of the user, group, or computer.

Windows 98 follows a particular order when reading the policy file:

1. Windows 98 checks whether the user is a member of any groups it has entries for. If the user is a member of some groups, all groups he is a member of are processed in order of the groups' priorities.

2. Windows 98 then checks to see whether there is an entry for the user logging in. If there is an entry for the user, Windows 98 applies the changes for that user.

3. If there are no entries for that user or no groups are processed, the entry for Default User is applied.

4. After applying the user policy, Windows 98 applies a computer policy.

5. If there is an entry for your current computer name, it will be applied; otherwise, the entry for Default Computer is applied.

There is no way to create policies for groups of computers. All computers on the same domain or server use the same default policy.

If some or all of the computers on the network are not processing the groups in the policy file, make sure group policies were installed on the client computers following the procedure described earlier in this chapter. If group policies were not installed, clients should be processing the default user policy. If this policy is not being implemented, check the location of the policy file and its structure. The priority of the groups is determined by their order in the Group Priority dialog box under the Options menu. The list is processed from the bottom up; conflicting settings in the highest group override those from lower groups. Only policy entries for groups of which the user is a member are applied.

Using Policy Template Files

A system policies template file contains entries that will appear as system policy options when you load the template in the System Policy Editor. As this chapter has already described, the default system policy template is the template file `Windows.adm`, stored in the `Windows\INF` directory. The template file is a text file with a particular structure. You can use a text editor to create your own template file that refers to specific Registry settings you'd like to override. The following list describes some keywords and their use within a policy file. You won't need to memorize this list for the Windows 98 exam, but the following keywords will give you an idea of the format of system policy template files:

- ◆ **CLASS.** This is the largest section in the policy files. The class must be either User or Machine.

- ◆ **!! (two exclamation marks).** This identifies the next word as a variable or string that must be defined in the STRINGS section at the end of the policy file. Strings are defined with the following structure:

  ```
  StringName="String value"
  ```

- ◆ **CATEGORY and END CATEGORY.** These keywords enclose each category in the policy editor structure. These are the expanding branches of the file and can be nested within each other as follows:

  ```
  CATEGORY !!CategoryOne
        CATEGORY !!CategoryTwo
          CATEGORY !!CategoryThree
          ...
          ...
          END CATEGORY  ; CategoryThree
      END CATEGORY    ; CategoryTwo
  END CATEGORY      ; CategoryOne
  ```

- ◆ **KEYNAME.** Each category contains a KEYNAME or Registry key path that starts immediately after HKEY_LOCAL_MACHINE or HKEY_CURRENT_USER. This determines where in the Registry changes should be made. The following is an example of a KEYNAME:

  ```
  KEYNAME
  System\CurrentControlSet\Services\Control\FileSystem
  ```

- ◆ **POLICY.** This is used to define the check boxes that are displayed.

◆ **VALUENAME.** This is the name of the Registry value you want to change. VALUENAME always is contained within a PART.

◆ **PART.** This defines individual items displayed in the Settings section of the Policy Editor at the bottom of the window. The following is an example of a PART statement:

```
PART !!CPL_Display_Disable CHECKBOX
    VALUENAME NoDispCPL
END PART
```

PARTS can be of the following types:

- **TEXT.** Used for display text. The following is an example of this PART type:

  ```
  PART !!NetworkTourPath_TIP TEXT END PART
  ```

- **NUMERIC.** Used for values to be written to the Registry as REG_DWORD types. The following is an example of this PART type:

  ```
  PART !!SearchMode1 NUMERIC
      VALUENAME SearchMode
      MIN 0 MAX 7 DEFAULT 0
      END PART
  ```

- **DROPDOWNLIST.** Used for list boxes and values. The following is an example of this PART type:

  ```
  PART !!MyPolicy DROPDOWNLIST
      VALUENAME ValueToBeChanged
        ITEMLIST
          NAME "One" VALUE NUMERIC 1
          NAME "Two" VALUE NUMERIC 2
          NAME "Three" VALUE NUMERIC 3
          NAME "Four" VALUE NUMERIC 4
        END ITEMLIST
  END PART
  ```

- **COMBOBOX.** Used for list boxes with a text field that can be overridden. Suggestions in the drop-down list are in the following format:

  ```
  SUGGESTIONS
      Red Yellow Pink "Royal Blue"
  END SUGGESTIONS
  ```

- **EDITTEXT.** Used for string data to be written to the Registry with a type of REG_SZ.

- **REQUIRED.** Can be added to make data entry mandatory.

- **EXPANDABLETEXT.** Used for string data that includes replaceable strings such as %SYSTEMROOT%. This is stored in the Registry with a type of REG_EXPAND_SZ.

- **CHECKBOX.** Used for values set to 0 or 1. The following is an example of this:

```
PART !!DomainLogonConfirmation CHECKBOX
     KEYNAME Network\Logon
     VALUENAME DomainLogonMessage
END PART
```

PARTS can contain the following values:

- **MAXLEN.** Used to set a maximum length for typed strings.

- **MIN and MAX.** Used to set boundaries on NUMERIC data types.

- **DEFAULT.** Used to set a default value for text or numeric data types.

- **DEFCHECKED.** Causes check boxes to be enabled by default.

- **VALUEON and VALUEOFF.** Similar to CHECKBOX, except this is used when ON and OFF values are not 1 and 0. The following is an example:

```
POLICY !!HideDrives
     VALUENAME "NoDrives"
     VALUEON NUMERIC 67108863  ; low 26 bits on
➥ (1 bit per drive)
END POLICY
```

- ◆ **ACTIONLISTON and ACTIONLISTOFF.** Used to display alternating action lists if a check box is on or off.

If you want to know more about the structure of template files, consult the *Windows 98 Resource Kit*.

SYSTEM POLICY EDITOR REGISTRY MODE

You can use the System Policy Editor to edit the Registry directly (as opposed to specifying system policy settings that will override the Registry). When you are using the System Policy Editor in Registry mode, the settings are not saved to a policy file but are instead saved directly to the Registry.

To operate the System Policy Editor in Registry mode, pull down the File menu and select Open Registry. The System Policy Editor appears the same in Registry mode as it does in Policy mode. You'll see a computer icon for computer settings and a user icon for user settings.

You can also edit other computers' Registries using the System Policy Editor in Registry mode. Select Connect in the File menu and enter the name of a Windows 95/98 computer. Note that this is a Remote Administration function. The remote Registry service should be installed on both PCs, and the remote PC should have Remote Administration enabled in the Remote Administration tab of the Passwords Control Panel. See Chapter 5 for more information about enabling Remote Administration.

NOTE **A Registry Interface** When you're working in Registry mode, the System Policy Editor doesn't really have anything to do with system policies. Instead, it acts as a user interface to the Registry, and is thus similar to Control Panel or Registry Editor.

WORKING WITH HARDWARE PROFILES

Create hardware profiles.

A *hardware profile* is a bundle of configuration information related to the hardware installed on your PC. A hardware profile provides Windows 98 with information on which hardware drivers should load at startup.

The classic scenario for hardware profiles is a laptop computer that is sometimes in a docked state (attached to a home docking station) and sometimes in an undocked state. Through hardware profiles, you can define a separate set of hardware components for the docked laptop and the undocked laptop.

Hardware profiles also can be used on desktop computers to enable certain hardware components. You can disable your network card, for example, when you want to use your modem; this might follow some strict security rule on your network.

You always have at least one hardware profile, usually called Original Configuration. To create a new hardware profile, choose the Hardware Profiles tab in the System Control Panel (see Figure 6.6).

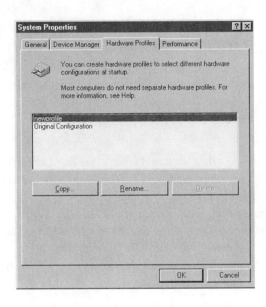

FIGURE 6.6

You can create hardware profiles using the Hardware Profiles tab in the System Properties Control Panel.

To create a new profile, select an existing profile (such as Original Configuration) and click Copy. (You can also rename an existing profile, as well as delete a hardware profile, as you can see in Figure 6.6).

To configure the new hardware profile, log off, add or remove any hardware, and then log on again. You should see a dialog box asking which hardware profile you'd like to use. Choose the new hardware profile. (Windows 98 will attempt to determine which hardware profile to use based on the hardware information it accumulates at startup. If Windows 98 can't determine which profile to use, the dialog box will appear, asking you to choose a profile.) After you have logged on with the new profile, Windows 98 will already have adjusted to configuration of Plug and Play hardware available at startup. Additional changes to your hardware configuration will be saved with your hardware profile.

See Exercise 6.3 for a step-by-step description of how to implement hardware profiles in Windows 98.

You can use Device Manager to disable or remove hardware from the active hardware profile. (See Chapter 4, "Installing and Configuring Hardware," for more information about Device Manager.) The Device Manager tab of the System Control Panel is illustrated in Figure 6.7.

NOTE

Hardware Profiles and Plug and Play Microsoft insists that if a portable computer that will support two docking states is fully Plug and Play compliant, you won't need hardware profiles because the computer will be able to ascertain complete device information at startup.

EXAM TIP

Coverage Alert The distinction between disabling and removing a device is important, and you may see a question on this distinction in the Windows 98 MCSE exam.

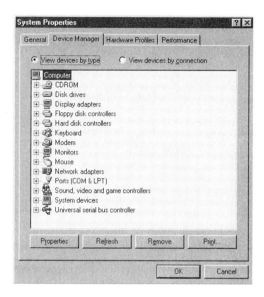

FIGURE 6.7
You can use Device Manager to enable or disable hardware.

The Properties dialog box (click on Properties to reach this dialog box) for each non-essential device includes a small subtree called Device Usage. This section lets you disable the device for the active hardware profile. In some cases, you may also have the option of *removing* the device from the active hardware profile (see Figure 6.8).

Note the distinction between disabling and removing a device. If you *disable* a non-Plug and Play device, you prevent the device from loading when the system starts, but you do not free the resources assigned to the device. If you *remove* a non-Plug and Play device, you prevent the driver from loading and also free any resources assigned to the device. According to Microsoft, resources are freed automatically when you disable a Plug and Play device.

When deleting hardware profiles, you cannot delete your current profile. Regardless of which profile you use, your data remains the same. It is important to keep it safe by backing it up.

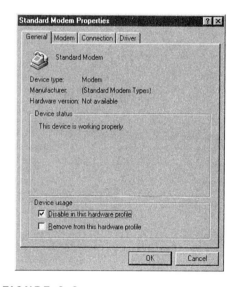

FIGURE 6.8
A Device Properties dialog box offers Device Usage settings.

CASE STUDY: ENKLIN COLLEGE

ESSENCE OF THE CASE

Here are the essential elements of the case:

- Access to applications should be based on a student's major, year in college, and courses the student is involved with.

- Two Windows 98 computers should be configured to run only Microsoft Office and Internet Explorer.

- Each student at the college has his own logon identification to the Windows NT Domain. Additionally, each student is a member of a global group designated as his year in college, another group as his declared major, and groups for each course he attended.

- Server Operators and a global group called Troubleshooters should be exempt from any machine restrictions.

SCENARIO

Enklin College, a small community college in middle Tennessee, would like to control its students' ability to perform certain actions on the computers in the public lab.

ANALYSIS

System policies would need to be created based on students' years in school, majors, and courses they attended. Group priority would have to be adjusted based on the resources and activities granted to the students through the policies.

The two Windows 98 machines that are to run only Microsoft Office and Internet Explorer would need computer policies so that no matter who logs on, those machines would have the same look and feel for each user.

Server Operators and Troubleshooters would require their own system policy to allow them to be exempt from any system policies on the computers throughout the domain.

CHAPTER SUMMARY

KEY TERMS

- user profiles
- roaming profiles
- local profiles
- mandatory profiles

This chapter described some important Windows 98 features that you can use to configure and manage the user environment. You learned about the following features:

◆ **User profiles.** A *user profile* is a collection of user-specific settings that create a custom user environment. With user profiles, each user can have his own wallpaper, shortcuts, and Start menu. A network-based user profile, called a *roaming profile*, is downloaded to the Windows 98 machine at startup.

CHAPTER SUMMARY

Roaming profiles allow the user to *roam* to other computers on the network and still receive the customized user profile settings at startup. A *mandatory profile* is like a roaming profile except that a user cannot resave profile settings—the system reverts to a preconfigured profile each time it starts.

◆ **System policies.** *System policies* are configuration settings that override settings defined in the Registry files system.dat and user.dat. You can use system policies to restrict a user's access to the operating system. For instance, you can hide Control Panel applications or disable Registry editing tools. You can also use system policies to enforce compliance with password policies or to preconfigure settings for network services. Windows 98 system policies are saved in a file called config.pol. By default, config.pol should be located in the Netlogon$ share of the primary domain controller. The System Policy Editor application lets you configure system policy settings.

◆ **Hardware profiles.** A *hardware profile* is a description of a hardware environment. A Windows 98 computer can have more than one hardware profile, which means that it can operate from within more than one operating environment. The best example of when to use a hardware profile is a laptop computer that is sometimes attached to a desktop docking station and sometimes operates without external devices. Windows 98 attempts to choose the correct hardware profile automatically at startup. If Windows 98 cannot determine which hardware profile to use, it prompts you to choose a hardware profile. On a fully Plug and Play–compliant system, hardware profiles may not be necessary (Microsoft says they *aren't* necessary) because the system will respond automatically to changes in the hardware environment.

System policies, user profiles, and hardware profiles are powerful tools for customizing the user environment and shaping Windows 98 to fill the needs of your organization.

KEY TERMS (CONTINUED)

- system policies
- user policies
- group policies
- computer policies
- hardware profiles
- Device Manager

APPLY YOUR KNOWLEDGE

Exercises

6.1 Implementing User Profiles

This exercise shows you how to implement user profiles. It is based on a standalone workstation, so all profiles and users are local to the Microsoft Windows 98 machine. If your workstation is configured to log on to a domain or NetWare server, you will want to add two test users to your NetWare server or NT domain.

Estimated Time: 25 minutes

1. From Start choose Settings, Control Panel.

2. In Control Panel, choose Passwords.

3. From the Passwords applet, choose the User Profiles tab. From this tab, choose the option that allows users to customize their preferences and desktop settings.

4. At the bottom of the User Profiles tab, select both options: Include Desktop Icons and Include Start Menu and Program Groups.

5. Choose OK and reboot your PC.

6. After you reboot, log on to Windows 98 as Fred.

7. It is noted that you have not logged on to this PC before; you are prompted to save your settings. Choose Yes.

8. Right-click on your desktop and choose Properties.

9. Change your screensaver, color scheme, and wallpaper settings for Fred and then exit the Display applet.

10. From the Start button menu, choose Log of Fred.

11. Now log on as Sally. Again, as a new user, you are prompted to save your settings. Choose Yes.

12. Notice that Fred's settings are not displayed. Log off as Sally and log back on as Fred.

13. Notice that Fred's environment is restored.

6.2 Enabling System Policies on Windows 98

System policies can be used to manage users, groups, and computers in Windows 98. This exercise will create a local system policy for a test user on your Windows 98 machine. Before implementing policies, recall that profiles must be enabled on your Windows 98 machine. To enable profiles, open the Passwords applet in Control Panel and choose the Profiles tab. Select the following option: Users Can Customize Their Preferences and Desktop Settings. Windows Switches to Your Personal Settings When You Log On. You can select either one or two of the profile sub-settings for this exercise.

Estimated Time: 30 minutes

1. From the Start menu, select Programs, Accessories, System Tools, System Policy Editor. If System Policy Editor is not installed on your PC, install System Policy Editor using the procedure described earlier in this chapter.

2. When the System Policy Editor opens, create a new policy file by choosing File, New Policy.

3. The Default User and Computer are displayed. Add a test user to the system policy. From the Edit menu, select Add User, or click the New User Button from the toolbar.

4. The Add User dialog box appears. Because this policy is local, you can make up a new user that will log on to this system. Type in the name Sally and then click OK.

APPLY YOUR KNOWLEDGE

5. Double-click on Sally to display her account properties.

6. Click the plus sign (+) by Windows 98 System and several sub-categories will appear. From the list of sub-categories, click the plus sign by Shell.

7. Click the plus sign by Restrictions. From the list of available restrictions, confirm that there is a check mark in the following boxes:

   • Remove Run command

   • Remove Find command

   • No Entire Network in Network Neighborhood

   • Don't save settings on exit

> **Three Checkbox Settings** You may
> have noticed that a possible selection
> box originates as gray. When you click
> it, a check mark appears; if you click
> the box again, the check mark is gone
> and the box remains empty. The three
> settings are as follows: Gray (ignore
> this setting), check (implement this
> value), and clear or empty (clear this
> entry from the policy).

8. Click the minus sign (–) by Restrictions to hide that menu.

9. Click the plus sign by Control Panel and then the plus sign by Display.

10. Check the Restrict Display applet. You do not want Sally to change her display settings or her background page, so you should check the Hide Settings page and the Hide Background page

from the options at the bottom of the Policies dialog box for the Display applet.

11. Click the minus sign next to Display to hide that category.

12. Click the plus sign next to Network and check the Restrict Network applet to view its contents.

13. You do not want Sally to change anything in the Network applet so you should check the Display Control Panel option at the bottom of the Sally Properties.

14. Click the minus sign by Network and then click the plus sign by Passwords. Click the Restrict Passwords Control Panel to view its contents.

15. Check the Hide Remote Administration page and the Hide User Profiles page to prevent Sally from accessing these entries.

16. Click the minus symbol next to the Passwords applet, and then click the plus symbol by the Systems entry. Check the Restrict Systems Control Panel option to view its contents.

17. Check the following to restrict Sally from these entries:

   • Hide Hardware Profiles page

   • Hide File System button

   • Hide Virtual Memory button

18. Click the minus sign to Hide the System entries.

19. Click the plus sign by Desktop Display. Assign Sally the wallpaper display of bubbles.bmp and the color scheme of The Reds.

20. Click the minus sign to hide the Display properties, and then click the plus sign to view the Restrictions.

APPLY YOUR KNOWLEDGE

21. Check the Disable Registry Editing tools to keep Sally out of the Registry Editor and the System Policy Editor.

22. Click OK to approve your changes to the Sally Properties.

23. To save the policy, choose Save from the File menu, or click the disk button on the toolbar. The policy file should be saved in your Windows directory. The filename should be called `config.pol`.

24. After saving the file, you must update the Registry to alert it that the system policy file will be retrieved from the local machine rather than from a server. To do this, enter Registry mode by choosing Open Registry from the File menu.

25. The Default Computer and Default User icons are displayed. These icons represent the user and computer parts of the Registry that can be managed through the System Policy Editor.

> **WARNING**
>
> **Careful with the Registry!** Be extremely careful when editing the Registry through the System Policy Editor. It is possible to lock even yourself out of the Registry or cause damage to your system configuration if you incorrectly edit the Registry. It is recommended to make a backup copy of the Registry before making any changes to it.

26. Double-click the local computer to open its properties.

27. Click the plus sign by Windows 98 Network to view its properties. Click the plus sign by the Update category.

28. Check the Remote Update selection. In the Update mode, confirm that Manual (use specific path) is selected.

29. In the path for Manual Update, type in the path and the name of your policy file. For example, if your Windows directory is on drive C:, the path would read `C:\windows\config.pol`. It's crucial that this path be correct or else the policy file will not work.

30. Click OK. Close the System Policy Editor. When you are asked whether you want to save your changes to the Registry, confirm that you do.

31. Log off your computer and then log back on as Sally. Because Sally has never logged on to this computer before, you must confirm that "Sally" wants to keep her own preferences for this machine.

32. Notice that Sally's desktop appears with the `bubbles.bmp` and her color scheme is The Reds.

33. Click on the Start menu and notice that the Run and Find commands are gone as you specified in the system policy.

34. Right-click the desktop and choose Properties. The Display applet appears. Notice that the only tabs that are available are the Screensaver and the Appearance tab.

35. Right-click My Computer and then click the Performance tab. Click on Virtual Memory and then choose Let Me Specify My Own Virtual Memory Settings. Choose OK. Although Windows warns you that this is not recommended, choose Yes to continue.

36. In this policy you want to disable the Virtual Memory button. Click on the Virtual Memory button again and note that your changes have not been saved.

APPLY YOUR KNOWLEDGE

37. Log off as Sally and return as your regular user account. You can delete the `config.pol` from your Windows directory now. Also, clear the Registry Manual Update setting you set in step 29.

6.3   Creating a Hardware Profile on Windows 98

Hardware profiles allow you to use your Windows 98 machine in different environments. This exercise will show you how to create a hardware profile. This exercise will treat your Windows 98 machine as if it were a portable laptop. You will need one Windows 98 machine and a network card installed on your computer. If you do not have a network card, you can use a modem, sound card, or another device in your system.

Time Estimate: 15 minutes

1. From the Start menu, select Settings, Control Panel.

2. Open the Systems applet and choose Hardware Profiles.

3. Click Original Configuration, and click Copy.

4. In the Copy To field, name this profile Off the Network.

5. Close the System applet and the Control Panel and restart your machine.

6. When Windows 98 restarts, select the Off the Network profile.

7. Open the System applet again in Control Panel and choose the Device Manager tab.

8. Click the plus sign (+) next to the Network Adapter category and select your network adapter card.

9. Open the properties for your network adapter card.

10. From the Device Usage section, click the option to disable this device in this hardware profile.

11. Choose OK and exit the System applet.

12. Restart your computer and choose the Off the Network profile.

13. Test your profile by trying to use your network adapter card.

14. To delete the profile you've created, restart with the original configuration.

15. Open the Systems applet and choose the Hardware Profile tab.

16. Select the Off the Network profile and click Delete.

17. Confirm that you want to delete the profile and exit the Systems applet.

Review Questions

1. What is a user profile?

2. In a Windows NT domain, where are user profiles stored?

3. What are system policies?

4. In a NetWare environment, where are system policies stored?

5. Can policies be used to control a computer that is not on a network?

6. If a user is a member of more than one group in a domain and there is a policy for each group, what will happen?

APPLY YOUR KNOWLEDGE

7. What is a hardware profile?

8. What tool allows the creation of hardware profiles?

Exam Questions

1. Monique, the CEO of your company, is very upset that her user profile on her Windows 98 machine does not follow her to every Windows 98 computer she logs on to throughout your network. Which of the following may be a cause for the problem? Choose all that apply.

    A. Monique is not logging on to the network. If she does not log on to the computer, her roaming profile is not downloaded to that computer.

    B. Monique is logging on to public computers on which you have very strict computer policies that set up the environment for all users logging on to those computers.

    C. Monique is logging on to computers that do not have profiles enabled, so her profile is not downloaded to these computers.

    D. Monique is logging on to computers that are out of synch with the server's time. When she logs on to a computer whose time stamp is out of synch with the server's time, her profile is not uploaded to the server. You would need to create a logon script that synchronizes the Windows 98 system time with the NT domain controller's time.

2. Your boss comes to you with this problem: On his home computer, his kids keep getting into his checkbook software and playing with all the numbers. In addition, they are changing his colors and icons so each time he uses the computer he has trouble finding his applications. He wants to know if there is anything that you can do to help him alleviate the problem. Of the following, which is the best solution?

    A. Enable profiles for his home computer. This way the kids can have their own colors and icons, and your boss can keep his.

    B. Enable mandatory profiles for the kids; set up the Start menu so that only the applications they need to be involved with appear. This way the kids cannot change the environment or tinker with applications that they shouldn't be involved with.

    C. Enable system policies for the kids. With system policies, you are forced to use user profiles, so the kids will have their own colors and icons. Through policies, you can restrict the kids from running applications that they do not need to be involved with—even those that are not part of the Start menu.

    D. Enable a computer policy. With a computer policy, you could force the machine to look and feel the same for all users that will use the home computer.

3. You are the administrator for a Windows NT domain. Your clients include Windows NT Workstation and Windows 98 machines. You have enabled user profiles for your Windows 98 machines and completed the user profile path through User Manager for Domains. All of the profiles seem to be working on the NT Workstations, but not on the Windows 98 machines. You verify that profiles are enabled on the Windows 98 computers. What could be the problem?

APPLY YOUR KNOWLEDGE

A. User profiles for Windows 98 clients are actually stored in the users' home folders. You must create a home folder for each user.

B. Profiles for Windows 98 clients are not compatible with Windows NT Workstation. You must manually change the profile names from `ntuser.dat` to `user.dat` for each client.

C. To use profiles with Windows 98 through a Windows NT domain, you have to use the Profiles tab through the System applet with Windows NT Server.

D. Users have only read permission to their Profile folders on Windows NT Server. You need to change the permission to write so that the users can uploaded their changed profiles to the Windows NT Server.

4. You have created four system policy files, one each for the Sales, Marketing, Finance, and Managers groups. You have saved the policy files as Sales, Marketing, Finance, and Managers. For some reason, the policy files do not seem to be working. What do you suspect is the problem?

A. You do not need to create multiple policy files. Simply create one file called `config.pol` and add users and groups to that one policy file.

B. Policy files must be saved in the Policy share. You probably have not saved these policy files in the correct location.

C. You must save multiple policy files in the `Netlogon$` share as `Ntconfig1.pol`, `Ntconfig2.pol`, and so on.

D. You must save your Windows 98 policy in the `Winlogon` share on the PDC and enable load balancing for Windows 98.

5. You are the network administrator of a college. You would like to set up system policies that would restrict users' access to various programs and Control Panel applets based on their year in school. Your network consists of Windows NT Server as a PDC, three BDCs, two application servers, and all Windows 98 clients in the classrooms. There is one computer lab in the library that is open to all students from your school, students from a neighboring community college, and high school seniors who are enrolled in a program with your college. You need security in this lab as well. Of the following, which provides the best solution?

A. Create mandatory profiles, which restrict users from doing certain events on your computers.

B. Create computer policies, which restrict users from doing certain events on your computers.

C. Create system policies for each user in the domain, which restrict what access a user has to parts of the system.

D. Create system policies based on groups of users in the domain, which restrict what access they have to activities on the system.

6. You have created a computer policy that specifies a logon message for a Windows 98 machine called Workstation5. The policy is saved on your Windows NT Domain Controller. You now decide that you do not want the logon message on the Windows 98 computer. What is the correct solution?

A. Delete the system policy file off the Windows NT Server.

B. Delete the system policy file off the Windows 98 machine.

APPLY YOUR KNOWLEDGE

C. Edit the system policy off the server to remove the logon message.

D. Reinstall Windows 98.

7. You have created a system policy that controls the Start menu's Programs menu items. The system policy is saved on your domain controller. However, you now have two Programs groups on your Start menu. What do you suspect is the problem?

A. You need to restart your Windows 98 machine.

B. You need to restart your Windows NT Domain Controller.

C. You need to check the option to hide the Start menu subfolders from the Custom Folders option in the System Policy Editor.

D. You need to create a template that removes the Programs folder.

8. You are supporting the travelling sales staff. Several members of the sales staff report that when they are on the road they receive an error message about not being able to find a domain controller. They do not receive this message when they are in the office. What is causing the problem and what can you do to resolve it?

A. They are not on the LAN, so a domain controller cannot be found. Create a user profile to eliminate the network card usage when they are on the road.

B. They are not on the LAN, so a domain controller cannot be found. Create a hardware profile to eliminate the network card usage when they are on the road.

C. They are not on the LAN, so they will not be able to access system resources. Create a user profile that will allow access to system resources.

D. They are not on the LAN, so they will not be able to access system resources. Create a hardware profile that will allow access to system resources.

9. Martin has created a hardware profile for his machine that disables his sound card when he is on the road. He now decides that he would like to make this hardware profile his default startup profile. How can this be done?

A. Martin must move the hardware profile up in the list of hardware profiles through the System applet.

B. Martin must change the default profile Original Configuration to disable his sound card.

C. Martin must edit his system BIOS.

D. Martin must edit the `HKEY_LOCAL_MACHINE\ SYSTEM\CurrentControlSet\HardwareProfiles` setting.

10. You have created a local computer policy for your standalone Windows 98 machine. Your policy does not seem to be working. What do you suspect is the problem?

A. You cannot create system policies on standalone Windows 98 machines.

B. You must change the update category to a local path rather than the default path, which is to a server.

APPLY YOUR KNOWLEDGE

C. You have to edit the Registry to point the machine to the local system policy.

D. You have to create a hardware profile with a disabled network adapter card driver.

Answers to Review Questions

1. A user profile is a collection of settings that define how the computer looks and operates when a specific user logs on. User profile information is stored in a profile directory, either on a network share (in the case of a roaming or mandatory profile) or on a local computer. The profile directory contains the user.dat file (called user.man in the case of a mandatory profile) and other subfolders, files, and shortcuts, depending on the configuration settings you define in the User Profiles tab of the Passwords Control Panel. (For more information, refer to the section "Setting Up User Environments Through User Profiles.")

2. For Windows 98 users, user profiles on a Windows NT domain are stored in the user's home directory. (For more information, refer to the section "Setting Up User Environments Through User Profiles.")

3. System policies are settings that restrict users' activities on a system by overriding Registry settings at startup. Policies can control individual users, groups of users, or specific computers on a network. (For more information, refer to the section "Setting Up User Environments Through System Policies.")

4. System policies on a NetWare Server are stored in the sys\public directory. (For more information, refer to the section "Setting Up User Environments Through System Policies.")

5. Policies can be saved locally to control computers that are not on a network. The update path would have to be configured to reflect that policy is saved locally instead of on a remote server. (For more information, refer to the section "Setting Up User Environments Through System Policies.")

6. The Group Priority option will process the policy based on the order of the groups as designated through the group priority setting with the System Policy Editor. (For more information, refer to the section "Setting Up User Environments Through System Policies.")

7. A hardware profile allows a Windows 98 machine to be started with different hardware configurations. For example, a laptop may need a network card drive while logged onto the LAN in an office, but will not need the network card driver while away from the LAN. (For more information, refer to the section "Working with Hardware Profiles.")

8. Hardware profiles are created through the System applet in Control Panel. (For more information, refer to the section "Working with Hardware Profiles.")

APPLY YOUR KNOWLEDGE

Answers to Exam Questions

1. **A, B, C, D.** If Monique does not log on to the network, her profile will not be downloaded to her.

   If you have a computer policy enabled on a computer, the computer policy will override all users who are logging on to that computer.

   If the computer Monique is using is not configured to accept profiles, her profile will not be downloaded from the server.

   If the computers' time is incorrect, then the profile could be ignored when uploading to the server, making any changes null and void on Monique's profile, which is still sitting on the server. The next time she logs on to another PC, her profile would appear to be out of date. A logon script should be created that would set the local time of the Windows 98 machine with a time server. (For more information, refer to the section "Setting Up User Environments Through User Profiles.")

2. **C.** By enabling a system policy for the kids, you could create both the profile and the restrictions to affect only the kids and keep them out of places they should not be in the system. (For more information, refer to the section "Setting Up User Environments Through User Profiles.")

3. **A.** Through User Manager for Domains. It appears that all you must do is supply the path to where the profiles are to be stored. With Windows 98, however, the User Profile path setting does not apply. Profiles must be stored in each user's home directory, each user must have a home directory identified through User Manager for Domains. (For more information, refer to the section "Setting Up User Environments Through User Profiles.")

4. **A.** You do not need to create multiple policy files for Windows 98. You create one policy file and save this one `config.pol` file in the `Netlogon$` share. (For more information, refer to the section "Setting Up User Environments Through System Policies.")

5. **D.** System policies can restrict the activities of users on the system. Profiles are simply the way a computer looks and feels to the user. (For more information, refer to the section "Setting Up User Environments Through System Policies.")

6. **C.** To clear out any settings of a system policy, simply edit the policy file to reflect the changes you would like implemented for the policy. Deleting the policy would not work because the logon message has been downloaded to the computer's Registry. (For more information, refer to the section "Setting Up User Environments Through System Policies.")

7. **C.** If you are using a custom Programs folder, check the option to hide the Start menu subfolders; if you do not, you will see two Programs folders. (For more information, refer to the section "Setting Up User Environments Through System Policies.")

8. **B.** If a machine is configured to log on to the domain, it will always ask the user to log on to the domain. Creating a hardware profile to disable the network adapter card will help alleviate the network error messages the sales reps receive when they are on the road. (For more information, refer to the section "Working with Hardware Profiles.")

APPLY YOUR KNOWLEDGE

9. **B.** Martin would need to change the default profile Original Configuration and disable the sound card on this profile to disable the sound card with his default hardware settings. (For more information, refer to the section "Working with Hardware Profiles.")

10. **B.** To use system policies on a standalone machine, you must change the Remote Update category to reflect where the policy is being stored locally, rather than on a server. (For more information, refer to the section "Setting Up User Environments Through System Policies.")

Suggested Readings and Resources

1. *The Windows 98 Resource Kit*; Microsoft Press

2. *The Windows 98 Professional Reference*, Hallberg and Casad; New Riders

This chapter helps you to prepare for the Microsoft exam by covering the following objectives within the "Monitoring and Optimization" category:

Monitor system performance by using Net Watcher, System Monitor, and Resource Meter.

▶ Net Watcher allows you to administer remote shares, see what shared resources are in use, and disconnect users from specific resources. System Monitor allows you to see real-time activity on the system and how that activity affects overall performance. Resource Meter provides a fast way to check out the available resources on a Windows 98 machine. You will be tested on how to use the tools to optimize a Windows 98 computer.

Tune and optimize the system in a Microsoft environment and a mixed Microsoft and NetWare environment. Tasks include the following:

Optimizing the hard disk by using Disk Defragmenter and ScanDisk

Compressing data by using DriveSpace 3 and the Compression Agent

Updating drivers and applying service packs by using Windows Update and the Signature Verification Tool

Automating tasks by using Maintenance Wizard

Scheduling tasks by using Task Scheduler

Checking for corrupt files and extracting files from the installation media using the System File Checker

▶ This objective will test your knowledge of how to optimize the Windows 98 environment with the system tools provided with the operating system. Through these system tools, you should be able to diagnose, repair, or resolve issues that may affect Windows 98 overall performance.

CHAPTER 7

Monitoring and Optimization

▶ Windows 98 provides many tools for monitoring and optimizing system performance. The best way to prepare for the part of the exam focusing on these two main concepts is to study the material within this chapter. Challenge yourself with the review and exam questions, complete the exercises, and then invest some time with each specific system tool to make sure you understand its purpose and how to use it properly. Experiment with each Windows 98 tool until you attain a complete understanding of how the tool works and in what circumstance an administrator would want to use the tool.

INTRODUCTION

If you wanted to get the best performance out of your automobile, you would regularly take it in for oil changes and tune-ups, consider replacing or upgrading parts with higher-performance parts, and pamper it with any number of gifts to make its life better. The same rules apply to your computer and its hard drive. The unfortunate thing is that your computer is usually ignored unless something goes wrong (which is also true for some people and their automobiles).

This chapter looks at what you can do to maintain your computer and its hard drive and achieve the best performance possible. The topics that will be covered deal with monitoring, tuning, and optimizing your system. The tools you will use to monitor your system include Net Watcher for monitoring network connections and System Monitor for monitoring your overall system. The tools you will use to tune and optimize your system include Disk Defragmenter and ScanDisk for maintaining hard drive health and performance, and DriveSpace and Compression Agent for managing compressed drives. These tools will be examined to show you how to diagnose and prevent system performance problems. You'll also learn about automating tasks and updating and replacing system files.

MONITORING YOUR WINDOWS 98 SYSTEM

Monitor system performance by using Net Watcher, System Monitor, and Resource Meter.

The only way you will ever know that you have a problem with your computer, short of a failure in the system, is to monitor its performance. The first topic in this chapter is how you can use Net Watcher, System Monitor, and Resource Meter to track your computer's use and performance. Net Watcher and System Monitor can also monitor other computers on your network.

Monitoring Network Resources Using Net Watcher

Windows 98's Net Watcher application allows you to see who is currently attached to your computer from other locations on your network. Net Watcher also lets you track open files, create new shared folders, and stop sharing folders.

Net Watcher is a valuable tool for monitoring shared resources. Although it is possible to create and remove shares using other tools, such as through Explorer or through the DOS prompt (as described in previous chapters), Net Watcher lets you view all the shares from one convenient interface. Net Watcher can help you provide better security because it lets you monitor the files that are open at any moment and what users are connected to those files. Net Watcher can also help you provide better performance because it helps you monitor the effect of user connections and file service activity on the Windows 98 machine (see the following note).

Later sections describe how to use Net Watcher to perform the following actions:

◆ Connect to other computers

◆ Monitor shared folders

◆ Work with shared folders

◆ Monitor users

◆ Monitor open files

Connecting to Other Computers

You can use Net Watcher to view network connections to resources on your own computer, or you can connect to another computer and use Net Watcher to monitor the remote computer's resources.

Before you can use Net Watcher to view another computer, you must enable remote administration on both computers and be an administrator for the remote computer. See Chapter 5, "Managing Resources in Windows 98," for more information about Windows 95/98 remote administration. If the remote computer has implemented user-level access control, you have to be included on the Remote Administration tab of the Passwords icon of Control Panel,

NOTE

Net Watcher as Watchdog Users connecting to your computer will adversely affect its performance. The more files that are accessed, the larger they are, and the longer the length of time they are kept open, the more your computer will be affected.

Microsoft has not imposed file sharing limits on Windows 98, so technically you can have everyone on your network connect to your computer. If those people wanted to maintain a high level of activity on multiple files, you would quickly realize that Windows 98 wasn't designed for this type of file sharing. Windows 98's File and Printer Sharing services are low-performance and were designed for low activity, rare access, or minimal numbers of users. Net Watcher lets you track some of this activity on your computer.

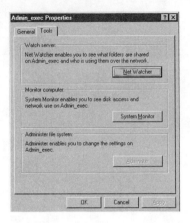

FIGURE 7.1
Net Watcher can be launched from the Tools tab of a computer's Properties sheet in Network Neighborhood.

or you have to be a member of a group that has been included on the Remote Administration list. If the other computer is using share-level access control, you will need to know the password that was used to set up remote administration.

After you are an administrator for the other computer, you can access it in either of two ways. You can access the other computer by launching Net Watcher through the computer's Properties dialog box in Network Neighborhood (see Figure 7.1) or by opening Net Watcher in the Accessories, System Tools program group and choosing Select Server from Net Watcher's Administer menu.

Net Watcher lets you view shares and current connections to shares (see Figure 7.2). Net Watcher's View menu lets you view network share information by connection, shared folder, or open file.

Monitoring Shared Folders

Net Watcher can give you a list of shared folders that are currently available on your system. This is an extremely useful feature because the folders that are shared could be buried under several layers of folders.

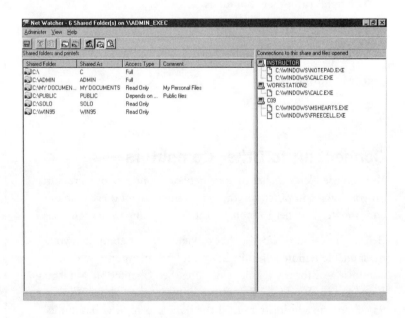

FIGURE 7.2
Net Watcher provides you with a list of shared folders, as well as who is accessing them.

Not only does Net Watcher provide a list of shared folders, but it also tells you what the share name is and the access level granted to the folder (only when you select View, Details—refer to Figure 7.2). The usefulness of this screen is enhanced when you select one of your shared folders because a list of connected computers appears in the right pane. This list of connected computers also shows any open files that are maintained by that computer.

You should keep a watchful eye on the number of folders that are shared on your computer. Each shared folder uses a small amount of your computer's sharing resources, and an excessive number of shared folders will affect network performance.

In addition to monitoring shared folders, Net Watcher also lets you share folders and change the properties of shared folders.

Working with Shared Folders

Before adding a new shared folder, stopping the sharing of a folder, or changing the settings for an established shared folder, you must switch to the Shared Folder view by selecting View, By Shared Folder.

To add a new shared folder, select Administer, Add Shared Folder. When you do this, you will be prompted for a path to the folder. You can either type in a path or click the Browse button. If you're sharing a folder on a remote computer through remote administration, you can browse the resources through the hidden administrative drive shares such as C$ (see Figure 7.3). After choosing a directory to work with, you will see the standard Share Directory dialog box. See Chapter 1, "Planning," and Chapter 5 for more information about sharing resources.

To change the properties of a shared folder, select the folder from the list of shared folders and then choose Administer, Shared Folder Properties. This brings up the sharing settings for that folder. You can change any of the settings, such as the allowed users or the share password, and then close the dialog by clicking OK.

To stop sharing a folder, select the shared folder from the list of shared folders and select Administer, Stop Sharing Folder. This will stop the folder from being shared with other people on the network.

> **EXAM TIP**
>
> **Net Watcher Shares** As you prepare for the Windows 98 exam, remember that you can add and remove shares from within Net Watcher. You may see a question on this.

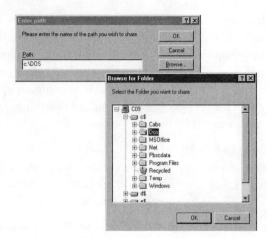

FIGURE 7.3
Net Watcher can browse through remote hard
drives by accessing the administrative shares.

Monitoring Users

In order to monitor your system by connected users, select View, By
Connections. When you switch to this view, you will see a list of
users who are currently connected to your computer, as shown in
Figure 7.4. In Details view, you also see the names of the computers
that they are using to establish the connections and the number of
shares and open files that they are accessing. The last two detail
columns that are listed are Connected Time and Idle Time. When
you select a user, you see the list of shared folders that that person is
accessing, as well as the list of open files.

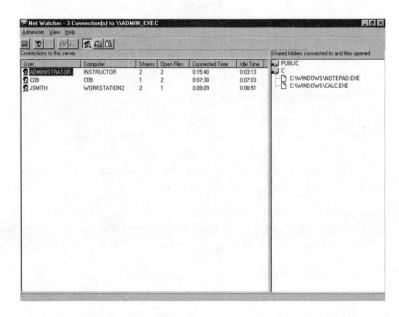

FIGURE 7.4
Net Watcher lets you track activity by user.

When using Net Watcher as a maintenance tool, you can examine the number of users who are connected to your computer and the number and types of files they are accessing. Windows 98 will suffer from a performance degradation if it must maintain a large number of idle open sessions. When viewing by connection in Net Watcher, you can track these sessions and close sessions that are nonessential.

To close a session, disconnect the user by selecting the user and then selecting Administer, Disconnect User.

You have now examined your network usage by shared folder and by connected user. The third way you can monitor your network is by the files that are actually in use.

Monitoring Open Files

When users access files on your computer, they have to read or write the files from or to your hard drive. During the read and write processes, these files are open for either input or output. Some files that you work with, such as applications, will remain open for extended periods of time. Net Watcher will list all your open files when you select View, By Open Files.

When viewing open files, you will see who is accessing the files, through what share name, and the type of access they are using for the file (read or write), as shown in Figure 7.5. In a sharing environment, open files play a larger role in performance degradation than the number of connected users does.

If you find that you have too many open files, and you think performance might be suffering, the only thing you can do is stop sharing. As long as you are sharing resources, other users will be able to open your files.

Net Watcher's main focus as an application is to let you see who is connecting to what resources on your computer. Its role in your computer's routine maintenance is to let you see what type of activity is currently occurring on your shared resources. This information helps you decide if you're sharing too many folders and should cut back in order to improve local performance. In order to determine how badly local performance is suffering, use System Monitor.

> **WARNING**
>
> **Must Disconnect and Reconnect**
> If you change the permissions assigned to a user who is currently accessing a shared folder, the effect of those permissions won't be noticeable until the user disconnects and reconnects to the folder. To force the user to reauthenticate, you should manually disconnect him using Net Watcher. If the user doesn't have any open files, he shouldn't notice the interruption and should automatically reconnect.

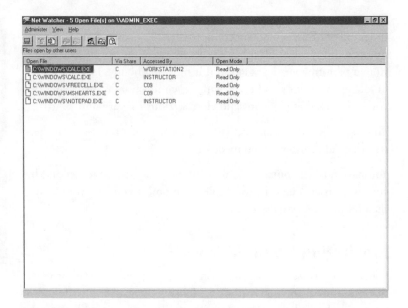

FIGURE 7.5
High activity on your computer is caused by
open files, not connected users.

Monitoring System Performance Using System Monitor

System Monitor tracks performance statistics about your computer
and displays the information in three different chart formats. This
information lets you see what areas of your computer are performing
properly and which areas are performing only marginally. System
Monitor can be found under Start, Programs, Accessories, System
Tools. In exploring the use of System Monitor as a maintenance
tool, you will examine the following:

◆ How System Monitor gathers information

◆ How to remotely monitor a computer's performance

◆ The different ways to view information

◆ Adding objects to the monitor screen

◆ Key counters to watch in system maintenance

Seeing Where the Information Comes From

Your computer is constantly keeping track of a series of performance
statistics, but this information is displayed only if you request it. The

statistics are kept in the Registry in the HKEY_DYN_DATA\PerfStats\ StatData key (see Figure 7.6). In this key you will see a series of values such as KERNEL\CPUUsage, whose value is a hexadecimal number. This number is usually displayed as a decimal value in the System Monitor charts. Your Registry always keeps these performance statistics up-to-date for you.

Running System Monitor Remotely

System Monitor may be used to monitor your own computer or another computer on your network. To monitor another computer on your network, you need to ensure that the following conditions have been met:

◆ You have administrative privileges on the target computer (refer to Chapter 5).

◆ The target computer is currently on the network (refer to Chapter 3, "Windows 98 Networking").

◆ The target computer has been set for user-level access control (refer to Chapter 1).

◆ Both computers have the Remote Registry service installed (refer to Chapter 5).

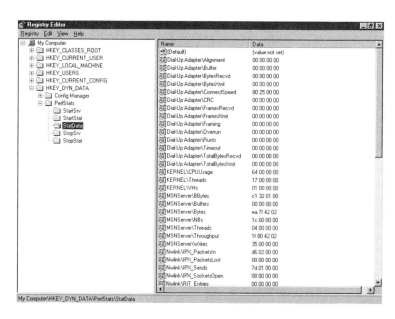

FIGURE 7.6
All the performance counters are stored in the Dynamic Data section of the Registry.

All of these requirements are actually the requirements for Remote Registry Editing. Because all the System Monitor counters are stored in the Registry, and because System Monitor simply reads the values of these counters from the Registry, in order to use System Monitor to monitor another computer on the network, you need to be able to read that Registry. To view the other computer, select File, Connect and type in the name of the computer you want to connect to.

Viewing Information

There are three different ways to view the information in System Monitor (to switch between chart types, use the View menu):

◆ Line charts

◆ Bar charts

◆ Numeric charts

Line charts display an area graph for each counter you add to the System Monitor window. As you add more counters, System Monitor decreases the size of each graph to display all the graphs in a single window (see Figure 7.7). If you select one of the graphs, System Monitor shows you the name of the counter, as well as the last and peak values for the counter over the graph period. Line charts are great tools if you want to get a feel for how the values interrelate. For instance, when free memory decreases, disk access increases due to increased access to the swap file or page file. A line chart will demonstrate this visually. Line charts make tracking exact numbers somewhat more difficult, especially if you're tracking a large number of counters, because each chart will be very small.

Bar charts provide another way to view the data that is being collected. Bar charts display a moving bar on a horizontal scale, as shown in Figure 7.8. Whenever the value peaks, System Monitor leaves a marker on the scale until it reaches the seventh reading, at which time it decreases to the current value. The advantages of bar charts are that the numeric value of the counter is easier to read, and they allow you to see how the value has decreased over the last seven readings. This chart walks a fine line between line charts and numeric charts.

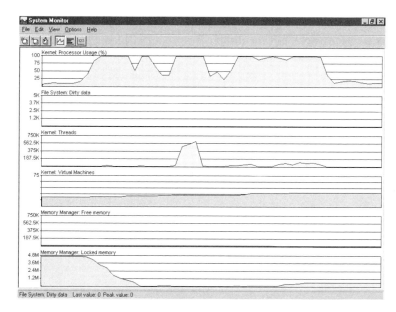

FIGURE 7.7
Line charts make examining relationships between counters easier.

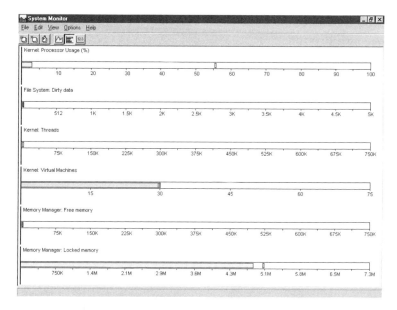

FIGURE 7.8
Bar charts make interpreting numbers much easier than with line charts.

Numeric charts give you the greatest number of counters monitored at any given time, but the display is more limited (see Figure 7.9). If you select one of the numbers displayed in the main window, the status bar at the bottom of the window provides additional information, such as the last and peak values. The advantage of the numeric chart is that it is very easy to see the exact value of the counter.

As with most programs, each view has its strong points and its weaknesses. If you are familiar with all three of the views, you can choose the view that will best allow you to access the information you need. You might even feel that the best way to gather your information is to switch between the different views while System Monitor is running. Doing this will let you draw on the best features of each view.

Adding Counters to Be Monitored

The first time you open System Monitor, it will be charting the processor usage on a line chart. Any changes you make will automatically be saved for the next time you open System Monitor. These changes could be the selection of a different view or the addition of a counter to be monitored.

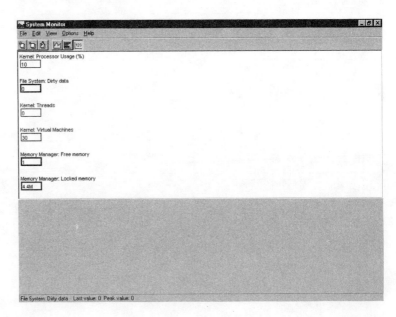

FIGURE 7.9
Numeric charts make getting the correct value easy, but the display is more limited.

To add a new counter, select Edit, Add Item. You will see a screen that lets you select a specific information category. After you select a category, the items available for monitoring in that category will appear in the box on the right. If you're unsure of what an item is for, select the item and click the Explain button. You see the dialog box shown in Figure 7.10.

The Edit menu has two additional commands for your counters:

◆ Remove Item

◆ Edit Item

When you select Remove Item, you will see a list of counters that you are currently tracking, and you have the option of removing one or more of them. Edit Item presents you with the same list of installed counters, and you may choose one of them to edit. When you edit a counter, you can change the color that is used to draw it and decide whether it should have a dynamic (automatic) scale or a fixed scale (see Figure 7.11). This window displays the current top of the scale. If the scale is fixed, you can set the value of the top of the scale.

Key Counters to Watch in System Maintenance

Not all of System Monitor's counters will always be valuable to you. In certain instances (for example, while you are trying to diagnose the reason for a performance loss), you might only care about a small number of counters. This section helps you identify how some of the counters may be used to monitor performance.

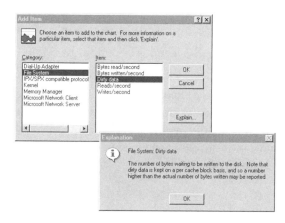

FIGURE 7.10

You can select new components to be monitored from a list of counters.

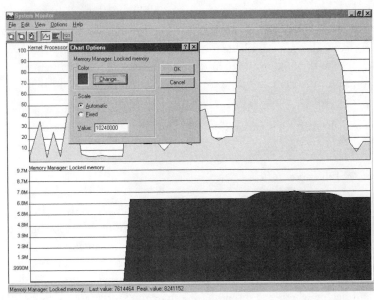

FIGURE 7.11
For readability, you might want to change to
scales on your charts or assign different colors.

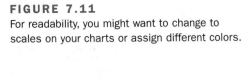

Counter Names Intuitive If a question on the Windows 98 MCSE exam asks about a System Monitor counter you don't recognize, don't panic. The names for the counters are very descriptive. If you read the problem carefully, you can often figure the best counter to use just by its name.

This section describes counters from the folowing categories: Dial-Up Adapter, File System, IPX/SPX-compatible protocol, Kernel, Memory Manager, Microsoft Network Client, and Microsoft Network Server. You will see why you might care about some of these counters and the types of performance problems you will be trying to diagnose.

Here are the counters in the Dial-Up Adapter category and why they are important:

◆ **Bytes Received/Second.** Gives you an idea of the rate of incoming data to your system. You will be able to take the rated speed of your modem and compare this value on extended reads to see if you are achieving speeds close to the registered limits.

◆ **Bytes Transmitted/Second.** The same as Bytes Received/Second, except that it works with transmitted data.

◆ **Connection Speed.** Reports the negotiated line speed between your modem and the target modem. If the speed is far below the speed that either modem supports, you might want to examine the line itself, because there might be an excessive amount of line noise.

◆ **CRC Errors.** Should not occur with any regularity. If these errors occur regularly, you should look for either a hardware failure or excessive line noise.

When monitoring the file system, in addition to the tracking reads and writes per second, you might want to track dirty data. *Dirty data* is sometimes referred to as *lazy writes*. It represents the number of bytes of data currently residing in RAM that are waiting to be written to disk. The actual number is the number of cache blocks waiting to be written, which might be higher than the number of bytes. The more dirty data on your system, the more efficient disk caching is. The drawback of this efficiency is that more data is volatile in the event of a power outage or system crash.

A key measure of the utilization of the IPX/SPX-compatible protocol on your computer and your network servers is the total number of open sockets. Each socket represents a file connection from your computer to the server. A higher-than-normal number of open sockets might indicate that the server or your computer isn't closing off the connections properly. This will eventually impede the performance of both the server and your computer.

When monitoring the Kernel, the most obvious counter to monitor is Processor Usage, which displays a percentage utilization of the processor. It's acceptable for the processor to experience small peaks (even as high as 100 percent) for brief periods of time. For this counter, performance problems would be indicated if the processor achieves and maintains a high level of utilization. An example of high utilization is 70 to 80 percent utilization for several minutes.

The Memory Manager is responsible for several key counters:

◆ **Disk Cache Size.** The total size of the disk cache for reading data from your hard drive. The larger the size of the disk cache, the faster and more productive disk reads are.

◆ **Free Memory.** The amount of free or available RAM on your system. If your RAM falls to too low of a level, Windows 98 attempts to use the dynamic swap file.

◆ **Locked Memory.** Memory that the operating system has deemed special. This memory is special because whatever else happens on the computer, this information is kept in RAM and is never sent to the page or swap file.

NOTE **Dial-Up Networking Counters** Most of the counters that affect Dial-Up Networking are installed when you add the Dial-Up Networking 1.2 system update.

◆ **Page Faults.** Indicates that there is a problem accessing information that an application has stored in RAM. This isn't really a problem, but rather a signal to the rest of the operating system that the information has been swapped with physical RAM and is stored in the swap file on the computer's hard drive. When attempting to obtain that piece of information, the computer will do a quick check to see if it is in physical memory. If not, it generates a page fault. The page fault will trigger the loading of the information from the hard drive.

Page faults also apply to all applications that haven't been opened. For example, Windows 98 will determine whether the application that you are opening is in RAM yet. If not, it will generate a page fault and load the application. If your computer is suffering from an excess number of page faults, you should be noticing very slow performance. Excess page faults are a signal that too much information is being swapped to your hard drive. The best way to prevent information from being swapped to your hard drive is to add more RAM to the system.

◆ **Page-outs.** Information that is written specifically to the Windows 98 swap file. The lower the number, the less you're using the swap file, and the more you're using RAM.

◆ **Swapfile in Use.** Represents the amount of the swap file you are currently using.

◆ **Swapfile Size**. The current dynamic size of the swap file.

Microsoft Network Client System Monitor counters tend to focus on the speed of access across your network. These counters include the following:

◆ **Bytes Read/Second.** The number of raw bytes that are read by the network client per second. Compare this to the theoretical 100Mbps or 12.5Mbps for your network.

◆ **Bytes Written/Second.** Similar to Bytes Read/Second, but it represents data sent to the server. If either of these numbers is too low, you might want to consider upgrading to a faster network card.

◆ **Sessions.** The number of network conversations you have open. If you aren't closing off network sessions properly, this number will continue to grow and will cause performance problems for both the server and your workstation. If you have sessions that are not being closed off properly, this is probably the result of a particular application. To find out which application, you will have to monitor the sessions while working with the various applications on your computer.

The Microsoft Client for NetWare Networks counters, like the Microsoft Network Client counters, focus on network access speed:

◆ **Dirty Bytes in Cache.** The number of bytes of data that have been cached by the redirector (network client) waiting to be written to the hard drive.

◆ **BURST and NCP Packets Dropped.** The number of packets that are lost in transit on the network.

◆ **Requests Pending.** The number of requests that your redirector wants to make, but is waiting for the server to process.

When your computer is running File and Printer Sharing for Microsoft Networks, it is a Microsoft Network Server. Here are some of the counters you might want to keep an eye on:

◆ **Bytes Read/Sec.** The number of bytes of data that have been transferred to your computer from across the network. This is similar to the Bytes Read/sec on the client.

◆ **Bytes Written/Sec.** The number of bytes that the server has transferred to clients on the network or written to the network.

◆ **Memory.** Represents the total amount of memory that the server services are using on your computer.

◆ **NBs.** The number of network buffers that have been allocated to handle talking to network clients. The more buffers, the faster the communication.

◆ **Server Threads.** The number of threads, or execution segments, that Windows 98 is executing for the file and printer sharing.

Microsoft shows the counters for the File and Printer Sharing services for NetWare Networks under the heading of Server. Here are some of the counters in this category you might want to track:

◆ **Bytes Throughput/Second.** The number of bytes of data that are handled by the File and Printer Sharing service.

◆ **Cache Memory.** The amount of memory that is reserved to handle the server's burst buffers.

◆ **Packets Dropped.** The number of packets that are lost on the network.

◆ **Total Heap.** Tracks the total amount of memory that is used by the server.

◆ **Transactions/Second.** Records the total number of requests that the server responds to for the clients on the network.

If you notice that any of these counters have started reporting numbers that deviate from the norm, this might indicate a problem with performance. The only way you will know what is normal for you is to monitor the counters for a period of time when you think everything is working.

Monitoring System Performance Using Resource Meter: Monitoring Resource Memory

Windows 98's Resource Meter is a very simple tool that displays the amount of free memory allocated to three Windows 98 core system components: the System (Kernel) component, the User component, and the GDI component (see Figure 7.12). These core components provide services for applications running on your system.

The functions provided by each of these core components are as follows:

◆ **User.** Handles user input, such as input from a mouse or keyboard, and manages some aspects of output to the user interface, such as menus, icons, and windows.

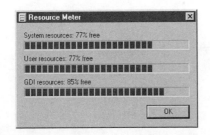

FIGURE 7.12
Resource Meter displays resources allocated to Windows 98's System, User, and GDI components.

♦ **System (Kernel).** Supports basic operating system services, such as exception handling, system I/O, task scheduling, and virtual memory management.

♦ **Graphics Device Interface (GDI).** Provides a graphical subsystem that supports screen graphics and graphic output to other devices such as printers.

If your system is running slow, check Resource Meter to see if any of these components is running out of available resources. A low reading for %free resources for one of the core components could indicate a problem with that component.

To start Resource Meter, perform the tasks outlined in Step by Step 7.1.

STEP BY STEP

7.1 Starting Resource Meter

1. Click on the Start menu.

2. Choose Programs, Accessories, System Tools.

3. Select Resource Meter.

4. You may see a dialog box warning you that Resource Meter uses system resources when it is running. Click on OK to open Resource Meter.

5. Resource Meter appears on your screen (refer to Figure 7.12). Click OK to minimize Resource Meter. It will appear as an icon beside the system clock.

> **NOTE** **Might Need to Install** If you can't find Resource Meter with the System Tools, you may need to install it using the Windows Setup tab of the Add/ Remove Programs Control Panel.

Monitoring

The preceding sections discussed three important monitoring tools:

♦ **Net Watcher.** Lets you monitor shared resources and user access on the local computer and on other Windows 95/98 computers on the network. You can also use Net Watcher to add or remove shares. Net Watcher saves time for the administrator because it collects information on shared resources into a single interface and it lets the administrator conveniently administer resources on other computers from a single location.

◆ **System Monitor.** Lets you track several indicators of system usage. System Monitor helps you search out system bottlenecks.

◆ **Resource Meter.** Tracks key resource memory components. Resource Meter displays the free memory allocated to the System, User, and GDI (Graphics Device Interface) components. If your system is running slow, Resource Meter is a quick first step that can help you isolate a possible cause.

As you prepare for the Windows 98 exam, make sure you know how and when to use these important monitoring tools.

Optimizing Disks

Tune and optimize the system in a Microsoft environment and a mixed Microsoft and NetWare environment.

Windows 98 includes several tools you can use to optimize and maintain your hard disks, and Microsoft makes a point of mentioning most of these tools in the objectives list for the Windows 98 exam. Each of the following optimization tools is examined in following subsections:

◆ Disk Defragmenter

◆ ScanDisk

◆ DriveSpace 3

◆ Compression Agent

◆ Disk Cleanup

For more on managing hard disk resources, refer to Chapter 5.

Optimizing Disks Using Disk Defragmenter

All hard drives, as a matter of course, eventually become fragmented. A fragmented drive has files on it that have been broken into pieces. The job of Disk Defragmenter is to reassemble each file into a single piece.

Files become fragmented through normal use of your hard drive. When your hard drive is new, it has no files. As you add a new file, it is easy for Windows 98 to save the file in free space that is large enough to hold the entire file. As you delete files, you invariably leave holes in the used space. As you continue to work with your hard disk, the contiguous free space areas get smaller and smaller—even the little areas of free space that once held files. Every time you attempt to save a file to your hard disk, Windows 98 will attempt to write the file to the largest area of free space on your disk. However, there will quickly come a time when you attempt to save files that will not fit in the largest free areas. When this happens, Windows 98 writes part of the file in the largest area and leaves a pointer at the end of the file that indicates where the rest of the file is stored. The file is now fragmented.

Now enter the defragmentation program. It slowly and methodically moves each file on your disk to a new location, thereby leaving a hole that can be used to move another file into. The program continues with this process, from the first sector of your hard disk to the last. As it moves through your disk, it slowly creates a block of free space that moves through your disk until it is at the end of the disk and the job is done.

The disk defragmentation program that is included with Windows 98 is Disk Defragmenter. It can be found under Start, Programs, Accessories, System Tools. When you open Disk Defragmenter, it asks you which drive you want to work with, as shown in Figure 7.13. Select the drive from the drop-down menu or choose All Hard Drives to defragment all drives in order.

Select a drive to defragment. The Settings button invokes the Disk Defragmenter Settings dialog box (see Figure 7.14). The Disk Defragmenter Settings dialog box lets you select whether you want the defragmenter to rearrange your program files so the programs will start faster. You can also choose whether you want to check the

FIGURE 7.13
Choose the drive you want to defragment.

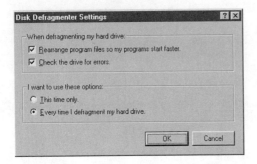

FIGURE 7.14
The Disk Defragmenter Settings dialog box lets you select (among other things) whether you want the defragmenter to rearrange your program files so the programs will start faster.

drive for errors during the defragmentation process. The Disk Defrag error check option allows ScanDisk algorithms to check the areas of the drive that are being read from and written to. This provides a level of safety for the data that is being moved around. If you had just completed a full ScanDisk of the drive before defragmenting, you could uncheck this check box—otherwise, you should leave the check mark in the box. Prior to using any process that works with the data over your entire drive, you should run ScanDisk to ensure that the medium you are working with is free of errors.

To finish off the Settings options, Windows 98 asks whether you want to use the options every time or only for this session. The choices are as follows:

◆ **This Time Only.** Next time, use the defaults again: This option discards your settings changes.

◆ **Every Time I Defragment My Hard Drive.** This option preserves your settings changes for all future defragmentations.

After you have made your changes to the way Disk Defragmenter will perform the defragmentation, close the dialog box by clicking OK. Now start the defragmentation process by clicking OK in the Select Drive dialog box (refer to Figure 7.13).

Upon doing so, the defragmenter will display a bar that indicates the progress of the defragmentation as a percentage, as shown in Figure 7.15. If you would like to see a more detailed description of what is going on, click Show Details.

When you click Show Details, you see a large window that displays each cluster on your hard disk as a box, as shown in Figure 7.16.

Each box is color-coded based on the type of data. This Details window has four buttons:

◆ **Stop.** Stops the defragmentation process and lets you confirm your decision, select a different drive, or exit the program.

◆ **Pause.** Temporarily halts the defragmentation process until you click the Resume button.

◆ **Legend.** Displays the legend, which describes the color-coded boxes used in the Defragmenting Drive window.

◆ **Hide Details.** Switches you back to the summary of the defragmentation status (refer to Figure 7.15).

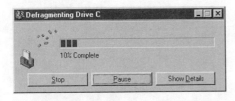

FIGURE 7.15
The default user interface is a status bar that indicates the overall defragmentation of your hard drive.

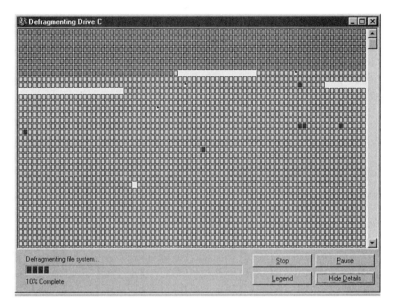

With the Details screen visible, you can watch Windows 98 move clusters of data from one section of your hard drive to another. You will see each read and write, and Windows 98 will move the view of the screen to keep pace with where it is performing the defragmentation. If you would like to see what type of data is represented by each color block, you can bring up the legend. Some of the data markers in the Defragmenting Drive windows are as follows:

◆ **Optimized (Defragmented) Data.** Data that has already been processed.

◆ **Data That Will Not Be Moved.** Windows 98 maintains some open files and knows of other files that applications don't want to see moved. These clusters are left in place.

◆ **Bad (Damaged) Area of the Disk.** Windows 98 marks these clusters as damaged and won't use them to store any other data.

When Disk Defragmenter has completed its job, you should see some improvement in hard disk performance. The difference will be more noticeable on systems that were badly fragmented.

In order to keep your computer working at its highest performance level at all times, you should perform a full defragmentation once a month. If your hard drive doesn't have a large amount of free space, you might want to perform defragmentations more often. The less free space you have, the quicker your files become fragmented.

Before you defragment your hard drive or perform any task that works with large amounts of data on your hard drive, consider scanning your hard drive for errors with ScanDisk.

Optimizing Disks Using ScanDisk for Windows

ScanDisk is a variation of the MS-DOS utility for checking your hard drive for errors in the file and directory structure as well as errors with the actual medium. The utility now ships in two forms with Windows 98: SCANDSKW.EXE is designed to work within the Windows 98 GUI, and SCANDISK.EXE is a command-line version that is designed to be used when the Windows 98 GUI has not been loaded. This section examines ScanDisk for Windows. An upcoming section, "Optimizing Disks Using SCANDISK.EXE (the Command-Line Version)," addresses the version ScanDisk uses when the GUI has not loaded.

To open ScanDisk for Windows, select Start, Programs, Accessories, System Tools, ScanDisk. You can choose a hard drive to scan, a type of scan, and whether you want to be notified of errors, as shown in Figure 7.17.

FIGURE 7.17
ScanDisk lets you choose the type of scan you want to perform.

It is wise to run a scan of your drive every time your computer freezes and requires you to reboot it. (Windows 98 often runs the DOS-based version of ScanDisk automatically when the system restarts after a failure.) You should also run a scan of your drive prior to installing applications that will load files on the majority of your hard drive. In addition, it is wise to get in the habit of checking your drives once a month to prevent possible corruption of your data and keep your drives performing at peak efficiency. The scans performed by ScanDisk will not damage your data. They will, however, prevent data that is already damaged from further corrupting other data on your hard drive.

The following subsections discuss some ScanDisk options.

Choosing a Scan Type

ScanDisk can perform two types of scans:

◆ **Standard Scan Type**. Performs a check on the file allocation table. This scan makes sure that the structure of the file allocation table is proper. This step is vital, because the file allocation table holds pointers to the start of every file on your hard drive. If you don't know where the files start, you won't be able to read them.

◆ **Thorough Scan Type**. Also performs a check of the file allocation table. After doing this, the thorough scan follows up with a surface scan. The *surface scan* accesses every cluster on your hard drive to ensure that each is functioning properly. If the surface scan uncovers any bad clusters, ScanDisk attempts to move the data to a new area and map out the bad clusters on your hard drive. The thorough scan also checks each file for invalid information, such as invalid dates and names.

When conducting a thorough, or surface, scan, you can configure a few additional options by clicking the Options button. The Surface Scan Options dialog box appears (see Figure 7.18).

The following list details these additional options:

◆ **System and Data Areas.** Allows ScanDisk to scan both the boot sector and data areas of the drive. This is the default option.

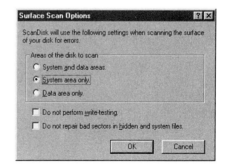

FIGURE 7.18
ScanDisk supports some additional options for thorough scans.

◆ **System Area Only.** Checks only the boot sector and file allocation table areas of the hard disk. If there is an error in these areas of the disk, you probably will have to reformat or replace the damaged hard disk.

◆ **Data Area Only.** Moves the damaged data to a new area of the disk if the data hasn't been damaged to the point of being unreadable.

◆ **Do Not Perform Write-Testing.** Causes ScanDisk to read the contents of each sector of your hard drive, but ScanDisk doesn't write the data back to the disk to complete the verification of the hard drive's clusters. This option assumes that if you can read the data from the disk, the disk must be working well enough to hold the data written to it. The actual process of writing the data back proves that the area of the disk works.

◆ **Do Not Repair Bad Sectors in Hidden and System Files.** Rather than attempting to recover the data and moving it to a new location on the hard drive, Windows 98 leaves it where it is. Moving the data from its original location prevents some programs that expect to find files in specific locations from working properly.

If you don't want Windows 98 to prompt you about correcting each type of file that it might find, you might want to select the Automatically Fix Errors check box in the ScanDisk window (refer to Figure 7.17). When this option is selected, all errors encountered are fixed automatically.

After you've chosen your scan type, click on Start to start scanning the disk. Or, for additional options, click on Advanced. It is a good idea to close any open applications before running ScanDisk.

Applying Advanced Options

Regardless of the type of scan that ScanDisk performs, you may configure some advanced options by clicking the Advanced button (refer to Figure 7.17). The screen shown in Figure 7.19 appears.

The advanced options are as follows:

◆ Display Summary

◆ Lost File Fragments

FIGURE 7.19
The ScanDisk Advanced Options dialog box lets you set options prior to the scan, which prevents ScanDisk from having to prompt you for options during the scan.

◆ Log File

◆ Check Files For

◆ Cross-Linked Files

◆ Check Host Drive First

◆ Report MS-DOS Mode Name Length Errors

Displaying a Summary

ScanDisk can be configured to display a summary at the following times:

◆ Always Display a ScanDisk Summary

◆ Never Display a ScanDisk Summary

◆ Display a ScanDisk Summary Only If Errors Were Found During the Scan

Handling Lost File Fragments

Files are stored on a FAT (File Allocation Table) partition using a linked cluster directory structure. This means that the FAT stores the location of the first cluster of the file. The end of each cluster points to the beginning of the next cluster of files. Occasionally something goes wrong with this system, and in the middle of a file, a cluster in one file starts to point to a cluster used by another file. When this happens, the last clusters of the original file are left floating freely on the disk. These are lost file fragments. You may do one of the following things with lost file fragments:

◆ **Free (Delete) the File Fragments.** In most cases you will not find any useful information in the file fragments, so you should delete them.

◆ **Convert to Files.** Causes all the file fragments to be saved in a folder on the root of your hard drive, and the files will be numbered sequentially (such as FILE0001).

Recording a Log File

These options let you configure how the log file will be managed on your computers. You have the following options:

- ◆ Replace the Log Each Time ScanDisk Is Run
- ◆ Append to the Log Each Time ScanDisk Is Run
- ◆ Bypass Saving Any Log File at All

Checking File Settings

These options let you tell ScanDisk to check files for the following invalid settings:

- ◆ **Invalid Filenames.** Where the name might be corrupted through an error on the drive. ScanDisk lets you give the file a different name.

- ◆ **Invalid Dates and Times.** Causes ScanDisk to set the date and time for the file to today's current date and time. Some applications won't work with the file if the date and time are invalid.

- ◆ **Duplicate Names.** Checks for duplicate file names.

Dealing with Cross-Linked Files

As mentioned earlier, sometimes the linked directory structure of files becomes confused. When this happens, the files are referred to as *cross-linked files*. The files have two starting points that share a common ending point. In this case, it is possible that both files are now corrupted. You can do the following with cross-linked files:

- ◆ **Delete Both Files.** Work on the assumption that both files are probably damaged.

- ◆ **Make Copies of Both of the Potential Files.** There is a chance that one of the files is still okay, and only the second file is corrupted.

- ◆ **Ignore These Files and Deal with the Error Later.** It is generally not a good idea to ignore cross-linked files.

Other Options

Other options in the ScanDisk Advanced Options dialog box include the following:

◆ **Check Host Drive First.** If you have selected a compressed drive, ScanDisk will check the compressed drive's host drive first. Refer to Chapter 5 for more information about disk compression and host drives.

◆ **Report MS-DOS Mode Name Length Errors**. Deselected by default.

Click OK to exit the ScanDisk Advanced Options dialog box.

Optimizing Disks Using SCANDISK.EXE (the Command-Line Version)

In addition to the Windows version of ScanDisk, Microsoft provides you with a command-line version of ScanDisk. It can be used outside of the Windows 98 GUI to fix errors in compressed drives, or when your system has been rebooted from a system hang. Windows 98 runs this version of ScanDisk automatically in the event of a system hang or an unexpected shutdown.

If you try to run the DOS-based SCANDISK.EXE from the Windows Run dialog box, Windows will start the Windows-based ScanDisk instead. Step by Step 7.2 describes how to run the ScanDisk command-line version.

STEP BY STEP

7.2 Running ScanDisk Command-Line Version

1. Start your computer in MS-DOS mode (choose Shutdown in the Start menu and select the option button labeled Restart in MS-DOS mode).

2. When the command prompt appears, type `scandisk`.

3. If the active drive is a compressed drive, ScanDisk will ask if you want to scan the host drive first. Press Enter to scan the host drive, or move to No using the keyboard arrow keys.

4. ScanDisk first performs a number of checks that test the file structure, and then asks if you'd like to perform a surface scan. (See the discussion of the thorough scan type earlier in this chapter.) Choose Yes to perform a surface scan, or choose No if you don't want to perform a surface scan.

5. When the scan is complete, choose Next Drive to scan the next drive, or choose View Log to view a report of the ScanDisk session. Choose Exit to exit ScanDisk.

Optimizing Disks Using DriveSpace 3

Disk compression was discussed in Chapter 5. In that chapter you saw that files are compressed on your drive into Compressed Volume Files (CVFs). The act of writing the file into a CVF forces you to run a compression algorithm. Running the compression algorithm costs time on your computer. If the level of compression that you receive shrinks the file sufficiently, the smaller file will take less time to write to your hard drive. If you don't receive a high compression level, the file will take the same amount of time to write to your hard drive, and the time taken to execute the compression algorithm was wasted on the computer.

In most cases, the only time compression will act as a performance-enhancing tool is when you have a hard drive with a slow access time and a fast processor with large amounts of RAM.

To start Windows 98's compression utility, DriveSpace 3, select Start, Programs, Accessories, System Tools, DriveSpace. You can also compress a drive by right-clicking on the drive, choosing Properties, and selecting the Compression tab. Note that you cannot use DriveSpace 3 on FAT32 drives.

Refer to Chapter 5 for more information about using DriveSpace 3 in Windows 98. For an example of disk compression, see Exercise 7.3, found later in this chapter.

EXAM TIP

Heads-Up!   Remember that DriveSpace 3 disk compression doesn't work on FAT32 drives.

Optimizing Disks Using Compression Agent

Compressing a drive saves disk space, but it almost always exacts a performance penalty because Windows 98 must continually translate data to and from the compressed format as you read and write to the disk. Windows 98's Compression Agent lets you choose how much compression you want to apply to the data. The greater the degree of compression, the longer the read/write translation takes, but the more free disk space you'll have. The balance point for the compression versus performance trade-off depends on the type of data you're compressing, the performance of your hardware, and your own personal preferences. Compression Agent lets you apply additional compression to some or all the files on a disk in order to reach the optimum ratio of space and performance.

Windows 98 actually supports three levels of disk compression:

◆ **Standard.** Provides more compression than previous DriveSpace versions, but not as much as the following two levels.

◆ **HiPack.** More compressed than standard. Uses the same encoding format as standard.

◆ **UltraPack.** Provides the most compression and, consequently, the slowest performance.

By default, when you compress your drive using the DriveSpace utility (see preceding section), the drive will be compressed with standard compression. You cannot use Compression Agent unless your drive is already compressed. You can then use Compression Agent to increase the compression on some or all of the files on a compressed drive. Or, you can use Compression Agent to reduce the level of compression on files that have already been compressed to higher levels.

To start Compression Agent, select Start, Programs, Accessories, System Tools, Compression Agent. The Compression Agent main window is shown in Figure 7.20. Note that the display showing space gained and lost for each compression level shows zeros before you run Compression Agent. When you start the recompression, the columns will start to show the space gained (when the recompression increases space) and the space lost (when the recompression reduces compression).

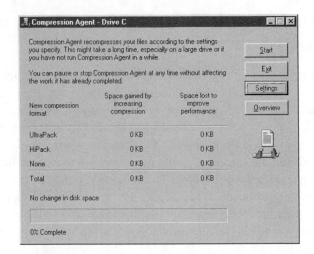

FIGURE 7.20
Compression Agent optimizes disk compression.

Compression Agent will recompress the drive according to settings you specify. Click the Settings button in the Compression Agent window to invoke the Compression Agent Settings dialog box (see Figure 7.21). The dialog box lets you specify rules for which files Compression Agent should recompress and what level of compression to use for those files. Note that the Compression Agent Settings dialog box basically offers some options for when to use the UltraPack level and lets you choose whether to use HiPack for the remainder of the files.

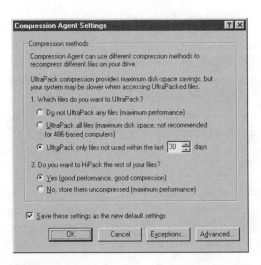

FIGURE 7.21
The Compression Agent Settings dialog box lets you choose compression level settings.

The Advanced button in the Compression Agent Settings dialog box offers some options that limit the decompression applied to a drive. Specifically, you can tell Compression Agent not to reduce the compression level for any file if the amount of free disk space is less than a predetermined level, and you can specify not to unpack any UltraPacked files.

The Exceptions button in the Compression Agent Settings dialog box lets you designate a specific compression level for a specific file, folder, or file extension.

When you have defined your recompression settings, choose the Start button in the Compression Agent window (refer to Figure 7.20) to start Compression Agent.

Optimizing Disks Using Disk Cleanup

A useful disk tool that isn't mentioned directly in the exam objectives for the Windows 98 exam is the Disk Cleanup tool. Disk Cleanup includes a number of features you can use to free up space on your hard drive. Actually, Disk Cleanup is really a collection of cleanup options that could also be carried out manually without the help of Disk Cleanup tool. Disk Cleanup adds convenience by combining these tools into a single interface. You can configure the Disk Cleanup utility to perform a series of cleanup tasks, then either perform the cleanup or schedule a routine cleanup using Task Scheduler or Maintenance Wizard (described later in this chapter). Some of the cleanup tasks performed by the Disk Cleanup tool include the following:

◆ Emptying the Recycling Bin

◆ Deleting specific types of files, such as temporary Internet files or downloadable program files

◆ Deleting Windows components that you don't use

◆ Deleting programs you don't use

◆ Converting a FAT16 drive to FAT32

The Settings tab in the Disk Cleanup dialog box lets you configure the Disk Cleanup tool to run automatically when the drive is low on disk space.

Optimizing Disks

The hard drive is an extremely important feature in the real life of any network administrator, and Microsoft makes no secret of its desire to ensure that anyone who becomes an MCSE should know how to maintain, optimize, and troubleshoot hard drives. You can expect the Windows 98 exam to include questions on how and when to use the following tools:

◆ **ScanDisk.** A Windows 98 utility that searches for and corrects disk errors.

◆ **Disk Defragmenter.** Windows 98's built-in disk defragmenter utility.

◆ **Compression Agent.** A utility that optimizes disk compression hard drives.

◆ **Disk Cleanup.** A utility that performs routine cleanup tasks to free disk space. Disk Cleanup isn't referenced directly in the Windows 98 exam objectives, but it is included with the three preceding utilities in the set of disk maintenance tools provided with Maintenance Wizard, so you should know what it is and what it does.

Refer to Chapter 5 for more information about compressing, configuring, and maintaining hard disks in Windows 98.

SCHEDULING AND AUTOMATING TASKS

One part of optimization is reducing the total expense of operating a PC in a production environment. Microsoft has recently placed increased emphasis on lowering maintenance costs, and, as part of this low-maintenance-cost strategy, Microsoft includes the Task Scheduler automation tool with Windows 98. Task Scheduler is similar to the System Agent tool included with the Windows 95 Plus Pack. For setting up routine disk maintenance, Windows 98 also includes a wizard called Maintenance Wizard. You'll learn about Task Scheduler and Maintenance Wizard in the following two sections.

Task Scheduler

Task Scheduler is a Windows 98 utility that runs in the background and automatically executes routine tasks. Step by Step 7.3 describes how to schedule a task using Task Scheduler.

STEP BY STEP

7.3 Scheduling a Task

1. Select Start, Programs, Accessories, System Tools, Scheduled tasks.

2. When you first start Task Scheduler, you'll see that it is preconfigured to run ScanDisk, Disk Defragmenter, and Disk Cleanup (see Figure 7.22). You can schedule these tasks, or you can add a new task to Task Scheduler (see step 3).

3. To add a new scheduled task, double-click on the Add Scheduled Task icon in the Scheduled Tasks window. The Add Scheduled Task icon will invoke the Scheduled Task Wizard, which will lead you through a series of screens defining configuring the new Scheduled Task entry.

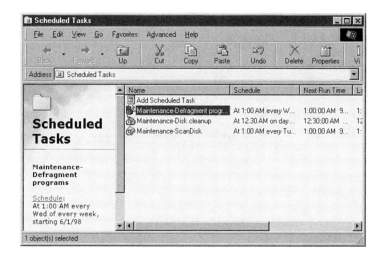

FIGURE 7.22
Click on the Add Scheduled Task icon in the Task Scheduler main window to schedule a new task.

You can use Task Scheduler to execute any of the following:

- Program files such as .exe and .com files

- Windows application files with registered file types. For instance, you could open a Microsoft Word .doc file from Task Scheduler.

- MS-DOS batch files (.bat files)

- Windows Scripting Host scripts, such as .js and .vbs scripts.

The Scheduled Task Wizard lets you specify a time interval of daily, weekly, or monthly scheduling. If you want to execute the task more often, or if you want to schedule a precise completion time, click on the Advanced button in the Task Properties Schedule tab.

4. To view or edit the schedule for a task, right-click on the task in the Task Scheduler window and choose Properties. The Task tab of the Task Properties dialog box (see Figure 7.23) defines settings such as the path and filename of the program you want to run. The Schedule tab (see Figure 7.24) lets you define when the task will run. The Settings tab (see Figure 7.25) provides other useful settings. You can specify power management settings, such as whether to execute the specified task if the computer is running on batteries and idle-time settings, such as how long the computer should be idle before beginning the task. (The idle-time settings are useful if you only want the scheduled tasks—such as a defragmentation—when the computer isn't being used for something else).

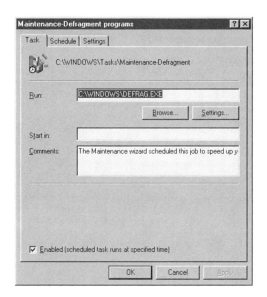

FIGURE 7.23
The Task Properties Task tab defines the path to the scheduled task—in this case, the Disk Defragmenter utility.

FIGURE 7.24
The Task Properties Schedule tab gives the time when the task will run.

FIGURE 7.25
The Task Properties Settings tab lets you configure task settings.

Maintenance Wizard

Maintenance Wizard is primarily an alternative front end for the
Task Scheduler. The main purpose of Maintenance Wizard is to let
you schedule the following tasks:

◆ Disk compression

◆ Disk Defragmenter

◆ ScanDisk

◆ Disk Cleanup

See the discussions of these maintenance tasks earlier in this chapter.
Maintenance Wizard's Custom option offers a few additional features. For instance, to make Windows start faster, you can disable
automatic startup for specific programs that presently start when
Windows starts.

To start Maintenance Wizard, select Start, Programs, Accessories,
System Tools, Maintenance Wizard. Maintenance Wizard will ask if
you'd like to perform maintenance now, or if you'd like to change
maintenance settings. To perform maintenance using the existing
maintenance settings, select Perform Maintenance Now. To change
maintenance settings, follow the procedure described in Step by
Step 7.4.

STEP BY STEP

7.4 Scheduling Maintenance or Changing Maintenance Settings

1. Select Start, Programs, Accessories, System Tools, Maintenance Wizard.

2. In the first Maintenance Wizard dialog box, choose the option button labeled Change My Maintenance Settings or Schedule.

3. Maintenance Wizard asks if you'd like to use the Express or the Custom maintenance setup. As you would guess, the Express method is faster, and the Custom method offers more options. Choose a method.

4. If you choose the Express method in step 3, Maintenance Wizard will offer you three optional time periods for running the maintenance tasks. Choose Nights (Midnight to 3:00 a.m.), Days (Noon to 3:00 p.m.), or Evenings (8:00 p.m. to 11:00 p.m.), and click on Next. In the next screen, choose whether you'd like to perform the maintenance for the first time when you exit Maintenance Wizard, and click on Finish. Maintenance Wizard will run Compression Agent, Disk Defragmenter, ScanDisk, and Disk Cleanup.

   If you choose the Custom method in step 3, Maintenance Wizard will guide you through a series of maintenance options. Choose a time for running maintenance tasks (as described in the preceding paragraph). In the Start Windows More Quickly screen, deselect programs currently configured to start when the system starts. The following screen lets you configure settings individually for Compression Agent, Disk Defragmenter, ScanDisk, and Disk Cleanup. In the final screen, choose whether you'd like to perform the maintenance for the first time when you exit Maintenance Wizard, and click on Finish.

VERIFYING AND UPDATING FILES

In keeping with Microsoft's strategy of optimizing the PC by reducing administration costs, Windows 98 adds tools designed to make it easier to discover and replace missing, corrupt, or outdated system files. Those tools include the following:

◆ Windows Update

◆ Signature Verification Tool

◆ System File Checker

You'll learn about these tools in the following sections. Chapter 8, "Troubleshooting Windows 98," describes additional tools and strategies you can use to troubleshoot system files.

Windows Update

Windows 98's Windows Update feature is really a shortcut to a Web site maintained by Microsoft where you'll find enhancements, patches, fixes, and new drivers for your Windows 98 installation. To connect to the Windows Update Web site (**http://windowsupdate.microsoft.com**), click on the Start button and select the Windows Update icon.

From the Windows Update site (see Figure 7.26), you can download a special ActiveX program that will automatically analyze your system and determine if any components need updating. You can add new components to your system, whether or not you elect to download this automatic ActiveX analysis program. To update your system, click Product Updates. The first time you access the Product Updates page, a dialog box will appear asking if you want Product Updates to analyze your system to determine what components have already been installed. If you click Yes, Product Updates will analyze your system and display a list of suggested upgrade options. If you click No, you'll still get a list of suggested components at the Windows Update site, but some of the components may be components you don't need. Browse through the component list and look for components you want to add to your system.

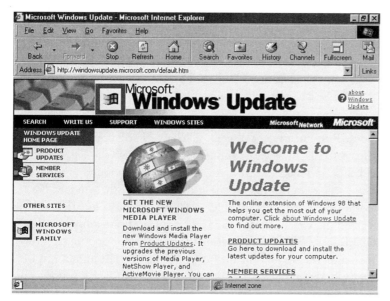

FIGURE 7.26
The Windows Update Web site lets you automatically update your Windows 98 installation.

The update list is divided into the following categories:

◆ Critical Updates

◆ Picks of the Month

◆ Recommended Updates

◆ Additional Windows Features

◆ Device Drivers

The Critical Updates are listed first. Microsoft recommends that you download any critical updates.

Signature Verification Tool

Microsoft maintains a quality standard for drivers that will be used with Windows 98. Windows drivers are tested by the Windows Hardware Quality Labs (WHQL), and drivers that pass the tests receive WHQL approval. All drivers that have passed the WHQL approval process receive a digital signature to verify that the driver meets the WHQL standard. The *signature* is a special string built into the file that acts as a kind of seal of approval. Certain system files also receive this digital signature.

Windows 98 includes a tool called the Signature Verification Tool (sigverif.exe). The Signature Verification Tool (see Figure 7.27) lets you search for signed files or unsigned files in a specific directory.

You can use the Signature Verification Tool to ensure that a file bears Microsoft's signature.

To start the Signature Verification Tool, click on the Start menu and choose Run, then type sigverif. Click on New Search in the Microsoft Signature Verification Tool window (refer to Figure 7.27) and click on Find Now to start a search. The files found in the search will appear in the file list at the bottom of the window. For additional information on a file, select the file in the file list and click on the Details button to invoke the Certificate Properties dialog box (see Figure 7.28). This dialog box provides additional information on the file and the file's digital signature. For instance, you can verify that no one has tampered with the file since it was signed.

Windows 98 provides for automatic signature checking when new drivers are installed. You can choose from three levels of signature checking:

◆ **Level 0.** No signature checking.

◆ **Level 1.** Checks to see if a new driver has passed WHQL approval. If a driver does not bear a valid signature, a dialog box appears warning you that the driver has failed the signature check.

◆ **Level 2.** Prohibits the installation of any drivers that fail the signature check.

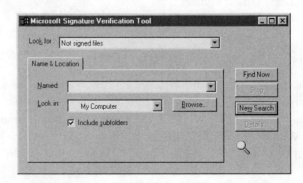

FIGURE 7.27
The Signature Verification Tool ensures that drivers on your system bear the WHQL digital signature.

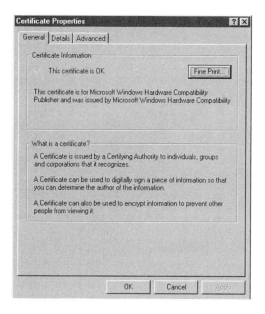

You can enable automatic digital signature checking through system policies. See Chapter 6, "Managing Profiles and System Policies," for more information about system policies. To enable digital signature checking through system policies, load the `Windows.adm` template and look for the default computer policy with the path `Windows98System\Install Device Drivers\Digital Signature Check`.

You can also set up signature checking using the Registry Editor. Set the value `HKEY_LOCAL_MACHINE\Software\Microsoft\Driver Signing` to a value of `00 00 00 00` for Level 0, `01 00 00 00` for Level 1, or `02 00 00 00` for Level 2.

System File Checker

System File Checker checks your system files and looks for missing or corrupt files. System File Checker can also track changes to your system files in a log file.

You can access System File Checker through the Microsoft System Information utility. To Start the Microsoft System Information, click on the Start menu and select Programs, Accessories, System Tools, System Information. From the Microsoft System Information main window, pull down the Tools menu and select System File Checker.

The System File Checker main window is shown in Figure 7.29.

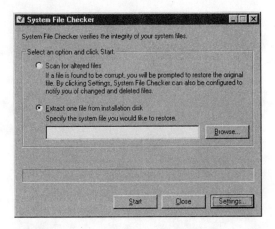

FIGURE 7.29
The System File Checker looks for missing and corrupt system files.

This window offers the following two options:

◆ **Scan for Altered Files.** Scans your hard drive for altered system files and prompts you to replace a file that has been changed or deleted.

◆ **Extract One File from Installation Disk.** If you know a certain system file is altered or missing, you can extract the original version of the file from the .cab files on the Windows 98 installation disk.

The Settings button invokes the System File Checker Settings dialog box, which lets you configure various settings. In the Settings tab (see Figure 7.30), you can elect to back up files before restoring. You can also dictate whether to log the results to a log file and whether to append to or overwrite an existing log file. The check boxes at the bottom of the Settings tab let you specify whether to check for changed and/or deleted files.

The Search Criteria tab in the System File Checker Settings dialog box lets you specify search criteria for the system file check. You can select folders you want to check, or you can add or remove file types from the search list. The Advanced tab (see Figure 7.31) lets you configure a verification data file. By default, a file called default.sfc supplies the baseline system file information that System File Checker will use to check the integrity of system files. In the Advanced tab, you can specify a different verification data file. Click on the Create button to create a new verification data file. Or, you can restore the settings used in the original default.sfc file by clicking on the Restore Defaults button.

FIGURE 7.30
Configure System File Checker settings in the Settings tab.

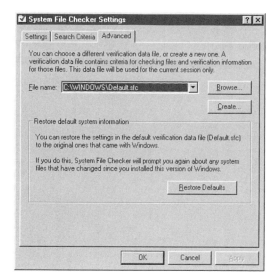

FIGURE 7.31
The Advanced tab of the System File Checker Settings dialog box lets you choose a verification data file.

CASE STUDY: SUCCESS TITLE COMPANY

ESSENCE OF THE CASE

Here are the essential elements in this case:

- System Monitoring must be done remotely.

- All machines are running Windows 98.

- Tina needs to be able to monitor the processor, memory, and occasionally the network card of a machine.

SCENARIO

Tina Volten of the Success Title Company is responsible for keeping 45 Windows 98 machines running at optimum performance. Tina would like to monitor system performance remotely with as little downtime as possible.

ANALYSIS

Each Windows 98 computer would need to have the Remote Registry Editing Service installed. Each Windows 98 machine would have to have Remote Administration enabled. Tina can monitor each Windows 98 machine through System Monitor and can connect to the remote machines.

CHAPTER SUMMARY

KEY TERMS

- Net Watcher
- System Monitor
- counters
- Resource Meter
- Disk Defragmenter
- ScanDisk
- cross-linked files
- DriveSpace 3
- Compression Agent
- Disk Cleanup
- Task Scheduler
- Windows Update
- Signature Verification Tool
- System File Checker

This chapter introduced some of Windows 98's monitoring and optimization tools. You learned about Net Watcher, System Monitor, and Resource Meter. This chapter also discussed the disk maintenance tools Disk Defragmenter, ScanDisk, DriveSpace 3, and Compression Agent. You also learned about automating maintenance tasks in Windows 98 using the Task Scheduler and Maintenance Wizard, and you learned how to keep your Windows 98 installation up-to-date using Windows Update and System File Checker.

Microsoft has been known to surprise exam takers, but in general, the most important things to know about these utilities for the exam are what they are, what they do, when to use them, and how to reach them. Many of the details for configuring particular settings are included with this chapter so that you can become familiar with these tools, but for the most part, the details of particular options are not as important as knowing which tool to use in a given situation.

APPLY YOUR KNOWLEDGE

Exercises

7.1   Optimizing the Hard Disk Using Disk Defragmenter for Windows 98

This exercise will use Disk Defragmenter to defragment your hard drive. You'll need one computer running Windows 98.

Estimated Time: 20 minutes

1. Click Start, then select Programs, Accessories, System Tools, and click on Disk Defragmenter.

2. Disk Defragmenter will start and you will be prompted to choose which drive to defragment. Choose your C: drive for this exercise.

3. Click on the Settings button. The Disk Defragmenter Settings dialog box will appear.

4. Make certain the two settings, Rearrange Program Files so My Programs Start Faster and Check the Drive for Errors, are selected.

5. The bottom section of the dialog box asks if you'd like these settings to be used for this session or for all future sessions. Accept the default of Every Time I Defragment My Hard Drive and click OK.

6. Click OK to begin defragmenting your hard disk.

7.2   Optimizing the Hard Disk by Using the Maintenance Wizard

Maintenance Wizard is a tool that allows you to schedule disk maintenance and to select what programs will start at system startup. This exercise will use Maintenance Wizard to schedule some tasks on your system.

Estimated Time: 20 minutes

1. Click Start and then select Programs, Accessories, System Tools and then click on Maintenance Wizard.

2. Maintenance Wizard starts and asks if you'd like to perform maintenance now or change your maintenance settings or schedule. For this exercise, choose Change My Maintenance settings or schedule and then click OK.

3. Maintenance Wizard continues and asks if you'd like to accept the most common maintenance settings or whether you'd like to customize your maintenance settings. For this exercise, choose custom, and then click Next.

4. The next dialog box prompts you to set a time that is most convenient to do the maintenance tasks. Choose a time during which your computer is likely to be turned on but not in use, and then choose next.

5. To start Windows more quickly, you can choose which programs will launch at startup time. Review the programs that are currently configured to launch each time you start Windows and clear the check mark next to any program that you don't want to launch when Windows starts. Choose next when you are ready to continue.

6. You are prompted to make a decision about running Compression Agent (or Disk Defragmenter, if you don't have a compressed drive). For this exercise, choose Yes.

7. Click on the Reschedule button to set a specific time to run Compression Agent (or Disk Defragmenter).

8. From the Schedule Task drop-down list, choose Weekly. From the Start Time drop-down list, choose to start the utility at 1:00 a.m. each Monday.

9. Click on the Advanced tab. From here you can also choose to start and end these settings on a given date. You can also choose to repeat the task every given hour or minute until a set time, or you can designate a duration. For this exercise, you won't need any special timings, so just choose Cancel.

10. Click on Settings to choose which drive you'd like to optimize.

11. Click OK to accept the settings.

12. Choose Next to continue with Maintenance Wizard.

13. Similar dialog boxes appear for Disk Defragmenter and ScanDisk. Click on Reschedule and choose the weekly option, at 1:00 a.m. each Tuesday.

14. Choose OK to accept the time. Click the Settings tab and choose a drive. For this exercise, choose Thorough for the type of test.

15. Check the box to have ScanDisk automatically fix any errors and then click OK.

16. Choose Next to continue.

17. Maintenance Wizard now asks if you'd like to delete any unnecessary files. Look through the proposed list of files that Maintenance Wizard will delete and make sure you're comfortable with all the choices. Choose Yes, and then click on the Reschedule button.

18. Choose to delete these files weekly at 1:00 a.m. each Wednesday. Click OK to accept these settings.

19. Click on the Settings button to choose exactly what types of files will be deleted from your PC. For this exercise, check the Recycle Bin files to delete these automatically as well.

20. Choose OK and then click Next to continue.

21. Maintenance Wizard displays the tasks you have created for your machine and the settings for each. Choose Finish to accept these settings.

7.3 Using DriveSpace 3 on a Floppy Disk

This exercise will utilize Windows 98's DriveSpace 3 on a floppy disk. Because compression is not allowed on FAT32 drives, a floppy will be used in lieu of a fixed drive. The procedure is nearly identical.

Estimated Time: 10 minutes

1. Insert a blank floppy disk into the floppy drive (drive A:).

2. Click on Start, then point to Programs, Accessories, System Tools, and then click on DriveSpace3.

3. The DriveSpace3 window appears, displaying a list of drives in your computer. Click once on Drive A:.

4. From the Drive menu, choose Compress. A dialog box will appear, showing the amount of free space before and after the compression.

5. Click Start to begin the compression. After the compression is complete, the status of the compressed drive will be displayed.

6. Click Close and then exit DriveSpace 3.

APPLY YOUR KNOWLEDGE

7.4 Updating Drivers and Service Packs via Windows Update

Windows Update is a utility that allows you to update your Windows 98 operating system and device drivers. This exercise walks you through the process of doing just that. This exercise may be somewhat slow if you do not have a fast Internet connection.

Estimated Time: 15–40 minutes

1. Connect to your ISP, either through your Dial-Up Networking connection or through your company's LAN.

2. Click on Start and then click on the Windows Update icon.

3. Your default Internet browser will launch Microsoft's Windows Update site.

4. Because this Web page will likely change from day to day, you will need to locate the section on the Web site that refers to Product Updates to update your version on Windows 98. When you find the link, choose it to continue.

5. You may be prompted that the program can determine what components have been installed on your computer and which updates you have received. For this exercise, click on OK.

6. After the program runs, the page will be refreshed with updates and add-ons for Windows 98. You can select which components should be added to your system through this Web site.

7. Review the components, and choose which components, if any, are applicable to your system and then download the selections. Remember that Microsoft recommends you download any Critical Updates.

8. After the download is complete, the updates will be installed and you may be prompted to restart your computer.

7.5 Automating Tasks Through Task Scheduler

Task Scheduler allows you to run any program, such as a maintenance type application, at any given time. The exercise will focus on Task Scheduler. You'll launch Calculator as an example.

Estimated Time: 15 minutes

1. Click on Start then point to Programs, Accessories, System tools, and then click on Scheduled Tasks.

2. The Scheduled Tasks dialog box appears. You may already have entries in the Scheduled Tasks dialog box from the Maintenance Wizard exercises earlier in this module.

3. Click on the Add Scheduled Task button and the Scheduled Task Wizard appears. Choose Next to continue.

4. A list of programs is presented that you can choose from. If the program you want to run is not in the list, you can browse your computer or Network to find the application you are looking for.

5. From the list of applications presented, choose Calculator for this exercise.

6. Choose Next to Continue.

7. If you'd like to assign a different name to the task, you can do so.

8. From the list of times to perform the task, choose When I Log On and then choose Next.

9. The task is confirmed to start each time you log on to your machine. Check the Open Advanced Properties for the Task checkbox and then choose Finish.

10. The Task Properties dialog box for Calculator appears. You can make more choices regarding the calculator task.

11. Click the Settings tab and review the settings for the Calculator tab. For this exercise, under Power Management, choose that the task should stop if battery mode begins.

12. Choose OK to finish.

13. To test the task, log out and log back on to your PC.

14. Finally, to delete this task, unless you want the calculator to start each time you log on, return to the Scheduled Tasks and right-click the calculator task and choose Delete.

15. Close the Scheduled Tasks dialog box to continue.

7.6 Using System File Checker

System File Checker will investigate your Windows System files and repair any files if necessary. This exercise walks you through these processes.

Estimated Time: 20 minutes

1. Click on Start, then point to Programs, Accessories, System Tools, and then click on System Information. The System Information program appears and displays some basic information about your PC.

2. From the Tools menu, choose System File Checker.

3 The System File Checker asks if you'd like to check the files, or extract a specific file from the 98 CD. For this exercise, choose Scan for Altered Files.

4. Click Start to begin the process.

5. The System File Checker will begin scanning your Windows System Files. If there is a problem with a file, you'll be alerted and prompted to replace the files from disk.

6. After the System File Checker is complete, click on the Details button for more information.

7. Review the results and click OK, then click OK again.

8. Click Close to close the System File Checker.

9. Exit the System Information utility.

7.7 Monitoring the System

This exercise will use System Monitor to monitor real-time activity on your Windows 98 machine.

Estimated Time: 15 minutes

1. Click Start, then point to Programs, Accessories, System Tools, and then click System Monitor.

2. The System Monitor will open in the Chart view. Notice that the processor is already being monitored.

3. From the Edit menu, choose Add Item. From the categories, choose Memory Manager; from Items, choose Page Faults to track how many page faults are generated through Virtual Memory pages being swapped to RAM.

4. From the Edit menu, choose Add Item. From the categories choose Kernel; from Items, choose Virtual Machines. Click OK.

5. Your chart is now displaying data about the activity of your system. From the Start menu, launch some applications, including a DOS prompt.

6. After you have launched several applications, switch back to the System Monitor. Note the activity these additional applications have on your system's performance.

7. From the toolbar, click on the button that will change the chart to a line chart.

8. From the toolbar, click on the button that will change the chart to a numerical expression.

9. Close the DOS prompt and then switch back to the System Monitor. Note the number of virtual machines.

10. Close additional applications and notice the effect that this has on the system.

11. From the File menu, choose Exit.

Review Questions

1. What are some Windows 98 tools that allow you to maintain and optimize the hard disk?

2. What is the purpose of the Disk Cleanup tool?

3. What Windows 98 tools manage data compression?

4. What Windows 98 feature allows you to update drivers and the operating system via the Internet?

5. What file types can be scheduled to run as tasks using Task Scheduler?

6. What Windows 98 tools can check the integrity of system files?

7. What Windows 98 tool can be used to view system performance on the local machine or on remote machines?

8. Why is monitoring a system important?

Exam Questions

1. Mike would like a tool that will help him eliminate unnecessary files from his PC. Of the following, what tools should Mike use?

A. Backup

B. System File Checker

C. DriveSpace 3

D. Disk Cleanup

2. Jane calls you to report that she was installing some new software when a message appeared on her Windows 98 machine asking for a newer version of a certain Windows 98 system module. What would you recommend Jane do?

A. Reinstall Windows 98.

B. Add the updated Windows module through Add/Remove Programs.

C. Use Computer Update Control Panel.

D. Use Windows Update.

3. Chris would like to schedule Microsoft Excel to start every Friday morning at 10:00 a.m. to remind him to compute the sales reps' commission reports. What is the best way to configure this?

A. Create a batch file and use the AT command.

B. Create an entry in the AT scheduler to trigger the program every seven days at 10:00 a.m.

APPLY YOUR KNOWLEDGE

  C. Add an Automated Task in Task Scheduler that launches Excel every Friday at 10:00 a.m.

  D. This cannot be done.

4. Karen calls to alert you that she accidentally deleted some files from her Windows directory, then she promptly emptied the Recycle Bin. Now she's getting weird messages whenever she tries to open certain programs, or connect to the network. What should Karen do?

  A. Reinstall Windows 98.

  B. Run the Windows Update utility.

  C. Run the System File Checker.

  D. Run the Undelete utility from the Systems folder.

5. Lee tells you that his computer almost always runs ScanDisk whenever he boots up. He would like to know what the problem is and how can he stop ScanDisk from running each time.

  A. Lee's computer is low on disk space. ScanDisk will always run until more than 20 percent of the disk is free.

  B. Lee's computer is low on memory. Because Windows 98 uses virtual memory, the disk has to be optimized so that virtual memory can operate at the fullest capacity. ScanDisk will continue to run each time until more memory has been added to his computer.

  C. Lee is not shutting his computer off properly. He needs to choose Start and Shut Down to eliminate the problem.

  D. ScanDisk will always run on Windows 98. Lee can disable ScanDisk through the System applet in Control Panel.

6. You are a consultant for King Manufacturing. King would like to automate routine disk maintenance to run at nighttime so as not to interfere with the daytime activity. What is your recommendation?

  A. Compress the drive; regular maintenance will occur automatically.

  B. Use Maintenance Wizard to automate the schedule for the desired tools.

  C. Use the AT command to schedule maintenance entries.

  D. Create a batch file that will trigger all of the maintenance tools to run at 1:00 a.m. each day.

7. You are a consultant for a law office. Your contact reports to you that several of the office's Windows 98 machines are running slow when they launch several applications. How can you monitor this problem to troubleshoot the issue?

  A. Launch the program on each machine and test out the machine by using it for approximately 30 minutes.

  B. Use the System Monitor while the program is launched. Track several key issues, such as the Kernel and memory.

  C. Use the 98 Diagnostics tool off the Windows 98 CD-ROM.

  D. Use the protocol analyzer to see if the machines are receiving too many network interrupts from the LAN.

8. You are an administrator of a small LAN. Several of your peers report to you that their machines are slow. How can you monitor the performance

of their machines through the network with a Windows 98 tool?

A. You cannot monitor system performance through the network.

B. You can monitor system performance through the network by using the Resource Meter tool with the option pack installed.

C. You can monitor system performance through the network by using the System Performance monitoring tool and choosing the remote computer to monitor.

D. You can monitor the system through the network only by using the Registry Editor and connecting to the remote Registry.

9. Sharon calls you because she is having trouble sharing a file off of her Windows 98 machine. How can you help Sharon share out the file? Choose the best answer.

A. Go to Sharon's machine and do it for her.

B. Use Net Watcher to share out the resource for her.

C. Use the Registry Editor to create the new share.

D. Map a drive to her C: drive and then share out the resource through Explorer.

10. You are considering moving resources off of users' Windows 98 machines to a Windows NT Server. How can you view what users are currently connected to the Windows 98 machine?

A. Use Windows NT Server Manager to view all of the users connected to Windows 98 machines.

B. Use Net Watcher to see what users are connected to the resources you are considering moving to the Windows NT Server.

C. You will have to visit each machine and see what users are connected to the resource.

D. Use the NET USERS \\server name command.

Answers to Review Questions

1. Some tools included with Windows 98 that allow you to maintain and optimize your hard disks are ScanDisk, Disk Defragmenter, DriveSpace 3, Compression Agent, and the Disk Cleanup utility. You can use Task Scheduler and Maintenance Wizard to automate disk maintenance tasks. (For more information, refer to the section "Optimizing Disks.")

2. Use Disk Cleanup to get rid of unnecessary files that may be using valuable disk space, such as temporary files, Internet cache files, and unneeded install files that are safe to delete. (For more information, refer to the section "Optimizing Disks.")

3. DriveSpace 3 is Windows 98's primary compression utility. After you compress your hard drive, you can change the level of compression by using Compression Agent. (For more information, refer to the section "Optimizing Disks.")

4. The Windows Update feature is responsible for updating automatically updating the operating system. (For more information, refer to the section "Verifying and Updating Files.")

APPLY YOUR KNOWLEDGE

5. You can schedule .exe files, .com files, .bat files, files with registered file types, and Windows scripts. (For more information, refer to the section "Scheduling and Automating Tasks.")

6. The System File Checker can check the integrity of system components. The System File Checker can be launched through the System Information utility included with Windows 98. (For more information, refer to the section "Verifying and Updating Files.")

7. System Monitor allows monitoring of system performance on both the local machine and remote machines. (For more information, refer to the section "Monitoring System Performance Using System Monitor.")

8. Monitoring system performance is crucial to effective planning, troubleshooting, and for planning system growth. (For more information, refer to the section "Monitoring System Performance Using System Monitor.")

Answers to Exam Questions

1. **D.** Disk Cleanup will help Mike eliminate unnecessary files from his hard disk. (For more information, refer to the section "Optimizing Disks.")

2. **D.** Jane should launch Windows Update to retrieve any service packs or updates for Windows 98. (For more information, refer to the section "Verifying and Updating Files.")

3. **C.** The Task Scheduler lets you launch a program at any time. (For more information, refer to the section "Scheduling and Automating Tasks.")

4. **C.** The System File Checker will check out her system files and prompt her to recover the missing or corrupted files from her Windows 98 installation source. (For more information, refer to the section "Verifying and Updating Files.")

5. **C.** If Lee is powering down his PC without going through the correct shutdown procedure, his PC will always run ScanDisk when he restarts. (For more information, refer to the section "Optimizing Disks.")

6. **B.** The easiest way to configure this for your client is through the Maintenance Wizard. You can choose the maintenance tools to run, when they are to run, and the settings that will be enforced for each tool. (For more information, refer to the section "Scheduling and Automating Tasks.")

7. **B.** Use the System Monitor to track down the system resources that may be causing the bottleneck while the application is running. (For more information, refer to the section "Monitoring System Performance Using System Monitor.")

8. **C.** Through System Monitor you can monitor remote computers as well as the local machine. (For more information, refer to the section "Monitoring System Performance Using System Monitor.")

9. **B.** Use Net Watcher to share out the resource for her. (For more information, refer to the section "Monitoring System Performance Using System Monitor.")

10. **B.** Use Net Watcher to view how many users currently are connected to the users' machines and to what resources on their machines. (For more information, refer to the section "Monitoring System Performance Using System Monitor.")

APPLY YOUR KNOWLEDGE

Suggested Readings and Resources

1. *The Windows 98 Resource Kit*; Microsoft Press

2. *The Windows 98 Professional Reference*, Hallberg and Casad; New Riders

This chapter helps you prepare for the Microsoft exam by covering the following objectives within the "Troubleshooting" category:

Diagnose and resolve installation failures. Tasks include the following:

> **Resolving file and driver version conflicts by using Version Conflict Manager and the Microsoft System Information Utility.**

▶ Your ability to solve installation failures will be tested on the Microsoft exam. You should have a working knowledge of the Version Conflict Manager and the Microsoft System Information Utility.

Diagnose and resolve boot process failures. Tasks include the following:

> **Editing configuration files by using System Configuration Utility.**

▶ System Configuration Utility will allow you to quickly edit and update your system files. A working knowledge of this new tool is essential to passing the Windows 98 exam.

Diagnose and resolve connectivity problems in a Microsoft environment and a mixed Microsoft and NetWare environment. Tools include the following:

> **WinIPCfg**
>
> **Net Watcher**
>
> **Ping**
>
> **Tracert**

▶ Troubleshooting Microsoft and NetWare networks is an important element in the Windows 98 exam. Know how and why to use the connectivity tools included with Windows 98.

CHAPTER 8

Troubleshooting Windows 98

OUTLINE

▶ To adequately prepare for this section of the exam, invest your time in troubleshooting problems arising from installation failures. Use the Version Conflict Manager and explore the Microsoft System Information Utility to retrieve information about different Windows 98 computers. Experiment with the System Configuration Utility to edit your startup and system files. Delve into the networking components of Windows 98 to understand how these work and what troubles can arise from incorrect configurations. These troubles can stem from failed resource access to incorrect protocol information. In short, know it all.

INTRODUCTION

In a complex operating system environment, troubleshooting technical problems or optimizing for performance is never an exact science. Although the number of possible hardware and software combinations (and resulting conflicts and configuration issues) on any given computer is virtually limitless, you can narrow the scope of any problems that may arise and, with luck, isolate the offending component(s), whether internal or external. Often the problems are a combination of both internal and external factors. Troubleshooting is your bread and butter as a network administrator, or as a Microsoft Certified Systems Engineer. Your users or clients are not really interested in how many tests you have passed, or how many trade journals you read. They want to know, "Can you fix my computer—NOW?!" To this end (and to prepare you to pass the Windows 98 exam), this chapter takes a close look at troubleshooting.

This chapter examines the following main topics:

◆ General troubleshooting guidelines

◆ Installation failures

◆ Boot process failures

◆ Connectivity problems

◆ Printing problems

◆ File system problems

◆ Resource access problems

◆ Application problems

◆ Hardware and hardware driver problems

GENERAL TROUBLESHOOTING GUIDELINES

You can follow a number of steps when attempting to isolate technical problems. Some are specific to Windows 98; others are just part of a logical approach to any problem:

1. Determine whether the problem occurs with regularity. If the problem is regular, your next step is to look for patterns and what factors are common to each occurrence of the problem. If the problem occurs randomly, it becomes more difficult to diagnose. You should note that, although a problem seems to occur randomly, it often is in fact occurring regularly—but the factors linking each occurrence may be very obscure. It is rare for computers to behave erratically for no reason, except in the case of intermittent hardware failures.

2. Determine whether the problem began after a particular change was made to the configuration of the operating system, such as a driver update, the addition of a new modem, or a new video resolution setting. If this is the case, try to determine how the new configuration and the problem may be related.

3. Use binary logic to isolate one variable at a time in your search for the failing component. If the operating system is suspect, for example, turn off all its advanced features simultaneously. If the problem goes away, refine your search, turning the features back on one at a time until the problem reoccurs. If turning off all the features does not solve the problem, you can likely look elsewhere (see step 4).

4. Determine as precisely as possible whether the problem seems to be clearly internal to Windows 98 or includes external software/hardware. Generally, installing Windows 98 on a new computer will not cause many problems, unless those problems are related to hardware incompatibilities. The situation always becomes more complex when an existing system's software and hardware are migrated to Windows 98. Windows 98 is then likely to inherit any existing problems with the computer as well as some potential new problems (such as Windows 3.1 applications that do not work properly under Windows 98). The best example of this methodology is booting into Safe mode, because this disables many if not all special features, drivers, and software of the operating system. If the problem goes away in Safe mode, the problem probably is limited to a few key configuration parameters.

5. Determine whether sequence is important to the problem. Is it a matter of the order in which things happen in the operating

system? This can point out conflicts between different applications, for example. Does one application fail only after another particular application has loaded?

6. Is this a known or common problem? Does it occur on other computers, or is it an isolated event? To find known problems, consult your available technical resources to learn potential solutions or to determine whether a known solution exists. Obviously, this is much easier to do if you can produce the problem on demand.

Although you cannot anticipate every potential problem that a system may encounter when Windows 98 is installed, certain courses of action are recommended for particular troubleshooting scenarios. Because every technical problem is in many ways unique to its operating environment, these suggestions neither are exhaustive nor guaranteed to work in a given situation. Table 8.1 shows some possible solutions for common problems. These solutions are intended to provide examples of applicable methodologies.

TABLE 8.1

TROUBLESHOOTING EXAMPLES

Problem	*Possible Solution*
Cannot print to a local printer.	Verify that the correct driver is installed, ensure that the printer's buffer is clear, and try printing directly to the LPT port from a DOS prompt.
Cannot print to a network printer.	Ensure that File and Printer Sharing is enabled at the remote computer; verify that you have correct network protocols configured.
Print jobs are not spooling properly.	Disable spooling in the Properties sheet of the printer, which will indicate whether spooling is in fact the problem; verify that enough disk space is available to hold the spooled print jobs.
Print jobs are garbled.	Disable EMF spooling; check whether Windows 3.1 printer drivers are being used.
Fatal Exception errors and GPFs.	Try Safe mode; try a standard VGA driver; run ScanDisk with a full surface scan to check for corrupted files.

continues

| TABLE 8.1 | *continued* |

TROUBLESHOOTING EXAMPLES

Problem	*Possible Solution*
Message that communications port is already in use when attempting to use a terminal program.	Verify that no fax manager software is running in the background, waiting for calls because this ties up the communications port.
A newly installed ISA device is not functioning.	Check the Device Manager for conflicts with existing devices (designated by a yellow exclamation mark).
CD-ROM drive is not listed as a drive in the Explorer or the Device Manager.	Most likely not a supported brand; install Real-mode driver support.
A device is malfunctioning; but when it is removed from Device Manager and redetected, the problem persists.	Edit the Registry, delete the associated key under `HKLM\Enum\Root\`, restart the computer, and run hardware detection again.

DIAGNOSING AND RESOLVING INSTALLATION FAILURES

Diagnose and resolve installation failures.

Windows 98 installation is usually successful; but on occasion problems do arise. These problems are often traceable to legacy hardware or poorly documented off-brand equipment. This section is directed toward helping you troubleshoot Windows 98 Setup. Your best weapon when troubleshooting Setup is a thorough understanding of the different phases of the Setup program. You may want to review some of the material covered in Chapter 2, "Installing Windows 98," before you study this chapter.

As Chapter 2 mentions, Windows 98 Setup includes a Safe Recovery feature that helps you recover from failed installations. If Setup fails before hardware detection, when you restart, you'll be asked whether you want to use Safe Recovery to resume the installation. If you opt to use Safe Detection, Setup will inspect the log file setuplog.txt to determine where the installation terminated. Setup will then skip the step that caused the failure and resume the installation. If you choose not to use Safe Recovery, Setup will start over with the installation.

If Setup fails during hardware detection, a log file called detcrash.log will be created (as discussed later in this section). detcrash.log gives Setup the information it needs to resume the hardware detection and bypass the step that caused the failure. If detcrash.log is present in the root directory of the boot partition, Setup will automatically switch to Safe mode. As you'll learn later in this section, a text-file equivalent of detcrash.log called detlog.txt is also created so that users can review hardware detection information.

Given Setup's elaborate recovery mechanisms, the best thing to do if Setup fails is to restart your system and let Setup try to work around the problem. As Chapter 2 mentioned, Microsoft recommends the following action (in this order) if Setup stops unexpectedly:

1. Press F3 or click on the Exit button.

2. Press Ctrl + Alt + Del.

3. Turn off your computer, wait 15 seconds, then restart.

If Safe Recovery does not solve your Setup problems, you can use Setup's log files to guide your troubleshooting. The Windows 98 Setup program creates the log files setuplog.txt and detlog.txt (if Setup fails during hardware detection). Another pair of files (netlog.txt and bootlog.txt) is created as Windows 98 starts up the first time. The following list looks at each of the log files in detail:

◆ **setuplog.txt.** setuplog.txt is an ASCII text file that contains a log of the installation process. As Windows 98 installation progresses, entries are written into setuplog.txt for each step in sequence. This file is used by Windows 98's Safe Recovery feature in case of setup failure, and you can use it to look for the source of Setup errors.

NOTE

Allow Automatic Hardware Detection Several Times If necessary, allow Windows 98 to attempt automatic hardware detection several times before giving up. Although it may seem that the computer is locking up at the same place each time, in fact it might not be the same thing causing the lockup each time. Setup remembers what it was doing the last time it locked up and it tries something else. Allow automatic hardware detection to do its job before choosing the manual route.

setuplog.txt is stored as a hidden file on the computer's root directory. Because new entries are added to setuplog.txt chronologically, start at the end of the file if you're trying to determine what caused the Windows 98 Setup program to fail.

◆ **detcrash.log.** detcrash.log is a binary file containing information on Windows 98 Setup's hardware detection process. When Setup fails during hardware detection, detcrash.log is created as a hidden file in the root directory of the installation drive. When you reboot, Setup will use the information in detcrash.log to restart the installation. An ASCII equivalent of detcrash.log, called detlog.txt, is also created.

◆ **detlog.txt.** This is an ASCII text file that contains a record of all devices found during the hardware detection phase of installation. If a device is found, the detected parameters are identified and recorded.

Do not confuse this with detcrash.log! If the hardware detection phase should cause the computer to stall or lock up, a binary file named detcrash.log is created. (See the discussion of detcrash.log earlier in this section.) Although detlog.txt is an ASCII file for you to read, the Windows 98 Setup program reads the binary information in detcrash.log to determine what steps were successfully completed.

detlog.txt is stored as a hidden file on the computer's root directory. Information is added to this file in the same order as the hardware detection phase. If you need to determine what caused the Windows 98 Setup program to fail or lock up, refer to the entries at the bottom of this file before restarting the system.

◆ **netlog.txt.** This is an ASCII text file that contains a record of all detected network components found during installation. The network detection phase consists of four parts. These correspond with the four class types of network configuration: network clients, network protocols, network adapters, and network services (such as file and print sharing).

netlog.txt is stored as a non-hidden file on the computer's root directory. Information is added to this file in the same order as the network detection phase. If you need to determine what caused the Windows 98 Setup program's failure to communicate across the network, refer to the entries in this file.

You will see where Windows 98 found the network adapter and identified which protocols, clients, and services to bind to the card. At the end of each line, you should see OK. If you see a line such as Couldn't determine..., or some other failure notice, you have found your problem.

◆ **bootlog.txt.** This is an ASCII text file that contains a record of the current startup process when starting Windows 98. When Windows 98 is started for the first time, bootlog.txt is created automatically. For subsequent reboots, you can create a bootlog.txt file by pressing F8 at startup (to invoke the Boot menu) and choosing the Boot menu option Logged (\bootlog.txt). You can also create a Boot log by running win.com from the command line and including the /b switch.

bootlog.txt records the Windows 98 components and drivers as they are loaded and initialized, and records the status of each step. The information in bootlog.txt is written in sequence during startup. You might need to examine the information closely to determine which error occurred. The Windows 98 Resource Kit has a good description of the sections within this file.

bootlog.txt is stored as a hidden file on the computer's root directory. Information is added to this file during the Windows 98 startup process. If you need to determine what caused Windows 98 to fail or lock up, refer to the entries within this file before restarting again. bootlog.txt seems to write everything twice. The first line will read something like Loading VXD=..., and the next line will read something like LoadSuccess VXD=.... In troubleshooting, it is important to see what loaded successfully, as well as what loaded unsuccessfully. bootlog.txt provides that information.

The following sections discuss some other topics related to installation troubleshooting. The next section discusses some general Setup troubleshooting issues. After that, you'll learn about a pair of tools that Microsoft specifically mentions in the installation troubleshooting exam objective: Version Conflict Manager and Microsoft System Information Utility.

EXAM TIP

Memorize These It is a good idea to learn the names and descriptions of the Windows 98 Setup and startup log files discussed in this section. The Windows 98 exam may ask which file to use for a specific troubleshooting scenario.

Troubleshooting General Setup Issues

The first step in troubleshooting Windows 98 setup issues is to get back to the basics. When installation fails early in the setup process, it is often related to one or more of the following issues:

◆ Is a disk management utility installed? If it is, can you safely remove it? This might entail a BIOS upgrade (if available) and quite possibly require using FDISK and repartitioning the drive. If this is the case, do you have a good backup?

◆ Is the disk compressed with a third-party utility? If so, can you safely uncompress the drive?

◆ Does Setup hang during the ScanDisk phase of installation? (An application is considered to be hung if it is still running, but not responding to any messages from the system.) If Setup does hang during the ScanDisk phase, you can manually run ScanDisk, and force a thorough inspection of the drive prior to Windows 98 installation.

◆ Have you disabled virus protection? Remember, it may be loading automatically from your previous OS, or it may be enabled in the computer's BIOS. Some anti-virus programs prevent writing to the boot sector of the hard disk. If this is the case, Windows 98 Setup will either fail to install, or will not load correctly. To correct this situation, you must disable the virus protection. After Windows 98 is properly installed, you can re-enable virus protection.

◆ Have you turned off power management? At times power management can cause problems (particularly if your computer decides to take a nap during some long-winded phase of Windows 98 Setup).

◆ Have you made certain that your computer does not have a virus? Run a current anti-virus program and check for viruses after booting from a known clean disk. (Don't forget to disable virus protection before restarting Setup.)

◆ SmartDrive can cause problems with some SCSI hard disks. By default, during Windows 98 Setup, Smart Drive is loaded, but double-buffering is turned off. To work around this situation, simply use the /c switch to run Setup without SmartDrive.

◆ What is being loaded from the `autoexec.bat` and `config.sys`? To see if `autoexec.bat` or `config.sys` may be causing the problem, perform the following steps:

1. Rename `autoexec.bat` by typing the following from the command line: **`ren c:\autoexec.bat autoexec.aaa`**.

2. Rename `config.sys` by typing the following from the command line: **`ren c:\config.sys config.aaa`**.

3. Restart the computer and run Windows 98 Setup again.

Version Conflict Manager

Windows 95 and Windows 98 both include vast collections of supporting files and drivers, some created by Microsoft and some distributed to Microsoft by vendors of specific devices. These files and drivers are constantly being updated, and at times several versions of a file or driver may be in simultaneous circulation. It isn't uncommon for Windows 98 Setup to discover that the version of a file already present on the computer is newer than the version that Setup is attempting to install. Compatibility, however, is also an important consideration. The files on the Windows 98 CD were developed and tested to function together, and the most reliable system is generally one with the fewest disruptions to the system of files that Windows 98 Setup is attempting to install. Setup is, therefore, occasionally faced with the situation of removing a newer version of a file in order to install the version included on the Windows 98 CD.

Rather than just deleting the newer (existing) version of the file that has caused a version conflict, Setup backs up the file to the `Windows\VCM` directory, and provides a tool called Version Conflict Manager to help you manage VCM directory files.

Windows 98's default strategy of replacing the newer (existing) version of the file with an older version present on the Windows 98 CD does not always circumvent version conflict problems, and in fact, it sometimes causes version conflict problems. If your Windows 98 installation experiences problems, or if an application or device doesn't run properly after you install Windows 98, the problem may be that Windows 98 Setup has replaced a file or driver with an older, incompatible version. Version Conflict Manager lets you restore a backed-up version of the file that was present before you installed Windows 98.

To start Version Conflict Manager, perform the tasks outlined in Step by Step 8.1.

STEP BY STEP

8.1 Starting Version Conflict Manager

1. Click on the Start menu and choose Programs, Accessories, System Tools.

2. Choose System Information from the System Tools group. This will open the Microsoft System Information utility, discussed in the next section.

3. From the Microsoft System Information Utility Tools menu, select Version Conflict Manager. The screen shown in Figure 8.1 appears.

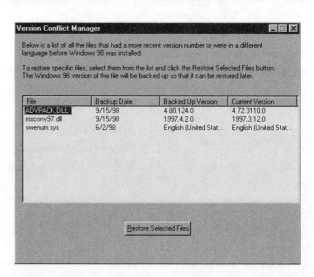

FIGURE 8.1
Version Conflict Manager lets you manage files that were replaced during installation even though they are more recent than the version on the Windows 98 CD.

From the main screen in Version Conflict Manager, you can select a file that was backed up because the version was more recent than the version of the file installed with Windows 98. Note that the Version Conflict Manager displays the backup date and the version numbers of the backed-up and current version of the file. Click the button labeled Restore Selected Files to restore the file(s) you select. When you restore a file, the current version of the file (the version you are replacing—the Windows 98 version) will be backed up in the Windows\VCM directory so you can restore it later if necessary.

> **NOTE**
>
> **VCM Manages Languages Conflicts**
> Version Conflict Manager also helps manage language conflicts, in which the language used for a particular file (the human language—English, Spanish, French, and so on) is different from the language specified for the Windows 98 installation.

Microsoft System Information Utility

Windows 98's setup and startup components can usually assign resources to all devices without conflicts. Sometimes, however, resource conflicts appear. One or more devices may be jumpered to the same resource settings, or a device may not be fully compatible with Windows 98 Plug and Play. Windows 98's Microsoft System Information Utility is a useful utility that provides a summary of system resources and how they're assigned. You can view information on hardware resources, Windows components, and various aspects of the software environment, such as drivers, 16- or 32-bit modules, running tasks, or OLE registration. You can use System Information Utility to find version conflicts.

To start Microsoft System Information Utility, click on the Start button and choose Programs, Accessories, System Tools, System Information. The Microsoft System Information Utility main screen appears (see Figure 8.2). System Information Utility is primarily a tool for displaying information, although the System Information Utility Tools menu lets you link to several of Windows 98's troubleshooting and configuration tools.

The settings displayed in System Information Utility appear in a tree-like format reminiscent of Explorer or Registry Editor. Figure 8.2 shows the Hardware Resources categories. Each category displays information relevant to the category's title. For instance, the IRQs category displays the interrupt request channel (IRQ) setting for each installed device. The Conflicts/Sharing category shows any hardware resources that are presently shared among multiple devices. If you are experiencing problems with a device, the Conflicts/Sharing view will show whether that device is sharing a resource with another device.

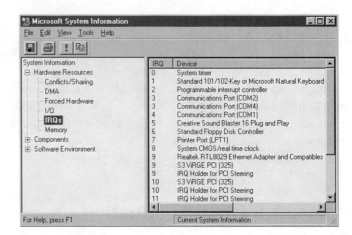

FIGURE 8.2

Microsoft System Information Utility provides a view of how hardware resources are allocated.

System Information Utility's Components tree (see Figure 8.3) shows system resources listed by component. You can view information on hardware resources, drivers, and Registry keys for various system components, such as display, multimedia, modems, ports, and storage devices.

The Software Environment tree (see Figure 8.4) shows information on drivers, modules, running tasks, startup programs, and OLE registration.

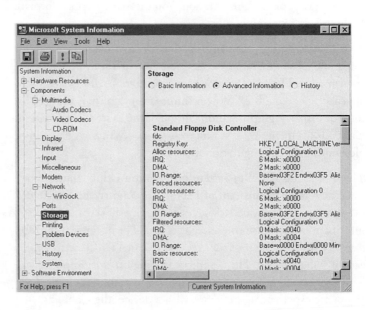

FIGURE 8.3

Microsoft System Information Utility's Components tree shows system resources listed by component.

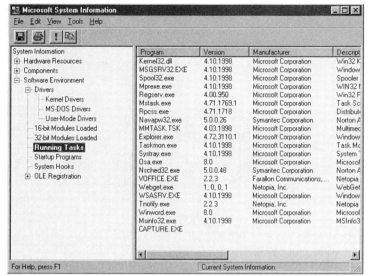

FIGURE 8.4
Microsoft System Information Utility's Software Environment tree provides information on drivers, modules, running tasks, OLE registrations, and other important settings.

System Information Utility is primarily an aid for troubleshooting, and Microsoft has conveniently linked System Information Utility to other troubleshooting utilities. The Tools menu provides a list of tools that you can launch directly from System Information Utility. Many of these tools are discussed elsewhere in this book. The following tools are included:

◆ **Windows Report Tool.** Takes a snapshot of your system configuration and lets you submit a report (along with system information) to technicians at Microsoft.

◆ **Update Wizard Uninstall.** Lets you uninstall packages installed through the Windows Update Wizard (refer to Chapter 7, "Monitoring and Optimization").

◆ **System File Checker.** (Refer to Chapter 7.)

◆ **Signature Verification Tool.** (Refer to Chapter 7.)

◆ **Registry Checker.** (Discussed later in this chapter.)

◆ **Automatic Skip Driver Agent.** Tracks device driver load failures during startup. Disables devices whose driver(s) fail to load.

◆ **Dr. Watson.** (Discussed later in this chapter.)

◆ **System Configuration Utility.** (Discussed later in this chapter.)

◆ **ScanDisk.** (Refer to Chapter 7.)

◆ **Version Conflict Manager.** (Discussed earlier in this chapter.)

EXAM TIP

Learn the New Utilities Windows 98 includes several new configuration, management, and troubleshooting utilities, including the utilities discussed in this chapter and some discussed in Chapter 7. It is a good idea to learn the names of these utilities and learn what they are used for.

Microsoft System Information Utility provides a good first stop for system troubleshooting. You can check for conflicts and verify that drivers are assigned to devices. You can also use the Export option in the File menu to create a text file with a complete report of system settings that a remote troubleshooter can use to analyze your system.

REVIEW   BREAK

General Troubleshooting

The preceding sections introduced some general troubleshooting guidelines and described some tools and strategies for addressing installation failures and version conflict problems. You won't be tested on the general troubleshooting guidelines for the Windows 98 exam, but these guidelines provide some insight about the troubleshooting process. Troubleshooting scenarios starts with the symptom, and you have to work backwards to the cause. Applying a consistent methodology will increase your effectiveness.

You will likely be tested on Version Conflict Manager and System Information Utility, however. Be sure you know how to use these tools.

DIAGNOSING AND RESOLVING BOOT PROCESS FAILURES

Diagnose and resolve boot process failures.

A large majority of the technical problems that arise under Windows 98 can be traced back to the configuration files and how these files control the boot process. Especially in upgrade situations, many settings that were necessary and that worked properly in a Windows 3.1 environment are either redundant or incompatible in a Windows 98 environment. Isolating which of these settings are redundant or incompatible with Windows 98 can be difficult. Windows 98 includes a number of features that will help you restart your system after a boot failure and find the source of the problem:

◆ The Startup menu

◆ The Startup disk

◆ Win.com switches

◆ System Configuration Utility

System Configuration Utility is a powerful new tool included with Windows 98 that acts as an interface to legacy Windows startup files such as autoexec.bat. and config.sys. Note that Microsoft calls special attention to System Configuration Utility in the Windows 98 MCSE exam objectives.

The Startup Menu

Pressing the Ctrl key when you boot your Windows 98 computer invokes the Windows 98 Startup menu, which provides a number of different modes in which Windows 98 can be booted. If the system fails to start normally, you may still be able to reboot into one of these alternative modes in order to troubleshoot the problem. The Startup menu options depend in part on the parameters specified in the msdos.sys file, but generally consist of the following:

◆ Normal mode

◆ Logged mode

◆ Safe mode

◆ Step-by-Step Confirmation mode

◆ Command-Prompt-Only mode

◆ Safe Mode Command-Prompt-Only mode

◆ Previous Version of MS-DOS

Normal Mode

This is the normal operation mode of Windows 98. If you boot to the Startup menu but then decide to complete the boot process and start Windows 98 under normal conditions, select this mode.

Logged Mode

When you select Logged mode, the entire boot process is logged to a file called `bootlog.txt`, which catalogs VxD initializations, driver loads, and various other boot-related events. `bootlog.txt` was described earlier in this chapter. You can use the boot log to determine where the boot failure occurs and what the system is doing at the time. Aside from the logging, the Logged mode performs a normal boot procedure (of course it will be a bit slower because it writes to the `bootlog.txt` file). `bootlog.txt` will normally be found in the root directory. You can load `bootlog.txt` into a text editor such as Notepad to examine the contents.

Safe Mode

Safe mode is likely the single most important troubleshooting tool available in Windows 98. In this mode, a number of key Windows 98 components and settings are disabled, including the following:

- `config.sys` and `autoexec.bat`
- The `[Boot]` and `[386Enh]` sections of `system.ini`
- The `Load=` and `Run=` parameters of `win.ini`
- The Startup program group
- The Registry
- All device drivers except the keyboard, mouse, and standard VGA video drivers

> **NOTE**
>
> **The inis and Windows 98** `win.ini` and `system.ini` are Windows 3.x configuration files that Windows 98 uses for compatibility with some Win16 applications.

Disabling these items allows the separation of fundamental operating system problems from those caused by a combination of software factors. In a situation in which the display is not functioning properly in Normal mode, for example, if the problem does not appear in Safe mode, the problem probably is video driver-related and is not due to a defective video card.

Similarly, you can use Safe mode to troubleshoot scenarios such as the following:

- GPFs (General Protection Faults)
- Application hangs
- A hang during the boot process
- A blank screen at boot time

Step-by-Step Confirmation Mode

This boot mode is similar to the F8 function of previous versions of MS-DOS; it permits the user to step through the various stages of the boot process and specify whether each should or should not be completed. This mode can be very useful when you are trying to isolate boot stages to determine which may be causing a given problem. You can also use it to view system responses to various parameters in config.sys and autoexec.bat, which otherwise are displayed far too quickly to read.

Command-Prompt-Only Mode

Command-Prompt-Only boot mode is similar to a normal boot of MS-DOS. Only config.sys, autoexec.bat, command.com, and the Registry are processed (along with any necessary disk compression drivers). This mode is useful in troubleshooting problems running MS-DOS applications in a VM under Windows 98. If the application functions in this mode but not inside Windows 98, the problem is likely due to a compatibility issue. If the application does not function in Command-Prompt-Only mode, the problem is likely a configuration problem in config.sys or autoexec.bat, or the application may be corrupt.

Safe Mode Command-Prompt-Only Mode

Safe Mode Command-Prompt-Only mode is similar to a Safe mode, except that command.com is processed. Also, Startup does not load himem.sys or ifshlp.sys and does not execute win.com to start the Windows interface. This mode is useful if your computer fails to boot properly in Safe mode. Safe Mode Command-Prompt-Only mode offers slightly different options from Safe mode, so you can use it for slightly different situations. For instance, you can use this mode if you don't want Windows to process win.com or himem.sys.

Previous Version of MS-DOS

Although the Previous Version of MS-DOS boot mode is not intended for troubleshooting, it can be used in situations in which particular MS-DOS–related functions worked in previous versions of MS-DOS but do not seem to function properly under Windows 98.

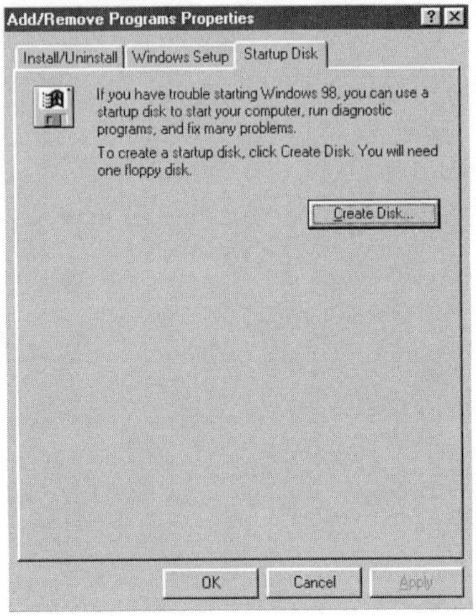

FIGURE 8.5
A Windows 98 Startup disk can be created at any time using the Startup Disk tab of the Add/Remove Programs Control Panel.

Of course, you can boot to a previous version only if you upgraded the computer from a previous version.

The Startup Disk

You can create the Startup disk at installation time or later through the Startup Disk tab of the Add/Remove Programs Control Panel (see Figure 8.5).

The disk serves as an emergency boot disk should the operating system fail to load. In addition to the boot files necessary to start Window 98 in Command-Prompt-Only mode, the Startup disk contains several tools you can use to troubleshoot boot problems. Some of those tools are as follows:

- **edit.com*.** Text editor. Makes changes to configuration files such as autoexec.bat and config.sys.
- **chkdsk.exe*.** Checks a disk drive and provides status information.
- **ext.exe*.** Extracts files.
- **format.com*.** Reformats a disk.
- **fdisk.exe.** Disk partition utility. (Refer to Chapter 5, "Managing Resources in Windows 98.")
- **scandisk.exe*.** Checks for disk errors. (Refer to Chapter 7.)
- **sys.com.** Transfers system files from one drive to another.
- **uninstall.exe*.** Uninstalls Windows 98 and restores previous system files (if you elected to save the system files at installation). (Refer to Chapter 2.)

NOTE   **edb.cab**   Files marked with an asterisk in the list in the right column are actually stored in compressed form in the file edb.cab on the Windows 98 Startup disk and then expanded during startup. edb.cab also contains other files you can use for configuring and troubleshooting.

The Windows 98 Startup disk also contains several real-mode CD-ROM drivers to enable support for a number of common CD-ROM drives.

If you can boot to the Windows 98 Startup disk, you can navigate through your hard drive to find a file that is interfering with the boot process. You can also troubleshoot your hard drive using ScanDisk, or even reformat and repartition your hard drive (start over) using format and fdisk. The CD-ROM drivers on the Startup disk will provide you with access to the Windows 98 installation

CD, in case you'd like to reinstall Windows 98 or copy files that are located on the CD.

The venerable sys.com utility, which originated in the days of MS-DOS, is still a very useful troubleshooting tool. sys.com transfers the system files `io.sys`, `msdos.sys`, and `command.com` from a source drive to a destination drive. These system files make a disk *bootable*. If one of these system files is deleted or corrupted on your hard drive, you can boot to the Windows 98 startup disk and transfer the system files from the Startup disk to the hard drive. For instance, you could boot to the Startup disk and type the following:

```
sys a: c:
```

`a:` is your floppy drive and `c:` is the active partition of your hard disk. Microsoft points out that if your hard drive is compressed, you need to transfer the system files to your host drive when using the `sys` command. Refer to Chapter 5 for more information about host drives on compressed partitions.

One very important point to remember, for general administration as well as for the Windows 98 MCSE exam, is that because of changes to the Windows 98 kernel to accommodate FAT32, many Windows 95 Startup disks are not usable in Windows 98. You should not bypass the Startup disk in Windows 98 installation (and fail to create one later) because you have a Windows 95 disk sitting around and you think it will still work. You should create a Windows 98 Startup disk when you upgrade to Windows 98. It is also a good idea to test the Startup disk before you need it. Place your Windows 98 Startup disk in the floppy drive and reboot your PC to ensure that the disk is operational.

Win.com Switches

Win.com includes support for a number of error-isolation switches. Although some are available from within Windows 98, you may have to specify them from the command prompt in situations in which Windows 98 fails to load. These switches are specified in the following format:

```
win /d:[f] [m] [n] [s] [v] [x]
```

The switches function as follows:

Switch	Function
f	Disables 32-bit file system drivers
m	Starts Windows 98 in Safe mode
n	Starts Safe mode with networking
s	Excludes the ROM address space between FOOO and 1MB from use by Windows 98
v	Tells Windows 98 that the ROM routine should handle disk interrupts
x	Excludes the adapter area from the area that Windows 98 scans when looking for unused disk space

You can use these switches independently or together as part of a single command.

If Windows 98 won't start normally, you may be able to boot to a system disk and run win.com using one or more of these switches to isolate the problem.

System Configuration Utility

Boot failures are often caused by drivers or settings invoked through one of the Windows Startup configuration files.

System Configuration Utility is an ingenious tool that lets you turn off or turn on specific entries in the Startup files autoexec.bat, config.sys, system.ini, or win.ini. You can also make other changes to the startup process that may help with diagnosing startup problems. The System Configuration Utility General tab is shown in Figure 8.6.

Note that, in addition to a normal startup, you can choose Diagnostic startup, or you can choose to selectively disable files. The tabs named for the Startup files (autoexec.bat, config.sys, system.ini, and win.ini) let you enable or disable specific statements within the file (see Figure 8.7).

You can also change the order of the statements within the file by using the Move Up and Move Down buttons. Or, you can add a new statement to the file or edit a statement by using the New and Edit buttons. The Startup tab (see Figure 8.8) lets you decide whether to load certain items at startup.

FIGURE 8.6
The System Configuration Utility's General tab lets you decide which Startup files you wish to execute.

FIGURE 8.7
System Configuration Utility lets you selectively enable or disable specific statements within a Startup file.

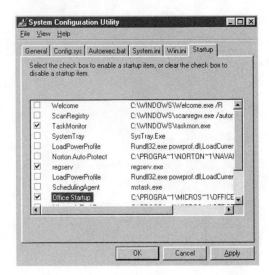

FIGURE 8.8
System Configuration Utility's Startup tab lets you decide whether to launch certain items at startup.

The Windows 95/98 Registry has largely eliminated the need for startup files such as autoexec.bat, config.sys, system.ini, and win.ini. In Windows 98, these files are primarily maintained for backward compatibility with older devices and applications. Nevertheless, the Startup files are still an occasional source of boot problems. System Configuration Utility provides a convenient interface for doing what was a standard troubleshooting procedure in earlier versions of Windows—selectively disabling specific statements in the Startup files to zero in on the source of a startup problem.

REVIEW   BREAK

Boot Process Failures

Windows 98 system problems often occur at startup. These problems are, of course, impossible to troubleshoot if you can't start your system. Windows 98 includes several methods for starting Windows that may help you diagnose a problem, or at least, start the system so you can pursue other troubleshooting remedies. The preceding sections discussed some of these options. The first step is usually to boot your system using the option boot modes of the Startup menu such as Safe mode or Step-by-Step Confirmation mode. The win.com switches are usually for subtler problems. System Configuration Utility is often useful for troubleshooting startup problems related to older devices and applications.

DIAGNOSING AND RESOLVING CONNECTIVITY PROBLEMS

Diagnose and resolve connectivity problems in a Microsoft environment and a mixed Microsoft and NetWare environment.

Connectivity problems can be some of the more vexatious issues to resolve in Windows 98. Part of the difficulty lies in trying to determine where a problem is occurring. Fortunately, Windows 98 has some good built-in tools to aid you in isolating and troubleshooting connectivity problems.

Using WinIPCfg

The TCP/IP protocol (refer to Chapter 3, "Windows 98 Networking") is an important and widely used networking protocol that is quickly becoming the standard for routed networks. Because TCP/IP is the protocol of the Internet, it is becoming nearly unavoidable—every network administrator or system engineer must at some point become familiar with configuring and troubleshooting TCP/IP. TCP/IP is relatively more difficult to configure than other common protocols, but TCP/IP also comes with a number of tools that will assist with configuring and verifying TCP/IP settings.

Windows 98's WinIPCfg utility (see Figure 8.9) is a Windows-based tool that provides a summary of TCP/IP information. To reach WinIPCfg, click Start, Run and enter `winipcfg` in the Run dialog box. You can use WinIPCfg to check your TCP/IP configuration settings. As shown in Figure 8.9, the initial IP Configuration window provides basic settings such as the adapter's MAC address, the IP address, the subnet mask, and the default gateway. (Refer to Chapter 3 for more information about these important TCP/IP settings.) The More Info button reveals additional settings, such as DHCP, WINS, and DNS server addresses, and settings for NetBIOS name resolution and IP routing.

If your TCP/IP connection is not working properly, you can use WinIPCfg to quickly check your TCP/IP settings. For instance, notice in Figure 8.9 that the setting for Default Gateway is blank. If the user of this PC could not connect to a computer on a different

FIGURE 8.9
The compact view of WinIPCfg reveals your IP address and subnet mask at a glance.

subnet, a glance at WinIPCfg would quickly reveal the missing Default Gateway setting as a probable cause of the problem. If your IP address is assigned by a DHCP server, the first item to check is whether an IP address has in fact been assigned to the machine. If the IP address box has 0.0.0.0 listed, you have not obtained an address and consequently cannot communicate with any other machine by using TCP/IP.

The Renew and Release buttons (refer to Figure 8.9) help you manage dynamic IP addresses assigned by a DHCP server on the network. See Chapter 3 for more on dynamic IP address assignment through DHCP. A DHCP server *leases* an IP address and accompanying IP settings to a DHCP client (such as a Windows 98 computer) for a predefined period. You can elect to renew or release the leased IP address using WinIPCfg's Renew and Release buttons.

Note that the drop-down box at the WinIPCfg's IP Configuration window provides the name of a network adapter. A fundamental concept of TCP/IP addressing is that an IP address is assigned to an adapter, not to a computer. If your computer has multiple network adapters, make sure the adapter for the connection you wish to troubleshoot is showing in the dropdown menu. It is possible for a computer to have more than one network adapter card. Each card would need its own IP address information. It is even more common for a PC to have one network card and also a modem that supports a connection to an Internet Service Provider (ISP). In that case, also, the computer would need two IP addresses. The modem address (which you may find under the heading PPP Adapter in WinIPCfg) would most likely be dynamically assigned, so if you aren't connected to the Internet when you check the address in WinIPCfg, you may see zeros for the IP address and subnet mask.

The following list describes some other settings available through WinIPCfg.exe (these TCP/IP settings are described in greater detail in Chapter 3):

◆ The first drop-down box lists the *adapters* configured in the machine. The adapter might be an Ethernet adapter, modem, or other device with an IP address bound to it.

◆ The *adapter address* in the case of an Ethernet card is a string of unique hexadecimal numbers that are hard coded into the device by the manufacturer. The adapter address is usually called the *physical address* or *MAC address*. If the adapter is a modem, a bogus number will be displayed in this box because a modem does not have such a number assigned to it.

◆ The *IP address* is a set of four decimal-separated values bound to the preceding adapter to enable communication between machines using this protocol. This number was either statically assigned to the machine when the protocol was configured, or it was dynamically allocated when the computer connected to the network.

◆ The subnet mask is also either statically assigned when you manually configure TCP/IP or it is dynamically obtained when you connect to a network with the computer. A *subnet mask* tells the computer whether the address of another machine is on the same local network, or whether it is on a remote network. Every computer configured with TCP/IP *must* have a subnet mask assigned.

◆ The *default gateway* tells the computer where to go to gain access to a remote network.

By clicking on the More Info button in WinIPCfg, you gain access to additional settings (see Figure 8.10).

These settings are explored in the following list:

◆ The *host name* is the name that identifies your computer in TCP/IP's native HOSTS file or DNS system. The host name is configured under Network Properties in Control Panel. This name must be unique to avoid conflict on the network.

◆ The *DNS Server* entry is the IP address of the server that provides name resolution for your machine. This server keeps a list of IP addresses and domain names for the network. A DNS server enables you to send message traffic to frodo.com, for example, instead of having to type in the IP address for it. If you can connect to a machine by typing in the IP address, but not by typing in the domain name, you might take a look at your DNS Server settings.

◆ The *Node Type* setting describes the method this computer will use for NetBIOS name resolution. Refer to Chapter 3 for more information about NetBIOS name resolution in

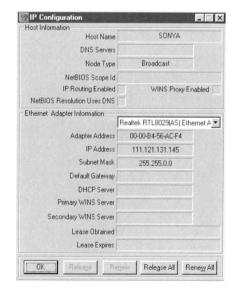

FIGURE 8.10

The expanded view of WinIPCfg enables you to release and to renew your IP address.

Windows 98. The NetBIOS Scope ID is a common identifier for a group of computers on a larger Internetwork that will communicate with each other using NetBIOS over TCP/IP.

◆ The boxes for IP Routing, NetBIOS Resolution Uses DNS, and WINS proxy reveal whether these settings are enabled for the TCP/IP connection. Refer to Chapter 3 for more on routing, WINS proxy, and NetBIOS resolution with DNS.

◆ The WINS Server entries provide the IP addresses of the primary and secondary WINS servers. A *WINS server* translates NetBIOS computer names into IP addresses. It maintains a database of computer names and maps them to IP addresses. If you can connect to a machine by typing in the IP address, but not by typing in the computer name, you might take a look at your WINS Server settings.

◆ If your IP address is handed out dynamically from a DHCP server, you will have lease information displayed in the two boxes near the bottom of the IP Configuration dialog box. When the server grants you an IP address for your machine, it also sets an expiration time for the address. This allows a greater number of computers to share a limited number of IP addresses. When one computer leaves the network, the address is still reserved for it until it is either released by the computer or expires due to age. It must be renewed prior to expiration; otherwise, the PC will drop off the network. If you are experiencing sporadic connectivity problems using TCP/IP, it might be due to the settings for lease expiration. The lease duration might need to be adjusted on the server, depending on your particular situation.

◆ The Release, Renew, Release All, Renew All buttons (refer to Figure 8.9) are helpful in troubleshooting IP address leasing problems. You can release the address, reboot the machine, and see whether it picks it back up. Also, you can attempt to renew the address and see whether you can obtain a renewal of your lease.

Verifying TCP/IP Connectivity with Ping

Ping is an important TCP/IP utility that bounces a signal to a specified network adapter, receives a reply from that adapter, and displays information on the reply. Ping is used on all TCP/IP networks to verify connectivity. When a computer is first added to the network, the network administrator uses Ping to ensure that the TCP/IP connection with other network computers is working. Later, if an application or process fails to complete a network connection, the network administrator can use Ping to test whether the failure was due to the network.

Ping is a command-prompt utility. To use Ping, you just need to go to the command prompt and type the following:

    Ping IPaddress

IPaddress is the dotted decimal IP address of the computer you want to ping (for example, 169.131.121.117). On networks that use DNS or NetBIOS name resolution, you can enter a host name or a NetBIOS name instead of an IP address.

A typical Ping reply is shown in Figure 8.11. Note that one ping command sends multiple signals and receives multiple replies. (The default in Windows 98 is four replies.)

You can use a special address called the *loopback address* to test whether TCP/IP is installed and running properly on the local computer. The loopback address is 127.0.0.1. Pinging the loopback address will verify that TCP/IP is operational on your computer:

    Ping 127.0.0.1

FIGURE 8.11

In Windows 98, the ping command results in four replies from the remote computer you just pinged.

NOTE

Everybody Pings TCP/IP utilities such as Ping are not limited to use with other Microsoft products. Ping is a very common utility on all TCP/IP networking systems, and it is possible to ping any TCP/IP host that supports Ping, including UNIX and Linux systems as well as NetWare, Macintosh, and other systems that are using TCP/IP.

A common routine for isolating connectivity problems and verifying connectivity on a TCP/IP network is as follows:

1. Ping the loopback address (127.0.0.1) to ensure that TCP/IP is operating properly on your system.

2. Ping the IP address of the local (your PC's) network adapter card. This will ensure that TCP/IP is bound to the adapter and will provide a check for duplicate IP addresses.

3. Ping the default gateway on your network. This verifies that the local subnet is functioning and that packets addressed to other subnets will reach the default gateway.

4. Ping a computer beyond the default gateway, to ensure that packets will be delivered to remote networks.

Depending on the problem, network administrators sometimes execute these steps sequentially, and they sometimes execute the steps in reverse order. (If step 4 works, for example, you have a pretty good idea steps 1–3 will work also.)

Verifying Internetworks with Tracert

Tracert is Microsoft's version of the standard UNIX TCP/IP utility traceroute. Tracert uses Internet Control Message Protocol (ICMP) echo packets to reveal the path that a packet would take from the source PC to a remote destination. The purpose of Tracert is to show the series of routers that forward a data packet to a particular destination. The number of router *hops* required to deliver the packet is a major factor in determining the speed of the connection. If your network experiences a slowdown, you can use Tracert to check whether the slowdown is caused by inefficient routing (which may be caused by a downed router somewhere).

The format for the Tracert command is as follows:

```
Tracert IPaddress
```

IPaddress is the IP address of the destination PC. On networks with name resolution, you can use a host name or NetBIOS name instead of an IP address.

You can use Tracert to verify the complete path from the source to a specified remote destination. A typical Tracert output is shown in

FIGURE 8.12
Tracert shows the path an ICMP echo packet takes through a series of routers.

Figure 8.12. Note that Tracert shows the host name and IP address of each router along the path.

The Tracert output displays the round-trip time in milliseconds required to reach a node at each hop. If the time exceeds the maximum Time To Live (TTL) for the packet, an asterisk appears, showing that the packet has timed out.

Microsoft points out that the Ping utility (described earlier in this chapter) rarely works over PPTP network connections. Another use of Tracert is to verify connectivity over PPTP connections.

Using Net Watcher

You can use the Net Watcher utility (refer to Chapter 7) to create or delete shared resources on remote computers, or monitor access to those resources. Remember, however, that Net Watcher is also an important tool for anyone troubleshooting connectivity problems in a networked environment.

By using Net Watcher, you can see at a glance who can connect to a Windows 98 machine, and who cannot. You can see what shares are created, and who is utilizing what files. The following factors are important when considering remote administration using Net Watcher:

◆ The remote computer must have File and Printer Sharing enabled.

◆ You can access only those remote systems that use the same security model you are using on your computer. (Share-level security computers cannot access user-level security computers, for example.)

◆ You can connect only to remote systems that use the same type of File and Printer Sharing (Microsoft or NetWare).

Net Watcher provides a quick means of correlating resources with users and computers. If a user is experiencing network problems, you can use Net Watcher to immediately determine which shares, or which files within a share, the user is connected to, and you can systematically remove shares or disconnects users to isolate the source of the problem. Refer to Chapter 7 for more information about Net Watcher.

Dial-Up Networking Problems

To troubleshoot Dial-Up Networking problems, the first places to start looking for the problem are in the Network Properties sheets for the Dial-Up Adapter, the Dial-Up Networking connection, the modem, and the application you want to use over the connection. This isolates your troubleshooting to the client computer. You then can start looking at problems that may be affecting the phone-line connection, such as a busy signal on the other end, a dead phone line, or the connection to the outgoing phone line. Finally, you can isolate the problem to the server-side computer. In this case, you may not have physical access to that computer and may need to rely on someone local to that computer to diagnose and fix any problems on the server.

Some of the problems you may encounter with Dial-Up Networking (DUN) occur with the following:

◆ **Modems.** Be sure your modem is installed properly to work with Windows 98. If the modem is external, make sure it is turned on. Also, be sure it is plugged in to the phone line.

◆ **Phone numbers.** Double-check the phone number you are dialing to be sure your modem is correctly dialing that number. If you need to enter a number for an outside line, be sure to enter it. If you have call waiting on your phone line, disable it. If you need to dial a long-distance number, be sure the entire number, including 1 + area code, is being dialed. Also, make sure the number you are dialing is for a modem or fax modem.

◆ **Protocols.** Make sure the Dial-Up Adapter is configured to use the same line protocol as the server-side computer. If, for example, you use DUN to connect one Windows 98 computer to another using the Dial-Up Networking Server software, and you are using PPP on one computer, make sure the other computer is also using PPP. Also, be sure both computers are using the same networking protocol, such as NetBEUI or IPX/SPX. If you use TCP/IP to connect to the Internet, make sure your TCP/IP settings, such as IP address, host names, and other configuration settings are correct.

◆ **Access permissions.** If you can connect to a remote server but cannot access user resources on that site, you may not have proper access privileges. Make sure you enter the correct password and that the server side is set up to allow you access to it.

◆ **Servers.** A common problem with the Dial-Up Networking Server is that it is not enabled. Enable it by opening the Dial-Up Networking folder and choosing Connections, Dial-Up Server. Choose the Allow Caller Access option.

◆ **Applications.** If your application does not function properly over Dial-Up Networking, you may have a slow connection or a bad connection, or your application may not be intended to function as remote-access software. Read the application's documentation to make sure it can operate as remote software, or contact its manufacturer for specific steps for making it work with Windows 98. One way to determine whether there is an application problem is to use the Windows 98 applet Hyper-Terminal. HyperTerminal is a bare-bones, no-frills communication program that seems to be able to connect when no other program can. If you can connect with HyperTerminal, chances are you have a configuration problem with your application.

> NOTE
>
> **Grabbing the Line** When you attempt to use an application that does not work with Windows 98 TAPI architecture and you have the Dial-Up Server enabled, your application will not be able to call out. If, for example, you use CompuServe WinCIM 2.01 or earlier software to dial CompuServe, you receive a `Cannot Initialize Port` message when Dial-Up Server is running. When this happens, just disable the Dial-Up Server until you are finished using the application.

DIAGNOSING AND RESOLVING PRINTING PROBLEMS

Diagnose and resolve printing problems in a Microsoft environment or a mixed Microsoft and NetWare environment.

Chapter 5 discussed how to configure and manage printers in Windows 98. One of the best ways to prepare to troubleshoot printing problems is to study the printing process and understand all the features of printing configuration. When you're faced with a printing problem, be prepared to work from the symptoms through the various elements of the printing process to an acceptable remedy.

Aside from the common low-tech printer problems discussed later in this section (out of paper, not connected, not plugged in), one of the most common printer problems—and one you're likely to see on the Windows 98 MCSE exam—concerns the spool data format. Windows 98 includes built-in support for the following data formats:

◆ **Enhanced Metafile Format (EMF).** An intermediate data format used by Windows 95/98 and Windows NT 4.0 computers.

◆ **RAW.** Raw printer data.

According to Microsoft, by default, all output to non-PostScript printers spools in EMF format. Output to Postscript printers spools in RAW format. The reality, though, may not be that simple. If you are having trouble printing to a PostScript printer, check the Spool data format to see if you could try setting the format to RAW. If you have trouble printing to a non-PostScript printer, you could also change the data format to RAW to see whether the problem relates to EMF file spooling. Microsoft contends that printing can take up to twice as much time using RAW format.

To check the Spool Data format, perform the tasks outlined in Step by Step 8.2.

STEP BY STEP

8.2 Checking the Spool Data Format

1. Right-click on the printer icon in the Printers folder and choose Properties.

2. In the Printer Properties dialog box, select the Details tab.

3. In the Details tab, click on the Spool Settings button. The Spool Settings dialog box appears (see Figure 8.13).

4. Click the down arrow beside the Spool Data Format box and select a different data format.

Another source of potential printing problems is MS-DOS applications. MS-DOS applications are typically designed to print directly to the printer, without print spooling and other components of Windows 98's modular printer architecture. Microsoft has devoted considerable attention to supporting printing from MS-DOS applications, and the way that DOS documents print in Windows 98 bears little resemblance to the way they printed in DOS. Each DOS application runs in a virtual machine, and each DOS application can print to a virtual printer port. The MS-DOS application thus *thinks* it is printing directly to the printer, but it is instead spooling print jobs directly to Windows 98's 32-bit print spooler. In most cases, this means faster printing and faster return of control to the DOS application. In some cases, however, if you are experiencing problems printing to MS-DOS applications, you may wish to disable spooling for MS-DOS print jobs.

To disable MS-DOS spooling, perform the tasks outlined in Step by Step 8.3.

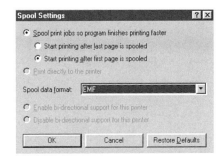

FIGURE 8.13
You can choose a different print data format in the Spool Settings dialog box.

STEP BY STEP

8.3 Disabling MS-DOS Spooling

1. Right-click on the Printer icon in the Printers folder and choose Properties.

2. In the Printer Properties dialog box, choose the Details tab.

3. In the Details tab, click on Port Settings.

4. In the Configure LPT Port dialog box (see Figure 8.14), uncheck Spool MS-DOS Print Jobs.

In spite of Windows 98's virtual printer features, some MS-DOS applications that expect to print to a local LPT port may still have trouble printing to a network printer. Windows 98's Capture Printer Port feature (handed down from Windows 95) lets you map a local printer port to a network printer. (This is yet another way of tricking an MS-DOS application into thinking it is printing to a local printer port.)

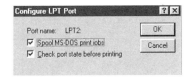

FIGURE 8.14
Use the Configure LPT Port dialog box to disable spooling for MS-DOS print jobs.

To map a local port to a network printer, perform the tasks outlined in Step by Step 8.4.

STEP BY STEP

8.4 Mapping a Local Port to a Network Printer

1. Right-click on the printer icon in the Printers folder and choose Properties.

2. In the Printer Properties dialog box, choose the Details tab.

3. Click on the button labeled Capture Printer Port.

4. In the Capture Printer Port dialog box (see Figure 8.15), choose a device name (LPT1, LPT2, and so on) and enter the UNC path to the network printer. Click on OK.

Another consideration in print performance is how quickly control is returned to the user after a print job is submitted. You can configure the print subsystem of Windows 98 to return control to the user after the first page of a print job is spooled or after the last page is spooled. This parameter can be configured from the Spool Settings dialog box (refer to Figure 8.13—click on the Spool Settings button on the Details tab of the Properties sheet for the printer in question). Choosing to return control after the first page shortens wait time but increases printing time and consumes more disk space; the inverse is true if control is returned after the last page is spooled. The Spool Settings dialog box also lets you turn off spooling altogether and print directly to the printer. Printing directly to the printer generally leads to less efficient performance than the spooling options, but this option can be an important troubleshooting tool if you suspect the problem may be related to spooling.

One way to remedy a printing problem is to use the Print Troubleshooter, which is available from the Windows 98 Help utility (search the index for printing; troubleshooting). You also can use the following guidelines to help clear up printer problems:

◆ Make sure the printer is turned on, full of paper, and is online.

◆ Check the printer cable and parallel port to make sure the printer is connected to the computer.

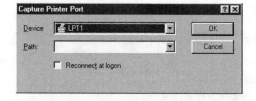

FIGURE 8.15
The Capture Printer Port dialog box lets you map a network printer to a local printer port.

◆ Open the Printers folder, right-click on the printer, and choose Properties. Make sure the settings are correct for your printer.

◆ Turn off Metafile Spooling. It may not work properly for all printers.

◆ Make sure you have the latest printer driver installed. Sometimes reinstalling the same printer driver fixes the problem. Contact the printer manufacturer to obtain a new printer driver for Windows 98, if available.

◆ Download a PostScript error handler to the printer if the problem is with a PostScript printer.

◆ View your resources, such as free disk space and free memory. For each print job, you need some free disk space for temporary files to be stored. Likewise, free memory address space is needed to process the print job. Close an idle application to free up some memory, if necessary.

◆ Attempt to print to the printer from another application. A quick test is to open Notepad, create a line of text, and print the file. If this works, the original application that failed to print may need to be configured for printing. If this does not work, you may need to reinstall the printer.

◆ Print to a file, then copy the file to a printer port to see whether the file prints to the printer. If this works, the problem is due to spooler or data transmission problems. If this does not work, the program or printer driver is at fault. Similarly, you can print a test page using the Print Test Page button in the General tab of the computer's Properties dialog box to test whether the problem is due to an application or the printer itself.

◆ Shut down and restart Windows 98. Similarly, turn the printer off for 15 seconds or so, and then turn it back on. Sometimes this clears memory buffers that at times get clogged with downloaded fonts on the computer and printer.

◆ If you cannot print a complex document, try removing some of the graphic elements in the document.

As you learned in Chapter 5, a network printer looks like a local printer in the Windows 98 Printers folder, but it is, in fact, a very different and requires a different form of troubleshooting. On Microsoft networks, a network printer is almost always a local printer somewhere else. The first question is whether the network printer works locally on the print server machine. Also, make sure that file and print sharing is configured on the print server machine and that the printer is shared. If the printer is properly configured, make sure the network connection from the workstation to the print server computer is functioning.

A good habit to develop is to document printer problems and distribute copies of the document to other users in your company or organization. Because most end users send a job to the printer sooner or later, the rate at which they experience a printer problem far outweighs many other problems they encounter. Having a document that end users can refer to might decrease the number of support calls you get for printer problems.

Diagnosing and Resolving File System Problems

Diagnose and resolve file system problems.

The first step to resolving file system problems is to ensure the computer is fully optimized and is using the proper drivers.

One of the main ways in which you can enhance performance and reliability in Windows 98 is by using 32-bit protected-mode device drivers. These drivers are designed to work faster and more efficiently in relaying data than older 16-bit drivers. A Windows 3.1 driver or MS-DOS–based driver should be used only if no 32-bit driver is available.

A number of ways exist to maximize the use of 32-bit drivers:

◆ Verify that the Performance tab in the System Control Panel shows all 32-bit components for the file system and for virtual memory (see Figure 8.16).

◆ If you are using non-Microsoft disk compression, the compression may be operating in Real mode. Make sure your disk compression software uses a 32-bit driver; obtain an update if necessary.

◆ Ensure that disk-partitioning software is not being used. If a local hard drive employs nonstandard or software-based partitioning, it likely will not be able to function with the 32-bit file system drivers of Windows 98.

The following sections discuss some other topics related to file system troubleshooting:

◆ Optimizing file system and disk performance

◆ Troubleshooting file system properties

◆ Understanding file system compatibility

For more information about Windows 98 file systems and disk management, refer to Chapter 1, "Planning," and Chapter 5.

Optimizing the File System for Desktop Performance

To ensure the highest file system performance, you can take a number of actions, including the following:

◆ Remove share.exe and smartdrv.exe from the autoexec.bat because these files are not needed in Windows 98 and take up memory needlessly.

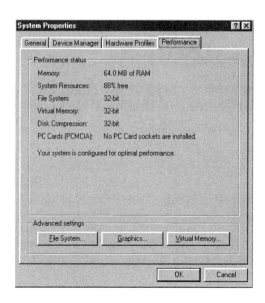

FIGURE 8.16
The Performance tab of System Properties provides a convenient summary of crucial information.

◆ If the Performance tab of the My Computer Properties sheet indicates that the file system is not using 32-bit drivers, check the ios.log to find the filename of the real-mode driver that may be preventing the use of 32-bit file system drivers.

◆ Use ScanDisk, Disk Cleanup, and Disk Defragmenter regularly (refer to Chapter 7).

Troubleshooting File System Properties

The center for configuring file system properties is the File System Properties dialog box. To access the File System Properties dialog box, select the Performance tab in the System Control Panel and click on the button labeled File System (refer to Figure 8.16). You can also reach the Performance tab by right-clicking on My Computer and choosing Properties. The File System Properties dialog box is shown in Figure 8.17.

For purposes of troubleshooting, the most important tabs are as follows:

◆ **Hard Disk.** The Hard Disk tab lets you define a role for your computer. You can also set read-ahead optimization to optimize reads from the hard disk.

◆ **Troubleshooting.** The Troubleshooting tab lets you enable and disable certain options that will help you discover the source of a file system problem.

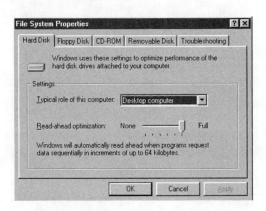

FIGURE 8.17
The File System Properties dialog box lets you configure some important file system settings.

The options provided by these important file system tabs are discussed in the following subsections.

Configuring the File System for Different Roles

Because computers can be optimized for different roles, including network performance, Windows 98 configures certain performance-related file system parameters according to the role the computer is expected to play. You can improve the performance of your computer (and therefore troubleshoot poor system performance) by ensuring that the computer is configured for a role that is consistent with its actual use. You can define the computer's role in the Hard Disk tab of the File System Properties dialog box (refer to Figure 8.17). The three possible configurations available under File System Properties are as follows:

◆ Desktop computer

◆ Mobile or docking system

◆ Network server

You'll find Registry settings relevant to file system role in the Registry key HKEY_LOCAL_MACHINE\Software\Microsoft\Windows\CurrentVersion\FS Templates. The following parameters are important to the file system role configuration:

◆ **PathCache.** The size of the cache VFAT uses to track most recently accessed folders. This affects performance by limiting the number of times the file system accesses the file allocation table to search for directory paths. The setting is 32 paths for a desktop, 16 for a laptop, and 64 for the server profile.

◆ **NameCache.** Stores the most recently accessed filenames. The setting is 8KB (or about 677 filenames) for a desktop, 4KB (or about 337 names) for a mobile system, and 16KB (or about 2,729 names) for a server profile.

The settings are calculated based on each configuration's needs. In the case of a network server, for example, due to its intensive file processing needs, both the listed settings would be at their maximum to increase efficiency in retrieving files. It is important to note that the PathCache and the NameCache settings use memory from the general system heap. Also, if you have a low-memory machine that is lightly utilized, you may consider using the mobile settings. Conversely, if you have a powerful machine and are heavily hitting the hard drive, you should consider using the network server profile.

Disabling File System Features

If you encounter difficulty with any applications and you suspect the file system might be involved, you can disable a number of file system features using the Troubleshooting tab in the File System Properties dialog box to isolate the problem (see Figure 8.18).

Disabling any of the file system features will result in performance degradation. You can, however, disable the following features:

◆ File sharing

◆ Long filename preservation for old programs

◆ Protected-mode hard disk interrupt handling

◆ Synchronous buffer commits

◆ 32-bit protected-mode disk drivers

◆ Write-behind caching

The following subsections discuss these troubleshooting options.

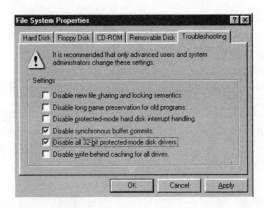

FIGURE 8.18
You can configure certain advanced file system features using the File System Properties Troubleshooting tab.

Disabling File Sharing

You can disable file sharing for applications that are incompatible with the way Windows 98 typically implements file sharing (use SHARE.EXE until the application is updated to support Windows 98 file sharing).

Disabling Long Filename Preservation for Old Programs

If an application requires the directory space used by LFNs in Windows 98, you might have to disable this support for older applications. However, if you turn this off here, you turn off the tunneling feature that preserves Long File Names for all old programs.

Disabling Protected-Mode Hard Disk Interrupt Handling

The Disable Protected-Mode Hard Disk Interrupt Handling option disables Windows 98 normal practice of intercepting all MS-DOS–level disk I/O requests and handling them with a 32-bit protected-mode driver. Disk performance is degraded, but compatibility with older applications is enhanced.

Disabling Synchronous Buffer Commits

If you disable the Synchronous Buffer Commits, the Commit File API initiates a write of dirty (uncommitted) buffers to disk. However, it does not wait for the write to complete. This means the data may not be on the disk when the API returns.

It almost sounds as though you could get some extra performance by using this option, but that is not the case for most programs and in fact may cause file integrity problems for any programs that expect data to be committed to disk. You should use this option only when you are troubleshooting. It is also a good idea to check with tech support before using this option.

Disabling All 32-Bit Protected-Mode Disk Drivers

If a hard drive is experiencing problems reading or writing information while Windows 98 is running, you can disable all 32-bit disk drivers to enhance compatibility with older applications. Once again, however, disk performance is degraded.

Disabling Write-Behind Caching

The Disable Write-Behind Caching for All Drives option is useful when data integrity is crucial and you cannot risk losing data in the write-behind cache when a power failure occurs. Write-behind caching causes Windows to wait until idle time to write disk changes, which may be too late if a power failure occurs and all cache items are lost. When write-behind is disabled, all write operations are performed immediately. Yet again, performance likely will be degraded.

Understanding File System Compatibility

Chapter 1 described the differences between Windows 98's native file systems FAT16 (also called just FAT) and FAT32, and also mentions the native Windows NT file system NTFS. If these file systems are used in the wrong situations, especially in a dual-boot scenario, you may not be able to access your file resources. Some important facts to remember are as follows:

NOTE

Know Dual-Boot Configuration Rules Be sure you know the rules for dual-boot configurations: Windows NT can't access FAT32, and Windows 98 can't access NTFS.

◆ FAT32 is compatible with Windows 98 and some late versions of Windows 95, but it isn't compatible with Windows NT, MS-DOS, or Windows 3.x. If you dual-boot from NT, 4.0 or earlier, or Windows 3.x, you won't be able to access FAT32 partitions.

◆ Windows NT's NTFS file system is not supported by Windows 98. If you dual-boot Windows NT and Windows 98, Windows 98 will not be able to access Windows NT partitions.

◆ Disk utilities designed for FAT16 do not work under FAT32. Windows 98's DriveSpace 3 compression utility does not work on FAT32 partitions.

◆ FAT32 does not support partitions smaller than 512MB.

◆ The active partition for a Windows NT/Windows 98 dual-boot must be a FAT16 partition.

Refer to Chapters 1 and 5 for more information about configuring, managing, and accessing FAT16 and FAT32 partitions in Windows 98.

DIAGNOSING AND RESOLVING RESOURCE ACCESS PROBLEMS

Diagnose and resolve resource access problems in a Microsoft environment or a mixed Microsoft and NetWare environment.

A clear understanding of Windows 98 architecture is needed when troubleshooting resource allocation and access problems. In addition to this general architecture coverage, the following sections provide an overview of virtual machines, multitasking, process, and threads in Windows 98. You also learn about how WIN16-based applications multitask under Windows 98, and more.

Multitasking: Preemptive and Cooperative

Windows 98 uses two types of multitasking, depending on the type of application:

- ◆ Preemptive multitasking
- ◆ Cooperative multitasking

Preemptive multitasking involves dividing the processor's capacity into time slices that are allocated according to the priority of the processes requiring them. Thus, one application processes for *x* number of milliseconds, and then may be interrupted by a process with a higher priority. However, periodically, all processes will get a bump up in priority to preclude them from becoming compute bound.

Cooperative multitasking also divides the processors time into slices, but is different in that it allows a given process to engage the processor until it voluntarily cedes its control to another process. The disadvantage of this type of multitasking is that a misbehaving application can monopolize the processor's time and effectively stop other processes from executing. Recognizing multitasking problems when they occur can save you from hours of frustration. If the computer seems to hang, for instance, you might suspect a hardware problem or a device conflict. But if you identify the misbehaving application,

> **N O T E**
>
> **WIN16 Uses Cooperative Multitasking** WIN16 Windows applications—the applications typically associated with the Windows 3.1 environment—use cooperative multitasking.

you might find a multitasking problem. If you are lucky, the software vendor will release an update to fix the problem you just diagnosed.

Multithreading

Multithreading is the capability of a process to create multiple threads, each having access to the memory space inhabited by its parent process. In this manner, the application can have two separate execution processes multitasked by the processor, creating the impression that the application is itself performing two tasks simultaneously. Word can repaginate a document and allow the user to type at the same time, for example. All multitasking is done at a thread level, with applications submitting either single or multiple threads, depending on the application type.

Virtual Machines

Windows 98 is capable of running three types of applications:

◆ MS-DOS 16-bit applications

◆ Windows 3.1 16-bit applications (also known as WIN16 applications)

◆ 32-bit Windows applications (also known as WIN32 applications; includes most Windows 95/98 and Windows NT software)

Windows 98 can run these varying applications because of a number of architectural design factors, the most important being the idea of *virtual machines (VMs)*. A VM is a virtual environment that appears to the application as a separate computer. In a single-tasking, single-threaded environment such as MS-DOS, in which only one application at a time is requesting the operating system's resources, managing those resources is much easier. In an environment such as Windows 98, which is intended to manage multiple applications that might be operating simultaneously, a much greater need for careful management of the system's resources exists. The computer remains primarily a single-task machine (one processor equals one task at a time, no matter how fast it performs those tasks). In this single-task environment, two processes requesting the use of a device at the exact same moment would be very problematic. Clearly, a procedure in place to arbitrate such requests is necessary.

Windows 98 implements this procedure through virtual machines. One VM (called the *System VM*) is home to all system processes, including Win32 applications and Win16 applications. Within the system VM are other VMs. Each 32-bit application runs in its own virtual machine, and all 16-bit Windows applications (because WIN16 applications are designed for cooperative multitasking) run in a single virtual machine. Each MS-DOS application runs in its own virtual machine.

Hardware Virtualization

Another important component in the creation of VMs is *hardware virtualization*. Old legacy MS-DOS, and (to a lesser extent) Windows 3.1 applications, often require direct access to the system hardware. This is something Windows 98 generally does not allow, which results in greater stability. To provide backward compatibility, the concept of hardware virtualization was created. By simulating the hardware environment in which the application is accustomed to running, all the devices are available when needed. This is implemented through software drivers called *VxDs (Virtual Device Drivers)*. These VxDs are responsible for arbitrating requests (often simultaneous) from running processes and queuing them so they do not conflict with each other or cause the device in question to fail because it is trying to do two things at once.

Internal Messaging

A message is generated each time a key is pressed or the mouse is clicked, effectively asking an application to do something. In a single-tasking environment, there is no question which application the keyboard or mouse input is intended for. In a multitasking environment, however, a more complex system of determination and delivery is required. Because you can have multiple applications onscreen simultaneously, where the mouse is clicked or what window is active when a key is pressed determines which application the message is intended for. After the intended application is targeted, the message is placed in the appropriate message queue to be processed.

16-Bit Applications' Resource Usage

WIN16 applications generally are those created for Windows 3.1. If possible, upgrade the application to a 32-bit version. If this is not feasible, however, you need to remember the following when troubleshooting WIN16 applications:

◆ Windows applications (including WIN32 applications) exist in the *System Virtual Machine*, which is a special VM designed to provide one hardware virtualization layer for all Windows software.

◆ Within this VM, WIN16 applications share a common address space. (This is necessary to maintain backward compatibility with the way Windows 3.1 applications are designed to interact.)

◆ WIN16 applications operate on a cooperative multitasking basis. (This also is due to the way applications were designed for Windows 3.1, which did not support preemptive multitasking.)

◆ A single message queue is used for all WIN16 applications.

◆ All WIN16 applications are single-threaded, because Windows 3.1 does not support multithreading.

◆ WIN16 applications generally load themselves into the virtualized space between 3GB and 4GB, and some also use a space between 0MB and 4MB to be able to share data with other WIN16 applications.

◆ WIN16 applications do not access the Registry because they are designed to use `.ini` files for their stored settings. However, Windows 98 can migrate certain settings from the `.ini` files into the Registry. The WIN16 applications can continue to access and modify the `.ini` files, and these modifications then can be migrated to the Registry.

◆ 16-bit applications are not designed to recognize or use LFNs because LFNs are not implemented in Windows 3.1.

◆ Whereas under Windows 3.1 system resource stacks are 64KB, these have been converted to 32-bit stacks in Windows 98, dramatically decreasing the likelihood of running out of system resources.

32-Bit Applications' Resource Usage

Windows 98 is designed to support and interact with 32-bit applications specifically designed for Windows 95/98 or Windows NT. These applications are best suited to take advantage of the architectural design features of Windows 95/98. These design features include the following:

◆ The capability to take advantage of Windows 98 flat 32-bit, 4GB memory address space. (WIN32 applications typically load into the 4MB to 2GB range of memory.)

◆ The capability to pass more information in a single 32-bit programming call than is possible with a single 16-bit programming call, thus increasing processing performance.

◆ The capability to submit multiple simultaneous threads for processing, allowing greater user productivity within the 32-bit application because the user does not need to wait for one task to finish to start another.

◆ The capability to take advantage of Windows 95/98 preemptive multitasking, which is more efficient and runs more smoothly than Windows 3.1 cooperative multitasking.

◆ More comprehensive protection from other applications because each WIN32 application is assigned its own separate address space that is not visible to other applications.

◆ A separate message queue for each thread in a WIN32 application, which prevents other applications from interfering with the receipt or processing of system messages.

◆ The capability to use the Registry to store all application settings on a generic or per-user basis.

◆ The capability of the application to uninstall itself more easily than previous application types, because all changes to the Registry can be tracked and rolled back in the case of uninstallation.

TROUBLESHOOTING APPLICATION PROBLEMS

Although applications should normally run without interruption, situations do arise when, due to either programming errors or incompatibilities, applications cease to function properly. Though not addressed directly within Microsoft's list of objectives for the Windows 98 exam, knowing how to handle application problems is important in being able to administer the operating system properly. The two main problems that occur with applications are General Protection Faults (GPFs) and application hangs.

Recognize General Protection Faults and How They Are Caused

A General Protection Fault (GPF) typically is caused by an application that attempts to violate system integrity in one of a number of ways:

◆ By making a request to read or write to a memory address space owned by another application.

◆ By attempting to access the system hardware directly.

◆ By attempting to interact with a failing hardware driver. (Drivers operate at Ring 0, and so can seriously impact the operating system.)

The GPF is generated when the operating system shuts down an offending application to prevent a system integrity violation. How the offending application is specifically handled depends on its application type.

Because MS-DOS applications reside in their own VM and have their own message queue, if they cause a GPF, a message is displayed and the application is terminated without impacting the rest of the operating system.

In the case of WIN16 applications, the procedure is somewhat more complex. Because WIN16 applications share both a common address space and a common message queue, when one application creates a

GPF, all others are suspended until the offending application is terminated. After this is done, the remaining applications resume processing.

Finally, with 32-bit applications, the procedure is quite straightforward. Because 32-bit applications exist in their own separate address space, and each has a separate message queue, a GPF in one 32-bit application in no way affects any other 16- or 32-bit programs. Only the offending program is terminated.

Troubleshooting Application Faults with Dr. Watson

Dr. Watson is a utility that tabulates information about the system at the time of an application fault. In order to tabulate this system information, Dr. Watson must be running at the time of the fault. If you know how to trigger the fault (for instance, if the fault always occurs when you open a specific application), start the Dr. Watson application, then trigger the fault. Dr. Watson will record the state of the software environment at the time of the failure. After the fault, the Details button in the error message dialog box will provide the information collected by Dr. Watson.

To start Dr. Watson, perform the tasks outlined in Step by Step 8.5.

STEP BY STEP

8.5 Starting Dr. Watson

1. Click on the Start menu and choose Programs, Accessories, System Tools.

2. Choose System Information from the System Tools menu.

3. In Microsoft System Information Utility, pull down the Tools menu and choose Dr. Watson.

Dr. Watson will start minimized in the system tray (next to the clock). When you click on the Dr. Watson icon, it will generate a snapshot of your system. After Dr. Watson records the system information, the Dr. Watson main window appears on your screen (see Figure 8.19). The default view is the standard view shown in this figure, showing the Diagnosis tab, which provides relevant diagnostic information based on the state of the system at the time the snapshot was recorded.

Note that the Diagnosis tab includes a space for the user to write a note to the support technician describing what was happening at the time of the failure. For additional information on the state of the system at the time of the snapshot, choose Advanced View in the View menu. Dr. Watson's Advanced view provides several tabs describing different aspects of the system at the time of the snapshot (see Figure 8.20).

When an application fault occurs, Dr. Watson saves the logged information to a file called `watsonxx.wlg` in the `\Windows\Drwatson` directory. *xx* (in `watsonxx.wlg`) is an incremented number. You can also save a snapshot to a file using the Save and Save As options in the Dr. Watson File menu. You can view the contents of a Dr. Watson log file by opening it using the Open Log File option in the Dr. Watson File menu. You can also open a Dr. Watson in Microsoft System Information Utility.

NOTE

Add a Shortcut to Dr. Watson If you know an application fault will occur again but you don't know how to reproduce it, Microsoft suggests that you add a shortcut to Dr. Watson to the Start, Programs, Startup folder for your computer or user profile. Putting a shortcut to Dr. Watson in the Startup folder will cause Dr. Watson to start automatically when the system starts.

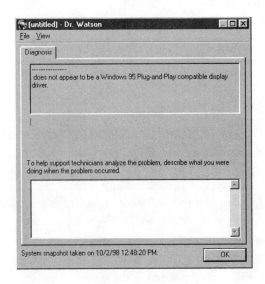

FIGURE 8.19

Dr. Watson's standard view shows the Diagnosis tab, which provides diagnostic information.

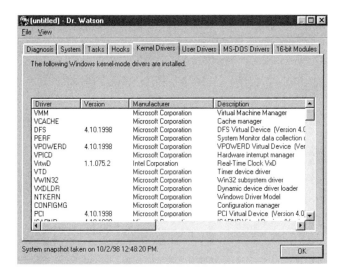

FIGURE 8.20
Dr. Watson's Advanced view provides additional tabs, showing the state of various components at the time of the snapshot.

Choose the Appropriate Course of Action When an Application Fails

Windows 98 lets you terminate a specific application without affecting other currently running processes. To terminate an application, press Ctrl + Alt + Delete, which opens a Close Program dialog box. Listed in this dialog box are all currently running tasks (including system processes not otherwise listed on the taskbar). You must then select a process (Not Responding usually is indicated in brackets next to the process name) and click on the End Task button. The operating system then attempts to terminate the process (which might take several seconds). Depending on the reason why the application is hung, you also might be presented with the option to wait a few seconds for the application to respond, and then to terminate the application if no response is received.

The following sections describe some considerations for when an application hangs, based on the application type:

- ◆ MS-DOS
- ◆ Windows 16-bit subsystem (WIN16)
- ◆ Windows 32-bit subsystem (WIN32)

MS-DOS Application

Ctrl + Alt + Del should work on an MS-DOS session because the MS-DOS application exists in its own VM and has its own message queue—a hung MS-DOS session does not affect the operation of any other process. An MS-DOS session also can be terminated from the Properties sheet of the session if the session is in a window.

16-Bit Windows Subsystem

As stated earlier, because WIN16 applications share a common memory address space and a common message queue, if a WIN16 process hangs while in the foreground, all other WIN16 processes cease to receive messages from the operating system and also appear hung.

This is due to a flag that is set for WIN16 processes, known as the *WIN16 mutex* (mutually exclusive). Because 16-bit code is considered *non-reentrant* (it cannot be used by more than one process at a time), a system must be in place to ensure that no two processes attempt to use the same piece of 16-bit code simultaneously. Under Windows 98, this is done by enforcing the rule that only the process that currently owns the rights to the WIN16 mutex can make requests to 16-bit API functions. When the given process is finished using the 16-bit code, it hands the mutex to the next process.

If an application hangs while it owns the WIN16 mutex, no other application can access 16-bit API functions. Thus, all 16-bit applications appear to hang. In addition, any 32-bit application that requires the use of a 16-bit API function (such as writing to the screen) also appears to hang. The application is still running but cannot make any updates to the screen, and thus appears to be inactive or unresponsive.

To remedy this situation, the 16-bit application that currently holds the mutex must be terminated through the means described previously. After this is done, the mutex should be reset and available for use by other processes.

32-Bit Windows Subsystem

Just testing to see whether you have been paying attention. A 32-bit application will not hang the system, because it will be preemptively

multitasked. In other words, control will be taken away from a misbehaving WIN32 application even if does not want to relinquish
control.

DIAGNOSING AND RESOLVING HARDWARE AND HARDWARE DRIVER PROBLEMS WITH SCANREG AND SCANREGW

Diagnose and resolve hardware device and device driver problems.

Windows 98 includes a utility called Registry Checker that helps
you back up, check, and maintain the Windows 98 Registry.
Microsoft mentions ScanReg and ScanRegW in the objective on
hardware device and device driver problems. Some types of devices
depend on configuration information in the Registry. If the Registry
is corrupt or misconfigured, the device might not function properly.
Similarly, if you add a device or a driver that writes to the Registry
incorrectly, you may compromise the Registry configuration.
Registry Checker checks the Registry for problems and can restore
the Registry if necessary. The Registry Checker utility is actually
comprised of two parts:

♦ **ScanReg.exe.** An MS-DOS–based, real-mode utility.

♦ **ScanRegW.exe.** A Windows–based, protected-mode utility.

ScanRegW.exe attempts to back up the Registry once per day during
a system startup. When Windows 98 restarts, ScanRegW.exe scans
Registry files and configuration files (user.dat, system.dat, win.ini,
and system.ini) to look for corruption. If no corruption is found,
ScanRegW.exe backs up the Registry and configuration files to a
CAB file in the Windows\Sysbackup folder. If ScanRegW.exe detects a
problem, it prompts you to restart your system.

When your system restarts, the MS-DOS–based utility ScanReg.exe
takes charge. First, ScanReg.exe attempts to replace the corrupt
Registry or configuration file with a working version from a previous
backup. If ScanReg.exe can't find a suitable backup copy, it will

NOTE

ScanReg and the Twin in the Window
You may consider it strange the Registry Checker's duties are divided among the utilities ScanReg.exe and ScanRegW.exe. When you think about it, though, you'll realize why Microsoft chose not to use a program running within Windows (ScanRegW.exe) to restore and repair a damaged Windows Registry. The philosophy seems to be to do as much of the routine business as possible within Windows, and then to use the MS-DOS–based ScanReg.exe (operating outside of Windows) to repair and restore the Registry itself. ScanReg.exe is also capable of performing some of the scanning and backup functions performed by ScanRegW.exe.

attempt to repair the Registry. ScanReg.exe can also perform optimization on the Registry if ScanRegW.exe detected a need for optimization during the last scan.

You can force a check of the Registry files by starting ScanRegW.exe directly. To start ScanRegW.exe, perform the tasks outlined in Step by Step 8.6.

STEP BY STEP

8.6 Starting ScanRegW.exe

1. Click on the Start menu and choose Programs, Accessories, System Tools.

2. Choose System Information in the System Tools group.

3. In Microsoft System Information Utility, pull down the Tools menu and select Registry Checker.

You can also start ScanRegW.exe by entering **scanregw** in the Start Menu's Run dialog box.

Refer to Chapter 5 for more information about saving, restoring, and configuring the Windows 98 Registry.

Case Study: Arizona Belt and Leather Company

ESSENCE OF THE CASE

Here are the essential elements in this case:

- There are 13 users, all using Windows 98.

- There is no centralized server, so all users are using share-level security for file and resource access.

- Most users are telemarketers and are not familiar with the inner workings of Windows 98.

- Users are having difficulty sharing out their data folders so that Mangers can access them.

- Some tool must be used to make shares easier to create and manage.

SCENARIO

Rachael, the Chief Information Officer for the Arizona Belt and Leather Company, would like to simplify how users share their data within their Windows 98 workgroup.

ANALYSIS

Net Watcher should be implemented so that Rachael can create and monitor shares throughout the entire network. Because share-level security is used, Rachael can assign and manage all passwords to the shared resources. Users will be monitored as to what share they are accessing through Net Watcher.

CHAPTER SUMMARY

KEY TERMS

- cooperative multitasking
- Enhanced Metafile Format (EMF)
- General Protection Fault (GPF)
- hardware virtualization
- IRQ
- Logged mode
- multitasking
- physical address (MAC address)
- Ping
- preemptive multitasking
- RAW data format
- Safe mode
- Safe Recovery
- Spool Data format
- spooler
- Startup disk
- Startup menu
- Step-by-Step Confirmation mode
- version conflict
- Virtual machine
- write-behind caching

This chapter discussed troubleshooting in Windows 98. You learned about some tools and strategies for troubleshooting Windows 98 PCs, and you learned about some common problems associated with Windows 98 computers. Specifically, this chapter looked at troubleshooting the following types of problems:

- ◆ Installation problems
- ◆ Boot process problems
- ◆ Network connectivity problems
- ◆ Printing problems
- ◆ File system problems
- ◆ Resource access problems
- ◆ Application problems
- ◆ Hardware device and device driver problems

When you take the Windows 98 exam, you may find that it isn't always apparent which questions are the troubleshooting questions. Troubleshooting draws from all your knowledge of configuring and managing Windows 98. So when you prepare for the troubleshooting portion of the Windows 98 exam, don't just think about this chapter—think about everything you've learned in this book and be prepared to apply it to solve problems in real situations.

|---|
| **APPLY YOUR KNOWLEDGE** |

Exercises

8.1   Exploring System Information Utility

This exercise will allow you to retrieve information about your system through System Information Utility. This information can be used to troubleshoot hardware conflicts, to help you to make decisions on hardware upgrades, and as a starting point when doing various types of troubleshooting on Windows 98 systems.

Estimated Time: 25 minutes

1. Click on the Start button and point to Programs, Accessories, System Tools.

2. From System Tools, click System Information. The Microsoft System Information Utility dialog box appears.

3. From the System Information Utility dialog box, note the processor type of your system and the amount of RAM on your system.

4. Click the plus sign (+) next to Hardware Resources. A list of categories appears. Click on Conflicts/Sharing.

5. Note any IRQs conflicting with other devices or being shared between devices.

6. Click on DMA. Note any DMA resources being used and any that are free.

7. Click on I/O. Note the I/O addresses for your computer's Floppy Disk Controller and keyboard.

8. Click on IRQ. Note what IRQ 4 is being used for. Also note the IRQ of your system's Printer Port.

9. Click on Memory. Note the memory range for your computer's video adapter.

10. Click the plus sign (+) next to Components.

11. Click on Input. Note the devices listed in this category.

12. Click on System.

13. Across the top of the system information, choose the option button for History. Note when the system board was originally configured according to the information displayed. Also note whether your system has a Plug and Play BIOS.

14. Click the plus sign (+) by Software Environment.

15. Click the plus sign (+) by the subcategory Drivers.

16. Click on the category Kernel Drivers. Note what VMM is responsible for.

17. Click on the category Running Tasks. Note the first program listed.

18. Click on the plus sign (+) next to the category labeled OLE Registration.

19. Click on INI File. Note the information displayed there.

20. Click on the Registry. Note the type of information displayed there.

21. Review why System Information Utility is useful for Windows 98 administrators, or help desk operators.

22. Keep Microsoft System Information Tool open for the next exercise.

APPLY YOUR KNOWLEDGE

8.2 Using Version Conflict Manager

This exercise will build the foundation for working with Microsoft's Version Conflict Manager. During installation, existing files that are replaced by older versions on the Windows 98 CD will be backed up. Version Conflict Manager is a way to restore these backed up files. Take caution; incorrect usage of this tool can override newer files with these older files.

Estimated Time: 10 minutes

1. If you have the Microsoft System Information Tool open from the last exercise, proceed with step 2. If not, open the System Information Utility through Programs, Accessories, System Tools.

2. Click the Tools menu, and the click Version Conflict Manager.

3. Version Conflict Manager will report a list of files that had a more recent version number before Windows 98 was installed. Note the oldest Backup Date of a file on your system.

4. Review why Version Conflict Manager is useful to administrators of Windows 98 and how this tool be dangerous to Windows 98.

5. Close out of Version Conflict Manger, but keep Microsoft System Information Utility open for the next exercise.

8.3 Troubleshooting the Boot Process Through Systems Configuration Utility

This exercise will allow you to manage and troubleshoot the boot process on a Windows 98 machine through System Configuration Utility. This utility allows you to interact with the boot process to see how the operating system is loaded. This tool can be used to inspect your startup environment and deduce what files may be causing problems.

Estimated Time: 15 minutes

1. If you have Microsoft System Information Tool open from the last exercise, proceed with step 2. If not, open System Information Utility through Programs, Accessories, System Tools.

2. Click the Tools menu and choose System Configuration Utility. The utility is displayed.

3. On the General tab, choose Diagnostic Startup and then click OK.

4. You are prompted to restart your machine to begin the diagnostics. Choose Yes to continue.

5. As Windows 98 restarts, the boot menu will be displayed. You must choose option 4, a step-by-step confirmation.

6. Each step of the startup is offered for you to accept the value or skip over the value for this boot up. Why would this be valuable for troubleshooting?

7. Accept all values and open System Configuration Utility again.

8. Choose Normal Startup and then click on the Config.sys tab.

9. From the Config.sys tab, you can select the variables in your config.sys file that should be processed on your machine, and in what order. In addition, you can add to the config.sys file or edit an existing line.

10. Click on the Autoexec.bat tab. Its choices are similar to those on the Config.sys tab.

APPLY YOUR KNOWLEDGE

11. Click on the System.ini tab. From here, note that there are different categories for each startup component, both system and hardware.

12. Click on the Win.ini tab and note the categories and the controls for each category.

13. Click the Startup tab and note the items that are selected to launch at startup time.

14. Exit System Configuration Utility and the Microsoft System Information Utility.

8.4   Diagnose and Resolve Connectivity Problems Using WinIPCfg

This exercise will explore the TCP/IP information utility, WinIPCfg. WinIPCfg allows you to retrieve your IP information for your computer. Often you'll need this information to troubleshoot connectivity problems to remote hosts. Of course, TCP/IP must be installed on your machine to complete this exercise.

Estimated Time: 15 minutes

1. Click on Start and choose Run.

2. Type in **WinIPCfg** and press Enter.

3. The IP Configuration is displayed for your first network adapter. Click the down arrow and select the network adapter card for your local network. If your first network adapter card is your modem or PPP adapter, you will most likely receive all zeros while your modem is offline. This is because your modem uses an IP address only when connecting to a dial-up server that dynamically assigns your modem an IP address. You may want to dial into your Internet connection if you are only working a modem adapter.

4. Note the following: your network adapter card's address (this is also the MAC address), your IP Address, the subnet mask, and the default gateway IP Address.

5. Click on More Info.

6. If you are using DHCP to obtain your IP address, note the IP Address of the DHCP server.

7. Note whether you have a primary or secondary WINS Server.

8. If you are using DHCP, note when your lease was obtained.

9. Note the expiration date of your lease.

10. If you are using DHCP to obtain an IP address, click the Release All button. Note whether your IP address changes.

11. Click the Renew All button. Note whether your IP address changes.

12. Click OK to close the IP Configuration Information dialog box.

8.5   Using Net Watcher to Troubleshoot Remote Resources

This exercise will allow you to administer a remote Windows 98 machine through Net Watcher. To complete this exercise successfully you will need two Windows 98 machines on a network. The target Windows 98 machine will need Remote Administration enabled, which can be done through the Passwords applet in Control Panel. Refer to Chapter 1 for more information about enabling Remote Administration.

Estimated Time: 15 minutes

APPLY YOUR KNOWLEDGE

1. Click Start then point to Programs, Accessories, System Tools.

2. From System Tools, click on Net Watcher.

3. Click the Administer menu and click Select Server.

4. Type in the machine name that you would like to administer, or click Browse and choose the server from the network list.

5. After you have made the connection to the target Windows 98 machine, Net Watcher displays a list of users connected to the machine and the resources that are currently being used.

6. Across the toolbar, there are buttons that allow you to quickly administer the remote machine. The last three buttons allow you to change views of the resources on the remote machine.

7. Click the button that represents the shares on the remote machine. The shares are listed with the path, share name, access type, and any comments on the share. As you click on each share, note the connections to the share.

8. Click on any share from the list and then click on the Stop Sharing button. The share will be removed from the list.

9. Click on the button to add a share. Enter the path of the folder you would like to share for the target machine, or browse the remote machine's resources to choose the folder you want to share out.

10. Click on Browse. The remote machine's resources are displayed for you to begin sharing out the resources.

11. Find a folder you would like to share for remote machine and click OK and OK again.

12. The Permissions dialog box appears. Add the permissions. If you are using share-level security, choose the access type and the password for the share. If you are using user-level security, assign the appropriate groups or users permission to the resource and choose OK.

13. Close Net Watcher.

14. Open Network Neighborhood and open the machine where the share was just added. Note whether the share is listed as a resource.

15. Close Network Neighborhood.

8.6 Troubleshooting TCP/IP Connectivity Problems with Ping and Tracert

This exercise will use two TCP/IP tools to confirm IP connections and trace the routes an IP packet will take to and from a remote host. Ping will be used to test that a connection can be made to the remote host; Tracert will be used to check the path that the connection is made through. TCP/IP must be installed on this machine, and you must be able to access the Internet or a remote host on your network.

Estimated Time: 10 minutes

1. Click Start, Run. Type in `WinIPCfg` to retrieve your IP information for this lab.

2. Click Start, then point to Programs, MS-DOS Prompt.

3. At the command prompt, type in `PING 127.0.0.1` and press Enter. Note the response you receive.

4. Now ping your own IP address. Note the response you receive.

APPLY YOUR KNOWLEDGE

5. Ping the IP address of your default gateway.

6. Ping the NetBIOS computer name of a machine on your network. For example, if there is a machine called Workstation5, you would enter **PING Workstation5**. Note the response.

7. Ping the name of your favorite Web site (if your network is connected to the Internet). If necessary, connect to the Internet via your dial-up ISP account, then ping your favorite Web site. Note the result.

8. Enter Tracert and the IP of a local machine on your network.

9. Enter Tracert to your favorite Web site.

> NOTE
>
> **Firewall Information** If you are behind a firewall, you may not get a response on the hops your IP packets are taking to that destination.

10. Exit out of the DOS Prompt.

8.7 Check for Corrupt Registry Files by Using ScanReg and ScanRegW

This exercise will use ScanReg to check the validity of the Registry. Registry problems can arise from incorrect hardware configuration, hardware failure, and corrupted files.

Estimated Time: 10 minutes

1. Click Start and point to Programs, MS-DOS Prompt.

2. At the command prompt, type in **scanreg/autorun** and press Enter. ScanReg will run and if it finds any errors will automatically fix the problem first by attempting to restore a backup copy of the Registry that was creating during the bootup.

3. At the command prompt, enter **scanregw**. This protected-mode version of ScanReg will launch a user interface. If no problems were found with the Registry you'll be asked if you'd like to back up the Registry again.

4. For this exercise, choose Yes. ScanregW will back up the Registry and report its status back to you.

5. Click OK to close ScanRegW.

Review Questions

1. What Windows 98 utility allows you to restore files and drivers that were backed up because they were replaced with earlier versions present on the Windows 98 CD?

2. What Windows 98 tool allows you to quickly gather system information?

3. What Windows 98 tool allows you to quickly and easily edit the configuration files of a PC running Windows 98?

4. If you would like to check your TCP/IP configuration, which Windows 98 tool will tell you all TCP/IP configuration, including your network card's MAC address?

5. How can you add shares to a remote Windows 98 machine?

APPLY YOUR KNOWLEDGE

6. Ping allows you to do what on a Windows 98 machine?

7. What is Tracert used for?

8. What Windows 98 tool automatically creates a daily backup copy of the Registry and key startup files?

9. If you cannot print to a remote Windows 98 print server, what are at least three things you should check?

10. What is the difference between user-level security and share-level security?

Exam Questions

1. Martin has just installed a new application on his Windows 98 machine. The new application is causing immense trouble with his older applications whenever this new version interacts with these applications. What should Martin do?

   A. Run the older 16-bit apps in separate memory address space.

   B. Run the new application in its own VDM, with limited access to the hardware.

   C. Use System Information Utility to restore the previous version of the application.

   D. Check Version Conflict Manager to see if files or drivers from the old application were replaced.

2. Mary is a consultant for the Holtz Marketing Firm. She needs to create a report on all the processors in each machine, and the amount of RAM in each Windows 98 machine. What Windows 98 tool will tell her this information?

   A. RegEdit

   B. System Information Utility

   C. 98 Diagnostics

   D. Microsoft SMS

3. You are configuring a Windows 98 machine that is failing during the boot up phase. You suspect an entry in the system.ini is the culprit. What tool will allow you to easily experiment with this win.ini file?

   A. Version Conflict Manager

   B. BootUp Examiner

   C. Microsoft System Information Utility

   D. System Configuration Utility

4. You are trying to connect to a remote host using TCP/IP. You suspect some IP information has been entered incorrectly on the local machine. Where can you retrieve IP addressing information? Choose all that apply.

   A. WinIPCfg

   B. Ping

   C. Network applet

   D. IPLOG.txt

5. You are trying to connect to a host on your network. You are certain that your IP address is correct, but you suspect that either the other computer's IP address is incorrect, or there may be a line down between your router and the remote machine. What can you do to check the connectivity to the remote machine?

   A. Confirm that the user has a physical connection and is logged into the network.

APPLY YOUR KNOWLEDGE

B. Use NBTSTAT –A against the remote machine's IP address.

C. Ping the IP address of the remote host.

D. Ping the IP address of the router.

6. You are a network administrator for a WAN. Users are complaining that to connect to the server in Phoenix it is taking much longer than usual. What can you do to evaluate the problem?

A. Ping the server in Phoenix.

B. Use Tracert against the IP address of the server in Phoenix.

C. Use FTP to connect to the server in Phoenix.

D. Use Net Watcher to monitor the connection with the server in Phoenix.

7. You are dual-booting between Windows 98 and Windows NT Workstation 4.0. Under Windows NT, you cannot see all of the partitions you have created under Windows 98. What do you suspect is the problem?

A. Windows NT does not see partitions that have not been made through Disk Administrator.

B. Windows NT cannot view FAT32 partitions.

C. Windows NT uses local security; you do not have permission to see the partition.

D. Windows NT needs to write a signature to the drive. This can be done through Disk Administrator.

8. John is trying to print to a remote Windows 98 print server but cannot. Of the following, which may be reasons why he cannot print to the remote printer shared off of a Windows 98 computer?

A. Incorrect protocols.

B. Incorrect permissions to access the printer.

C. Hardware problems with his network card.

D. The printer is paused.

APPLY YOUR KNOWLEDGE

Answers to Review Questions

1. Version Conflict Manager saves a backup copy of newer files that are replaced by older versions during application installation. Should you receive conflicts, you can restore these files with the Version Conflict Manager. (For more information, refer to the section "Troubleshooting Installation Problems.")

2. Microsoft System Information Utility allows you to quickly gather system information for troubleshooting. (For more information, refer to the section "Troubleshooting Installation Problems.")

3. Microsoft System Configuration Utility will allow you to edit your Startup files and to perform a diagnostic startup or a selective startup. (For more information, refer to the section "Diagnosing and Resolving Boot Process Failures.")

4. WinIPCfg retrieves IP addressing information. This information may be useful in tracking down connectivity problems to remote hosts. (For more information, refer to the section "Diagnosing and Resolving Connectivity Problems.")

5. Use Net Watcher to view, add, and monitor shares on a remote computer. In addition, Net Watcher can be used to see which users are connected to a remote share. (For more information, refer to the section "Diagnosing and Resolving Connectivity Problems.")

6. Check the ability of TCP/IP to connect to remote hosts. (For more information, refer to the section "Diagnosing and Resolving Connectivity Problems.")

7. To see the route an IP packet will take to a remote host. (For more information, refer to the section "Diagnosing and Resolving Connectivity Problems.")

8. The Registry Editor, consisting of the utilities ScanRegW.exe and ScanReg.exe. (For more information, refer to the section "Diagnosing and Resolving Hardware and Hardware Driver Problems with ScanReg and ScanRegW.")

9. Check the protocols that are in use, the physical connection to the network, and the permissions assigned on the printer. (For more information, refer to the section "Diagnosing and Resolving Printing Problems.")

10. User-level security is based on users with a Windows NT Domain or a NetWare environment; share-level access is based on passwords. (For more information, refer to Chapters 1 and 5.)

Answers to Exam Questions

1. **D.** Version Conflict Manager will keep the previous version of a software files if it is newer than the version whenever software has been updated on the machine. (For more information, refer to the section "Diagnosing and Resolving Installation Failures.")

2. **B.** System Information Utility is the Windows 98 resource Mary can run at each machine to get the information she needs for her report. Although Regedit will deliver the answers Mary needs, it would be much easier to collect that data through System Information Utility. (For more information, refer to the section "Diagnosing and Resolving Installation Failures.")

APPLY YOUR KNOWLEDGE

3. **D.** System Configuration Utility will allow you to edit all of the startup variables on a Windows 98 machine. (For more information, refer to the section "Diagnosing and Resolving Boot Process Failures.")

4. **A, C.** WinIPCfg will report back the IP addressing information about the local machine. The Network applet will display information about IP addressing if the address information was entered locally (refer to Chapter 3). (For more information, refer to the section "Diagnosing and Resolving Connectivity Problems.")

5. **C.** If you are trying to connect to a remote machine and are uncertain whether you have a connection to that machine, you can ping the IP address of the remote machine. (For more information, refer to the section "Diagnosing and Resolving Connectivity Problems.")

6. **B.** Tracert will trace the hops the IP packets will take along the route to the Phoenix server. It is possible that a router along the usual route has gone down, resulting in the development of a new route that may take longer than what has been experienced in the past. (For more information, refer to the section "Diagnosing and Resolving Connectivity Problems.")

7. **B.** Windows NT 4.0 cannot see FAT32 partitions without NT Service Pack 4 installed. (For more information, refer to the section "Diagnosing and Resolving File System Problems.")

8. **A, B, C.** Incorrect protocols will prevent John from connecting to the remote printer to print. If John does not have permissions to the printer, he will not be allowed to print. If John has hardware trouble with his network card, he will not be able to connect to the printer to print. (For more information, refer to the section "Diagnosing and Resolving Connectivity Problems.")

APPLY YOUR KNOWLEDGE

Suggested Readings and Resources

1. *The Windows 98 Resource Kit*; Microsoft Press

2. *The Windows 98 Professional Reference*, Hallberg and Casad; New Riders

FINAL REVIEW

Fast Facts

Study and Exam Prep Tips

Practice Exam

By now, you have studied the entire book and are preparing to take the Windows 98 exam. Selecting the correct solution to a given situation often comes down to eliminating the obviously wrong choices, and then choosing the right one from what is left. These exam tips will help you weed out some of the "distracter" answers you will see when you sit for your certification test. Rather than give you a bunch of facts you've read elsewhere in this book, the information herein reflects some of the author's experiences with the beta exam— some things you need to know. The information is categorized by objective. Note that this is not a substitution for studying the rest of the book and working on a Windows 98 machine. It is to help you focus your studies.

PLANNING

Develop an Appropriate Implementation Model for Specific Requirements in a Microsoft Environment and a Mixed Microsoft and NetWare Environment

Further considerations include choosing the appropriate file system and planning a workgroup.

Choosing the Appropriate File System

See Summary Table 1 for an outline of Windows 98 support for Windows file systems.

Fast Facts

SUMMARY TABLE 1
WINDOWS FILE SYSTEMS AND WINDOWS 98 SUPPORT

File System	Operating Systems Supported
FAT (FAT16)	Common to Windows 3.1, 95, 98, NT, and OS/2.
FAT32	New to Windows 98 and Windows 95 OSR/2. Not compatible with Windows 3.x, Windows NT, or OS/2.
NTFS	Not compatible with Windows 98. Windows NT's NTFS file system is not visible to Windows 98 in dual-boot situations.

Only FAT (also called FAT16) can be used as the active partition in a dual boot with Windows NT.

Planning a Workgroup

Make sure you know the effect of the workgroup name on browsing and joining a domain. It is also important to know the different ways you can log on to an existing domain (that is, Quick Logon, and Logon and Restore Connections.) Chapter 1, "Planning," discusses the *Planning a Workgroup* objective, but the issues that accompany the task of planning a workgroup are inseparable from the full discussion of Windows 98 networking provided in Chapter 3, "Windows 98 Networking."

Benefits of a Workgroup

◆ A workgroup allows the browsing of computers by workgroup (department).

◆ One system in each workgroup must use File and Printer Sharing, with the Master Browser enabled or automatic.

◆ Just because a Windows 98 system is logged on to a domain does not make it a member of the domain. Only Windows NT computers can be part of the domain.

◆ If the workgroup matches the domain name, then the Domain Master Browser is the workgroup master browser.

Logging On to a Domain

◆ Quick Logon does not test the mapped drives and remote shared drives. Only when they are needed is a connection established. There is no error if a server is unavailable.

◆ Logon and Restore Connections checks each connection during Startup and reports any errors.

Develop a Security Strategy in a Microsoft Environment and a Mixed Microsoft and NetWare Environment

Strategies include system policies, user profiles, File and Printer Sharing, and share-level access control or user-level access control.

System Policies

Make absolutely certain you have installed and configured system policies on a Windows 98 machine. Understanding this topic is crucial for passing this exam. Know what effect checking a box, clearing a box, and leaving a box grayed has on the policy. Be very familiar with the kinds of things you can enforce from system policies (such as forcing a logon to a network). Policies are applied only if the User Profiles feature is enabled.

Implications of Check Boxes in a Policy File

See Summary Table 2 for details about check boxes.

SUMMARY TABLE 2
IMPLICATIONS OF CHECK BOXES IN POLICY FILES

Check Box	Implication
Checked	This option overrides the current settings in the local Registry by enabling the feature.
Unchecked	This option overrides the current settings in the local Registry by disabling the feature.
Grayed	This option does not change the current settings in the local Registry; if the feature was enabled or disabled, it maintains its settings after the policy is run.

Type of Policies

See Summary Table 3 for details about system policies.

SUMMARY TABLE 3
SYSTEM POLICIES

Type of Policy	Application or Use
Specific user	Applies just to that user. That user is not subjected to group policies or default user policies.
Group	Easier to administer many users, especially when users change groups. If a user is a member of several groups, policy restrictions are applied in the order of the group's priorities.
Default user	Applies to all users that do not have a specific policy.
Computer	Applies just to that computer name. Any users on the system are affected. The computer is not subjected to the default computer policy in the file.
Default computer	Applies to all computers that do not have a specific policy.

Default Location of Policy Files

◆ **Primary logon for Windows NT domain**. The Windows 98 system policy file config.pol is on the Netlogon share of the primary domain controller. To enable load balancing, copy the policy file to each backup domain controller's Netlogon share and set the load balance option with the location of policy files.

◆ **Primary logon for Novell domain**. The system policy file config.pol is located in the public folder on the Logon server.

User Profiles

Windows 98 provides three types of user profiles:

◆ **Local.** Stored in the Windows\Profiles\username directory of the local computer. Applies only to the local computer.

◆ **Roaming.** Stored on the network and accessible from any network workstation.

◆ **Mandatory.** Same as roaming profiles except changes to the profile are not saved.

The user profile consists of a copy of the user.dat Registry file (renamed user.man in the case of manditory profiles) with personalized settings for the user, plus supporting folders, files, and shortcuts, depending on whether your computer is configured to include desktop and Start menu settings in the profile. Configure user profiles settings through the User Profiles tab of the Passwords Control Panel.

On a Windows NT Server domain, a roaming or mandatory user profile is stored in the user's home directory. On a NetWare server, roaming or mandatory user profiles are stored in the user's mail directory, unless the Windows 98 computer uses Microsoft Services for NetWare Directory Services, in which case the roaming or mandatory profile is stored in the user's home directory.

File and Printer Sharing

◆ You can install only one file and printer sharing service per computer. You can install file and printer sharing for either Microsoft or NetWare, but not both.

◆ If you do not have file and printer sharing installed, your machine cannot share resident files or locally attached printers with other computers in the workgroup or domain.

◆ File and printer sharing must be enabled to perform remote administration commands.

Share-Level Access Control or User-Level Access Control

◆ Share-level access control uses passwords—one for read-only and a different one for full access.

◆ User-level access control uses user and group permissions to control access and depends on a security provider such as NT computer or domain or a Novell server.

◆ To remotely administer another Windows 98 system, both systems must have the same share type.

◆ For remote Registry, you must have user-level access control.

> N O T E **Current Shares Removed** If you change from user-level to share-level access control, or vice versa, all current shares are removed.

INSTALLATION AND CONFIGURATION

Installation and Configuration is one of the main topics covered on the exam. In general, make sure you

know how much space Windows 98 requires for a typical installation, a compact installation, and a portable installation. Of course, the Custom Installation option of Setup allows more individualized control.

Install Windows 98

Installation options include Automated Windows Setup, New, Upgrade, Uninstall, and Dual-Boot combination with Microsoft Windows NT 4.0.

Automated Windows Setup

◆ Batch98 is used to create an installation script to set up Windows 98 with little user interaction.

◆ Use an installation script to select components during an install. This overrides any default settings.

◆ Use a different batch installation file for each configuration required.

New

This is a relatively straightforward topic. Just remember that the hard disk needs an active partition formatted with FAT or FAT32.

Upgrade

◆ Keeps the basic configuration settings of the old operating system if you're upgrading from Windows 95 or Windows 3.1x.

◆ Gives you the options of saving the old operating system files if you want to uninstall Windows 98.

◆ Can be manual or can use a Batch file.

You can upgrade over Windows 95, Windows 3.1, and Windows for Workgroups 3.1.1. You can install Windows 98 on a system running DOS 5.0 or later, but the installation does not automatically migrate settings and thus is not a true upgrade. You cannot run Windows 98 Setup from within Windows NT. You cannot upgrade operating systems like UNIX.

Uninstall

◆ If you saved the existing operating system files during Windows 98 Setup, you can uninstall Windows 98 by using the Uninstall tab of the Add/Remove Programs Control Panel.

◆ If you compressed the partition containing the previous operating system files or converted the partition to FAT32, you cannot successfully uninstall the old operating system.

Dual-Boot Combination with Microsoft Windows NT 4.0

The easiest way to do this is to install Windows 98 first, and then install Windows NT.

◆ Windows 98 does not work on an NTFS partition.

◆ Windows NT does not work on FAT32.

◆ Windows NT does not work if you use Windows 98 disk compression.

Configure Windows 98 Server Components

Server components include Microsoft Personal Web Server 4.0 and Dial-Up Networking Server.

Microsoft Personal Web Server 4.0

Remember that Windows 98 ships with a web server. This is a scaled-down version of IIS 4.0, used primarily for intranet purposes.

◆ Intranets

◆ Supports HTTP services

◆ Supports FTP services

Dial-Up Networking Server

◆ Only one dial-in at a time.

◆ Dial-in services can be disabled.

◆ Can use user-level security with an NT or Novell server.

◆ Users that dial in can access the Internet by using the remote network's default gateway in TCP/IP. Otherwise, only local network access is provided.

Dial-Up Networking is used for home systems or small networks with less need for security over dial-in systems.

Install and Configure the Network Components of Windows 98 in a Microsoft Environment and a Mixed Microsoft and NetWare Environment

Network components include Client for Microsoft Networks, Client for NetWare Networks, network adapters, File and Printer Sharing for Microsoft networks, File and Printer Sharing for NetWare networks, Service for NetWare Directory Services, Asynchronous

Transfer Mode, Virtual Private Networking and PPTP, and Browse Master.

Client for Microsoft Networks

◆ Must be primary login if roaming/mandatory profiles and system policies are to be implemented.

◆ Logon must be validated if a logon script is to be run.

Client for NetWare Networks

◆ Preferred servers in Novell are the main logon servers.

◆ Must be the primary login server if a logon script is to be run.

◆ Only keep Windows 98 common entries in a logon script. Keep map drives and capture printers.

Just make sure you are comfortable with all the tabs and check boxes when you are configuring the clients. You may want to brush up on things such as selecting the preferred server and logging on to an NT domain. For example, do you know how to make the client process login scripts?

Network Adapters

Network adapters are listed in the Add Adapter dialog box. You must be able to install adapters not listed and update drivers.

File and Printer Sharing for Microsoft Networks

◆ This allows other Windows 98, 95, 3.11, and 3.1 clients, as well as DOS clients, to access shared files and printers.

◆ Windows 3.1 and 3.11 can only browse up to eight-character share names.

◆ Windows 98 can only create up to 12-character share names.

◆ A computer name shows up in the browse list only if File and Printer Sharing is enabled and common protocol is used.

File and Printer Sharing for NetWare Networks

◆ For Novell DOS clients to see the Windows 98 system and its shares using SLIST, you must enable SAP advertising.

◆ All systems must have the same frame type to exchange data over IPX/SPX.

◆ Novell clients cannot log on to a Windows 98 system. They can only attach to it and access its shares.

Remember that only one File and Printer Sharing service can be running at any time.

Service for NetWare Directory Services (NDS)

◆ New to Windows 98, this service helps connect to Novell servers running NDS, such as Novell NetWare 4.x.

◆ NDS uses default context and preferred trees.

Asynchronous Transfer Mode (ATM) Components

To take advantage of ATM technology, Windows 98 includes components in the network icon to connect to an ATM network.

Virtual Private Networking and PPTP

◆ Using a dial-up adapter, Windows 98 connects with a VPN adapter instead of a modem.

◆ Communication is done over a secure channel.

◆ VPN piggybacks over a modem or LAN connection.

◆ PPTP is Point-to-Point Tunneling Protocol—one protocol inside another.

Browse Master

◆ All workgroups must have one Master browser in order to use the Network Neighborhood.

◆ A system running file and/or printer sharing has Master browser set to Automatic. It participates in the Master browser elections.

◆ Enabling Master browser on one system and disabling it on all other systems identifies which system is the Master browser.

◆ Setting the domain name as the workgroup name makes the Windows 98 system use the same Master browser as the domain.

◆ Only systems using the same protocol as your PC appear in your browse list.

◆ For File and Printer Sharing for Novell, you must enable SAP advertising before server names show up in the browse list.

Install and Configure Network Protocols in a Microsoft Environment and a Mixed Microsoft and NetWare Environment

Protocols are hit pretty hard on the exam, both directly and indirectly. Most of the questions are about TCP/IP and remote access using a default gateway. In general, make absolutely certain you know what each protocol is used for, and the advantages and disadvantages of each. The following sections address some of the more specific protocol issues on the exam.

NetBEUI

◆ Not routable; cannot access remote systems

◆ Can be used on a LAN or with Dial-Up Networking

◆ No configuration required

◆ Simple for small, single-segment networks

IPX/SPX-compatible Protocol

◆ IPX/SPX is used in NetWare environments.

◆ The NT equivalent is NWLink.

◆ IPX/SPX is a routable protocol.

◆ SAP advertising is used to display your server name and is shared to Novell system and the browse list.

◆ NetBIOS is not enabled by default with IPX/SPX. In the properties of IPX/SPX, there is a check box to enable NetBIOS over IPX/SPX.

◆ IPX/SPX and Novell use frame types. Two systems must have a common frame type in order to exchange data.

TCP/IP

TCP/IP is hit really hard on the exam; Microsoft asks all kinds of questions about it. A good background will aid you in the troubleshooting of scenario questions.

◆ TCP/IP is routable.

◆ A default gateway address is required to access remote systems.

◆ The default gateway address must be on the same segment.

◆ If your Windows 98 computer is configured to receive a dynamically assigned IP address, a DHCP server on the network can automatically distribute non-conflicting IP addresses and additional settings to clients, such as subnet mask, default gateway, and WINS.

◆ WINS server runs on an NT server and helps with NetBios name resolution. NetBIOS name resolution is used for each remote Microsoft and Novell server. NetBIOS is used for file or printer sharing, Network Neighborhood, and drive mappings. WINS is a dynamic tool.

◆ LMHOSTS is also used for NetBIOS name resolution or remote NetBIOS server, but this is a file that resides locally on each Windows 98 system in the Windows folder. LMHOSTS has no extension on its filename.

◆ DNS server runs on an NT or UNIX server and is used for HOSTS name resolution when using TCP/IP utilities such as Web or FTP services. Each computer has a host name and a domain name. A Fully Qualified Domain Name (FQDN) uses the host name and the domain name, such as www.microsoft.com.

◆ The HOSTS file is used just as DNS is for local and remote hosts' name resolution. This file resides in the Windows folder and has no filename extension.

Microsoft DLC

Basically, all you need to know is what it is used for (that is, some HP printers, connectivity to mainframes, and at times AS-400s).

Fast Infrared

◆ Fast Infrared is new to Windows 98.

◆ Fast Infrared is a protocol used by Infrared adapters to connect printers to the network.

Install and Configure Hardware Devices in a Microsoft Environment and a Mixed Microsoft and NetWare Environment

Hardware devices include modems, printers, Universal Serial Bus, multiple display support, IEEE 1394 FireWire, Infrared Data Association, Multilink, and power management scheme.

Modems

◆ The Modem Wizard is used to install a new modem.

◆ You can set a modem log in the Advanced Configuration tab to record possible errors.

◆ More recent modems require new drivers from their manufacturers.

Printers

◆ The Printer Wizard guides you through the installation of local and network printers.

◆ If you are printing to a network printer from a DOS application, you may need to map a local printer port to the network printer using the Capture Printer Port feature.

◆ In Windows 98, a *print device* is the machine that produces paper printed with text or graphics. A *printer* is the software drivers and configuration.

◆ PostScript printer drivers generate all types of scrambled text on non-PostScript printers.

◆ Windows 98 uses the EMF format for non-PostScript printers and the RAW format for PostScript printers.

◆ For slow applications, set the spooler to wait for all pages to be spooled before sending to the print device. This prevents print jobs from being mixed up.

◆ A banner page can be set to print before each print job to identify its origins.

◆ A separator page prints after each print job to identify the last page of the print job.

◆ For a PnP printer to be configured automatically, you must have a bidirectional port and an IEEE 1294-compliant cable.

◆ A network printer's drivers are downloaded to your Windows 98 system if they are compatible. Windows NT servers can have Windows 95/98-compatible drivers loaded and made available for shared printers. Each time a job is sent to a network printer, the print drivers are compared and downloaded if needed.

Universal Serial Bus (USB)

A lot of new devices support USB. Make sure you know the advantages and limits of USB. Contrast USB with conventional devices that require IRQ settings.

And you should be able to contrast USB with IEEE 1394 FireWire.

◆ USB devices do not require unique IRQs, DMAs, IOs, or base addresses.

◆ Standard connectors are used for all USB devices.

◆ USB devices can be BUS powered or self powered.

◆ USB devices can be connected directly to one another or through a USB hub.

◆ USB can handle up to 127 devices per port.

◆ USB can communicate at rates up to 12Mbps.

◆ You can get a USB keyboard, mouse, modem, and scanner, to name just a few devices.

Multiple Display Support

◆ PCI (Peripheral Component Interconnect) or AGP (Accelerated Graphics Port) video cards can be used.

◆ One card is the main device, with an additional card for each other monitor used.

IEEE 1394 FireWire

◆ New technology used for demanding digital video

◆ IEEE1394 FireWire is used for high-demand digital video with transmission rates of 150Mbps–400Mbps.

◆ Up to 63 devices

◆ Transmission rated up to 400Mbps

Infrared Data Association (IrDA)

IrDA provides faster transmission rates than the previous implementation of Infrared in Windows 95.

Multilink

- Two devices are connected as one to provide twice the bandwidth.

- Multilink uses modems and/or ISDN lines.

- Multilink and Callback do not work together.

Power Management Scheme

Windows 98 lets you configure a power management scheme through the Power Management Control Panel. A power management scheme enables you to configure the computer to turn off the monitor or hard drive and to put the system on standby after a predefined interval of inactivity. Power management is typically used for battery-powered laptops, but it also has application in desktop units. Not all hardware supports power management.

Install and Configure Microsoft Backup

- Remember that Windows 98 Backup now works with SCSI drives. It also works with QIC 40, 80, and 3010.

- If you have properly installed a compatible tape drive, Windows 98 will automatically detect the drive. If you change drives, you can select Redetect Tape Drive from the Tools menu if needed.

- You can back up your data to tape, floppy, or a networked drive.

- A *full backup* includes all the files selected and marks the files as being backed up.

- An *incremental backup* includes only the files that have been added or changed since the last backup and marks the files as being backed up. This

method is faster than a full backup. To restore, however, you must use all the backups.

- A *differential backup* includes only the files that have been added or changed since the last backup but does not mark the files as being backed up. This method is fastest when you need to restore. To restore you need use only the full backup and the last backup, which is cumulative.

CONFIGURING AND MANAGING RESOURCE ACCESS

This objective addresses assigning access permissions for shared folders; creating, sharing, and monitoring resources; setting up user environments using system policies and user profiles; backing up data and the Registry; restoring the Registry; managing hard disks; and creating hardware profiles.

Assign Access Permissions for Shared Folders in a Microsoft Environment and a Mixed Microsoft and NetWare Environment

Methods include passwords, user permissions, and group permissions.

Passwords

If your computer uses share-level security, you can assign a password to a shared folder. Right-click on a folder in Explorer and choose the Sharing tab. You can enter different passwords for Read-only access and Full access.

User Permissions

◆ Permission given to a specific username overrides any group permissions.

◆ For user permission, you must be using user-level security with a security provider such as NT or Novell server.

◆ Valid permissions are Read-only, Change, Full Control, and No Access. You can also customize access rights.

Group Permissions

◆ Group permissions, with the exception of No Access, are cumulative for users in multiple groups.

◆ For group permissions, you must be using user-level security with a security provider such as an NT computer or Novell server.

◆ Valid permissions are Read-only, Change, Full Control, and No Access.

Create, Share, and Monitor Resources

Resources include remote computers and network computers.

Remote Computers

Remember that you must be running user-level access control to install and configure many of the Remote management tools.

Network Printers

Most of this was already covered in "Printers" in general. Just make sure you keep in mind the RPC Printer, and how you would manage a network printer remotely.

◆ Everyone can see the list of print jobs.

◆ Only the owner of a print job and administrators can delete a print job.

◆ Administrators and owners of the printer can change the priority of a print job.

Set Up User Environments by Using User Profiles and System Policies

◆ User profiles are not automatically enabled in Windows 98.

◆ Profiles can be changed to mandatory by renaming user.dat to user.man.

◆ Roaming and mandatory profiles are stored in the user's home folder on an NT domain. Client for Microsoft must be the primary logon.

◆ Roaming and mandatory profiles are stored the user's mail folder on a Novell server unless you are using Microsoft Services for NetWare Directory Services, in which case the user's profile is stored in the home directory.

◆ User profiles must be enabled to use policies.

◆ The default location for the config.pol policy file on an NT Domain is the Netlogon share on the PDC. Only when Load Balancing is turned on does Windows 98 download policies from BDC.

◆ The default location for the config.pol system policy file on a Novell Server is the public directory on the SYS volume.

◆ Default user and default computer policies are not used if a specific user or computer has a policy.

◆ Group policies are not implemented if the Windows 98 system does not have group policies enabled with Groupol.dll.

◆ Remember that a gray box in the policy file means that policy does not change the current settings of the local Registry.

Back Up Data and the Registry, and Restore Data and the Registry

The Registry backup is very important. Understand the difference between exporting a folder and backing it up.

◆ Backing up the Registry includes the entire Registry.

◆ Exporting a Registry file (such as just one key or one subkey) can be used to back up a subsection of the Registry. The Registry file can then be merged back into the Registry.

◆ Windows 98's Registry Checker tools (ScanRegW.exe and ScanReg.exe) also can back up and restore the Registry.

Configure Hard Disks

Tasks include disk compression, partitioning, enabling large disk support, and converting to FAT32.

Disk Compression

◆ Windows 98 uses DriveSpace 3.0.

◆ 2GB is the largest partition that can be compressed using DriveSpace.

◆ A host drive is the location at which data is really stored. Drive C: is where the user accesses information. The host drive is usually hidden.

◆ NT is not compatible with DriveSpace 3.0.

◆ A FAT32 partition cannot be compressed using DriveSpace 3.0.

Partitioning

You use FDISK to create and manage partitions on a drive. Make sure you understand about extended DOS partitions, primary DOS partitions, and active partitions. This knowledge will be good for a few extra points on the exam.

◆ Only primary partitions can be active and bootable.

◆ Extended partitions can be subdivided into multiple logical drives.

◆ Windows 98 supports only one primary and one extended partition.

Enabling Large Disk Support

Know when Windows 98 offers support for FAT32. Be familiar with the FDISK Program and the size of partitions.

◆ FAT32 uses smaller clusters. 4KB clusters use up less space on the hard drive, allowing for more real storage.

◆ Windows 98's FDISK offers large disk support when a partition of 540MB or more is created.

◆ FAT32 is not compatible with Windows NT.

◆ FAT32 partitions cannot be compressed using DriveSpace.

Converting to FAT32

Understand how to convert from FAT to FAT32. Remember that you cannot dual boot with NT if the main drive is FAT32, and that you cannot convert back from FAT32 to FAT.

◆ The Convert utility does not reformat the partition and no data is lost. The Convert utility is found in the System Tools.

◆ Windows 98 can only convert from FAT to FAT32; it cannot convert from FAT32 back to FAT.

Create Hardware Profiles

In most cases, an administrator needs to implement two hardware configurations for the same system. An example would be a laptop with one hardware configuration for office use and one for out-of-the-office use.

◆ Hardware profiles are created in the Hardware Profiles tab of the System Control Panel.

◆ After a profile is created, you must reboot into that profile to make changes to it.

INTEGRATION AND INTEROPERABILITY

Some information pertaining to this objective is presented in the previous section on configuring network components.

Configure a Windows 98 Computer As a Client Computer in a Network That Contains a Windows NT 4.0 Domain

See the notes regarding configuring network components of a client computer. Also note that users of Windows 98 can log on to an NT domain, but that the Windows 98 system is not part of the domain.

Configure a Windows 98 Computer As a Client Computer in a NetWare Network

See the earlier notes regarding configuring network components of a client computer. Remember that a Windows 98 system can be a client to NT and Novell at the same time.

Configure a Windows 98 Computer for Remote Access by Using Various Methods in a Microsoft Environment or a Mixed Microsoft and NetWare Environment

Methods include Dial-Up Networking and proxy server.

Dial-Up Networking

Understand that the Dial-Up Networking tool in this case is the only client. Make sure you can integrate Multilink, as well as the VPN device and PPTP with Dial-Up Networking, into this section. This is basically a combination of Configuring Dial-Up Networking and TCP/IP.

◆ Dial-Up Networking can be used to connect to a corporate network or the Internet.

◆ A pair of modems or ISDN adapters can be used in a Multilink session to increase bandwidth.

◆ Connecting over TCP/IP allows access to the local area network.

◆ Selecting Use Remote Default Gateway allows access to the LAN and the Internet.

◆ A VPN (Virtual Private Network) allows a secure connection over the Internet through a modem or network connection.

Here again, it is mostly a matter of getting Dial-Up Networking installed properly, setting up the modem properly, and binding the appropriate protocols. It can get complicated, but mercifully is not hit too bad on the exam. Remember, if you do not have a modem installed, and you try to configure Dial-Up Networking, it will take you through the Add Modem Wizard first. Also, remember that in Windows NT, Dial-Up Networking is called RAS (Remote Access Service).

Proxy Server

The proxy server is not part of Windows 98. Here you need to know how to configure the proxy client in Windows 98 and the purpose of implementing proxy for security and access reasons.

◆ A proxy server can be set up to allow a Windows 98 system access to the Internet.

◆ The proxy client is installed on each Windows 98 system. The client can be configured manually, or you can have the proxy server configure it automatically, which updates each time the client connects.

◆ A proxy server can restrict connections based on Internet protocol (HTTP, FTP, Gopher, and so on), IP address, or Internet domain name.

MONITORING AND OPTIMIZATION

This area features several important concepts for you to consider.

Monitor System Performance by Using Net Watcher, System Monitor, and Resource Meter

Make sure you know the requirements to install and use Net Watcher. You should have a good feel for the kind of information you can obtain here.

◆ Net Watcher allows administrators to remotely monitor who is connected to a system and which folders are being accessed.

◆ Net Watcher can also be used to create or stop shares on a remote Windows 98 system.

◆ Both systems must be running the same access control: user-level or share-level.

◆ Remote administration must be enabled, and the user trying to monitor must have permission.

You do not need to know what each of the System Monitor's counters is, but you do need to experiment with System Monitor and have a solid feel for the kinds of information you can get from it.

◆ System Monitor is used to evaluate the system's performance.

◆ System Monitor can be used to detect possible bottlenecks.

◆ Remote monitoring can be done if remote administration is enabled and the user has permission.

◆ Only objects for the components that are installed are displayed.

◆ For network monitoring, you must install the remote Registry service.

◆ The kernel object and its usage are pivotal to Windows 98's performance. This is the counter to evaluate the processor's usage.

Tune and Optimize the System in a Microsoft Environment and a Mixed Microsoft and NetWare Environment

Tasks include using Disk Defragmenter and ScanDisk to optimize the hard disk, updating drivers, applying service packs, using the Maintenance Wizard to automate tasks, using the Task Scheduler, and checking for corrupt files with System File Checker.

Optimizing the Hard Disk by Using Disk Defragmenter and ScanDisk

Know when you would run the Disk Defragmenter, and why. You also need to remember that there are different ways to run the Disk Defragmenter, such as Full Defragmentation, Defragment Files, and Consolidate Free Space Only. Make sure you have a good feel for when you would use each option.

◆ Run the Defragmenter utility to collect all the files into a contiguous section of the hard drive, freeing up more space for storage.

◆ Run the Defragmenter utility to reorganize files so the application can start up faster.

◆ You should defragment the drive after moving or deleting a lot of files.

◆ Defragment the drive when file access and storage seems sluggish.

◆ Defragmenting just free space does not make access any faster but provides better storage for new files.

You should know what kinds of errors ScanDisk can detect and correct. You should also know the difference between a standard and thorough scan.

◆ Run ScanDisk to check for errors in files or surface errors on the hard drive.

◆ ScanDisk can find lost clusters and delete them.

◆ ScanDisk can fix cross-linked files.

◆ ScanDisk can mark bad sectors and prevent their future use as data storage.

◆ A thorough scan checks the surface of the drive.

Compressing Data by Using DriveSpace 3.0 and the Compression Agent

◆ DriveSpace 3.0 can be used to compress drives up to 2GB in size.

◆ DriveSpace 3.0 cannot be used with NTFS or FAT32 partitions.

◆ DriveSpace can use different compression ratios to improve access time (less compression) or improve storage capacity (more compression). Use Compression Agent to manage compression ratios.

◆ Not all files compress to the same ratio. Text files compress at higher ratios than program files.

Updating Drivers and Applying Service Packs by Using Windows Update and the Signature Verification Tool

Understand the system requirements to use Windows Update. Namely, access the Internet and registered software to get all updates. Have a basic understanding of the risk of Internet downloads and how the Signature Verification tool helps.

◆ New drivers for existing hardware.

◆ New components and fixes for Windows 98 system files.

◆ Internet connectivity is required to use System Update.

◆ System Update can scan your system and recommend which updates are necessary and which ones are optional.

◆ Your copy of Windows 98 must be registered with Microsoft for you to have access to all updates.

◆ The Signature Verification Tool is used to make sure the update has not been tampered with and the source is legitimate.

Automating Tasks by Using Maintenance Wizard

Be familiar with the tool and the difference between the Custom and Express options. Also remember that you cannot add other applications in this wizard.

◆ Compression Agent, Disk Defragmenter, ScanDisk, and DiskCleanup can be set up with Maintenance Wizard. No other utilities can be automated with this wizard.

◆ The Custom option allows you to select which components to load and what time of day to run them.

Scheduling Tasks by Using Task Scheduler

Task Scheduler executes the disk maintenance utilities configured through Maintenance Wizard (Compression Agent, Disk Defragmenter, ScanDisk, and DiskCleanup) and also lets you configure other applications to run without user intervention.

◆ Task Scheduler provides the same basic maintenance tools as provided by the Maintenance Wizard.

◆ Any other applications can be set up to start at a given time.

◆ Fully automated applications are preferred because no user interaction is required.

Checking for Corrupt Files and Extracting Files from the Installation Media by Using the System File Checker

Know how to find and replace corrupt system files using System File Checker.

◆ Windows 98 has CAB files, which contain compressed files used for installation and additional configuration.

◆ The System File Checker utility can be used to restore damaged files, as well as to view CAB file content.

TROUBLESHOOTING

Much of the Troubleshooting items have already been covered. On the exam, questions seem to fall into multiple objectives. This is particularly true of the scenario questions.

Diagnose and Resolve Installation Failures

Tasks include resolving file and driver version conflicts with Version Conflict Manager and the Microsoft System Information Utility.

Resolving File and Driver Version Conflicts by Using Version Conflict Manager and the Microsoft System Information Utility

◆ Version Conflict Manager backs up newer versions of files that were replaced by older versions during installation.

◆ Conflict Manager can replace files.

◆ Conflict Manager can verify and compare driver revision numbers and dates.

◆ The Microsoft System Information utility lists all 16- and 32-bit applications that are currently on the system.

◆ System Information can be used to produce reports about the system, assisting administrators and support personnel.

Diagnose and Resolve Boot Process Failures

Tasks include using the System Configuration Utility.

Editing Configuration Files by Using the System Configuration Utility

You'll see only a few basic types of boot-up issues with a Windows 98 machine. These include viruses, hardware problems, and Registry problems. In addition to these items, if you know how to use Safe Mode and the other Startup menu options to get the machine back up and running, then you have this objective well in hand. You also need to know how to create a boot disk.

◆ A Windows Startup disk contains the necessary files to start Windows 98 at a command prompt. You can create a startup disk from the Password icon in the Control Panel.

◆ Using SYS from the Startup disk, you can restore the boot sector on drive C:.

◆ The Startup disk is not unique to any computer; it can be used to troubleshoot several systems.

◆ Using Safe Mode, Windows 98 starts up without any extra device drivers and without network connectivity unless Safe Mode with Network Support is selected.

◆ System Configuration Utility lets you configure startup items and selectively enable, disable, and edit entries in the startup files autoexec.bat, config.sys, system.ini, and win.ini.

Diagnose and Resolve Connectivity Problems in a Microsoft Environment and a Mixed Microsoft and NetWare Environment

Tools include WinIPCfg, Net Watcher, Ping, and Tracert.

WinIPCfg

Make sure you are familiar with the information you obtain from WinIPCfg. Couple this with the information from the TCP/IP section and you will do well here.

◆ WinIPCfg displays current IP addresses and subnet masks for each network card and modem.

◆ Using the More Info button in the WinIPCfg dialog box, you will see the default gateway and other configuration settings for TCP/IP.

◆ WinIPCfg's Release and Renew are used with client machines that are configured by a DHCP server.

Net Watcher

It is important to know what you can do with Net Watcher, and what you cannot do with it. Make sure you understand the requirements for running Net Watcher. Refer to the Net Watcher explanation earlier in this chapter.

Ping

Ping is a command-line tool that allows you to troubleshoot network connections. You can use Ping to send a test packet to the specified address and then, if things are working properly, the packet is returned.

Tracert

Using Tracert, you can determine the path that your packets take to the remote host. Execute `TRACERT hostname`, in which *hostname* is the computer name or IP address of the computer whose route you want to trace. Tracert will return the different IP addresses the packet was routed through to reach the final destination. The results also include the number of hops needed to reach the destination. Execute `TRACERT` without any options to see a help file that describes all the Tracert switches.

Diagnose and Resolve Printing Problems in a Microsoft Environment and a Mixed Microsoft and NetWare Environment

See the earlier discussion on configuring printers.

Diagnose and Resolve File System Problems

Refer to the discussion on ScanDisk and Disk Defragmenter.

Diagnose and Resolve Resource Access Problems in a Microsoft Environment and a Mixed Microsoft and NetWare Environment

This topic was covered in the section on configuring clients and protocols.

Diagnose and Resolve Hardware Device and Device Driver Problems

Tasks include using ScanReg and ScanRegW to check for corrupt Registry files.

Checking for Corrupt Registry Files by Using ScanReg and ScanRegW

ScanReg and ScanRegW perform the Registry Editor functions in Windows 98.

- ScanRegW is a Windows-based utility that scans Registry and configuration files for corruption and backs up Registry and configuration files at startup.

- ScanReg is an MS-DOS-based utility that can scan the Registry and back up files. ScanReg can also restore a backup version of a Registry or configuration file if the file is found to be corrupt.

If no backup copy of the file is present, ScanReg will attempt to repair the corrupt file.

SUMMARY

The exam consists of several types of questions. The most common is a multiple-choice question that will describe a short scenario in which a typical user or administrator could be involved. There are typically four answers listed. Be very careful to read the full question and all of the answer options before answering. If the question requests the best answer, do not be surprised if *your* best answer is not listed. Think about the question in terms of the situation and how *Microsoft* would expect you to answer.

There is also a new type of question on the Windows 98 exam. It displays a dialog box with selections already made. The question prompts you to identify which box to check or uncheck in order to satisfy the requirements. Using the mouse, click on the appropriate check box as you would if it were a real dialog box.

If you are unsure about one of your answers, do not spend too much time on it. Simply mark that question and come back to it at the end of the exam. Keep your eye on the timer and be sure to complete the exam before the time runs out.

Here's hoping you do well on the exam. Your exam preparation and the review you've undertaken using this book, as well as your experience actually working with Windows 98 (a must), has appropriately prepared you. If you feel you need more exam-type practice, you are encouraged to take the practice exams in this book and to pick up a copy of Macmillan Publishing's *MCSE Test Prep: Windows 98* for exam 70-098. Study hard and good luck!

Study and Exam Prep Tips

This chapter provides you with some general guidelines for preparing for the exam. It is organized into three sections. The first section addresses your pre-exam preparation activities, covering general study tips. This is followed by an extended look at the Microsoft Certification exams, including a number of specific tips that apply to the Microsoft exam formats. Finally, it addresses changes in Microsoft's testing policies and how they might affect you.

To better understand the nature of preparation for the test, it is important to understand learning as a process. You probably are aware of how you best learn new material. Maybe outlining works best for you, or maybe you are a visual learner who needs to "see" things. Whatever your learning style, test preparation takes time. While it is obvious that you can't start studying for these exams the night before you take them, it is very important to understand that learning is a developmental process. Understanding the process helps you focus on what you know and what you have yet to learn.

Thinking about how you learn should help you recognize that learning takes place when we are able to match new information to old. You have some previous experience with computers and networking, and now you are preparing for this certification exam. Using this book, software, and supplementary materials will not just add incrementally to what you know. As you study, you actually change the organization of your knowledge to integrate this new information into your existing knowledge base. This will lead you to a more comprehensive understanding of the tasks and concepts outlined in the objectives and related to computing in general. Again, this happens as an iterative process rather than a singular event. Keep this model of

learning in mind as you prepare for the exam, and you will make better decisions on what to study and how much to study.

STUDY TIPS

There are many ways to approach studying, just as there are many different types of material to study. However, the tips that follow should work well for the type of material covered on the certification exams.

Study Strategies

Although individuals vary in the ways they learn information, some basic principles of learning apply to everyone. You should adopt some study strategies that take advantage of these principles. One of these principles is that learning can be broken into various depths. *Recognition* (of terms, for example) exemplifies a surface level of learning: You rely on a prompt of some sort to elicit recall. *Comprehension or understanding* (of the concepts behind the terms, for instance) represents a deeper level of learning. The ability to analyze a concept and apply your understanding of it in a new way or to address a unique setting represents further depth of learning.

Your learning strategy should enable you to know the material a level or two deeper than mere recognition. This will help you to do well on the exam(s). You will know the material so thoroughly that you can easily handle the recognition-level types of questions used in multiple-choice testing. You will also be able to apply your knowledge to solve novel problems.

Macro and Micro Study Strategies

One strategy that can lead to this deeper learning includes preparing an outline that covers all the objectives and subobjectives for the particular exam you are working on. You should then delve a bit further into the material and include a level or two of detail beyond the stated objectives and subobjectives for the exam. Finally, flesh out the outline by coming up with a statement of definition or a summary for each point in the outline.

This outline provides two approaches to studying. First, you can study the outline by focusing on the organization of the material. Work your way through the points and subpoints of your outline with the goal of learning how they relate to one another. For example, be sure you understand how each of the main objective areas is similar to and different from one another. Then do the same thing with the subobjectives. Also, be sure you know which subobjectives pertain to each objective area and how they relate to one another.

Next, you can work through the outline and focus on learning the details. Memorize and understand terms and their definitions, facts, rules and strategies, advantages and disadvantages, and so on. In this pass through the outline, attempt to learn detail as opposed to the big picture (the organizational information that you worked on in the first pass through the outline).

Research shows that attempting to assimilate both types of information at the same time seems to interfere with the overall learning process. Separate your studying into these two approaches, and you will perform better on the exam than if you attempt to study the material in a more conventional manner.

Active Study Strategies

In addition, the process of writing down and defining the objectives, subobjectives, terms, facts, and definitions promotes a more active learning strategy than merely reading the material does. In human information processing terms, writing forces you to engage in more active encoding of the information. Simply reading over it constitutes passive processing.

Next, determine whether you can apply the information you have learned by attempting to create examples and scenarios of your own. Think about how or where you could apply the concepts you are learning. Again, write down this information to process the facts and concepts in a more active fashion.

The hands-on nature of the Step by Step tutorials and the exercises at the end of the chapters provide further active learning opportunities that will reinforce concepts.

Common Sense Strategies

Finally, you should also follow common sense practices in studying: Study when you are alert, reduce or eliminate distractions, take breaks when you become fatigued, and so on.

Pre-Testing Yourself

Pre-testing allows you to assess how well you are learning. One of the most important aspects of learning is what has been called "meta-learning." Meta-learning has to do with realizing when you know something well or when you need to study some more. In other words, you recognize how well or how poorly you have learned the material you are studying. For most people, this can be difficult to assess objectively on their own. Therefore, practice tests are useful because they reveal more objectively what you have and have not learned. You should use this information to guide review and further studying. Developmental learning takes place as you cycle through studying, assessing how well you have learned, reviewing, and assessing again, until you feel you are ready to take the exam.

You may have noticed the practice exam included in this book. Use it as part of this process. In addition to the Practice Exam, the Top Score software on the CD-ROM also provides a variety of ways to test yourself before you take the actual exam. By using the Top Score Practice Exams, you can take an entire practice test. By using the Top Score Study Cards, you can take an entire practice exam or you can focus on a particular objective area, such as Planning, Troubleshooting, or Monitoring and Optimization. By using the Top Score Flash Cards, you can test your knowledge at a level beyond that of recognition; you must come up with the answers in your own words. The Flash Cards also enable you to test your knowledge of particular objective areas.

You should set a goal for your pre-testing. A reasonable goal would be to score consistently in the 90-percent range (or better). See Appendix D, "Using the Top Score Software," for more detailed explanation of the test engine.

EXAM PREP TIPS

Having mastered the subject matter, the final preparatory step is to understand how the exam will be presented. Make no mistake about it, a Microsoft Certified Professional (MCP) exam will challenge both your knowledge and your test-taking skills! This section starts with the basics of exam design, reviews a new type of exam format, and concludes with hints that are targeted to each of the exam formats.

The MCP Exam

Every MCP exam is released in one of two basic formats. What's being called *exam format* here is really little more than a combination of the overall exam structure and the presentation method for exam questions.

Each exam format utilizes the same types of questions. These types or styles of questions include multiple-rating (or scenario-based) questions, traditional multiple-choice questions, and simulation-based questions. It's important to understand the types of questions you will be asked and the actions required to properly answer them.

Understanding the exam formats is essential to good preparation because the format determines the number of questions presented, the difficulty of those questions, and the amount of time allowed to complete the exam.

Exam Format

There are two basic formats for the MCP exams: the traditional fixed-form exam and the adaptive form. As its name implies, the fixed-form exam presents a fixed set of questions during the exam session. The adaptive format, however, uses only a subset of questions drawn from a larger pool during any given exam session.

Fixed-Form

A fixed-form, computerized exam is based on a fixed set of exam questions. The individual questions are presented in random order during a test session. If you take the same exam more than once, you won't necessarily see the exact same questions. This is because two or three final forms are typically assembled for every fixed-form exam Microsoft releases. These are usually labeled Forms A, B, and C.

The final forms of a fixed-form exam are identical in terms of content coverage, number of questions, and allotted time, but the questions themselves are different. You may have noticed, however, that some of the same questions appear on, or rather are shared across, different final forms. When questions are shared across multiple final forms of an exam, the percentage of sharing is generally small. Many final forms share no questions, but some older exams may have ten to fifteen percent duplication of exam questions on the final exam forms.

Fixed-form exams also have a fixed time limit in which you must complete the exam. The Top Score software on the CD-ROM that accompanies this book provides fixed-form exams.

Finally, the score you achieve on a fixed-form exam (which is always reported for MCP exams on a scale of 0 to 1,000) is based on the number of questions you answer correctly. The exam passing score is the same for all final forms of a given fixed-form exam.

The typical format for the fixed-form exam is this:

◆ 50–60 questions

◆ 75–90 minute testing time

◆ Question review is allowed, including the opportunity to change your answers

Adaptive Form

An adaptive form exam has the same appearance as a fixed-form exam, but it differs in both how questions are selected for presentation and how many questions actually are presented. Although the statistics of adaptive testing are fairly complex, the process is concerned with determining your level of skill or ability with the exam subject matter. This ability assessment begins with the presentation of questions of varying levels of difficulty and ascertains at what difficulty level you can reliably answer them. Finally, the ability assessment determines if that ability level is above or below the level required to pass that exam.

Examinees at different levels of ability will then see quite different sets of questions. Examinees who demonstrate little expertise with the subject matter will continue to be presented with relatively easy questions. Examinees who demonstrate a high level of expertise will be presented progressively more-difficult questions. Both individuals may answer the same number of questions correctly, but because the higher-expertise examinee can correctly answer more-difficult questions, he or she will receive a higher score and is more likely to pass the exam.

The typical design for the adaptive form exam is this:

◆ 20–25 questions

◆ 90 minute testing time (although this is likely to be reduced to 45–60 minutes in the near future)

◆ Question review is not allowed, providing no opportunity to change your answers

The Adaptive Exam Process

Your first adaptive exam will be unlike any other testing experience you have had. In fact, many examinees have difficulty accepting the adaptive testing process because they feel they were not provided the opportunity to adequately demonstrate their full expertise.

You can take consolation in the fact that adaptive exams are painstakingly put together after months of data gathering and analysis and are just as valid as a fixed-form exam. The rigor introduced through the adaptive testing methodology means that there is nothing arbitrary about what you'll see! It is also a more efficient means of testing that requires less time to conduct and complete.

As you can see from Figure 1, a number of statistical measures drive the adaptive examination process. The one that's most immediately relevant to you is the ability estimate. Accompanying this test statistic are the standard error of measurement, the item characteristic curve, and the test information curve.

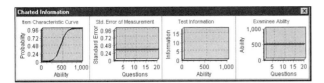

FIGURE 1
Microsoft's adaptive testing demonstration program.

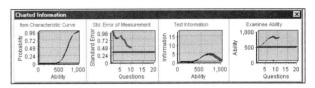

FIGURE 2
The changing statistics in an adaptive exam.

The standard error, which is the key factor in determining when an adaptive exam will terminate, reflects the degree of error in the exam ability estimate. The item characteristic curve reflects the probability of a correct response relative to examinee ability. Finally, the test information statistic provides a measure of the information contained in the set of questions the examinee has answered, again relative to the ability level of the individual examinee.

When you begin an adaptive exam, the standard error has already been assigned a target value below which it must drop for the exam to conclude. This target value reflects a particular level of statistical confidence in the process. The examinee ability is initially set to the mean possible exam score, which is 500 for MCP exams.

As the adaptive exam progresses, questions of varying difficulty are presented. Based on your pattern of responses to those questions, the ability estimate is recalculated. Simultaneously, the standard error estimate is refined from its first estimated value of one toward the target value. When the standard error reaches its target value, the exam terminates. Thus, the more consistently you answer questions of the same degree of difficulty, the more quickly the standard error estimate drops and the fewer questions you will end up seeing during the exam session. This situation is depicted in Figure 2.

As you might suspect, one good piece of advice for taking an adaptive exam is to treat every exam question as if it is the most important. The adaptive scoring algorithm is attempting to discover a pattern of responses

that reflects some level of proficiency with the subject matter. Incorrect responses almost guarantee that additional questions must be answered (unless, of course, you get every question wrong). This is because the scoring algorithm must adjust to information that is not consistent with the emerging pattern.

New Question Types

A variety of question types can appear on MCP exams. Examples of multiple-choice questions and scenario-based questions appear throughout this book and the Top Score software. Simulation-based questions are new to the MCP exam series.

Simulation Questions

Simulation-based questions reproduce the look and feel of key Microsoft product features for the purpose of testing. The simulation software used in MCP exams has been designed to look and act, as much as possible, just like the actual product. Consequently, answering simulation questions in an MCP exam entails completing one or more tasks just as if you were using the product itself.

The format of a typical Microsoft simulation question is straightforward. It presents a brief scenario or problem statement along with one or more tasks that must be completed to solve the problem. The next section provides an example of a simulation question for MCP exams.

A Typical Simulation Question

It sounds obvious, but the first step when you encounter a simulation is to carefully read the question (see Figure 3). Do not go straight to the simulation application! Assess the problem being presented and identify the conditions that make up the problem scenario. Note the tasks that must be performed or outcomes that must be achieved to answer the question, and then review any instructions on how to proceed.

The next step is to launch the simulator by using the button provided. After clicking the Show Simulation button, you will see a feature of the product, like the dialog box shown in Figure 4. The simulation application will partially cover the question text on many test center machines. Feel free to reposition the simulation or to move between the question text screen and the simulation using hot-keys and point-and-click navigation or even by clicking the simulation launch button again.

It is important to understand that your answer to the simulation question is not recorded until you move on to the next exam question. This gives you the added capability to close and reopen the simulation application (using the launch button) on the same question without losing any partial answer you may have made.

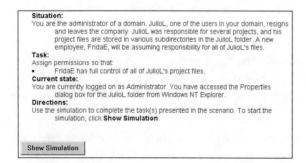

FIGURE 3
Typical MCP exam simulation question with directions.

FIGURE 4
Launching the simulation application.

The third step is to use the simulator as you would the actual product to solve the problem or perform the defined tasks. Again, the simulation software is designed to function, within reason, just as the product does. But don't expect the simulation to reproduce product behavior perfectly. Most importantly, do not allow yourself to become flustered if the simulation does not look or act exactly like the product. Figure 5 shows the solution to the sample simulation problem.

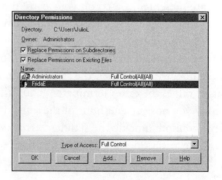

FIGURE 5
The solution to the simulation example.

There are two final points that will help you tackle simulation questions. First, respond only to what is being asked in the question. Do not solve problems that you are not asked to solve. Second, accept what is being asked of you. You may not entirely agree with conditions in the problem statement, the quality of the desired solution, or sufficiency of defined tasks to adequately solve the problem. Always remember that you are being tested on your ability to solve the problem as it has been presented.

The solution to the simulation problem shown in Figure 5 perfectly illustrates both of these points. As you'll recall from the question scenario (refer to Figure 3), you were asked to assign appropriate permissions to a new user called FridaE. You were not instructed to make any other changes in permissions. Thus, if you had modified or removed Administrator permissions, this item would have been scored wrong on an MCP exam.

Putting It All Together

Given all these different pieces of information, the task is now to assemble a set of tips that will help you successfully tackle the different types of MCP exams.

More Pre-Exam Preparation Tips

Generic exam preparation advice is always useful. Follow these general guidelines:

◆ Become familiar with the product. Hands-on experience is one of the keys to success on any MCP exam. Review the exercises and the Step by Step tutorials in the book.

◆ Review the current exam preparation guide on the Microsoft MCP Web site. The documentation Microsoft makes publicly available over the Web identifies the skills every exam is intended to test.

◆ Memorize foundational technical detail as appropriate. But remember, MCP exams are generally heavy on problem solving and application of knowledge more than they are on questions that require only rote memorization.

◆ Take any of the available practice tests. We recommend the one included in this book and those you can create using the Top Score software on the CD-ROM. While these are fixed-format exams, they provide preparation that is also valuable for taking an adaptive exam. Because of the nature of adaptive testing, it is not possible for these practice exams to be offered in the adaptive format. However, fixed-format exams provide the same types of questions as adaptive exams and are the most effective way to prepare for either type of exam. As a supplement to the material included with this book, try the free practice tests available on the Microsoft MCP Web site.

◆ Look on the Microsoft MCP Web site for samples and demonstration items. These tend to be particularly valuable for one significant reason: They allow you to become familiar with any new testing technologies before you encounter them on an MCP exam.

During the Exam Session

Similarly, the generic exam-taking advice you've heard for years applies when taking an MCP exam:

◆ Take a deep breath and try to relax when you first sit down for your exam. It is very important to control the pressure you may (naturally) feel when taking exams.

◆ You will be provided scratch paper. Take a moment to write down any factual information and technical detail that you committed to short-term memory.

◆ Carefully read all information and instruction screens. These displays have been put together to give you information relevant to the exam you are taking.

◆ Accept the Non-Disclosure Agreement and preliminary survey as part of the examination process. Complete them accurately and quickly move on.

◆ Read the exam questions carefully. Reread each question to identify all relevant detail.

◆ Tackle the questions in the order they are presented. Skipping around won't build your confidence; the clock is always counting down.

◆ Don't rush, but at the same time, don't linger on difficult questions. The questions vary in degree of difficulty. Don't let yourself be flustered by a particularly difficult or verbose question.

Fixed-Form Exams

Building from this basic preparation and test-taking advice, you also need to consider the challenges presented by the different exam designs. Because a fixed-form exam is composed of a fixed, finite set of questions, add these tips to your strategy for taking a fixed-form exam:

◆ Note the time allotted and the number of questions appearing on the exam you are taking. Make a rough calculation of how many minutes you can spend on each question, and use that number to pace yourself through the exam.

◆ Take advantage of the fact that you can return to and review skipped or previously answered questions. Mark the questions you can't answer confidently, noting the relative difficulty of each question on the scratch paper provided. When you reach the end of the exam, return to the more difficult questions.

◆ If there is session time remaining when you have completed all questions (and you aren't too fatigued!), review your answers. Pay particular attention to questions that seem to have a lot of detail or that required graphics.

◆ As for changing your answers, the rule of thumb here is *don't*! If you read the question carefully and completely and you felt like you knew the right answer, you probably did. Don't second-guess yourself. If, as you check your answers, one stands out as clearly incorrect, however, of course you should change it. But if you are at all unsure, go with your first impression.

Adaptive Exams

If you are planning to take an adaptive exam, keep these additional tips in mind:

◆ Read and answer every question with great care. When reading a question, identify every relevant detail, requirement, or task that must be performed and double-check your answer to be sure you have addressed every one of them.

◆ If you cannot answer a question, use the process of elimination to reduce the set of potential answers, and then take your best guess. Stupid mistakes invariably mean additional questions will be presented.

◆ Forget about reviewing questions and changing your answers. Once you leave a question, whether you've answered it or not, you cannot return to it. Do not skip any questions either. If you do, that question is counted as incorrect!

Simulation Questions

You may encounter simulation questions on either the fixed-form or adaptive form exam. If you do, keep these tips in mind:

◆ Avoid changing any simulation settings that don't pertain directly to the problem solution. Solve the problem you are being asked to solve and nothing more.

◆ Assume default settings when related information has not been provided. If something has not been mentioned or defined, it is a non-critical detail that does not factor in to the correct solution.

◆ Be sure your entries are syntactically correct, paying particular attention to your spelling. Enter relevant information just as the product would require it.

◆ Close all simulation application windows after you complete the simulation tasks. The testing system software is designed to trap errors that could result when using the simulation application, but trust yourself over the testing software.

◆ If simulations are part of a fixed-form exam, you can return to skipped or previously answered questions and change your answer. However, if you choose to change your answer to a simulation question, or if you even attempt to review the settings you've made in the simulation application, your previous response to that simulation question will be deleted. If simulations are part of an adaptive exam, you cannot return to previous questions.

FINAL CONSIDERATIONS

Finally, a number of changes in the MCP program will impact how frequently you can repeat an exam and what you will see when you do.

◆ Microsoft has instituted a new exam retake policy. This new rule is "two and two, then one and two." That is, you can attempt any exam twice with no restrictions on the time between attempts. But after the second attempt, you must wait two weeks before you can attempt that exam again. After that, you will be required to wait two weeks between subsequent attempts. Plan to pass the exam in two attempts; if that's not possible, increase your time horizon for receiving an MCP credential.

◆ New questions are being seeded into the MCP exams. After performance data has been gathered on new questions, they will replace older questions on all exam forms. This means that the questions appearing on exams will change regularly.

◆ Many of the current MCP exams will be republished in adaptive format in the coming months. Prepare yourself for this significant change in testing format, as it is entirely likely that this will become the new preferred MCP exam format.

These changes mean that the brute-force strategies for passing MCP exams may soon completely lose their viability. So if you don't pass an exam on the first or second attempt, it is entirely possible that the exam will change significantly in form. It could be updated from fixed-form to adaptive form, or it might have a different set of questions or question types.

The intention of Microsoft is clearly not to make the exams more difficult by introducing unwanted change. Their intent is to create and maintain valid measures of the technical skills and knowledge associated with the different MCP credentials. Preparing for an MCP exam has always involved not only studying the subject matter, but also planning for the testing experience itself. With these changes, this is now more true than ever.

Practice Exam

This appendix consists of 82 questions that are representative of what you should expect on the actual exam. You will find the answers at the end of the element. It is strongly suggested that when you take this practice exam, you treat it just as you would the actual exam at the test center: Time yourself, read carefully, and answer all the questions to the best of your ability.

EXAM QUESTIONS

1. You would like to configure five Windows 98 computers to participate in a small peer-to-peer environment. Of the following, which best describes the network environment you would like to create?

   A. Windows NT domain

   B. Windows 98 workgroup

   C. Windows 98 internetwork

   D. Windows 98 clients in a NetWare environment

2. You have installed Windows 98 on four computers and connected these four computers to an Ethernet hub. You cannot see any of the computers through network neighborhood. Of the following, which could you check in an effort to discover the problem? Choose all that apply.

   A. Incorrect protocol(s) and/or configuration

   B. Network card failure

   C. File and printer sharing service configuration

   D. Client for Microsoft Networks status

3. You are the consultant for the Alcoa Boat Company. Alcoa would like to configure its Windows 98 machines to log in to a Windows NT Server domain. The NT Server is using TCP/IP only. What network components are required for the Windows 98 computer to log in to the domain? Choose all that apply.

   A. Client for Microsoft Network

   B. TCP/IP

   C. TCP/IP with a dynamically assigned IP address

   D. File and Printer Sharing for Microsoft Networks

4. Of the following, which best describes Windows 98 acting as a DHCP client?

   A. The DHCP client receives a permanent IP address from a DHCP server.

   B. The DHCP client receives a temporary IP address from a DHCP server.

   C. The DHCP client must be configured to log in to the Windows NT domain to receive a permanent IP address.

   D. The DHCP client must be configured to log in to the Windows NT domain to receive a temporary IP address.

5. You are the MIS director for an insurance agency. Your network is configured as a Windows NT domain using TCP/IP only. Most of your users are using Windows 98 and are configured to log in to the domain. Several users are complaining that connecting to servers on the network takes

longer than it should. What Windows NT service could you implement throughout your network to increase speed when connecting to hosts on the network?

A. NetBIOS

B. WINS

C. GSNW

D. FPNW

6. You have been contracted to deal with security issues on a network. The client is running a Windows NT domain with all Windows 98 workstations configured to log in to the domain. The first security problem you encounter is that users are sharing passwords to access resources on the Windows 98 machines. Of the following, which are valid ways to eliminate the security breech on this network?

A. Move all shared resources to a Windows NT server.

B. Make users choose more difficult passwords.

C. Use only share-level security on the Windows 98 machines.

D. Use only user-level security on the Windows 98 machines.

7. Todd is using a Windows 98 machine that is configured to log in to both a NetWare server and a Windows NT domain. He would like to share out resources on the workgroup so he has added the File and Printer Sharing for Microsoft Networks. Whenever he tries to add the File and Printer Sharing for *NetWare* Networks, however, he is not allowed to add the service. What do you suspect is the problem?

A. Todd is not logged in to a NetWare server.

B. Todd is not a supervisor.

C. Todd is only allowed one instance of a File and Printer Sharing service.

D. Todd needs to restart the machine before he can add an additional File and Printer Sharing service.

8. What Microsoft client will allow a Windows 98 machine to log in to a NetWare server?

A. The Client for Microsoft Networks

B. The Microsoft Client for NetWare Networks

C. Client32 for NetWare

D. IPX/SPX

9. Ann Marie reports that although she can see and connect to other computers in Network Neighborhood, she cannot see her own computer. She would like to know why. Which of the following is the answer to Ann Marie's problem?

A. Ann Marie is looking at Network Neighborhood through her own computer. Her computer would not show up in Network Neighborhood.

B. Ann Marie has not installed a File and Printer Sharing service.

C. Ann Marie has not shared out any files or printers.

D. Ann Marie is not an administrator.

10. Robert complains that his profile changes are not being saved. He is using Windows 98 and his profile is following him from machine to machine. Of the following, which can be a valid answer to Robert's problem?

A. Robert has a mandatory profile.

B. Robert does not have a roaming profile.

C. Robert does not have write permissions to the Windows 98 .dat files.

D. Robert has to restart his machine to update the roaming profile to the server.

11. Nancy would like to create some way to disperse the company's phone list, employee manuals, and health insurance update information through her company's Windows 98 network. What would you recommend for Nancy?

    A. Use email delivery of the information.

    B. Create an intranet with Windows 98's Internet Information Server.

    C. Create an intranet with Windows 98's Personal Web Server.

    D. Create a public folder and share it out with all of the necessary documents.

12. Jane is about to install Windows 98 on her Windows 95 computer. She is concerned about losing her profile settings during the upgrade. Is this a valid concern?

    A. No. Profile settings are saved to the `95.dat` file and can be upgraded into Windows 98 without any difficulty.

    B. No. Profile settings are carried over to Windows 98 during the upgrade.

    C. Yes. Profiles settings cannot be converted to Windows 98 because of the major restructuring to the Windows 98 Registry.

    D. Yes. Profiles settings cannot be converted to Windows 98 unless the user requests that profiles be backed up and then restored as part of the Windows 98 setup program.

13. How does Windows 98 detect hardware during the installation? Choose all that apply.

    A. Plug and Play.

    B. Through test POSTs (Power On Self Tests).

    C. Manual query of `config.sys`, `autoexec.bat`, and areas of memory to detect legacy hardware.

    D. Hardware is not detected during the installation, but rather after the installation is complete.

14. Harold is trying to install Windows 98 on his home computer. He has 16MB of RAM, a 386DX/20, 300MB of free space, and CD-ROM and floppy drives. He is having trouble installing Windows 98. What do you suspect is the problem?

    A. Harold does not have enough RAM.

    B. Harold does not have a powerful enough processor.

    C. Harold does not have enough free space.

    D. Harold does not have at least a 4-speed CD-ROM drive.

15. Donald is installing Windows 98 for the first time. He is confused as to whether he should keep a backup copy of his old system files. Of the following, which is a valid reason to keep the older operating systems files?

    A. In case Donald would like to remove Windows 98 and return to Windows 95

    B. In case Donald would like to dual-boot between Windows 98 and Windows 95

    C. In case Donald will later require his groups from Windows 95

    D. In case Donald would like to upgrade to Windows NT

16. You are the consultant for a printing company. The help desk supports users on Windows 98 and on Windows NT Workstation. The help desk

personnel would like to configure their Windows 98 machines to boot to both Windows 98 and to Windows NT Workstation. Can this be done?

A. No. Windows 98 and Windows NT cannot exist on the machine.

B. No. Windows 98 and Windows NT cannot exist on the same machine due to file system conflicts.

C. Yes. Windows NT and Windows 98 can exist on the same machine as long as the Windows 98 installation is done before that of Windows NT. Each OS should be contained within its own partition due to file system conflicts.

D. Yes. Windows NT and Windows 98 can exist on the same machine as long as the Windows 98 installation is done before that of Windows NT. Each OS's system files should be contained within its own folder due to file system conflicts.

17. You have just added a new drive to your Windows 98 computer, which is configured to dual-boot with Windows NT Workstation 4.0. You use FDISK to format the 4GB drive as a single partition. When you open NT's Disk Administrator, however, the drive is unrecognized. What do you suspect is the problem?

A. Windows NT is limited to FAT drives no larger than 2GB.

B. Windows NT is limited to FAT drives on the master disk only.

C. Windows NT cannot see FAT32 without Service Pack 4.

D. Windows NT must be restarted for the new drive to show up in Disk Administrator.

18. You are about to install Windows 98 on a freshly formatted drive but you cannot access your CD-ROM drive. What do you suspect is the problem?

A. You do not have the CD-ROM drivers loaded.

B. Your CD-ROM drive is not compatible with Windows 98.

C. You have not marked the primary partition as active.

D. You have to restart the computer with your Windows 98 CD in the CD-ROM drive.

19. A worried user reports that as she is installing Windows 98, the machine appears to be hung and has stopped responding. What action should the user take to continue with the installation?

A. Do nothing. Windows 98 will continue after a timeout value of 20 minutes.

B. As a first step, restart the computer and allow the setup to continue.

C. Restart the computer, press F8 at the Now Starting Windows 98 message, and choose Safe mode.

D. Restart the computer and then restart the installation process.

20. You have just installed Windows 98 on your PC. Windows 98 detected all of your hardware except for a second network driver in the machine. Upon further investigation you learn that the network card is not Plug and Play compatible. What can you do to configure the card and add it to the computer?

A. Windows 98 cannot use cards that are not Plug and Play compatible.

B. Use the Add Legacy Hardware Wizard in Control Panel.

C. You will have to manually add the card by using a setup program for the network card to assign or confirm resources and then you will have to add the card through the Network applet with a compatible driver.

D. The network card needs to be converted to Plug and Play by the manufacturer.

21. Mary has just added a new modem to her Windows 98 machine. The modem's package described the modem as Plug and Play compliant and Windows 98 compliant, yet when Mary added the hardware, Windows 98 did not detect the hardware. What do you suspect is the problem?

A. The modem is not Plug and Play compliant, but legacy hardware.

B. The modem is Plug and Play, but Mary's computer does not have a Plug and Play BIOS.

C. The modem is Plug and Play compliant, but Mary's computer does not a have a driver for this modem.

D. The modem will not be detected until Mary opens the Add New Modems Wizard.

22. Don and Frank are about to add an older legacy sound card to their Windows 98 machine. Don thinks that the card will not work with Windows 98 because this sound card is not Plug and Play compliant. Frank believes that the card will work with Windows 98, albeit not through Plug and Play, but it can still be added and configured to work with Windows 98. Who is correct and why?

A. Don is correct. Only Plug and Play devices can be added to Windows 98.

B. Frank is correct. The bus enumerator in Windows 98 will detect the hardware and list it as unknown hardware. This is Windows 98's pseudo-detection mode.

C. Don is correct. Sound cards, joysticks, and MIDI devices cannot be added to Windows 98 unless they are Plug and Play compliant.

D. Frank is correct. Legacy hardware can be added to Windows 98 through the Add Remove Hardware Wizard in Control Panel.

23. Robert has just added a network card to his Windows 98 computer. The card is not Plug and Play compatible. The card has to use IRQ 11, which is currently being used by another device in the system. Where can Robert find which device is using IRQ 11 and change that IRQ if necessary?

A. Device Manager

B. Windows 98 Diagnostics

C. System Information Monitor

D. Help, search for Hardware

24. Heidi has been exploring the Device Manager and has discovered that her joystick has a yellow exclamation point through the device. What does this mean?

A. Her joystick is not Plug and Play enabled.

B. Her joystick is conflicting with another device.

C. Her joystick is broken; Windows 98 has detected this and marked the device for removal after next boot.

D. Her joystick is not Windows 98 compliant and has been marked for removal.

25. You are the consultant for a small manufacturing firm. The manager there would like to have a hard copy report of all devices throughout each Windows 98 computer. What would be a fast way to provide this information to your client?

    A. Search the Registry and export each key where the device is listed.

    B. Use Windows 98 Diagnostics to create the report and print it out.

    C. Use the Device Manager to create and print such a report.

    D. There is no quick and easy way to do this within Windows 98.

26. Mark is adding several USB devices to his Windows 98 machine. He can't seem to connect two of the devices to the machine no matter where he puts the devices in the daisy-chain order. His first device is serving as a bus-powered hub. What do you suspect is the problem? Choose all that apply.

    A. You cannot connect a bus-powered hub to another bus-powered hub. His second device is probably a second bus-powered hub.

    B. A bus-powered hub cannot support more than four downstream ports. He may have more than four devices downstream from this bus-powered hub.

    C. His USB devices are conflicting with IRQs in the system.

    D. His USB devices won't be detected until he restarts the system.

27. You are the Windows 98 support person for an accounting company. Henry, your employer, would like to work with multilink but does not have a good grasp on the concept. Which of the following best describes multilink?

A. Multilink is the ability to combine two modems of identical make and model for faster dial-up connections.

B. Multilink is the ability to combine numerous modems of varying makes, models, and even speeds for fast dial-up connections.

C. Multilink is the ability to share out a modem across a network. Only NetBEUI and IPX/SPX can be used, however.

D. Multilink is the ability to share out a modem across a network. Only TCP/IP can be used, however.

28. Marcy Jane complains that her PC is always "asleep" whenever she returns from lunch. She wants you to remove this feature from her Windows 98 machine. How can this be done for her?

    A. Create a hardware profile that has this feature disabled.

    B. Disable the Power Management scheme through the System Applet in Control Panel.

    C. Disable the Power Management scheme in the Display applet in Control Panel.

    D. Use the Always On scheme in the Power Management applet through Control Panel.

29. Rebecca has just added a Plug and Play printer to her Windows 98 machine. She is certain that all the hardware and her printer and computer are Plug and Play compliant, but Windows 98 does not connect to the printer to install the print device. What do you suspect is the problem?

    A. The printer has to be set up for Plug and Play compliance through some interface or card at the printer.

B. Rebecca needs to restart her Windows 98 computer while holding down the Shift key for printer Plug and Play detection to occur.

C. Rebecca probably does not have the correct parallel cable. She needs an IEEE 1284-compliant cable to detect her printer.

D. Windows 98 does not offer Plug and Play compatibility on printers.

30. You typically print large manuals to your company's shared printer. Other users on the network complain that they have to wait for your job to print before theirs will—even though your manuals sometimes take several minutes between some pages due to graphics on the pages. What can you do to be more considerate of your peers' printing? Choose the best answer.

A. Use the Spooling option to not print until the last page is spooled.

B. Use the Spooling option to not print complex graphics and then print those pages out last.

C. Do not print these large jobs until the end of the day.

D. Schedule these jobs to print at nighttime.

31. You have just created a Windows 98 peer-to-peer network and would like to start sharing out resources on this network but are concerned about security. What choice do you have with access to resources on a Windows 98 network?

A. Share-level security only. Users access resources based on their passwords to those resources.

B. User-level security only. Users access resources based on their logon identification.

C. Share-level or user-level. You can mix and match your security model as you see fit.

D. There is no available security to resources on a Windows 98 network. All users have full control to any shares on a Windows 98 LAN.

32. You would like to enable user-level security for a few Windows 98 machines that are sharing out resources. How can this be done with Windows 98?

A. You must create a `users.pwl` file and point the Windows 98 machine to this `.pwl` file through the Passwords applet.

B. You must have a Windows NT server, an NT workstation, or a Novell NetWare server. You then can enable user-level security through the Network applet.

C. You must be logged in as an NT Administrator or a NetWare Supervisor and then enable this through the Security applet in Control Panel.

D. Windows 95 will automatically enable your machine to use user-level security when you log in to a Windows NT domain; NetWare user-level security must be enabled through the Security applet in Control Panel.

33. You are a consultant for a small accounting firm. The firm would like to share out resources on its Windows 98 workgroup. The firm is worried, however, about using share-level security. Of the following, which are valid concerns with share-level security?

A. Whoever learns of the password has access to the resources.

B. Passwords can be no longer than five characters.

C. Password management can become tedious because users will have to remember the passwords that allow them access to each resource.

D. Passwords are stored in the `.pwl` file, which can be opened with Notepad, so all passwords can be discovered.

34. Lee and Sheri are creating a Windows 98 workgroup. They are trying to decide what level of security they can use. Lee thinks that all they can use is share-level security because they do not have a domain or a NetWare server to authenticate logon requests. Sheri thinks they can use user-level security because they do have an NT workstation in their workgroup. Who is right and why?

    A. Lee is correct. User-level security requires a Windows NT domain or a NetWare server.

    B. Sheri is correct. User-level security can be accomplished with the File and Printer Sharing for Microsoft Networks—if all `.pwl` files are stored on a shared directory on an NTFS file system.

    C. Lee is correct. Windows 98 can read NTFS partitions, which all NT workstations use, so it is not possible to use an NT workstation as a security provider.

    D. Sheri is correct. Windows 98 can be configured, through the Network applet, to use a Windows NT workstation as a security provider.

35. You have created several shares on a Windows 98 machine that is using user-level security. A share called Sales has been set up so that the Sales group has change permissions and the Managers group has read permissions. You learn that Alice, a member of the Managers group, has change permission to the folder. Why? Choose the best answer.

    A. You have set up permissions incorrectly.

    B. She is also a member of the Sales group.

C. You originally had the share set with The World equals Full Control permission. She needs to log out and back on to the LAN.

D. She has learned the password to the share.

36. You are the network administrator for a Windows 98 LAN. Ralph reports that he is trying to use the DriveSpace 3 tool to compress his D: drive, but is unable to. What do you suspect is the problem?

    A. Ralph is not logged on as an administrator.

    B. Ralph's D: drive has not been formatted. Only formatted drives can be compressed.

    C. Ralph is using a FAT16 drive. Only FAT32 drives can be compressed.

    D. Ralph is using a FAT32 drive. Only FAT16 drives can be compressed.

37. You are the consultant for a manufacturing company. Its executives have asked you to configure their hard disk into two partitions. One partition will house the Windows 98 operating system and applications; the second partition is to be used for data only. How can you create these two partitions within Windows 98?

    A. Use Disk Administrator and create two primary partitions.

    B. Use FDISK to create two primary partitions.

    C. Use Disk Administrator to create a primary partition as well as an extended partition with one logical partition inside it.

    D. Use FDISK to create one primary partition as well as an extended with one logical drive inside it.

38. What is the difference between a primary partition and a logical drive in regard to Windows 98?

A. A primary partition must be at least 2GB and has to be formatted with FAT32.

B. A primary partition can be marked as active, while a logical drive refers to a partition within an extended partition.

C. A primary partition is the active partition on the drive; a logical drive is also called a CVF, or compressed volume file.

D. A primary partition is the active drive, whereas the logical drive can be marked as active if you are dual booting between Windows 98 and Windows NT Server.

39. You receive a call from a troubled user. He explains that while trying to create a partition on his new hard disk within Windows 98's FDISK he received the message to enable large disk support. Why is this important?

A. The user is using a drive larger than 512MB. This message enables the FAT32 file system to see drives larger than 512 when it formats the drive.

B. The user is using a SCSI drive. All SCSI drives must use the large disk support feature to enable sector translation.

C. The user has disabled all 32-bit disk controller drivers. By enabling large disk support the user will re-enable all 32-bit disk controller drivers.

D. The user is using a controller card that is not WD-1003 compatible.

40. Sharon reports that she is having some trouble with all the data on her partition. The partition, you learn, has been formatted with FAT and was recently scanned by a disk utility program designed for Windows 3.11. Why do you think Sharon is having problems on her FAT drive?

A. Windows 98 does not support FAT partitions. Sharon should convert the drive to FAT32 with drive converter tool.

B. Windows 98 supports FAT; however, the Windows 3.11 utility probably destroyed her long filenames on that drive because the program is not long filename aware.

C. Windows 98 occasionally loses data on FAT partition. Sharon should recover from backup.

D. Sharon needs to restart her machine and then run the Windows 3.11 utility on the drive to restore the long filenames from the checkfiles in the temp directory.

41. Tom and Nancy are sharing a Windows 98 computer that is not on a network. Tom does not like that Nancy changes the desktop color each time she uses the computer. What can be done to make them both happy?

A. Enable user profiles through the Passwords applet.

B. Enable user profiles through the Security applet.

C. Enable user profiles through the Network applet, client for Microsoft Networks.

D. User profiles cannot be enabled on a computer that is not networked.

42. Where are roaming user profiles for Windows 98 users stored on a Windows NT server?

A. In the `%Systemroot%\Profiles` directory

B. In the `Netlogon` share

C. In each user's home folder

D. In the `Winnt\System32\repl\import\scripts` directory

43. You are configuring a Windows 98 machine to use roaming user profiles. What command must you add to the Windows NT logon scripts to ensure that profiles will be updated when a user logs off of a Windows 98 machine?

    A. `Net time \\timeserver /set /yes`

    B. `Net time = \\timeserver /set /yes / autoconfig`

    C. `Net time = \\timeserver /GMT`

    D. Use load balancing

44. You have been hired by the Holtz Manufacturing company to manage its Windows 98 network. You immediately notice that users are editing the Registry, not logging in to the network, changing the display settings, and doing other trouble-causing antics. What can you do to immediately halt this inappropriate activity?

    A. Implement logon scripts that restrict users from engaging in these activities.

    B. Implement profiles that restrict users from engaging in these activities.

    C. Implement system policies that restrict users from engaging in these activities.

    D. Implement mandatory profiles.

45. You have created a computer policy that includes a logon banner to warn users about unofficial usage of this computer. The computer policy, however, does not seem to work when you just logged on to the computer. What do you suspect is the problem?

    A. The first time you log on to the computer specified in the computer policy, the Registry settings are downloaded into the computer. The actual restrictions will appear the next time you log on to the machine.

    B. The first time you log on to the computer specified in the computer policy, the Registry settings are downloaded into the computer. The actual restrictions will appear the next time you restart the machine.

    C. You are not using the correct protocol for the computer.

    D. Logon messages do not work with Windows 98 computers

46. Where are users' profiles stored on a NetWare 3.x server?

    A. In each user's home folder.

    B. In each user's mail ID folder.

    C. In the `Sys\public` directory.

    D. You cannot use roaming profiles with NetWare servers.

47. You would like to create a profile for all of the Sales users that prevents them from changing their profiles. How can this be done with Windows 98?

    A. Change the `user.dat` to `user.perm`.

    B. Change the `user.dat` to `user.man`.

    C. You must create a system policy to include all of the restrictions on the user to prevent them from changing the profile.

    D. You must create a system policy and include the restriction to not save changes on exit.

48. You have just created system policies for your users on Windows 98 that are configured to log in to your Windows NT domain. None of your policies seems to be working. What do you suspect is the problem?

    A. You have not saved the system policy to each user's home folder.

B. You have not saved the system policy to your `%systemroot%\system32\repl\` folder.

C. You have not saved the system policy to your `%systemroot%\system32\repl\import\scripts` folder.

D. You have not named your policy `config.pol`.

49. You have created a system policy for all users in the Sales group. You have successfully saved the policy to the correct location on your Windows NT server. However, whenever a sales rep logs on to a Windows NT workstation, the policy file is ignored. What is the problem?

A. You have not selected the option to use load balancing.

B. The Windows 98 policy is not enforced on Windows NT workstations.

C. Windows NT workstations do not use system policies.

D. Windows NT workstations require that policies used for both Windows 98 and NT be stored in `%systemroot%` on each NT Server.

50. Mark and Janet would like to create system policies on their Windows 98 computer, which is not connected to a network. They have saved the policy to their Windows directory, but the policy is still not being enforced. What do you suspect is the problem?

A. You cannot use policies on a standalone computer.

B. Policies have to be saved in a folder called `Netlogon`.

C. Within Policy Editor, Mark and Jane need to point the Network, Update path to manual (rather than remote) and enter the local path of `C:\windows\config.pol` where their policy file resides.

D. Mark and Jane need to restart the computer before the policy will be enforced.

51. What log file does Setup use in the event of a failed installation to determine where the setup terminated?

A. `Setup.log`

B. `Setuplog.log`

C. `Setuplog.txt`

D. `Setup.txt`

52. What log file does Setup inspect when the setup crashes during the detection of hardware?

A. `Setuplog.txt`

B. `Detcrash.log`

C. `Detcrashlog.txt`

D. `98detect.log`

53. Roxanne is installing Windows 98 on her PC. Setup seems to have frozen up during the hardware detection phase. What should Roxanne do?

A. Continue to wait; Windows 98 will create a workaround for the problem.

B. Restart the setup process.

C. Power off the machine for approximately 15 seconds and then restart the computer.

D. Restart the computer and run ScanDisk.

54. You are troubleshooting a hardware failure on a Windows 98 computer. You suspect that two devices have been assigned to the same IRQ through jumper settings on the cards. What tool will enable you to confirm your suspicions?

A. Version Conflict Manager

B. Systems Information Utility

C. Setup

D. Windows 98 Diagnostics

55. You are troubleshooting a Windows 98 machine that crashes each time you start up the system. You'd like to boot into Safe mode for additional troubleshooting. How do you do this?

   A. Hold down the Shift key when you start Windows 98.

   B. Press F8 when the message `Starting Windows 98` appears and then choose Safe mode or press F5.

   C. Press F1 when the message `Starting Windows 98` appears and then choose Safe mode.

   D. You cannot enter into Safe mode manually. The system will prompt you for Safe mode if the Registry is corrupt.

56. When you installed Windows 98, you created an Emergency Startup Disk for troubleshooting. You have, however, misplaced this startup disk and would like to create another one. How can you do this within Windows 98?

   A. Run setup /ox.

   B. Create a startup disk through the Add/Remove Programs applet.

   C. Create a startup disk through the Systems applet.

   D. Run Setup and choose Create a Startup Disk Only.

57. Marcy is having trouble booting up her Windows 98 machine. She suspects that the problem lies in her `config.sys` file. How can she quickly and easily edit the file within Windows 98? Choose the best answer.

   A. REM out any suspect statements in her `config.sys` file.

B. Choose the step-by-step confirmation during the boot-up phase.

C. Hold down the Shift key as Windows 98 boots and she'll be prompted for each entry in her `config.sys` file.

D. Use the System Configuration utility to edit her `config.sys` file.

58. Todd and Sharon are troubleshooting a Windows 98 computer that is having trouble connecting to a remote TCP/IP host. The two users would like to somehow test the connection from their machine to the remote host. They want to ensure that they can connect to the remote machine or see if the remote machine is even responding. What tool will allow them to do this?

   A. Ping

   B. Ipconfig

   C. Ipconfig /all

   D. WinIPCfg

59. Zack has configured his Windows 98 machine to use DHCP to obtain an IP address. What tools within Windows 98 will allow Zack to view his IP address?

   A. Ipconfig

   B. Ipconfig /all

   C. WinIPCfg

   D. Net Watcher

60. You are the consultant for an advertising agency. Several users would like to create shares on their Windows 98 machines. How can you do this from your machine on the fifth floor to their machines on the seventeenth floor?

   A. Use Server Manager

   B. Use Regedit

C. Use Net Watcher

D. Use Explorer

61. A user complains that all of her data from her D: drive seems to be missing. You learned that she was trying to convert the drive to FAT32, but is uncertain if she did it properly. What do you suspect is the problem?

   A. She formatted her drive.

   B. She used FAT32 Drive Converter without running ScanDisk first.

   C. She used the FAT32 Drive Converter with the Format Drive option.

   D. She has not yet restarted her machine after running the FAT32 converter.

62. Bob is having trouble saving files to his hard disk. He notices that there are many temporary files and even some install files on his hard disk that probably shouldn't be there. Bob is hesitant to delete the files because he doesn't know which ones may be needed for later usage by the system. What tool should Bob use to clean up his disk in this instance?

   A. ScanDisk

   B. ScanDisk with /t option to delete temp files

   C. Disk Cleanup

   D. FAT32 Converter to wipe out unneeded files

63. Marcy is trying to compress her D: drive but is unsuccessful. She has compressed her C: drive. What do you suspect is the problem?

   A. Her C: and D: drives are both on the same disk. Marcy can only have one compressed partition per disk.

   B. Only administrators can compress partitions. Marcy is not logged on as an administrator when she is trying to compress her D: drive.

   C. Marcy is trying to compress a FAT32 partition. Her C: drive is FAT.

   D. Only one drive at a time can be compressed. Marcy has not rebooted after compressing the C: drive.

64. You are the consultant for a large printing company. All of the sales staff is using Windows 98. Robert, the sales manager, has read an article on the Internet about enhancements to Windows 98 that are provided by Microsoft. He would like you to install these enhancements on all of the sales staff's Windows 98 computers. How would you go about this task?

   A. Use the Windows Update tool to update the operating system.

   B. Use the Add/Remove Programs and then choose Browse to get to the Internet.

   C. Reinstall Windows 98 with the newer release of the enhancements.

   D. Use the System applet to update the operating system.

65. You are helping a friend set up his Windows 98 machine. He understands the importance of running system maintenance tools on a regular schedule, but he doesn't want to have to be in front of the PC to launch the tools. How can you help your friend? Choose the best answer.

   A. Use the AT Scheduler to launch the tools automatically.

   B. Use the System Scheduler to schedule the tasks to run automatically.

C. Create a batch file to start the tools whenever he logs in to the machine.

D. Windows 98 does not provide this functionality.

66. Gloria suspects that something is wrong with her Windows 98 Registry. She asks you to check out her Registry files for her. How can this be done within Windows 98?

A. Use the System File Checker.

B. Check out the properties of the `*.dat` files.

C. Boot into Safe mode with Last Known Good configuration.

D. Use the Registry Checker.

67. You are the consultant for a hospital. The hospital staff would like to use FAT32 on their drives, but have heard that not all operating systems can read FAT32. Their main concern is that when they share out resources from the Windows 98 computers that other operating systems will not be able to connect to folders shared off of a FAT32 drive. Is this a valid concern?

A. Yes. Only operating systems that can read FAT32 will be able to connect to the shares.

B. Yes. Only operating systems that have the FAT32 remote agent installed can connect to the shares.

C. No. All operating systems receive the FAT32 remote agent when they attempt to connect to the share off of a FAT32 drive.

D. No. The rules of FAT32 apply only to the local drive. Remote operating systems can connect to the shares off of a FAT32 partition.

68. What Windows 98 file controls the boot-up sequence and variables?

A. `win.ini`

B. `msdos.sys`

C. `boot.ini`

D. `config.sys`

69. A user reports that whenever he turns on his computer, ScanDisk runs automatically. He would like to know why this is occurring. Choose the best answer.

A. He has a bad hard disk.

B. His machine has been spiked by an electrical surge.

C. He is powering off his machine incorrectly.

D. He has his machine set for the wrong voltage.

70. You have created a partition under Windows 98 and formatted this partition with FAT32. When you boot the machine into Windows NT Workstation 4.0, you cannot see the FAT32 partition. Why?

A. You need to open Disk Administrator in NT Workstation to recognize the FAT32 partitions.

B. You need to restart NT Workstation.

C. NT Workstation cannot recognize FAT32 partitions.

D. You have created the FAT32 partition in an extended drive. NT cannot see partitions in extended drives that were not created through either Disk Administrator or the Windows NT Setup program.

71. You are a consultant for a credit bureau. You would like to check the amount of RAM on each Windows 98 machine as well as the processor type. Which Windows 98 tool will allow you to quickly gather this information?

    A. REGEDIT

    B. Microsoft Systems Configuration Utility

    C. SMS

    D. 98 Diagnostics

72. Users are complaining that they are having trouble connecting to a Windows NT server. All users are using DHCP to receive an IP address and you have confirmed that the NT server does have a valid, working IP address. What Windows 98 tool should you use to retrieve the IP information for the Windows 98 clients?

    A. WinIPFG

    B. WinIpconfig /all

    C. IPCFG

    D. WinIPCfg

73. You are the administrator for a Windows 98 workgroup. A user reports that some users are able to alter resources that they should only have read access to. She thinks she has incorrectly set the permissions on the share resource. What Windows 98 tool can you use to remotely view her share permissions?

    A. Net Watcher

    B. Systems Configuration Utility

    C. Explorer

    D. Remote Registry Editing

74. A user is trying to connect to a server in Phoenix, but cannot. You are using TCP/IP on all of your Windows NT servers and on your Windows 98 clients. What tool should you use to test the connectivity of the remote IP address?

    A. Ping the loopback address.

    B. Ping the local machine.

    C. Ping the router.

    D. Ping the remote host.

75. Users are complaining that it is taking an unusually long time to connect to a server in Baltimore from their Windows 98 machines. You suspect that the delay is caused by the route the packets are taking to the remote server. What TCP/IP tool can you use to confirm your suspicions?

    A. A firewall

    B. MS Proxy Server

    C. Tracert

    D. Trace route

76. What tools on Windows 98 can reveal the IRQ settings for all devices on your computer?

    A. Microsoft Systems Information Utility

    B. Device Manager

    C. Ports applet

    D. Setup

77. You would like to configure Windows 98 to use DHCP for IP address assignment. Where is the value set within Windows 98?

    A. Control Panel, System

    B. Control Panel, Network

    C. Registry Editor

    D. Policy Editor

78. You have manually assigned an IP address to your Windows 98 machine, but you cannot connect to the network. You suspect that you have an incorrect IP address, so you change the computer to use DHCP. Where can you now retrieve your IP settings? Choose the best answer.

    A. At the DHCP server

    B. Through the Registry

    C. By pinging your machine name from another machine on the network

    D. Through WinIPCfg

79. You are attempting to connect to a remote Windows 98 machine to share out a folder for a user in your Windows NT domain. You are a domain administrator, but you still cannot access her remote machine to create the share. You can ping her machine and see it in Network Neighborhood. What do you suspect is the problem?

    A. The remote machine is using share-level security.

    B. The remote machine is using user-level security.

    C. The remote machine does not have remote administration enabled.

    D. The remote machine does not have remote Registry editing enabled.

80. What is the difference between ScanReg and ScanRegW?

    A. ScanReg is launched from the DOS prompt; ScanRegW is launched from within Windows 98.

    B. ScanReg is launched automatically each time you start Windows 98; ScanRegW is launched only when you enter Safe mode.

C. ScanReg is used to verify the validity of the operating system; ScanRegW uses the wipe command to wipe out older entries.

D. There is no difference between the two.

81. You are a consultant for an advertising agency. Users at this agency would like to somehow connect to their desktops to access clients' work while at home. How can this be configured through Windows 98?

    A. Use the RAS client and the RAS server service within Windows 98.

    B. Use the RAS server service within Windows 98 and the remote dial-up networking client.

    C. Configure the Windows 98 machine to accept phone calls and then configure the remote Windows 98 machine to dial into the dial-up server through Dial-Up Networking.

    D. Windows 98 does not allow remote clients to dial in.

82. Of the following, which best describes a proxy server?

    A. A server that automatically assigns an IP address to a host for Web browsing.

    B. A server that acts as a go-between for the client and the Internet.

    C. A server that resolves fully qualified domain names to an IP address for Internet browsing.

    D. A server that resolves NetBIOS names to an IP address for Internet browsing.

ANSWERS AND EXPLANATIONS

1. **B.** With a small LAN of only five computers working in a peer-to-peer environment, a workgroup is the best solution.

2. **A, B, C, D.** Incorrect protocols and the configuration thereof can prevent you from participating on the network. A network card failure would prevent network access. The lack of a file and printer sharing service on the computers will prevent any network activity; the lack of a client will prevent network activity.

3. **A, B.** The Client for Microsoft Networks must be installed and configured to log in to the Windows NT domain. An IP address is also required in this situation—the IP address does not have to be from a DHCP server.

4. **B.** The DHCP client receives a temporary IP address from a DHCP server.

5. **B.** A WINS server can be added to a Windows NT server. WINS can be used to resolve NetBIOS names to IP addresses for connectivity. By adding a centralized source for NetBIOS to IP address information, you reduce traffic and increase speed on the network.

6. **A, D.** By moving all shares to a server, users will not be using passwords to connect to shares. By using user-level security, users are assigned access not by passwords but by their identification in the domain or NetWare environment.

7. **C.** Todd is only allowed one instance of a file and printer sharing service. This is because Windows 98 acts as a server only for Microsoft networks or for NetWare networks.

8. **B.** The Microsoft Client for NetWare Networks allows you to configure a Windows 98 machine to log in to a NetWare server.

9. **B.** Ann Marie has not installed a File and Printer Sharing service. Without File and Printer Sharing turned on, there is no reason why Ann Marie's computer should show up in Network Neighborhood.

10. **A.** Robert has a mandatory profile that does not save the changes made to his profile whenever he logs off.

11. **C.** Nancy should create an intranet with Windows 98's Personal Web Server. Through the Personal Web Server, Nancy could create an intranet that would allow her to publish her documentation without having to reprint her manuals, phone books, and other information each time there is a change to the documents. This would also save on the expense of printing the information.

12. **B.** Because profile settings are part of Windows 95's Registry, they will be carried over and preserved to Windows 98.

13. **A, C.** Windows 98 uses Plug and Play as well as manual query of `config.sys`, `autoexec.bat`, and areas of memory to detect legacy hardware.

14. **B.** Harold needs at least a 486 to install Windows 98.

15. **A.** Donald should keep the older operating systems files in case he would like to remove Windows 98 and return to Windows 95.

16. **D.** Yes. You can install Windows 98 and Windows NT Workstation on the same disk. It's recommended that Windows 98 is installed before Windows NT. In addition, each operating system's system files must be kept in different folders.

17. **C.** Windows NT cannot see FAT32 partitions without NT Service Pack 4.

18. **A.** Don't forget to load your CD-ROM device drives from DOS, and any tools such as MSCDEX.exe, to access your CD-ROM drive.

19. **B.** Restart the computer and allow Windows 98 to work around the problem.

20. **C.** Add the legacy card through the Network applet with the updated driver from the manufacturer.

21. **B.** Mary's computer must have a Plug and Play BIOS for the system to detect the Plug and Play device.

22. **D.** Windows 98 allows legacy hardware to be added to Windows 98 through the Add New Hardware Wizard in the Control Panel.

23. **A.** Device Manager allows you to interact with all the system resources your devices may be using and to configure the usage of the system resources as you see fit.

24. **B.** Heidi's joystick is conflicting with another device and Device Manager has added that alert so Heidi can attempt to resolve the problem.

25. **C.** Device Manager allows you to print out all the information about your installed hardware.

26. **A, B.** The rules of USB prevent you from adding two bus-powered hubs directly into one another. It's also possible that Mark has more than four downstream ports.

27. **B.** Multilink allows you to connect many dissimilar modems to your Windows 98 machine for faster connectivity.

28. **D.** Marcy Jane's computer has been configured to use a power management scheme. Simply use the power management scheme of Always On to alleviate this problem.

29. **C.** If the printer and her computer are Plug and Play compliant, then the problem must be between the two. She needs a bidirectional printer cable, which will be clearly marked on the cable as IEEE 1284 compliant.

30. **A.** By not printing until the last page is spooled, your entire document will be in the language your printer expects when it is ready to print.

Others can use the printer while your job is still rasterizing. Waiting to print the jobs at the end of the day would work, but this solution is not the best choice for this question.

31. **A.** When using a Windows 98-only network, you can use only share-level security.

32. **B.** To use user-level security, you must have a security provider. A valid security provider may be a Windows NT domain, a NetWare server, a Windows NT server, or even a Windows NT workstation.

33. **A, C.** Passwords allow access to all resources. As users learn the passwords to resources, they have that level of access to the resource—whether you want them to or not. The more resources you offer on the network, the more passwords users must remember.

34. **D.** Sheri is correct. A Windows NT workstation can be identified through the Network applet as a security provider.

35. **B.** Alice is also a member of the Sales group, so she will have change permission.

36. **D.** FAT32 drives cannot be compressed.

37. **D.** Use FDISK to create the primary partition, and then create the extended partition that will house the logical drive.

38. **B.** A primary partition can be marked as active; a logical drive is simply a partition within an extended partition.

39. **A.** Large disk support enables FAT32 drives to go beyond the 512MB limit.

40. **B.** The Windows 3.11 utility probably destroyed the data on that drive because the program is not long filename aware.

41. **A.** Profiles are enabled through the Passwords applet.

42. **C.** Roaming profiles are stored in each user's home folder.

43. **A.** `net time \\timeserver /set /yes` will set the local computer time to be in sync with the time-server so that profiles are updated and time stamped properly.

44. **C.** System policies will police the activities users are allowed to engage in.

45. **A.** Computer policies are first downloaded to the local machine and then enforced.

46. **B.** Profiles on a NetWare server are stored in each user's mail ID folder.

47. **B.** Change the `user.dat` to `user.man` to make the profile mandatory.

48. **C.** Policies on a network must be saved to the `Netlogon` share on a Windows NT server. The path is `%systemroot%\system32\repl\import\ scripts.`

49. **B.** Policies created for Windows 98 do not work with Windows NT due to the differences in the Registries.

50. **C.** They need to edit their Registries through Policy Editor and point their computers to the locally stored `config.pol`.

51. **C.** `Setuplog.txt` is used by Setup to determine what caused the machine to stop responding during the setup.

52. **B.** `Detcrash.log` is used by Setup if a crash occurs during the hardware detection phase.

53. **C.** Roxanne should power off the computer and then start back up. Setup will continue after it examines the `detcrash.log` file.

54. **B.** The Systems Information Utility is a tool that allows you to check out the system resources that are in use by hardware installed on your Windows 98 machine.

55. **B.** By pressing F8 when the message `Now Starting Windows 98` appears, you can choose to boot into Safe mode or use F5.

56. **B.** Add/Remove Programs offers the Startup Disk tab.

57. **D.** The System Configuration utility allows you to edit your `autoexec.abt`, `config.sys`, `system.ini`, and `win.ini` files.

58. **A.** Ping can be used to test the connection to the remote machine. The syntax from a DOS prompt would be `PING ip_address_of_remote-machine.`

59. **A, B, C.** Ipconfig will reveal the IP address, subnet mask, and default gateway; Ipconfig /all will reveal all IP address information assigned by DHCP; and WinIPCfg will reveal the same information through a GUI.

60. **C.** Net Watcher allows you to create and edit the remote shares on a Windows 98 computer.

61. **A.** She has formatted her drive. If she had converted her drive, her data would have still been present. Choices B, C, and D are not applicable to this question.

62. **C.** Disk Cleanup will free up disk space for Bob by wiping out any unneeded files.

63. **C.** Marcy is trying to compress a FAT32 drive. A FAT32 partition cannot be compressed due to the cluster size on that drive.

64. **A.** The Windows Update tool will connect to the Microsoft Windows Update site and provide the option to update Windows 98 system files and enhancements.

65. **B.** The System Scheduler will allow you to create a schedule to run any programs at given times.

66. **D.** Use the Registry Checker to check out the validity of her Registry files.

67. **D.** FAT32 can be accessed through the network. The rule that other operating systems are not able to see FAT32 partitions applies only to a dual-boot situation on the local computer.

68. **B.** The `Msdos.sys` file is used to control the boot-up process for Windows 98 computers.

69. **C.** He is powering off his computer incorrectly. If he is simply turning off his machine by pushing the on/off switch, then ScanDisk will run automatically the next time the machine is powered on.

70. **C.** NT Workstation cannot recognize FAT32 partitions.

71. **B.** The Microsoft Systems Configuration utility is a tool that allows you to retrieve information about all aspects of your system.

72. **D.** Use WinIPCfg to retrieve IP information on Windows 98.

73. **A.** Net Watcher can be used to connect to remote Windows 98 computers to view and create shares, as well as monitor users' network activity to that computer.

74. **D.** Ping the remote host to see if you can make a connection to the remote host.

75. **C.** Tracert will trace the route packets are taking to the remote server.

76. **A, B.** The Microsoft System Information utility and the Device Manager both can report system resources such as IRQ usage.

77. **B.** To configure your Windows 98 machines to retrieve an IP address, automatically accept this default value in the TCP/IP properties within the Network applet.

78. **D.** Although the other choices would reveal your IP address information, WinIPCfg is the easiest method to use to retrieve your IP address settings.

79. **C.** The remote machine must have remote administration enabled through the Passwords applet.

81. **C.** Configure the Windows 98 machine as a dial-up server through Dial-Up Networking. Configure the remote Windows 98 machine to dial into this server through Dial-Up networking.

82. **B.** A proxy server acts as a go-between, or proxy, for the IP client and the Internet. Most proxy servers can control and track where users go on the Internet. Some proxy servers offer client caching, which keeps frequent Web sites in cache so these Web pages are loaded faster for the client.

PART

III

APPENDIXES

Glossary

A

adapter Network Interface Card, also known as NIC. Also the term is used to describe dial-up adapters or SCSI adapters. *See* NIC.

Add/Remove Hardware Wizard A Windows utility, or Help Wizard, that walks you step by step through the process of adding or removing hardware from a system.

All Selected Files backup A backup of all files specified in a file set and changes the archive bit.

ATM Asynchronous Transfer Mode. A high-speed data transfer protocol.

automated setup The process of simplifying the installation of Windows 98 on many machines by creating batch scripts that can control the setup process.

B

Backup A Windows 98 utility that stores data in a compressed format to be used as a backup.

backup browser A computer that receives the browse list from the master browser and responds to browse requests from computers on the network.

backup set A backed-up copy of data files along with the preferences that were set up for that backup session.

Backup utility A Windows 98 program that allows you to back up and restore data.

Batch Files A text-based program used to run several commands consecutively.

binding A connection between a protocol and a network adapter.

bootlog.txt An ASCII filename containing a log of the most recent startup process of Windows 98.

browser election Used to determine which computer will become the master browser.

C

CGI Common Gateway Interface. This interface allows for an application to be written to a certain standard to run when a Web page is accessed. CGI is considered slower than and is the predecessor to ISAPI.

CHAP Challenge Handshake Authentication Protocol. A security protocol used to encrypt authentication between servers and clients during a RAS session.

class A network address Category for all IP addresses that start with a particular first octet from 1 to 126 (for example, 107.0.0.0). This means that a class A address might have as many as 16,777,216 IP hosts. 127 is also a class A network address, but is reserved.

class B network address   Category for the first two octets of an IP address from 128.1 to 191.255 (for example, 145.170.0.0). This allows up to 65,536 hosts.

class C network address   Category for the first three octets from 192.0.1 to 223.255.254 (for example, 208.192.235.0). This allows a maximum of 256 hosts on a class C network.

client   A networking functionality built into Windows 98 that allows a Windows 98 computer to be on many different types of networks at the same time.

cluster   The minimum amount of space on a drive that can be allocated to a file.

COM port   Short for communications port, a port connected to the motherboard that allows data to pass into and out of a computer..

config.pol   An optional part of the Registry that contains policy information related to the system and user settings.

Context   Defines your position in relation to the NDS tree. For example, Jim is the sales manager for the Eastern Division of the Widget Company.

cross-linked files   Two or more files that erroneously reference the same cluster on a drive.

CVF   Compressed Volume File. A file that stores data and the structure of a compressed drive.

D

Default Computer   An icon in the System Policy Editor that shows the computer settings applied to the computer regardless of the user who has logged on to the computer. Changes that are implemented are stored in the computer's system.dat file.

Default User   An icon in the System Policy Editor that shows the user settings for each user regardless of the computer that a user logged on to. The changes that are implemented are stored in the user's user.dat file.

Defragmenter   A disk utility used to place file clusters into a contiguous chain.

detcrash.log   A binary file created by Windows 98 if Setup fails during the hardware detection phase. Subsequently used when Setup is rerun.

detlog.txt   An ASCII file containing a list of hardware devices found by Windows 98 during the hardware detection phase of Setup.

device driver   Program or code written for a specific piece of hardware to allow it to interface with Windows 98.

Device Manager   A Windows 98 utility that enables you to view and change a system's hardware configuration.

DHCP   Dynamic Host Configuration Protocol. Used to dynamically assign IP addresses and other TCP/IP configuration information to computers.

Dial-Up Networking   A Windows feature enabling you to connect to remote servers using a modem and telephone lines. This service is used for remote access to network services such as file and printer sharing, electronic mail, scheduling, SQL database access, and other resources. Increasingly popular for users accessing the Internet.

dial-up server   Allows Windows 98 to receive modem calls and allows remote users to access resources.

Disk Cleanup   A disk utility used to remove older temporary files from the hard drive.

disk compression   The process of increasing available space on a drive by storing data in packed format, reducing the space required by a file.

Disk Defragmenter   A utility that moves files and free space to contiguous clusters on a drive.

distribution team   The people you assemble in order to implement Windows 98 on all systems in an organization.

DMF   Distribution Media Format. A file format used on Windows 98 setup disks to allow more data on each floppy disk. Such disks cannot be copied with standard methods.

DNS   A domain name server that is used to resolve host names to IP addresses.

domain controller   A Windows NT server that stores and authenticates a list of users. Can be primary or backup.

DoubleSpace   A disk compression utility that comes with MS-DOS 6.0.

driver   A program that allows a piece of hardware to communicate with the operating system.

DriveSpace   A disk compression utility that comes with MS-DOS 6.2, Windows 95, and Windows 98. The latest is DriveSpace 3. Compresses the data on the computer's hard disk to make more space on the disk.

E

ECP   Extended Capabilities Port. A feature that allows Windows 98 to use data compression to speed the flow of data to a printer.

EMF   Enhanced Metafile. A print format using a graphic file that allows control to return to an application more quickly than does RAW print format.

Extract   A disk utility that can read the content of source CAB files and extract those files.

F

FAT   File Allocation Table. Maintains the structure of files and folders on a drive. It is used by DOS, Windows 95, Windows 98, and Windows NT. Also known as FAT16.

FAT32   The file system provided by OEMs through Windows 98 and the OSR2 release of Windows 95. Accessible only through Windows 98 and Windows 95 OSR2. FAT32 uses smaller cluster sizes to store data, thus saving disk space.

fax modem   A device attached to a computer that can send and receive text and images through telephone lines. The fax modem offers the functionality of a fax machine, but all documents are electronic.

FDISK   A utility used to create and delete partitions, mark drives as active, and retrieve disk configuration information.

file and printer sharing   A network setting that, when enabled, allows you to share your resources with others, and allows you to use any of their resources for which you have authority to access.

file system   The organization of files and folders on a drive. For Windows 98 computers, the file system is either FAT16 or FAT32. For NT, it is either FAT16 or NTFS.

fragmentation   The scattering of pieces of files across a drive in non-contiguous clusters. Increases the time required to read and write to a disk.

frame type   Used with the IPX/SPX protocol. Both the workstation and the server must be using the same frame type to communicate.

free space   Clusters on a drive that have not been assigned to a file, or have not been allocated for system use.

FSD File System Driver. Enables I/O requests to be sent to and from installed file systems.

FTP File Transfer Protocol. File transfer can be controlled by user name or can allow anonymous connections.

Full backup All selected files are backed up.

G

gateway A device used to pass packets to remote subnets based on their network IDs.

GUI Graphical user interface. A generic term in the context of how an operating system is displayed.

H

Hardware/Software Compatibility List A list of hardware and software supported by and tested with Windows 98.

hidden share A share that has been hidden from view in the browse list by adding a dollar sign ($) to the end of the share name.

host drive A drive that contains a compressed volume file (CVF).

HOSTS file A static file used to resolve TCP/IP host names to IP addresses.

HTTP Hypertext Transport Protocol. The World Wide Web uses HTTP to create and publish Web pages. *Hypertext* refers to links in the text that when selected jump to other locations on the Web.

I

ICM Image Color Matching. A color-matching specification that can determine how a screen image will look when printed.

IEEE 1394 specification The specification that offers a much faster bus with greater bandwidth for demanding digital video.

IFS Installable File System. A file system with which the operating system may work.

IFS Manager The IFS Manager is responsible for analyzing incoming I/O requests from applications and other processors and then determining which file system driver can fulfill requests most effectively.

IIS Internet Information Server. Microsoft's full Internet Web server. It supports HTTP, FTP, and Gopher.

Implementation model The guidelines you follow when installing and configuring Windows 98.

Incremental backup Only the files that have changed since the last backup are copied.

IP address A unique 32-bit, four-section decimal number to uniquely identify each host on a TCP/IP network.

IPX/SPX Internetwork Packet Exchange/Sequenced Packet Exchange. The protocol designed by NetWare for communication in a NetWare network environment. *NWLink* is the Windows NT–compatible version of the protocol.

IrDA Infrared specification for peripheral communication. The IrDA can be used in a wireless network environment.

ISAPI   Internet Server Application Programming Interface. This is an extension of the Internet server that allows an application to run on the Web server.

ISP   Internet service provider. Provides users with access to the Internet through a direct line. The ISP is responsible for assigning the IP address, a subnet mask, a default gateway, and in most cases, a DNS server.

J

job   The current configuration of the backup utility with the list of selected files.

K

Kernel   The part of the Windows 98 operating system that handles memory management.

L

Legacy   Refers to older cards. Usually not Plug and Play. Must be configured manually using jumpers or dip switches.

LFN   Long filename. A file or folder that is longer than the 8.3 standard naming convention. Can be up to 255 characters in Windows 98 and 260 characters maximum for both the path and the filename.

LMHOSTS file   A static file used to resolve NetBIOS names to IP addresses.

local resources   Resources available on your computer.

logical errors   Problems with the data and organization of files stored on a drive.

M

master browser   A computer system in the network that keeps a list of all computers, shares, servers, and domains on a network.

minidrivers   Printer drivers that are supplied by printer manufacturers (and sometimes Microsoft) and talk directly to printers.

modemlog.txt   A log file of all modem commands sent and responses received over a phone line.

multilink   Windows 98's ability to utilize two phone lines merged as one for data communication over a modem.

multiple display support   Windows 98's ability to make use of up to nine individual monitors to display information.

N

name resolution   A process used on the network for resolving a computer's address as a computer's name, to support the process of finding and connecting to other computers.

NDIS   Network Driver Interface Specification.   The layer that wraps itself around the network device driver to allow communication with the protocol layers and the hardware. NDIS 3.1 adds Plug and Play capabilities.

NDS   NetWare Directory Services.   A user database designed by Novell. It allows a single point of network administration for users, computers, and other objects.

Net Watcher   Windows 98 tool that enables you to see who is currently connected to your shared folders. The Net Watcher provides information about who is currently connected to your computer and to what folder.

NetBEUI   NetBIOS Extended User Interface. A small, fast networking protocol used in LANs.

NetBIOS   Network Basic Input/Output System. An application program interface that provides application programs, such as Windows Explorer, with a set of rules. These rules are used as a guideline to conduct communication between nodes on a network.

`netlog.txt`   An ASCII file containing a list of all network components found during the Windows 98 installation.

NETSETUP   A utility that copies Windows 98 files to a network for the purpose of installing to other computers over the network.

New and Changed Files backup   A backup of only those files that have changed since the last All Selected Files backup. Changes the archive bit. Also known as an *Incremental backup*.

NIC   Network Interface Card. The peripheral hardware device that provides transport access for network packets.

O

OEM   Original Equipment Manufacturer. A supplier or vendor of new computers.

on-the-fly compression   Compression and expansion of files by the operating system, which is transparent to the user. The process of disk compression replaces repetitive patterns that take up space in a given piece of data with a token taking up less space.

OSR2   The Original Equipment Manufacturer Service Release 2 version of Windows 95. OSR2 comes installed on new computers.

P

PAP   Password Authentication Protocol. Uses cleartext passwords between servers and clients in a RAS environment.

physical errors   Problems with the surface of an actual hardware device or floppy drive.

Ping   A command-line utility that is the most widely used utility for simple troubleshooting. It sends a network packet to the destination host in search of a response.

Plug and Play   A technology that allows a piece of hardware to automatically be detected and configured.

Plug and Play printers   Printers that can be automatically configured by Windows 98.

Point-to-Point Tunneling Protocol (PPTP)   An advanced method of networking that allows secure access, via a Virtual Private Network (VPN), to remote networks across the Internet. PPTP places data from one protocol into TCP/IP, thus hiding or encrypting data over the network. A non-routable protocol that can be routed through PPTP over a WAN.

POLEDIT.EXE   The System Policy Editor that allows an administrator to edit system policies that are stored in the `config.pol` file.

port   Each Winsock service is uniquely identified by the port that it uses. There are default ports that are universally implemented in TCP/IP.

Power Management Scheme   Windows 98's use of new technology that allows you to turn a computer on or off and not have to wait for a shut0down or power-on interval.

PPP   Point-to-Point Protocol. This protocol is widely used on the Internet to connect systems. Because it is supported by UNIX– and Intel–based systems, it is very practical.

ppolog.txt   A log file containing information about how the software layers of PPP have processed a Dial-Up Networking call.

printer spool   Storage of data to be printed. Can be configured for RAW or EMF format.

Protected mode   An operating system processing mode in which address spaces are protected from each other. 32-bit Windows applications run in protected mode.

protocol   A type of language two or more computers would use to communicate.

proxy client   The proxy client intercepts any Winsock requests and redirects them to the proxy Server.

proxy server   Microsoft's proxy server handles Internet requests on behalf of clients.

Pull model   A broadcast model in which clients request setup or configuration information from server.

Push model   A broadcast model in which servers send setup or configuration information to clients.

PWS   Peer Web Server. Designed for small groups that need to share information with HTTP or FTP. PWS also supports ISAPI and CGI.

R

RAS   A service that provides remote networking for telecommuters.

RAW   A printer-dependent print format in which processing occurs in the foreground, keeping control from the user or application.

Real mode   An operating system processing mode in which address spaces of applications are not protected from each other; 16-bit applications run in Real mode.

REGEDIT.EXE   A utility that provides the ability to view and edit the system Registry.

Registry   A database in which Windows 98 stores configuration information for hardware and software. The Registry in Windows 98 is stored in two files: user.dat and system.dat.

remote administration   The ability of administrators to view and maintain Windows 98 system configurations across a network. The goal of remote administration is to give someone on the network full access to the local file system and to allow remote changes to file and printer sharing settings.

remote resources   Resources available to other users through the network.

Restore   A Windows 98 utility that restores to its original format compressed data created by the Backup utility.

S

Safe recovery   Restart of the Windows 98 Setup program after a failure, allowing Setup to use previous log files to continue installation.

ScanDisk   A utility that checks hard drives and floppy drives for logical and physical errors, and then attempts to repair those errors.

sector allocation granularity   Process of disk compression that involves changing the way data is stored on a hard drive by circumventing the often large amounts of wasted space created under a normal FAT file system.

server   Refers to any computer on the network that shares resources. A computer that runs administrative software that controls access to all or part of a network and its resources. Servers can also be peer servers such as Windows 98 systems with file and printer sharing turned on, or file servers, such as NT.

server-based A group of computers that assigns rights based on a list of users stored on a central computer.

service An application that executes in the background. Services load after Windows 98 boots. They often tend to give additional network functionality in the form of a server application.

Service for NetWare Directory Services NDS is a NetWare mechanism that allows administrators to group users and servers into more manageable pieces on Novell 4.x servers.

setuplog.txt An ASCII file containing setup information. Created during Windows 98 installation.

share *(verb)* To allow others to access a resource. *(noun)* A resource, such as a directory or print queue, that others can access.

shared resource A computer resource, such as a file, folder, or printer, for which you are providing access to other users.

Shared Windows 98 An installation of Windows 98 on a network so that it can be shared by clients to reduce the amount of required hard disk space.

share-level access control The user assigns a password to a specific resource in share-level access control. Depending on the password used, a user may have read-only or full control.

share-level security A type of security in which a password is assigned to a resource. Anyone who knows the password can access the resource.

Signature Verification Tool A system by which the source of a Web site can be authenticated.

SMB Server Message Block. A file-sharing protocol. Its main function is to allow a user, or more specifically a system, to access a remote file transparently.

SMTP Simple Mail Transfer Protocol. An ASCII message format commonly used for mail sent on the Internet.

SPAP Shiva Password Authentication Protocol. A two-way (reversible) encryption mechanism employed by Shiva.

Subnet mask A TCP/IP parameter that distinguishes between the network ID and host ID portions of an IP address.

System Configuration Utility A tool used to change the startup components and edit system files.

system files Files that are used to run Windows 98's main components.

System Information Utility A tool used to view current environment settings. Offers links to additional tools to perform diagnostic tests and configuration changes.

System Monitor A utility that allows you to view various Windows 98 resources, both on a local machine and on remote computers across a network.

system policies A single file on a server that is processed when users log on to the network. This file contains a list of settings or restrictions that apply to the users at logon. After the entries are read, they are merged into the Registry.

System Policy Editor Much of the security that Windows 98 is capable of is implemented through system policies, which are created by the System Policy Editor. Use the System Policy Editor to create system policy users, groups of users, and computers.

system.dao A backup of the system.dat file created by Windows 98 after the last successful startup.

system.dat One of two files that make up the Registry. This is the Registry file that contains the hardware and computer-specific settings for a workstation. By default, this file is located in the Windows SYSTEM directory. system.dat contains machine-specific data. *See also* user.dat.

T

TAPI   Telephony Application Program Interface. A standard set of procedures used for modem communications.

task   An action or application that performs an activity.

TCP/IP   Transmission Control Protocol/Internet Protocol. A widely used networking protocol, popular because of the Internet.

tree   In the NDS structure, a tree provides a focal starting point, or *encapsulation*, much like a company name provides recognition for an employee.

troubleshooting wizards   Wizards available through Windows Help that will walk you step by step through the procedures to correct common system problems.

U

UNC   Universal Naming Convention. The full name of a resource on the network.

unidrivers   Windows 98 printer drivers that act as an interface between applications and minidrivers. The two unidrivers are PostScript and non-PostScript.

unified browsing   All computers that can be browsed by Windows 98 are displayed together in the Network Neighborhood.

unimodem   Unimodem stands for *universal modem* and refers to the basic modem driver components that Microsoft provides with Windows 98.

Unimodem/V   Unimodem/V stands for *Unimodem/Voice*, which is a driver that allows for shared fax servers to operate over your network.

USB   Universal Serial Bus. A bidirectional, isochronous, dynamically attachable serial interface for adding peripheral devices. This is a new port and bus type that removes the limitations of available resources and expansion slots. USB can handle up to 127 devices.

user profile   A profile that enables users to keep personalized settings on a computer. If the computer is used by multiple users, each user can have her own settings.

user.dao   A backup of the user.dat file created by Windows 98 after the last successful startup.

user.dat   The file that contains user configuration settings used to implement user profiles either locally or on a network. This is one of the two files that make up the Registry. *See also* system.dat.

user-level access control   In user-level access control, specific users are given rights to a specific resource. A network server (NetWare or Microsoft) is required as a security provider, which provides a list of authorized users.

user-level security   A type of security in which rights to resources are granted on a user-by-user basis. No additional passwords are assigned to the resource. Access information is stored in a central account database located on a server.

V

Version Conflict Manager   A tool to verify the version of current driver files with backup copies.

VPN   Virtual Private Network. Allows communication from a remote client already configured with secure access. It accepts network packets only from its PPTP clients and discards all others.

W

warm boot   Restarting a computer by pressing the Ctrl + Alt + Del keys.

Windows Update   A utility that connects to a Microsoft Web site to compare and update software components.

WinIPCfg   An IP-configuration utility that displays IP settings and enables a user to change some of those settings.

Winsock   An application interface that TCP/IP utilities and application use to communicate.

write-behind caching   A process by which data isn't written immediately to disk but is written when the processor is otherwise idle. Write-behind caching improves disk performance by writing data to cache until the processor can commit the cache to disk.

Overview of the Certification Process

You must pass rigorous certification exams to become a Microsoft Certified Professional. These certification exams provide a valid and reliable measure of your technical proficiency and expertise. The closed-book exams are developed in consultation with computer industry professionals who have on-the-job experience with Microsoft products in the workplace. These exams are conducted by an independent organization—Sylvan Prometric—at more than 1,200 Authorized Prometric Testing Centers around the world.

Currently Microsoft offers six types of certification, based on specific areas of expertise:

◆ **Microsoft Certified Professional (MCP).** Persons who attain this certification are qualified to provide installation, configuration, and support for users of at least one Microsoft desktop operating system, such as Windows NT Workstation. In addition, candidates can take elective exams to develop areas of specialization. MCP is the initial or first level of expertise.

◆ **Microsoft Certified Professional + Internet (MCP+Internet).** Persons who attain this certification are qualified to plan security, install and configure server products, manage server resources, extend service to run CGI scripts or ISAPI scripts, monitor and analyze performance, and troubleshoot problems. The expertise required is similar to that of an MCP with a focus on the Internet.

◆ **Microsoft Certified Systems Engineer (MCSE).** Persons who attain this certification are qualified to effectively plan, implement, maintain, and support information systems with Microsoft Windows NT and other Microsoft advanced systems and workgroup products, such as Microsoft Office and Microsoft BackOffice. MCSE is a second level of expertise.

◆ **Microsoft Certified Systems Engineer + Internet (MCSE+Internet).** Persons who attain this certification are qualified in the core MCSE areas and are qualified to enhance, deploy, and manage sophisticated intranet and Internet solutions that include a browser, proxy server, host servers, database, and messaging and commerce components. In addition, an MCSE+Internet–certified professional will be able to manage and analyze Web sites.

◆ **Microsoft Certified Solution Developer (MCSD).** Persons who attain this certification are qualified to design and develop custom business solutions by using Microsoft development tools, technologies, and platforms, including Microsoft Office and Microsoft BackOffice. MCSD is a second level of expertise with a focus on software development.

◆ **Microsoft Certified Trainer (MCT).** Persons who attain this certification are instructionally and technically qualified by Microsoft to deliver

Microsoft Education Courses at Microsoft-authorized sites. An MCT must be employed by a Microsoft Solution Provider Authorized Technical Education Center or a Microsoft Authorized Academic Training site.

> **N O T E**
>
> **Stay in Touch**   For up-to-date information about each type of certification, visit the Microsoft Training and Certification World Wide Web site at http://www.microsoft.com/train_cert. You must have an Internet account and a WWW browser to access this information. You also can call the following sources:
>
> - Microsoft Certified Professional Program:
>   800-636-7544
>
> - Sylvan Prometric Testing Centers:
>   800-755-EXAM
>
> - Microsoft Online Institute (MOLI):
>   800-449-9333

How to Become a Microsoft Certified Professional (MCP)

To become an MCP, you must pass one operating system exam. The following list contains the names and exam numbers of all the operating system exams that will qualify you for your MCP certification (a * denotes an exam that is scheduled to be retired):

◆ Implementing and Supporting Microsoft Windows 95, #70-064 (formerly #70-063)

◆ Implementing and Supporting Microsoft Windows NT Workstation 4.02, #70-073

◆ Implementing and Supporting Microsoft Windows NT Workstation 3.51, #70-042*

◆ Implementing and Supporting Microsoft Windows NT Server 4.0, #70-067

◆ Implementing and Supporting Microsoft Windows NT Server 3.51, #70-043*

◆ Microsoft Windows for Workgroups 3.11–Desktop, #70-048*

◆ Microsoft Windows 3.1, #70-030*

◆ Microsoft Windows Architecture I, #70-160

◆ Microsoft Windows Architecture II, #70-161

How to Become a Microsoft Certified Professional + Internet (MCP+Internet)

To become an MCP with a specialty in Internet technology, you must pass the following three exams:

◆ Internetworking Microsoft TCP/IP on Microsoft Windows NT 4.0, #70-059

◆ Implementing and Supporting Microsoft Windows NT Server 4.0, #70-067

◆ Implementing and Supporting Microsoft Internet Information Server 3.0 and Microsoft Index Server 1.1, #70-077

   OR Implementing and Supporting Microsoft Internet Information Server 4.0, #70-087

How to Become a Microsoft Certified Systems Engineer (MCSE)

MCSE candidates must pass four operating system exams and two elective exams. The MCSE certification path is divided into two tracks: the Windows NT 3.51 track and the Windows NT 4.0 track.

The following lists show the core requirements (four operating system exams) for the Windows NT 3.51 track, the core requirements for the Windows NT 4.0 track, and the elective courses (two exams) you can choose from for either track.

The four Windows NT 3.51 track core requirements for MCSE certification are:

- Implementing and Supporting Microsoft Windows NT Server 3.51, #70-043*

- Implementing and Supporting Microsoft Windows NT Workstation 3.51, #70-042*

- Microsoft Windows 3.1, #70-030*

  OR Microsoft Windows for Workgroups 3.11, #70-048*

  OR Implementing and Supporting Microsoft Windows 95, #70-064

  OR Implementing and Supporting Microsoft Windows 98, #70-098

- Networking Essentials, #70-058

The four Windows NT 4.0 track core requirements for MCSE certification are:

- Implementing and Supporting Microsoft Windows NT Server 4.0, #70-067

- Implementing and Supporting Microsoft Windows NT Server 4.0 in the Enterprise, #70-068

- Microsoft Windows 3.1, #70-030*

  OR Microsoft Windows for Workgroups 3.11, #70-048*

  OR Implementing and Supporting Microsoft Windows 95, #70-064

  OR Implementing and Supporting Microsoft Windows NT Workstation 4.0, #70-073

  OR Implementing and Supporting Microsoft Windows 98, #70-098

- Networking Essentials, #70-058

For both the Windows NT 3.51 and the Windows NT 4.0 track, you must pass two of the following elective exams for MCSE certification:

- Implementing and Supporting Microsoft SNA Server 3.0, #70-013

  OR Implementing and Supporting Microsoft SNA Server 4.0, #70-085

- Implementing and Supporting Microsoft Systems Management Server 1.0, #70-014*

  OR Implementing and Supporting Microsoft Systems Management Server 1.2, #70-018

  OR Implementing and Supporting Microsoft Systems Management Server 2.0, #70-086

- Microsoft SQL Server 4.2 Database Implementation, #70-021

  OR Implementing a Database Design on Microsoft SQL Server 6.5, #70-027

  OR Implementing a Database Design on Microsoft SQL Server 7.0, #70-029

- Microsoft SQL Server 4.2 Database Administration for Microsoft Windows NT, #70-022

OR System Administration for Microsoft SQL Server 6.5 (or 6.0), #70-026

OR System Administration for Microsoft SQL Server 7.0, #70-028

◆ Microsoft Mail for PC Networks 3.2-Enterprise, #70-037

◆ Internetworking with Microsoft TCP/IP on Microsoft Windows NT (3.5–3.51), #70-053

OR Internetworking with Microsoft TCP/IP on Microsoft Windows NT 4.0, #70-059

◆ Implementing and Supporting Microsoft Exchange Server 4.0, #70-075*

OR Implementing and Supporting Microsoft Exchange Server 5.0, #70-076

OR Implementing and Supporting Microsoft Exchange Server 5.5, #70-081

◆ Implementing and Supporting Microsoft Internet Information Server 3.0 and Microsoft Index Server 1.1, #70-077

OR Implementing and Supporting Microsoft Internet Information Server 4.0, #70-087

◆ Implementing and Supporting Microsoft Proxy Server 1.0, #70-078

OR Implementing and Supporting Microsoft Proxy Server 2.0, #70-088

◆ Implementing and Supporting Microsoft Internet Explorer 4.0 by Using the Internet Explorer Resource Kit, #70-079

How to Become a Microsoft Certified Systems Engineer + Internet (MCSE+Internet)

MCSE+Internet candidates must pass seven operating system exams and two elective exams. The following lists show the core requirements and the elective courses (of which you need to pass two exams).

The seven MCSE+Internet core exams required for certification are:

◆ Networking Essentials, #70-058

◆ Internetworking with Microsoft TCP/IP on Microsoft Windows NT 4.0, #70-059

◆ Implementing and Supporting Microsoft Windows 95, #70-064

OR Implementing and Supporting Microsoft Windows NT Workstation 4.0, #70-073

OR Implementing and Supporting Microsoft Windows 98, #70-098

◆ Implementing and Supporting Microsoft Windows NT Server 4.0, #70-067

◆ Implementing and Supporting Microsoft Windows NT Server 4.0 in the Enterprise, #70-068

◆ Implementing and Supporting Microsoft Internet Information Server 3.0 and Microsoft Index Server 1.1, #70-077

OR Implementing and Supporting Microsoft Internet Information Server 4.0, #70-087

◆ Implementing and Supporting Microsoft Internet Explorer 4.0 by Using the Internet Explorer Resource Kit, #70-079

You must also pass two of the following elective exams:

◆ System Administration for Microsoft SQL Server 6.5, #70-026

◆ Implementing a Database Design on Microsoft SQL Server 6.5, #70-027

◆ Implementing and Supporting Web Sites Using Microsoft Site Server 3.0, #70-056

◆ Implementing and Supporting Microsoft Exchange Server 5.0, #70-076

   OR Implementing and Supporting Microsoft Exchange Server 5.5, #70-081

◆ Implementing and Supporting Microsoft Proxy Server 1.0, #70-078

   OR Implementing and Supporting Microsoft Proxy Server 2.0, #70-088

◆ Implementing and Supporting Microsoft SNA Server 4.0, #70-085

How to Become a Microsoft Certified Solution Developer (MCSD)

MCSD candidates must pass two core technology exams and two elective exams. The following lists show the required technology exams, plus the elective exams that apply toward obtaining the MCSD.

You must pass the following two core technology exams to qualify for MCSD certification:

◆ Microsoft Windows Architecture I, #70-160

◆ Microsoft Windows Architecture II, #70-161

You must also pass two of the following elective exams to become an MCSD:

◆ Microsoft SQL Server 4.2 Database Implementation, #70-021

   OR Implementing a Database Design on Microsoft SQL Server 6.5, #70-027

   OR Implementing a Database Design on Microsoft SQL Server 7.0, #70-029

◆ Developing Applications with C++ Using the Microsoft Foundation Class Library, #70-024

◆ Implementing OLE in Microsoft Foundation Class Applications, #70-025

◆ Programming with Microsoft Visual Basic 4.0, #70-065

   OR Developing Applications with Microsoft Visual Basic 5.0, #70-165

◆ Microsoft Access 2.0 for Windows-Application Development, #70-051

   OR Microsoft Access for Windows 95 and the Microsoft Access Development Toolkit, #70-069

◆ Developing Applications with Microsoft Excel 5.0 Using Visual Basic for Applications, #70-052

◆ Programming in Microsoft Visual FoxPro 3.0 for Windows, #70-054

Becoming a Microsoft Certified Trainer (MCT)

To understand the requirements and process for becoming a Microsoft Certified Trainer (MCT), you need to obtain the Microsoft Certified Trainer Guide document from the following Web site:

```
http://www.microsoft.com/train_cert/mct/
```

From this page, you can read the document as Web pages, or you can display or download it as a Word file.

The MCT Guide explains the four-step process of becoming an MCT. The general steps for the MCT certification are described here:

1. Complete and mail a Microsoft Certified Trainer application to Microsoft. You must include proof of your skills for presenting instructional material. The options for doing so are described in the MCT Guide.

2. Obtain and study the Microsoft Trainer Kit for the Microsoft Official Curricula (MOC) course(s) for which you want to be certified. You can order Microsoft Trainer Kits by calling 800-688-0496 in North America. Other regions should review the MCT Guide for information on how to order a Trainer Kit.

3. Pass the Microsoft certification exam for the product for which you want to be certified to teach.

4. Attend the Microsoft Official Curriculum (MOC) course for which you want to be certified. You do this so that you can understand how the course is structured, how labs are completed, and how the course flows.

> **WARNING**
>
> **Be Sure to Get the MCT Guide!**
> You should consider the preceding steps to be a general overview of the MCT certification process. The precise steps that you need to take are described in detail on the Web site mentioned earlier. Do not mistakenly believe the preceding steps make up the actual process you need to take.

If you are interested in becoming an MCT, you can receive more information by visiting the Microsoft Certified Training (MCT) Web site at `http://www.microsoft.com/train_cert/mct/` or call 800-688-0496.

What's on the CD-ROM

This appendix offers a brief rundown of what you'll find on the CD-ROM that comes with this book. For a more detailed description of the newly developed Top Score test engine, exclusive to Macmillan Computer Publishing, see Appendix D, "Using the Top Score Software."

TOP SCORE

Top Score is a test engine developed exclusively for Macmillan Computer Publishing. It is, we believe, the best test engine available because it closely emulates the format of the standard Microsoft exams. In addition to providing a means of evaluating your knowledge of the exam material, Top Score features several innovations that help you to improve your mastery of the subject matter. For example, the practice tests allow you to check your score by exam area or category, which helps you determine which topics you need to study further. Other modes allow you to obtain immediate feedback on your response to a question, explanation of the correct answer, and even hyperlinks to the chapter in an electronic version of the book where the topic of the question is covered. Again, for a complete description of the benefits of Top Score, see Appendix D.

Before you attempt to run the Top Score software, make sure that autorun is enabled. If you prefer not to use autorun, you can run the application from the CD by double-clicking the START.EXE file from within Explorer.

EXCLUSIVE ELECTRONIC VERSION OF TEXT

As alluded to above, the CD-ROM also contains the electronic version of this book in Portable Document Format (PDF). In addition to the links to the book that are built into the Top Score engine, you can use that version of the book to help you search for terms you need to study or other book elements. The electronic version comes complete with all figures as they appear in the book.

COPYRIGHT INFORMATION AND DISCLAIMER

Macmillan Computer Publishing's Top Score test engine: Copyright 1998 New Riders Publishing. All rights reserved. Made in U.S.A.

Using the Top Score Software

GETTING STARTED

The installation procedure is very simple and typical of Windows 95 or Window NT 4 installations.

1. Put the CD into the CD-ROM drive. The autorun function starts, and after a moment, you see a CD-ROM Setup dialog box asking you if you are ready to proceed.

2. Click OK, and you are prompted for the location of the directory in which the program can install a small log file. Choose the default (C:\Program Files\), or type the name of another drive and directory, or select the drive and directory where you want it placed. Then click OK.

3. The next prompt asks you to select a start menu name. If you like the default name, click OK. If not, enter the name you would like to use. The Setup process runs its course.

When setup is complete, icons are displayed in the MCSE Top Score Software Explorer window that is open. For an overview of the CD's contents, double-click the CD-ROM Contents icon.

If you reach this point, you have successfully installed the exam(s). If you have another CD, repeat this process to install additional exams.

INSTRUCTIONS ON USING THE TOP SCORE SOFTWARE

Top Score software consists of the following three applications:

◆ Practice Exams

◆ Study Cards

◆ Flash Cards

The Practice Exams application provides exams that simulate the Microsoft certification exams. The Study Cards serve as a study aid organized around specific exam objectives. Both are in multiple-choice format. Flash Cards are another study aid that require responses to open-ended questions, which test your knowledge of the material at a level deeper than that of recognition memory.

To start the Study Cards, Practice Exams, or Flash Cards applications, follow these steps:

1. Begin from the overview of the CD contents (double-click the CD-ROM Contents icon). The left window provides you with options for obtaining further information on any of the Top Score applications, as well as a way to launch them.

2. Click a "book" icon, and a listing of related topics appears below it in Explorer fashion.

3. Click an application name. This displays more detailed information for that application in the right window.

4. To start an application, click its book icon. Then click on the Starting the Program option. Do this for Practice Exams, for example. Information appears in the right window. Click on the button for the exam, and the opening screens of the application appear.

Further details on using each of the applications follow.

Using Top Score Practice Exams

The Practice Exams interface is simple and straightforward. Its design simulates the look and feel of the Microsoft certification exams. To begin a practice exam, click the button for the exam name. After a moment, you see an opening screen similar to the one shown in Figure D.1.

Click on the Next button to see a disclaimer and copyright screen. Read the information, and then click Top Score's Start button. A notice appears, indicating that the program is randomly selecting questions for the practice exam from the exam database (see Figure D.2). Each practice exam contains the same number of items as the official Microsoft exam. The items are selected from a larger set of 150–900 questions. The random selection of questions from the database takes some time to retrieve. Don't reboot; your machine is not hung!

> **NOTE**
>
> **Some Exams Follow a New Format**
> The number of questions will be the same for traditional exams. However, this will not be the case for exams that incorporate the new "adaptive testing" format. In that format, there is no set number of questions. See the chapter entitled "Study and Exam Prep Tips" in the Final Review section of the book for more details on this new format.

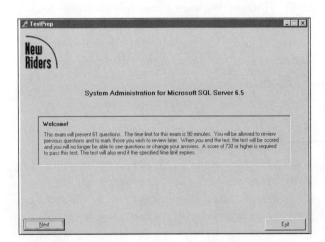

FIGURE D.1
Top Score Practice Exams opening screen.

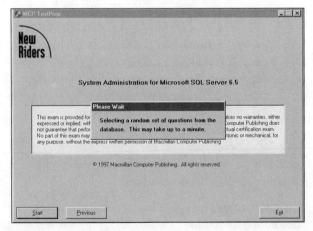

FIGURE D.2
Top Score's Please Wait notice.

After the questions have been selected, the first test item appears. See Figure D.3 for an example of a test item screen.

Notice several important features of this window. The question number and the total number of retrieved questions appears in the top-left corner of the window in the control bar. Immediately below that is a check box labeled Mark, which enables you to mark any exam item you would like to return to later. Across the screen from the Mark check box, you see the total time remaining for the exam.

The test question is located in a colored section (it's gray in the figure). Directly below the test question, in the white area, are response choices. Be sure to note that immediately below the responses are instructions about how to respond, including the number of responses required. You will notice that question items requiring a single response, such as that shown in Figure D.3, have radio buttons. Items requiring multiple responses have check boxes (see Figure D.4).

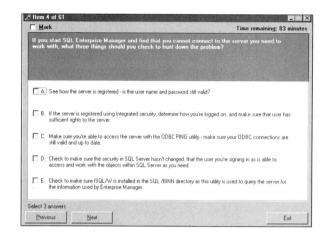

FIGURE D.4
A Top Score test item requiring multiple responses.

Some questions and some responses do not appear on the screen in their entirety. You will recognize such items because a scroll bar appears to the right of the question item or response. Use the scroll bar to reveal the rest of the question or response item.

The buttons at the bottom of the window enable you to move back to a previous test item, proceed to the next test item, or exit Top Score Practice Exams.

Some items require you to examine additional information referred to as *exhibits*. These screens typically include graphs, diagrams, or other types of visual information that you will need in order to respond to the test question. You can access Exhibits by clicking the Exhibit button, also located at the bottom of the window.

After you complete the practice test by moving through all of the test questions for your exam, you arrive at a summary screen titled Item Review (see Figure D.5).

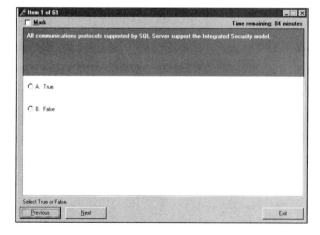

FIGURE D.3
A Top Score test item requiring a single response.

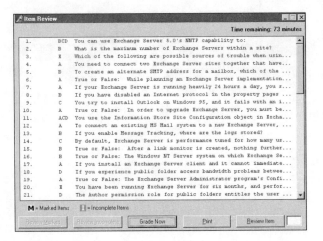

FIGURE D.5
The Top Score Item Review window.

This window enables you to see all the question numbers, your response(s) to each item, any questions you have marked, and any you've left incomplete. The buttons at the bottom of the screen enable you to review all the marked items and incomplete items in numeric order.

If you want to review a specific marked or incomplete item, simply type the desired item number in the box in the lower-right corner of the window and click the Review Item button. This takes you to that particular item. After you review the item, you can respond to the question. Notice that this window also offers the Next and Previous options. You can also select the Item Review button to return to the Item Review window.

> **NOTE**
> **Your Time Is Limited** If you exceed the time allotted for the test, you do not have the opportunity to review any marked or incomplete items. The program will move on to the next screen.

After you complete your review of the practice test questions, click the Grade Now button to find out how you did. An Examination Score Report is generated for your practice test (see Figure D.6). This report provides you with the required score for this particular certification exam, your score on the practice test, and a grade. The report also breaks down your performance on the practice test by the specific objectives for the exam. Click the Print button to print out the results of your performance.

You also have the option of reviewing those items that you answered incorrectly. Click the Show Me What I Missed button to view a summary of those items. You can print out that information if you need further practice or review; such printouts can be used to guide your use of Study Cards and Flash Cards.

Using Top Score Study Cards

To start the software, begin from the overview of the CD contents. Click the Study Cards icon to see a listing of topics. Clicking Study Cards brings up more detailed information for this application in the right window.

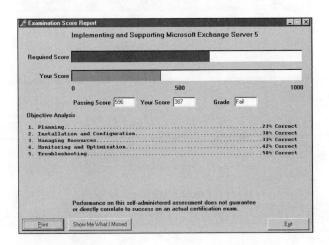

FIGURE D.6
The Top Score Examination Score Report window.

To launch Study Cards, click on Starting the Program. In the right window, click on the button for the exam in which you are interested. After a moment, an initial screen similar to that of the Practice Exams appears.

Click on the Next button to see the first Study Cards screen (see Figure D.7).

The interface for Study Cards is very similar to that of Practice Exams. However, several important options enable you to prepare for an exam. The Study Cards material is organized according to the specific objectives for each exam. You can opt to receive questions on all the objectives, or you can use the check boxes to request questions on a limited set of objectives. For example, if you have already completed a Practice Exam and your score report indicates that you need work on Planning, you can choose to cover only the Planning objectives for your Study Cards session.

You can also determine the number of questions presented by typing the number of questions you want into the option box at the right of the screen. You can control the amount of time you will be allowed for a review by typing the number of minutes into the Time Limit option box immediately below the one for the number of questions.

When you're ready, click the Start Test button, and Study Cards randomly selects the indicated number of questions from the question database. A dialog box appears, informing you that this process could take some time. After the questions are selected, the first item appears, in a format similar to that in Figure D.8.

Respond to the questions in the same manner you did for the Practice Exam questions. Radio buttons signify that a single answer is required, while check boxes indicate that multiple answers are expected.

Notice the menu options at the top of the window. You can pull down the File menu to exit from the program. The Edit menu contains commands for the copy function and even allows you to copy questions to the Windows clipboard.

Should you feel the urge to take some notes on a particular question, you can do so via the Options menu. When you pull it down, choose Open Notes, and Notepad opens. Type any notes you want to save for later reference. The Options menu also allows you to start over with another exam.

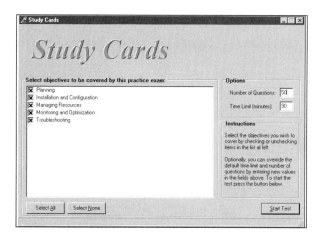

FIGURE D.7
The first Study Cards screen.

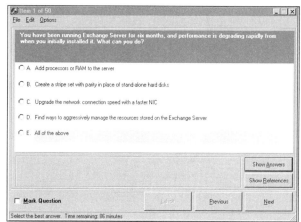

FIGURE D.8
A Study Cards item.

The Study Cards application provides you with immediate feedback of whether you answered the question correctly. Click the Show Answers button to see the correct answer, and it appears highlighted on the screen as shown in Figure D.9.

Study Cards also includes Item Review, Score Report, and Show Me What I Missed features that function the same as those in the Practice Exams application.

Using Top Score Flash Cards

Flash Cards offer a third way to use the exam question database. The Flash Cards items do not offer you multiple-choice answers to choose from; instead, they require you to respond in a short answer/essay format. Flash Cards are intended to help you learn the material well enough to respond with the correct answers in your own words, rather than just by recognizing the correct answer. If you have the depth of knowledge to answer questions without prompting, you will certainly be prepared to pass a multiple-choice exam.

You start the Flash Cards application in the same way you did Practice Exams and Study Cards. Click the Flash Cards icon, and then click Start the Program.

Click the button for the exam you are interested in, and the opening screen appears. It looks similar to the example shown in Figure D.10.

You can choose Flash Cards according to the various objectives, as you did Study Cards. Simply select the objectives you want to cover, enter the number of questions you want, and enter the amount of time you want to limit yourself to. Click the Start Test button to start the Flash Cards session, and you see a dialog box notifying you that questions are being selected.

The Flash Cards items appear in an interface similar to that of Practice Exams and Study Cards (see Figure D.11).

Notice, however, that although a question is presented, no possible answers appear. You type your answer in the white space below the question (see Figure D.12).

Compare your answer to the correct answer by clicking the Show Answers button (see Figure D.13).

You can also use the Show Reference button in the same manner as described earlier in the Study Cards sections.

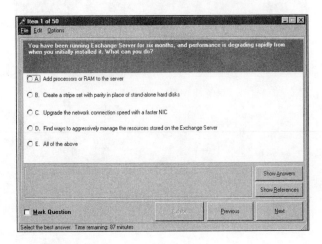

FIGURE D.9
The correct answer is highlighted.

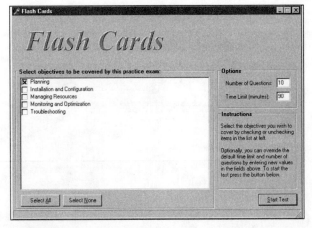

FIGURE D.10
The Flash Cards opening screen.

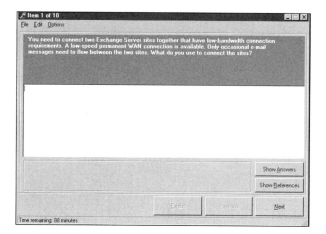

FIGURE D.11
A Flash Cards item.

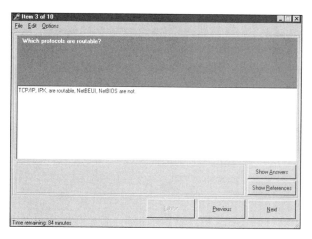

FIGURE D.12
A typed answer in Flash Cards.

The pull-down menus provide nearly the same functionality as those in Study Cards, with the exception of a Paste command on the Edit menu instead of the Copy Question command.

Flash Cards provide simple feedback; they do not include an Item Review or Score Report. They are intended to provide you with an alternative way of assessing your level of knowledge that will encourage you to learn the information more thoroughly than other methods do.

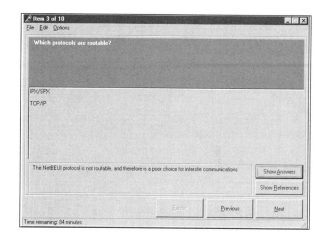

FIGURE D.13
The correct answer is shown.

SUMMARY

The Top Score software's suite of applications provides you with several approaches to exam preparation. Use Practice Exams to do just that—practice taking exams, not only to assess your learning, but also to prepare yourself for the test-taking situation. Use Study Cards and Flash Cards as tools for more focused assessment and review and to reinforce the knowledge you are gaining. You will find that these three applications are the perfect way to finish off your exam preparation.

Index

S

TRAINING GUIDES
THE NEXT GENERATION

MCSE Training Guide: Networking Essentials, Second Edition

1-56205-919-X, $49.99, 9/98

MCSE Training Guide: TCP/IP, Second Edition

1-56205-920-3, $49.99, 11/98

MCSE Training Guide: Windows NT Server 4, Second Edition

1-56205-916-5, $49.99, 9/98

MCSE Training Guide: SQL Server 7 Administration

0-7357-0003-6, $49.99, Q2/99

MCSE Training Guide: Windows NT Server 4 Enterprise, Second Edition

1-56205-917-3, $49.99, 9/98

MCSE Training Guide: SQL Server 7 Design and Implementation

0-7357-0004-4, $49.99, Q2/99

MCSE Training Guide: Windows NT Workstation 4, Second Edition

1-56205-918-1, $49.99, 9/98

MCSD Training Guide: Solution Architectures

0-7357-0026-5, $49.99, Q2/99

MCSE Training Guide: Windows 98

1-56205-890-8, $49.99, 1/99

MCSD Training Guide: Visual Basic 6

0-7357-0002-8, $49.99, Q1/99

TRAINING GUIDES
FIRST EDITIONS
Your Quality Elective Solution

MCSE Training Guide: Systems Management Server 1.2, 1-56205-748-0

MCSE Training Guide: SQL Server 6.5 Administration, 1-56205-726-X

MCSE Training Guide: SQL Server 6.5 Design and Implementation, 1-56205-830-4

MCSE Training Guide: Windows 95, 70-064 Exam, 1-56205-880-0

MCSE Training Guide: Exchange Server 5, 1-56205-824-X

MCSE Training Guide: Internet Explorer 4, 1-56205-889-4

MCSE Training Guide: Microsoft Exchange Server 5.5, 1-56205-899-1

MCSE Training Guide: IIS 4, 1-56205-823-1

MCSD Training Guide: Visual Basic 5, 1-56205-850-9

MCSD Training Guide: Microsoft Access, 1-56205-771-5

FAST TRACK SERIES

The Accelerated Path to Certification Success

Fast Tracks provide an easy way to review the key elements of each certification technology without being bogged down with elementary-level information.

These guides are perfect for when you already have real-world, hands-on experience. They're the ideal enhancement to training courses, test simulators, and comprehensive training guides. *No fluff—simply what you really need to pass the exam!*

LEARN IT FAST

Part I contains only the essential information you need to pass the test. With over 200 pages of information, it is a concise review for the more experienced MCSE candidate.

REVIEW IT EVEN FASTER

Part II averages 50–75 pages, and takes you through the test and into the real-world use of the technology, with chapters on:

1) Fast Facts Review Section
2) Hotlists of Exam-Critical Concepts
3) Sample Test Questions
4) The Insider's Spin (on taking the exam)
5) Did You Know? (real-world applications for the technology covered in the exam)

MCSE Fast Track:
Networking Essentials

1-56205-939-4,
$19.99, 9/98

MCSE Fast Track:
Windows 98

0-7357-0016-8,
$19.99, 12/98

MCSE Fast Track:
Windows NT Server 4

1-56205-935-1,
$19.99, 9/98

MCSE Fast Track:
Windows NT Server 4
Enterprise

1-56205-940-8,
$19.99, 9/98

MCSE Fast Track:
Windows NT
Workstation 4

1-56205-938-6,
$19.99, 9/98

MCSE Fast Track:
TCP/IP

1-56205-937-8,
$19.99, 9/98

MCSE Fast Track:
Internet Information
Server 4

1-56205-936-X,
$19.99, 9/98

MCSD Fast Track:
Visual Basic 6,
Exam 70-175

0-7357-0018-4,
$19.99, 12/98

MCSD Fast Track:
Visual Basic 6,
Exam 70-176

0-7357-0019-2,
$19.99, 12/98

TESTPREP SERIES

Practice and cram with the new, revised Second Edition TestPreps

Questions. Questions. And more questions. That's what you'll find in our New Riders *TestPreps*. They're great practice books when you reach the final stage of studying for the exam. We recommend them as supplements to our *Training Guides*.

What makes these study tools unique is that the questions are the primary focus of each book. All the text in these books supports and explains the answers to the questions.

- ✓ **Scenario-based questions** challenge your experience.

- ✓ **Multiple-choice questions** prep you for the exam.

- ✓ **Fact-based questions** test your product knowledge.

- ✓ **Exam strategies** assist you in test preparation.

- ✓ **Complete yet concise explanations of answers** make for better retention.

- ✓ **Two practice exams** prepare you for the real thing.

- ✓ **Fast Facts** offer you everything you need to review in the testing center parking lot.

Practice, practice, practice, pass with New Riders TestPreps!

MCSE TestPrep: Networking Essentials, Second Edition

0-7357-0010-9, $19.99, 12/98

MCSE TestPrep: TCP/IP, Second Edition

0-7357-0025-7, $19.99, 12/98

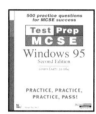

MCSE TestPrep: Windows 95, Second Edition

0-7357-0011-7, $19.99, 12/98

MCSE TestPrep: Windows 98

1-56205-922-X, $19.99, 11/98

MCSE TestPrep: Windows NT Server 4, Second Edition

0-7357-0012-5, $19.99, 12/98

MCSE TestPrep: Windows NT Server 4 Enterprise, Second Edition

0-7357-0009-5, $19.99, 11/98

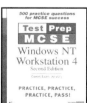

MCSE TestPrep: Windows NT Workstation 4, Second Edition

0-7357-0008-7, $19.99, 12/98

FIRST EDITIONS

MCSE TestPrep: SQL Server 6.5 Administration, 0-7897-1597-X

MCSE TestPrep: SQL Server 6.5 Design and Implementation, 1-56205-915-7

MCSE TestPrep: Windows 95 70-64 Exam, 0-7897-1609-7

MCSE TestPrep: Internet Explorer 4, 0-7897-1654-2

MCSE TestPrep: Exchange Server 5.5, 0-7897-1611-9

MCSE TestPrep: IIS 4.0, 0-7897-1610-0

How to Contact Us

IF YOU NEED THE LATEST UPDATES ON A TITLE THAT YOU'VE PURCHASED:

1) Visit our Web site at www.newriders.com.

2) Click on the DOWNLOADS link, and enter your book's ISBN number, which is located on the back cover in the bottom right corner.

3) In the DOWNLOADS section, you'll find available updates that are linked to the book page.

IF YOU ARE HAVING TECHNICAL PROBLEMS WITH THE BOOK OR THE CD THAT IS INCLUDED:

1) Check the book's information page on our Web site according to the instructions listed above, or

2) Email us at support@mcp.com, or

3) Fax us at (317) 817-7488 attn: Tech Support.

IF YOU HAVE NON-SUPPORT RELATED COMMENTS ABOUT ANY OF OUR CERTIFICATION PRODUCTS:

1) Email us at certification@mcp.com, or

2) Write to us at New Riders, 201 W. 103rd St., Indianapolis, IN 46290-1097, or

3) Fax us at (317) 581-4663.

IF YOU ARE OUTSIDE THE UNITED STATES AND NEED TO FIND A DISTRIBUTOR IN YOUR AREA:

Please contact our international department at international@mcp.com.

IF YOU WANT TO PREVIEW ANY OF OUR CERTIFICATION BOOKS FOR CLASSROOM USE:

Email us at pr@mcp.com. Your message should include your name, title, training company or school, department, address, phone number, office days/hours, text in use, and enrollment. Send these details along with your request for desk/examination copies and/or additional information.

WE WANT TO KNOW WHAT YOU THINK

To better serve you, we would like your opinion on the content and quality of this book. Please complete this card and mail it to us or fax it to 317-581-4663.

Name _____

Address _____

City _____ State _____ Zip _____

Phone _____ Email Address _____

Occupation _____

Which certification exams have you already passed? _____
_____
_____
_____

Which certification exams do you plan to take? _____
_____
_____
_____

What influenced your purchase of this book?
❏ Recommendation   ❏ Cover Design
❏ Table of Contents   ❏ Index
❏ Magazine Review   ❏ Advertisement
❏ Reputation of New Riders ❏ Author Name

How would you rate the contents of this book?
❏ Excellent   ❏ Very Good
❏ Good   ❏ Fair
❏ Below Average   ❏ Poor

What other types of certification products will you buy/have you bought to help you prepare for the exam?
❏ Quick reference books   ❏ Testing software
❏ Study guides   ❏ Other

What do you like most about this book? Check all that apply.
❏ Content   ❏ Writing Style
❏ Accuracy   ❏ Examples
❏ Listings   ❏ Design
❏ Index   ❏ Page Count
❏ Price   ❏ Illustrations

What do you like least about this book? Check all that apply.
❏ Content   ❏ Writing Style
❏ Accuracy   ❏ Examples
❏ Listings   ❏ Design
❏ Index   ❏ Page Count
❏ Price   ❏ Illustrations

What would be a useful follow-up book to this one for you?_____

Where did you purchase this book? _____

Can you name a similar book that you like better than this one, or one that is as good? Why?_____
_____
_____

How many New Riders books do you own? _____

What are your favorite certification or general computer book titles? _____
_____

What other titles would you like to see us develop?_____
_____

Any comments for us? _____
_____
_____
_____

Fold here and tape to mail

Place
Stamp
Here

New Riders
201 W. 103rd St.
Indianapolis, IN 46290